# Encyclopedia of
# COUNSELING

## Who Else Wants To Say, "I Passed"?

With more questions and answers than any other edition, the *Encyclopedia of Counseling*, Fourth Edition, is still the only book you need to pass the NCE, CPCE, and other counseling exams. Every chapter has new and updated material and is still written in Dr. Rosenthal's lively, user-friendly style counselors know and love. The book's new and improved coverage incorporates a range of vital topics, including social media, group work in career counseling, private practice and nonprofit work, addictions, neurocounseling, research trends, the *DSM-5*, the new ACA and NBCC codes of ethics, and much, much more.

**Howard Rosenthal, EdD, CCMHC, HS-BCP, LPC, MAC, NCC,** is professor and coordinator of the human services program at St. Louis Community College at Florissant Valley and is the author of numerous successful publications on counseling, counselor training, test anxiety, and test preparation.

# Encyclopedia of
# COUNSELING

## Fourth Edition

Master Review and Tutorial for the
National Counselor Examination,
State Counseling Exams, and
the Counselor Preparation
Comprehensive Examination

# Howard Rosenthal

Routledge
Taylor & Francis Group

NEW YORK AND LONDON

Fourth edition published 2017
by Routledge
711 Third Avenue, New York, NY 10017

and by Routledge
2 Park Square, Milton Park, Abingdon, Oxon, OX14 4RN

*Routledge is an imprint of the Taylor & Francis Group, an informa business*

First edition published by Routledge 1993
Second edition published by Routledge 2002
Third edition published by Routledge 2008

*Library of Congress Cataloging in Publication Data*
Names: Rosenthal, Howard, 1952- author.
Title: Encyclopedia of counseling : master review and tutorial for the national counselor examination, state counseling exams, and the counselor preparation comprehensive examination / Howard Rosenthal.
Description: Fourth edition. | New York, NY : Routledge, 2017. | Includes bibliographical references and index.
Identifiers: LCCN 2016032107| ISBN 9781138942646 (hardback : alk. paper) | ISBN 9781138942653 (pbk. : alk. paper) | ISBN 9781315671499 (ebook)
Subjects: LCSH: Counseling psychology--Examinations, questions, etc. | Counseling psychology--Examinations--Study guides.
Classification: LCC BF636.6 .R67 2017 | DDC 158.3076--dc23
LC record available at https://lccn.loc.gov/2016032107

ISBN: 978-1-138-94264-6 (hbk)
ISBN: 978-1-138-94265-3 (pbk)
ISBN: 978-1-315-67149-9 (ebk)

Typeset in New Caledonia and Friz Quadrata
by Saxon Graphics Ltd, Derby

# Contents

# Figures

# Preface to the Fourth Edition:
# The Legend of
# The Purple Book

The year was 1993. Bill Clinton had set up shop in the Oval Office, a movie named *Jurassic Park* featuring genetically engineered dinosaurs was making inroads at the box office, and I was working like a man possessed to complete my secret project.

This was going to be the dragon slayer. Never again would any counselor need to fear a minor, major, or even a comprehensive exam for a license or certification. My ultimate study guide would even the score. Like a scientist building a satellite in his or her basement, I worked late at night and into the wee hours of the morning to complete this arduous task of building the perfect beast. On one occasion I was so engrossed in my writing I nearly missed Thanksgiving dinner. But that didn't matter. Truth be told, I didn't need the major hit of tryptophan from the turkey to make me sleepy, ergo slowing down the progress to finish my city-upon-a-hill study guide.

The culminating project featured 900 easy-to-understand, perfectly crafted, tutorial questions and answers, all written in an upbeat manner. Finally, I was convinced my manuscript was ready for prime time. Yes, I was well aware of the fact that I might never sell the book, but I convinced myself that if I encountered a worst-case scenario, I would put copies of my masterpiece in three ring notebooks and loan them to counselors and students.

Like a 10-year old kid who purchased a baseball glove merely because it was the same brand that Mickey Mantle used, I sent the book off for publication to a company who published all the books drafted by one of my counseling heroes, only to have the editor, who perused this would-be icon, reject it! The editor insisted that exam prep texts needed to be serious tomes (my translation, sleep therapy!).

He was put off by the fact that my book broke all the rules and was written in a folksy, upbeat, reader-friendly tone that actually made studying fun. In other words, my argument for the book was precisely his argument against it.

But what was I thinking? Five years earlier, Dr. Joseph W. Hollis, a counselor of note and the owner of Accelerated Development Inc., had published my first book on suicide prevention and later a cassette tape exam prep guide that I had created. I would send my document to him. It just made sense. My initial idea to pen the work manifested itself when faithful cassette listeners wanted to know where they could purchase my book.

Joe was a prince of a guy who was totally down to earth. Since he always relied on handwritten communication he sent me a longhand letter praising the merits of my manuscript. He was, nevertheless, not smitten with my *Ultimate Study Guide* title. Instead, he felt that the work was so comprehensive that I should call it the *Encyclopedia of Counseling*. Although the book didn't truly fit the mold of a typical volume touted as an encyclopedia, Joe was correct that my manuscript was remarkably in-depth, complete, and nearly all-inclusive. Moreover, I used a little creative visualization and decided that the words "author of the *Encyclopedia of Counseling*" would give my professional resume a shot of high-powered adrenaline, so I readily said yes to his novel idea for a title.

Now you are probably thinking that I'm going to say that the sales of the *Encyclopedia* took off like a jet fighter plane on steroids, but that would be a total lie. In reality, the text came out of the starting blocks with all the vigor of a tortoise with ankle weights strapped to its feet. But fortunately, as time went by, that slow-moving tortoise began to gain some serious speed.

The turning point seemed to occur when one day I received a call on my answering machine from a graduate counseling professor asking where her students could purchase "The Purple Book." Before I could respond to the caller I punched up my email only to discover a message from a counselor who just received her master's degree, who also wanted to buy a copy of "The Purple Book." What in the world was The Purple Book? I punched the term into a search engine and discovered **that counselors writing on Internet discussion groups and chat rooms from coast-to-coast were talking about *my* book!**

The only explanation was that my friend, that slow-moving tortoise, put the pedal to the metal and kicked into passing gear. A grass-roots movement began to take hold that I, as the author, didn't even see happening. Permit me to explain. Beginning with the second edition of the *Encyclopedia of Counseling* we used a purple cover. (The first edition used a green, black, and white color scheme with a hint of gray.) At about the same time my book was coming of age, a pharmaceutical company, AstraZenica, was advertising a drug called Nexium for heartburn and billed it as "The Purple Pill." Counselors put a twist on the ad and my *Encyclopedia of Counseling* had become The Purple Book.

Why was the book becoming so popular? Simple, I actually made exam prep (dare I say it) fun and easy to understand. That's right, studying became enjoyable. I never believed that education needed to be dry, dull, and boring, and my book went on to prove it. *The greatest exam secret is that studying and exam prep can actually be a pleasant experience and something you will look forward to doing.*

My style in the *Encyclopedia* (um excuse me, I mean The Purple Book) is upbeat and at times humorous. For years now I have been in meetings or conferences where I have heard professors remark, "I'm not here to entertain the students." I often heard the exact same thing from professors when I was a student. But I decided to take the road less traveled. I typically stroll into classes that I am teaching on the first day and tell my students, "A lot of educators will tell you they aren't here to entertain you, but actually, I am here to entertain you!" I embrace that same great philosophy in this very book.

The *Encyclopedia* was (and still is) merely my entertaining and engaging teaching style in print and readers were loving every minute of it (and still do). How do I know? Great question! I could tell you that on many occasions I punched the keyword counseling into Amazon's search or other top booksellers' websites and there I spied the *Encyclopedia* sitting pretty within the top five spots ... often at number one! In 2010, the Routledge Counseling and Psychotherapy catalog listed the *Encyclopedia* as the number one seller in the *Top Ten List*. In 2011 it captured the number two spot, beating works by many of the top counseling and psychology authors in the world.

At one point the *Encyclopedia* was posted on Amazon as the number two seller in St. Louis, Missouri, which is near my home town. Who ever heard of an aging, professional work dominating the book charts, and blowing the socks off popular trade books written by celebrities or local sports stars—even if it was just for a limited period of time? After all, this book was, and is, an academic publication. It is decidedly not the kind of publication Oprah wants to showcase in an interview for her book club. However, if you happen to be reading this Oprah …

(And just in case you mumbled, "Big deal, of course the text sold well, he said St. Louis is near his home town. Counselors probably purchased the book because they knew Rosenthal personally." Let me set the record straight and share with you that all the sales records I have been able to amass to reveal that my book sells much *better* outside St. Louis, and even beyond the borders of the state of Missouri, than it does in my own back yard.)

Yes success leaves clues, but here is my most-convincing argument. Over the years I've received numerous emails from readers who have suggested that they were sad when their study process ended. Say what? Seriously? Yes, seriously! That's correct; you read it right, counselors were enjoying the exam preparation process so much that they didn't want it to end. Some readers even used the word grieving to describe their reaction. Others actually uttered the F word … yep, fun, to describe the process.

I'll tell you something I find really humorous. Most reader reviews commenting on The Purple Book are overwhelmingly positive. But I specifically remember a critical reviewer who commented that, "The beginning of the book reads like an infomercial." Hello, is anybody in there? I want my opening remarks to sound similar to an infomercial! Why? Because I want you to have supreme confidence in my ability to take you from here to wherever you want to go, whether that is tackling the CPCE, the NCE, your licensing exam, or getting a mind-blowing high score on your graduate comps. This book is too important for the future of your career to put down. So yes indeed, I am intentionally selling you on the notion of using it. The work has helped countless people reach their goals. Just recently, I discovered that a Chinese version will be released in the future. Nevertheless, if you harbor even a shadow of doubt, just go to my website (www.howardrosenthal.com) and read a seemingly endless string of testimonials, all I might add, with real names.

**The Encyclopedia works! This book delivers the goods and it actually makes studying enjoyable.**

# A COUNSELING SUPERSTAR THAT KEEPS GETTING BETTER WITH AGE

Some things just get better with age. This new version of the *Encyclopedia* is even bigger, better, and more refined than any of its three markedly successful predecessors. Each section has been improved, with every single question having been reviewed to determine if it should be updated, tweaked, or deleted and replaced.

I'm happy to say that the *Encyclopedia* still reads like a novel but imparts information like a postgraduate seminar.

# WHY THIS BOOK SUCCESSFULLY PREPARES YOU FOR STATE LICENSING, CERTIFICATION, COMPREHENSIVE EXAMS, COURSE WORK, OR SUCCESSFUL COUNSELING

- Tutorial format includes 1,000 questions and answers to expand your knowledge.
- Plenty of repetition promotes learning even if you have been out of school for an extended period of time.
- Key concepts are explained in several different ways.
- Covers all major areas commonly found on counselor licensing, certification, and exit exams—highly recommended for comps including oral and written boards.
- Chock-full of memory devices and special hints for tackling tough exam questions you won't find elsewhere.
- Easy-to-use index conveniently lists topics by question number.
- Lively, folksy, conversational style promotes confidence, reduces test anxiety, and actually makes studying enjoyable.
- Text is specifically designed for the busy professional or student who must make maximum use of study time.
- Can be combined with my highly effective *Vital Information and Review Questions* audio CD study guide preparation program and my *Human Services Dictionary* to create the ultimate preparation package. There is also an *Encyclopedia of Counseling* Exam Prep App (for iPhone/iPad and android phone/tablet) for mini-study sessions on the go.
- Includes an updated "Final Overview and Last-Minute Super-Review Boot Camp" section that helps optimize exam preparation.

(Several prepublication readers insisted that they would pay the full price for the book, just to get their hands on this single chapter! Yeah, it's really that good.)

## WHO ELSE WANTS TO SAY, "I PASSED!"?

This National Counselor Examination (NCE) and Counselor Preparation Comprehensive Examination (CPCE) guide is still here, very much alive and still thriving after a host of its competitors bit the dust years ago. Many of the testimonials I've received indicated that this book was superior to books, courses, and seminars costing up to *10 times the price of this work*. The results of this work speak for themselves. Although this Routledge academic bestseller can serve as a powerful stand-alone study guide, it works best when it is combined with my popular audio exam preparation programs. In the early 1990s when I began banging out the manuscript for this book on my primitive, technologically prehistoric computer (it didn't even sport a hard drive) I never dreamed that one day counselors would be contacting me on a daily basis to thank me for helping them snare professional credentialing.

Why revise a winner like this book? Simply to update every section with tons of revisions, and a boatload of additional information, including:

- Fifty additional tutorial questions and answers to bring the new grand total up to 1,000.
- A new, seriously beefed-up, Last-Minute Super-Review Boot Camp chapter.

New sections:
- 10 Major Career Theories on the Head of a Pin
- 11 Current Trends in Counseling Research
- Quick Guide to the New 2014 ACA Ethics
- 27 Hints for Tackling *DSM-5/ICD* Questions on Your Exams
- What You Need to Know About the Emerging Neuroscience and Counseling Revolution.

All of the aforementioned additions contain valuable information to raise your NCE, CPCE, or other exam score, and, fine tune it to a new, higher level of perfection.

So if you are going my way I have just one important question: Will you be my next testimonial?

Have a great day and best wishes on your exam.

*Dr. Howard Rosenthal*

# Acknowledgments

It's here! The ultimate weapon against test anxiety—a user-friendly exam preparation guide that has no archetype, except for the previous editions. The ideas, information, and the style are my own, though it would be impossible to complete a complex work such as this on a solo basis. I would be remiss if I did not acknowledge the tremendous assistance afforded by others. To make this text a hairline shorter I am limiting my comments primarily to individuals who helped me with the current edition.

First, hats off to my wife, Patricia, for her continued support. After all, trying to navigate through a house inundated with behavioral science books piled knee high isn't exactly most people's idea of a good time! Thanks to my sons Paul and Patrick who assisted with computer and technical issues. Paul, in fact, built the computer I am keyboarding on right now.

Next I must mention my brother Wayne Rosenthal, who fancies the challenge of a complex statistical problem.

Then, of course, there's Carolyn Duncan, who literally put her reputation (as well as her professional career) on the line by being the first person to test the merits of the initial edition of this book on an actual licensing exam. She passed, I might add, and with more than flying colors, paving the way for literally thousands of counselors who would come after her.

A warm hand clasp goes out to literally scores of counselors who have contacted me to thank me for writing the book (and providing me with the motivation to write a newer, bigger, and better version) and those who had ideas to make it even better.

Professor Julie Graul was a great help due to her vast knowledge in the area of human growth and development, and Dr. Baorong Guo for her statistical expertise. My Routledge editor, Anna Moore, and her editorial assistant, Nina Guttapalle, are always there brimming with optimism to assist me when I need it most.

Last, credit goes out to a very special gentleman, Dr. Joseph Hollis, a counselor who reached the pinnacle of success in our field. Joe believed in the *Encyclopedia of Counseling* and my companion audio program and helped to bring the original edition of this landmark preparation guide to print.

# The National Counselor Examination for Licensure and Certification (NCE) at a Glance

- The examination is created and administered by the National Board for Certified Counselors (NBCC). Exam development began in 1982.
- Counselors who receive a passing score and meet NBCC's requirements secure the Nationally Certified Counselor Credential (NCC). Some states require a passing score on the test as a part of their licensing process.
- The exam is composed of 200 multiple-choice questions. Only 160 of the questions are graded. Forty questions are being field-tested to see if they might be appropriate for future versions of the exam. Thus, the highest possible score from the exam is 160.
- A four-hour time limit is set for taking the exam.
- The examination is based on eight Counseling and Related Educational Programs (CACREP) core content areas:

    1. Human Growth and Development: 12 questions
    2. Social and Cultural Diversity: 11 questions (smallest exam content area)
    3. Helping Relationships: 36 questions (largest exam content area)
    4. Group Work: 16 questions
    5. Career Development: 20 questions
    6. Assessment: 20 questions
    7. Research and Program Evaluation: 16 questions
    8. Professional Orientation and Ethical Practice: 29 questions

Five work behavior areas determine the domains, context or work setting related to each question:

1. Fundamental Counseling Issues: 32 questions
2. Counseling Process: 45 questions
3. Diagnostic and Assessment Services: 25 questions
4. Professional Practice: 38 questions
5. Professional Development, Supervision, and Consultation: 20 questions

# The Counselor Preparation Comprehensive Examination (CPCE) at a Glance

- The CPCE is researched, developed, and distributed by the Research and Assessment Corporation for Counseling (RAAC) and the Center for Credentialing and Education (CCE). The aforementioned entities are affiliate corporations of the National Board for Certified Counselors (NBCC).
- The CPCE was first used in 1997.
- At this point in time nearly four hundred programs across virtually every state use this instrument created to standardize the measurement of students in counseling programs.
- Exam questions are compiled from major texts used in counselor education programs by master's as well as doctoral-level professionals.
- The CPCE is not a licensing or alternative credential exam. Eligibility for the exam is determined by your educational institution.
- The exam is often dubbed as "an exit exam" and in many instances it is used as a graduation requirement. In some programs the CPCE can be substituted for writing a thesis or scholarly paper. Always check with your graduate advisor pertaining to your institution for higher learning.
- The exam is composed of 136 graded questions out of 160 questions on the exam. Twenty-four items not identified to the person taking the exam are being field-tested. The exam illuminates strengths and weaknesses in the various areas of counseling. The highest possible score is 136.
- A four-hour time limit is set for taking the exam.

The CPCE is based on the exam same eight content areas as the NCE:

1. Human Growth and Development: 20 questions (17 graded)
2. Social and cultural Diversity: 20 questions (17 graded)
3. Helping Relationships: 20 questions (17 graded)
4. Group Work: 20 questions (17 graded)
5. Career Development: 20 questions (17 graded)
6. Assessment: 20 questions (17 graded)
7. Research and Program evaluation: 20 questions (17 graded)
8. Professional Orientation and Ethical Practice: 20 questions (17 graded)

# Historic NBCC Announcement Could Impact Your Career

On November 17, 2014, NBCC President and CEO, Dr. Thomas W. Clawson, sent out an e-mail "to share a historic change regarding future NBCC application requirements."

First, let me be 101% crystal clear that this change will not—I repeat **will not**—affect your current NBCC status. Any counselor who currently has NBCC certification simply needs to pay their fees, complete their Continuing Education Units (CEUs), and comply with NBCC's Code of Ethics.

The new change concerns national certification applications received by NBCC **after January 1, 2022.** After the aforementioned date, applicants must possess a master's degree or higher from a graduate program accredited by the Council for Accreditation of Counseling & Related Programs (CACREP).

Dr. Clawson reminds us in the memo that counselors now have licensure laws in all 50 states, the District of Columbia, and Puerto Rico. That said, NBCC has heard comments from numerous counselors who have had difficulty when moving to another state or attempting to meet eligibility requirements for federal programs. According to Dr. Clawson, inconsistent educational standards are fueling this problem. NBCC believes that, "embracing one accreditation, will help solve these issues."

CACREP has provided educational standards for school counseling, addictions, and clinical mental health in approximately three hundred colleges and universities. CACREP now accredits over seven hundred programs.

Dr. Clawson readily admits he personally graduated with counseling degrees before CACREP and he holds a counselor's license as well as NCC status.

ACA is backing NBCC's new position.

Will your exam have a question on this issue? Well, as you may have guessed I'm not psychic, but I'd say there is a fighting chance your exam just might mention it.

But look at it this way: even if your exam does not, this change could impact your career, that of your colleagues, and individuals you are counseling.

# 1

## Study Guides:
## My Own Humble Beginnings

*In the report card of life, nobody gets a mark for effort.*
—Andrew Salter, father of
conditioned reflex therapy

It sounded like a barking dog, only a heck of a lot louder, though I certainly knew they didn't allow animals in the halls. After all, this was an institution for higher learning. As I rounded the corner I was no longer perplexed. The ruckus emanated from one Dr. Jack Furbis, head of the illustrious history department. He was red as a beet, perhaps even a tad purple, as I watched him read a fellow student the riot act. As he displayed his true colors I could see why the greater part of the student body referred to him as Dr. Vegetable Head.

> Listen to me; those study guides are worthless... and... and, they are cheating. Yes, they're trash, pure trash mister. If I had my way it would be illegal for the bookstore to sell that junk.

Two things ran through my mind. The first was that I thanked my lucky stars that I didn't have Doc Vegetable Head for a course. The second was that my curiosity about these so-called study guides was piqued. I wanted to find out just exactly what those devilish treatises contained.

The woman who ran the bookstore knew exactly where I could find the works responsible for Doc Furbis's elevated blood pressure. They were conveniently located in the section designated "Study Guides."

Seemingly, these purveyors of grade cards made in heaven covered every conceivable subject. Some analyzed short stories and novels. Others explained how to pass the Graduate Record Examination (GRE) or a civil service test to secure employment at the post office. Another described how to pass an exam in order to receive advanced placement in college biology.

All I could say to myself was: "Thanks for the find, Dr. Furbis. These study guides are terrific." I walked away with no less than four on that prophetic day—one for statistics, one for American history, and a couple of others pertaining to psychology and sociology.

For the next 18 years I doubt whether I came within shouting distance of a bona fide study guide, but then it happened. As part of my work in supervising some students for state counselor licensure I felt that in addition to providing guidance related to their clients it was my moral duty as their so-called licensing supervisor to help them prepare for the written exam that would be staring them square in the face when they finished their 3,000 hours of supervision with yours truly.

To be sure, the rumors were already starting to fly, and believe me, they were anything but pleasant.

"It's a bear… I've never seen anything like it… the hardest test I ever took in my life."

"We never covered any of that stuff in my counseling courses, that's for sure."

"Honestly, I never heard of half of the terms on the exam; I have no idea how I passed it."

One counselor, who was treating clients for anxiety disorders, told me she was beginning to experience panic attacks herself and was having nightmares based on rumors and the anticipation of actually having to take the monster—excuse me, I mean the test!

The test responsible for the horrendous intimidation was the National Counselor Examination for Licensure and Certification (NCE), which was and is the test used to evaluate counselors for the status of National Certified Counselor (NCC). Many states use this exam as the test for state counselor licensing; for example, the Licensed Professional Counselor (LPC) credential. The NCE and the NCC were creations of the National Board for Certified Counselors (NBCC). One thing you discover in a hurry when you investigate counselor licensure and certification requirements is that the field is inundated with alphabet soup acronyms.

The interesting thing is that it is unethical for persons who have taken the exam to reveal any of the questions on the test. The way I figure it, the NBCC can breathe easy knowing that, at least in my case, the individuals I conversed with were so intimidated by the exam that it could have been written in a foreign language. In case I haven't made my point, allow me to be a bit more explicit: The examinees I spoke with were so threatened by the test that they couldn't even verbalize what they found so difficult; hence, they were in no danger whatsoever of revealing anything concrete—so much for the issue of test ethics violations.

Frankly, I was perplexed by the whole issue. For starters, I recalled that, much to my chagrin, I personally had taken the test. You see, when licensing came to my state, Missouri, I was grandfathered in, based on the fact that I had NCC status. I found out via the counselor licensing board that Missouri, like many other states, did not have a licensing test and thus was using the NCE. I even discovered that in Missouri the examinee could kill two birds with one stone, if you will, by scoring high enough to secure NCC as well as state licensure. In other words, since the NCE was the test used to determine NCC status, you could snare NCC.

My memory of the test was hardly a catastrophic one. Though I could remember truly struggling with a number of the questions, I was not mortified by them. True, I had several advantages. One was that I was doing some supervision of helpers and college teaching at the time. This might have meant that I was more familiar with a number of principles than your average, everyday counselor on the street, in an agency, or in private practice. Another issue was that the test was supposedly evolving, which was most likely a very diplomatic way of saying that it was getting more difficult with each update or version! Moreover, the required score to put a license number after your John Hancock was creeping up. Thus, the bottom line was that although my experience with the test had not been a negative one, I realized that times change and I needed to dip into my resources for a little accurate empathy to help those who would need to tangle with the NCE or one of its derivatives. I say one of its derivatives inasmuch as many states are using the NCE as a licensing instrument. Those states that are not doing so will still look to the NCE for guidance. Therefore, even if your state does not use the NCE per se, there is a very good chance that your exam will be very similar, to say the least.

Armed with this information I concluded that the answer to my supervisees' dilemma was just a bookstore away. I imagined that I'd zip over to the nearest bookseller, peruse the study guide section, and return with a text on the NCE. I even rationalized that on the one-in-a-million chance that Dr. Furbis was taking in the bestseller list that day, he still wouldn't recognize me behind the extra-dark sunglasses I made a point of wearing.

I had it all figured out. It was going to be easy—except for one minor snafu I hadn't counted on: namely, that the store didn't carry a book intended for LPC or NCE study. I was shocked. Since my glorious college days it seemed that the authors of these study guides had added nearly every title under the sun **except a book to help with counselor licensure and certification.** I was sure there was a mistake, yet the woman at the checkout counter assured me her faithful computer indicated that the store did not carry such a work. In disbelief I hit every major, minor, college, and university bookstore in our town (and believe me, there were plenty of them) without a success. I even offered to let them order it from out of town ("I don't mind the six-week wait," I told them) but was informed that I couldn't purchase a book that didn't exist. Tired and weary from having book dealers' doors slammed in my face, I assumed a depressed posture and headed home empty handed. I got in my car, fired it up, put the car in gear, and popped a tape in my cassette deck and a giant light labeled "insight" lit up in my head.

## AUDIO DOCTOR TO THE RESCUE

It has been said that genius is often right in front of your nose, but in this case it was tugging at my ear lobes. A number of years earlier when I had to tangle with oral and written boards for my doctorate, I had recorded what I felt was key information onto cassette tapes. These cassettes then turned my home stereo, portable cassette player, boombox, and Walkman into veritable teaching machines. Best of all, I used the tape player in my car in order to convert boring traffic jams into worthwhile learning experiences. To be sure, I was the only road warrior traveling Highway 40 West who was using stalled tractor trailers as an excuse to learn that negative reinforcement was not the same thing as punishment. A bit eccentric, perhaps, but I breezed through my oral and written boards. I thus geared up to produce some cassette tapes for my students. Yet there was one little problem—I had no idea what was on the test!

Since I was a National Certified Counselor myself, I picked up the phone and called NBCC to see if they could point me in the right direction. Sure enough, they did. Within minutes after terminating my telephone conversation I was ordering a copy of *How to Prepare: Your Guide to the National Counselor Examination*. Though this booklet, published by NCC, explicitly states that the guide is not intended to enhance your performance on the exam, I would advise anyone taking the test to secure a copy. (Note: NBCC currently calls this the *NBCC's Official Preparation Guide for the National Counselor Examination for Licensure and Certification*.) The booklet gives vital information regarding the nature and format of the exam. There is also a practice test replete with answers. In my case, the work clarified the eight basic areas of the exam (more on that later) and gave me a fine bibliography that the authors refer to as "potential references."

I then returned to my local college bookstores (still hiding behind my extra-dark shades, of course!) and began buying every brand of study guide available that helps students prepare for the Graduate Record Examination (GRE) in psychology. Using somewhat superficial logic, I assumed that there would be at least a moderate amount of overlap between the two disciplines (i.e., counseling and psychology). Sure the NCE was in the big leagues, the test intended for those who already possessed a master's or a doctorate. Nevertheless, I hypothesized that many principles of behavior were relevant at all levels of education, though the postgraduate version might be a tad more precise or complex than the explanation given to students who had only completed a bachelor's degree.

As I perused these guides there was something else I was trying to master, and that was the thinking process of the experts who put these types of tests together (the idea being that I could ultimately think like these folks). I could make some very good educated guesses about the questions my supervisees might have to reckon with come NCE time.

As I studied the guides, I began to actually feel that I was beginning to think like these authors. It then occurred to me that perhaps something else was transpiring. That "something else" was that the repetitive nature of the questions which appeared in study guides a, b, and c was not necessarily indicative of the authors' respective cognitions. I began to see instead that the tendency for certain issues to appear again and again was most likely an indication that these were key points in the mind of almost any behavioral science scholar. Thus, armed to the teeth with an arsenal of GRE study guides, NCE-recommended textbooks, and a stack of books that represented my own 12-year stint in college, I headed for my trusty tape recorder.

Again, I took to the streets and cruised over the highways and byways of America's heartland listening to myself babble on hour after hour. A trip to the office was no longer a trip to the office. Instead it became a lecture about Albert Ellis's rational-emotive behavior therapy, Jung's analytic psychology, or a few hints on distinguishing the statistical mean from the median or perhaps the mode.

While I was supporting my tape addiction, some of my students had enrolled in courses given by companies which marketed programs that were specifically intended to help students prepare for licensing or certification exams. From everything I heard and saw (i.e., the materials) the programs were doing a fine job. My only concerns were (1) the programs had pretty stiff price tags (e.g., one student I knew attended one which cost over $600—ouch!) and (2) many of them required the future licensed counselor to travel to the city where the seminar was being held. The combined cost of the seminar plus travel, room, and board added up to a fairly sizable chunk of change, not to mention the inconvenience. I spoke with a number of busy professionals who said they just couldn't fit such programs into their schedules. Others didn't want to break into their piggy banks.

I therefore continued to fine tune my tapes, analyzing feedback I received from a number of individuals. My final product consisted of nearly nine hours of material. Four of the tapes consisted of vital information and lecture material geared specifically toward the eight areas of the exam. Two of the tapes contained an innovative 225-question review which was like a practice test. I say "innovative" because I used the questions to convey information. For example, I might say, "Perls is the father of gestalt therapy. Who is the father of the Person-Centered Approach?" Moreover, on most of the questions I chose to expand on the answer, thus providing the listener with information which could conceivably help the person answer a number of other questions on the actual exam.

My tape program became an instant success and, since its inception, has been updated and expanded on several occasions. The current audio CD version has more than four times the information included in the initial tape series. If you have not yet secured the audio program and are interested in doing so—and by all means you should be—you can call the publisher toll free at 1-800-634-7064. The audio program contains lively lectures on all exam areas, over 300 audio tutorial questions and answers, and is intended to supplement this book. And to answer your question in advance: No, it's not merely me reading this text into a microphone!

Mission accomplished—well, not quite. You see, about the same time my original tapes went on to the publisher my friendly college bookstore called to report that a miracle had taken place: They had several new books specifically intended to help counselors prepare for the state licensing and certification exams. I have little doubt that I was the first on my block to own and read these books. Quite frankly, I felt the books were well written and very helpful.

Why this book then, you may ask? It's an excellent question, indeed. The first and foremost reason is that the above-referenced works, as well as the preparation booklet by NBCC, do not include explanations of the answers. Thus, the reader of such works may well pick the correct answer to a test question but may have answered it correctly for the wrong reason. This reminds me of something I once heard a prolific self-help writer comment on during a lecture. He stated that people would write him and tell him they were helped tremendously by using the principles he outlined in his books. Unfortunately, when they went on to explain, it was obvious they were not following the advice set forth in his books, and they certainly weren't practicing anything that remotely resembled his self-improvement theories!

You've probably heard the story about the chemistry professor. First he puts a worm in a beaker of water and allows it to swim around. Next he places the worm in a beaker of alcohol and it disintegrates. The professor then turns to the class and asks the students to describe what they learned. "It's obvious," responds a student, "If you drink a lot of alcohol you'll never get worms."

And so I become a man with a mission—a mission to write a worm-free study guide. Now let's see what's in it for bookworms like you.

## WHY THIS NEW BREED OF ENCYCLOPEDIA CAN BENEFIT ALL MENTAL HEALTH PROFESSIONALS

Now I must be honest with you and share the fact that there was another impetus for this book. From all reports, the tapes were a raving success. I began receiving calls and letters from across the country praising the merits of my audio study program. Many of the tape users began asking the same question, namely: "How can I get a copy of your book to go along with the tapes?" Unfortunately, I had to tell them that there was no book. Listeners liked my folksy, conversational, and sometimes humorous tutorial teaching style on the tapes, and now they wanted to see it in print. I knew the tape users were telling me the truth about the style because I had previously used this style successfully in an earlier book (*Not With My Life I Don't: Preventing Your Suicide and That of Others*, Accelerated Development Publishers, 1988).

As I began the monumental task of putting together this text, I kept adding more and more critical information until it became obvious that this work would go well beyond the boundaries of an ordinary study guide. I ultimately created a master review and tutorial. But let's give credit where credit is due. Joseph W. Hollis, a remarkable man who owned Accelerated Development, and was a pioneer in the counseling movement, insisted that I had actually written an *Encyclopedia of Counseling*, and that we ought to go with that as the title. The idea immediately caught my fancy and the rest as they say is history. Certainly this book still will serve as a superb guide for counselors (or study groups) who must take exit exams—the CPCE— are seeking state licensing or national board certification, but it is not limited to this purpose. As this text now stands, it also will assist psychologists, psychiatrists, social workers, crisis workers, pastoral counselors, psychiatric nurses, educators, human service workers, guidance personnel, and any other mental health professional preparing for course work, oral or written boards, or licensing and certification. It makes an ideal text to supplement advanced human services classes, graduate seminars, and practicum or internship experiences. Moreover, you will discover that it neatly summarizes an amazing amount of key material. Hence, you'll find that it is the perfect refresher course if you have been out of school for an extended period of time.

Simply put: You don't need to be studying for licensure or certification to benefit from this book. **Here is a book that belongs on the shelf of every serious mental health professionals' personal library.** Nevertheless, if you are worried about taking a test or exam of any sort, you can secure support merely by turning the page.

# 2

---

# How to End Exam Worries

*Counselor: I feel like I'm not going to pass the National Counselor Examination.*

*Counselor's supervisor: Now, now. You know that as mental health professionals we advocate positive thinking.*

*Counselor: Okay, I'm positive I won't pass the National Counselor Examination.*

"I'm not a happy camper," remarked Jeff Nelson, a 43-year-old clinical director for a not-for-profit counseling center. In an attempt to display my best accurate empathy I nodded affirmatively and reached over the counter and pulled a red gum ball from the gum ball machine. "Come on, have one, the red ones are the best, honest. These are the same ones we give the kids under ten and they swear by the red ones. Some say they're better than counseling, even play therapy, for curing depression."

**Jeff:**   No thanks, I'm trying to quit. Besides, I'm hooked on the sugarless stuff now. Anyway, I was fine until I got sand kicked in my face.

**Author:**  Sand! (furrows brow.) You mean sand as in beaches, sand traps on golf courses, and that sort of thing?

**Jeff:**  Oh, I'm sure you've heard this one before. I'm sitting on the beach, minding my own business when this big, beefy type kicks sand in my face. He's big and hairy and goes by the name of NCE.

**Author:**  And let me guess, the dude packs about 200 Council for the Accreditation and Related Educational Programs (CACREP) content area questions to help balloon up his deltoids and to peak his biceps up to the size of Mount Rushmore.

**Jeff:**  Ah, so you know this guy. And um, you've heard this tale of woe before.

**Author:**  Yes, of course, I've heard it—it's the Charles Atlas parable. But this is the counseling version where the bully wears his NCE/CACREP trunks. Look, let's get to the point since you're not my client and I'm not getting paid to listen to this saga. How many points did you flunk the licensure test by?

**Jeff:**  One.

**Author:**  You flunked the test by one point?

**Jeff:**  One measly point.

**Author:**  How much did you study?

**Jeff:**  Hey, come on now. You know I got my doctorate from a powerful program. And I know all that stuff.

**Author:**  Oh really. Who is the father of guidance?

**Jeff:**  Well um, it's Freud, I guess. Isn't it?

**Author:**  Sorry Charlie, I mean Jeff. Can you tell me the difference between a Type I and a Type II statistical error?

**Jeff:**  Say, I said I knew the material; I didn't say I was a statistical genius or anything.

**Author:**  Yeah, I agree you needn't be a statistical genius to pass the state licensure exam, but you need to know that an ANOVA isn't a constellation of stars. Explain the alloplastic–autoplastic dilemma in multicultural counseling.

**Jeff:**  Explain who?

**Author:**  Jeff look, I'm your friend, right? And you want me to be honest with you, right? Well, Jeff, you didn't study, and to be brutally frank with you—you didn't deserve to pass the licensing exam. In fact, it's hard to believe you scored as high as you did. Did you get some extra points for spelling your name correctly or something?

**Jeff:**     I really didn't think I had to study. I thought I knew the material.

**Author:**     Oh, you weren't alone. I heard that 39 out of the 88 people who took the test with you failed.

**Jeff:**     So let's cut the small talk. I'll take a copy of your *Encyclopedia*, your audio exam prep program, and, um, a couple of those gum balls—red, of course—hey you're not really going to use this dialogue in your new study guide book, are you?

Yes Jeff, I decided to use the dialogue. The salient point is that most people who wish to snare LPC/NCC credentials will need to study for the test. It's nice to have a degree from an Ivy League school but it's no guarantee you will pass the NCE. I decided to include this story because it is not atypical—Jeff is not the only examinee who hypothesized that he knew the material.

When I talk with counselors who have signed up to take the NCE, the CPCE, or, for that matter, any other exam, I can't help thinking about the age-old adage that asserts that a little knowledge is a dangerous thing. Sure you've heard of Pavlov and maybe you even remember that his name is associated with classical conditioning. But can you discern a conditioned stimulus from an unconditioned response? And yes, you know what a counseling experiment is but can you ferret out the DV from the IV? Of course, you'll need to recall what DV and IV stand for. I could go on but I think the point is obvious: A little bit of knowledge is a dangerous thing because it may give you false confidence, ergo you won't study, ergo you may not pass your exam.

## WHAT'S DIFFERENT ABOUT THIS MASTER REVIEW AND TUTORIAL?

The answer: a lot of things. For one thing, it will give you 1,100 questions with which to grapple. Unlike traditional study guides, however, many of the questions are "ringers" in the sense that they are purposely loaded with valuable information to help you successfully answer other questions on an exam. So, just as an example, I might say, "William Glasser is the father of the new reality therapy with choice theory. Who is the father of gestalt therapy?" Thus, the questions themselves impart key information. Often, this will be information that will help you answer future questions that are a tad more difficult. This means that the most effective method of using this study guide is to begin with question number 1 and work through all the questions in order without skipping any.

As you can see this is a lot different from many study guides. Many will begin with a practice test so you can assess your level of knowledge. This study guide remains a new breed. It decidedly does not include a practice pretest or posttest. Instead, each question is intended to teach you key points and hence is a learning experience.

As a bonus there is a wealth of repetition when explaining critical information. **Unlike many resources this text will often not limit itself to one description. Often five or six different definitions or explanations will be provided in regard to "must-know" concepts.** I'd rather have you accuse me of being redundant than miss a question due to a lack of understanding. If you use this book and/or my audio program and get sick of me telling you this or that, then you can safely assume that you really know the material.

Now here is a factor I cannot overstate. **To get the most out of this study guide you absolutely, positively must read the answers to each question.** Here again, this could differ from other study guides you have utilized. I intentionally expand on many of the answers so that the information could conceivably help you answer several actual questions on an actual exam. When it is appropriate (and not obvious) I shall explain why the other three choices are incorrect and go on to explicate their relevance (or lack of it!) to the question at hand.

## WHY THIS BOOK (DARE I SAY IT?) ACTUALLY MAKES EXAM PREP ENJOYABLE

I have gone out of my way to make the material interesting by adding a little levity and even outright humor when possible. I'll tell you a little secret I learned from having lectured to over 100,000 people on the topic of mental health—it's not what you say that grabs the audience, but rather the way you say it. In this book I have pulled out all the stops and used my vast lecturing experience to ensure that you won't be recommending this book to your clients as sleep therapy!

You have my word as a gentleman, a scholar, and a fellow counselor that I have done everything in my power to keep the answers lively and chock-full of relevant information (a mighty difficult task, indeed). So just in case you still aren't certain you understand, let me state forthrightly that you must read each and every answer if you want the maximum benefit from this study guide (yes, even when you answered the question correctly). I personally don't believe that counseling or counselor education needs to be dry, dull, or boring and the material herein reflects this position.

## HOW TO IMPROVE YOUR MEMORY IN ONE EVENING

Another unique factor in this study guide is the use of mnemonic or so-called memory devices. For some people, some of the time, memory devices can make a remarkable difference. In fact, I have discovered that, very often, memory devices are so powerful that an individual can literally be taught to remember something in seconds when he or she has struggled with it for years. Skeptical? Fine, then consider this example from my own life. For years, I couldn't remember whether the word that means letterhead was stationary or stationery. Imagine the embarrassment of being armed to the teeth with 12 years of post-high school education, four college degrees, and a full-fledged doctorate, and yet my memos to my secretaries invariably used the word *letterhead* for fear I would use "stationary." Incidentally, repeatedly looking the word up in the dictionary did not seem to help the situation. Then I discovered this highly effective, yet incredibly simple memory trick. The word is spelled with the suffix -*ery* when referring to a letterhead and -*ary* when describing a motionless or fixed state. The word *letter* (as in letterhead) has an *e* and so does the stationery when it is used to describe writing materials. Hence, when you want stationery to mean a letterhead you use the version spelled -*ery* since letter is spelled with an *e*.

The trick is simply used to associate the difficult-to-recall principle with something (or some things) that you can easily recall. At times these associations may be very serious ones, and at other times it may be easier to use those that seem foolish. The secret is to play around with associations to discover which ones work best for you.

Try this one on for size. Whose picture is on a 5-dollar bill? If you know, that's wonderful; you certainly don't need a mnemonic device. If you don't know, why not consider this: A Lincoln is a large car and will hold approximately five people. I doubt whether you will ever forget it again. Each time I pull a five-spot out of my pocket now I mentally see those five people seated comfortably in a Lincoln. A Lincoln would hold more than one person (imagine a 1-dollar bill), but it certainly would be mighty tough to squeeze 10 or 20 persons into the vehicle (imagine a 10- or 20-dollar bill).

Now let me zero in on an example from our own field. For a number of years now I've been mentioning Ivan Pavlov's famous classical conditioning experiment in the classes I teach. The problem is that come test time the material seems very complex. The students can't seem to remember whether the UCS is the bell or a light, the meat, the dog's nickname, or perhaps the name of the dog's second cousin. Maybe some unusually honest reader can remember struggling with UCS, CS, CR, and UCR questions in the past or, worse yet, is dreading the possibility that one could actually make its way into an oral or written board or, God forbid, the NCE or CPCE. Well relax, I've got a few tricks up my sleeve and judging by my college students, not to mention the glut of testimonials I receive, apparently they work.

You see, for the last several years when I covered this material in my class I included a memory device. I told the class to remember that in the U.S. we eat a lot of meat. In fact, I went a step further and said to the students three or four times: "Class, repeat after me. In the U.S. we eat a lot of meat. Again: In the U.S. we eat a lot of meat." Why? Because in Pavlov's landmark experiment the US, or UCS as it is sometimes written, is the meat.

Corny? You bet it is. Childish? Perhaps. But I must inform you that nobody—that means zip, zero, not a soul—has missed the UCS question since I've been teaching this memory association! This study guide, unlike any before it, includes a veritable treasure chest of memory goodies.

You'll discover two really neat things as you read my memory devices. The first is that even if you forget the memory device, you will usually remember the principle you wish to recall. You could forget that a Lincoln is a large car which holds approximately five people, yet you will in all probability remember that a 5-dollar bill sports a shot of Lincoln's mug. The second factor you might notice is that you feel that my memory suggestion is too stupid, too complex, too irrelevant, or, ironically, just too confusing to remember! Nevertheless, I'm willing to bet that very often any suggestion which is inappropriate for you will give you an idea for a memory device that does indeed make sense to you. Remember: A memory device only has to make sense to you; nobody else. Now let us take a passing look at some questions and answers.

## A PASSING LOOK AT QUESTIONS AND ANSWERS WITH SOME GOOD NEWS FOR PERFECTIONISTS

**Question:** I am certain you have answered this question a thousand times. Should I use the *Encyclopedia* or your audio program to prepare for my comprehensive exam?

**Answer:** Neither!

**Question:** I don't get it. What exactly do you mean?

**Answer:** First, let me commend you on your estimate that I have answered this question a thousand times, but truth be told your guess might be a tad on the low side. Think about it. If you are taking any comprehensive exam, it could be the most important career-focused exam you will ever take. In fact, experts in the field refer to exams like the CPCE and the NCE as high-stakes exams because such measures have a profound impact on your future. While a driver's license, another example of a high-stakes exam, can keep you from driving if you don't pass, the counseling exams can keep you from graduating or practicing counseling. I thus say flatly: Arm yourself to the teeth. Although both my *Encyclopedia of Counseling* and my *Vital Information and Review Questions for the NCE, CPCE, and State Counseling Exams* audio program can both be used as stellar stand-alone or independent study guides, they work best as a team. Now, if you take this Purple Book, combine it with my audio program, and add my popular work the *Human Services Dictionary*, with definitions purposely worded to help take the sting out of tough exam questions, you have a real powerhouse. Most stores and websites market all three as a package and give you a nice discount over the piecemeal price to boot. I can tell you that nearly 90% of the buyers who purchase their materials on my own website (www.howardrosenthal.com) do purchase the entire package.

**Question:** Why would I want your audio program? Isn't it just you reading the *Encyclopedia* into a microphone?

**Answer:** Absolutely not! I present the material in a completely different way with lively lectures on each of the core exam areas. Next, I treat you to several hundred tutorial audio questions/answers that are different than in the book.

**Question:** Frankly I couldn't care less about counselor licensing, certification, the NCE, or the CPCE. I'm a clinical psychology major taking an advanced graduate course in psychotherapeutic strategies. Can your questions and answers help me?

**Answer:** This may come as a shock to you, but I've discovered that Freud, Jung, Wolpe, Rogers, Glasser, and nearly anyone else's theory you could possibly name remains the same whether you learn it in the school of counseling, psychology, psychiatry, social work, or education. Onward!

**Question:** I am concerned about snaring my counselor's license. What can I expect when I finally meet the NCE face to face?

**Answer:** The NCE is composed of 200 questions. In order to answer each question you will be given four alternative responses or answer choices. Your task will be to pick the best possible answer stem.

**Question:** Is there ever more than one correct answer?

**Answer:** No. You will simply take a number two pencil and blacken the alternative of your choice (i.e., a, b, c, or d) on the answer sheet or on the computer screen—that's right I said the computer screen. In many places you can take the entire exam via computer and will receive immediate results regarding your score. The system is generally set up so you can mark questions you wish to skip and then come back to them at a later time. Often the computer version is administered in a setting which has nothing to do with counseling, for example, a tax office or accounting firm. If another individual is in the room he or she could be taking another licensing exam that is totally unrelated to our profession.

**Question:** I contacted my state licensing bureau and was told I would need to take the NCE at an AMP center. Just what exactly is an AMP center?

**Answer:** AMP literally stands for Applied Measurement Professionals, Inc. AMP is an assessment-chain network with nearly two hundred locations where you can take your exam. The exam is never administered on major holidays. And, oh yes, a word to the wise: Be on time. If you arrive more than 15 minutes late, you will not be able to take the exam. I would personally try to find the center a few days prior to the actual exam just to be sure you know where it is at. You can generally schedule an exam merely by going to www.goamp.com and clicking "candidates." If you need additional information on exam scheduling, you can contact Applied Measurement Professionals (AMP), 18000 W. 105th St., Olathe, KS 66061-4650 or call them at 913-895-4600. You could also fax them at 913-895-4650

**Question:** Is there a penalty for guessing?

**Answer:** No. If a sane person doesn't know the answer on the NCE (or for that matter on the CPCE) then he or she should guess.

**Question:** I can't wait another minute. What's the good news for perfectionists?

**Answer:** All right, as I said earlier, the NCE consists of 200 generic counseling questions. Forty of the items are being field-tested to ascertain their appropriateness for future use.

**Question:** Now wait a minute. Let me get this straight. Are you saying that I don't need a perfect score on the test to get a perfect score?

**Answer:** That's right! You will be scored on just 160 items. Again, 40 items are simply put there for field-testing.

**Question:** Hey that's cool! How will I know which items are being field-tested?

**Answer:** Simply put, you won't. You should therefore do your best on all the 160 items on the CPCE or 200 items on the NCE. The good news, nevertheless, is that as a perfectionist, you can keep in mind that you could conceivably miss 40 items on the NCE and still receive a perfect score. Counselors say to me: "I'm so upset. I bet I missed 40 or 50 questions on the exam" and I reply with something like, "that's terrific, it's possible you achieved one of the highest scores ever posted on the exam!" Well, are you breathing any easier yet?

**Questions:** My graduate advisor told me that in order to graduate with a master's degree in counseling my program requires that students take the CPCE from the Center for Credentialing & Education, Inc. (CCE). Does this exam contain any questions that are being field-tested?

**Answer:** You bet it does. The CPCE, or Counselor Preparation Comprehensive Examination, is a shorter test than the NCE, but retains the same a, b, c, d answer format. On the NCE you will answer 200 questions; 160 are graded. On the CPCE you answer 160 questions and 136 are graded. Unlike the NCE, the CPCE will have the same number of questions in each of the eight CACREP areas (i.e., 20 per section). Only 17 questions per area are scored. Three questions in each area are being field-tested or "pretested." So if you crunch the numbers you will discover that 24 questions on the CPCE are not actually being graded. Needless to say, just like the NCE, you won't know which questions fall into this category, so do your best on each question. To put it a different way, a perfect score on the CPCE would be 136.

**Question:** I keep hearing about the eight CACREP areas covered on the NCE and the CPCE. Can you tell me precisely what they are?

**Answer:** Sure, the NCE covers Human Growth and Development (12 items); Social and Cultural Diversity (11 items); Helping Relationships (36 items); Group Work (16 items); Career

Development (20 items); Assessment (20 items); Research and Program Evaluation (16 items); and Professional Orientation and Ethical Practice (29 items). The content areas on the CPCE are exactly the same; however, all of the eight areas would have 20 questions. Note: Additional research into the tasks performed by professional counselors could result in new areas or a different number of areas. Hence, professional counselors taking the NCE or the CPCE should *always* contact NBCC, their state licensing board, or their graduate advisor before sitting for either exam.

**Question:** Wait a minute, let's get back to the National Counselor Examination. I was reading another counseling book and it gave a completely different statistical breakdown of the test. What gives?

**Answer:** From 1989 to 1993 NBCC performed an occupational analysis or so-called work behavior study. In 1993, a published book version entitled *A Work Behavior Analysis of Professional Counselors* was released. Another study was conducted in the year 2000. Most recently, NBCC announced that a new analysis was conducted and it would begin impacting the NCE versions in October and December of 2012. The research revealed that counselors' tasks fall into five primary work behavior areas, or clusters. If we examine the questions from this standpoint (which is no doubt what was quoted in the counseling book of which you speak) then there are: 32 items pertaining to Fundamental Counseling Issues; 45 items regarding the Counseling Process; 25 items related to Diagnostic and Assessment Services; 38 items highlighting Professional Practice; and 20 items concerning Professional Development, Supervision and Consultation. Again, add 'em up and presto, you'll get a perfect score of 160 again. Thus each question on the exam addresses a content area as well as a work behavior area. These numbers can change with the administration of the NCE, hence I insist that you check with NBCC or your state licensing bureau prior to taking the examination. Work behavior areas do not apply if you are taking the CPCE.

**Question:** Now I'm really confused! How could a question on the NCE seemingly cover a content area and a work behavior area at the same time?

**Answer:** With great difficulty! No seriously. An exam question might ask about a consultant or supervisor who is working with a counselor conducting a psychoeducational group. Thus the content area is "group work" but the practice area covered would be "Professional Development Supervision and Consultation." **Personally, I wouldn't waste any precious energy trying to figure out the content/context practice areas when you are actually taking the exam. Just focus on answering the question correctly. My feeling is that if you know the material, it won't matter which category or domain is being showcased.**

**Question:** Let's say I take the NCE and flunk it. Won't I be taking the same test if I take the exam next time it is given?

**Answer:** Wishful thinking, but the answer is an unequivocal "no." A new form or version of the test will be given. NBCC will allow you to repeat the test three times in a two-year period. After that you will need to repeat the application process as if you had never taken the exam. And oh yes, do something about that attitude problem of yours!

**Question:** I want to be licensed as a clinical psychologist. Will I need to pass the National Counselor Examination?

**Answer:** No. In order to obtain a psychology licensure for independent practice in any state in the United States or any province in Canada, you will need to pass the Examination for Professional Practice in Psychology (EPPP). A lot of folks have used this text to help prepare for this exam and I think that is blow-away awesome. Nevertheless, this book does not cover all the topics tested on the EPPP, such as psychopharmacology, physiological psychology, abnormal psychology, or industrial/organizational psychology. Moreover, the EPPP focuses on the American Psychological Association (APA) ethics, and not those set forth by the American Counseling Association (ACA), and the National Board for Certified Counselors (NBCC). The bottom line is that although the *Encyclopedia of Counseling* might be a terrific help for those taking the EPPP, I would never recommend it as your primary study guide.

**Question:** I am a social worker, will the *Encyclopedia* help me get licensed?

**Answer:** I had to chuckle when I read your question. I was presenting at a mental health organization and two fellows came up to thank me for getting them licensed. Imagine my surprise when they guided me into their office to proudly show off their Licensed Clinical Social Work (LCSW) credentials! Here again, like psychology, since the areas of this book and the thrust of the questions and answers may not meet the needs of a social worker, I would advise you to never use it as your sole exam prep guide. I'd say the aforementioned guys lucked out big time. Now, that said, yes the *Encyclopedia* certainly could be used to supplement a program targeted toward a social work license. Social workers will need to contend with examinations established by the Association of Social Work Boards (ASWB).

**Question:** Will this book totally prepare me for NBCC's National Clinical Mental Health Counseling Examination (NCMHCE)?

**Answer:** The NCMHCE is a totally different animal. My answer would be the same as my responses to using this text for a psychology or social work tests. Supplement yes … complete exam prep guide … no.

**Question:** Any suggestions for securing the Human Services-Board Certified Practitioner (HS-BCP) credential?

**Answer:** Of course. I will put in a shameless plug for my *Encyclopedia of Human Services, Master Review and Tutorial for the Human Services-Board Certified Practitioner Examination (HS-BCPE)*. The text is more or less a clone of this book except it is targeted toward the discipline of human services. Readers call it the green book as opposed to The Purple Book.

**Question:** Any suggestions for an acute case of test anxiety?

**Answer:** Yes, read the questions and answers in this book and call me in the morning. Seriously, you can begin by studying the review questions and answers in this book. Exposure to a fearful stimulus often lessens its impact. Generally, the more you study and the more you know, the more confident you will become. Remember that confidence is the sworn enemy of test anxiety.

**Question:** What if I review all the questions in this book, listen to your audio program, and still suffer from test anxiety; then what?

**Answer:** Think about it for a moment. What would you suggest to a client? You would probably prescribe relaxation training, systematic desensitization, biofeedback, or perhaps hypnosis. As a counselor, why not try using relaxation techniques, self-systematic desensitization, or even self-hypnosis on yourself? And if all the aforementioned strategies fail, try seeing another counselor for help. Intervention in this area is generally extremely effective. As a professional counselor myself I can tell you that I've helped numerous individuals who were plagued with this difficulty. A counselor also can help you investigate other reasons for your difficulty such as a dire fear of failure, an aversion to success, or a high tendency to be self-critical. You can also secure a copy of my special test anxiety prevention audio program that is chock-full of hints to help you. The program includes a complete creative visualization/guided imagery specifically designed to starve the life out of your test terror. The test anxiety prevention audio material can be purchased by itself and is included when you purchase my complete audio study package. Again, the number to order is: 1-800-634-7064.

**Question:** Are there any other exam preparation materials you recommend?

**Answer:** I'm constantly combing the field for materials that will help you score higher on the exam. My current recommendations are always posted on my website (www.howardrosenthal.com). In addition to your graduate textbooks and sources cited by the CPCE or NBCC literature, I recommend the classic by Nicholas A. Vacc and Larry Loesch titled *Professional Orientation to Counseling*. I am also a fan of *Mastering the National Counselor Exam and the Counselor Preparation Comprehensive Exam* by former ACA president Bradley T. Erford, Danica G. Hays, and Stephanie Crockett. Textbooks written by Gerald Corey and Samuel Gladding are generally extremely helpful. Last, but certainly not least, I have also received wonderful reviews from counselors who supplement my materials with the prep guides and online programs created by Dr. Linton Hutchinson. His website is www.counselingexam.com.

**Question:** Just checking, do you have some sort of financial arrangement with the authors you just mentioned?

**Answer:** No, in fact these folks probably have no clue they are even mentioned in this book! I've just seen and heard good things about their materials.

**Question:** Say I answer four questions in a row with a "c." Should I shy away from answering the next question with "c" even if I firmly believe that "c" is the correct answer? In other words, how many a's, b's, c's, or d's in a row is too many?

**Answer:** A fine question, indeed. The answer is that one question on the real test, as well as my test herein, is not related to the next question. Thus, you should not waste one iota of your time worrying about how many a's, b's, c's, or d's you have marked.

**Question:** What if I am disabled or need special accommodations for the exam?

**Answer:** NBCC or AMP will attempt to make special provisions for your situation. However, you must make your request in writing at the time you send in your application to take the exam. In the case of the CPCE I suggest speaking with the folks at your educational institution.

**Question:** Just what constitutes a passing score on the NCE, and is it true that the exam is graded on a curve?

**Answer:** Truthfully, I hate to quote you a score because the exact figure I quote you could be incorrect and indeed the passing score varies. But, here are a few hints. NBCC does not grade on a curve. The test is graded using a modified Anghoff procedure that is based on the competency of the group taking the exam as well as the questions that are randomly picked for that particular version of the exam. The procedure uses a group of counseling professionals who make a judgment regarding the likelihood of a minimally qualified counselor answering each question correctly. Thus, a passing score will often vary from exam to exam. Over the years the so-called cutoff score or minimum raw score needed to pass has been as low as the mid-80s and as high as a hairline over 100. Here again, these are just ballpark figures. State licensing boards often use different cutoff scores, and thus you must call your state licensing board for further information. The minimum score is comparable no matter which version of the test you take, so theoretically it doesn't matter which version you receive or when you take the test.

**Question:** Do you mean that I could pass with a score of 97 but if I took the test at a different time that same score would not be high enough to pass?

**Answer:** Absolutely. What is passing on one version of the exam would not necessarily be passing when the test is administered again. Again, NBCC asserts that it is not easier to pass one version than another despite the fact that you could pass with a lower score. Eighty to eighty-five percent of the counselors who take the exam pass. Without getting too technical, a passing score is generally achieved by answering *approximately* 60–70% of the questions correctly. Translation: You'll need to correctly answer *approximately* 90–110 questions out of the 160 to pass the NCE. At this point in time, it is up to your institution to decide what constitutes a passing grade on the CPCE. Put this book down right now and call your advisor. On second thought, read the next question and then contact your advisor because CPCE takers will also want to know one more important fact.

**Question:** You only seem to be focused on a counselor's total score. A friend of mine who took the NCE said she received numerous scores.

**Answer:** Your friend is telling you the truth. The NCE yields 14 scores. You will receive one for each of the eight content areas, one for each of the five work practice or context areas, and finally one overall score. As of this date only the overall score on the NCE counts. Translation: You could do poorly on several areas of the exam and still pass the test. The CPCE could be a different story! Some graduate schools who use the CPCE as an exit exam require you to take another exam (possibly created by the educational institution) if you score below a certain level on a score on any of the CACREP areas. Say, for example, you scored very low on Human Growth and Development, then the school might require you to attend a seminar or repeat a course and then pass an exam created by your graduate school in this particular area. In addition, your institution might add extra exam components such as essay questions or questions from a specialty area such as addictions counseling. This is something that can obviously differ from one institution to another. I insist that you meet with your advisor before taking the CPCE or any exit exam.

**Question:** Is this study guide affiliated with the NBCC or the CCE in any manner?

**Answer:** No.

**Question:** I am scared to death of timed tests, and I've heard I will be taking a timed exam. Is there anything you can tell me to keep me from catastrophizing over this?

**Answer:** Well, a course of rational-emotive behavior therapy might be helpful, but let's start with something a little simpler first. On the NCE, for example, you will have four hours to complete the exam, or 1.2 minutes per question. Nearly everybody who takes the test finishes in less than four hours. In fact, NBCC insists that most folks finish in less than three hours. The CPCE, an achievement test, is also a four-hour instrument. Since it has fewer questions than the NCE (160 versus 200) you may be able to cruise at an even lower speed if you wish. In plain old statistical terms, you have 1.5 minutes per question, not counting the time it will take you to fill out a short demographic questionnaire included for CCE research purposes. My advice to you is **relax, read each question carefully, and take your time—time is not an issue to be overly concerned about when you are taking most comprehensive exams**. Most persons will discover that they have enough time to check over responses to make certain that a careless error has not been made. **Again, whether you are taking the NCE or the CPCE you have four hours to complete your exam. I have corresponded with literally thousands of counselors who have tackled**

**these exams and have rarely encountered anybody who did not have time to finish. Take your time!**

**Question:** Will I be allowed to smoke during the examination?

**Answer:** No. Perhaps this would be a good time to sell your stock in the tobacco companies and give up cancer sticks.

**Question:** After glancing at your study guide it seems that some of the questions actually have more than one correct answer. For example, I saw a question in which I felt that choices "a" and "b" were both appropriate responses. What gives?

**Answer:** This is what is known in the trade as a "best answer" question. Questions of this nature seem to be the calling card for folks who construct comprehensive exam questions. Although several answers may seem correct, your job is to ferret out the finest or the so-called best response. **On some versions of these exams you will have so many questions of this type that it might seem like virtually the entire exam is composed of best response or best plan of action questions. Expect to wrestle with lots of these and you probably won't be disappointed.** Moreover, I cannot stress too strongly that you should read each question very carefully. Words like "always," "never," and "most" can change the meaning of a question. Pay special attention to such words, which are used to qualify the precise nature of the question. Also be prepared to tackle "negative" or so-called "reverse type" questions. Questions of this ilk will emphasize that you mark the response which is the only one which is incorrect. For example: "All of the following are behavior therapy techniques except…" or "Transference is not…."

**Question:** I've heard that some questions on the NCE, the CPCE, and other major behavioral science exams are based on "analogy questions." Can you clarify this strategy?

**Answer:** Certainly. If you crack your trusty dictionary you will discover that the word *analogy* basically refers to the similarities between things which are otherwise different. An analogy can be used to explain something by comparing it to something different, yet similar. It's actually a lot simpler than you might think. Take this example: "Binet is to IQ as _____ is to REBT." Your answer choices are: a. Glasser, b. Rogers, c. Berne, and d. Ellis. The answer in this case would be "d." The logic here is that Binet is considered a pioneer in the formation of the IQ test. Ellis, on the other hand, is the pioneer of REBT. If it's still a tad foggy in your mind, don't lose any sleep over it. This guide is literally inundated with analogy-type questions so that you will not have any surprises whatsoever come test time.

**Question:** Do you absolutely, positively guarantee you'll cover every single possible question that I'll tangle with on the NCE, CPCE, or other major examinations? After all, you have a lot of questions in this text!

**Answer:** I absolutely, positively can guarantee you that **I will not cover every possible question that you will have to tangle with on the NCE or CPCE.** No ethical person or company marketing a book, audio program, or study guide would ever make such an outlandish promise. The idea here is to make you familiar with the major concepts and principles and theorists in the eight major content areas. I have no idea exactly what questions you will see on your exam. In fact, the chances of seeing a question on an exam which is identical (i.e., word for word) to my questions is highly unlikely. If you do take the exam and see a question identical to mine, then it's probably your lucky day. You'll no doubt pass the test, and I'd suggest you head out to buy a lottery ticket after completion of the exam! **The questions in this preparation guide can be thought of as triggering devices to help you review and expand your knowledge in a given area. They are not intended to be the questions you will see on the exam.**

**Question:** Okay, I can see why your questions would not be identical to those utilized on various versions of the NCE or CPCE. Is it safe to say that your questions are very similar to those I will encounter on quizzes, classroom tests, the NCE, or CPCE?

**Answer:** Well, yes and no. Please allow me to explain. In many cases, yes—my questions and answer choices will probably be strikingly similar to the types of questions you will find on your state licensing, graduate exit, or certification exam. In other cases this will *not* be the situation inasmuch as many of my questions and their respective answer choices are intended to convey pertinent information. Many, if not most of my questions, are intended to teach you key material that will help you take the sting out of some of the tough questions you could encounter on counseling examinations. Let me make it perfectly clear, however, that on the real test the questions are decidedly not worded to teach you key information. On the real exam, for example, you will not find a question such as: "The mean is the arithmetic average. Which statement best describes the mode?" In this book, nevertheless, questions like this are commonplace. Moreover, on many of the questions I have even picked the incorrect answers for the purpose of teaching you something. Again, the major purpose of this guide is to help you learn, and based on the tremendous amount of positive feedback I've received I'd say the paradigm is working!

**Question:** What would you say about an individual who answers all the questions in this book, but fails to read the answer explanation?

**Answer:** I guess I'd have to say the person had a self-defeating personality. I can in no way overemphasize that you absolutely must read each and every answer if you want to get the most out of this program of study. The answers clearly give vital, additional information that you will not learn merely by reading the question (yes, even if you answered the question correctly). Have I made myself clear?

**Question:** Do you absolutely, positively guarantee that you personally agree with every answer you share with readers in this book?

**Answer:** Just curious, what exactly is this hang-up you have about asking those "absolutely, positively guarantee" questions regarding the material in this book? In any event—and this will probably seem like the most bizarre statement I will make in this entire text—the answer to your question is no!

Before you have me involuntarily committed, please indulge me while I share an incredible story which will help clarify my position. A famous counselor was once told by the publishers of an IQ test that they were using several paragraphs from his book to construct questions for their test. Needless to say, he was flattered. He thus asked to see the material they had chosen and the questions. After he answered the questions he was shocked (perhaps horrified would be a better description) to discover that according to *their correct answers* he had missed three out of the five questions on his own material! Need I say more?

In a similar fashion I once disagreed with a couple of the answers to sample comprehensive exam questions distributed by a professional organization. I then enlisted the assistance of several experts in that particular subject area who also disagreed. Was I, along with my fellow cohorts, correct, while the individuals who drafted the questions for this particular exam wrong? Surprisingly enough, not necessarily: Imagine putting together the dream team of Carl R. Rogers, Albert Ellis, and Sigmund Freud and asking each of them the best way to treat a given client. I think you'll agree that you would come up with three diametrically opposed answers. Even the top experts in the world can disagree. An expert may even change his or her theory or an ethical code changes while a book is going to print.

In addition, experts can change their own position over the years. Remember when physicians told us to stop eating butter and start eating heart-healthy margarine? Today we're back to "eat butter, it's a lot healthier."

For many years dietary cholesterol was the ultimate villain. As of late, not so much.

Just the other day a woman contacted me and said, "I just love your materials but I really disagreed with the statement concerning blank, blank about such and such." Imagine her surprise when I responded with, "So do I."

Here is my point. I'd say that 99% of the time I agree with the answers I'm giving you in this book and the terminology I am using. Nevertheless, on a few rare occasions, I don't necessarily agree with the answer or perhaps the verbiage being espoused. However, since it represents what is being championed by the major textbooks, theorists, and publications in the field, it is most likely to be the correct answer on your exam. To quote a brochure disseminated via the CCE depicting the CPCE: "Each question was developed based on information found in the most commonly used textbooks." According to the CCE, all counselor education programs were surveyed and more than one hundred programs shared the references used in their courses. Next, master's level and doctoral-level professionals constructed the questions. Hence, on rare occasions, my own personal opinion is not only irrelevant, but would lower your score, which is the last thing you need.

**Question:** You really seem to push those so-called memory devices of yours. Isn't that, well, a bit gimmicky? I mean isn't rote memory fairly useless if you don't really comprehend the material?

**Answer:** Yes, finally we agree on something. I am totally against you using memory devices—or any learning strategy for that matter—if you do not use them to understand the principles. Even my two African gray parrots can listen to a phrase out of a graduate text in counseling and repeat it back from rote memory. (Well, perhaps I'm exaggerating just a bit, but at least they are trying.) On the other hand, you must be able to remember a principle to explain its usefulness in the field of counseling. Hence, I have provided the reader with a wealth of memory devices as well as a lot of repetition. In reference to your position that the memory techniques are gimmicky, I'd advise you to reserve judgment until you have personally given them a whirl. Remember that in everyday life, science is often described as what works! You must be able to recall a principle to understand it.

**Question:** Is it all right to skip questions or entire sections of this book?

**Answer:** I certainly would not advise it for counselors seeking professional credentials. You see, this book is designed so that the information you learn from any given question will help you answer later questions. The knowledge in this guide is cumulative. Thus, for best results, answer the questions in numerical sequence. If, however, you are merely using this test to brush up for a lesser exam or perhaps to study for a pop quiz, you might wish to concentrate on a relevant section or utilize the *user-friendly* index, which conveniently lists key topics and theorists *by question number*.

**Question:** After glancing at your questions I can honestly say that many of them seem incredibly simple while others look extremely difficult. Is this a typical response?

**Answer:** Congratulations, you're normal. That's precisely what most people studying for the exam would say. Now what's the *DSM* going to say about that?

**Question:** I'd like to pick your brain for a moment. After you decided on the critical material for a question, did you consult an authoritative source to help you construct the best possible questions and answers?

**Answer:** One source, one source, surely you jest? Numerous times during the preparation of this guide I couldn't walk across the room to my computer to continue keyboarding without tripping over a 2-foot pile of behavioral science literature. Luckily, my family hasn't thrown me out of the house—yet! Many times, I consulted 10–20 reference books and enough Internet sites to capsize a cruise ship before constructing a single question. My goal was to find a simple explanation you could understand. I used dictionaries, journals, references, study guides, newsletters, journal articles, consultations with experts, scholarly websites and textbooks from the fields of counseling, psychology, psychiatry, social work, human services, management, mathematics, statistics, education, and sociology, to name a few. I then became eclectic and used the best of every source, not to mention my own knowledge and creative teaching skills, to create a synthesis that would make the material easy to assimilate. And by all means, when you don't comprehend an answer or a principle, look it up in another source. A study guide is never intended to be your sole source of information.

**Question:** I also have your audio preparation program. What is the best way to combine the study materials? Do I read a chapter and then listen to the corresponding material in the audio program, or would it be best to read this entire book first, and then the listen to the audio program, or would the opposite work best?

**Answer:** I have heard from literally thousands of counselors nationwide now and can tell you that there is no single best method. Some use the audio program concurrently with this book, occasionally looking up a definition here and there in the *Human Services Dictionary*. Many of these counselors have racked up some seriously high scores. On the other side of the coin, I've heard from a high number of counselors that insist they studied just one program at a time and posted mind-blowing high scores. Let intuition be your guide. My only advice would be that the sooner you begin studying for the exam the better, and that short study sessions (say about 20 minutes) are generally superior to marathon study sessions that seem to go on ad infinitum.

**Question:** I consider myself an auditory learner and have gained a wealth of material by listening to your audio program. Can you give me a good reason to wade through your questions and answers in this book?

**Answer:** Certainly. No matter how strongly you protest to your state licensing board, NBCC, or graduate faculty that you are an auditory learner, you will still be tangling with the NCE or CPCE via pencil and paper or on a computer screen. This book gives you hundreds of chances to prepare for the task that awaits you. It also contains explanations and questions that are distinctly different from the audio program. Statistics from my own website indicate that nearly 90% of the counselors who buy my books use my audio program as well.

**Question:** Any advice for those of us who must experience an oral exam?

**Answer:** First, remember that one-word answers are a no-no. You must impress upon your board of examiners that you understand the material. I'd also be prepared to argue against a given theoretical position. If, for example, you are asked to explicate on the merits of behaviorism, I'd be prepared to find fault with behaviorism and point out the merits of an opposing view such as psychoanalysis. Some states may utilize a procedure which involves an oral exam (that often focuses on specific state ethics or state laws known as a jurisprudence exam) for persons seeking licensure. And, needless to say, if you are working on your doctorate you generally will need to pass your oral boards before you can write a dissertation.

**Question:** Do all states have counselor licensing?

**Answer:** As of this writing, all 50 states plus the District of Columbia, and Puerto Rico have credentialing legislation. Again, most states (currently 36) rely on the NBCC test (the NCE). Indiana, Massachusetts, New Hampshire, and Rhode Island use the NCMHCE. Still others (currently nine states) will give you your choice of the NCE or the NCMHCE. Thus, if you already have Certified Clinical Mental Health Counselor (CCMHC) status, contact your state licensing board. Three states (Ohio, Texas, and Virginia) have their own exams. My materials seem to work well for those exams as well.

**Question:** How many state-credentialed counselors are there in the United States, and do these counselors need continuing education units to retain their status?

**Answer:** In the United States there are over 120,000 licensed counselors. Your state may also have a continuing education requirement. Here, again, the requirement varies from state to state. Counselors with NCC status must complete 100 contact hours of continuing education every five years or take the NCE again to remain certified. Approximately 52,000 counselors currently have NBCC certification.

**Question:** I'm dreaming about opening a private practice where most of my clients will use some sort of insurance or managed care plan. If I secure my NCC will I still need a state counselor's license?

**Answer:** Sorry to inform you, but the NCC credential alone— although it is a valuable credential—will not cut the mustard. You need a state counselor's license. It is possible that there is an insurance company or a managed care firm somewhere that would accept the certification without the license, but I can tell you that in over 25 years I've never come across one. I'm not saying it's impossible, just extremely unlikely. If you are serious about making your private practice go on your own, you'll need to be state licensed.

**Question:** I've heard that all the questions on a given topic are grouped together. For example, all the group work questions would be in one section, while all the helping relationships questions would be in another. Is this information accurate?

**Answer:** When I wrote the first edition of the *Encyclopedia* that was true. However, on the new NCE the questions are *not* grouped together in sections. Hence, question number one could be on ethics, question two on career counseling, and question three on appraisal. Nevertheless, the questions and answers herein are presented in sections so the material will flow smoothly for learning purposes. If you know the material, it won't matter one iota where it appears on the exam.

**Question:** Speaking of the "helping relationships" section, I notice you supply the reader with an awesome 200 questions and answers rather than the generous number of 100 supplied for each of the other sections. Do you consider this the most important section?

**Answer:** No. This format did, however, allow me to provide you with a brief cook's tour of the major principles related to the most popular schools of counseling. Moreover, according to the most recent statistical breakdown of the NCE, there are 36 questions related to this area, making it the most emphasized content area on the exam. The second largest area, checking in at a hefty 29 items, is professional orientation and ethics, so don't gloss over it either.

**Question:** Please be honest with me Dr. Rosenthal. Couldn't I personally look up and secure all of the information in this book without purchasing and reading the text?

**Answer:** Absolutely, but it would most likely take you hundreds of hours, you'd need to consult hundreds of sources, and it could conceivably take you years. Read just one chapter and you'll see what I mean!

**Question:** I was flipping through this book and saw quite a few questions that said **test hint**. What's the story on these?

**Answer:** First, let me say that everybody who performs well on a comprehensive exam studies a ton (and yes, I do mean a ton) of stuff that won't be on the exam! Just what is that ton of stuff? Well nobody knows because it depends on the exam you are taking and then on which version of the test you happen to be blessed with on exam day. Just think of all the extra material you soak up as exam insurance. Okay, so here's the scoop. Although all of the material in this text is relevant, when I tell you that something is a **test hint** or a **key exam reminder** or something similar to that, then there is an excellent chance (though still not 100%) it will appear on your version of a comprehensive exam. Because these topics are so crucial, I'll do anything to get your attention. So I won't be too redundant, I won't use the terms *test hint* or *key exam* reminder every time. I'll shake things up and **bold face it**, underline it, *italicize it*, WRITE IT USING ALL CAPITAL LETTERS, shout it off a rooftop at you using a megaphone, whatever it takes to get your full attention. It would be your former English professor's worst style nightmare, but you're going to love it!

**Question:** I'm scared to death of math. Will I be required to perform calculations on the NCE or CPCE?

**Answer:** Yes, but the calculations will generally be very simple. It is not necessary to memorize inferential statistical formulas (e.g., to compute a $t$ test) for the exam. You'll also be provided with a few sheets of scratch paper to assist you or to write the letters SOS and fly it at half mast. Just kidding of course. **Counselors who score exceptionally high often use the scratch paper to draw a normal curve with typical scores such as percentiles, t-scores, z-scores, Stanines, and IQ scores before they begin answering exam questions. I have personally used this strategy in my own career. Practice drawing it at home several times using the bell-shaped curve shown in the Graphical Representations section of this very text.**

**Question:** What should I do the night before the big exam?

**Answer:** Take in a show, have a nice dinner, take a leisurely drive in the country, or anything else you enjoy. Get a good night's sleep, but whatever you decide to do, *don't cram*. Study for a reasonable period of time during each study session and always do it well in advance of the exam—and well in advance does not mean the night before the test! Most counselors will benefit from a *brief review* of all the major concepts a night or two prior to the exam. The super-review boot camp included in this text combined with the review in my audio program would be ideal.

**Question:** Your practice questions often present the reader with an answer choice that encompasses the answers presented by two choices (e.g., choice "d" includes "a" and "c"). Is this format used on the NCE or the CPCE at this time?

**Answer:** Again, nobody can tell you precisely what is on the exam; however, at this point in time it is safe to say that you might, notice I said might, indeed encounter a few answers of this genre on the exam. On other exam versions you will not find a single question of this ilk. But to reiterate: Never mark more than one answer choice or stem!

**Question:** Will the exam always include the theorist's first name. For example, would an answer stem say "Sigmund Freud" or just "Freud"?

**Answer:** To repeat, I don't have a crystal ball and thus cannot tell you precisely what is or is not on the exam. Sample questions created via NBCC and the CCE instrument guides indicate that some questions or answers might only include the last name of a well-known theorist or figure in the field (e.g., Freud). On the other hand, don't be surprised if you encounter an entire version of the test with no theorists' names. One question might say something like, "A behaviorist would most likely ... ." A second question could read, "A cognitive counselor leading a group usually ...."

**Question:** If I need additional information how do I contact the NBCC or the CCE?

**Answer:** First, remember that if you are taking a pencil and paper version of the exam it can take six to eight weeks after your exam to get your score, and the **NBCC does not provide you with information regarding your score over the telephone.** If you wish to contact them for other reasons try: National Board for Certified Counselors, 3 Terrace Way, Greensboro, NC 27403–3660, USA. Phone: (336) 547-0607. Their website is: www.nbcc.org. **Graduate students should never contact the CCE directly, instead please contact your graduate advisor or the individual responsible for administering the CPCE.**

**Question:** Any last words of wisdom?

**Answer:** Yes, if this book saves you one measly point on the exam and you pass, then it was worth my writing it and your time wading through the numerous questions and answers. I'll be certain to include MA, M.Ed and LPC, NCC (whatever applies) after your name the next time I write or e-mail you!

# 3

## Human Growth
## and Development

*How old would you be if you didn't know how old you were?*
—Satchel Paige, baseball legend

*It's never too late to have a happy childhood*
—Wayne W. Dyer, counselor and self-help advocate

1. Freud's stages are psychosexual while Erik Erikson's stages are

   a. psychometric.
   b. psychodiagnostic.
   c. psychopharmacological.
   d. psychosocial.

Let's begin with an easy one. Only one choice fits the bill here. The Freudian stages (oral, anal, phallic, latency, and genital) emphasize sexuality. Erik Erikson's eight stages (e.g., trust versus mistrust or integrity versus despair) focus on social relationships and thus are described as psychosocial. To mention the other answer choices is to dispose of them. Psychometric simply refers to mental testing or measurement. Psychodiagnostic pertains to the study of personality through interpretation of behavior or nonverbal cues. In counseling, per se, it also can mean that the counselor uses the aforementioned factors or tests to label the client (e.g., using the *DSM*, a book listing the symptoms and descriptions for mental disorders) in a diagnostic category. Psychopharmacology studies the effects that medications or drugs have on psychological functions.                    **(d)**

2.    In Freud's psychodynamic theory instincts are emphasized. Erik Erikson is an ego psychologist. Ego psychologists

   a.    emphasize id processes.
   b.    refute the concept of the superego.
   c.    believe in man's powers of reasoning to control behavior.
   d.    are sometimes known as radical behaviorists.

**Your first Rosenthal reminder: Psychodynamic theories focus on unconscious processes rather than cognitive factors when counseling clients.** To say that the id is the bad boy of Freudian theory is to put it mildly! The id is the seat of sex and aggression. It is not rational or logical, and it is void of time orientation. The id is chaotic and concerned only with the body, not with the outside world. Freud emphasized the importance of the id, while Erikson stressed ego functions. The ego is logical, rational, and utilizes the power of reasoning and control to keep impulses in check. Simply put, ego psychologists, unlike the strict Freudians, accent the ego and the power of control. The term *superego* in choice "b" refers to the moralistic and idealistic portion of the personality. The behaviorists, mentioned in choice "d," do not believe in concepts like the id, the ego, and the superego. In fact, radical behaviorists do not believe in mental constructs such as "the mind" nor do they believe in consciousness. The behaviorist generally feels that if it can't be measured then it doesn't exist.                    **(c)**

3.   The only psychoanalyst who created a developmental theory which encompasses the entire life span was

   a.   Erik Erikson.
   b.   Milton H. Erickson.
   c.   A. A. Brill.
   d.   Jean Piaget, who created the four stage theory.

In Freudian theory, the final stage (i.e., the genital stage) begins at age 12 and is said to continue throughout one's life span. **Many scholars do not feel that Freud's theory truly covers the entire life span.** They find it difficult to believe that a crisis at age 12 remains the central issue until senility sets in! Erik Erikson, also a psychoanalyst and a disciple of Freud's, created a theory with eight stages in which each stage represents a psychosocial crisis or a turning point. Since the final stage does not even begin until age 60, most personality theorists believe that his theory actually covers the entire life of an individual. As for the other choices, Brill is analytic and will be discussed in the section on career theory. Milton H. Erickson, not to be confused with Erik Erikson, has a "c" in his name and is generally associated with brief psychotherapy and innovative techniques in hypnosis. Jean Piaget is the leading name in cognitive development in children. His four-stage cognitive development theory is based on epigenesis or the notion that successfully completing a previous stage is necessary for the stages that transpire next.                                                **(a)**

4.   The statement "the ego is dependent on the id" would most likely reflect the work of

   a.   Erik Erikson.
   b.   Sigmund Freud, who created psychodynamic theory.
   c.   Jay Haley.
   d.   Arnold Lazarus, William Perry, and Robert Kegan.

In Freudian theory the id is also called the pleasure principle and houses the animalistic instincts. The ego, which is known as the reality principle, is pressured by the id to succumb to pleasure or gratification regardless of consequences. Erik Erikson, an ego psychologist, would not emphasize the role of the id, but rather the power of control or the ego. Jay Haley is known for his work in strategic and problem-solving therapy, often utilizing the technique of paradox. He claims to have acquired a wealth of information by studying the work of Milton H. Erickson, who is mentioned in the previous question. Arnold Lazarus is considered a pioneer in the behavior therapy movement, especially in regard to the use of systematic desensitization, a technique which helps clients cope with phobias. Today his name is associated with multimodal therapy. **Exam hint:** (Throughout this text I will be giving you a wealth of exam hints. In fact, this edition contains considerably more exam hints than any earlier edition. These hints will often espouse concepts that go beyond merely answering the question because I have this uncanny notion that the extra information can boost your exam score. On occasion, I will repeat myself (often using a different explanation) because the concept is a tad fuzzy to grasp or just to make certain it won't appear to be a foreign language if the material is presented in a unique manner on the exam. Okay, enough filibustering, time for the first hint). **Robert Perry is known for his ideas related to adult cognitive development; especially regarding college students.** For exam purposes I would commit to memory the fact that Perry stresses a concept known as **dualistic thinking** common to teens in which things are conceptualized as good or bad or right and wrong. Dualism has also been referred to as black and white thinking with virtually no ambiguity. Noted counseling author Ed Neukrug shares the fact that students in this stage assume that a professor has "the answer." As they enter adulthood and move into **relativistic thinking** the individual now has the ability to perceive that not everything is right or wrong, but an answer can exist relative to a specific situation. In essence there is more than one way to view the world. Finally, Robert Kegan is another well-known figure in the area of adult cognitive development. Kegan's model stresses interpersonal development. Kegan's theory is billed as a "constructive model of development, meaning that individuals construct reality throughout the life span."                    **(b)**

5.    Jean Piaget's idiographic approach created his theory with four stages. The correct order from stage 1 to stage 4 is

a.    formal operations, concrete operations, preoperations, sensorimotor.
b.    formal operations, preoperations, concrete operations, sensorimotor.
c.    sensorimotor, preoperations, concrete operations, formal operations.
d.    concrete operations, sensorimotor, preoperations, formal operations.

**Idiographic approaches to theories such as Freud and Piaget examine individuals (not groups of people) in depth. Idiographic theories can be contrasted with nomothetic approaches such as behaviorism or the *DSM* where large numbers of people are studied to create general principles that apply to the population. Onward! Piaget was adamant that the order of the stages remains the same for any culture, although the age of the individual could vary.** It is time for your first memory device. It would make sense that Piaget's first stage emphasizes the senses and the child's motoric skills, hence the name *sensorimotor stage*. I can remember the last stage by reminding myself that people seem to be more formal as they get older. The final stage is of course formal operations. As for the other two stages, the stage with "pre" (i.e., preoperations) must come before the remaining stage which is concrete operations. Do not automatically assume that my memory devices will be the best ones for you. Instead, experiment with different ideas. The memory strategies presented here are simply ones which my students and I have found helpful.                                                     **(c)**

6.    Some behavioral scientists have been critical of Swiss child psychologist Jean Piaget's developmental research inasmuch as

a.    he utilized the *t* test too frequently.
b.    he failed to check for Type I or alpha errors.
c.    he worked primarily with minority children.

d.   his findings were often derived from observing his own children.

Piaget was trained as a biologist and then worked with Alfred Binet in France. Binet created the first intelligence test. Piaget's research methods, though very innovative, could be classified as informal ones. He sometimes utilized games and interviews. Who were his subjects? Well, often they were Lucienne, Laurent, and Jaqueline: his own children. Some researchers have been critical of his methods. Answer choice "a" is incorrect, as a $t$ test is a parametric statistical test used in formal experiments to determine whether there is a significant difference between two groups. The "t" in $t$ test should be written with a lower-case $t$ and is technically utilized to ascertain if the means of the groups are significantly different from each other. When using the $t$ test the groups must be normally distributed. Some books will refer to the $t$ test as the Student's $t$. Choice "b" will be discussed in much greater detail in the section on research and evaluation. This choice is incorrect inasmuch as Piaget generally did not rely on statistical experiments that would be impacted by type 1 or alpha errors.                                                      **(d)**

7.   A tall skinny pitcher of water is emptied into a small squatty pitcher. A child indicates that she feels the small pitcher has less water. The child has not yet mastered

a.   symbolic schema.
b.   conservation.
c.   androgynous psychosocial issues.
d.   trust versus mistrust.

This is a must-know principle for any major test in counseling! In Piaget's theory the term *conservation* refers to the notion that a substance's weight, mass, and volume remain the same even if it changes shape. According to Piaget, the child masters conservation and the concept of reversibility during the concrete operations stage (ages 7–11 years). Now here is a super memory device. Both conservation and the ability to count mentally (i.e., without matching something up to something else physically) both occur in the concrete operational thought stage. Fortunately, conservation, counting, and concrete operations all start with a "c." How convenient! And you thought memorizing these principles was going to be difficult. The other answer choices are ridiculous, and that's putting it mildly. In Piaget's theory, symbolic schema is a cognitive structure that grows with life experience. A schema is merely a system which permits the child to test out things in the physical world. Choice "c," androgynous, is a term which implies that humans have characteristics of both sexes. (The Greek word *andros* means man while the Greek word for women is *gyne*.) And, of course, by now you know that trust versus mistrust is Erikson's first psychosocial stage.    **(b)**

8.    In Piagetian literature, conservation would most likely refer to

   a.    volume or mass.
   b.    defenses of the ego.
   c.    the sensorimotor intelligence stage.
   d.    a specific psychosexual stage of life.

If you missed this question go back to square one! The answer given for question 7 clearly explains this principle. Again, a child who has not mastered conservation does not think in a very flexible manner. A child, for example, is shown a pie cut into two pieces. Next, the same pie is cut into 10 pieces. If the child has not mastered conservation he or she will say that the pie that is now cut into 10 pieces is bigger than when it was cut into just two pieces. You can't fool a child who has mastered conservation, however. This child will know that the pie has not changed in volume and mass. In general, the statistical research of David Elkind supports Piaget's notions regarding conservation. Piaget and Elkind report that mass is the first and most easily understood concept. The mastery of weight is next, and finally the notion of volume can be comprehended. (A good memory device might be MV, such as in most valuable player. The "M," or mass, will come first and the "V," or volume, will be the final letter. The "W," or weight, can be squeezed in-between.)    **(a)**

9.    A child masters conservation in the Piagetian stage known as

    a.    formal operations—12 years and older.
    b.    concrete operations—ages 7–11 years.
    c.    preoperations—ages 2–7 years.
    d.    sensorimotor intelligence—birth to 2 years.

Remember your memory device: conservation begins with a "c" and so does concrete operations. The other three stages proposed by Jean Piaget do not begin with a "c."    **(b)**

10.    _____ expanded on Piaget's conceptualization of moral development.

    a.    Erik Erikson
    b.    Lev Vygotsky
    c.    Lawrence Kohlberg
    d.    John B. Watson

Choice "b" provides another key name. **Vygotsky disagreed with Piaget's notion that developmental stages take place naturally. Vygotsky insisted that the stages unfold due to educational intervention. Kohlberg (the correct answer) is perhaps the leading theorist in moral development. Kohlberg used stories to determine the level of moral development in children.** Kohlberg's, Erikson's, and Maslow's theories are said to be epigenetic in nature. *Epigenetic* is a biological term borrowed from embryology. This principle states that each stage emerges from the one before it. The process follows a given order and is systematic. **Recently, the definition has focused on the fact that environmental factors can influence genetic expression.** Watson, choice "d," is the father of American behaviorism and coined the term *behaviorism* in 1912.    **(c)**

11.  According to Jean Piaget, a child masters the concept of reversibility in the third stage, known as concrete operations or concrete operational thought. This notion suggests

    a.  that heavier objects are more difficult for a child to lift.
    b.  the child is ambidextrous.
    c.  the child is more cognizant of mass than weight.
    d.  one can undo an action, hence an object (say a glass of water) can return to its initial shape.

Choice "d" is the definition of reversibility. The word *ambidextrous*, in choice "b," refers to an individual's ability to use both hands equally well to perform tasks.    **(d)**

12.  During a thunderstorm, a 6-year-old child in Piaget's stage of preoperational thought (stage 2) says, "The rain is following me." This is an example of

    a.  egocentrism.
    b.  conservation.
    c.  centration.
    d.  abstract thought.

Expect to see a question on the test like this one and you can't go wrong. This is the typical or prototype question you will come across in order to ascertain whether you are familiar with the Piagetian concept of egocentrism. By egocentrism, Piaget was not really implying the child is self-centered. Instead, egocentrism conveys the fact that the child cannot view the world from the vantage point of someone else. Choice "d" mentions abstract thought, which does not occur until Piaget's final or fourth stage known as formal operations.    **(a)**

13.  Lawrence Kohlberg suggested

    a.  a single level of morality.
    b.  two levels of morality.
    c.  three levels of morality.
    d.  preoperational thought as the basis for all morality.

Kohlberg's theory has three levels of moral development: the preconventional, conventional, and postconventional (the latter is referred to in some texts as the personal integrity or morality of self-accepted principles level). Each level can be broken down further into two stages.  **(c)**

14.  The Heinz dilemma is to Kohlberg's theory as

    a.  a brick is to a house.
    b.  Freud is to Jung.
    c.  the Menninger Clinic is to biofeedback.
    d.  a typing test is to the level of typing skill mastered.

This is your first chance to wrestle with an analogy-type question. The **Heinz dilemma** is one method used by Lawrence Kohlberg to assess the level and stage of moral development in an individual. The story goes like this:

> A woman in Europe was dying of cancer. Only one drug (a form of radium) could save her. It was discovered by a local druggist. The druggist was charging $2,000, which was ten times his cost to make the drug. The woman's husband, Heinz, could not raise the money and even if he borrowed from his friends, he could only come up with approximately half the sum. He asked the druggist to reduce the price or let him pay the bill later since his wife was dying but the druggist said, "No." The husband was thus desperate and broke into the store to steal the drug. Should the husband have done that? Why?

The individual's reason for the decision (rather than the decision itself) allowed Kohlberg to evaluate the person's stage of moral development. In short, the reasoning utilized to solve a moral dilemma such as the Heinz dilemma could be used to assess moral development. Kohlberg's stages and levels are said to apply to all persons and not merely to those living in the U.S. Thus, it is evident that the Heinz dilemma is most like choice "d," a typing test. C. G. Jung, mentioned in choice "b," is the father of analytic psychology. Freud is the father of psychoanalysis. And lastly, the Menninger Psychiatric Clinic is a traditional psychoanalytic foothold as well as the site of landmark work in the area of biofeedback, which is a technique utilized to help individuals learn to control bodily processes more effectively using electronic devices. And, oh yes, before you go out and have a good cry, let me emphasize that the story of Heinz is fictional and simply used as a research tool. **(d)**

15. The term *identity crisis* comes from the work of

    a. counselors who stress RS involvement issues with clients.
    b. Erikson.
    c. Adler.
    d. Jung.

    Let's deal with choice "a" first, although it is incorrect. **RS in our field means religious and spiritual. Addressing RS issues in counseling has increased in the last several years. In fact, the number of counselors who consider themselves spiritual (though not necessarily religious) is also climbing. RS factors are often examined by counselors who are attempting to integrate the practice of "positive psychology" into their work. Positive psychology is hot right now and I suspect you could see a question about it on your exam. The term, coined by Abraham Maslow and popularized by learned helplessness syndrome pioneer Martin Seligman, refers to the study of human strengths such as joy, wisdom, altruism, the ability to love, happiness, and wisdom. Keep in mind that I use the correct as well as correct answers to teach you key material.** Now back to the correct answer for this question: Erik Erikson (b) felt that, in an attempt to find out who they really are, adolescents will experiment with various roles. Choice "c" refers to another name you should know, Alfred Adler, the founder of individual psychology, which stresses the inferiority complex. **(b)**

16. Kohlberg's three levels of morality are

    a. preconventional, conventional, postconventional.
    b. formal, preformal, self-accepted.

    c.    self-accepted, other directed, authority directed.

    d.    preconventional, formal, authority directed.

In the preconventional level the child responds to consequences. In this stage reward and punishment (i.e., selfish motives) greatly influence the behavior. In the conventional level the individual wants to meet the standards of the family, society, and even the nation. Kohlberg felt that many people never reach the final level of postconventional or self-accepted morality. A person who reaches this level is concerned with universal, ethical principles of justice, dignity, and equality of human rights. Kohlberg's research indicated that under 40% of his middle-class urban males had reached the postconventional level. Ghandi, Socrates, and Martin Luther King Jr. have been cited as examples of individuals who have reached this level, in which the common good of society is a key issue.    **(a)**

17.    Trust versus mistrust is

    a.    an Adlerian notion of morality.

    b.    Erikson's first stage of psychosocial development.

    c.    essentially equivalent to Piaget's concept of egocentrism.

    d.    the basis of morality according to Kohlberg.

Erik Erikson proposed eight stages in the formation of the ego identity and this is the first. This stage corresponds to Freud's initial oral-sensory stage (birth to approximately 1 year). Each of Erikson's stages is described using bipolar or opposing tendencies. Although Jean Piaget and Erikson are the most prominent stage theorists, you should also become familiar with the work of Harry Stack Sullivan, who postulated the stages of infancy, childhood, the juvenile era, preadolescence, early adolescence, and late adolescence. Sullivan's theory, known as the psychiatry of interpersonal relations, is similar to Erikson's theory in that biological determination is seen as less important than interpersonal issues and the sociocultural demands of society. Again, Sullivan focuses on social influences.    **(b)**

18. A person who has successfully mastered Erikson's first seven stages would be ready to enter Erikson's final or eighth stage,

    a. generativity versus stagnation.
    b. initiative versus guilt.
    c. identity crisis of the later years.
    d. integrity versus despair.

    Each stage is seen as a psychosocial crisis or a turning point. Erik Erikson did not imply that the person either totally succeeds or fails. Instead, he says that the individual leans toward a given alternative (e.g., integrity or despair). The final stage begins at about age 60. An individual who has successfully mastered all the stages feels a sense of integrity in the sense that his or her life has been worthwhile. **(d)**

19. In Kohlberg's first or preconventional level, the individual's moral behavior is guided by

    a. psychosexual urges.
    b. consequences.
    c. periodic fugue states.
    d. counterconditioning.

    In the consequences stage (called premoral), an M&M, treat, or removal of a favorite toy is more important than societal expectations and the law. In choice "c" the term *fugue state* refers to an individual who experiences memory loss (amnesia) and leaves home, often with the intention of changing his or her job and identity. What does this have to do with answering the question regarding Lawrence Kohlberg, you ask? Nothing, that's decidedly why it's the wrong answer! In choice "d" you are confronted with the word *counterconditioning*. This is a behavioristic technique in which the goal is to weaken or eliminate a learned response by pairing it with a stronger or desirable response. Systematic desensitization is a good example, but more on that later. **(b)**

20. Kohlberg's second level of morality is known as conventional morality. This level is characterized by

    a.   psychosexual urges.
    b.   a desire to live up to society's expectations.
    c.   a desire to conform.
    d.   b and c.

    At the conventional level the individual wishes to conform to the roles in society so that authority and social order can prevail. Kohlberg felt that attempts to upgrade the morals of our youth have failed and he has referred to some character-building education programs as "Mickey Mouse stuff!"          **(d)**

21. Kohlberg's highest level of morality is termed *postconventional morality*. Here the individual

    a.   must truly contend with psychosexual urges.
    b.   has the so-called "good boy/good girl" orientation.
    c.   has self-imposed morals and ethics.
    d.   a and b.

    Only one answer is correct here, folks. Postconventional morality is the highest level where the individual creates his or her own moral principles rather than those set by society or family. It has been called a *prior to society perspective*. Choice "a" reflects the Freudian theory, while choice "b" is stage 3 of Kohlberg's theory, which occurs at the conventional level. In the "good boy/good girl orientation" the person is concerned with approbation and the ability to please others in order to achieve recognition.   **(c)**

22. According to Lawrence Kohlberg, level 3, which is postconventional or self-accepted moral principles,

    a.   refers to the naive hedonism stage.
    b.   operates on the premise that rewards guide morals.
    c.   a and b.
    d.   is the highest level of morality. However, some people never reach this level.

Hedonism mentioned in choice "a" occurs in stage 2 of the preconventional level. Here the child says to himself, "If I'm nice others will be nice to me and I'll get what I want." Choice "b" actually refers to the first stage of the preconventional level, which is the punishment versus obedience orientation.    **(d)**

23.  The zone of proximal development

    a.  was pioneered by Lev Vygotsky.
    b.  was pioneered by Jean Piaget and Lawrence Kohlberg.
    c.  emphasized organ inferiority.
    d.  a, b, and c.

**The zone of proximal development describes the difference between a child's performance without a teacher versus that which he or she is capable of with an instructor, and was pioneered by Vygotsky.** In choice "c" the concept of organ inferiority is mentioned. This term is primarily associated with the work of Alfred Adler, who created individual psychology.    **(a)**

24.  Freud and Erikson

    a.  could be classified as behaviorists.
    b.  could be classified as maturationists.
    c.  agreed that developmental stages are psychosexual.
    d.  were prime movers in the dialectical behavior therapy or DBT movement.

In the behavioral sciences, the concept of the maturation hypothesis (also known as the maturation theory) suggests that behavior is guided exclusively via hereditary factors, but that certain behaviors will not manifest themselves until the necessary stimuli are present in the environment. In addition, the theory suggests that the individual's neural development must be at a certain level of maturity for the behavior to unfold. A counselor who believes in this concept strives to unleash inborn abilities, instincts, and drives. The client's childhood and the past are seen as important therapeutic topics. In reference to choice "d"

**DBT focuses heavily on mindfulness (being aware of your own state of mind and the environment) and was created by Marsha M. Linehan and is useful for clients harboring feelings of self-harm and suicide. It is also useful with substance abuse issues**.    **(b)**

25.    John Bowlby, the British psychiatrist, is most closely associated with

    a.    the work of psychologist and pediatrician, Arnold Gesell, a maturationist.
    b.    developmental stage theories.
    c.    bonding and attachment.
    d.    the unconscious mind.

**Arnold Gesell was a pioneer in terms of using a one-way mirror for observing children. Maturationists such as Gesell feel that development is primarily determined via genetics/heredity. Hence, a child must be ready before he or she can accept a certain level of education (e.g., kindergarten).** Bowlby's name starts with a "B," as does the word *bonding*. Aren't memory devices wonderful? John Bowlby saw bonding and attachment as having survival value, or what is often called adaptive significance. Bowlby insisted that in order to lead a normal social life the child must bond with an adult before the age of 3. If the bond is severed at an early age, it is known as "object loss," and this is said to be the breeding ground for abnormal behavior, or what is often called psychopathology. Margaret Mahler calls the child's absolute dependence on the female caretaker "symbiosis." Difficulties in the symbiotic relationship can result in adult psychosis. Mahler's theory is known as separation-individual theory of child development. **(c)**

26.    In which Eriksonian stage does the midlife crisis occur?

    a.    Generativity versus stagnation.
    b.    Integrity versus despair.
    c.    a and b.
    d.    Erikson's stages do not address midlife issues.

Most theorists believe that the midlife crisis occurs between ages 35 and 45 for men and about five years earlier for women, when the individual realizes his or her life is half over. Persons often need to face the fact that they have not achieved their goals or aspirations. Incidentally, the word *generativity* refers to the ability to be productive and happy by looking outside one's self and being concerned with other people. Some exams may refer to this stage as "generativity versus self-absorption." Daniel Levinson, who wrote *Seasons of a Man's Life* and *Seasons of a Woman's Life*, viewed the midlife crisis as somewhat positive, pointing out that individuals who do not face it may indeed stagnate or become stale during their fifties. In other words, avoiding or bypassing the crisis can lead to lack of vitality in later years.                                                                      **(a)**

27. The researcher who is well known for his work with maternal deprivation and isolation in rhesus monkeys is

   a.   Harry Harlow.
   b.   John Bowlby.
   c.   Lawrence Kohlberg.
   d.   all of the above.

Harlow's work is now well-known in the social sciences. Harlow believed that attachment was an innate tendency and not one which is learned. Monkeys placed in isolation developed autistic abnormal behavior. When these monkeys were placed in cages with normally reared monkeys some remission of the dysfunctional behavior was noted. Evidence that this is true in man comes from the work of René Spitz, who noted that children reared in impersonal institutions (and hence experienced maternal deprivation between the sixth and eighth months of life) cried more, experienced difficulty sleeping, and had more health-related difficulties. Spitz called this "anaclitic depression." These infants would ultimately experience great difficulty forming close relationships.                                          **(a)**

28. The statement: "Males are better than females when performing mathematical calculations" is

   a. false.
   b. true due to genetics.
   c. true only in middle-aged men.
   d. true according to research by Eleanor Maccoby and Carol Jacklin.

   Maccoby and Jacklin reviewed the literature and found very few differences that could be attributed to genetics and biological factors. The literature suggests that, where males outperformed females in mathematics, they did not do so until high school or perhaps college. Thus, the major impetus for sex-role differences may come from child-rearing patterns rather than bodily chemistry.  **(d)**

29. The Eriksonian stage that focuses heavily on sharing your life with another person is

   a. actually the major theme in all of Erikson's eight stages.
   b. generativity versus stagnation—ages 35–60 years.
   c. intimacy versus isolation—ages 23–34 years.
   d. a critical factor which Erikson fails to mention.

   If you didn't know the answer, did you guess? Yes, of course I'm being serious. Remember no penalty is assessed for guessing on the NCE/CPCE. An educated guess based on the fact that intimacy implies sharing one's life would have landed you a correct answer here. Counselors need to be aware that an individual who fails to do well in this stage may conclude that he or she can depend on no one but the self.  **(c)**

30. We often refer to individuals as conformists. Which of these individuals would most likely conform to his or her peers?

   a. A 19-year-old male college student.
   b. A 23-year-old male drummer in a rock band.

c.    A 57-year-old female stockbroker.
d.    A 13-year-old male middle school student.

Conformity seems to peak in the early teens.    **(d)**

31.    In Harry Harlow's experiments with baby monkeys

a.    a wire surrogate mother was favored by most young monkeys over a terry-cloth version.
b.    the baby monkey was more likely to cling to a terry-cloth surrogate mother than a wire surrogate mother.
c.    female monkeys had a tendency to drink large quantities of alcohol.
d.    male monkeys had a tendency to drink large quantities of alcohol.

Infant monkeys preferred the terry-cloth mothers to wire mothers even though the wire mothers were equipped to dispense milk. Harlow concluded that "contact comfort" is important in the development of the infant's attachment to his or her mother. A 165-day experiment revealed that the monkeys were spending an average of 1.5 hours per day with the wire mother and 16 hours with the terry-cloth mother. John Bowlby, mentioned previously, would say that in humans the parents act as a "releaser stimulus" to elicit relief from hunger and tension through holding.    **(b)**

32.    Freud postulated the psychosexual stages:

a.    id, ego, and superego.
b.    oral, anal, phallic, latency, and genital.
c.    eros, thanatos, regression, and superego.
d.    manifest, latent, oral, and phallic.

Choice "a" depicts Freud's structural theory of the mind as being composed of the id, the ego, and the superego. In choice "c" the word *eros* refers to the Freudian concept of the life instinct while *thanatos* refers to the self-destructive death instinct. Analysis is just brimming with verbiage borrowed from Greek mythology. The term *regression* is used to describe clients who return to an earlier stage of development. In choice "d" you should familiarize yourself with the terms *manifest* and *latent*, which in psychoanalysis refer to the nature of a dream. Manifest content describes the dream material as it is presented to the dreamer. Latent content (which is seen as far more important by the Freudians) refers to the hidden meaning of the dream.   **(b)**

33.  In adolescence

    a.   females commit suicide more than males.
    b.   suicide is a concern but statistically very rare.
    c.   the teens who talk about suicide are not serious.
    d.   males commit suicide more often than females, but females attempt suicide more often.

**Males commit suicide more often than females. This answer would apply not just to adolescence but to nearly all age brackets.** One theory is that males are more successful in killing themselves because they use firearms whereas females rely on less lethal methods. Choice "b" is false inasmuch as suicide is generally the tenth or eleventh leading cause of death in the U.S. as well as the second or third leading killer of teens each year. And as far as choice "c" is concerned, a counselor should always take it seriously when a client of any age threatens suicide. The truth is that the vast majority of those who have killed themselves have communicated the intent to do so in some manner. So take clients' suicide threats seriously. Have I made myself clear?                                                     **(d)**

34.  In the general U.S. population

    a.   the suicide rate is 2/100,000.
    b.   suicide occurs at the beginning of a depressive episode, but rarely after the depression lifts.
    c.   suicide rates tend to increase with age.
    d.   suicide occurs at the beginning of a depressive episode, but rarely after the depression lifts, and suicide rates tend to increase with age.

**Choice "b" is way off the mark. Suicidal clients often make attempts after the depression begins to lift!** Official statistics indicate about 41,000 suicides each year in the United States. Suicidologists (and yes there is such a word!) believe that the actual number may be closer to 75,000 due to complications in accurately coding the cases. Choice "a" reflects the approximate suicide rate in African American females, which checks in as the lowest of any racial gender. The overall suicide rate in the United States in any given year is about 12/100,000. Interestingly enough, personality measures such as the MMPI-2 and the Rorschach are not good predictors of suicide or for that matter of suicide attempts. In essence, test profiles of suicidal individuals generally are not distinguishable from those of persons who are not suicidal.                                                        **(c)**

35.  The fear of death

   a.   is greatest during middle age.
   b.   is an almost exclusively male phenomenon.
   c.   is the number one psychiatric problem in the geriatric years.
   d.   surprisingly enough occurs in the teen years.

In Erikson's stages the individual would accept the finality of life better during the final ego identity versus despair stage rather than in the middle-age years.                                             **(a)**

36.  In Freudian theory, attachment is a major factor

   a.   in the preconscious mind.
   b.   in the mind of the child in latency.
   c.   which evolves primarily during the oral age.
   d.   a and b.

Choice "c" would make sense from a logical standpoint, because the oral stage is the first Freudian psychosexual stage and occurs while the child is still an infant (i.e., the stage goes from birth to 1 year). As mentioned earlier, attachments in human as well as animal studies indicate that the bonding process takes place early in life.                                    **(c)**

37.  When comparing girls to boys, it could be noted that, in general

a.   girls grow up to smile more.
b.   girls are using more feeling words by age 2.
c.   girls are better able to read people without verbal cues at any age.
d.   all of the above.

Boys, on the other hand, are sometimes more physically active and aggressive.                                    **(d)**

38.  The Freudian developmental stage which "least" emphasizes sexuality is

a.   oral.
b.   anal.
c.   phallic.
d.   latency.

Here's an easy one. Remember how I mentioned in question 32 that the word *latent* refers to the hidden meaning of the dream? Well in the developmental stages the sexual drive seems hidden (or at least not very prominent) during latency. Sexual interests are replaced by social interests like sports, learning, and hobbies. Now this is very important: Latency is the only Freudian developmental stage which is not primarily psychosexual in nature. It occurs roughly between ages 6 and 12.         **(d)**

39.  In terms of parenting young children

a.   boys are punished more than girls.
b.   girls are punished more than boys.
c.   boys and girls are treated in a similar fashion.
d.   boys show more empathy toward others.

**Hint:** Before you sit for the NCE/CPCE or written or oral boards, take a moment to review the major theories and research related to child rearing. Stanley Coopersmith, for example, found that child-rearing methods seem to have a tremendous impact on self-esteem. A study he conducted indicated that, surprisingly enough, children with high self-esteem were punished just as often as kids with low self-esteem. The children with high self-esteem, however, were provided with a clear understanding of what was morally right and wrong. This was not usually the case in children with low self-esteem. The children with high self-esteem actually had more rules than the kids with low self-esteem. When the child with high self-esteem was punished the emphasis was on the behavior being bad and not the child. Parents of children with high self-esteem were more democratic in the sense that they would listen to the child's arguments and then explain the purpose of the rules. The Coopersmith study utilized middle-class boys, aged 10–12.    **(a)**

40.    When developmental theorists speak of nature or nurture they really mean

  a.    how much heredity or environment interact to influence development.
  b.    that the focus is skewed in favor of biological attributes.
  c.    a and b.
  d.    a theory proposed by B. F. Skinner's colleagues.

In this question the word *nature* refers to heredity and genetic makeup, while *nurture* refers to the environment. The age-old argument is whether heredity or environment has the greatest impact on the person's development. **This is the old nature versus nurture or heredity versus environment controversy.** Today theorists shy away from an extremist position and admit that both factors play a major role. Just for the record, choice "d" mentioned B. F. Skinner, who was the prime mover in the behavioristic psychology movement. Behaviorists, like Skinner, tend to emphasize the power of environment. **Today, clinical applications of Skinnerian principles (and those set forth**

**by other prominent behaviorists) are called ABA or applied behavior analysis.** **(a)**

41. Stage theorists assume

    a. qualitative changes between stages occur.
    b. differences surely exist but usually can't be measured.
    c. that humanistic psychology is the only model which truly supports the stage viewpoint.
    d. b and c.

Choice "b" is incorrect inasmuch as differences can often be measured. Just ask any behaviorist! Choice "c" makes no sense because analysts (who are not considered humanistic) such as Freud and Erikson have supported the stage theory viewpoint. **(a)**

42. Development

    a. begins at birth.
    b. begins during the first trimester of pregnancy.
    c. is a continuous process which begins at conception.
    d. a and c.

Developmental psychologists are fond of looking at prenatal influences (i.e., smoking or alcohol consumption) that affect the fetus before birth. **(c)**

43. Development is cephalocaudal, which means

    a. foot to head.
    b. head to foot.
    c. limbs receive the highest level of nourishment.
    d. b and c.

The head of the fetus develops earlier than the legs. Cephalocaudal simply refers to bodily proportions between the head and tail. **(b)**

44.  Heredity is the transmission of traits from parents to their offspring and

a.  assumes the normal person has 23 pairs of chromosomes.
b.  assumes that heredity characteristics are transmitted by chromosomes.
c.  assumes that genes composed of DNA hold a genetic code.
d.  all of the above.

Here is a vest-pocket definition of heredity (choices "a," "b," and "c"). You should also be familiar with the term *heritability*, which is the portion of a trait that can be explained via genetic factors.                                                          **(d)**

45.  Piaget's final stage is known as the formal operational stage. In this stage

a.  abstract thinking emerges.
b.  problems can be solved using deduction.
c.  a and b.
d.  the child has mastered abstract thinking but still feels helpless.

Again, unfortunately, Piaget felt a large number of individuals never really reach this stage; hence, the difficulty with subjects like algebra, physics, and geometry. Another characteristic of the formal operations stage is that the child can think in terms of multiple hypotheses. If you ask a child to answer a question such as, "Why did someone shoot the president?" a child who has mastered formal operations (approximately age 11 and beyond) will give several hypotheses while a child in the previous stages would most likely be satisfied with one explanation. For exam purposes, remember that abstract concepts of time (e.g., what was life like 500 years ago?) or distance (e.g., how far is 600 miles?) can only be comprehended via abstract thinking, which occurs in this stage. Answer "d" is incorrect inasmuch as Piaget felt that when the child eventually reached the final stage he or she would be ready for adulthood and would not experience child-like feelings of helplessness,                      **(c)**

46. Kohlberg lists _____ stages of moral development which fall into _____ levels.

    a. 6; 3
    b. 6; 6
    c. 3; 6
    d. 3; 3

    Here is a vest-pocket review of the stages and levels. **Preconventional** level with stage 1: punishment/obedience orientation and stage 2: naive hedonism (also called instrumental or egotistic) orientation. The entire first level is sometimes called the "premoral level." **Conventional** level with stage 3: good boy/good girl orientation and stage 4: authority, law, and order orientation. This entire level is often known as "morality of conventional rules and conformity." **Postconventional** level with stage 5: democratically accepted law or "social contract" and stage 6: principles of self-conscience and universal ethics. The last level is sometimes termed the "morality of self-accepted principles level."                                                    **(a)**

47. A person who lives by his or her individual conscience and universal ethical principles

    a. has, according to Kohlberg, reached the highest stage of moral development.
    b. is in the preconventional level.
    c. is in the postconventional level of self-accepted moral principles.
    d. a and c.

    Still confused? Review answer given in question 46.          **(d)**

48. Freud's Oedipus complex (or Oedipus stage)

    a. is the stage in which fantasies of sexual relations with the opposite-sex parent occur.
    b. occurs during the phallic stage.

c.   a and b.

d.   is a concept Freud ultimately eliminated from his theory.

The Oedipus complex or phase is the most controversial part of
Freud's theory and choices "a" and "b" roughly describe it. The
Oedipus complex—the boy's secret wish to marry his mother,
paired with rage toward his father—is said to occur between
ages 3 and 5. Looking for a good memory device? Well here it is.
The Oedipus complex occurs during the phallic stage and both
words conveniently contain the letter "p." Some tests may
actually refer to this stage as the phallic–oedipal stage. Freud
chose the name based on the Greek myth in which Oedipus, the
mythical king of Thebes, unknowingly killed his father and
married his mother.                                    **(c)**

49.   In girls the Oedipus complex may be referred to as

a.   systematic desensitization.
b.   covert desensitization.
c.   in vivo desensitization.
d.   the Electra complex.

In the Oedipus complex in boys and the Electra complex in girls
(grounded in the Greek myth of Electra), the female child
fantasizes about sexual relations with the parent of the opposite
sex. This creates tension since this is generally not possible.
Hence the child is said to have a fantasy in which he or she
wishes to kill the parent of the opposite sex. Freud went on to
hypothesize that eventually the child identifies with the parent
of the same sex. This leads to internalization of parental values,
and thus the conscience or superego is born. As for choices "a,"
"b," and "c," they are all behavioral terms and hence incorrect.
The term *covert* in choice "b" refers to any psychological process
which cannot be directly observed, while in choice "c" I introduce
you to "in vivo," which means the client is exposed to an actual
situation which might prove frightful or difficult. The word
*desensitization* refers to behavior therapy techniques that help
to ameliorate anxiety reactions.                       **(d)**

50.  The correct order of the Freudian psychosexual or libidinal stages is:

    a.  oral, anal, phallic, latency, and genital.
    b.  oral, anal, genital, phallic, and latency.
    c.  oral, phallic, latency, genital, and anal.
    d.  phallic, genital, latency, oral, and anal.

Freud is the father of psychoanalysis, which is the most comprehensive theory of personality and therapy ever devised. **Libidinal merely means related to libido which is the sexual impulse or desire.**                                    **(a)**

51.  Eleanor Gibson researched the matter of depth perception in children by utilizing

    a.  Piaget's concept of conservation.
    b.  Erikson's trust versus mistrust paradigm.
    c.  Piaget's formal operations.
    d.  an apparatus known as a visual cliff.

It seems no child development book is complete without a picture of an infant crawling toward an experimenter on a visual cliff. The visual cliff is a device which utilizes a glass sheet which simulates a drop-off. Interestingly enough, by the sixth month of life most infants will not attempt to cross the drop-off, thus indicating that depth perception in humans is inherent (i.e., an inborn or so-called innate trait). By approximately 8 months of age the child begins to show stranger anxiety, meaning that he or she can discriminate a familiar person from a person who is unknown. **(d)**

52.  Theorists who believe that development merely consists of quantitative changes are referred to as

    a.  organismic theorists.
    b.  statistical developmentalists.
    c.  empiricists.
    d.  all of the above.

Empiricism grew out of the philosophy of John Locke in the 1600s and is sometimes referred to as associationism. According to this theory, scientists can learn only from objective facts. The word *empiricism* comes from the Greek word meaning *experience*. This philosophy adheres to the principle that experience is the source for acquiring knowledge. Remember that empiricism is often said to be the forerunner of behaviorism and you could pick up a point on the test you'll be taking. Choice "a" mentions the organismic viewpoint, which is slanted toward qualitative rather than quantitative factors that can be measured empirically. Strictly speaking, organismic psychologists do not believe in a mind–body distinction. Since empiricists believe developmental changes can be measured and the organicists feel that change can be internal, the two views are sometimes said to be opposing viewpoints.                                                          **(c)**

53.  An empiricist view of development would be

   a.   psychometric.
   b.   behavioristic.
   c.   against the use of formal statistical testing.
   d.   a and c.

Here again, the empiricist view is behavioristic. Using a little logic you can see that answer "c" is false inasmuch as some behaviorists have literally gone on record as saying, "if you can't measure it then it doesn't exist!" In case I still haven't made myself clear, behavioristic empiricist researchers value statistical studies and emphasize the role of the environment. Organismic supporters feel the individual's actions are more important than the environment in terms of one's development.                              **(b)**

54.  In the famous experiment by Harry Harlow, frightened monkeys raised via cloth and wire mothers

   a.   showed marked borderline personality traits.
   b.   surprisingly enough became quite friendly.
   c.   demonstrated a distinct lack of emotion.
   d.   ran over and clung to the cloth and wire surrogate mothers.

When given the choice of two cloth-covered mothers—one that provided milk and one that did not—the infant monkeys chose the one that gave milk. In a later experiment, Harlow and a colleague discovered that a warm mother and a mother who rocked were superior to a cool mother or a mother who did not rock. **Ultimately, Harlow discovered that contact was even more important than milk and that monkeys preferred terry-cloth mothers over wire-frame mothers even when both dispensed milk.**                           **(d)**

55.    A theorist who views developmental changes as quantitative is said to be an empiricist. The antithesis of this position holds that developmental strides are qualitative. What is the name given to this position?

    a.    Behaviorism.
    b.    Organicism.
    c.    Statistical developmentalism.
    d.    all of the above.

The term *organismic* also has been used to describe gestalt psychologists, such as Kurt Goldstein, who emphasize a holistic model.                                                            **(b)**

56.    In Piaget's developmental theory, reflexes play the greatest role in the

    a.    sensorimotor stage.
    b.    formal operational stage.
    c.    preoperational stage.
    d.    acquisition of conservation.

It would make sense that the child would use reflexes in the first stage, which is termed *sensorimotor intelligence*. Piaget has said that the term *practical intelligence* captures the gist of this stage. Piaget emphasized the concept of "object permanence" here. A child who is beyond approximately 8 months of age will search for an object that is no longer in sight (e.g., hidden behind a parent's back or under a blanket). The child learns that objects have an existence even when the child is not interacting with them.                                                              **(a)**

57.  A mother hides a toy behind her back and a young child does not believe the toy exists anymore. The child has not mastered

   a.  object permanence.
   b.  reflexive response.
   c.  representational thought.
   d.  a and c.

The child who has not mastered object permanence is still a victim of "out of sight, out of mind." The child, needless to say, needs representational thought to master object permanence, which is also called object constancy. During this initial stage the child learns the concept of time (i.e., that one event takes place before or after another) and causality (e.g., that a hand can move an object).                                                              **(d)**

58.  The schema (i.e., a mental representation of the real world) of permanency and constancy of objects occurs in the

   a.  sensorimotor stage—birth to 2 years.
   b.  preoperational stage—ages 2–7 years.
   c.  concrete operational stage—ages 7–12 years.
   d.  formal operational stage—12 years and beyond.

It's the sensorimotor stage. If you missed this question take a break; you've probably been studying too long! After a little rest and relaxation, review questions 56 and 57. Incidentally, around the second month of age the child begins to smile in response to a face or a mask that resembles a face.                                                              **(a)**

59.  John Bowlby has asserted that

   a.  attachment is not instinctual.
   b.  attachment is best explained via the Skinnerian principle.
   c.  a and b.

d.    conduct disorders and other forms of psychopathology can result from inadequate attachment and bonding in early childhood.

Remember, Bowlby starts with a "b" and so does bonding. Bowlby, a British psychoanalyst, felt that mothers should be the primary caretakers, while the father's role is to support the mother emotionally rather than nurturing the child himself. Although this view was well accepted when it was proposed in the early 1950s, most counselors probably would not agree with it today.    **(d)**

60.    The Harlow experiments utilizing monkeys demonstrated that animals placed in isolation during the first few months of life

a.    still developed in a normal fashion.
b.    still related very well with animals reared normally.
c.    appeared to be autistic.
d.    were fixated in concrete operational thought patterns.

People with autism often have trouble communicating with others and forming close social bonds.    **(c)**

61.    According to the Freudians, if a child is severely traumatized, he or she may _____ a given psychosexual stage.

a.    skip
b.    become fixated at
c.    ignore
d.    a and c

Here is a must-know term for any major exam. In psychoanalytic theory the word *fixation* implies that the individual is unable to go from one developmental stage to the next. The person literally becomes stuck (or fixated) in a stage where he or she feels safe. Therefore, when life becomes too traumatic, emotional development can come to a screeching halt, although physical and cognitive processes may continue at a normal pace.    **(b)**

62.  An expert who has reviewed the literature on videos and violence
     would conclude that

     a.   watching violence tends to make children more aggressive.
     b.   watching violence tends to make children less aggressive.
     c.   reality TV shows or videos have no impact on a child's
          behavior.
     d.   what adults see as violent, children perceive as caring.

     Experiments have demonstrated that even nursery school age
     children display more violent behavior after observing violence.
     Other researchers emphasize that the more we see, hear, and
     read about violence, the less it bothers us; ergo, we behave in a
     more violent manner.                                          **(a)**

63.  A counselor who utilizes the term *instinctual* technically means

     a.   behavior results from unconscious aggression.
     b.   women will show the behavior to a higher degree than
          men.
     c.   a and b.
     d.   behavior that manifests itself in all normal members of a
          given species.

     Instincts (e.g., hunger) are species-specific innate behaviors that
     do not need to be practiced or learned. Instincts are not learned
     behavioral responses.                                         **(d)**

64.  The word *ethology*, which is often associated with the work of
     Konrad Lorenz, refers to

     a.   Piaget's famous case study methodology.
     b.   the study of animals' behavior in their natural environment.
     c.   studies on monkeys raised in Skinnerian air cribs.
     d.   all of the above.

     The study of ethology was developed by European zoologists who
     tried to explain behavior using Darwinian theory. Today, when
     counselors refer to ethology, it concerns field research utilizing

animals (e.g., birds or fish). The term *comparative psychology* refers to laboratory research using animals and attempts to generalize the findings to humans. Konrad Lorenz is best known for his work on the process of imprinting, an instinctual behavior in goslings and other animals in which the infant instinctively follows the first moving object it encounters, which is usually the mother. Lorenz used himself as the first moving object, and the newborn geese followed him around instead of following the real mother! This illustrates the principle of "critical periods," which states that certain behaviors must be learned at an early time in the animal's development. Otherwise, the behaviors will never be learned at all. Just for the record, choice "c" mentions Burrhus Frederic Skinner's air crib, which was a relatively bacteria-free, covered crib that Skinner relied on to help raise his daughter! Skinner is famous for his operant conditioning model. It will be examined in greater depth in future questions.    **(b)**

65.  A child who focuses exclusively on a clown's red nose but ignores the clown's other features would be illustrating the Piagetian concept of

    a.   egocentrism.
    b.   centration.
    c.   formal abstract reasoning.
    d.   deductive processes.

Centration occurs in the preoperational stage and is characterized by focusing on a key feature of a given object or situation while not noticing the rest of it. Egocentrism in choice "a" refers to the preoperational child's inability to see the world from anyone else's vantage point. Piaget and his colleague Barbel Inhelder showed children a model mountain from all sides. The children then sat in front of the model and were asked to pick a picture that best described what the experimenter was seeing. The experimenter was sitting in a different location. Children continually picked pictures of their own view. The abstract reasoning in choice "c" takes place in the final formal operational stage. Deductive thinking processes in choice "d" allow an individual to apply general reasoning to specific situations.    **(b)**

66.   Piaget felt

   a.   that homework depresses the elementary child's IQ.
   b.   strongly that the implementation of Glasser's concepts in *Schools Without Failure* should be made mandatory in all elementary settings.
   c.   that teachers should lecture a minimum of four hours daily.
   d.   that teachers should lecture less, as children in concrete operations learn best via their own actions and experimentation.

The only correct answer is "d" inasmuch as Piaget felt that before the final stage (i.e., formal operations, which begins at age 11 or 12) a child learns best from his or her own actions, not lectures, and his or her interactions and communications with peers rather than adults. Piaget, nevertheless, was quick to point out that he did not consider himself an educator but rather a genetic epistemologist. Epistemology is a branch of philosophy that attempts to examine how we know what we know. William Glasser in choice "b" is the Father of reality therapy with choice theory.                                              **(d)**

67.   Piaget's preoperational stage

   a.   is the final stage, which includes abstract reasoning.
   b.   includes mastering conservation.
   c.   includes the acquisition of a symbolic schema.
   d.   all of the above.

Symbolic mental processes allow language and symbolism in play to occur. A milk carton can easily become a spaceship or a pie plate can become the steering wheel of an automobile. The preoperational stage occurs from ages 2 to 7 years. If you erroneously felt any of the other choices were correct review all the previous questions related to Piagetian theory.        **(c)**

68.    Sigmund Freud and Erik Erikson agreed that

    a.    each developmental stage needed to be resolved before an individual could move on to the next stage.

    b.    developmental stages are primarily psychosexual.

    c.    developmental stages are primarily psychosocial.

    d.    a person can proceed to a higher stage even if a lower stage is unsolved.

Freud felt that the stages were psychosexual and his disciple Erikson felt that they were psychosocial, yet both agreed that individuals must resolve one stage before forging on to the next. Another well-known figure in developmental processes is **Robert J. Havinghurst, who proposed developmental tasks for infancy and early childhood** (e.g., learning to walk or eat solid foods); **tasks for middle childhood, ages 6–12 years** (e.g., learning to get along with peers or developing a conscience); **tasks of adolescence, ages 12–18 years** (e.g., preparing for marriage and an economic career); **tasks of early adulthood ages, 19–30 years** (e.g., selecting a mate and starting a family); **tasks of middle-age ages, 30–60 years** (e.g., assisting teenage children to become responsible adults and developing leisure-time activities); and **tasks of later maturity, age 60 and beyond** (e.g., dealing with the death of a spouse and adjusting to retirement). Another popular stage theorist is Jane Loevinger, who focused on **ego development** via seven stages and two transitions, the highest level being "integrated" (being similar to Maslow's self-actualized individual or Kohlberg's self-accepted universal principles stage).    **(a)**

69.    The tendency for adult females in the United States to wear high heels is best explained by

    a.    the principle of negative reinforcement.

    b.    sex-role socialization.

    c.    Lorenz's studies on imprinting.

    d.    ethological data.

In the past the belief was that the differences between men and women were the result of biological factors. However, most counselors today feel that the child "learns" gender identity and male/female roles. Sandra Bem has spoken out against gender stereotyping (e.g., a woman's place is in the home) and feels that when males and females are not guided by traditional sex roles individuals can be more androgynous and hence more productive. Choice "a," negative reinforcement, is a behavioristic term. Negative reinforcement occurs when the removal of a stimulus increases the probability that an antecedent behavior will occur. **Never forget: All reinforcers—positive and negative—increase the probability that a behavior will occur.** In positive reinforcement the addition of a stimulus strengthens or increases a behavior. If you still don't understand, relax, there's plenty more in the Helping Relationships section of this guide.    **(b)**

70. The sequence of object loss, which goes from protest to despair to detachment, best describes the work of

    a.   Freud.
    b.   Adler on birth order.
    c.   Erikson.
    d.   Bowlby.

    In psychoanalysis the term *object* describes the target of one's love. Bowlby felt that if the child was unable to bond with an adult by age 3 he or she would be incapable of having normal social relationships as an adult.    **(d)**

71. A counselor who is seeing a 15-year-old boy who is not doing well in public speaking class would need to keep in mind that

    a.   in general, boys possess better verbal skills than girls.
    b.   in general, girls possess better verbal skills than boys.
    c.   in general, boys have better visual–perceptual skills and are more active and aggressive than girls.
    d.   b and c.

The correct response is "d," since choices "b" and "c" are both evident according to the research of Eleanor Maccoby and Carol Jacklin. Although I previously stated that most sex-role differences are the result of learning, not biological factors, the tendency for boys to be more aggressive is probably one of the behavioral differences that can be attributed to biological attributes. Actually, this is a very tricky question indeed. Assuming you could separate fact from male/female fiction, you still might have marked choice "b" feeling that choice "c" was irrelevant in terms of counseling the client. My feeling is that "c" nevertheless is relevant since you might wish to emphasize positive qualities that the client possesses. Thus, if you marked choice "b," give yourself a grade of A-, or convince yourself that I'm just plain wrong. After all, that's what makes baseball games, political elections, oral and written boards, or even licensing and certification exams. Of course, since you're dealing with your perfectionism in a rational manner, it really won't matter now, will it?                                                      **(d)**

72. Two brothers begin screaming at each other during a family counseling session. The term that best describes the phenomenon is

    a.   the primal scene.
    b.   preconscious psychic processes.
    c.   sibling rivalry.
    d.   BASIC-ID.

In counseling, sibling rivalry refers to competition between siblings (i.e., a brother and a brother, a brother and a sister, or a sister and a sister). The "primal scene" noted in choice "a" is a psychoanalytic concept that suggests that a young child witnesses his parents having sexual intercourse or is seduced by a parent. The incident, whether real or imagined, is said to provide impetus for later neuroses. Choice "b" is also an analytic term and is known as the "foreconscious" in some textbooks. The preconscious mind is deeper than the conscious but not as deep as the unconscious. Preconscious material is not conscious but can be recalled without the use of special psychoanalytic techniques. This will be examined in more detail in the Helping Relationships section. The final choice, BASIC-ID, is an acronym posited by behaviorist Arnold Lazarus who feels his approach to counseling is multimodal, relying on a variety of therapeutic techniques. BASIC-ID stands for: Behavior, Affective Responses, Sensations, Imagery, Cognitions, Interpersonal Relationships, and Drugs.                                                    **(c)**

73.  A preschool child's concept of causality is said to be animistic. This means the child attributes human characteristics to inanimate objects. Thus, the child may fantasize that an automobile or a rock is talking to him. This concept is best related to

    a.  Jung's concepts of anima, animus.
    b.  Freud's wish fulfillment.
    c.  Piaget's preoperational period, ages 2–7 years.
    d.  ego identity.

Animism occurs when a child acts as if nonliving objects have lifelike abilities and tendencies. Choice "a" mentions two concepts of the Swiss psychiatrist C. G. Jung, the father of analytic psychology. The anima represents the female characteristics of the personality while the animus represents the male characteristics. (Two super memory devices are that men generally have muscles [ani"mus"] and ma means mother, who is female [ani"ma"].) Jung calls the anima and the animus "archetypes," which are inherited unconscious factors. Choice "b," wish fulfillment, is a Freudian notion that dreams and slips of the tongue are actually wish fulfillments. The term *ego identity*, used in choice "d," is most often associated with Erikson's fifth stage: identity versus role confusion. When an adolescent is able to integrate all of his or her previous roles into a single self-concept, the person has achieved ego identity. An inability to accomplish this task results in role confusion, which is known as an identity crisis.                                       **(c)**

74. Elementary school counseling and guidance services

    a. have been popular since the early 1900s.
    b. became popular during World War II.
    c. are a fairly new development which did not begin to gain momentum until the 1960s.
    d. none of the above.

Choice "a" would be true for secondary school counseling and guidance fueled by the work of Frank Parsons. Elementary school counseling services increased rapidly in the 1960s. Now let's turn our attention to elementary school counseling. **Three key reasons have been cited for the slow development of elementary school counseling. First, the majority of people believed that schoolteachers could double as counselors. Second, counseling was conceptualized as focusing on vocational issues. This would not be a primary issue in the elementary years. Finally, secondary schools utilized social workers and psychologists who would intervene if emotional problems were still an issue as the child got older.** In the 1980s some state departments of education made elementary school counselors mandatory and needless to say the number of jobs in this area flourished. Surprisingly, middle school/junior high counseling is an even more recent phenomenon than elementary school counseling. Except for the fact that these children (ages 10 to 14, also known as bubblegummers!) experience more anxiety than their elementary or high school counterparts, we know less about this population than any other in the K–12 system. There are over 260,000 school counselors in the United States.                                                **(c)**

75. Research related to elementary school counselors indicates that

    a. counselors of this ilk work hard, but just don't seem to have an impact on youngsters' lives.
    b. these counselors are effective, do make a difference in children's lives, and more counselors should be employed.
    c. counselors of this ilk could be helpful if they would engage in more consultation work.

d.    these counselors should be used primarily as disciplinarians, but this is not happening in most districts.

In reference to choice "c" elementary counselors do indeed perform a host of useful consultation services with teachers and other professionals. Elementary school counseling has been defined as the *only organized profession* to work with individuals from a purely preventive and developmental standpoint. Let's hear it for all those wonderful elementary school counselors out there!                                                                                    **(b)**

76.    According to the Yale research by Daniel J. Levinson

a.    Erikson's generativity versus stagnation stage simply doesn't exist.
b.    80% of the men in the study experienced moderate to severe midlife crises.
c.    an "age 30 crisis" occurs in men when they feel it will soon be too late to make later changes.
d.    b and c.

Levinson and his colleagues were surprised to discover that adult developmental transitions in white-collar and blue-collar men seemed to be relatively universal. Gail Sheehy has pointed out that both men and women tend to experience typical crises, or so-called "passages," and each passage can be utilized to reach one's potential.                                                                                    **(d)**

77.    Erikson's middle-age stage (ages 35–60) is known as generativity versus stagnation. Generativity refers to

a.    the ability to do creative work or raise a family.
b.    the opposite of stagnation.
c.    the productive ability to create a career, family, and leisure time.
d.    all of the above.

Choice "d" gives you a thumbnail sketch of Erikson's seventh (or second-to-last) stage. A person who does not master this stage well becomes self-centered; hence, you also will see the stage termed "generativity versus self-absorption." A nice memory device here is that "generativity" sounds like "generation" and a successful individual in this stage plans for the next generation. Robert J. Havinghurst, mentioned earlier, would refer to this stage as the middle adult years (he also mentions young adult and old adult periods). Havinghurst, who created a developmental tasks theory, feels that the middle adult should achieve civic responsibility, maintain a home, guide adolescents, develop leisure, adjust to bodily changes, learn to relate to a spouse, and adjust to aging parents. Good advice, but if it seems a little dated, it is; 1952 vintage. The 1950s were the golden years for developmental psychology.                                    **(d)**

78.  A person who can look back on his or her life with few regrets feels

    a.  the burden of senile psychosis.
    b.  ego-integrity in Erikson's integrity versus despair stage.
    c.  despair, which is the sense that he or she has wasted life's precious opportunities.
    d.  the burden of generalized anxiety disorder as described in the *Diagnostic and Statistical Manual of Mental Disorders* (*DSM*), published by the American Psychiatric Association (APA).

According to Erikson, successful resolution of the integrity versus despair stage results in the belief that one's life served a purpose. Choice "a" introduces the term *senile psychosis*, which is decidedly incorrect but a relevant term nevertheless. The word *psychosis* refers to a break from reality which can include hallucinations, delusions, and thought disorders. In senile psychosis this condition is brought on via old age. At times, the term will be used in a looser sense to imply a loss of memory. Choice "d" throws out two other "must-know" new terms. In counseling, anxiety (or *generalized anxiety*) refers to fear, dread, or apprehension without being able to pinpoint the exact reason for the feeling. Anxiety is in contrast to a phobia, in which the client can pinpoint the cause or source of fear (e.g., riding an elevator). The *DSM* is a manual used to classify and label mental disorders so that all mental health practitioners will mean roughly the same thing (i.e., regarding symptomatology, etc.) when they classify a client. The branch of medicine which concerns itself with the classification of disease is known as "nosology." Thus counselors use the *DSM* as their primary nosological guide. **(b)**

79. Sensorimotor is to Piaget as oral is to Freud, and as _____ is to Erikson.

    a. integrity versus despair
    b. Kohlberg
    c. trust versus mistrust
    d. play therapy

This is the analogy question mentioned earlier, and identifying the correct answer is actually quite simple. The question matches Piaget's name to his first stage (i.e., sensorimotor) and Freud's name to his first stage (i.e., oral). Thus you will match Erikson's name to his first stage, which is trust versus mistrust. **Play therapy (choice "d") and art therapy are often preferable to traditional counseling and therapy because cultural differences have less impact on these types of intervention.** **(c)**

80. Which theorist was most concerned with maternal deprivation?

    a. A. Lazarus.
    b. H. Harlow.
    c. J. Wolpe.
    d. A. Ellis.

Harry Harlow was born in 1905 and died in 1981. He is best known for his work with rhesus monkeys at the University of Wisconsin. He used surrogate mothers made from terry cloth and others made of wood and wire. Although the terry-cloth mother was preferred, those raised by surrogates were more timid and had difficulty mating. Choice "c" mentions Joseph Wolpe, who pioneered the technique of systematic desensitization, a behavioristic technique used in both individual and group settings to ameliorate phobic reactions. Albert Ellis (choice "d") was a New York clinical psychologist who developed a form of treatment known as rational-emotive behavior Therapy (REBT), which teaches clients to think in a more scientific and logical manner. Ellis was originally trained as an analyst and was a very prolific writer.    **(b)**

81.    When development comes to a halt, counselors say that the client

a.    has "learned helplessness" syndrome.
b.    suffers from a phobia.
c.    suffers from fixation.
d.    is displaying the risky shift phenomenon.

This is primarily an analytic concept. Sigmund Freud felt that frustration and anxiety are normal when passing through a developmental stage, but when they become too powerful emotional growth will literally stop and the person becomes stuck (fixated) in the current stage. Learned helplessness in choice "a" connotes a pattern in which a person is exposed to situations that he or she is truly powerless to change and then begins to believe he or she has no control over the environment. Such a person can become easily depressed. This concept is generally associated with the work of positive psychology pioneer Martin E. P. Seligman, who experimentally induced learned helplessness in dogs via giving them electric shocks while placed in a harness. These dogs—unlike untrained dogs—did not even try to escape the painful shocks when the harnesses were removed. Choice "b" is phobia, which is a known persistent fear, such as a fear of furry animals or flying in an airplane. **Key exam hint: In counseling, a phobia is often distinguished from anxiety. In an anxiety reaction, the client is unaware of the source of the fear.** The final choice, risky shift phenomenon, describes the fact that a group decision is typically more liberal than the average decision of an individual group member prior to participation in the group. Simply put, the individual's initial stance will generally be more conservative than the group's decision. **(c)**

82. Kohlberg proposed three levels of morality. Freud, on the other hand, felt morality developed from the

    a.   superego.
    b.   ego.
    c.   id.
    d.   eros.

    Eric Berne, the father of transactional analysis, put Freudian lingo in everyday language and spoke of the Parent ego state, which is roughly equivalent to the superego. The Parent ego state is filled with the shoulds, oughts, and musts which often guide our morality. **(a)**

83. Which theorist would be most likely to say that aggression is an inborn tendency?

    a.   Carl Rogers.
    b.   B. F. Skinner.
    c.   Frank Parsons, the father of guidance.
    d.   Konrad Lorenz.

    Bad news, folks; Konrad Lorenz compared us to the wolf or the baboon and claimed that we are naturally aggressive. According to Lorenz, aggressiveness is part of our evolution and was necessary for survival. The solution according to Lorenz is for us to utilize catharsis and get our anger out, using methods such as competitive sports. Choices "a" and "c" cite two of the most influential names in the history of counseling. Carl Ransom Rogers created nondirective counseling, later called client-centered counseling, and more recently, person-centered counseling. **Frank Parsons has been called the father of guidance.** In the early 1900s Parsons set up centers to help individuals in search of work. **(d)**

84. The statement "bad behavior is punished, good behavior is not" is most closely associated with

    a.    Kohlberg's premoral stage at the preconventional level.
    b.    Kohlberg's conventional level.
    c.    the work of Carl Jung.
    d.    Piaget's autonomous stage, which begins at about age 8.

    In the initial stage, morality is guided by a fear of punishment. Choice "d" is concerned with the Piagetian conceptualization of moral development. Piaget suggested two major stages: the heteronomous stage and the autonomous stage, which begins at approximately age 10. Heteronomous morality occurs between ages 4 and 7, when the child views rules as absolutes that result in punishment. Autonomous morality is characterized by the child's perception that rules are relative and can be altered or changed.                                                    **(a)**

85. A critical period

    a.    makes imprinting possible.
    b.    emphasizes manifest dream content.
    c.    signifies a special time when a behavior must be learned or the behavior won't be learned at all.
    d.    a and c.

    A critical period is a time when an organism is susceptible to a specific developmental process. A critical period marks the importance of heredity and environment on development. In humans, for example, language acquisition is thought to begin at around age 2 and ends at about age 14. For more on imprinting, see the next question.                                                         **(d)**

86. Imprinting—rapid learning during a critical period of development—is an instinct in which a newborn will follow a moving object. The primary work in this area was done by

    a.    Erik Erikson.
    b.    Milton H. Erickson.

c.    Konrad Lorenz.
d.    Harry Harlow.

Some behavioral scientists refer to instinctual behavior as "species-specific," meaning that the behavioral trait occurs in every member of the species. The behavior is unlearned and universal.    **(c)**

87.    Marital satisfaction

a.    is usually highest when a child is old enough to leave home.
b.    often decreases with parenthood and often improves after a child leaves home.
c.    correlates high with performance IQ.
d.    is highest among couples who have seven or more college-educated children.

Many studies agree that in general marital satisfaction is highest at the time of the wedding. Newer research tends to illuminate the fact that the oft-quoted statistic which suggests that 50% of all marriages end in divorce is inflated.    **(b)**

88.    Maslow, a humanistic psychologist, is famous for his "hierarchy of needs," which postulates

a.    lower-order physiological and safety needs and higher-order needs, such as self-actualization.
b.    that psychopathology rests within the id.
c.    that unconscious drives control self-actualization.
d.    that stimulus-response (S-R) psychology dictates behavioral attributes.

Answers "b," "c," and "d" are necessarily incorrect inasmuch as Abraham Maslow rejected both analytic psychology and behaviorism (though he adhered to its tenets early in his career); he felt they dehumanized men and women. Maslow's theory has been dubbed "humanistic psychology," or a "third force" psychology. Maslow felt the person first needs to satisfy immediate or basic needs such as food and water. Next, safety and security must be dealt with. Next, a need for love, affection, and belonging emerges. The highest level or ultimate goal is termed self-actualization, meaning the person becomes all he or she can be. A word to the wise: Some tests may refer to higher-order needs (i.e., any need which is not physiological) as "metaneeds." Maslow's writings helped spawn the human potential movement, popular during the 1960s and 1970s.    **(a)**

89.    To research the dilemma of self-actualization, Maslow

    a.    used goslings as did Konrad Lorenz.
    b.    psychoanalyzed over 400 neurotics.
    c.    worked exclusively with schizophrenics in residential settings.
    d.    interviewed the best people he could find who escaped "the psychology of the average."

You didn't mark choice "a," did you? Imagine trying to learn about self-actualization from studying baby goslings! No, Maslow didn't utilize goslings, nor did he turn to persons with severe psychological problems. Maslow said if you research the "psychopathology of the average" you will have a sick theory of human behavior! The answer: work with those who have transcended the so-called average or normal existence.    **(d)**

90.    Piaget is

    a.    a maturationist.
    b.    a behaviorist.
    c.    a structuralist who believes stage changes are qualitative.
    d.    cognitive-behavioral.

According to the structuralist viewpoint, each stage is a way of making sense out of the world. Choice "d," cognitive-behavioral, generally applies to counselors who emphasize thought processes in terms of their impact on emotions as well as behavioristic strategies (e.g., reinforcement or homework assignments).    **(c)**

91.    _____ factors cause Down syndrome, the most common type known as trisomy 21.

   a.    Environmental
   b.    Genetic (conditions passed through genes)
   c.    Chemical dependency
   d.    Unconscious

Persons with Down syndrome—also referred to as Down's syndrome—have a broad facial profile and short stature. Down syndrome, which is the result of a chromosomal abnormality (such as trisomy 21, three chromosomes on chromosome 21) results in an IQ hovering between 50 and 80 (100 is normal). The intelligence aspect can be influenced by early intervention, the environment, proper medical care, and dedicated educators. **Other genetic or hereditary conditions include**: **phenylketonuria (PKU)**, which is an amino acid metabolic difficulty that causes intellectual or physical disabilities unless the baby is placed on a special diet; **Klinefelter's syndrome**, in which a male has an extra X chromosome (i.e., XXY), is tall, has a high-pitched voice, an IQ approximately 10 points below the norm, shows no masculinity at puberty, and may be infertile; and **Turner's syndrome**, where a female has no gonads or sex hormones and is unable to have children. **Hemophilia** is a condition where blood coagulation is such that even a tiny injury could cause severe bleeding. Finally, **sickle cell anemia**, otherwise known as **sickle cell disease (SCD)**, afflicts primarily African Americans and causes anemia, pain, short stature, reduced life span, and organ damage.      **(b)**

92.    Piaget referred to the act of taking in new information as assimilation. This results in accommodation, which is a modification of the child's cognitive structures (schemas) to deal with the new information. In Piagetian nomenclature, the balance between assimilation and accommodation is called

   a.    counterbalancing.
   b.    equilibration.
   c.    balance theory.
   d.    ABA design.

Choice "a" refers to an experimental process in which a researcher varies the order of conditions to eliminate irrelevant variables such as fatigue or practice effects. Choice "c," balance theory, suggests that individuals avoid inconsistent or incompatible beliefs. In other words, people prefer consistent beliefs. This is sometimes known as the tendency to maintain "cognitive consistency." ABA design, noted in choice "d," is experimental and research lingo. The A stands for the baseline, which is the behavior before an experimental or treatment procedure is introduced. B is the treatment. After the treatment is implemented the occurrence of A (the behavior in question) is measured to see if a change is evident.                                    **(b)**

93.  There are behavioral, structural, and maturational theories of development. The maturational viewpoint utilizes the plant growth analogy, in which the mind is seen as being driven by instincts while the environment provides nourishment, thus placing limits on development. Counselors who are maturationists

    a.  conduct therapy in the here and now.
    b.  focus primarily on nonverbal behavior.
    c.  believe group work is most effective.
    d.  allow clients to work through early conflicts.

Counselors of this persuasion allow the client to work through the old painful material. Theoretically, the counselor acts almost like a perfect nonjudgmental parent. And thus the client can explore the situation in a safe, therapeutic relationship. Psychoanalysts and psychodynamic therapists fall into this category.                                    **(d)**

94.  Ritualistic behaviors, which are common to all members of a species, are known as

    a.  hysteria.
    b.  pica.
    c.  fixed-action patterns elicited by sign stimuli.
    d.  dysfunctional repetition.

Theoretically, a fixed-action pattern (abbreviated FAP) will result whenever a releaser in the environment is present. The preprogrammed action, or sequence of behavior, will not vary. In choice "a" the word *hysteria* is presented. Hysteria, a historical term today known as somatization disorder, is said to occur when an individual displays an organic symptom (e.g., blindness, paralysis, or deafness) yet no physiological causes are evident. Choice "b," pica, is a condition in which a person wishes to eat items that are not food (i.e., the item has no nutritional value) such as consuming a pencil or perhaps a watch band. Just in case you're wondering, fast-food consumption is not considered a sign of pica in our society—yet!                              **(c)**

95.  Robert Kegan speaks of a "holding environment" in counseling in which

   a.   the client is urged to relive a traumatic experience in an encounter group.
   b.   biofeedback training is highly recommended.
   c.   the client can make meaning in the face of a crisis and can find new direction.
   d.   the activity of meaning making is discouraged.

Choice "d" is necessarily incorrect inasmuch as Kegan encourages "meaning making." Kegan suggests six stages of life span development: incorporative, impulsive, imperial, interpersonal, institutional, and interindividual.                              **(c)**

96.  Most experts in the field of counseling agree that

   a.   no one theory completely explains developmental processes; thus, counselors ought to be familiar with all the major theories.
   b.   Eriksonian theory should be used by counselors practicing virtually any modality.
   c.   a counselor who incorporates Piaget's stages into his or her thinking would not necessarily need knowledge of rival therapeutic viewpoints.

d.   a realistic counselor needs to pick one developmental theory in the same manner that he or she picks a psychotherapeutic persuasion.

Since each theorist's work has a slant to it (e.g., Freud—psychosexual factors; Kohlberg—moral factors; Piaget—intellectual/cognitive factors, etc.) a well-rounded counselor will necessarily need a basic knowledge of all the popular theories. **(a)**

97.   Equilibration is

a.   a term which emphasizes the equality between the sexes.
b.   performed via the id according to the Freudians.
c.   a synonym for concrete operational thought.
d.   the balance between what one takes in (assimilation) and that which is changed (accommodation).

In case you haven't caught on, I'm banking on the fact that repetition can do wonders for your exam review. So one more time, just for the record: Equilibration (or equilibrium) occurs when the child achieves a balance. When new information is presented which the child's current cognitive structures, known as "schemas," cannot process, a condition referred to as "disequilibrium" sets in. The child therefore changes the schemas to accommodate the novel information, and equilibration or equilibrium is mastered.   **(d)**

98.   A counselor is working with a family who just lost everything in a fire. The counselor will ideally focus on

a.   Maslow's higher-order needs, such as self-actualization.
b.   building accurate empathy of family members.
c.   Maslow's lower-order needs, such as physiological and safety needs.
d.   the identified patient.

Maslow, a pioneer in third force or humanistic psychology, suggested the following hierarchy of needs: survival, security, safety, love, self-esteem, and self-actualization. The assumption is that lower-order needs must be fulfilled before the individual can be concerned with higher-order needs.                     **(c)**

99.  The anal retentive personality is

    a.   charitable.
    b.   stingy.
    c.   kind.
    d.   thinks very little about money matters.

To put it bluntly, the anal retentive character is said to be cheap!                                                  **(b)**

100.  From a Freudian perspective, a client who has a problem with alcoholism and excessive smoking would be

    a.   considered an oral character.
    b.   considered an anal character.
    c.   considered a genital character.
    d.   fixated at the latency stage.

Here is where good old common sense comes in handy. The oral region of the body (i.e., the mouth) would be the portion of the body most closely related to smoking and alcoholism.        **(a)**

# 4

## Social and Cultural Diversity

*Society is the sworn enemy of mental health.*

—Andrew Salter, father of
conditioned reflex therapy

**Something to keep in mind: This exam topic sports the fewest questions if you are taking the NCE and constitutes the most difficult section for those taking the CPCE. Your experience, or as it has become popular to say on web user groups—your mileage—may vary!**

101. America has been called the most diverse country on the face of our planet. Counseling a client from a different social and/or cultural background is known as

    a.  cross-cultural counseling.
    b.  multicultural counseling.
    c.  intercultural counseling.
    d.  all of the above.

Although "b" is the term we hear most often, choices "a," "b," and "c" are roughly synonymous and hence mean approximately the same thing when you encounter them in the literature. **Some research indicates that clients from minorities have been misdiagnosed, misunderstood, and found counseling less helpful than those from the majority culture. Clients from minority cultures tend to seek out counseling less and drop out sooner. Nevertheless, a culturally competent counselor can be successful regardless of the client's background. Thus, this is an important area of study.** The ACA division that deals explicitly with this topic is the Association for Multicultural Counseling and Development (AMCD). The division is intended to raise cultural, racial, and ethnic understanding and empathy. Multicultural counseling—which emphasizes respect for differences—has been dubbed as the "fourth force of counseling theory." **Key exam hint: The term *multicultural* implies that we champion the idea of celebrating diversity and this can be age, sexual orientation, religion, social class, country of origin, race, and even health status. Some exams use the term *cultural pluralism* to suggest that a minority cultural group will keep their own unique cultural values, yet they still participate in the wider or dominant culture.**          **(d)**

102. Culture refers to

    a.   customs shared by a group which distinguish it from other groups.
    b.   values shared by a group that are learned from others in the group.
    c.   attitudes, beliefs, art, and language which characterize members of a group often passed from generation to generation.
    d.   all of the above.

The sum of choices "a," "b," and "c" add up to a wonderful little definition of culture. A person's culture can really be delineated by those customs which set him or her apart from another culture. Immigrants or persons who must live in a culture which is different from their native culture often experience "culture conflict." By definition culture conflict manifests itself whenever a person experiences conflicting thoughts, feelings, or behaviors due to divided cultural loyalties (i.e., loyalty to two or more cultures). Culture conflict also can describe the difficulties which arise when persons of different cultures live in the same geographical area. How will you know which definition of cultural conflict applies to a test question? Well, the only good answer is that you must read every question very carefully in order to ferret out the context of the question. **Hint**: The term *macroculture* or *majority culture* on comprehensive exams refers to the dominant culture or the culture that is accepted by the majority of citizens in a given society. When an exam uses the term *privilege*, it is referring to the fact that some individuals have an unearned advantage, giving that person dominance, access to resources, and therefore power. Ideally, this power should be shared with others who don't have it (i.e., to empower others) rather than discriminating against those who do not.                                                                **(d)**

103. Our culture is more diverse than in the past. Multicultural counselors often work with persons who are culturally different. This means the client

    a.    is culturally biased.
    b.    suffers from the diagnosis of cultural relativity.
    c.    belongs to a different culture from the helper.
    d.    presents problems which deal only with culturally charged issues.

Here is a very important distinction. Multicultural counselors work with the entire range of human difficulties just like other counselors. Yes, multicultural counselors do indeed deal frequently with cultural issues and therefore choices "a" and "b" could be true, but they are decidedly not the best answers. Choice "d" is easy enough to eliminate if you read it carefully and noted the word *only*. Let's zero in for a moment on the term noted in choice "b," *cultural relativity*, also described as *cultural relativism* on some exams. Cultural relativity connotes that a behavior cannot be assessed as good or bad except within the context of a given culture. The behavior must be evaluated relative to the culture. In the United States, for example, teen pregnancy prior to marriage is sometimes considered a negative behavior and viewed as a difficulty. In other parts of the world premarital pregnancy may be seen as something which is positive because it establishes the woman's fertility. Such a woman may even be described as more "marriageable." **The multicultural counselor must assess the client's behavior based on the client's own culture—not merely based on the counselor's culture. The meaning or desirability of a given behavior, trait, or act is based on the culture.** It is said that effective counselors must transcend the "culture-bound values" barrier in which the counselor is "bound" to his or her own values and tries to impose them on clients.    **(c)**

104.  In order to diagnose clients from a different culture

   a.   the counselor ideally will need some information regarding the specifics of the culture.
   b.   the counselor will find the *DSM* useless.
   c.   the counselor should rely heavily on cultural epoch theory.
   d.   NBCC ethics prohibit the use of *DSM* diagnosis.

Some of the literature in this area distinguishes "material culture" (e.g., books, paintings, homes, and tools) from what is termed "nonmaterial culture" (e.g., customs, values, humor, social ideas, or traditions). Some exams will refer to material culture items as "artifacts." In any case, the current trend in counseling suggests that the counselor must understand cultural factors. This trend is known as "cultural awareness" and it is contrasted by a position of "cultural tunnel vision." A good cross-cultural counselor will not impose his or her values on a client from a different cultural perspective. Another term you may see on an exam is *culture epoch theory*, which suggests that all cultures—like children— pass through the same stages of development in terms of evolving and maturing. Recently, multicultural experts have come to believe this is not a valid notion. (I guess that eliminates choice "c" as the best answer!) In regard to choice "d," ethics stipulate that counselors must incorporate "culturally relevant techniques into their practice" and should acquire "cultural sensitivity" to client populations served. The appropriateness of a given *DSM* diagnosis is not specifically addressed. Nevertheless, experts seem to agree on the fact that the *DSM* is most applicable to those of European descent.    **(a)**

105. In the United States, each socioeconomic group represents

     a.   a separate race.
     b.   a separate culture.
     c.   the concept of color blindness.
     d.   a separate national culture.

Choice "a," race, refers to the identification of individuals via distinct physical or bodily (somatic) characteristics such as skin color or facial features. The assumption is thus made that a given **race is based on genetic origin**. Many racial groups can be distinguished from others by virtue of biological attributes such as their looks. Social scientists have questioned whether race is indeed a valid concept since it is sometimes questionable as to what constitutes a given race. Choice "c," color blindness, is said to take place when you ignore the person's race, culture or color. Keep in mind that is is not . . . I repeat . . . not necessarily a good thing in the counseling process and is often viewed as the direct opposite of good multicultural helping. Choice "d," *national culture*, is a term used to describe the cultural patterns common to a given country. Nevertheless, keep in mind that in reality there is the "ideal culture," which is the way individuals are supposed to behave, as well as the "real culture," which encompasses all behaviors within the culture, even those which are illicit or frowned upon. When a group of persons vehemently opposes the values of the culture, they are said to be members of a "counterculture."    **(b)**

106. Which therapist was not instrumental in the early years of the social psychology movement?

     a.   Freud.
     b.   Durkheim.

c. McDougall.
d. Berne.

What's a social psych question doing in a chapter on social and cultural foundations? Well, hold your horses, I'll get to that soon enough. Eric Berne, the father of transactional analysis (choice "d"), is the only answer which makes sense here. Here's why. Sigmund Freud (choice "a") is known for his influential 1921 book, *Group Psychology and the Analysis of the Ego*, which suggested that the group was held together by a bond between the leader and the group members that was seen as somewhat analogous to a hypnotist and his or her subject. This is a bit far-fetched according to some, but clearly indicative of Freud's fascination with the power of hypnosis. The Frenchman Emile Durkheim (choice "b") is considered one of the founders of modern sociology. His principles were first outlined in his 1895 work, *Rules of Sociological Method*. He is also well-known for his research into suicide, which culminated in another literary work, *Suicide*, two years later. Durkheim is said to have taken group phenomena beyond the armchair-speculation stage into formal research. William McDougall (choice "c") is the father of "hormic psychology," a Darwinian viewpoint which suggested that individuals in or out of groups are driven by innate, inherited tendencies. Although this approach began to lose ground after the behaviorist movement picked up steam, McDougall is well-remembered for his 1908 landmark work, *Introduction to Social Psychology*. He also believed in the concept of eugenics or the notion that genetics (e.g., selective breeding of those with high intelligence) would improve the gene pool and the human condition. Unfortunately, this position has often been viewed in a negative light and has been dubbed as "scientific rascism." **(d)**

107. _____ and _____ would say that regardless of culture, humans have an instinct to fight.

a. Maslow; Rogers
b. Ellis; Harper
c. Freud; Lorenz
d. Glasser; Rogers

Freud believed that man was basically driven by the instincts of sex and aggression. Lorenz—partially basing his theory on the fact that certain tropical fish will attack an alternate target even when the actual target of aggression is removed—is another believer in the so-called "innate aggression theory." I find this logic a tad fishy when applied to the genus *Homo sapiens*. P.S. McDougall, mentioned in the previous question, could also join the ranks of Freud and Lorenz as an "instinct theorist."     **(c)**

108. _____ believe that aggression is learned. Thus, a child who witnesses aggressive behavior in adults may imitate the aggressive behavior.

   a.   Instinct theorists
   b.   Innate aggression theorists
   c.   Social learning theorists
   d.   Followers of Erik Erikson

If you marked choices "a" or "b" then it's crystal clear that you are not reading the answers carefully enough. Review the last question. The social learning theory contradicts the "innate/ instinct aggression theory" by emphasizing the environment rather than genetics or inborn tendencies. This model is generally associated with the work of Albert Bandura and his associates, who noted that children who viewed live or filmed aggression imitated the behavior. **This is known as social learning theory or observational learning.** The phenomenon is greatest when the adult is admired, powerful, or well liked. Hmmm. I wonder how many television personalities, rock stars, and sports figures are keeping abreast of the findings in social psychology. Just for the record, adolescents often model angry or aggressive parents, even in homes where the parents discourage hostile behavior.     **(c)**

109. The APGA, which became the AACD until 1992 and is now the ACA, contributed to the growth of cross-cultural counseling by

    a.  the 1972 formation of the Association for Non-White Concerns in Personnel and Guidance, later known as the Association for Multicultural Counseling and Development.
    b.  the 1972 ethic which made it unethical to see culturally different clients without three hours of relevant graduate work in this area.
    c.  the 1972 ethic which required a 3,000-hour practicum in order to work with culturally different clients.
    d.  urging nonwhites to take graduate counseling courses.

    The Civil Rights Act of 1964 (P.L. 88–352) prohibiting discrimination for reasons of gender, race, religion, or national origin was instrumental in terms of setting the stage for minority concerns.                                                              **(a)**

110. Daniel Levinson proposed a controversial stage-crisis view theory with several major life transitions. He

    a.  is the father of multicultural counseling.
    b.  wrote the 1978 classic *Seasons of a Man's Life* and the 1997 sequel *Seasons of a Woman's Life*.
    c.  postulated a midlife crisis for men between ages 40 and 45 and for women approximately five years earlier.
    d.  b and c.

    Middle-aged readers: listen up! Subsequent research indicates that Levinson's theory of a midlife crisis for men or for women doesn't really hold water. Levinson's theory, originally derived by interviewing 40 middle-aged men from different backgrounds, suggested three major transitions. Levinson provides no statistical analysis. The first transition is known as *early adult transition* and is said to occur between the ages of 17 and 22. In this stage the individual makes decisions about college, the military, and breaking away from one's parents. This is the "leaving the family stage." A dream of the ideal adult life is formulated. Next, he proposes the *age 30 transition* (ages 28–33) in which the person attempts to make the dream a reality. After this stage the man experiences a *settling down* period. Next comes the *midlife transition* (ages 40–45 or approximately five years earlier for women). This stage is seen as stressful. The person questions his dream and acknowledges that goals may not be met. Moreover, one's mortality becomes an issue (i.e., being young vs. being old). An age 50 transition occurs. The final transition is *later adulthood* (ages 60–65) where the individual makes peace with the world. **Levinson's theory is now viewed as biased against women (i.e., gender bias) since it does not truly deal adequately with women's development proposing that women receive fulfillment by meeting the needs of their husbands and families. To put it a different way, men dream or have visions, goals, and aspirations about occupations and women dream about their marriage and family and often lack long-term goals.**         **(d)**

111. The three factors which enhance interpersonal attraction are:

   a.  assertiveness, anxiety, ego strength.
   b.  close proximity, physical attraction, similar beliefs.
   c.  culture, race, assertiveness.
   d.  ego strength, anxiety, race.

Social psychology has a lot to say about attraction! **Proxemics, or the study of proximity, relates to personal space, interpersonal distance, and territoriality.** Leon Festinger discovered that friendship and attraction were highest for apartment dwellers living next door to each other. **Social psychologists refer to the tendency for people who are in close proximity (say working at the same office or living close) to be attracted to each other as *propinquity*.** The attraction waned even among people living two or three doors away. Although we like attractive people, the research shows that we generally end up with mates who are on our own level of attractiveness. Studies have literally shown that voters prefer attractive candidates though they are unaware of their bias. I often do a mini-experiment in my classes in which I pass out a picture of a very attractive individual and one who is very plain.

I then ask the class to rate both individuals in regard to IQ and salary. True to the research, my class generally gives the good-looking individual an inflated IQ and salary. Studies also indicate that attractive people fare better in legal altercations (yes, even when they have committed a crime). Moreover, they are more likely to receive help during a time of need, and they are better able to sway the opinions of an audience. Compliments, or what some of the literature refers to as "rewardingness" (a genuine caring), could also be added to the list of factors which help to intensify attraction. Finally, **reciprocity of attraction or liking suggests we are attracted to people who like us and find us attractive. For long-term relationships, the matching hypothesis asserts we very often pick a partner who roughly matches our level of attractiveness.**          **(b)**

112. The term *contextualism* implies that

    a.    multicultural counseling is the oldest subspecialty in the profession.
    b.    behavior must be assessed in the context of the culture in which the behavior occurs.
    c.    the notion of worldview is highly inaccurate.
    d.    projective tests are more accurate than objective measures when performing cross-cultural counseling.

    Let's dispense of choice "a" by pointing out that although Frank Parsons, the father of guidance, acknowledged the significance of culture, it did not really begin to emerge as a true, accepted subspecialty until the 1970s. A person's perception of his or her relationship to the world as a whole is often termed a *worldview*. Choice "b" is a textbook definition of contextualism.          **(b)**

113. Carol Gilligan, although she was an assistant to Lawrence Kohlberg, was critical of his theory of moral development

    a.    as she felt it was too psychoanalytic.
    b.    as she felt it was too behavioristic.
    c.    as she felt it was not applicable to African Americans.
    d.    as she felt it was more applicable to males than females.

According to Gilligan, Kohlberg's theory did not delineate the notion that women place more emphasis on caregiving and personal responsibility than do men, who focus more on individual rights and justice.   **(d)**

114. _____ helped to popularize the multicultural counseling movement.

    a.   Arthur Jensen's views on IQ testing (also known as Jensenism)
    b.   The civil rights movement
    c.   Jung's feeling that all men and women from all cultures possess a collective unconscious
    d.   The *Tarasoff* duty

First, remember that intercultural counseling means the same thing as multicultural counseling if the term pops up on your exam. Jensen, choice "a," tried to prove that African Americans had lower IQs due to genetic factors, while the *Tarasoff* case, mentioned in choice "d," resulted in the counselor's duty to warn and protect an intended victim who might be the target of danger or violence.   **(b)**

115. When a counselor speaks of a probable outcome in a case, he or she is technically referring to

    a.   the prognosis.
    b.   the diagnosis.
    c.   the intervention.
    d.   attending behavior.

Prognosis refers to the probability that one can recover from a condition. When charting in a client's file the counselor would do well to discuss the length of treatment and the status expected at the end of treatment.   **(a)**

116. When a counselor speaks of what he or she believes must transpire from a psychotherapeutic standpoint, he or she technically is referring to

    a.    recommendations.
    b.    the diagnosis.
    c.    the prognosis.
    d.    the notion of transference.

One difficulty with formal diagnosis (i.e., using the *Diagnostic and Statistical Manual* (*DSM*) of the American Psychiatric Association) is that a given diagnosis does not imply or recommend a given treatment process. The *DSM* will *not* tell you, for example, to treat a major depression with reality therapy or an adjustment disorder with anxious mood using a client-centered approach. **(a)**

117. The 1971 famous Stanford Prison experiment conducted by Philip Zimbardo demonstrated that

    a.    passivity is the norm for most individuals.
    b.    assertive behavior is clearly the healthiest behavioral alternative.
    c.    it takes people several weeks to change their behavior.
    d.    people conform to social roles.

In this landmark research Zimbardo turned the basement of the Stanford University Psychology Building into a mock prison . . . not a misprint! Zimbardo randomly picked students to become guards as well as prisoners. The prisoners *and* the guards played their roles . . . well, let us just say . . . too well! Guards hurled insults at prisoners, were mean, hostile, sadistic, and abusive. The prisoners became passive. The experiment, slated to last two weeks, was shut down after merely six days as prisoners were harassed by the guards at such a high level (e.g., forced to clean the toilet facilities with their bare hands) they were becoming anxious, depressed, and stressed out. The experiment partially explains how the atrocities of the Holocaust could have been perpetrated and some of the behaviors noted at Abu Ghraib prison. **An interesting footnote: In 1973 the American**

**Psychological Association (APA) ruled the experiment as ethical, but today this would not be the case. Even Zimbardo went on record as saying that nobody in this country should ever be a part of an experiment like this ever again—shining a spotlight on the positive that some experts felt that the experiment resulted in better, more-stringent ethical guidelines.** **(d)**

118. A wealth of research demonstrates that

   a. surprisingly enough, African Americans generally request Asian American counselors.
   b. surprisingly enough, Asian Americans generally request African American counselors.
   c. in most instances, clients prefer a counselor of the same race and a similar cultural background.
   d. in most instances, clients prefer a counselor of the same race, yet a different culture.

In multicultural counseling, "likes attract." Social psychologists who have studied attraction tell us that similarity increases attraction. The phrase "in most instances" was intentional. Research demonstrates that if the other person is a member of a different nationality, race, or culture but is perceived as "similar" (i.e., more like you than someone of the same race and culture), then you still will be more attracted to the individual perceived as "similar" despite race or cultural barriers. **(c)**

119. The frustration-aggression theory is associated with

   a. Albert Ellis.
   b. Robert Havinghurst, who created the idea of the developmental task concept.
   c. Eric Berne, the creator of transactional analysis (TA).
   d. John Dollard and Neal Miller.

Frustration occurs when an individual is blocked so that he or she cannot reach an intended goal (or the goal is removed). The Dollard/Miller hypothesis asserts that frustration leads to aggression. Albert Ellis (note choice "a"), the father of rational-emotive behavior therapy (REBT), does not agree with the frustration-aggression theory. He feels that unfortunately many clients do indeed believe that frustration causes aggression. Ellis maintains that this dynamic is due to the client's irrational thought process (i.e., actually believing it is true) rather than some automatic response pattern. Some social psychologists believe that when individuals lose their identity (sometimes called "deindividuation") they are likely to become aggressive or violent. It has been found that the presence of weapons raises the level of violence as well as the probability that violence will occur. Counselors need to keep this in mind when dealing with suicidal and homicidal clients.                                    **(d)**

120. A popular cognitive consistency or balance theory in social psychology is _____ cognitive dissonance theory.

   a.   Dollard and Miller's
   b.   Crites and Roe's
   c.   Festinger's
   d.   Holland and Super's

Choices "b" and "d" are names primarily associated with the career counseling movement. **The concept of balance theory suggests that people strive for consistency/balance in terms of their belief systems. Simply put, individuals attempt to reduce or eliminate inconsistent or incompatible actions and beliefs.** A state of incompatibility is known as "dissonance," which literally means discord. Leon Festinger, in 1957, suggested that individuals are motivated to reduce tension and discomfort, thus putting an end to the dissonance. A statement like, "I'd rather smoke three packs of cigarettes a day and enjoy myself than quit and live an extra year or two," would be an example of cognitive dissonance in action. The person in this example has "changed the balance" by making his or her thinking consistent. **People don't like inconsistency in their thoughts or attitudes versus behavior.** Dissonance is often reduced using denial. Thus the individual who says "Sure I smoke, but the research which suggests it is harmful is not accurate" is also practicing cognitive dissonance, since he or she is using a form of denial.   **(c)**

121. Culture is really a set of rules, procedures, ideas, and values shared by members of a society. Culture is said to be normative. This implies that

    a.   one culture will have norms which differ only slightly from another.
    b.   culture excludes customs.
    c.   culture provides individuals with standards of conduct.
    d.   culture is never socially learned.

    Cultures often differ markedly from each other, and most experts would agree that the customs are nearly always learned and shared with members of the society.   **(c)**

122. A statistical norm measures actual conduct, while a cultural norm

    a.   describes how people are supposed to act.
    b.   has little to do with expectations.
    c.   is irrelevant when counseling a client.
    d.   all of the above.

    Choice "b" is the direct antithesis of the correct alternative choice "a." Some multicultural practitioners suggest that culture is really a system of norms. Here is an important distinction: A statistical norm measures actual conduct, while a cultural norm describes the expectations of how one should act.   **(a)**

123. Mores are beliefs and social customs

    a.   regarding the rightness or wrongness of behavior.
    b.   which should be the central focus in multicultural counseling.
    c.   that are conscious decisions made by persons in power.
    d.   that are identical with the folkways in the culture.

Mores—the plural of *mos*, which is rarely used in the literature—develop as a given group decides what is good and bad for the welfare of the people. **People are generally punished for violating the mores.** On an exam you may be asked to distinguish "folkways" (see choice "d") from mores. Folkways, like mores, describe correct, normal, or habitual behavior. The difference is that breaking folkways generally results in embarrassment, while breaking mores causes harm to others or threatens the existence of the group. If, for example, you are an American and you drink a large bowl of soup directly from a soup bowl rather than using a spoon, then you have violated an American folkway. Your behavior won't really win you friends or positively influence people, but you won't be asked to spend time in a maximum security correction facility either. If, on the other hand, you kill three people and rob a bank, you have violated mores and your behavior could indeed result in serious punishment. Some of the literature does not attempt to describe mores as a separate entity but rather as a type of folkway, and thus choice "d" isn't really that far off the mark. If you're looking for a simple memory device, why not try the fact that "mores" begins with an "m" as does the word "morals." Mores are behaviors that are based on morals. If you drink your soup out of a large bowl or pot, you may be in violation of an American folkway or in dire need of a course in etiquette, though I doubt whether your friends will classify you as immoral! Keep in mind that in other cultures a behavior such as this might not be in violation of a folkway. For example, in some Japanese cultures it is considered good table manners to drink soup out of a bowl as if it were a cup. As I pointed out earlier, when I mentioned the concept of cultural relativism, a behavior can only be judged within the context of a person's culture.                                      **(a)**

124. _____ was the first pioneer to focus heavily on sociocultural issues.

   a.   Mark Savickas, a major figure in career construction theory relying on narrative therapy,
   b.   Alfred Adler, the father of individual psychology,

c.    Maxie Maultsby, the father of rational behavior therapy (RBT),

d.    Frank Parsons, the father of guidance,

Frank Parsons and his associates are considered the first social reformers concerned with guidance in the United States. He wrote *Choosing a Vocation*.                                                   **(d)**

125.  A counselor who is part of a research study will be counseling clients in the polar regions and then at a point near the equator. Her primary concern will be

a.    universal culture.
b.    national culture.
c.    ecological culture.
d.    b and c.

Clemmont Vontress suggested that multicultural counselors would do well to remember that we are all part of a universal culture (choice "a"). We all have similar or universal needs (e.g., the hierarchy proposed by Maslow) and requirements for food, water, air, and sleep regardless of our cultural affiliation. Vontress noted that universal culture can be distinguished from national, regional, racio-ethnic, and ecological culture. Ecological culture implies that cultural norms are often the result of practical and survival behaviors related to the climate or the resources in a given physical or geological environment. Eating, drinking, clothing, and shelter behaviors would clearly be different in the polar regions than at the equator, desert region, or New York City. From a personal standpoint the counselor's primary concern would probably be the ecological culture, and choice "b" (national culture) would no doubt run a close second.    **(d)**

126.  Biological similarities and sameness are indicated by

a.    ecological culture.
b.    mores.
c.    regional and national culture.
d.    universal culture.

The Human Genome Project has verified that biologically we are all more alike than different. The adept multicultural counselor will always keep in mind that he or she—like the client—is a product of universal culture.    **(d)**

127. Early vocalization in infants

    a.   is more complex in African American babies.
    b.   is more complex in white babies.
    c.   is nearly identical in all cultures around the globe.
    d.   is the finest indicator of elementary school performance.

From one side of the globe to the other, the initial sounds made by babies are very similar. The cultural environment then strengthens certain verbalizations via the process of reinforcement. The first word usually is spoken after approximately one year of life. The child may use one- or two-word phrases (e.g., "me eat" or "I Betty") initially. These are known as "holophrases." Initially, the child's language is egocentric. By the fourth year most children can construct simple sentences. Anne Fernald of Stanford University discovered that by age 2 there can be a six-month language gap between children who are living in poverty and those who are not. This could be dubbed as socioeconomic status or SES on the exam. Clearly, more research is necessary and Fernald is quick to point out that this difference at a young age does not translate to destiny. Lack of environmental stimulation in any socioeconomic bracket (referred to as an "unstimulating" environment on some exams) does indeed hinder vocalization development.    **(c)**

128. In the 1920s, Emory Bogardus developed a social distance scale, which evaluated

    a.   socioeconomic trends.
    b.   how an individual felt toward other ethnic groups.
    c.   disadvantaged youth.
    d.   language barriers between African Americans and Asian Americans.

Ethnicity can be defined as that which pertains to a large group of individuals who are categorized by national, religious, linguistic, or cultural attributes. Measurement of attitudinal attributes began in the 1920s. The Bogardus data were indicative of negative attitudes toward a number of groups, including African Americans, Jews, Mexicans, and Turks. A replication of the study in 1947 revealed that the negative attitudes still prevailed. **Wanting to keep a social distance from a certain group of people is seen as a form of prejudice.** **(b)**

129. According to the foot-in-the-door compliance technique, which has two distinct steps, a counselor who needs to make a home visit to a resistant client's home

    a.   should conduct the interview from the porch.
    b.   should double-bind the client.
    c.   should ask to come in the home.
    d.   should exude accurate empathy, but never ask to enter the home.

Choices "a," "b," and "d" could be utilized; nonetheless, they do not describe the "foot-in-the-door" obedience technique. The phenomenon asserts that when a person agrees to a less-repugnant request (step 1), then he or she will be more likely to comply with a request which is even more distasteful (step 2). Thus, a counselor who first asks to come in the house (a small request) and receives an answer of "yes," can then, for example, ask for medical information (a bigger request or so-called target request) related to a possible case of child abuse. Social science researchers report that trivial commitments lead to a so-called "momentum of compliance." The notion is generally related to a 1966 study by Jonathan Freedman and Scott Fraser in which housewives who were first asked to sign a safe-driving petition were more apt to comply with the request to put a large "Drive Carefully" sign on their front lawns. The moral of the experiment is to always ask for a small favor and you'll have a better chance of getting a person to say "yes" when you ask for a bigger favor. Could a memory device which takes advantage of the fact that Freedman and Fraser start with an "f" like the word *foot* help you to remember the researchers whose often-quoted studies support this principle?                                          **(c)**

130. Most countries have an official language, a stated viewpoint, and a central government. This is reflected mainly by

    a.  national culture.
    b.  human culture.
    c.  regional culture.
    d.  ecological culture.

    **Hint:** Although choice "b" is not the correct answer, don't let it throw you if your exam refers to "universal culture" as "human culture." The above statement best describes national culture. Big business and high-tech media are lessening the gap between national cultures. In this day and age an individual living on the opposite side of the earth could be wearing the same prestigious pair of designer jeans as you. Thus, some experts have suggested that traditional cultures will eventually be supplanted by a "unified world culture" or a "unified global culture." **As of late, the term third culture kid (TCK) has been used to describe children raised primarily in a culture that is different than their parents' culture during their formative years.**     **(a)**

131. Whereas a culture is defined primarily via norms and values, a society differs from a culture in that a society

    a.  is defined as a set of mores.
    b.  has a distinct lack of norms.
    c.  is a self-perpetuating independent group which occupies a definitive territory.
    d.  none of the above.

    The boundaries of a culture and a society are not the same. **Cultures operate within societies; however, all members of a given society may not share the same culture.**     **(c)**

132. Ethnocentrism

    a.  uses one's own culture as a yardstick to measure all others.
    b.  means race.
    c.  is a genetic term.
    d.  all of the above.

Statements like "superior race," "savages," "backward people," or "the chosen few" capture the essence of the concept of ethnocentrism. In short, all societies are ethnocentric in the sense that they use their own views as a standard of reference and view themselves as superior. **Again, ethnocentrism conveys the notion that one's own group is superior.**    (a)

133. All of these statements are ethnocentric *except*

    a.  You can't trust anyone over the age of 40.
    b.  Americans are generous.
    c.  Blue-collar workers are mean and selfish.
    d.  The Gross Domestic Product in the United States exceeds the figure in Mexico.

Ethnocentrism is based on opinion while choice "d" is fact. Ethnocentrism was clearly expressed in the World War II joke which suggested that Hitler couldn't build a race of supermen because Superman could only be an American.    **(d)**

134. Ethnocentrism

    a.  is not universal.
    b.  promotes a sense of patriotism and national sovereignty.
    c.  promotes stability and pride, yet danger in the nuclear age.
    d.  b and c.

According to researchers Robert LeVine and Donald Campbell you can scratch off choice "a," because **ethnocentrism is truly a universal phenomenon in which an ethnic group tries to prove it is superior**. The U.S. government (as well as others) engages in choice "b" (a form of ethnocentrism) deliberately.

Choice "c" reminds us of the ultimate danger in trying to prove sovereignty in a nuclear age. **Key concept: Expect to see the term *acculturation* on exams related to multicultural studies. The term suggests that ethnic and racial minorities integrate or adopt cultural beliefs and customs from the majority or dominant culture. Assimilation is said to occur when the individual has such a high level of acculturation that he or she becomes part of the dominant, macro, or majority culture. A quick final thought: On occasion, the opposite can occur. Persons of the dominant culture like (or even think it is cool) to dress, talk, or follow customs set forth via a minority culture.** **(d)**

135. Regardless of culture, the popular individual

    a.  has good social skills.
    b.  values race over ethnicity.
    c.  dresses in the latest styles.
    d.  never possesses a modal personality.

My best guess would be that most of you correctly chose the best alternative (choice "a") based on common sense. So save your money on clothes (choice "c") and fine tune your social skills! The only thing which might have made the question difficult was the introduction of the term *modal personality* in choice "d." The term—derived from the statistical concept of the mode, used to describe the score which occurs most frequently—refers to a composite personality, which is the most typical profile of a given group of people. **A modal personality is the personality which is characteristic or typical of the group in question.**    **(a)**

136. Social exchange theory postulates that

    a.  a relationship will endure if both parties are assertive.
    b.  a relationship will endure if the rewards are greater than the costs.
    c.  a relationship will endure if both parties are sexually attracted to each other.
    d.  men work harder to keep a relationship strong.

Social exchange theory assumes that rewards are things or factors we like, while costs are things we dislike. The theory assumes that a positive relationship is characterized by "profit." Reward minus cost equals profit. Some counselors are understandably turned off by this "vest-pocket definition of relationships" based on behavioral psychology and economic theory. A client who says to a family member "As long as I pay the bills, you'll do your chores" is basing a relationship on rewards and costs. An alternative explanation of relationships is provided by the "complementarity theory," which states that a relationship becomes stronger as the two people's personality needs mesh. The word *complementary* indicates that one personality can make up what is lacking or missing in the other personality. For example, according to this theory, a dominant man and a non dominant woman would have a fine chance of relating well toward each other. **(b)**

137. Balance theory postulates

   a.   a move from cognitive consistency to inconsistency.
   b.   a move from cognitive inconsistency to consistency.
   c.   a tendency to achieve a balanced cognitive state.
   d.   b and c.

   **Here's a mini-review: Inconsistent thoughts are often referred to as "dissonance." Most counselors agree that dissonance is a distasteful state of mind which the individual will attempt to change.** **(d)**

138. Most individuals believe that people whom they perceive as attractive

   a.   are nonassertive.
   b.   are aggressive.
   c.   have other positive traits.
   d.   are socially adept but not very intelligent.

   This can cause the professional counselor difficulty if he or she tends to minimize a client's problems merely because he or she is good looking. For example, a thought such as "with looks like that she is no doubt the life of the party" demonstrates how the counselor erroneously assumes that a woman who is good looking will have good social skills and feel comfortable at a social gathering. Clients—like books—cannot be judged by their covers, yet this tendency is quite common.                    **(c)**

139. A counselor who works primarily with older adults needs to be aware that

   a.   too many counselors choose gerontology as their specialty.
   b.   individuals over 65 tend to overuse hotline and helpline crisis counseling services.
   c.   surprisingly, attractiveness is a fine predictor of retirement adjustment.
   d.   surprisingly, financial security and health are the best predictors of retirement adjustment.

Yes, an old adage which suggests that money can help buy happiness might just have a grain of truth. Here's why. Approximately 9.5% of all Americans age 65 and older have an income below the poverty level! The prevailing feeling is that counselors of the future will be increasingly forced to deal with an older population as the U.S. population in general ages (the so-called "Age Wave"). In 1900 only 4% of the U.S. population was over 65; as of this writing the total is over 13% and growing, If I were you, another question I'd expect to see on my exam would relate to myths which impact upon counselors working with the aged. Two of the most popular myths are that: (a) IQ scores (intelligence) drops markedly as folks age—in reality, IQ scores remain fairly stable over the life span; and (b) the elderly are incapable of sex. In regard to the former, some exam questions could disagree with this generalization slightly, as **the theory of "terminal drop" or "terminal decline" postulates that a dramatic decrease in intellectual functioning does occur, but even according to this theory, it only occurs during the final five years of life. It usually centers around verbal skills**. Counseling seniors will become more common in the future: the human life expectancy has almost doubled since the early 1900s when the average hovered below 50 years of age. Are you old if you have reached the big four-O? Certainly not in my estimation; however, employment agencies often view those who are over 40 as "older" and thus those who fit into this age bracket experience longer periods of unemployment than folks who are under 40. **Counseling clients over the age of 65 is often called gerontological counseling or therapy. Helpers often just say I work in "gero" for short.**        **(d)**

140. Most experts would agree that a multicultural counselor's diagnosis

    a.    must be performed without regard to cultural issues.
    b.    must be done within a cultural context.
    c.    a and b.
    d.    none of the above.

    The "cultural approach to normality" suggests that the behavior of the majority of the people defines what is considered "normal." An important point to note, however, is that deviant behavior, such as in the case of a very powerful leader or a genius, may be lauded.        **(b)**

141. A counselor who is seeing a client from a different culture would most likely expect _____ social conformity than he or she would from a client from his or her own culture.

    a.    less
    b.    more
    c.    the same
    d.    more realistic

    We demand more rigid standards from our own culture.    **(a)**

142. In terms of diagnosis,

    a.    a client's behavior could be sane and appropriate in one culture, yet disturbed and bizarre in another.
    b.    culture is irrelevant in children under 14.

c.    culture is an issue with males, but not with females.
d.    culture is an issue with females, but not with males.

Again, the concept of "cultural relativism" implies that one's behavior can only be evaluated in relation to the culture. **Behavior in one culture cannot be judged by that which is considered normal in another culture.** Behavioral scientists have thus attempted to create "cultural-free" diagnostic instruments, but as of this date none has been totally effective.    **(a)**

143. In the United States, a frequent practice is to see a perfect stranger for therapy.

a.    This trend seems to be true in any area of the world.
b.    This is true for Licensed Professional Counselors (LPCs) but not true for Licensed Clinical Social Workers (LCSWs).
c.    This is true for LPCs and LCSWs but not licensed clinical psychologists.
d.    In other cultures it would not be the norm to see a stranger and receive pay for providing help.

In E. Fuller Torrey's thought-provoking book *The Mind Game: Witch Doctors and Psychiatrists* he explains that in Nigeria, helpers have accepted a female client as a wife in lieu of a fee! He also notes that in other cultures a therapist cannot accept a fee unless the treatment is successful.    **(d)**

144. According to the cognitive dissonance theory of Leon Festinger, a woman has an approach–approach conflict. She has her choice of a beautiful silver watch and an equally stunning gold watch. Both are different brands. She feels the silver model will be perfect for some of her jewelry and outfits while the gold is ideal for other jewelry and modes of dress. She chooses the silver watch.

a.    She will feel intense guilt.
b.    She will read positive reviews on the silver watch—and possibly negative reviews about the gold model—after the

purchase to justify her behavior and reduce post-decisional dissonance.

c.   According to the theory she will remain a tad ambivalent about her choice.

d.   She will be angry because in reality she wanted both watches, but could not afford them.

Although all the choices are plausible, choice "b" best expresses the tendency to justify behavior to create a state of "consonance" (a fancy word for harmony) between attitudes and behavior. Hence, if a test report states that the watch is a good buy, the belief and the behavior are consistent. In case you haven't picked it up yet, I'm betting you'll see at least one question regarding cognitive dissonance on your exam.                    **(b)**

145.   A woman who is being robbed

a.   would probably get the most assistance in a crowd with a large number of bystanders.

b.   would find that the number of people who would respond to her distress actually decreases as the number of bystanders increases.

c.   would rarely have a bystander from a different race try to help her.

d.   none of the above.

Here is a principle which is often quoted: The number of people who will help a victim in distress decreases, and the time it will take to intervene increases, as the number of bystanders increases. **This phenomenon is billed as the bystander effect or bystander apathy. Everybody assumes somebody else will step in and take charge. This is referred to as diffusion of responsibility.** The converse, or helping an individual in distress, is generally called "**altruism**" or basically an unselfish concern for others. Altruism could conceivably apply in a psychological sense when you are working with groups and a client is the victim of scapegoating and you step in as the leader to emotionally protect this client.                    **(b)**

146. A counselor reading this book says, "I couldn't care less about passing my comprehensive exam." This

   a.   is displacement.
   b.   is an attempt to reduce dissonance via consistent cognitions.
   c.   is an attempt to reduce dissonance by denial, thus minimizing tension.
   d.   is projection.

Choices "a" and "d" are ego defense mechanisms. This topic is covered in the Helping Relationships section of this book. Choice "b" is incorrect since reading this book to pass the exam and not caring about passing are "inconsistent." **(c)**

147. The statement "Even though my car is old and doesn't run well, it sure keeps my insurance payments low"

   a.   is displacement.
   b.   is an attempt to reduce dissonance via consistent cognitions.
   c.   is projection.
   d.   would never reduce dissonance in an individual.

This also could be described as the "sweet lemon" variety of rationalization (see the Helping Relationships section of this book). **(b)**

148. In the case of an individual who purchased a $50,000 watch, cognitive dissonance theory postulates that

   a.   he or she might ignore positive information regarding other models and secure a lot of information regarding the $50,000 platinum model.
   b.   he or she might sell the $50,000 watch immediately following the purchase.
   c.   he or she might focus heavily on negative information regarding rival models.
   d.   a and c.

This is a tough question since the alternatives are a bit complex. **Remember: cognitive dissonance theory predicts that the person will look for things which are consistent with his or her behavior.** Is choice "a" consistent? Of course; yet choice "c" is also possible since the individual could ignore positive attributes of the competition (i.e., choice "a") or maximize their negative features (i.e., choice "c"). Counselors should keep in mind that consistency is considered a desirable personality trait in most cultures.                                                   **(d)**

149. In the United States, middle- and upper-class citizens seem to want a counselor who

    a.   will give them "a good talking to."
    b.   gives a specific and steady stream of advice.
    c.   helps them work it out on their own.
    d.   is highly authoritarian and autocratic.

The theory here is that *most* middle- and upper-class citizens are taught that independence is a virtue. The person would not want to be dependent on a therapist, parents, or others, as is implied in choices "a," "b," and "d."                                            **(c)**

150. In a traditional culture which places a high premium on authority figures,

    a.   passivity on the part of the counselor would be viewed in a negative manner.
    b.   a client would be disappointed if he or she did not receive advice.
    c.   assigning homework and teaching on the part of the counselor would be appropriate.
    d.   all of the above.

An active-directive model works best with persons who respond well to an authority figure.                                            **(d)**

151. Cognitive dissonance research deals mainly with

    a.  attraction.
    b.  cognition and attitude formation.
    c.  cognitions and emotion.
    d.  none of the above.

The notion is that the discrepancies or inconsistencies that create tension are caused by cognitions and attitudes. **(b)**

152. Parents who do not tolerate or use aggression when raising children produce

    a.  less-aggressive children.
    b.  more-aggressive children.
    c.  passive-aggressive children.
    d.  passive-dependent children.

Children who are abused by their parents are more likely to be abusers when they have children of their own. **Remember that counselors are legally required to report child abuse, neglect, sexual abuse, or exploitation.** (a)

153. Overall, Rogerian person-centered counseling

    a.  is rarely utilized in cross-cultural counseling.
    b.  is too nondirective for intercultural counseling.
    c.  a and b.
    d.  has been used more than other models to help promote understanding between cultures and races.

In the 1970s, Rogers conducted workshops to enhance cross-cultural communication. People from all over the world participated. Person-centered techniques are popular in Japan. Person-centered therapy is nonjudgmental and thus is considered a superb modality for multicultural/multiracial usage. The exception (mentioned earlier) could occur when counseling an ethnic or racial group that demands structure or authority from a helper. Low-income clients generally view the helper as an advice giver. Estimates indicate that approximately 50% of all ethnic minority clients quit counseling after the first session feeling they will not secure what they want from the helper.    **(d)**

154. In intercultural/multicultural counseling the term *therapeutic surrender* means

    a.    nothing—it is not a valid term.
    b.    most therapists will give up in 16 sessions or less if progress is not evident.
    c.    the client psychologically surrenders himself or herself to a counselor from a different culture and becomes open with feelings and thoughts.
    d.    the therapist assumes a passive therapeutic stance.

    Therapeutic surrender occurs when a client is able to trust the counselor and self-discloses. Contrary to choice "a," the term is used frequently in intercultural counseling.    **(c)**

155. The literature suggests these factors as helpful in promoting therapeutic surrender:

    a.    an analysis of cognitive dissonance.
    b.    rapport, trust, listening, conquering client resistance, and self-disclosure.
    c.    paradoxing the client.
    d.    analyzing flight-to-health defense mechanism variables.

    Choice "d" is an analytic concept which asserts that the client has improved too rapidly and the real difficulty (i.e., unconscious conflicts) has not been resolved. A similar term, *flight from reality*, is used when the client resorts to psychosis (i.e., losing touch with reality) to avoid dealing with current life difficulties.    **(b)**

156. In terms of trust and therapeutic surrender,

    a.    it is easier to trust people from one's own culture.
    b.    lower-income people often don't trust others from a higher social class.

c.   lower-income clients may feel that they will end up as losers dealing with a counselor from a higher social class.
d.   all of the above.

Language barriers, on the part of the client or the counselor, intensify the difficulty of therapeutic surrender. One good technique is to steer clear of slang or fancy therapeutic jargon and try to speak in a clear, concise, and direct manner.     **(d)**

157. A(n) _____ client would most likely have the most difficulty with self-disclosure when speaking to a white counselor.

a.   white female
b.   African American female
c.   African American male
d.   upper-class white male

Males in general sometimes have difficulty expressing feelings. According to the literature, African American males are especially hesitant about revealing themselves to whites.     **(c)**

158. According to assimilation-contrast theory, a client will perceive a counselor's statement that is somewhat like his or her own beliefs as even more similar (i.e., an assimilation error). He or she would perceive any dissimilar attitudes as

a.   even more dissimilar (i.e., a contrast error).
b.   standardization.
c.   similar to his or her own.
d.   paraphrasing.

In any case, if a counselor is highly regarded and trustworthy, his or her statements will be better accepted than if the helper has poor credibility.     **(a)**

159. When counseling a client from a different culture, a common error is made when negative transference

a.   is interpreted as positive transference.

b.   is interpreted as therapeutic resistance.

c.   is interpreted as white privilege.

d.   none of the above.

Okay, there are some terms you just have to know for this section of the exam and one of those terms (note choice "c") is *white privilege*. The term has been used to focus on the special advantages, privileges, and opportunities that nonwhites don't have. Since transference relates to incidents which occurred prior to treatment, such issues must be distinguished from the current helping relationship. This is sometimes difficult to accomplish.     **(b)**

160.  Counselors who have good listening skills

a.   facilitate therapeutic surrender.

b.   hinder therapeutic surrender.

c.   often have a monolithic perspective.

d.   are too nondirective to promote therapeutic surrender.

Let's place choice "c" under our trusty microscopes for just a moment. **A monolithic perspective indicates that the counselor perceives all the people in a given group (say African Americans or Latino/a Americans) as being identical**—hey, not a good thing folks! Counselors are urged to adopt an individualistic, rather than a monolithic, perspective. Good listening facilitates any type of helping.     **(a)**

161.  Counselors can more easily advise

a.   clients from their own culture.

b.   clients from a different culture.

c.   clients of a different race.

d.   clients utilizing ethnocentric statements.

To persuade someone is easiest when he or she has similar views, ideas, and background to one's own. It is entirely possible that a client of a different culture has been taught not to trust persons with the counselor's cultural background.     **(a)**

162. It's easiest to empathize with

    a.    a client who is similar to you.
    b.    a client who is dissimilar to you.
    c.    Latino/a clients.
    d.    Asian American male clients.

Clients who have counselors of the same ethnicity tend to stay in counseling longer. See the previous question if this question seemed a tad difficult—ditto! And for exam purposes please do not forget that when we speak of Latino/a clients, we need to include individuals from the Dominican Republic (i.e., Dominicans) who now number nearly a million and a half people in the U.S.                                                                 **(a)**

163. In cross-cultural counseling, structuring is very important. This concept asserts that counseling is most effective

    a.    when structured exercises are utilized.
    b.    when a counselor takes an active–directive stance.
    c.    when nondirective procedures are emphasized.
    d.    when the nature and structure of the counseling situation is described during the initial session.

Structure has a number of meanings in the field of professional counseling (see the Group Counseling and Group Work section of this book for additional meanings). In the context of multicultural counseling, structure indicates that the counselor will explain the role of the helper as well as the role of the helpee. This helps ward off embarrassment and further enhances the effectiveness of the counseling process. The greater the social/cultural gap, the more important the need for structuring. Despite the merits of the Rogerian model, some would claim that it falls short of the ideal paradigm when a high degree of structure is the treatment of choice. As mentioned earlier, clients from other cultures can harbor gross misconceptions of what represents the helping process.                                          **(d)**

164. A client from another culture will

    a.    talk to the counselor the same as he or she would to a peer.
    b.    speak to the counselor differently from the way he or she would when speaking to someone of his or her own background.
    c.    generally use slang on purpose to confuse the counselor.
    d.    generally play dumb to receive the counselor's sympathy.

Often individuals are courteous and polite with those who are of the same cultural origin, but are suspicious and don't trust outsiders.                                                                              **(b)**

165. An African American client tells a white counselor that the dance she went to last night was "bad," though she literally means it was good. The counselor's misunderstanding could best be described as a

    a.    client of color error.
    b.    cognitive dissonance error.
    c.    connotative error.
    d.    confounding variable.

I was corresponding with a counselor in China who has a good working knowledge of the English language. Nevertheless, on occasion she would write back and say, "When you said it was really cool, did you mean it was stylish or great, or were you talking about the temperature in your area of the U.S.?" According to some experts in this field, the three major barriers to intercultural counseling are culture-bound values (mentioned earlier), class-bound values, and language differences. **Connotation applies to the emotional content of a word, which is different from the true or dictionary definition.** The tendency for words to convey different connotations is often referred to as a "semantic differential." Choice "d," a confounding variable, is an extraneous variable which is not purposely introduced by an experimenter conducting research. This difficulty is inherent in correlational data. One more quick quip here: The term "people of color" refers to Asian Americans or Asian Pacific Americans, Latino/a

Americans, African Americans, Native Americans, and those who are multiracial. By approximately 2043 these groups will eventually outnumber whites of European descent in the United States, and as I complete this sentence the U.S. has experienced several years where white births were the minority.                                    **(c)**

166. A monolingual U.S. counselor

   a.   speaks only English.
   b.   speaks English and Spanish.
   c.   works as a counseling interpreter.
   d.   fits the definition of bilingual.

Mono literally means "one" or "single." Persons who are bilingual (i.e., speak two languages) can be employed as counselors or interpreters to facilitate efficacious intervention. In order to reduce the difficulty introduced by "semantic differential" and "connotative errors"—mentioned in the answer to the previous question—the bilingual counselor would ideally be bicultural (i.e., have familiarity with the culture of the counselor and the client).                                                                **(a)**

167. _____ was a prime factor in the history of multicultural counseling.

   a.   Frankl's experience in a concentration camp
   b.   Perl's use of the German concept of gestalt
   c.   Freud's visits to the United States
   d.   The 1954 Supreme Court decision, *Brown v. the Board of Education*, which outlawed public school segregation

Choice "a" mentions Viktor Frankl, the father of logotherapy, an existential form of treatment which stresses "healing through meaning." Choice "b" mentions Fritz Perls, the father of gestalt therapy, which attempts to ameliorate a mind/body split supposedly responsible for emotional distress. *Gestalt* is a German word which roughly means the "whole" form, figure, or configuration. The final alternative is correct. Desegregation created culturally different populations for school counselors.          **(d)**

168. Multicultural counseling promotes

    a.    eclecticism.
    b.    rigidity.
    c.    psychodynamic models.
    d.    neurolinguistic programming (NLP).

Most experts would insist that choice "a" is best inasmuch as intercultural counselors need to be flexible. An "eclectic" position (i.e., selecting treatment intervention strategies from diverse counseling models) would generally come closest to meeting this requirement.                    **(a)**

169. Multicultural counselors often adhere to the emic viewpoint. The word *emic*

    a.    is associated with the Supreme Court decision of 1954 outlawing segregation.
    b.    suggests that all clients are alike regardless of culture.
    c.    is associated with rational behavior therapy (RBT).
    d.    is a "culture-specific" perspective, from the word phonemic meaning sounds in a particular language.

J. G. Draguns suggested the emic–etic distinction in cross-cultural counseling. **Emic can be defined as an insider's perception of the culture. A researcher or counselor using an emic frame of reference wants to know what somebody participating in the culture thinks. The emic viewpoint emphasizes that each client is an individual with individual differences, while the etic view adheres to the theory that humans are humans—regardless of background and culture—thus, the same theories and techniques can be applied to any client the counselor helps.** Hence, a counselor who values the "emic" view will try to help clients by understanding the client's specific culture, while **the "etic" counselor emphasizes the sameness among clients—a universalism perspective—that literally transcends cultural boundaries.** Universal helping principles transcend culture. The "etic" counselor would not alter his or her technique when working with a client from a different culture or a minority group. **Distinctions such as etic/emic are often easiest to remember if you rely on a memory device. Can you come up with one?** **(d)**

170. A practicum supervisor who says to his or her supervisee "You can deal with your Asian American clients the same as you deal with anybody else" is espousing the

    a.    emic viewpoint.
    b.    alloplastic viewpoint.
    c.    etic viewpoint, derived from the term *phonetic* referring to sounds that remain the same in any language.
    d.    autoplastic viewpoint.

    Here's help for those of you who came up empty handed in terms of snaring a suitable memory device (and hence may have struggled with the question). I like to remember that "etic," which sports a "t," and sounds remarkably similar to "etiquette," is similar in the sense that when practicing etiquette we practice good manners with all individuals whether they are African American, white, Asian American, and so on. Likewise, counselors who espouse the etic viewpoint will use the **same strategies and techniques on virtually any client**. In this case, for example, the Asian American client will be treated no differently from an American, a Native American, a French Canadian, or for that matter anybody else. Actually the etic distinction also reminds me of the educational concept of "mainstreaming," which asserts that all children—including those with disabilities—can benefit from placement in a regular classroom. But just when you thought the coast was clear you were confronted with another distinction or dilemma (see choices "b" and "d") for the multicultural helper.    **(c)**

171. The statement "All humans, from all cultures, all races, and all nations, are more alike than different" is based on the

    a.    emic viewpoint.
    b.    alloplastic viewpoint.

c.    etic viewpoint.
d.    autoplastic viewpoint.

If you chose an alternative other than "c," then you need to reread answers to questions 169 and 170.          **(c)**

172. A counselor is confronted with his or her first Native American client. Native Americans (also called American Indians on some exams) are descendants of the original inhabitants of North America. After the initial session, the counselor secures several books which delineate the cultural aspects of Native American life. She discovers that there are over 560 federally recognized tribes in the United States. This counselor most likely believes in the

a.    emic viewpoint.
b.    alloplastic viewpoint.
c.    etic viewpoint.
d.    autoplastic viewpoint.

The "emic" view holds that an approach which is culturally specific is generally the most effective.          **(a)**

173. An Asian American counselor says to an African American client, "If you're unhappy with the system, get out there and rebel. You can change the system." This is the _____ viewpoint for coping with the environment.

a.    emic
b.    alloplastic
c.    etic
d.    autoplastic

This question is testing your knowledge of the autoplastic/ alloplastic dilemma in intercultural helping. The "autoplastic" view asserts that change comes from the self such as thoughts and behaviors, while the "alloplastic" conceptualization is that the client can cope best by changing or altering external factors in the environment (as alluded to in this question). Memory devices, anyone?          **(b)**

174. A young Latino male is the victim of discrimination. His counselor remarks, "I hear what you are saying and I will help you change your thinking so this will not have such a profound impact on you." In this case the counselor had suggested

    a.  an alloplastic method of coping.
    b.  an autoplastic method of coping.
    c.  the emic–etic distinction.
    d.  the emic viewpoint.

    Try this memory device on for size. The word *auto* generally refers to changing the "self" rather than altering the environment. Consider the technique of "autosuggestion" or "autohypnosis," or how about the act of writing an "autobiography"? In each of the aforementioned cases, the person works to create the project, solve the difficulty, or, simply put, change the self. In the "autoplastic" approach the counselor helps the client change him- or herself (as in this question). And if you think of a more elegant memory device—then I say "go for it!" It will come in mighty handy on the test date!     **(b)**

175. You are counseling a client from a different culture. She cannot move her right arm, but has been examined by some of the finest physicians and they cannot find any physical reason for her condition. The irony is that she is there to work on some personal issues but states forthrightly that the total lack of mobility in her arm does not bother her and thus is not an issue to deal with in the counseling sessions. The most likely explanation would be

    a.  she is displaying malingering.
    b.  she was severely abused as a young child.
    c.  she is suicidal.
    d.  she has a conversion disorder with la belle indifference.

    The fact that you are counseling a client from a different culture is irrelevant. A conversion disorder is evident when a person displays symptoms (generally neurological) which cannot be accounted for via medical exams. In essence, a medical diagnosis shows no reason for the individual's condition. **Clients with** conversion disorders sometimes display la belle indifference also called belle indifference, meaning they do not seem to be bothered or concerned by their condition. The person is not intentionally creating the symptoms, hence the implication is the condition is fueled by stress and emotions rather than physical factors. Counseling, biofeedback, and relaxation therapy might be helpful. The psychodynamic perspective suggests the person's symptom serves a purpose. A person who saw a very frightening scene and presently can't see would exemplify this position since the individual is no longer worried she will see something scary. Choice "a", malingering, occurs when a person fakes a physical or emotional illness to avoid work, military duty, or prison. We just don't have the evidence to make that diagnosis in this question. Needless to say, she could be misdiagnosed, but the question fails to address this possibility.                    **(d)**

176. Positive transference is to love or affection, as negative transference is to hostility, and as ambivalent transference is to

    a.    anger.
    b.    hate.
    c.    uncertainty.
    d.    admiration.

    *Ambivalent transference*, a term popular in multicultural counseling settings, occurs when the client rapidly shifts his or her emotional attitude toward the counselor based on learning and experiences related to authority figures from the past. The Helping Relationships section of this book goes into more depth regarding the notion of transference.                    **(c)**

177. The word *personalism* in the context of multicultural counseling means

    a.    all people must adjust to environmental and geological demands.
    b.    the counselor must adjust to the client's cultural mores.
    c.    a counselor who personalizes the treatment is most effective.

d.   biologically speaking, there is no reason why humans must adjust to environmental demands.

Culture must mold itself such that individuals can best thrive and survive in a given environment. Personalism implies that the counselor will make the best progress if he or she sees the client primarily as a person who has learned a set of survival skills rather than as a diseased patient. Fierce environmental conditions, such as living in a desert or a poverty-stricken neighborhood, cause individuals to cooperate with each other more and stick together as a group. This, nevertheless, can cause problems for the counselor who has never lived in an impoverished neighborhood or a desert and hence is seen as an outsider. The "person," who has lived in a poor area or the desert, will want to check out the counselor's authenticity as a "person," and a counselor who keeps his or her "professional distance" runs the risk of being seen as superficial. A comment such as, "You don't care about me, you just care about your paychecks (or "the agency," or "the court," or "your stupid report," etc.) indicates that the multicultural counselor is being perceived as remote and not very personal. This could create problems for the counselor since (a) in the United States "professionalism" is stressed more than "personalism" in the sense that a good counselor is not "supposed" to get very close to clients and if (b) the counselor has not necessarily grown up in a culture that stresses such a high level of interpersonal cooperation.                                    **(a)**

178. A client whose counselor pushes the alloplastic viewpoint may believe his counselor is simply

    a.   too Rogerian.
    b.   attacking the system.
    c.   too Freudian.
    d.   too cognitive.

The salient point here is that generally a synthesis, rather than a pure alloplastic or autoplastic position, will be the most effective.                                    **(b)**

179. Good multicultural counselors are

    a.   flexible.
    b.   rigid.
    c.   utilize Eric Berne's transactional analysis (TA), Fritz Perl's gestalt therapy, and/or William Glasser's reality therapy in nearly every case.
    d.   generally behavioristic.

Although choices "c" and "d" are not the best choices, a case could certainly be made for using these modalities in an intercultural helping relationship. Transactional analysis (TA), reality therapy, and behavioral interventions all stress "contracting." The process of contracting has its merits in cross-cultural situations because it keeps the counselor from shoving a dose of his or her own cultural values down the clients throat (i.e., the client has input before signing or agreeing with the contract). Furthermore, TA has been praised for illuminating cultural and ethnic injunctions. On the other hand, TA lingo is often complex for a client with a different background. Quite unlike behaviorism, gestalt therapy is a superb modality for cultures that need to liberate their feelings. In addition, it is helpful when working with a population which emphasizes nonverbal communication. The danger in utilizing gestalt comes from pushing techniques (i.e., trying to insist upon them before clients are ready for them) that emphasize the expression of feelings on a cultural or ethnic group which views the expression of feelings as a sign of weakness. Practitioners are warned that behaviorism (choice "d") is not a panacea in multicultural work inasmuch as some cultures do not value assertiveness. **Every brand of therapy has its merits and its disadvantages: It is therefore best if the multicultural counselor remains flexible.**                    **(a)**

180. A client remarks, "Hey, I'm African American and it's nearly impossible to hide it." This is illustrative of the fact that

    a.   race is not the same as ethnicity.
    b.   race and ethnicity are virtually identical.

c.    a connotative impediment exists.
d.    severe ambivalent transference exists.

This question attempts to see whether you can discern race from ethnicity. The assumption here is that you can generally see racial differences since they are the result of genetics. If a client really made this type of statement, the counselor might wish to deal directly with the racial issue. The counselor could inquire, "In what way do you feel that the fact that I'm white and you're African American will affect the counseling process?" Experts often assert that a question of this nature should be asked no later than the second session. Choice "d" would not be totally outlandish, although the question does not provide enough information to make it the best choice.    **(a)**

181. Experts in the field of multicultural counseling feel that the counselor's training

a.    must come from an APA-approved graduate program.
b.    must come from a supervisor who is from a different culture than the graduate student.
c.    should be broad and interdisciplinary.
d.    need not include rational-emotive behavior therapy (REBT).

Choice "d," rational-emotive behavior therapy (REBT) certainly can be helpful when counseling clients from another culture because it does not stress mental illness. The perception of the REBT practitioner as a "teacher" makes the process of helping more palatable to some populations. Choice "c" is the best answer. An adept multicultural helper ideally would study topics which go beyond traditional counseling theory. Some educators have even suggested that an exchange program in which counselors study in foreign universities could be beneficial.    **(c)**

182. Doing cross-cultural counseling

a.    makes counselors increasingly aware of cultural differences.

b.    allows counselors to see that culture is merely a matter of semantics.
c.    is different since clients are more likely to return for help after the first session.
d.    allows counselors to ignore the concept of pluralism.

Choice "c" is incorrect. Preliminary studies, as I hinted at earlier, indicate that clients from other cultures do not use counseling as often as they could. Moreover, the dropout rate is premature, perhaps 20% higher after the initial session than relationships which are not intercultural. The concept of "pluralism" literally means that an individual exists in more than one category. A condition known as "separatism" exists when a group of people totally withdraw from the political majority. Pluralism presents a less-extreme option. Cultural pluralism occurs when persons of a cultural heritage retain their traditions and differences, yet cooperate in regard to social, political, and economic matters. In counseling per se, the term suggests that certain categories of individuals (e.g., women, older adults, minorities, alternative cultures, or the disabled) often need special services. An Asian American, for example, could feel torn between adhering to Asian culture while trying to become more Americanized. The counselor must show respect for these individuals in order to do effective treatment; hence, the notion of pluralism cannot be ignored.    **(a)**

183.    Floyd Henry Allport created the concept of social facilitation. According to this theory, an individual who is given the task of memorizing a list of numbers will

a.    perform better if he or she is alone.
b.    perform better if he or she is part of a group.
c.    perform better if he or she has undergone psychotherapy.
d.    perform better if he or she is an auditory learner.

This is indeed an interesting phenomenon. The presence of other persons (e.g., coworkers, other athletes, fellow students) improves an individual's performance even when there is no verbal interaction!    **(b)**

184. In social psychology, the sleeper effect asserts that

    a.  sleep learning facilitates social skills.
    b.  after a period of time, one forgets the communicator but remembers the message.
    c.  after a period of time, one remembers the communicator but forgets the message.
    d.  REM sleep facilitates insight.

Perhaps more importantly, the so-called sleeper effect asserts that when you are attempting to change someone's opinion the change may not occur immediately after the verbal exchange. In other words, when a counselor provides guidance to a client a **delay** may occur before the client accepts the message. **The communication may have more impact after some time has passed.**                                                             **(b)**

185. In 1908, books by _____ helped to introduce social psychology in America.

    a.  Moreno and Yalom
    b.  Holland and Roe
    c.  Barber and Salter
    d.  McDougall and Ross

William McDougall wrote *Introduction to Social Psychology*, which expounded on his "hormic psychology" position that individual as well as group behavior is the result of inherited tendencies to seek goals. Edward Alsworth Ross authored *Social Psychology*. Other famous names noted in the alternatives include Jacob Moreno, who pioneered psychodrama and coined the term *group therapy*; Irvin Yalom, an existentialist, well known for his strides in group work, existential therapy, and death and dying; John Holland, who stressed that a person's occupational environment should be congruent with his or her personality type; Anne Roe, who postulated that jobs can compensate for unmet childhood needs; T. X. Barber, who espoused a cognitive theory of hypnotism; and Andrew Salter, a pioneer in the behavior therapy creating a paradigm dubbed conditioned reflex therapy, and a behavioristic theory of hypnosis, and autohypnosis.                                              **(d)**

186. _____ is associated with obedience and authority.

    a.   Stanley Milgram, a noted psychologist,
    b.   Arthur Janov, who created primal scream therapy,
    c.   A. T. Beck, a cognitive therapy pioneer,
    d.   Robert Harper, a pioneer in the REBT bibliotherapy movement,

In one of the most shocking and frightening investigations of all time, Milgram discovered that people who were told to give others powerful electric shocks did so on command. Subjects were told that they were to punish a learner strapped to an electric chair when he gave an incorrect answer. Out of 40 experimental subjects, only 14 refused to go to the highest level of shock (i.e., in excess of 435 volts)! And get this—in some of the experiments the persons administering the shocks (which, unbeknownst to them, were unreal) were actually given a 45-volt shock themselves so they could feel the intensity of this punishment. So much for accurate empathy! Even when the subjects heard the person receiving the shocks screaming they often continued to raise the level of voltage when told to do so. This principle is often used to explain "obedience to authority" in social situations such as the Salem witch hunts or Nazi war crimes. Fortunately, follow-up research indicated that most of the individuals who participated in the Milgram experiment did not feel they were harmed by the experience.                  **(a)**

187. Milgram discovered that normal people would administer seemingly fatal electric shocks to others when instructions to do so were given by a person perceived as

    a.   a peer.
    b.   an equal.
    c.   an individual from another culture.
    d.   an authority figure.

Prior to the experiment, psychiatrists predicted that only 1% would administer the highest level of shock. In reality, 65% dished out "fatal shock punishment" in response to an incorrect answer. If the experimental authority figure was in the room, the tendency to obey was higher than if he or she was not physically present. In a related study by Leonard Bickman, individuals told to give a dime or a paper bag to a stranger did so twice as often when the person giving the orders was dressed as a guard rather than a peer. Do uniforms and mode of dress have an impact? You better believe it!                                   **(d)**

188. The tendency to affiliate with others

     a.   is highest in the middle child.
     b.   is highest in children with *DSM* diagnoses.
     c.   is highest in firstborns and only children.
     d.   is based on hormonal output.

In the behavioral sciences the word *affiliation* refers to the need one has to associate with others. Choice "c" correctly reflects the landmark research of Stanley Schachter, which concluded that the need to affiliate decreases for later-born children.     **(c)**

189. A client tells his counselor that he has a choice of entering one of two prestigious PhD counseling programs. Kurt Lewin would call this an

     a.   approach–avoidance conflict.
     b.   approach–approach conflict.
     c.   avoidance–avoidance conflict.
     d.   avoidance vector.

Choices "a," "b," and "c" indicate the three basic categories of conflict which result in frustration. In the approach–approach format (suggested in this question) the individual is presented with two equally attractive options simultaneously. Of the three types, counselors believe that approach–approach is the easiest to help clients cope with since in most cases (unlike the situation presented in this question) the client can attempt both options:

first one, then the other. Moreover, approach–approach conflicts typically instill less anxiety than the other two types.    **(b)**

190. When a person has two negative alternatives, it is called an

    a.    approach–approach conflict.
    b.    approach vector.
    c.    avoidance–avoidance conflict.
    d.    avoidance cohesiveness.

When a client says, "I don't know whether to pay the hefty fine or go to jail," he is struggling with an avoidance–avoidance conflict in which both choices are undesirable, to say the least. Clients in this position often daydream, flee from the situation, or regress instead of confronting the choices. The client also may waver or vacillate when he or she comes close to making a choice.    **(c)**

191. A male client tells his counselor that he is attracted to "a gorgeous woman who is violent and chemically dependent." This creates an

    a.    approach–avoidance conflict.
    b.    avoidance–avoidance conflict.
    c.    avoidance of life space.
    d.    approach affiliation.

The approach–avoidance conflict presents a positive factor (a woman he finds attractive) with a negative factor (she is a substance abuser prone to violent behavior) at the same time. Most counselors would agree this is the toughest type of conflict for the client to tackle as it generates the highest level of frustration.    **(a)**

192. According to Charles Osgood and Percy Tannenbaum's congruity theory, a client will accept suggestions more readily if

    a.    the client likes the counselor.
    b.    the client dislikes the counselor.
    c.    the client distrusts the counselor.

d.  the counselor is in a higher economic bracket.

Here again, the tendency is based on "balance theory." If you like your counselor, your tendency to accept a suggestion would be balanced (i.e., consistent with your opinion). If you did not like or trust the counselor, then accepting his or her suggestions would produce an imbalance (i.e., an inconsistent attitude).  **(a)**

193.  An adept multicultural counselor

    a.  generally believes in the melting pot concept.
    b.  has a strong ethnocentric worldview.
    c.  will not ask the client for information related to religion or level of faith development.
    d.  usually supports the salad bowl model of diversity.

Choices "a," "b," and "c" are all characteristics of **ineffective multicultural helpers** leaving choice "d" as the lone hero. The melting pot concept—that different cultures assimilate or melt into the dominant culture—has been deemed a myth. The ethnocentric position holds that a given culture is the best or superior to others. The concept can also mean that the counselor falsely believes that the client views the world in the same manner as the helper. Efficacious helpers do attempt to elicit information regarding the client's religious and spiritual life. In the salad bowl analogy—preferred over the antiquated melting pot notion— people are mixed together, but like lettuce and tomatoes in a salad, they retain their unique cultural identity.  **(d)**

194.  A classic experiment in social psychology was conducted by the social psychologist Muzafer Sherif et al. at a boys' summer camp near Robbers' Cave, Oklahoma. The important finding in this study was that

    a.  most people cooperate in a social setting.
    b.  competition plays a small role in most of our lives.
    c.  a and b.
    d.  a cooperative, or so-called superordinate, goal attained only by working in a joint manner, can bring two hostile

groups together, thus reducing competition and enhancing cooperation.

Sometimes loosely called the **Robbers' Cave Experiment**, this study set up two distinct groups of 11-year-old boys who were hostile toward each other. The study concluded that the most effective way to reduce hostility between groups was to give them an alternative, a **superordinate goal**, which required a joint effort and could not be accomplished by a single group.        **(d)**

195. Sex-role stereotyping would imply that

   a.   a counselor would only consider traditional feminine careers for his female client.
   b.   a male counselor would rate a female client's emotional status differently than he would a male client's.
   c.   female clients are treated the same as male clients.
   d.   choices a and b.

**According to studies, male and female counselors can display prejudice toward women.** Prejudice means that we are negative or have a rigid, inflexible attitude toward a given group of people and can often act on our unfavorable thoughts. Moreover, the prejudiced individual often "prejudges" others without substantial evidence. Choices "a" and "b" are illustrative of stereotyping in which the counselor has generalized feelings about a given group (in this case, women). Unfortunately, research would suggest that the response in choice "a" might well be a typical one. In a study released in 1970 by Nancy K. Schlossberg and John J. Pietrofesa, counselor trainees and professors were instructed to help a female counselee choose between an engineering and a teaching career. All the counselor trainees tried to steer her clear of engineering, typically a masculine career. **According to the study females were as biased as males.** Horrors! As for choice "b," I can only say "ditto." A 1970 study by Inge K. Broverman, Donald M. Broverman, Frank E. Clarkson, Paul S. Rosenkrantz, and Susan Raymond Vogel found that all the therapists who filled out a questionnaire used a different standard of mental health when rating men from the one they used for women. Women and other minorities are sometimes said to be victims of a "caste system." The term *caste system* implies that there are fixed layers of superiority and inferiority which you are born into and thus cannot escape. **Please make it a priority to keep up with the literature in these key areas. This guide is not intended to do justice to these topics.** **(d)**

196. The statement "whites are better than African Americans" illustrates

    a.    a weakening of the caste system in the U.S.
    b.    racism.
    c.    sexism.
    d.    codependency.

Choice "a" is definitely wrong since the view that whites are better than African Americans is indicative of a caste system mentality (see the answer to the previous question). Choice "d," codependency, is a term which grew mainly out of the chemical dependency and addiction treatment movement. The word has various definitions, although it mainly refers to an individual who is emotionally involved with a chemically dependent person (perhaps even members of his or her family) and/or is addicted to a relationship with another person or drugs. "Racism," the correct answer, occurs when an assumption is made that some races are better than others. Hence, the race which feels superior can deny the other race rights and respect. *Sexism* is an analogous term. In sexism, one sex assumes that the other is inherently inferior. **(b)**

197. In terms of research related to affiliation

    a.    misery loves miserable company.
    b.    firstborns are more likely to affiliate than other children born later.
    c.    people affiliate in an attempt to lower fear.
    d.    all of the above.

Often the statement is made that misery loves more than company; it loves miserable company. Stanley Schachter set up an experiment in which subjects were informed that they were going to receive a very painful electrical shock (high anxiety) or a very weak one which would merely tingle. The subjects were told that they could wait alone for 10 minutes before receiving the shock or wait with others participating in the study. Of those subjects who were told they would receive a mere "tingle" only one third chose to wait with others, while over 62% of the high-anxiety group decided to do so. Follow-up research seems to indicate that a person with high anxiety will not choose to be with others unless the other individuals are in a similar situation. Philip Zimbardo discovered in a 1961 study that males placed in extremely embarrassing situations in which they would need to act like infants were much less willing to affiliate with others going through the same thing. One interpretation would be that individuals are more comfortable sharing real fear than anxiety which could result in embarrassment or shame. This research is somewhat similar to Leon Festinger's theory of social comparison, which postulates that people have a need to compare themselves with others to assess their own abilities and options. The theory further asserts that we will compare ourselves to others who are basically similar to us. **Important reminder: Researchers in the field of counseling are somewhat critical of most psychosocial experiments since the experimental situations are often artificial and the studies lack external validity, which is the ability to help understand behavior outside the experimental setting. (d)**

198. Six persons attend a counseling group. After the group, five members praise the merits of a group activity assigned by the group leader. The sixth person, who has heard the opinion of the other five people, felt the activity was useless and boring. According to studies on social behavior, about one third of the time the sixth individual would most likely tell the other five that

    a.    he totally disagreed with their assessment.
    b.    he too felt the group activity was very helpful.
    c.    he really wasn't certain how he felt about the activity.
    d.    a and c.

**This question is illustrative of an Asch situation.** Experiments by Solomon Asch and Muzafer Sherif would predict that the person would most likely "sell out" and agree with the other five. In one study Asch discovered that approximately 35% of the persons tested in a perceptual activity gave an answer which was clearly incorrect in order to conform! Social researchers consistently have discovered that people will conform to an obviously incorrect unanimous decision one third of the time. Moreover, studies indicate that as few as three other people can produce conformity in a social setting. Who conforms the most? The answer includes individuals who are authoritarian and thus are heavily influenced by authority figures, people who are external approval seekers, and persons who feel that outside external factors control them.                                      **(b)**

199. The client who would most likely engage in introspection would be a

    a.  52-year-old, single, African American male school administrator.
    b.  49-year-old, white homeless male.
    c.  40-year-old, divorced white female who is out of work and has three children.
    d.  19-year-old Latina mother on welfare with two children.

The key to this question is to focus on social class rather than acculturation (i.e., integrating one's own cultural beliefs and behaviors with the dominant culture), minority status, or sex. Clients in higher social classes have more time to "look within themselves" (introspect) since they need not dwell as much on external survival needs.                                      **(a)**

200. A Japanese client who was reluctant to look you in the eye during her counseling session would most likely be displaying

    a.  severe negative transference.
    b.  positive transference.
    c.  normal behavior within the context of her culture.
    d.  ambivalent transference.

Here is where knowledge of culture would come in handy. In some Asian cultures children are often brought up to believe that it is a sign of respect to avoid eye contact with an authority figure. In addition, in some cultures it is considered proper to talk no more than is necessary, which of course is not congruent with the way most Americans think. Moreover, some Asian Americans have been taught that it is shameful to brag or to express one's own desires, ambitions, or strong feelings. This background could well present a roadblock for a counselor operating under a paradigm that stresses abreaction. Some Asian Americans have been brought up to believe that all problems are solved only within the privacy of family meetings. If mental illness does exist, it is considered a genetic flaw and a family secret. Hence, some Asian Americans may place a high premium on self-control, which is an issue that can be examined in counseling. Derald Wing Sue and David Sue suggested that Asian Americans may respond best to brief therapy that is directive and structured with specific problem-solving goals. Often our somewhat scientific approaches to counseling really reflect what mainstream American society views as real or scientific. Some Latinos/as may value folk healing, which is very spiritual and can include elements such as going into a trancelike state and talking with God. Approximately 65% of the Latinos/as in the United States are of Mexican heritage according to the 2014 U.S. Census Bureau.                                **(c)**

# 5

## Counseling and Helping Relationships

*The curious paradox is that when I accept myself just as I am, then I can change.*
— Carl R. Rogers, father of person-centered counseling

**Special note to readers: This chapter contains considerably more information on psychoanalytic theory and behaviorism than you need to know to pass the NCE or the CPCE. Why in the world would I include this information? Excellent question! Unfortunately, both theories contain a wealth of information and the few questions your exam might incorporate could come from any of the material I have discussed herein. Don't think of it as overkill, but rather exam score insurance! On many comprehensive exams this section will be the largest section of the exam. Translation: It will have the biggest impact on your score! Moreover, other exams such as your comps and courses that cover these topics could indeed require the depth of material provided.**

**Key exam reminder** related to *all* theories of counseling and the helping relationship: The 2005 and 2014 American Counseling

Association (ACA) Code of Ethics stipulates that there must be scientific, empirical research, or a theory-based foundation for the use of *any* technique or treatment modality. This does not imply, however, that the technique or modality has been supported by a true experiment with random selection of subjects since that would exclude a host of viable strategies. If a client requests an approach that does not meet this new standard the counselor is obligated to tell the client that this approach is "unproven" or "developing" and thus could result in potential risk or harm. If after a thorough discussion the client fails to change his or her mind the counselor would have a responsibility to provide a referral. The ethics committee focused on this issue after discovering that some counselors rely on techniques that are based on the counselor's own bias, or perhaps a fad, rather than supporting research or an accepted theory. An example cited by ACA as an unproven approach is conversion/reparative therapy. Conversion/reparative therapy or sexual orientation change is intended to convert those in the LBGTQ community to heterosexuality. Although conversion/reparative therapy is not specifically mentioned as banned in the body of the ACA ethical guidelines document, subsequent articles quoting experts from the ACA task force indicate that it does fall in the "unproven" category. Moreover, the task force noted that it did not include this new ethical position to specifically target conversion/reparative therapy. At this point, there is no list (nor has one ever existed) that delineates precisely what techniques and approaches are unproven, although some task-force members did consider this option. Some task-force members feared that such a list could cause difficulties if an unproven technique was left out or manifested itself after the document was completed. The idea of creating a website with a list of proven strategies and those which might cause harm is being considered. For now, counselors who have any doubts regarding an approach are advised to consult an expert such as a former professor or a colleague. Consultation is extremely important. Counselors are also urged to turn to resources such as the ACA website, textbooks, professional journals, and newsletters, attend workshops, and keep in contact with persons who can act as consultants. Finally, this new ethical position does not prohibit the use of eclectic/integrative counseling (i.e., ideas from two or more different theories) as long as each approach meets these ACA ethical guidelines. This makes logical sense since the eclectic/integrative theoretical stance is used by more counselors (as well as social workers, psychologists, and psychiatrists) as their primary theoretical orientation than any other single approach (e.g., Rogerian, psychodynamic, humanistic, gestalt, systems, or cognitive). Almost 40% of all counselors now consider themselves eclectic/integrative.

**General hint: Is it traditional counseling (including brief therapy) or is it crisis intervention/crisis counseling? If a question on your exam implies that the goal is to return the person to their original level of functioning prior to the tragedy or crisis then it is crisis intervention/counseling since the symptoms are the result of the crisis. Counseling and therapy routinely attempt to deal with issues that go well beyond factors surrounding a crisis. For example, according to the 20/20 Consensus, the official unified definition of counseling states: "Counseling is a professional relationship that empowers diverse individuals, families, and groups to accomplish mental health, wellness, education, and career goals."**

201. Sigmund Freud is the father of psychoanalysis, which is both a form of treatment and a very comprehensive personality theory. According to Freud's theory, inborn drives (mainly sexual) help form the personality. _____ and _____, who originally worked with Freud, created individual psychology and analytic psychology, respectively.

    a.    Carl Jung; Alfred Adler
    b.    Alfred Adler; Carl Jung
    c.    Josef Breuer; A. A. Brill
    d.    Alfred Adler; Rollo May

Alfred Adler was the father of **individual psychology**, and Carl Gustav Jung (correctly pronounced "Yung") founded **analytic psychology**. But a word of caution is in order here: read all test questions carefully. Since the question utilizes the word *respectively* Adler's name (i.e., individual psychology) must come before Jung's name (i.e., analytic psychology), hence choice "a" is false. The question itself also emphasizes the key point that psychoanalysis is both a form of therapy as well as a theory of personality. Josef Breuer was a Viennese neurologist who taught

Freud the value of the talking cure, which is also termed *catharsis*. Brill's name is usually associated with the impact that Freudian theory has on career choice, and Rollo May was a prime mover in the existential counseling movement.                    **(b)**

202. Eric Berne's transactional analysis (TA) posits three ego states: the Child, the Adult, and the Parent. These roughly correspond to Freud's structural theory that includes

     a.   oral, anal, and phallic.
     b.   unconscious, preconscious, and conscious.
     c.   a and b.
     d.   id, ego, and superego.

     I must emphasize that neither Freud nor Berne characterized these ego states as biological entities. That is to say, a neurologist could not open up an individual's brain and map out the id or dissect the Parent ego state. Instead, the id, ego, and superego, and the Child, Adult, and Parent are hypothetical constructs used to explain the function of the personality. In Freudian theory, as well as in TA, experts in the field often refer to the aforementioned entities as the "structural theory." You will recall that the entities in choice "a" (oral, anal, and phallic) are the names of Freud's first three psychosexual stages. The unconscious, preconscious, and conscious noted in choice "b" relates to Freud's **topographic notion** that the mind has depth like an iceberg. The word *topography* means mapping, in this case that the Freudians have mapped the mind.          **(d)**

203. In transactional analysis (TA), the _____ is the conscience, or ego state concerned with moral behavior, while in Freudian theory it is the _____.

     a.   Adult, unconscious
     b.   Parent, ego
     c.   Parent, superego
     d.   Parent, id

**Hint:** Read test questions of this ilk very carefully. If I had a dollar for every instance that a counselor read conscience as conscious (or vice versa) I'd surely have a larger bank balance! Don't be a victim—read the question carefully. Eric Berne's TA utilizes popular terminology. The Parent ego state has been likened to Freud's superego. If a child has nurturing caretakers, he or she is said to develop "nurturing parent" qualities such as being nonjudgmental and sympathetic to others. The Parent ego state, however, may be filled with prejudicial and critical messages. Persons who fall into this category will tend to be intimidating, bossy, or know-it-alls. An individual whose caretaker left or died at an early age might be plagued with what TA refers to as the "incomplete parent." This person could expect others to parent him or her throughout life, or might use the lack of parenting as an excuse for poor behavior. ("Of course, I can't keep a job; I never had a mother to teach me how." TA calls this the game of "Wooden Leg.")                                    **(c)**

204. Freud felt that successful resolution of the Oedipus complex led to the development of the superego. This is accomplished by

   a.   identification with the aggressor, the parent of the same sex.
   b.   analysis during the childhood years.
   c.   identification with the parent of the opposite sex, the aggressor.
   d.   transference.

Oedipus means "swollen feet" and comes from the Greek tragedy by Sophocles. In the story Oedipus is unaware that he has killed his father and married his mother. According to Freudian theory, the child's libido or sex energy is directed toward the parent of the opposite sex. The child, nevertheless, realizes that retaliation would result if he (or she in the case of the Electra complex) would act on these impulses. The child thus strives for identification with the parent of the same sex to achieve vicarious sexual satisfaction. Now I must be honest and remind you that many behavioral scientists find this notion a bit far-fetched. The word *transference* in choice "d" is also a psychoanalytic concept. Transference implies that the client displaces emotion felt toward a parent onto the analyst, counselor, or therapist.                                              **(a)**

205. Freudians refer to the ego as

   a.   the executive administrator of the personality and the reality principle.
   b.   the guardian angel of the mind.
   c.   the pleasure principle.
   d.   the seat of libido.

Some scholars refer to the ego as the "executive administrator" since it governs or acts as a police officer to control the impulses from the id (instincts) and the superego (the conscience). The ego is a mediator. The ego is also called the reality principle and houses the individual's identity. Choices "d" and "c" describes the id. And just in case you chose choice "b," I can only say, "the guardian angel of the mind"—get serious, I just made it up! **(a)**

206. Freud's theory speaks of Eros and Thanatos. A client who threatens a self-destructive act is being ruled primarily by

   a.   Eros.
   b.   Eros and the id.
   c.   Thanatos.
   d.   both Eros and Thanatos.

Is it Greek or is it Freudian theory? You decide. Eros is the Greek god of the love of life. To the Freudians this means self-preservation. *Thanatos* is the Greek word for death. Later Freudian writings use the word to describe a death wish or what is sometimes called the death instinct. Today we call specialists who study death thanatologists.                                        **(c)**

207. The id is present at birth and never matures. It operates mainly out of awareness to satisfy instinctual needs according to the

   a.   reality principle.
   b.   notion of transference.

c.    Eros principle.
d.    pleasure principle, suggesting humans desire instinct gratification such for libido, sex, or the elimination of hunger or thirst.

**The id is the pleasure principle, the ego is the reality principle, and the superego is the ego ideal. Some exams will call it the pleasure–pain principle... relax... you've got this... it means precisely the same thing!**    **(d)**

208. If you think of the mind as a seesaw, then the fulcrum or balancing apparatus would be the

a.    id, which has no concept of rationality or time.
b.    ego.
c.    superego, which judges behavior as right or wrong.
d.    BASIC-ID.

**Freud felt the human mind was composed of three key components: the id, ego, and the superego.** If you missed this one, review the answer to question 205. Counselor educators often utilize the seesaw or fulcrum analogy when explaining the relationship of the id, ego, and superego. **The ego or reality principle attempts to balance the id and the superego.(b)**

209. A therapist who says to a patient "Say whatever comes to mind" is practicing

a.    directive counseling.
b.    transactional analysis.
c.    paraphrasing.
d.    free association.

Free association is literally defined as instructing the client to say whatever comes to mind even if it seems silly or embarrassing. Nothing the client says is censored by the helper. True to the tinsel town version, classical analysts have the client (known as an analysand) lie on a couch and free associate. The analyst remains out of sight. This is more or less the antithesis of directive approaches (choice "a") in which the client is asked to discuss certain material. Paraphrasing (choice "c") results whenever a counselor restates a client's message in the counselor's own words.                                                   **(d)**

210. The superego contains the ego ideal. The superego strives for _____, rather than _____ like the id.

   a.   perfection; pleasure
   b.   pleasure; perfection
   c.   morals; ethics
   d.   logic; reality

The superego is more concerned with the ideal and personal aspirations than what is real. The superego is composed of values, morals, and ideals of parents, caretakers, and society. And oh yes, as for choice "c," the id, ethical—with the possible exception of handling biological needs like hunger and thirst—never! The id is chaotic and has no sense of time.              **(a)**

211. All of these theorists could be associated with the analytic movement *except:*

   a.   Freud.
   b.   Jung.
   c.   Adler.
   d.   Wolpe.

Talk about a coincidence: Earlier today a counselor preparing for her exam emailed me to say I had the wrong answer to this question since choices "a," "b," and "c" are all correct. She failed to notice the word "except." **Read this question very carefully.** This is the so-called reverse- or negative-type question, and questions of this ilk do appear on the NCE/CPCE and other major exams. Questions of this nature ask you to ferret out the "incorrect" rather than the "correct" response. In this case, all of the choices except "d" name therapists in the psychoanalytic movement. Joseph Wolpe developed a paradigm known as "systematic desensitization," which is useful when trying to weaken (i.e., desensitize) a client's response to an anxiety-producing stimuli. **Systematic desensitization is a form of behavior therapy. It is based on Pavlov's classical conditioning. Other treatment modalities covered in this chapter that are derived from classical conditioning include: assertiveness training, flooding (aka flooding with response prevention), implosive therapy, and sensate focus.** **(d)**

212. Most scholars would assert that Freud's 1900 work entitled *The Interpretation of Dreams* was his most influential. Dreams have

    a.    manifest and latent content.
    b.    preconscious and unconscious factors.
    c.    id and ego.
    d.    superego and id.

    For Freud, the dream was the royal road to knowledge of the unconscious activities of the mind. **According to Freud, the dream is composed of a surface meaning, which is the manifest content, and then a hidden meaning or so-called latent content.** In therapy, dream work consists of deciphering the hidden meaning of the dream (e.g., symbolism) so the individual can be aware of unconscious motives, impulses, desires, and conflicts. **(a)**

213. When a client projects unconscious feelings toward the therapist that he or she originally had toward a significant other, it is called

    a.    free association.
    b.    insight.
    c.    transference.
    d.    resistance.

    Some counselors feel that transference is actually a form of projection, displacement, and repetition in which the client treats the counselor in the same manner as he or she would an authority figure from the past (e.g., a mother, a father, a caretaker, or significant other). Just for review purposes, choice "a," free association, is an analytic technique in which the client is instructed to say whatever comes to mind. Choice "b," insight, refers to the process of making a client aware of something which was previously unknown. This increases self-knowledge. Insight is often described as a novel sudden understanding of a problem. Choice "d" is resistance. Psychoanalysts believe that a client who is resistant will be reluctant to bring unconscious ideas into the conscious mind. Nonanalytic counselors generally utilize the term in a looser context and use the word to describe clients who are fighting the helping process in any manner.  **(c)**

214. Which case is *not* associated with the psychodynamic movement?

    a.    Little Hans.
    b.    Little Albert.
    c.    Anna O.
    d.    Daniel Paul Schreber.

Little Albert was a famous case associated with the work of John Broadus Watson, who pioneered American behaviorism. In 1920, John Watson and his graduate student, who later became his wife, Rosalie Rayner conditioned a 9-month-old boy named Albert to be afraid of furry objects. First Albert was exposed to a white rat. Initially the child was not afraid of the rat: however, Watson and Rayner would strike a steel bar, which created a loud noise whenever the child would get near the animal. This created a conditioned (i.e., learned) fear in the child. This experiment has been used to demonstrate the behavioristic concept that fears are learned rather than the analytic concept that they are somehow the result of an unconscious process. Incidentally, rumor has it that Albert (who was used to prove that Pavlovian conditioning could instill a fear in humans) was never cured of his experimentally induced affliction. Horrors! Choices "a," "c," and "d" refer to landmark psychoanalytic cases, which are often cited in the literature. The 1880s case of Anna O. (actually a client named Berta Pappenheim) was considered the first psychoanalytic patient. Anna O. was a patient of Freud's colleague Josef Breuer. She suffered from symptoms without an organic basis, which was termed *hysteria*. In hypnosis she would remember painful events, which she was unable to recall while awake. Talking about these traumatic events brought about relief and this became the talking cure or catharsis. Although Freud became disenchanted with hypnosis, his association with Breuer led him to his basic premise of psychoanalysis; namely, that techniques which could produce cathartic material were highly therapeutic. The case of Little Hans is often used to contrast behavior therapy (Little Albert) with psychoanalysis. It reflects the data in Freud's 1909 paper, "An Analysis of a Phobia in a Five-Year-Old Boy," in which this child's fear of going into the streets and perhaps even having a horse bite him were explained using psychoanalytic constructs such as the Oedipus complex and castration anxiety. Thus, Little Hans reflects psychoanalytic explanations of behavior, while Little Albert is indicative of the behaviorist paradigm. Daniel Paul Schreber has been called the "most frequently quoted case in modern psychiatry." In 1903, Schreber—after spending nine years in a mental hospital—wrote *Memoirs of a Nervous Patient* also titled *Memoirs of My Nervous Illness*. His family was rather wealthy and bought almost every copy in circulation. Nevertheless, Freud got his hands on one and in 1911 published *Psychoanalytical Notes upon an Autobiographical Account of a Case of Paranoia*. Schreber's major delusion was that he would be transformed into a woman, become God's mate, and produce a healthier race. Freud felt that Schreber might have been struggling with unconscious issues of homosexuality.                                    **(b)**

215. In contrast with classical psychoanalysis, psychodynamic counseling or therapy

    a.  utilizes fewer sessions per week.
    b.  does not utilize the couch.
    c.  is performed face to face.
    d.  all of the above.

Classical psychoanalysis is quite lengthy—three to five sessions per week for several years is not unusual—not to mention expensive. A complete analysis could cost well over $100,000 in some parts of the United States and virtually no forms of insurance or managed care will pay for this type of treatment. Psychodynamic therapy and counseling make use of analytic principles (e.g., the unconscious mind) but rely on fewer sessions per week to make it a bit more practical. Psychodynamic therapists generally dispense with the couch and sit face to face as in other forms of counseling and therapy. Freud once commented in regard to the merits of the couch that he could not stand to be stared at for many hours during the day. Moreover, he felt the couch could enhance the free-association process.                                                                    **(d)**

216. Talking about difficulties in order to purge emotions and feelings is a curative process known as

     a.   catharsis and/or abreaction.
     b.   resistance.
     c.   accurate empathy.
     d.   reflection of emotional content.

Hard-core analysts often prefer the word *abreaction* to the nontechnical term *catharsis*. Other writers use the word *catharsis* to connote mild purging of emotion, and *abreaction* when the repressed emotional outburst is very powerful and violent. Freud and Breuer initially used the term to describe highly charged repressed emotions, which were released during the hypnotic process. When all is said and done, most exams will do as I have done here and use the terms in a synonymous fashion. Choice "c," accurate empathy, means that the counselor can truly understand what the client is feeling or experiencing. Reflection of emotional content (choice "d") is accomplished when the counselor restates the client's verbalization in such a manner that the client becomes more aware of his or her emotions. Choices "c" and "d" are emphasized very heavily in the nondirective (later called client-centered and then person-centered) approach to counseling. **Rogerians do not emphasize diagnosis nor giving advice.**                                                            **(a)**

217. Id, ego, superego is to structural theory as _____ is to topographical theory.

    a.  Child, Adult, Parent
    b.  abreaction, catharsis, introspection
    c.  ego ideal
    d.  unconscious, preconscious, conscious

    First, let me explain why choice "a" is incorrect. Id, ego, and superego refer to Freud's structural theory of the personality while Child, Adult, and Parent is the structural model proposed by Eric Berne, father of transactional analysis. The question, nevertheless, does not ask you to compare the id, ego, and superego to another structural theory; it asks you to compare it to the components in the topographical theory. Remember, the one where the mind is seen as an iceberg? The term *introspection* introduced in choice "b" describes any process in which the client attempts to describe his or her own internal thoughts, feelings, and ideas.                                              **(d)**

218. The most controversial aspect of Freud's theory is

    a.  catharsis.
    b.  the Oedipus complex.
    c.  the notion of the preconscious mind.
    d.  the interpretation of dreams.

    The Oedipus complex is known as the Electra complex when it occurs in females. Also be aware that the most important concept in Freud's theory is the unconscious mind.                  **(b)**

219. Evidence for the unconscious mind comes from all of these *except:*

    a.  Hypnosis.
    b.  Slips of the tongue and humor.
    c.  Dreams.
    d.  Subjective units of distress scale.

Subjective Units of Disturbance Scale (SUDS) is a concept used in forming a hierarchy to perform Wolpe's systematic desensitization: a behavior therapy technique for curbing phobic reactions, anxiety, and avoidance responses to innocuous situations. The SUDS is created via the process of introspection by rating the anxiety associated with the situation. Generally, the scale most counselors use is 0 to 100, with 100 being the most threatening situation. The counselor can ask a client to rate imagined situations on the subjective units of disturbance scale so that a treatment hierarchy can be formulated. Just for the record, slips of the tongue (choice "b"), or what Freud called "the psychopathology of everyday life," will be technically referred to as "parapraxis" on some exams.                    **(d)**

220. In a counseling session, a counselor asked a patient to recall what transpired three months ago to trigger her depression. There was silence for about two and one-half minutes. The client then began to remember. This exchange most likely illustrates the function of the

   a.   preconscious mind.
   b.   ego ideal.
   c.   conscious mind.
   d.   unconscious mind.

The rationale here is simple enough. The conscious mind is aware of the immediate environment. The preconscious mind is capable of bringing ideas, images, and thoughts into awareness with minimal difficulty (e.g., in this question the memory of what transpired several months ago to trigger the client's depression). Thus, the preconscious can access information from the conscious as well as the unconscious mind. The unconscious, on the other hand, is composed of material which is normally unknown or hidden from the client. Thus, if the hypothetical client in this question had said, "Isn't that strange I can't remember what happened to trigger the depression," the correct answer would be choice "d," the unconscious mind (assuming, of course, the memory loss was not due to biological factors). And—strictly for the sake of repetition—the ego ideal of the superego is the perfect self or ideal self that the person judges himself or herself against.    **(a)**

221. Unconscious processes, which serve to minimize anxiety and protect the self from severe id or superego demands, are called

    a.    slips of the tongue.
    b.    ego defense mechanisms.
    c.    id defense processes.
    d.    latent dream material.

The id strives for immediate satisfaction, while the superego is ready and willing to punish the ego via guilt if the id is allowed to act on such impulses. This creates tension and a certain degree of pressure within the personality. The ego controls the tension and relieves anxiety utilizing "ego defense mechanisms." Simply put, ego defense mechanisms are unconscious strategies, which distort reality and are based on self-deception to protect our self-image. Although this concept has its roots in Freud's psychoanalysis, counselors of most persuasions now agree that defense mechanisms are relevant when studying the personality. Counselors who are not psychoanalytic, nevertheless, may not agree with the theoretical conceptualization that such behavior is the result of id, ego, and superego processes.    **(b)**

222. Most therapists agree that ego defense mechanisms are unconscious and deny or distort reality. Rationalization, compensation, repression, projection, reaction formation, identification, introjection, denial, and displacement are ego defense mechanisms. According to Freudians, the most important defense mechanism is

    a.    repression.
    b.    reaction formation
    c.    denial.
    d.    sublimation

Freud saw defense mechanisms as an unconscious method a person uses to protect him- or herself from anxiety. Freudians feel that repression is the kingpin or granddaddy of ego defense mechanisms. A child who is sexually abused, for example, may repress (i.e., truly forget) the incident. In later life, the repression that served to protect the person and "helped her through the distasteful incident at the time" can cause emotional problems. **Psychoanalytically trained counselors thus attempt to help the client recall the repressed memory and make it conscious so it can be dealt with. This is called insight and is often curative.** Choice "b," reaction formation, occurs when a person can't accept a given impulse and thus behaves in the opposite manner. Choice "c," denial, is similar to repression except that it is a conscious act. An individual who says "I refuse to think about it" is displaying suppression or denial. Sublimation, in choice "d," is present when a person acts out an unconscious impulse in a socially acceptable way. Hence, a very aggressive individual might pursue a career in boxing, wrestling, or football.                                                    **(a)**

223. Suppression differs from repression in that

    a.    suppression is stronger.
    b.    repression only occurs in children.
    c.    repression is automatic or involuntary.
    d.    all of the above.

    If you missed this one, review question 222. Some exams refer to suppression as denial.                                              **(c)**

224. An aggressive person who becomes a professional boxer because he or she is sadistic is displaying

    a.    suppression.
    b.    rationalization.
    c.    sublimation.
    d.    displacement.

    Again, if you missed this question review the question and answer for 222. A rationalization (choice "b") is simply an intellectual excuse to minimize hurt feelings. A student who says "Hey, I'm glad I didn't get good grades, only nerds get good grades" is practicing classical rationalization. The person who rationalizes will tend to interpret his thoughts and feelings in a positive or favorable manner. Choice "d", displacement—another defense mechanism—occurs when an impulse is unleashed at a safe target. The prototype example (which you could easily come across on a host of mental health exams) would be the man who is furious with his boss but is afraid to show it and so he comes home and kicks the family dog. One hopes that the family dog will have good enough sense to bite him back!   **(c)**

225. An advertising agency secretly imbeds the word *SEX* into newspaper ads intended to advertise the center's chemical dependency program. This is the practice of

   a.   sublimation.
   b.   repression.
   c.   introjection.
   d.   none of the above.

Okay, fess up: did you choose "a"? I'll bet you're not the only one! Let me say this in a way so you'll never miss this type of tricky question again: Sublimation is not the same as subliminal. Sublimation is a defense mechanism, while subliminal perception supposedly occurs when you perceive something unconsciously and thus it has an impact on your behavior. I say "supposedly" because the American Psychological Association (APA) has taken the position that subliminal perception is not effective. The opposite stance has been taken by Wilson Bryan Key who has written books such as *Subliminal Seduction* and *Media Sexploitation* in which he points out how advertisers and others have relied on this technique. So, a word to the wise: Read each exam question carefully. Here you will note that the question is describing a subliminal activity, yet the word *subliminal* is not an answer choice, making choice "d" the only correct answer. Choice "c," introjection, takes place when a child accepts a parent's, caretaker's, or significant other's values as his or her own. In the case of this defense mechanism, a sexually abused child might attempt to sexually abuse other children.   **(d)**

226. A man receives a nickel an hour pay raise. He was expecting a 1 dollar per hour raise. He is furious but nonassertive. He thus smiles and thanks his boss. That night he yells at his wife for no apparent reason. This is an example of

    a.    displacement.
    b.    denial.
    c.    identification.
    d     a Type II error.

    Here the man yells at his wife instead of kicking the family dog. This is displacement par excellence. Identification (choice "c") is also a defense mechanism, which results when a person identifies with a cause or a successful person with the unconscious hope that he or she will be perceived as successful or worthwhile. Another possibility is that the identification with the other person serves to lower the fear or anxiety toward that person. Finally, a Type II or so-called beta error is a statistical term, which means that a researcher has accepted a null hypothesis (i.e., that there is no difference between an experimental group and a group not receiving any experimental treatment) when it is false. There are plenty more questions of this sort when you reach the sections on statistics and research methodology.    **(a)**

227. A student tells a college counselor that he is not upset by a grade of "F" in physical education that marred his fourth-year perfect 4.0 average, inasmuch as "straight A students are eggheads." This demonstrates

    a.    introjection.
    b.    reaction formation.
    c.    sour grapes rationalization.
    d.    sweet lemon rationalization.

    Remember the fable in which the fox couldn't secure the grapes so he said they were probably sour anyway? Well here's the human equivalent affectionately known as the sour grapes variety of rationalization. "I didn't really want it anyway" is the way this one is usually expressed. Choice "d" depicts the "sweet lemon" variety of rationalization. Here the person tells you how wonderful a distasteful set of circumstances really is. Thus, in rationalization the person either underrates a reward (sour grapes) or overrates a reward (sweet lemon) to protect the self from a bruised ego.     **(c)**

228.  A master's level counselor lands an entry-level counseling job in an agency in a warm climate. Her office is not air conditioned, but the counselor insists she likes this because sweating really helps to keep her weight in check. This illuminates

   a.   sour grapes rationalization.
   b.   sweet lemon rationalization.
   c.   repression.
   d.   sublimation.

Review the previous question if you missed this. And here's a wonderful memory device. In our society we overrate the value of (or at least overeat) sweets in our diet. In the sweet lemon variety of rationalization the person overrates the situation. In this question the counselor is essentially saying, "Oh, gee, I just love to sweat, it keeps the water weight off of me and keeps my weight down." Right; and lemons taste sweet—dream on!     **(b)**

229.  A teenager who had his heart set on winning a tennis match broke his arm in an auto accident. He sends in an entry form to play in the competition which begins just days after the accident. His behavior is influenced by

   a.   denial.
   b.   displacement of anger.
   c.   sublimation.
   d.   organ inferiority.

This is classic denial. The tennis player is failing to face reality. Organ inferiority (choice "d") is usually associated with the work of Alfred Adler, who pioneered a theory known as "individual psychology."     **(a)**

230. _____ is like looking in a mirror but thinking you are looking out a window.

    a.   Repression
    b.   Sour grapes rationalization
    c.   Projection
    d.   Denial

    Simply put, the person who engages in projection attributes unacceptable qualities of his or her own to others. All of the answer choices are considered defense mechanisms.          **(c)**

231. Mark is obsessed with stamping out pornography. He is unconsciously involved in this cause so that he can view the material. This is

    a.   reaction formation.
    b.   introjection.
    c.   projection.
    d.   rationalization.

    In reaction formation the person acts the opposite of the way he or she actually feels. An adult living with a very elderly parent, for example, may spend all his or her time caring for the parent when in reality the individual unconsciously would like to see the elderly person die.          **(a)**

232. Ted has always felt inferior intellectually. He currently works out at the gym at least four hours daily and is taking massive doses of dangerous steroids to build his muscles. The ego defense mechanism in action here is

    a.   reaction formation.
    b.   compensation.
    c.   projection.
    d.   rationalization.

    Compensation is evident when an individual attempts to develop or overdevelop a positive trait to make up for a limitation (i.e., a perceived inferiority). The person secretly hopes that others will focus on the positives rather than the negative factors. **(b)**

233. Jane feels very inferior. She is now president of the board at a shelter for the homeless. She seems to be obsessed with her work for the agency and spends every spare minute trying to help the cause. When asked to introduce herself in virtually any social situation, Jane invariably responds with, "I'm the president of the board for the homeless shelter." Jane is engaging in

    a.   projection.
    b.   displacement.
    c.   introjection.
    d.   identification.

    If this is unclear review the explanation under question 226. **(d)**

234. A client who has incorporated his father's values into his thought patterns is a product of

    a.   introjection.
    b.   repression.
    c.   rationalization.
    d.   displacement.

    Yes, by the time you're finished wrestling with this set of questions you will definitely know your defense mechanisms! Sometimes introjection causes the person to accept an aggressor's values. A prisoner of war might incorporate the value system of the enemy after a period of time. **(a)**

235. The client's tendency to inhibit or fight against the therapeutic process is known as

    a.   resistance.
    b.   sublimation.
    c.   projection.
    d.   individuation.

A client who refuses to follow a counselor's directives such as a homework assignment or completing a battery of tests would be a typical example of resistance, or what counselors call the "resistant client."                                                       **(a)**

236. Freud has been called the most significant theorist in the entire history of psychology. His greatest contribution was his conceptualization of the unconscious mind. Critics, however, contend that

   a.   he was too concerned with the totem and the taboo.
   b.   he failed to emphasize sex.
   c.   many aspects of his theory are difficult to test from a scientific standpoint.
   d.   he was pro female.

How can concepts like the id, ego, or unconscious conflicts be directly measured? The answer is that for the most part, they can't. This has been a major criticism of Freud's theory. Choice "a" alludes to Freud's writings on the totem (an object that represents a family or group), the taboo, and the dread of incest. Freud felt that even primitive peoples feared incestuous relationships. The dread of incest is not instilled merely via modern societal sanctions. **Freud's psychoanalysis is the oldest major form of therapy.**                          **(c)**

237. The purpose of interpretation in counseling is to

   a.   help the therapist appear genuine.
   b.   make the clients aware of their unconscious processes.
   c.   make clients aware of nonverbal behaviors.
   d.   help clients understand feelings and behaviors related to childhood.

This is the kind of question that separates the men from the boys and the women from the girls. It is what is known as a "best answer" type of question. Although choices "c" and "d" are not necessarily incorrect, choice "b" is a textbook definition of interpretation.                                                        **(b)**

238. Organ inferiority relates mainly to the work of

    a. C. G. Jung's analytical psychology.
    b. Alfred Adler's individual psychology.
    c. Sigmund Freud's psychoanalytic theory.
    d. Josef Breuer's work on hysteria.

The term *individual* stresses the unique qualities we each possess. Individual psychology is keen on analyzing organ inferiority and methods in which the individual attempts to compensate for it. It is interesting to note that Alfred Adler was a very sickly child. Because of rickets (a disease caused by the absence of vitamin D, the so-called sunshine vitamin) Adler could not walk until age 4. He was then the victim of pneumonia as well as a series of accidents. Thus, for Adler, the major psychological goal is to escape deep-seated feelings of inferiority. Could Adler's theory reflect his own childhood? You decide. **(b)**

239. When a client becomes aware of a factor in his or her life that was heretofore unknown, counselors refer to it as

    a. individual psychology.
    b. confrontation.
    c. transference neurosis.
    d. insight.

Insight is the "aha, now I understand" phenomenon. Technically, the term *insight* is equated with the work of the gestalt psychologist Wolfgang Kohler. From 1913 to 1919 Kohler spent time on the island of Tenerife (the largest of the Canary Islands) where he studied chimpanzees and the great apes. In a somewhat landmark experiment one of Kohler's subjects, a rather intelligent chimp named Sultan, needed to secure a dish of food placed outside the cage. The chimp had two sticks but neither would reach the food. Finally, via trial and error, the chimp put the two sticks together to create a longer stick and the problem was suddenly solved (insight took place). In another famous experiment a banana was suspended from the ceiling of the cage, and the chimp needed to stack boxes and stand on them to reach the banana. When the chimp saw the value of using the box or the stick as a tool, Kohler called it an insight experience. His 1925 book *The Mentality of Apes* took the information beyond the Canary Islands to its rightful place in the therapy room. According to some theorists three types of learning exist: reinforcement (operant conditioning), association (classical conditioning), and insight. I can just hear you saying, "Okay Dr. Rosenthal, will I really need to know the cute little stories about the sticks and the bananas to pass my comprehensive exam?" Answer, "I certainly doubt it, but once in a while it's nice to learn something just for the sake of learning something fascinating."     **(d)**

240. C. G. Jung, the founder of analytic psychology, said men operate on logic or the _____ principle, while women are intuitive, operating on the _____ principle.

   a.   Eros; Thanatos
   b.   Logos; Eros
   c.   reality; pleasure
   d.   transference; countertransference

   Logos implies logic, while eros refers to intuition. Choice "d" uses the terminology, transference and countertransference. In transference, the assumption is that the client will relate to the therapist or counselor as he or she has done to significant others. The Freudians are fond of speaking of a "transference neurosis" in which the client is attached to the counselor as if he or she is a substitute parent. Countertransference (also commonly spelled with a hyphen) is said to be evident when the counselor's strong feelings or attachment to the client are strong enough to hinder the treatment process.     **(b)**

241. Jung used drawings balanced around a center point to analyze himself, his clients, and dreams. He called them

   a.   mandalas.
   b.   projective drawings.
   c.   unconscious automatic writing.
   d.   eidetic imagery.

Jung, the father of analytic psychology, borrowed the term *mandala* from Hindu writings in which the mandala was the symbol of meditation. In Jung's writings the mandala also can stand for a magic protective circle that represents self-unification. A bit mystical, isn't it? Perhaps that is why poets, philosophers, and those with an interest in religion often valued Jung's work more so than did psychiatrists. Choice "d" is a word you will often run across in child psychology and development tests. Eidetic imagery—which usually is gone by the time a child reaches adolescence—is the ability to remember the most minute details of a scene or a picture for an extended period of time. Laypersons will say that such a child has a "photographic memory," though the clinical term is "eidetikers." **(a)**

242. _____ emphasized the drive for superiority.

a. Jung
b. Adler
c. Constructivist therapists
d. Freud and Jung

Okay, here's a prime example where I am using an incorrect answer, choice "c" to teach you key material. The newer constructivist theories of intervention stress that it is imperative that we as helpers understand the client's view (also known as constructs) to explain his or her problems. Two popular classes of constructivist therapy include brief therapy, which examines what worked for a client in the past, and narrative therapy, which looks at the stories in the client's life and attempts to rewrite or reconstruct the stories when necessary. Alfred Adler, the father of individual psychology, initially felt that aggressive drives were responsible for most human behaviors. He then altered the theory slightly and said that the major factor was the "will to power." Finally, he concluded that it was the "striving for superiority" or a thirst for perfection that motivated behavior. (**Note:** The drive for superiority did not imply that the person wanted to dominate others or become a political figure or one of the ruling class.) **(b)**

243. The statement "Sibling interaction may have more impact than parent–child interaction" describes

    a.    Sigmund Freud's theory.
    b.    Alfred Adler's theory.
    c.    insight.
    d.    Carl Jung's theory.

Adler, who broke with Freud in 1911, went on to found a number of child guidance clinics in which he was able to observe children's behavior directly. One criticism of Freud has been that his child development theories were not based on extensive research or observations of children's behavior.     **(b)**

244. In contrast with Freud, the neo-Freudians emphasized

    a.    baseline measures.
    b.    social factors.
    c.    unconditional positive regard.
    d.    insight.

This is a must-know concept. It is hard to imagine a comprehensive exam that would not touch on this issue. Neo-Freudians such as Alfred Adler, Karen Horney, Erik Erikson, Harry Stack Sullivan, and Erich Fromm stressed the importance of cultural (social) issues and, of course, interpersonal (social) relations. Choice "a" is decidedly incorrect inasmuch as *baseline* is a behaviorist term. (Remember the behaviorists—the rivals of the analysts!) Baseline—sometimes written as two words—indicates the frequency that a behavior is manifested prior to, or in the absence of, treatment. Unconditional positive regard (choice "c") is a concept popularized by the late great therapist Carl R. Rogers, who felt that the counselor must care for the client even when the counselor is uncomfortable or disagrees with the client's position. In essence, the counselor accepts the client just the way he or she is without any stipulations.     **(b)**

245. The terms *introversion* and *extroversion* are associated with

    a.    psychoanalysis.
    b.    Freud.
    c.    Adler.
    d.    Jung.

Introversion meant a turning in of the libido. Thus, an introverted individual is his or her own primary source of pleasure. Such a person will generally shy away from social situations if possible. Extroversion, on the other hand, is the tendency to find satisfaction and pleasure in other people. The extrovert seeks external rewards. The introversion–extroversion distinction deals with inward or outward directiveness. Why not try the simplest of memory devices to remember this principle? You can remember that the "in" as in introvert looks "in" or with "in" himself or herself for satisfaction. Of course, an extrovert would be the opposite and look to external factors like social situations. Another idea might be to equate the "e," the first letter in extroversion, with the "e" which is the first letter in external. **(d)**

246. The personality types of the Myers–Briggs Type Indicator (MBTI) are associated with the work of

    a.    psychoanalysis.
    b.    Sigmund Freud.
    c.    Afred Adler.
    d.    Carl G. Jung.

This test, based on Volume 6 of Jung's collected works *Psychological Types* from the 1920s, is literally given to several million persons each year! The Myers–Briggs Type Indicator is said to be the most widely used measure of personality preferences and dispositions. The measure can be used to assess upper elementary children age 12 and over all the way through adulthood and yields a four-letter code, or "type," based on four bipolar scales. The bipolar preference scales are **extroversion/ introversion**; **sensing** (i.e., current perception)**/intuition** (i.e., future abstractions and possibilities); **thinking/feeling**; and

**judging** (i.e., organizing and controlling the outside world)/
**perceiving** (i.e., observing events).                              **(d)**

247. One of Adler's students, Rudolph Dreikurs,

   a.   created the TAT.
   b.   was the first to discuss the use of group therapy in private practice.
   c.   was a noted Freud hater.
   d.   created the hierarchy of needs.

Dreikurs also introduced Adlerian principles to the treatment of children in the school setting. The Thematic Apperception Test (TAT) mentioned in choice "a" is a projective test in which the client is shown a series of pictures and asked to tell a story. The TAT was introduced in Henry Murray's 1938 work *Explorations in Personality*. Murray called the study of the personality "personology." As for choice "c," I believe I'd go with Andrew Salter, who wrote *The Case Against Psychoanalysis*. Salter did groundbreaking work in behavior therapy, which led to the formation of assertiveness training. This information appeared in the 1949 classic *Conditioned Reflex Therapy*. In reference to choice "d," it was Abraham Maslow and not Alfred Adler who created the hierarchy of needs.                              **(b)**

248. Adler emphasized that people wish to belong. This is known as

   a.   superiority.
   b.   social connectedness.
   c.   the collective unconscious.
   d.   animus.

The Adlerian theory (choice "b") suggests that we need one another. The collective unconscious in choice "c" is a term coined by C. G. Jung, which implies that all humans have "collected" universal inherited, unconscious neural patterns. **(b)**

249. Adler was one of the first therapists who relied on paradox. Using this strategy, a client (who was a student in a counselor

preparation program) who was afraid to give a presentation in front of his counseling class for fear he might shake and embarrass himself would be instructed to

a. exaggerate the behavior and really do a thorough job shaking in front of the class.
b. practice relaxation techniques for 10–20 minutes before the speech.
c. practice rational self-talk.
d. practice rational thinking.

Paradoxical techniques also are associated with the work of Viktor Frankl, who pioneered logotherapy, a form of existential treatment. Paradoxical strategies often seem to defy logic as the client is instructed to intensify or purposely engage in the maladaptive behavior. Paradoxical interventions are often the direct antithesis of common sense directives such as choice "b." Paradoxical methods have become very popular with family therapists due to the work of Jay Haley and Milton H. Erickson. Currently, this technique is popular with family therapists who believe it reduces a family's resistance to change. Choices "c" and "d" are almost always associated with the so-called cognitive therapies, especially rational-emotive behavior psychotherapy. **(a)**

250. C. J. Jung felt that society caused men to deny their feminine side known as _____ and women to deny their masculine side known as _____.

a. Eros; Thanatos
b. animus; anima
c. anima; animus
d. yin; yang

These terms were introduced in the section on human growth and development, but just for review purposes and for those who never studied Latin: You can remember that anima is the feminine term as it ends in "ma," and needless to say, it is common to refer to one's mother as "ma." Choice "d" notes the Chinese Taoist philosophy in which the yin is the passive feminine force in the universe, which is contrasted by the yang, the masculine force.                                            **(c)**

251. Jung spoke of a collective unconscious common to all men and women. The material that makes up the collective unconscious, which is passed from generation to generation, is known as

    a.    a hierarchy of needs.
    b.    instinctual.
    c.    paradox.
    d.    archetypes.

    This is easy to remember if you keep the word *archaic* in mind. An archetype is actually a primal universal symbol, which means the same thing to all men and women (e.g., the cross). Jung perused literature and found that certain archetypes have appeared in fables, myths, dreams, and religious writings since the beginning of recorded history.                          **(d)**

252. Common archetypes include

    a.    the persona—the mask or role we present to others to hide our true self.
    b.    animus, anima, and self.
    c.    shadow—the mask behind the persona, which contains id-like material, denied, yet desired.
    d.    all of the above.

    The shadow noted in choice "c" is often called the dark side of the personality, though it is not necessarily negative. Jung noted that the shadow encompasses everything an individual refused to acknowledge. The shadow represents the unconscious opposite of the individual's conscious expression. Hence, a shy, retired individual might have recurring dreams that he or she is very outgoing, verbal, and popular. In addition to dreams, the basic nature of the shadow is also evident when an individual engages in projection. The clinical assumption is made that projection will decrease and individuation will increase as therapy renders shadow behaviors conscious.          **(d)**

253. A client is demonstrating inconsistent behavior. She is smiling but says that she is very sad about what she did. When her counselor points this out to her, the counselor's verbal response is known as

    a.  active listening.
    b.  confrontation.
    c.  accurate empathy.
    d.  summarization.

    Confrontation could also relate solely to verbal behavior. For example, a counselor might confront a client about what he says he is doing in his life versus what he is truly doing. The essence of confrontation is to illuminate discrepancies between the client's and the helper's conceptualization of a given situation. **Choice "c," accurate empathy, occurs when a counselor is able to experience the client's point of view in terms of feelings and cognitions. Empathy is a subjective understanding of the client in the here and now. Again, empathy deals with the client's perception rather than your own.** Summarization, mentioned in choice "d," transpires whenever a counselor brings together the ideas discussed during a period of dialogue. A counselor might also ask the client to summarize to be certain that he or she has actually grasped the meaning of an exchange. Some counselors believe that summarization should occur at the end of each session or after several sessions.                     **(b)**

254. During a professional staff meeting, a counselor says he is worried that if techniques are implemented to stop a 6-year-old boy from sucking his thumb, then he will begin biting his nails or stuttering. The counselor

    a.  is using ACT or acceptance and commitment therapy, a mindfulness-based behavior therapy.
    b.  is using Donald Meichenbaum's cognitive behavior modification.
    c.  is most likely a behaviorist concerned with symptom substitution.
    d.  is most likely an analytically trained counselor concerned with symptom substitution.

Choice "a," ACT, is a type of therapy created by Steve Hayes in 1986 which does not (yes not) focus on symptom reduction. ACT wants clients to take … well … effective action in their lives. The goal is to perceive feelings and thoughts as harmless, albeit uncomfortable. As soon as something is perceived as a symptom it seems pathological. According to ACT most of us will experience psychological suffering as a result of our own mental processes. Therapy is aimed at helping clients to stop struggling with their private experiences and to assist them in taking action toward the life they want. ACT suggests that struggling with negative feelings makes them worse. Okay, switching gears: The answer to the present question can only be choice "d" inasmuch as symptom substitution is a psychoanalytic concept. According to the theory, if you merely deal with the symptom another symptom will manifest itself since the real problem is in the unconscious mind. **Behaviorists do strive for symptom reduction and do not believe in the concept of symptom substitution.**                              **(d)**

255. An eclectic counselor

   a.   is analytic.
   b.   is behavioristic.
   c.   attempts to choose the best theoretical approach based on the client's attributes, resources, and situation.
   d.   insists on including all family members in the treatment.

An eclectic counselor uses theories and techniques from several models of intervention, rather than simply relying on one. An eclectic counselor, for example, would not say, "I'm a Rogerian," or "I see myself as a strict behavior therapist." The eclectic counselor uses "the best from every approach." Research indicates that about approximately half of all therapists claim to be eclectic, and a number of studies indicate eclecticism is on the rise.     **(c)**

256. The word *eclectic* is most closely associated with

   a.   Frederick C. Thorne.
   b.   Sigmund Freud.

c.  Jean Piaget.

d.  Burrhus Frederic Skinner.

It is very important to note that Thorne felt that true eclecticism was much more than "a hodgepodge of facts"; it needed to be rigidly scientific. Thorne preferred the term *psychological case handling* rather than *psychotherapy*, as he felt the efficacy of psychotherapy had not been scientifically demonstrated.  **(a)**

257.  A counselor who is obsessed with the fact that a client missed his or her session is the victim of

a.  cognitive dissonance.

b.  transference.

c.  countertransference.

d.  positive transference.

In countertransference the counselor's past is projected onto the client and the helper's objectivity suffers markedly. A counselor who falls in love with a client or feels extreme anger toward a client is generally considered a victim of countertransference. Choice "a," cognitive dissonance, suggests that humans will feel quite uncomfortable if they have two incompatible or inconsistent beliefs and thus the person will be motivated to reduce the dissonance.  **(c)**

258.  Lifestyle, birth order, and family constellation are emphasized by

a.  Freud.

b.  Jung.

c.  Adler.

d.  Thorne and Lazarus.

Adlerians believe that our lifestyle is a predictable self-fulfilling prophecy based on our psychological feelings about ourselves. Adler stressed the importance of birth order in the family constellation (e.g., the firstborn/oldest child could be dethroned by a later child who gets most of the attention; thus the firstborn would be prone to experience feelings of inferiority). Firstborns often go to great lengths to please their parents. A second child will often try to compete with a firstborn child and often surpasses the first child's performance. A middle child (or children) will often feel that he or she is being treated unfairly. Middle children are sometimes seen as being quite manipulative. The youngest child or baby in the family can be pampered or spoiled. The good news is that they often excel by modeling/imitating the older children's behavior. The concept of birth order has been criticized by some theorists such as Wayne Dyer, famous for his self-improvement book *Your Erroneous Zones,* which outsold every book written in the decade of the 1970s!                    **(c)**

259. A counselor who remarks that firstborn children are usually conservative but display leadership qualities is most likely

    a.    a Freudian who believes in the unconscious mind.

    b.    an Adlerian who believes behavior must be studied in a social context; never in isolation.

    c.    a Rogerian who stresses the importance of the therapeutic relationship.

    d.    a behavior modifier using a behavioral contract.

You can well imagine why the current family therapy movement has roots in Adlerian theory. Adlerians stress that clients long for a feeling of belonging and strive for perfection. Adlerians—like REBT practitioners—are didactic and use homework assignments. The Adlerian counselor often asks the client: What would life be like if you were functioning in an ideal manner? Then the counselor asks the client to act "as if" he or she did not have the problem. Now that's what I call a dramatic therapeutic strategy!                    **(b)**

260. Existentialism is to logotherapy as _____ is to behaviorism.

    a.    operants

    b.    associationism

    c.    Skinner

    d.    Socrates

Don't panic—this is simply an analogy-type question. Let's think this one out together so you can discover how choice "b" checks in as the correct answer. The first word in the question gives us a significant clue. That is to say, "existentialism" is a type of philosophy. Now existentialism (the philosophy) is compared to "logotherapy," which is a brand of psychotherapy. The question then mentions behaviorism, which is a type of psychology and more loosely defined as a brand of treatment. So, the question tells you that logotherapy grew out of the philosophy of existentialism and then asks you to fill in the blank with the philosophy which led to the formation of behaviorism. Skinner and his concept of operants are behavioristic to be sure; however, neither of them is a philosophy. The answer is associationism, which asserts that ideas are held together by associations. Now here's a super hint. Although associationism had its roots in an essay written by Aristotle on the nature of memory, most exams will list John Locke, David Hume, James Mill, or David Hartley as the pioneers. My guess: Look for the name John Locke come exam time. **(b)**

261. B. F. Skinner's reinforcement theory elaborated on

    a.   Edward Thorndike's law of effect.
    b.   Alfred Adler's concept of lifestyle.
    c.   Arnold Lazarus's concept of the BASIC-ID used in the multimodal therapeutic approach that is eclectic and holistic.
    d.   symptom substitution.

The "law of effect" simply asserts that responses accompanied by satisfaction (i.e., it pleases you) will be repeated, while those which produce unpleasantness or discomfort will be stamped out. Just a quick quip in regard to choice "c": Lazarus worked very closely with Joseph Wolpe—and thus his multimodal approach—although it is very holistic, meaning that the approach emphasizes the whole person—has a strong behavioral treatment slant. When practicing multimodal therapy the counselor focuses on seven key modalities or areas of the client's functioning: **B** = behavior including acts, habits, and reactions; **A** = affective responses such as emotions, feelings, and mood; **S** = sensations, including hearing, touch, sight, smell, and taste; **I** = images/the way we perceive ourselves, including memories and dreams; **C** = cognitions such as our thoughts, insights, and even our philosophy of life; **I** = interpersonal relationships (i.e., the way we interact with others); and **D** = drugs, that would include alcohol, legal, illegal, and prescription drug usage, diet and nutritional supplementation.    **(a)**

262.  Classical conditioning relates to the work of

a.   E. G. Williamson.
b.   B. F. Skinner.
c.   Viktor Frankl, who created logotherapy.
d.   Ivan Pavlov.

Interestingly enough, Pavlov won a Nobel Prize not for his work in classical conditioning but for his research on the digestive system. Choice "a," E. G. Williamson, is the father of the so-called Minnesota Viewpoint. Popular some years ago, especially with career counselors, this approach attempts to match the client's traits with a career. A word to the wise: Many exams will bill this as the "trait-factor" approach.    **(d)**

263.  An association that naturally exists, such as an animal salivating (an unconditioned response known as a UR or UCR) when food is presented, is called

a.   an operant.
b.   a conditioned stimulus (CS).
c.   an unconditioned stimulus (UCS).
d.   an acquisition period.

Let me see if I can make this simple for you so that every time you see some form of the word *conditioned* or *conditioning* you don't feel intimidated. From now on, whenever you see the word *conditioned*, substitute the word *learned*. When you see the word *unconditioned* substitute the word *unlearned*. Now this question becomes a heck of a lot easier, since salivating is an "unlearned" association. The dog need not sign up for a graduate course in behaviorism to learn this response. So, for review purposes: conditioned = learned; unconditioned = unlearned. Choice "d," the acquisition period, refers to the time it takes to learn or acquire a given behavior. If it takes a mentally challenged child two hours to learn to write his name, then two hours would be the acquisition period. **(c)**

264. Skinner's operant conditioning is also referred to as

    a.    instrumental learning.
    b.    classical conditioning.
    c.    cognitive learning.
    d.    learning via insight.

One possible memory device here would be that Skinner's last name has an "i" as does the word *instrumental*, whereas the word *Pavlov* doesn't. **(a)**

265. Respondent behavior refers to

    a.    reflexes.
    b.    operants.
    c.    a type of phobia.
    d.    punishment.

Okay, so you didn't fall in love with my memory device for the last question. Never fear; here's another way to go about it. Pavlov's theory involves mainly "reflexes," such as in the experiment where the dog salivates. The word *reflex* begins with an "r" and so does the word *respondent*. The bottom line: Pavlovian conditioning is respondent while Skinner's is instrumental/operant. P.S. Please don't read this if you get confused easily, but the term *respondent* is generally accredited to Skinner, although it applies to the theoretical notions of Pavlovian conditioning. **(a)**

266. All reinforcers

    a.   are plastic tokens.
    b.   tend to increase the probability that a behavior will occur.
    c.   are secondary.
    d.   do not raise behavior since negative reinforcement lowers
         behavior.

I can't say this too strongly: All reinforcers—yep, both positive
and negative—raise the probability that an antecedent (prior)
behavior will occur. In a situation where we have positive
reinforcement, something is added following an operant
(behavior). Now this is going to sound a little complicated, but
here goes. It is possible to use positive reinforcers to reduce or
eliminate an undesirable target behavior. Here's how. Using a
procedure known as "differential reinforcement of other
behavior" (DRO), the counselor positively reinforces an
individual for engaging in a healthy alternative behavior. The
assumption is that as the alternative desirable behavior increases
via reinforcement, the client will not display the inappropriate
target behavior as frequently. In the case of negative
reinforcement, something is taken away after the behavior
occurs. As for the incorrect choices, a secondary reinforcer is a
neutral stimulus, such as a plastic token, which becomes
reinforcing by association. Thus, a plastic token could be
exchanged for known reinforcers (like a trip to a major league
baseball game for adolescent clients in a treatment center).  **(b)**

267. Negative reinforcement requires the withdrawal of an aversive
     (negative) stimulus to increase the likelihood that a behavior will
     occur. Negative reinforcement is not used as often as positive
     reinforcement and

    a.   is really the same as punishment.
    b.   effectively lowers the frequency of behavior in young
         children.
    c.   is not the same thing as punishment.
    d.   is a psychodynamic conceptualization.

A comprehensive test that includes questions on behavior modification but does not have a question similar to this one would be about as likely as an orange containing lemon juice. In case my analogy is a bit too sarcastic (or sour) for your taste, the salient point is that you must understand this concept. **Negative reinforcement is not punishment. All reinforcers raise or strengthen the probability that a behavior will occur; punishment lowers it. In the case of a negative reinforcer, it generally provides relief. If you ingest a pain pill and it relieves pain you are more apt to take it again when you are plagued with pain since it gave you relief.** Now, what about punishment? It doesn't take a master's or a doctorate in counseling to grasp the notion that when you were punished as a child the probability of that particular behavior generally decreased for a period of time. I say "for a period of time" since most behavior modifiers feel punishment temporarily suppresses the behavior. This seems to be the case in humans and, according to B. F. Skinner, in rats. This would certainly seem to dethrone choice "b" as the correct response. **Advanced exam reminder:** Some tests *will discriminate* between positive and negative punishment. Positive punishment is said to occur when something is added after a behavior and the behavior decreases, while negative punishment takes place when a stimulus is removed following the behavior and the response decreases. **(c)**

268. Punishment

    a.  is the same as negative reinforcement.
    b.  is much more effective than reinforcement.
    c.  decreases the probability that a behavior will occur.
    d.  is used extensively in reality therapy.

A little review never hurt anybody. To set the record straight, behavior modifiers value reinforcement over punishment. William Glasser, M.D., the father of reality therapy, lists eight steps for effective treatment, of which step 7 admonishes "not to punish." **(c)**

269. In Pavlov's famous experiment using dogs, the bell was the
_____ and the meat was the _____.

    a.    CS; UCS
    b.    UCS; CS
    c.    CR; UCS
    d.    UCS; CR

Ah, remember my memory device from the beginning of this
book. It went like this: "In the U.S. we eat a lot of meat." Say it
aloud three or four times. I doubt whether you will ever forget
it. In the Pavlovian experiment, the US (which is sometimes
written UCS) is the unconditioned (think unlearned) stimulus,
or the meat. The CS is the conditioned or learned stimulus. **(a)**

270. The most effective time interval (temporal relation) between the
CS and the US

    a.    is irrelevant—it does not influence the learning process.
    b.    is 5 seconds.
    c.    is the .05 level according to social scientists.
    d.    is .5 or half a second.

As the interval exceeds 0.5 seconds, more trials are needed for
effective conditioning. How will you remember that the CS
comes before the US? Just remember that "c" (as in CS) comes
before "u" (as in UCS) in the alphabet. Nice! Or better still,
common sense would dictate that the reinforcer (the meat/US)
would come after the bell (the CS) to reinforce it. Now I'm going
to share something with you that will help you on difficult exam
questions. When the CS is delayed until the US occurs, the
procedure is known as "delay conditioning." If, however, the CS
terminates before the occurrence of the US, it is termed "trace
conditioning." Here's a slick and easy-to-use memory device.
Trace begins with "t" and so does termination. In trace
conditioning, the CS will terminate prior to the onset of the US
(or UCS as it will be abbreviated on some exams). **(d)**

271. Many researchers have tried putting the UCS (the meat) before the CS (the bell). This usually results in

    a.   increased learning.
    b.   anger on the part of the dog.
    c.   experimental neurosis.
    d.   no conditioning.

    Whether you put the cart before the horse, "u" before "c" in the alphabet, or the UCS before the CS, it just doesn't work. **This is called backward conditioning. Generally backward conditioning is ineffective and doesn't work. On a similar note, if the bell and the meat are presented at the exact same time—and this is called simultaneous conditioning— conditioning will not occur.** Some exams refer to the typical classical conditioning process where the CS comes before the UCS as "forward conditioning" to distinguish it from "backward conditioning," or "simultaneous conditioning."          **(d)**

272. Several graduate students in counseling trained a poodle to salivate to a child's toy horn using Pavlov's classical conditioning paradigm. One day the department chairman was driving across campus and honked his horn. Much to the chagrin of the students, the poodle elicited a salivation response. What had happened?

    a.   experimental neurosis had obviously set in.
    b.   extinction.
    c.   stimulus generalization or what Pavlov termed irradiation.
    d.   stimulus discrimination.

    Rule 1 for handling those lengthy questions on your exam: ignore all the irrelevant information. Whether it was the department chairman driving across the campus or the dean of students riding his bicycle with two flat tires is about as relevant to answering the question as the price of tea in New York City! Stimulus generalization, also called "second-order conditioning," occurs when a stimulus similar to the CS (in this instance, the bell) produces the same reaction. Hence, a car horn, a piano key, or a buzzer on a stove timer could conceivably produce the same reaction as the bell. Remember when I mentioned Little Albert's learned fear of white rats? The tendency for him to display fear with other furry white animals or a Santa Claus mask is illustrative of the principle of stimulus generalization. **A quick quip: A conditioned response is not as powerful as an unconditioned response or UR. Hence, a dog salivates when it sees meat. Now you condition the dog to salivate to a bell. Again, this is called a conditioned (learned) response or CR. The CR or learned response will be present, but still will not be as powerful as the original UR. And finally: the response we see in stimulus generalization is weaker than the response produced by the original conditioning. So, in theory, although Little Albert was afraid of a Santa Claus mask, his fear response would still be less intense than his fear of a white rat. (c)**

273. The department chairman found the poodle's response (see question 272) to his automobile horn humorous. He thus instructed the graduate students to train the dog to salivate only to his car horn and not the original toy bell. Indeed the graduate students were able to perform this task. The poodle was now demonstrating

   a. experimental neurosis.
   b. irradiation.
   c. pica.
   d. stimulus discrimination.

Stimulus discrimination is nearly the opposite of stimulus generalization. Here the learning process is "fine tuned," if you will, to respond only to a specific stimulus. In this example, the dog would be taught to salivate only when the department chairman sounds the horn in his vehicle. A piano key, a buzzer on a stove, or the original toy bell would not elicit (i.e., cause) the reaction. Stimulus discrimination is at times referred to as "stimulus differentiation" in some of the literature. Pica, choice "c", is the tendency for humans to eat objects that are non food, non nutritive items, such as chewing on a pencil or lead paint (the latter of which can cause irreversible brain damage). Some people believe pica is a psychological difficulty while other experts insist it occurs due to a lack of minerals in the diet.   **(d)**

274. The department chair was further amused by the poodle's tendency to be able to discriminate one CS from another (see question 273). He thus told the students to teach the dog to salivate only to the horn on his Ford but not one on a graduate student's Chevrolet truck. In reality, the horns on the two vehicles sounded nearly identical. The training was seemingly unsuccessful inasmuch as the dog merely took to very loud barking. In this case

    a.   experimental neurosis set in.
    b.   irradiation became a reality.
    c.   borderline personality traits no doubt played a role.
    d.   a covert process confounded the experiment.

    "Stop it, you're driving this dog crazy" would be the correct response to this question. Pavlov termed this phenomenon "experimental neurosis." When the differentiation process becomes too tough because the stimuli are almost identical, the dog will show signs of emotional disturbance. **Reminder:** On questions of this nature, some exams will refer to the CS as the NS, or "neutral stimulus," and the UCS as the "reinforcing" or "charged stimulus."   **(a)**

275. In one experiment, a dog was conditioned to salivate to a bell paired with a fast-food cheeseburger. The researcher then kept ringing the bell without giving the dog the cheeseburger. This is known as

    a.   instrumental learning via shaping.
    b.   positive reinforcement.
    c.   extinction, and the salivation will disappear.
    d.   negative reinforcement.

    This may be a doggy way to learn about classical Pavlovian respondent conditioning, but I believe it is effective. In this case the layperson might say that ringing a bell and not reinforcing the dog with a fast-food cheeseburger is animal cruelty. The professional will see it as classical extinction, not to be confused with operant extinction. Extinction occurs when the CS is "not" reinforced via the US. Most experts believe that the CR is not eliminated but is suppressed, or what is generally called "inhibited." The rationale for this position is that if the animal is given a rest, the CR (i.e., the salivation in this example) will reappear, though it will be weaker. This phenomenon has been called "spontaneous recovery." In Skinnerian or operant conditioning, extinction connotes that reinforcement is withheld and eventually the behavior will be extinguished (eliminated).                           **(c)**

276. John B. Watson's name is associated with

   a.   Little Hans.
   b.   Anna O.
   c.   Little Albert.
   d.   b and c.

The significance of the Little Albert case was that it demonstrated that fears were "learned" and not the result of some unconscious conflict.                                                    **(c)**

277. During a family counseling session, a 6-year-old girl repeatedly sticks her tongue out at the counselor, who is obviously ignoring the behavior. The counselor is practicing

   a.   negative reinforcement,
   b.   chaining.
   c.   reciprocal inhibition.
   d.   extinction.

A word to the wise experimenter or counselor: Some research demonstrates that when using extinction the behavior will get worse before it is eliminated. This tendency technically is called a response burst or an extinction burst. Fortunately, the "burst," or increase in the frequency of behavior, is temporary. In plain everyday English then, this counselor can expect the little girl's behavior—in this case sticking out her tongue—to get worse before it gets better. Ignoring a behavior is a common method of extinction as is the practice of time-out, where the client or student is isolated from reinforcement. Just for the record, the response burst is generally a major ethical consideration for therapists who are attempting to extinguish self-abusive or self-mutilating behaviors. Choice "b," *chaining*, is also a behavioristic term. A chain is a sequence of behaviors in which one response renders a cue that the next response is to occur. When you are writing a sentence and place a period at the end it is a cue that you're next letter will be an upper-case letter. In behavior modification simple behaviors are learned and then "chained" so that a complex behavior can take place. A chain is really just a series of operants joined together by reinforcers.  **(d)**

278. In general, behavior modification strategies are based heavily on _____, while behavior therapy emphasizes _____.

    a.   instrumental conditioning; classical conditioning
    b.   Pavlovian principles; Skinnerian principles
    c.   Skinnerian principles; Pavlovian principles
    d.   a and c

    Technically, behavior modification is Skinnerian (i.e., operant, instrumental), while behavior therapy is Pavlovian (i.e., classical, respondent).  **(d)**

279. A behavioristic counselor decides upon aversive conditioning as the treatment of choice for a gentleman who wishes to give up smoking. The counselor begins by taking a baseline. This is accomplished

    a.   using hypnosis.
    b.   by charting the occurrence of the behavior prior to any therapeutic intervention.
    c.   using a biofeedback device.
    d.   by counterconditioning.

The baseline indicates the frequency of the behavior untreated and is sometimes signified in the literature on a chart using an upper-case letter A.    **(b)**

280. The first studies, which demonstrated that animals could indeed be conditioned to control autonomic processes, were conducted by

a.    Edward Thorndike.
b.    Joseph Wolpe.
c.    Neal Miller.
d.    Ivan Pavlov.

In a study that perhaps challenged a 100-year-old psychological doctrine, Neal Miller and Ali Banuazizi showed that by utilizing rewards rats could be trained to alter heart rate and intestinal contractions. Prior to this experiment it was thought that automatic or "autonomic" bodily processes (such as heart rate, intestinal contractions, or blood pressure) could not be controlled. Today, counselors often use the technique of biofeedback (i.e., hooking the client to a sophisticated electronic device that provides biological feedback) to help clients control autonomic responses. Edward Thorndike, mentioned in choice "a," postulated the "law of effect," which is also known as "trial and error learning." This theory assumes that satisfying associations related to a given behavior will cause it to be "stamped in," while those associated with annoying consequences are "stamped out." And here is an important point: Practice per se does not ensure effective learning. The practice must yield a reward.    **(c)**

281. The significance of the Little Albert experiment by John B. Watson and Rosalie Rayner was that

a.    a phobia could be a learned behavior.
b.    it provided concrete proof that Skinner's model was correct.
c.    it provided concrete proof that Pavlov's model was correct.
d.    none of the above.

The psychoanalytic or Freudian theory espoused the notion that a fear was the result of an unconscious conflict. This is why analytic psychology is often called "depth psychology." Something is assumed to be wrong deep below the level of awareness. **The key take-away message from Watson's Little Albert experiment was that a fear was not due to psychopathology deep within the unconscious mind, but rather learning.** **(a)**

282. John B. Watson is to cause as Mary Cover Jones is to

    a.   cure.
    b.   Skinner.
    c.   Piaget.
    d.   NLP.

John B. Watson demonstrated that a phobic reaction was "learned," while Mary Cover Jones demonstrated that "learning" could serve as a treatment for a phobic reaction. Neurolinguistic programming (NLP) is the brainchild of linguistics professor John Grinder and mathematician/computer expert John Bandler. These outsiders to the helping professions watched expert helpers, most notably, Virginia Satir, Milton H. Erickson, and Fritz Perls to discover what these therapists really did rather than what they said they did. **(a)**

283. In the famous Little Albert experiment, a child was conditioned to fear a harmless white furry animal. Historical accounts indicate that the child also began to fear a Santa Claus mask. This would demonstrate

    a.   two *DSM* diagnoses which often co-occur: panic disorder and agoraphobia.
    b.   stimulus generalization.
    c.   an adjustment reaction.
    d.   stimulus discrimination.

In choice "a" the term agoraphobia refers to a fear of leaving home. The fear might take place in a wide open space, a public place, or a closed place such as an airplane, bus etc. where having a panic might prove awkward and embarrassing. The person feels trapped and can becomes worried about escaping. But, to answer the actual question: This is simple enough to remember, **since in stimulus generalization the fear "generalizes."** In other words, a Santa Claus mask is white and furry and somewhat similar to a furry white animal, and hence produces the same fearful reaction in the child. **(b)**

284. A counselor who says he or she practices depth psychology technically bases his or her treatment on

    a.    Pavlov's dogs.
    b.    Mary Cover Jones.
    c.    John B. Watson.
    d.    Freud's topographic hypothesis.

The process of elimination can work wonders here. Even if you couldn't distinguish Freud's topographic theory from a hole in the ground you could answer this question by eliminating choices "a," "b," and "c" based on the fact that Pavlov, Jones, and Watson were pioneers in the behaviorist movement. **(d)**

285. When a counselor refers to a counseling paradigm, she really means

    a.    she is nondirective.
    b.    she is very directive.
    c.    a treatment model.
    d.    she is not a depth psychologist.

You must be familiar with the word *paradigm*, which is utilized excessively in this field. A paradigm is a "model." Choice "a" is used to describe a counselor who allows the client to explore thoughts and feelings with a minimum of direction. This approach, which was initially popularized via the work of Carl R. Rogers, is also called the "client-centered" or the "person-centered" approach. This is often contrasted with the directive position (choice "b") in which the therapist leads the client to discuss certain topics and provides "direct suggestions" about how the client should think, act, or behave. And here is a wonderful **exam tip:** Many tests will use the term *active therapy* or "active-directive" therapy to delineate the directive paradigm. **(c)**

286. A man says, "My life has been lousy for the past six months." The counselor replies, "Can you tell me specifically what has made life so bad for the last six months?" The counselor is

   a.   using interpretation.
   b.   using summarization.
   c.   using concreteness.
   d.   using a depth psychology paradigm.

Concreteness is also known as "specificity" in some of the literature. The counselor uses the principle of concreteness in an attempt to eliminate vague language. Choice "a," interpretation, is highly valued in analytic and psychodynamic modalities, although it is used in other schools of counseling. Interpretation is said to take place when the counselor uncovers a deeper meaning regarding a client's situation. Most counselor educators believe that the counselor must wait until counselor–client trust is established; otherwise the client is more likely to reject the interpretation. This notion has been called "the timing of interpretation." **(c)**

287. A client who is having panic attacks is told to practice relaxing his jaw muscle for three minutes per day. The counselor here is using

   a.   concreteness.
   b.   a directive.
   c.   interpretation.
   d.   parroting.

When used in the context of counseling, a directive is merely a suggestion. Choice "d" is a no-no in effective counseling. Parroting is a misuse of paraphrasing. In parroting, the counselor restates the client's message back verbatim. The problem? Well, research shows parroting is for the birds! Clients who were victims of parroting were bored and uncomfortable during the session, and sometimes felt angry toward the counselor. **(b)**

288. _____ is a biofeedback device.

    a.    A bathroom scale
    b.    A DVD player
    c.    A digital clock
    d.    An analyst's couch

Biofeedback does not change the client, it merely provides the client and helper with biological information such that the client can master self-regulation. A scale and a mirror are two simple examples. In counseling, biofeedback devices are used primarily to teach clients to relax or to control autonomic (i.e., automatic) nervous system functions such as blood pressure, pulse rate, or hand temperature (often called thermal training). Currently, the practice is popular to help clients with attention deficit hyperactivity disorder (ADHD). In the case of ADHD, not all experts are convinced it is valuable. When biofeedback targets the brain the term neurofeedback (NFB) has become popular. **(a)**

289. Johnny just loves M&Ms but doesn't do his homework. The school counselor thus instructs Johnny's mom to give the child a bag of M&Ms every night after he finishes his homework. This is an example of

    a.    punishment.
    b.    biofeedback.
    c.    a Pavlovian strategy.
    d.    positive reinforcement.

The idea of any reinforcer (positive or negative) is to increase or strengthen the behavior. In this case something is added to the behavior so it would be "positive reinforcement." At first a behavior modifier will reinforce every behavior. This is known as a continuous schedule of reinforcement. After a while the client will be given a schedule of reinforcement that does not reinforce every desirable action. This process is sometimes referred to as "thinning," or an intermittent schedule of reinforcement.   **(d)**

290. Genuineness, or congruence, is really

    a.    identical to concreteness.
    b.    selective empathy.
    c.    the counselor's ability to be himself or herself.
    d.    an archaic Freudian notion.

The counselor who is congruent is real and authentic. This is a counselor who is not playing a role and is not putting up a facade.   **(c)**

291. Empathy is

    a.    the ability to understand the client's world and to communicate this to the client.
    b.    behavioristic.
    c.    a and b.
    d.    the same as sympathy.

Robert Carkhuff is very well known for his creation of a five-point scale intended to measure empathy, genuineness, concreteness, and respect. Many counselor educators consider empathy the most important factor in the counseling relationship. When using the Carkhuff scale, a rating of 1 is the poorest and a rating of 5 is the most desirable. A rating of 3 is considered the minimum level of acceptance. Choice "d" is incorrect. Empathy is the ability to experience the client's subjective world. Sympathy is compassion.   **(a)**

292. When something is added following an operant, it is known as a _____, and when something is taken away it is called a _____.

    a.    negative reinforcer; positive reinforcer
    b.    positive reinforcer; negative reinforcer

c.    extinction; shaping
d.    classical conditioning; operant conditioning

If you're getting sick of the word *operant* don't blame me, it's B. F. Skinner's label. Any behavior which is not elicited by an obvious stimulus is an operant. Most behaviors are indeed operants. Skinner differentiated operants from "respondents." A respondent is the consequence of a known stimulus. A dog salivating to food or the pupil in your eye enlarging when you walk into a dark room are examples of respondents. Now you know why Pavlovian conditioning has been called "respondent conditioning."

**Simple examples of negative reinforcement:**

- A depressed client takes an antidepressant medication and the depression is eliminated. She is more apt to take the medicine again.
- A client has a headache and ingests a pain medication. The pain subsides. Here again, the client is more likely to take the medicine in the future.
- A child cleans her room and her mother's nagging goes away. Mom's nagging is the negative reinforcer.

**In each instance the behavior increased or strenthened (e.g., more likely to clean a room or take a medicine) because a so-called negative reinforcer is removed or eliminated.**                                                        **(b)**

293.    After a dog is conditioned using the well-known experiment of Pavlov, a light is paired with the bell (the CS). In a short period of time the light alone would elicit the salivation. This is called

a.    extinction.
b.    token reinforcement.
c.    biofeedback.
d.    higher-order conditioning.

When a new stimulus is associated or "paired" with the CS and the new stimulus takes on the power of the CS, behaviorists refer to the phenomenon as "higher-order conditioning." In this case, the light (which is an NS or neutral stimulus) has taken on the power of the bell. Choice "b" occurs when a token (something which represents a reinforcer) is given after a desirable behavior. The token—which often just looks like a plastic coin—can be exchanged for the primary (i.e., actual) reinforcer. And here's a **very helpful hint:** Some exams refer to the items or activities which can be purchased with the tokens as "back-up reinforcers."                                    **(d)**

294. A counselor decides to use biofeedback training to help a client raise the temperature in his right hand to ward off migraines. He would utilize

    a.   a temperature trainer.
    b.   EMG feedback.
    c.   EEG neurofeedback.
    d.   EKG feedback.

Again, here is a question that separates the men from the boys and the women from the girls. To answer it correctly, you'd need a lucky guess or a smattering of knowledge regarding physiological alphabet soup nomenclature. The Menninger Clinic discovered that a very high percentage of individuals could ward off migraine headaches via raising the temperature in their hand. The technique is simply known as biofeedback "temperature training" or "thermal training." (Yes, that's right, the most complex sounding choice is not always the correct choice!) In essence, a biofeedback temperature trainer is just an extremely precise, high-priced thermometer. As for the wrong answers, EMG means electromyogram and is used to measure muscle tension. A person who is tensing a given muscle group could have an EMG biofeedback device hooked directly to the problem area. New evidence indicates EMG might actually be superior to the old standby—temperature training—when used to control migraines. The EEG or electroencephalogram biofeedback, again often dubbed as neurofeedback, is used to monitor brain waves. EEG training often focuses on the production of alpha waves, which is 8–12 cycles per second. An individual in an alpha state is awake but extremely relaxed. Lastly, EKG, or electrocardiogram, provides data on the heart. **(a)**

295. A counselor discovered that a client became nervous and often experienced panic attacks when she would tense her frontalis muscle over her eyes. The counselor wanted direct muscle feedback and thus would rely on

   a.   the Jacobson relaxation method.
   b.   GSR feedback.
   c.   EMG feedback.
   d.   a simple yet effective mood ring.

No reason for a complex memory device here folks. Why not remember that the "M" in EMG refers to muscle? Edmund Jacobson (choice "a") was a physiologist who developed a relaxation technique in which muscle groups are alternately tensed and relaxed until the whole body is in a state of relaxation. Due to simplicity and efficacy, the Jacobson Method rapidly became the darling of the behavior therapy movement. Choice "b" is the acronym for galvanic skin response, which—although it is a method of biofeedback—provides electrical skin resistance. The role of GSR and emotion is still a bit vague and thus it is not a very popular form of biofeedback treatment. As far as choice "d" is concerned, a tad of common sense should tell you that if a $1.29 mood ring was really effective, no one would ever spend in excess of 90 bucks an hour for biofeedback training! **(c)**

296. According to the Premack principle, an efficient reinforcer is what the client himself or herself likes to do. Thus, in this procedure

   a.   a lower-probability behavior is reinforced by a higher-probability behavior.
   b.   a higher-probability behavior is reinforced by a lower-probability behavior.
   c.   a and b are paradoxically both effective.
   d.   none of the above.

For test purposes know the acronyms LPB (low-probability behavior) and HPB (high-probability behavior). The principle asserts that any HPB can be used as a reinforcer for any LPB. The principle is sometimes called "Grandma's Rule" or "Grandma's Law." The chances are good that you experienced this one yourself at a young age. It went something like, "If you eat your veggies, then I let you have dessert."  **(a)**

297. A counselor who wanted to teach a client to produce alpha waves for relaxation would utilize

   a.   EMG feedback.
   b.   GSR feedback.
   c.   EEG feedback.
   d.   EKG feedback.

EEG is used to secure feedback related to brain wave rhythms.**(c)**

298. A reinforcement schedule gives the guidelines or rules for reinforcement. If a reinforcer is given every time a desired response occurs, it is known as

   a.   an intermittent schedule.
   b.   an extinction schedule.
   c.   continuous reinforcement.
   d.   thinning.

This is easy enough to remember. In continuous reinforcement you "continue" to provide the reinforcement **each time the target behavior occurs**. Continuous reinforcement is not necessarily the most practical or the most effective. Most human behaviors are reinforced effectively via the principle of intermittent reinforcement (choice "a"). In this format, the target behavior is reinforced only after the behavior manifests itself several times or for a given time interval. The exam you are taking may refer to intermittent reinforcement as "partial reinforcement," or thinning, which literally indicates that the behavior is only reinforced a portion of the time.  **(c)**

299. The two basic classes of intermittent reinforcement schedules
     are the _____, based on the number of responses and the
     _____, based on the time elapsed.

    a.   ratio; interval
    b.   interval; ratio
    c.   continuous; ratio
    d.   interval; continuous

The two basic classes of intermittent or partial reinforcement
are ratio and interval. You can remember that "interval" is based
on time rather than the number of responses, since in this society
we use the phrase "time interval." (**Note**: The terms *fixed* and
*variable* are often used with *ratio* and *interval*. "Fixed" implies
that the reinforcement always takes place after a fixed time or
number of responses, while "variable" implies that an average
number of responses or times may be used.)                    **(a)**

300. The most difficult intermittent schedule to extinguish is the

    a.   fixed ratio, for example giving a child an M&M for each five
        math problems she completes.
    b.   fixed interval, which describes the way most agency
        counselors are paid (e.g., one time per month, although the
        amount of work may vary from month to month).
    c.   variable interval.
    d.   variable ratio.

The memory device I use for the correct answer (variable ratio)
is VR, which reminds me of the vocational rehabilitation agency.
I remember that this agency is better than an agency going by FI
(fixed interval) etc. Perhaps you can think of a memory device
based on something personal in your life. Just for the record,
choice "b," fixed interval or FI, is the most ineffective of the
bunch.

**Final gems of wisdom related to schedules of
reinforcement:**

**Variable schedules are more effective than fixed schedules. Ratio schedules are more effective than interval schedules.**

**(Most effective) VR, VI, FR, FI (Least effective)    (d)**

301. Joseph Wolpe created systematic desensitization, a form of reciprocal inhibition based on counterconditioning. His strategy has been used in individual and group settings. When using his technique, the acronym SUDS stands for

    a.  standard units of dysfunction.
    b.  a given hierarchy of dysfunction.
    c.  subjective units of disturbance scale.
    d.  standard units of distress scale.

The subjective units of distress (aka subjective units of disturbance), or SUDS for short, is used to help create choice "b," the anxiety hierarchy. In the SUDS, 0 is used to convey a totally relaxed state, while 100 is the most anxiety-producing state a client can imagine. The SUDS helps therapists keep the levels in the hierarchy equidistant from each other. Wolpe's systematic desensitization is a popular treatment of choice for phobias and situations which produce high anxiety. The procedure, nonetheless, is not extremely effective for clients experiencing free-floating anxiety (i.e., a fear not connected to a given stimulus or situation). It is based on Pavlov's classical conditioning paradigm. **Special note is added for readers considering systematic desensitization for the reduction of test anxiety. Please be aware that it is not necessary or desirable to eliminate all anxiety in order to score well on your comprehensive exam. According to the "Yerkes–Dodson Law," a moderate amount of arousal actually improves performance! Thus, mild anxiety often can be a plus, since it keeps arousal at a moderate level. (High arousal is more appropriate for simple tasks rather than complex ones, such as a licensing exam.) So why bring the matter up? First, we do so to show you that a small amount of test anxiety could actually be beneficial, and second,**

**because most major exams for psychology majors will include a question on the "Yerkes–Dodson Law."**    **(c)**

302. A stimulus which accompanies a primary reinforcer takes on reinforcement properties of its own. This is known as

    a.    a primary reinforcer.
    b.    covert processing.
    c.    secondary reinforcement.
    d.    SUDS.

What's the most popular secondary reinforcer in the world? My guess: It is money. Money in and of itself isn't reinforcing. Can you eat it? Can you enjoy a conversation with it? Have you ever taken a 5-dollar bill out on a date? Money gets its power for the reinforcers you can acquire from having money. When a stimulus accompanies a reinforcer it can literally acquire reinforcement properties of its own like an actual or so-called primary reinforcer. When this occurs it is termed as "secondary reinforcement." The classical example is the mother who feeds her baby while talking. Plastic tokens or gold stars that can be exchanged for an actual reinforcer (say a piece of pie or a trip to the baseball game) are secondary reinforcers. Agencies that use tokens as a system of behavior modification are often dubbed as "token economies." In a short period of time the talking becomes a secondary reinforcer and provides some degree of satisfaction for the child. Half of the battle to pass a test on behaviorism is to be familiar with the lingo, or what scholars call the "nomenclature" or naming process. To further complicate this process some exams will split hairs and call reinforcing stimuli like money or tokens **generalized reinforcers**. Choice "b," covert, is a term which means that the behavior is not observable. In behavior therapy then, a covert process is usually a client's thought or a visualization. A "covert" behavior is roughly the opposite of an "overt" behavior, which is an *observable* behavior. Direct treatment of an overt behavior is called "in vivo treatment."    **(c)**

303. A teenager in a residential facility has earned enough tokens to buy his favorite brand of candy bar. The candy bar is

    a.   a negative reinforcer.
    b.   a back-up reinforcer.
    c.   an average stimulus.
    d.   a conditioned reinforcer.

    A back-up reinforcer is the best answer here since by definition a back-up reinforcer is an item or an activity which can be purchased using tokens. A strict behaviorist would assert that choice "d" is incorrect because back-up reinforcers are often unconditioned.                                            **(b)**

304. An alcoholic is given Antabuse, which is a drug that causes nausea when paired with alcohol. This technique is called

    a.   systematic desensitization.
    b.   biofeedback.
    c.   back-up reinforcement.
    d.   aversive conditioning.

    The idea here is to pair the alcohol with an aversive, somewhat unpleasant stimulus to reduce the satisfaction of drinking it. Ethical dilemmas are common when using this technique. Some smoking clinics, for example, that used electric shock as a noxious aversive stimulus have been shut down. Imagine a client who comes to the clinic and experiences a heart attack from the treatment process! Some clients have died from Antabuse (Disulfuram). Techniques like these are known as "in vivo aversive conditioning" since they are not performed in the imagination.                                            **(d)**

305. A counselor decides to treat a client's phobia of flying utilizing Wolpe's technique of systematic desensitization. The first step in the anxiety hierarchy items would be

    a.   imagining that she is calling the airlines for reservations.
    b.   imagining that she is boarding the plane.

c.   imagining a flight in an airplane.
d.   an actual flight in an airplane.

In systematic desensitization the order of the hierarchy is from least anxiety-arousing to the most anxiety-evoking items. Behaviorists note that the ideal hierarchy has 10–15 evenly spaced items. Therefore, in everyday plain English, to a person who has a fear of flying, imagining a phone call to secure reservations is certainly less anxiety-producing than imagining a flight, boarding a plane, or soaring through the sky in a supersonic jet airplane. **What we know now**: Joseph Wolpe assumed his systematic desensitization was based on Pavlov's respondent conditioning and was effective due to counterconditioning. But additional research used "dismantling theory" where a technique is deconstructed. In this instance it was discovered that systematic desensitization would work without the relaxation! The verdict: The strategy was working because of extinction and not counter-conditioning. A similar discovery was made when it was discovered that Francine Shapiro's **EMDR or eye movement desensitization and reprocessing (a popular treatment for traumas such as post-traumatic stress disorder (PTSD))** could produce results without the eye movement. Here again, extinction is thought to be the curative factor.          **(a)**

306.  A counselor utilizes role-playing combined with a hierarchy of situations in which the client is ordinarily nonassertive. Assertiveness trainers refer to this as

a.   conscious rehearsal.
b.   behavioral rehearsal.
c.   fixed role therapy.
d.   a and b.

Behavioral rehearsal (the correct answer) is the act of practicing a behavior in a counseling session that can be beneficial in the client's life (such as asking for a raise). The counselor in this case might also switch roles and model assertive behavior for the client. Choice "c," fixed role therapy, refers to the treatment model created by psychologist George A. Kelly. In this approach the client is given a sketch of a person or a fixed role. He or she is instructed to read the script at least three times a day and to act, think, and verbalize like the person in the script. Kelly's approach is quite systematic and has been called the "psychology of personal constructs" after his work of the same name.     **(b)**

307. Systematic desensitization consists of these orderly steps:

    a.    autogenic training, desensitization in the imagination, and construction of the hierarchy.
    b.    relaxation training, construction of anxiety hierarchy, in vivo desensitization, and desensitization in imagination.
    c.    relaxation training, desensitization in imagination, and construction of hierarchy.
    d.    relaxation training, construction of anxiety hierarchy, desensitization in imagination, and in vivo desensitization.

Several important points need to be mentioned here. The first is that your exam may refer to desensitization in imagination as "interposition." (Interposition is technically a perceptual term which implies that one item conceals or covers another. Thus, in this case, the relaxation obscures the anxiety of the imagined scene in the hierarchy.) The second point is that it is best if hierarchy items are evenly spaced using the SUDS. If items are too far apart, moving up the hierarchy could prove nearly impossible. On the other hand, if items are spaced too close together, then the helping process will be unusually slow, and behaviorists place a premium on rapid, efficacious treatment. Lastly, the "in vivo" stage implies that the client will actually expose himself or herself to the scary situations in the hierarchy. Experts believe that "in vivo" experiences should not begin until the client has been desensitized to 75% of the hierarchy items.     **(d)**

308. _____ is behavioral sex therapy.

    a.    Classical vegotherapy
    b.    Orgone box therapy
    c.    Conditioned reflex therapy
    d.    Sensate focus

Sensate focus is a form of behavioral sex therapy developed by William H. Masters and Virginia Johnson of St. Louis, Missouri. Like Wolpe's systematic desensitization, this approach relies on counterconditioning. A couple is told to engage in touching and caressing (to lower anxiety levels) on a graduated basis until intercourse is possible. Choices "a" and "b" illuminate the work of Wilhelm Reich, who felt that repeated sexual gratification was necessary for the cure of emotional maladies. Reich's orgone box was a device which the client would sit in to increase orgone life energy. Ultimately the FDA outlawed the orgone boxes and Reich died in jail. Today scholars are still arguing whether Reich was a madman or a genius. Conditioned reflex therapy (choice "c"), created by Andrew Salter, set the stage for modern assertiveness training. Some call Salter, who hated the psychoanalytic model, the father of behavior therapy.          **(d)**

309. A counselor has an obese client imagine that he is terribly sick after eating a high-caloric, high-fat meal. The client then imagines a pleasant scene in which his eating is desirable. This technique is called

   a.   behavioral rehearsal.
   b.   in vivo sensitization.
   c.   covert sensitization.
   d.   in vivo desensitization.

Even if you did not know what any of the choices meant you could still get the question correct! Yes really! You could simply remember that the only answer that mentions the imagination is the one with the word *covert*. This would constitute an educated guess. Keep in mind when answering behavior therapy questions that the word *desensitization* means to make one less sensitive while the word *sensitization* implies that one is made more sensitive to a stimulus. A counselor who tells an alcoholic to imagine that a drink nauseates him would be relying on "covert sensitization." The client is then instructed to imagine a relief scene such as an enjoyable feeling when the alcohol is removed and replaced with a glass of water. Antabuse (mentioned in earlier questions) could be used for the "in vivo sensitization of a client."                                                                                  **(c)**

310. One distinction between flooding (also known as "deliberate exposure with response prevention" in recent literature) and implosive therapy is that

     a.    implosive therapy is always conducted in the imagination.
     b.    flooding is always conducted in the imagination.
     c.    flooding is always safer.
     d.    implosive therapy is physically more dangerous.

     **Here's a superb memory device: implosive therapy begins with an "i" and so does the word *imagination*.** Nice! Implosive therapy (the brainchild of T. G. Stampfl) is always conducted using the imagination and sometimes relies on psychoanalytic symbolism. **Flooding, which is similar, usually occurs when the client is genuinely exposed to the feared stimulus. Flooding is also called "deliberate exposure with response prevention."** Here is how flooding works. Take a man who is afraid of snakes because he feels they will bite him. Using flooding, the client would be exposed to the snake for nearly an hour without the dreaded snake bite. Research has demonstrated that in vivo procedures like flooding are extremely effective in cases of agoraphobia (a fear of open places) and obsessive-compulsive disorders (OCD). Recent findings suggest that in some instances flooding outperforms systematic desensitization as a treatment for phobias. A single longer session seems to work better than several short sessions. Flooding and implosive therapy do not necessarily utilize relaxation nor do they introduce the fearful stimuli gradually. Both techniques assume that avoiding the fear serves to intensify it and that anticipation of catastrophe (e.g., physical pain or loss of control) initially caused the symptom in question. **Caution: flooding and implosive therapy do not work in every case. Cases have been cited in which the prolonged exposure to the feared stimuli actually tended to exacerbate the anxiety!**                                                                     **(a)**

311. Behavior therapists often shy away from punishment because

    a.  ACA ethics forbid the use of this technique.
    b.  NBCC ethics prohibit the use of operant conditioning.
    c.  extinction works more quickly.
    d.  the effects of punishment are usually temporary and it teaches aggression.

The great behavior modifier B. F. Skinner did not believe punishment was very effective. He felt that after the punishment was administered the behavior would manifest itself once again. Positive measures are seen as more effective than punishment. If punishment is used, remember that it does not cause the person (or other animal for that matter) to unlearn the behavior, and it should be used along with positive reinforcing measures.  **(d)**

312. A neophyte counselor discovers that her clients invariably give yes and no answers to her questions. The problem is most likely that

    a.  the counselor is sympathetic rather than empathetic.
    b.  the counselor is utilizing too many closed-ended questions.
    c.  the counselor's timing is poor in terms of interpretation.
    d.  she is summarizing too early in the counseling process.

A closed-ended question can be answered with "yes" or "no." If a counselor asks, "Is your depression lifting?" the client can easily respond with a "yes" or a "no." **Counselors prefer open-ended questions, which produce more information.** If the aforementioned counselor wanted to rephrase the question in an open-ended manner, she could ask, "Can you tell me about the things in your life you find so depressing?"  **(b)**

313. A client remarks that he was just dumped by his girlfriend. The counselor responds, "Oh, you poor dear. It must be terrible! How can you go on living?" This is an example of

    a.  EMDR.
    b.  accurate empathy.

c.    confrontation.
d.    sympathy.

This is sympathy, not to mention some of the most horrendous therapy one could imagine! Sympathy often implies pity, while accurate empathy is the ability to experience another person's subjective experience. Just for the record EMDR, choice "a," stands for eye movement desensitization and reprocessing, a technique created by Francine Shapiro to deal with traumatic memories. In the spring of 1987 Shapiro—then a graduate psychology student—accidentally noticed that disturbing memories began to abate when she was moving her eyes back and forth while strolling through the park. She then tested her theory on other clients having them follow her finger to induce the eye movements. Prior to Joseph Wolpe's death he noted that this model could be beneficial. EMDR helps clients deal with anxiety, traumatic memories, and PTSD.                              **(d)**

314.  A neophyte counselor is afraid he will say the wrong thing. He thus keeps repeating the client's statements verbatim when he responds. This is known as

a.    desirable attending behavior.
b.    parroting and is not recommended.
c.    level 3 on the empathy scale.
d.    paradoxical intention.

In the movie *Final Analysis* Richard Gere takes a young woman to dinner and explains how easy it is to be a therapist. You simply listen to the client, he basically explains to his dinner companion, and then you repeat their final words. Sorry, Rich, but the tinsel town version could be a tad oversimplified. The client doesn't really need to pay big bucks for this type of help; parroting can be accomplished simply by talking into a digital recorder. If you parrot a client, the client's response may be something like, "Yes, I just said that!" Parroting can cause the client to feel angry and uneasy. In the counseling profession, the term *attending* (choice "a") refers to behaviors on the part of the counselor which indicate that he or she is truly engaged in active listening skills.

Examples would be good eye contact or the old standby "umhum." Choice "c" is another must-know concept for nearly any major counseling test. Robert R. Carkhuff suggests a "scale for measurement" in regard to "empathic understanding in interpersonal processes." In a nutshell it reads like this: Level 1—not attending or detracting significantly from the client's verbal and behavioral expressions; Level 2—subtracts noticeable affect from the communication; Level 3—feelings expressed by the client are basically interchangeable with the client's meaning and affect; Level 4—counselor adds noticeably to the client's affect; Level 5—counselor adds significantly to the client's surface and underlying feelings, even in the client's deepest moments. If all of this sounds like a foreign language because you've never heard it before, you can now remove the cotton you placed in your ears during your graduate days, or better still, pick up a copy of Carkhuff's 1969 book *Helping and Human Relations*.                                                **(b)**

315. Viktor Frankl is the father of logotherapy, which is based on existentialism. Logotherapy means

    a.   healing through meaning.
    b.   healing through the unconscious.
    c.   logic cures.
    d.   all of the above.

Frankl also has been thought of as the father of paradoxical intention. Paradoxical intention is implemented by advising the client to purposely exaggerate a dysfunctional behavior in the imagination. You might find it a bit paradoxical (no pun intended) that a technique which comes from logotherapy—which is clearly a brand of helping based on existential philosophy—is now generally categorized as a behavioristic technique. Recently, counselors have gone beyond the paradoxical imagination and actually prescribe that the client engages in the dysfunctional behavior. (For example, a person with OCD (obsessive-compulsive disorder) might be instructed to wash his or her hands 51 times per day instead of the usual 45 times.)        **(a)**

316. All of these philosophers are existentialists *except:*

   a.  Plato and Epictetus.
   b.  Sartre, Buber, Binswanger, and Boss.
   c.  Kierkegaard, Nietzsche, and Tillich.
   d.  Heidegger, Dostoevsky, and Jaspers.

   Existentialism is considered a humanistic form of helping in which the counselor helps the client discover meaning in his or her life by doing a deed (e.g., an accomplishment), experiencing a value (e.g., love), or suffering (e.g., Frankl discovered that even being held hostage in a concentration camp could not take away his dignity). Existential counseling rejects analysis and behaviorism for being deterministic and simplistic. The existential viewpoint developed as a reaction to the analytic and behavioral schools and stresses growth and self-actualization. Frankl stressed that individuals have choices in their lives and one cannot blame others or childhood circumstances for a lack of fulfillment. The name Epictetus (in choice "a") is often quoted in regard to rational-emotive behavior therapy (REBT), created by New York clinical psychologist Albert Ellis. **Ellis is considered the founding father of the cognitive behavior therapy (CBT) movement.** In the first century AD, the Stoic philosopher Epictetus said, "Men are disturbed not by things, but of the view which they take of them." This statement captures the major premise of REBT. **Important exam hint:** REBT was formerly known as rational-emotive therapy (RET).          **(a)**

317. Although behavior therapy purports to be highly scientific, it has been criticized on the grounds that it is simplistic, and does not deal with underlying causes. Existential therapy, on the other hand, has been criticized for

   a.  being too short-term.
   b.  overemphasizing techniques.
   c.  ignoring group strategies.
   d.  being too vague regarding techniques and procedures.

Existential counseling is more of a philosophy of helping than a grab bag of specific intervention strategies. Critics charge that it is not a systematic approach to treatment. The behaviorists assert that it is abstract and not scientific. The approach rejects traditional diagnosis and assessment procedures.    **(d)**

318. Existentialists focus primarily on

    a.    the teenage years.
    b.    the client's perception in the here and now.
    c.    childhood traumas.
    d.    uplifting childhood memories.

The focus is on what the person can ultimately become. The present and even the future are emphasized. The key to change is seen as self-determination.    **(b)**

319. Existential counselors as well as Rogerian person-centered counselors adhere to what Martin Buber called the I–Thou relationship, which asserts that

    a.    the counselor is seen as a highly trained expert with answers.
    b.    the relationship is vertical.
    c.    the relationship is horizontal.
    d.    empathy is not necessary.

A horizontal relationship (e.g., I–Thou) assumes equality between persons. In a vertical relationship the counselor is viewed as an expert. Choice "d" is incorrect, as the existentialists stress nonthreatening empathy as necessary for successful therapy.    **(c)**

320. Frankl is an existentialist. So are

    a.    Ellis and Perls.
    b.    Perls and Stampfl.
    c.    Yalom and May.
    d.    Janov and Beck.

Rollo May introduced existential therapy in the United States. Irvin Yalom, another existentialist, is noted for his work in group therapy. In his book *Love's Executioner*, he reveals his approach to treatment with some of his most intriguing clients. Other names that appear in the answer choices to this question include: Fritz Perls, the father of gestalt therapy; Albert Ellis, who pioneered rational-emotive behavior therapy (REBT); Arthur Janov, noted for his primal scream therapy; and Aaron T. Beck, whose cognitive therapy (CT) or cognitive behavior therapy (CBT) resembles REBT and focuses on automatic thoughts leading to depression. Beck is praised for his **cognitive triad of depression**. It asserts that the depressed individual: (1) feels worthless and has a negative view of himself or herself; (2) has a negative view of the world as unfair; (3) feels the future as hopeless. If the name Stampfl doesn't ring a bell, review question 310.                                                    **(c)**

321. Existentialists speak of three worlds, the *Umwelt* or the _____ world, the *Mitwelt* or the _____ world, and the *Eigenwelt* or the _____ world.

    a.   unconscious; preconscious; conscious
    b.   id; ego; superego
    c.   self-identity; relationship; physical
    d.   physical; relationship; identity

Try this if you are searching for a memory device. *Mitwelt* has the prefix "mi," which sounds like "my" as in "my wife" or "my brother" or "my son"; the "my" shows possessiveness indicative of a "relationship." *Eigenwelt* sounds suspiciously like the word *identity*. By a process of elimination you would not need a memory device for the remaining term *Umwelt* (the physical and biological system).                                                    **(d)**

322. Frankl's experience in Nazi concentration camps taught him

    a.   the value of stimulus-response (S-R) psychological paradigms.
    b.   that you can't control the environment, but you can control your response.

c.   that blaming others can be truly therapeutic.
d.   the value of active-directive counseling.

From 1942 to 1945 Viktor Frankl was a prisoner in German concentration camps, including Auschwitz and Dachau. Several of his relatives died in the camps. Frankl felt, nonetheless, that suffering would be transformed into achievement and creativity.     **(b)**

323.  Existential counselors emphasize the client's

a.   free choice, decision, and will.
b.   transference.
c.   slips of tongue.
d.   latent dream symbolism.

Logotherapists often use the term *noogenic neurosis*, which is the frustration of the will to meaning. The counselor assists the client to find meaning in life so the client can write his or her own life story by making meaningful choices. When exploring the meaning of life some anxiety is normal. Moreover, death is not seen as an evil concept but rather an entity which gives meaning to the process of life. Choices "b," "c," and "d" are all psychoanalytic and therefore totally wrong.     **(a)**

324.  Existential theorists speak of phenomenology, which refers to the client's internal personal experience of events, and ontology, which is

a.   mental visualization for the treatment of cancer.
b.   the impact of cancer on emotions.
c.   a cancerous growth in the brain.
d.   the philosophy of being and existing.

The metaphysical study of life experience is called ontology. Please do not confuse this with "oncology" (hinted at in choice "c") which is the medical study of tumors.     **(d)**

325. Viktor Frankl is to logotherapy as William Glasser is to

   a.   rational therapy.
   b.   reality therapy.
   c.   rational-emotive imagery.
   d.   RBT.

Frankl is the father of logotherapy; Glasser is the father of reality therapy. Rational imagery (choice "c") is a technique used by rational-emotive behavior therapists in which the client is to imagine that he or she is in a situation which has traditionally caused emotional disturbance. The client then imagines changing the feelings via rational, logical, scientific thought. Choice "d" refers to rational behavior therapy (some exams call it rational self-counseling), created by psychiatrist Maxie C. Maultsby, Jr., who studied with Albert Ellis. This approach relies on REBT; however, the client performs a written self-analysis. Maultsby claims the technique is well-suited to problems of substance abuse, and it is highly recommended as a method of multicultural counseling.          **(b)**

326. Reality therapy has incorporated

   a.   control theory, later referred to as choice theory.
   b.   rational imagery.
   c.   TA principles.
   d.   rolfing.

Reality therapy exam questions often use the abbreviation BCP, which means that perception controls our behavior. Choice theory asserts than the only person whose behavior we can control is our own. According to choice theory, our behavior is our best attempt to control our world to satisfy our wants and needs. The final choice, rolfing, is not a traditional form of talk therapy but rather a type of deep muscle massage which is assumed to have an impact on the person's emotional state.  **(a)**

327. All of these statements regarding reality therapy are true *except:*

    a.    The client's childhood is explored.
    b.    Excuses are not accepted.
    c.    The unconscious is avoided.
    d.    Therapy is concerned primarily with the here and now.

According to choice theory the person's childhood may have contributed to the problem. However, the past is never really the problem. The client's childhood is usually not explored, and if the client brings it up, the reality therapist will often try to emphasize childhood successes, feeling that an analysis of the difficulties could actually reinforce maladaptive patterns. Reality therapy is a present moment form of counseling which focuses on the here and now. According to a strict behaviorist, the environment controls behavior. According to Glasser, the individual controls the environment. **(a)**

328. A counselor who repeats what a client has stated in the counselor's own words is using

    a.    contracting.
    b.    confrontation.
    c.    paraphrasing.
    d.    parroting.

Communications experts agree that paraphrasing has taken place when a client's thoughts and feelings are restated in the counselor's own words. Contracting (choice "a") with a client in a verbal or written manner is a technique favored by behavior therapists. In reality therapy, a plan is created to help the client master his or her target behaviors. **(c)**

329. Most experts would agree that _____ is most threatening for clients as well as counselors.

    a.    paraphrasing by the counselor
    b.    open-ended questions
    c.    role rehearsal
    d.    silence

Veteran counselors believe that some of the most valuable verbalizations occur after a period of silence. Silence gives the client time to assimilate the counseling process and is helpful in nondirective therapies because it coaxes the client to direct the session.                                                                **(d)**

330. When the past is discussed in reality therapy, the focus is on

    a.    failures.
    b.    irrational internal verbalizations.
    c.    transference issues.
    d.    successful behaviors.

Glasser believes that dwelling on past failures can reinforce a negative self-concept, or what reality therapists have termed the "failure identity."                                                      **(d)**

331. Glasser's position on mental illness is that

    a.    it is best explained by *DSM* guidelines.
    b.    diagnostic labels give clients permission to act sick or irresponsible.
    c.    it is best explained by *ICD* categories.
    d.    it is the result of a deep internal conflict.

Reality therapy has little use for the formal diagnostic process, or what is known in clinical circles as "nosology." The *Diagnostic and Statistical Manual* (*DSM*) of the American Psychiatric Association and the *International Classification of Disease* (*ICD*) provide the guidelines for diagnosis of clients. Glasser rejected this traditional medical model of disease.                        **(b)**

332. The relationship that the therapist has with the client in reality therapy is

    a.    detached but very empathic.
    b.    like that of a warm caring mother.
    c.    like that of a friend who asks what is wrong.
    d.    friendly, nevertheless punishment is used when it is appropriate.

Unlike the detached psychoanalyst, the reality therapist literally makes friends with the client. This is the first of eight steps utilized in this model. Step 7 is refusing to use punishment, making choice "d" a no go here.                    **(c)**

333. Glasser's theory was popularized in educational circles after he wrote

    a.    *Choice Theory.*
    b.    *The Interpretation of Dreams.*
    c.    *Positive Addiction.*
    d.    *Schools Without Failure.*

Glasser also authored choices "a" and "c" as well as his original 1965 classic *Reality Therapy*, and an update of the theory in his 2000 book *Reality Therapy in Action*. Choice "b" has nothing to do with reality therapy but generally is quoted as Freud's most influential work, often dubbed as "the Bible of Psychoanalysis."                    **(d)**

334. Glasser suggested eight steps in the reality therapy process. The final step asserts

    a.    that the client and counselor be persistent and never give up.
    b.    that some problems will not respond to any known plan of action.
    c.    that counselors should contract with the client for no more than five counseling sessions.
    d.    that a client who does not respond to the first seven steps is most likely a borderline personality.

Even when the client wants to give up, the therapist does not. Glasser's theory has been criticized on the basis that it is too simplistic. Unlike most of the other schools of thought discussed in this guide, Reality therapy has not been included in some texts and dictionaries of psychology.                    **(a)**

335. According to Glasser, a positive addiction might be

 a. jogging.
 b. gambling.
 c. playing the office football pool.
 d. playing professional football.

Negative addictions like alcoholism and drug abuse are often mentioned in mental health literature. Glasser stressed that people can be addicted to positive behaviors and this helps to instill self-confidence. A positive addiction must be a noncompetitive activity which can be performed alone for about one hour each day. Moreover, the person can see that performing the activity will lead to personal improvement. Lastly, the person needs to be capable of performing the activity without becoming self-critical.    **(a)**

336. When a counselor reviews what has transpired in past counseling sessions he or she is using

 a. paraphrasing.
 b. reflection.
 c. summarization.
 d. confrontation.

When a counselor summarizes, he or she is bringing together a number of ideas. This summarization also could deal strictly with the material in a single session of counseling. Summarization constitutes a "synthesis" regarding the general tone or feeling of the helping process. Allen Ivey recommends summarization at two or three points during each session and at the close of the session. Summarization is really the ability to condense the material to capture the essence of the therapeutic exchange.  **(c)**

337. Glasser felt the responsible person will have a _____ identity.

 a. failure
 b. success
 c. diffused
 d. crisis-oriented

The individual who possesses a success identity feels worthy and significant to others. Identity is a person's most important psychological need. A person who is irresponsible, and thus frustrated in an attempt to feel loved and worthwhile, will develop a failure identity and a faulty perception of reality. The client is encouraged to assume responsibility for his or her own happiness (i.e., by learning to fulfill personal needs without depriving others of their need fulfillment).          **(b)**

338. William Glasser, M.D., is to reality therapy as Albert Ellis, Ph.D., is to

    a.    rational-emotive behavior therapy (REBT).
    b.    transactional analysis (TA).
    c.    assertiveness training (AT).
    d.    gestalt therapy.

Analytically trained New York clinical psychologist Ellis is the father of REBT, which assumes that the client's emotional disturbance is the result of irrational thoughts and ideas. The cure is a high dose of rational thinking.          **(a)**

339. In Albert Ellis's rational-emotive behavior therapy, the client is taught to change cognitions, also known as

    a.    self-talk.
    b.    internal verbalizations.
    c.    impulses.
    d.    a and b.

The credo here is a simple one: Talk sense to yourself. When you change your thinking you can change your life.          **(d)**

340. The philosopher most closely related to REBT would be

    a.    Buber.
    b.    Epictetus.
    c.    Locke.
    d.    Jaspers.

Epictetus, a stoic philosopher who suggested we feel the way we think, said: "People are disturbed not by things, but by the views they take of them." In addition to Epictetus, Ellis also mentioned Alfred Korzybski, the founder of general semantics, and Karen Horney, who first recognized the "tyranny of the shoulds" when reflecting on the creation of Ellis's REBT theory. Ellis was quick to quote a statement from *Hamlet*: "There's nothing either good or bad but thinking makes it so." Buber and Jaspers are associated with existential therapy, while Locke's work resembled closely what later came to be known as behaviorism.    **(b)**

341. REBT suggests the ABC theory of personality in which A is the _____, B is the _____, and C is the _____.

    a.    affect; belief; control
    b.    activating event; belief system; emotional consequence
    c.    affect; behavior; control
    d.    authenticity; belief; emotional consequence

What constitutes an irrational and unhealthy "belief system?" Ex-analyst Albert Ellis (please emphasize *ex* inasmuch as Ellis felt that psychoanalysis was slow and often very ineffective) gave these examples of irrational thinking: It is absolutely necessary to be loved or approved of by every significant person in your life; you must be thoroughly competent in all areas of your life to consider yourself worthwhile; some people are bad and wicked and thus should be punished for their actions; it is awful or catastrophic when things are not the way you want them to be; unhappiness is caused externally by other things and people; an individual's past determines his or her happiness; it is terrible if a perfect solution to every problem cannot be found; and, you need someone stronger than yourself to lean on.    **(b)**

342. The ABC theory of personality postulates that the intervention that occurs at D, _____ leads to E, _____.

    a.    the dogmatic attitude; effective behavior
    b.    direct living; evaluation

c. disputing the irrational behavior at B; a new emotional consequence

d. the emotional disease; a new emotional consequence

Some of the literature by Ellis refers to E as a "new effect" or "an effective new philosophy of life." The theory, then, is that you create your own present emotional and behavioral difficulties. And talk about optimistic: Ellis believes that no matter how bad life seems, you always—that's right, *always*—have the power to ameliorate intense feelings of despair, anxiety, and hostility. **(c)**

343. A counselor instructs her client to read *A Guide to Rational Living* by Albert Ellis and Robert Harper. This is an example of

a. bibliotherapy.
b. countertransference.
c. musturbation.
d. concreteness.

Bibliotherapy is the use of books or writings pertaining to self-improvement. *A Guide to Rational Living,* affectionately known as "the Guide," is Ellis's best-known work. The title of his 1988 work *How to Stubbornly Refuse to Make Yourself Miserable about Anything—Yes, Anything!* captures the essence of his theory. To state that Ellis is a prolific writer would be to put it mildly. He has authored or served as a co-author for 80 books and approximately 1,200 articles! Choice "c" uses the term *musturbation,* coined by Ellis. Musturbation occurs when a client uses too many shoulds, oughts, and musts in his or her thinking. Some exams may refer to this as "absolutist thinking." **(a)**

344. Shoulds and oughts are _____ according to Ellis.

a. musturbations
b. masturbations
c. awfulizations
d. rational

When a preference becomes a dogmatic must or should, then you can bet that the client is in for a case of emotional disturbance. Choice "c" is a word commonly used in REBT. Awfulizing or catastrophizing is the act of telling yourself how difficult, terrible, and horrendous a given situation really is. And by the way, if you marked choice "b" you better sign up for a sex ed course. Ellis, also known for his work in sexology, humorously insisted that musturbation is more pernicious than masturbation.    **(a)**

345. A client says, "I lost my job and it's the most terrible thing in the world." This client is engaging in

   a.   rational self-talk.
   b.   self-induced empathy.
   c.   cognitive restructuring.
   d.   awfulizing and terriblizing, also known as catastrophizing.

Choice "d" would occur at point B, the belief system, in the ABC model of personality. Choice "c," cognitive restructuring, usually refers to Donald Meichenbaum's approach, which is similar to REBT. Restructuring takes place when the client begins thinking in a healthy new way using different internal dialogue. Choice "a" is the most inappropriate answer since Ellis considers awfulizing or terriblizing "irrational" unhealthy behavior.    **(d)**

346. Bibliotherapy is a form of

   a.   psychodynamic intervention.
   b.   homework.
   c.   displacement.
   d.   musturbation.

Yes, homework. I'm sure the word rings a bell if you think back to graduate school. In the context of counseling, homework takes place whenever the counselor gives the client an assignment which is to be done outside the counseling session. Bibliotherapy is a prime example. Therapies that basically "teach" the client (e.g., REBT) are known as "didactic" models of treatment.    **(b)**

347. Ellis feels that _____ is at the core of emotional disturbance.

   a.   a trauma before age 5
   b.   a current traumatic activating event
   c.   irrational thinking at point B
   d.   repression of key feelings

Choice "a" is really somewhat humorous in light of the fact that Ellis noted that at a very early age he decided his mother wasn't eligible for any prizes of mental health. While a more analytically inclined therapist might have viewed Ellis's childhood as traumatic, Ellis merely told himself that his mother was a fallible human being and he did not have to be disturbed by her behavior. Ellis believes you can be happy even if you are the survivor of numerous childhood traumas. For exam purposes please keep in mind that Ellis, Glasser, and the behaviorists put little stock in the notion of transference.                    **(c)**

348. Therapeutic cognitive restructuring really refers to

   a.   refuting irrational ideas and replacing them with rational ones.
   b.   keeping a journal of irrational thoughts.
   c.   allowing the client to purge feelings.
   d.   uncovering relevant unconscious material.

This is the process of changing your thoughts ergo your feelings via self-talk, or what Ellis often called internal verbalizations. REBT clients often receive emotional control cards from their therapist that delineate irrational ideas and what one can think rationally to combat these unhealthy thoughts. The act of changing the client's mode of thinking is sometimes called cognitive disputation. REBT therapists also use imaginal disputation (i.e., imagery to help with the process) and urge clients to behave in different patterns (i.e., behavioral disputation).                    **(a)**

349. Ellis most likely would not be impressed with a behaviorist's new animal study related to the psychotherapeutic process since

    a.    he does not believe in the scientific method.
    b.    the study would not take transference into account.
    c.    Ellis thoroughly dislikes hypothesis testing.
    d.    only humans think in declarations (internal sentences that can cause or ward off emotional discord).

As far as choice "a" is concerned it is incorrect inasmuch as Ellis firmly believed that his theory promotes scientific thinking, and lower animals may be incapable of such thought. Ellis described what he called the ABC theory of personality. At point A, there is an activating event; at point B, the person's belief system; and at point C, the emotional consequence. According to Ellis, most therapies can be faulted for not emphasizing irrational beliefs at point B. Such theories wrongly assert that A causes C. Choice "d" reveals the gist of REBT. **(d)**

350. Internal verbalizations are to REBT as _____ are to Glasser's choice theory.

    a.    contracting
    b.    pictures in your mind
    c.    lack of punishment
    d.    a therapeutic plan

A matter of semantics? Perhaps. Glasser insists that behavior is internally motivated and we choose our actions. **(b)**

351. Albert Ellis is to REBT as Maxie C. Maultsby, Jr., is to

    a.    RBT.
    b.    AT.
    c.    TA.
    d.    S-R research.

Maultsby is the father of rational-behavior therapy (RBT), which is similar to REBT but emphasizes a written self-analysis.

Maultsby's technique is said to work well for multicultural counseling and group therapy. In group work the counselor has a didactic or a teaching role in which participants are taught to apply the techniques to their own lives. The leader encourages equal group participation for all members and gives reading assignments (i.e., bibliotherapy) between the sessions. All in all, the leader is highly directive and uses RBT as a model for self-help. Like REBT, RBT utilizes rational-emotive imagery on a regular basis. Choice "d" describes an old abbreviation of stimulus-response behavioral psychology. REBT and RBT are not fond of this model because it asserts that a stimulus (or what Ellis has basically termed an *activating event* at point A) causes a response (or what Ellis calls the *consequence* at point C). The S-R stimulus-response model, according to Ellis, is guilty of leaving out B, the client's belief system. Thus, although Ellis might concede that the S-R paradigm explains rat behavior, it is inadequate when applied to human beings. The S-R model also has been called the "applied behavior analysis" or "radical behaviorism" by B. F. Skinner. Radical behaviorism makes the assumption that the environment maintains and supports behavior and that only overt behaviors are the subject of treatment. The treatment? You guessed it—Skinnerian operant conditioning, of course. **(a)**

352. Aaron T. Beck, an ex-psychoanalytic psychiatrist who created the Beck Depression Inventory (BDI), a self-report questionnaire, also developed an approach known as cognitive therapy. Although cognitive therapy is similar to REBT, Beck insisted that

   a. dysfunctional ideas are too absolute and broad though not necessarily irrational.
   b. the Oedipus complex is central to the treatment process.
   c. cognitive therapy is contraindicated in cases of phobia.
   d. cognitive therapy is contraindicated in cases of anxiety.

Choices "c" and "d" are incorrect. Beck's contention was that depression is the result of a cognitive triad of negative beliefs regarding oneself, one's future, and one's experience. Beck's model has indeed been shown to be applicable in cases of phobia and anxiety. Since Beck disliked the term *irrational ideas*, he emphasized "rules" or "formulas of living" which cause unhappiness, and he suggested new rules which the client can test. His daughter Judy Beck is now helping to popularize this approach. Note: Some exams use the word *metacognition* to describe an individual's tendency to be aware of his or her own cognitions or cognitive abilities. **Beck's approach could show up as cognitive therapy (CT), or cognitive behavior therapy (CBT) on exam questions. Beck, like the Adlerians, was a fan of asking clients to engage in Socratic questioning, such as: "Could I be misrepresenting this situation?" Or "Am I focusing too much on the negative aspects of the relationship?" Socratic questioning helps clients challenge unrealistic thought patterns.** Hundreds of studies attest to the fact that CBT is extremely helpful.　　　　**(a)**

353. The cognitive therapist most closely associated with the concept of stress inoculation treatment is

    a.　Albert Ellis.
    b.　Donald Meichenbaum.
    c.　Maxie C. Maultsby, Jr.
    d.　Aaron T. Beck.

Meichenbaum's approach is called "self-instructional training." Implementation of his so-called stress-inoculation technique has three basic phases. First the client is involved in an "educational phase." Here the client is taught to monitor the impact of inner dialogue on behavior. Next clients are taught to rehearse new self-talk. This is the "rehearsal phase." Finally, the "application phase" is where new inner dialogue is attempted during actual stress-producing situations. Counselor educators often classify approaches which dwell on cognition, while emphasizing behavioral strategies for change (e.g., REBT, RBT, self-instructional therapy) as "cognitive-behavioral approaches" to helping.　　　　**(b)**

354. Eric Berne created transactional analysis (TA). The model was popularized via his books *Games People Play* and *What Do You Say After You Say Hello?* TA therapists are most likely to incorporate _____ in the treatment process.

    a.   Meichenbaum's self-instructional therapy
    b.   reality therapy
    c.   gestalt therapy
    d.   vegotherapy

    Choice "c," the correct answer, may seem to make about as much sense as trying to mix water and oil since TA, from a pure standpoint of classification, is a cognitive approach, while gestalt is experiential. The well-known counselor educator Gerald Corey suggested that this marriage made in therapeutic heaven was actually positive inasmuch as gestalt therapy emphasized the affective exploration that was missing from TA, which was too intellectual. In other words, one emphasized what was missing in the other.                                              **(c)**

355. Berne suggested three ego states: the Parent, the Adult, and the Child (P-A-C). The Parent ego state is composed of values internalized from significant others in childhood. TA therapists speak of two functions in the Parent ego state, the

    a.   Nurturing Parent and the Critical Parent.
    b.   Critical Parent and the Repressed Parent.
    c.   Reactive Parent and the Active Parent.
    d.   Passive Parent and the Active Parent.

    The Parent ego state is the synthesis of the messages received from parental figures and significant others, incorporated into the personality. Also known as the "exteropsyche," **the Parent ego state bears a very strong resemblance to Freud's superego**. When a counselor analyzes out of which ego state a client is primarily operating, it is known as "structural analysis." When a counselor analyzes an ego state within an ego state (e.g., the Critical Parent or the Nurturing Parent) it is known as "second-order structural analysis." A statement like "Get some rest honey, you've been studying the NCE material for a long time and you deserve the rest" is an example of the Nurturing Parent. The Nurturing Parent is sympathetic, caring, and protective. The Critical Parent, on the other hand, might remark, "You should get off your duff and study that NCE material; how in the heck do you plan on passing?" The Critical Parent is the master of the shoulds, oughts, and musts. On occasion, you will see the parent broken down into another part, the Prejudicial Parent. The Prejudicial Parent is opinionated with biases not based on fact. "Women should always wear dresses to work" or "a real man enlists in the marines" would be examples. The death or absence of a parent can result in what TA counselors call an "Incomplete Parent state."                                  **(a)**

356. The Adult ego state

    a.   contains the "shoulds" and "oughts."
    b.   is the seat of feelings.
    c.   is like Freud's superego.
    d.   processes facts and does not focus on feelings.

**The Adult corresponds to Freud's ego.** It is also known as the "neopsyche." It is rational, logical, and does not focus on feelings. Choices "a" and "c" describe the Parent ego state.  **(d)**

357. The Child ego state is like the little kid within. The child may manifest itself as

    a.   the Natural Child.
    b.   the Adapted Child.
    c.   the Little Professor.
    d.   all of the above.

**The Child state, sometimes called the "archaeopsyche," resembles Freud's id.** The Natural Child is what the person would be naturally: spontaneous, impulsive, and untrained. The Little Professor is creative and intuitive. The Little Professor acts on hunches, often without the necessary information. The Adapted Child learns how to comply to avoid a parental slap on the hand. Messages we receive from parents to form the ego states are called "injunctions" and cause us to make certain early life decisions. Hence, if an early message was "I wish you would have never been born," then the decision might be, "If my life gets very stressful, I'll just kill myself." **Hint:** Describing the client using the P-A-C conceptualization is known as "structural analysis." **(d)**

358. TA is a cognitive model of therapy which asserts that healthy communication transactions

    a.    occur where vectors of communication run parallel.
    b.    are known as crossed transactions.
    c.    are always between the Child and Adult ego states.
    d.    are always empathic.

Choice "a" is a "complementary" transaction in which you get an appropriate, predicted response. The "crossed transaction" (note choice "b") would occur when vectors from a message sent and a message received do not run parallel. (For example, I send a message from my Adult to your Adult and you respond from your Adult to my Child.) Crossed transactions result in a deadlock of communication or a host of hurtful feelings. This principle probably won't be difficult to remember. We generally say it is not a good thing when individuals work at "cross" purposes. In TA a "crossed transaction" is not conducive to healthy communication. **Note:** See Graphical Representations (Chapter 13). TA therapists often use diagrams or pictorial representations in the treatment process. **(a)**

359. TA life positions were made famous by Tom Harris's book *I'm OK—You're OK*. The title of the book illuminates a healthy life position. The life position tells the counselor how a person goes about receiving strokes or recognition. A person categorized by the position "I'm OK—You're Not OK"

    a.    is generally self-abusive.
    b.    blames others for misery.
    c.    generally engages in self-mutilation.
    d.    is generally suicidal.

Tom Harris suggested four basic life positions. Choices "a," "c," and "d" are indicative of the "I'm Not OK—You're OK" position. A self-abusive person is sometimes known as a "masochistic personality" in the older literature. In an extreme case this position would lead the person to suicide. According to Harris the "I'm OK—You're OK" orientation is what successful winners choose. "I'm OK—You're Not OK" is the position taken by adolescent delinquents and adult criminals. Such persons feel victimized and are often paranoid. In extreme cases this person may see homicidal behavior as an acceptable solution to life's problems. "I'm Not OK—You're Not OK" is the most pessimistic position. This position could result in schizoid behavior and, in a worst-case scenario, the tendency to kill someone else and then take one's own life.                                            **(b)**

360. A man yells at his wife and then slaps her, stating that she does nothing around the house. The woman begins crying and he puts his arm around her to comfort her. He then begins crying and says that he doesn't know how he can continue doing all the housework because it is too difficult. A TA therapist who analyzes the situation using Stephen Karpman's drama triangle would say

   a.   the man is stuck in the "I'm Not OK—You're Not OK" life position.
   b.   the Critical Parent is dominating.
   c.   the man is obviously an adult child of an alcoholic.
   d.   the man has moved from the persecutor, to the rescuer, to the victim role.

Karpman suggested that only three roles are necessary for manipulative drama: persecutor, rescuer, and victim. A drama is similar to a TA "game," yet it has a greater number of events and the person switches roles during the course of the interaction. In TA, a game is a transaction with a concealed motive. Games prevent honest intimate discussion, and one player is always left with negative feelings. Games have a predictable outcome as a result of ulterior transactions. An ulterior transaction occurs when a disguised message is sent. **Hint:** The act of looking at the consequences of games is known as "game analysis."          **(d)**

361. A TA counselor and a strict behaviorist are both in the same case conference to staff a client. Which technique would the two most likely agree on when formulating a plan of action?

    a.   Empty chair technique.
    b.   Ego state analysis.
    c.   Contracting.
    d.   Formal assertiveness training.

    Using choice "a," the empty chair technique, the person imagines that another individual is in a chair in front of him or her, and then the client talks to the person. The technique is popular in TA as well as in the gestalt model. Contracting, nevertheless, is the only technique listed that is used readily by TA and behavior therapists.                                                                    **(c)**

362. A game is composed of transactions which end in a bad feeling for at least one player. Games are said to prevent true intimacy. Which other statement is true of games?

    a.   In a first-degree game someone gets seriously hurt.
    b.   In a first-degree game the harm is minimal, but the level of harm is quite serious in a third-degree game.
    c.   For a game to occur, three people must be involved.
    d.   Games always involve parallel vectors of communication.

    It is easy to remember that the higher the number the greater the hurt. For example, a second-degree game is more hurtful than a first-degree. In the first-degree game the hurt is innocuous; in the second-degree game the hurt is more serious; while in third-degree games the hurt can be permanent or on occasion deadly. And, oh yes, as far as choice "d" is concerned: Some exams will refer to parallel vectors of communication as "complementary transactions."                                              **(b)**

363. Unpleasant feelings after a person creates a game are called

    a.   rackets.
    b.   life scripts.

c.    the Little Professor.

d.    an analysis of variance.

When a client manipulates others to experience a childhood feeling, the result is called a "racket." (**Note:** in TA the experience of trying to secure these feelings is known as "collecting trading stamps.") Choice "b," or the life script, is a person's ongoing drama which dictates how a person will live his or her life. Claude Steiner has written extensively on scripts. His book *Scripts People Live* suggests three basic unhealthy scripts: no love, no mind, and no joy. It is like a theatrical plot based on early parental messages (often called injunctions in TA). Choice "d," abbreviated ANOVA, is a statistical technique used to determine differences between two or more means. Hold your horses, we'll get to statistics soon enough. **Does domestic violence have a script? Well, I guess the answer is kind of, sort of. According to Dr. Leonore Walker, who researched women in abusive relationships, there is a *cycle of violence* with three phases. First, there is a tension-building phase where arguments erupt very easily. Many women have dubbed this as the "walking on eggshells phase." Then there is the battering or acute incident phase where the actual fight or abuse, sexual abuse, or, worse yet, homicide occurs. Finally, there is a makeup phase (often referred to as the honeymoon phase) characterized by romantic moonlight dinners, the "I'll never do it again" lines, and the deliveries from the local flower shops. As time goes by the couple goes through the phases more rapidly and the honeymoon phase may not even exist.**                        **(a)**

364.  According to Eric Berne a life script is actually

a.    an ulterior transaction.

b.    an ego state.

c.    a life drama or plot based on unconscious decisions made early in life.

d.    a series of parallel transactions.

A script could apply to a family or even a country. The process of ferreting out the client's script is called "script analysis." Some popular life script categories include: the **never scripts**, or a person who never feels he or she will succeed; the **always scripts**, of individuals who will always remain a given way; **after scripts**, that result in a way a person believes he or she will behave after a certain event occurs; **open-ended scripts**, in which the person has no direction or plan; **until scripts**, in which the client is not allowed to feel good until a certain accomplishment or event arrives; and **desirable scripts/less desirable scripts**. Steiner, mentioned in the previous answer, analyzes the script of TA pioneer Eric Berne in his book! Ulterior transactions (choice "a") contain hidden transactions as two or more ego states are operating at the same time. For example, a man may say to a woman, "Would you like a ride in my new car?" She says. "Yes, I'd love to." This seems like a healthy (i.e., parallel) transaction from his Adult to her Adult ego state, and she responds in the same manner. He may, however, have a secret, covert, ulterior message if he is a game player. The ulterior message which goes from his Child to hers could be, "Wanna make out in my car?" Her ulterior answer—her Child to his Child—is, "Sure, I'd love to make out with you." Critics charge that script analysis relies too heavily on psychoanalytic principles.                                                          **(c)**

365. Eric Berne is to TA as Fritz Perls is to

   a.   the empty chair technique.
   b.   gestalt therapy.
   c.   the underdog.
   d.   the top dog.

Berne is the father of transactional analysis, while Frederick S. Perls created gestalt therapy. In some books he is called Fritz Perls or Fritz. All the other concepts apply to gestalt therapy. Perls saw the "top dog" as the Critical Parent portion of the personality which is very authoritarian and quick to use "shoulds" and "oughts." The "underdog" was seen as weak, powerless, passive, and full of excuses. These splits in the personality would wage civil war within the individual. In gestalt therapy, the empty chair technique could be employed so the individual could work on these opposing feelings. That is to say, the person could be the top dog in one chair and the underdog in the other. **(b)**

366. Empathy and counselor effectiveness scales reflect the work of

   a.   Perls and Berne.
   b.   Ellis and Harper.
   c.   Prochaska's transtheoretical model (TTM).
   d.   Carkhuff and Gazda.

In an attempt to isolate the factors associated with positive therapeutic outcomes, counselor educators generally state that the counselor must possess distinct qualities. In the literature these are known as the "core dimensions." According to research by Charles Truax and Kevin Mitchell, an effective counselor is authentic and genuine, not phony; gives positive regard through acceptance; and has accurate empathic understanding. As mentioned earlier, the Carkhuff scale rates the counselor from 1 to 5. The higher the rating the better the counselor is facilitating client growth. Gazda suggested a "Global Scale for Rating Helper Responses." On this scale a 1.0 response does not attend to the client's needs. The counselor may discredit or even scold the client. In case I haven't made myself clear, this is a response which is not helpful in any sense. A 2.0 response, although better than a 1.0, is superficial and deals only partially with surface feelings. The 3.0 response does facilitate growth. Although a 3.0 response is limited primarily to surface feelings, the counselor does not distort the content in his or her reflections. A 4.0 is evident when the counselor goes beyond reflection and deals with underlying feelings and meaning. Choice "c" is referring to the **transtheoretical model of change**. According to James O. Prochaska, the steps needed for change include: **precontemplation** (the person is not ready to change or acknowledge the issue), **contemplation** (the person is ambivalent or getting ready to change), **preparation** (the person comes up with ideas how to change), **action** (the individual takes steps to improve), and the final stage,

**maintenance** (relies on behaviors to prevent relapse and to perpetuate the new behaviors).                                    **(d)**

367. The acronym NLP is an abbreviation of

    a.   Bandler and Grinder's neurolinguistic programming.
    b.   new language programs for computer therapy.
    c.   new language psychotherapy software.
    d.   neurological psychotherapy.

This model (neurolinguistic programming; choice "a"), supposedly based somewhat on what Milton H. Erickson, Fritz Perls, and Virginia Satir really did in their sessions, makes some incredible claims, such as the ability to cure a longstanding phobia in less time than it takes to conduct a typical counseling session! Perhaps the two most popular techniques used by NLP practitioners are "reframing" and "anchoring." When using reframing the counselor helps the client to perceive a given situation in a new light so as to produce a new emotional reaction to it (e.g., a glass of water is not half empty; it is really half full). In anchoring, a desirable emotional state is evoked via an outside stimulus such as a touch or a sound or a specific bodily motion. This is similar to classical conditioning or the concept of a posthypnotic suggestion (i.e., a suggestion which works after you leave the hypnotist's office). A client with a phobia of cats, for example, might squeeze his left arm when he comes in contact with a cat, and this would bring out an emotion other than fear. If you are taking an exam which is slanted toward this model, then you must read *Structure of Magic I* and *Structure of Magic II* by John Bandler and John Grinder. This approach has been very popular with business people (especially sales persons) and emphasizes the importance of eye movements in determining a person's "representational system" for storing information, such as hearing, seeing, or feeling. I have no doubt that the fellow who has made the most money from this approach, however, is not a licensed therapist but rather Anthony (Tony) Robbins, who expanded on NLP and whose various *Personal Power* series have outsold any other motivational product in history. Tony—a dynamic speaker by any standard—sports a high school education.                          **(a)**

368. A gestalt therapist is most likely going to deal with a client's projection via

    a.    playing the projection technique.
    b.    the empty chair technique.
    c.    converting questions to statements.
    d.    a behavioral contract.

Choices "a," "b," and "c" are all techniques used frequently in gestalt therapy, but remember that you are searching for the best answer. Projection is an ego defense mechanism in which you see something in others that you cannot accept about yourself. Gestalt hits this head-on, and in "playing the projection" the counselor literally asks you to act like this person you dislike. Choice "c" would work thusly: A client might say, "Don't all people in a group feel scared during the initial session of group counseling?" The client is asked to turn the question into an "I statement," in this case, "I feel scared during this initial session of group counseling." In gestalt this is known as "taking responsibility for a feeling or situation." Often, the gestalt counselor literally asks the client to say this. For example, "I feel scared during this initial session of group counseling and I take responsibility for being scared." **(a)**

369. A client says she has a tingling sensation in her hands each time she talks about the probability of marriage. A gestalt therapist would most likely

    a.    ask the client to recount a dream.
    b.    urge the client to engage in thought stopping.
    c.    prescribe relaxation homework.
    d.    urge the client to stay with the feeling.

Gestalt therapy is concerned primarily with the here and now. When a client tries to avoid a feeling the counselor urges the client to face it or "stay with the feeling" if you will. Perls believed this is necessary for growth. Choice "a," dream work, is an integral part of the gestalt approach to counseling. The client is told to recount the dream "as if it is happening in the present."

Everything—yes everything—in the dream is considered a projection of the self. So if the client is being chased by a mean monster in the dream, the client might be asked to "become the monster." The gestalt model emphasizes experience rather than interpretation, which makes it especially attractive for group intervention.     **(d)**

370. Gestalt therapists sometimes utilize the exaggeration experiment which most closely resembles

    a.    successive approximations.
    b.    paradox as practiced by Frankl, Haley, or Erickson.
    c.    free association.
    d.    paraphrasing with emotional reflection.

As opposed to the other three therapists (in choice "b"), Perls emphasized the exaggeration in regard to present moment verbal and nonverbal behavior in the here and now. A gestalt therapist might say, "What is your left hand doing?" (In gestalt, "what" questions are seen as more valuable than "why" questions.) After the client responds, the therapist might add, "Can you exaggerate that movement in your left hand?" Choice "a" is an operant behavior modification term which suggests that a behavior is gradually accomplished by reinforcing "successive steps" until the target behavior is reached. This technique also is known as "shaping" or "shaping using successive approximations."     **(b)**

371. A client undergoing gestalt therapy who states "It is difficult to get a job in New York City" would be asked by the counselor to

    a.    go to the O*NET online website (www.onetonline.org) which is the replacement for the *DOT* and is now the nation's primary source of occupational information.
    b.    change the verbalization to an "I" statement.
    c.    read the *OOH*.
    d.    take the Strong Interest Inventory (SII).

A goal of gestalt is to eliminate "*it* talk" and replace it with "I statements." The other choices all relate to career counseling.

**Dr. Howard's helpful history hint:** The *DOT* (*Dictionary of Occupational Titles*) was a popular comprehensive career counseling reference created by the U.S. Department of Labor in 1938. The final official edition, which listed 13,000 occupations, was last published by the government in March, 1999 as a two-volume set as a companion to O*NET (Occupational Information Network). The O*NET is an online database which replaced the *DOT*. The *OOH* (choice "c") stands for the *Occupational Outlook Handbook*. It was first published in 1949 by the U.S. Department of Labor and is now revised every two years. The text attempts to depict projected job trends. It also delineates earnings, necessary training and education for a job, as well as working conditions and what workers in a given job actually do. The *Strong* (formerly the Strong Campbell Interest Inventory or SCII) is the most popular interest inventory, and it is based on the theory of John Holland. **(b)**

372. Gestalt therapy, a paradigm that focuses on awareness in the here and now incorporates

    a.    psychodrama.
    b.    Aaron Beck's cognitive therapy, which asserts that maladaptive thinking creates emotional disturbance and thus clients should record dysfunctional thoughts.
    c.    conditioned reflex therapy.
    d.    client-centered therapy.

Psychodrama incorporates role-playing into the treatment process. A client, for example, might act out an especially painful incident in his or her life. Psychodrama was invented by Jacob L. Moreno, who first coined the term *group therapy* in 1931. Gestalt therapists emphasize experiments and exercises. **(a)**

373. According to gestalt therapists, a client who is angry at his wife for leaving him, and who makes a suicide attempt, would be engaging in

    a.    sublimation.
    b.    a panic reaction.

    c.    retroflection.
    d.    repression.

Retroflection is the act of doing to yourself what you really wish to do to someone else. The psychoanalysts often say that the person who wishes to kill him- or herself really wants to kill someone else. True? Perhaps. Statistics now indicate that in cases of suicide, four out of every 100 begin with the person killing someone else!     **(c)**

374. Gestalt means

    a.    a group.
    b.    a form, figure, or configuration unified as a whole.
    c.    a dyad.
    d.    visual acuity.

Although there is no exact English translation, choice "b" roughly describes the nature of the concept. Gestalt also can imply that the integrated whole is greater than the sum of its parts. Growth takes place when the client has integrated disowned parts of the personality and reconnected with them.     **(b)**

375. Perls suggested _____ which must be peeled away to reach emotional stability.

    a.    four layers of neurosis
    b.    three layers of neurosis
    c.    two layers of neurosis
    d.    five layers of neurosis

Perls likened the process of therapy to that of peeling an onion. The person has a phony layer, a phobic layer (fear that others will reject his or her uniqueness), an impasse layer (the person feels struck), the implosive layer (willingness to expose the true self), and the explosive layer (person has relief due to authenticity).     **(d)**

376. In gestalt therapy unexpressed emotions are known as

    a.   unfinished business.
    b.   the emerging gestalt.
    c.   form/figure language.
    d.   the top dog.

Here is a key term in gestalt therapy. When an unexpressed feeling of resentment, rage, guilt, anxiety, or other emotion interferes with present situations and causes difficulties, it is known as "unfinished business." Just in case it comes up on your exam, Perls borrowed the term *Gestalt* from the system of psychology proposed by Max Wertheimer of Germany in the 1920s which emphasized that the whole is greater than the sum of the parts. The original gestalt psychologists studied perceptual phenomena (e.g., figure/ground relationships). The three most common principles relating to gestalt psychology are first, "insight learning" (discussed earlier in this book) as discovered by Wolfgang Kohler. Second, Bluma Zeigarnik's well-known "Zeigarnik effect," which suggests that motivated people tend to experience tension due to unfinished tasks, and thus they recall unfinished activities better. Thus, if you sincerely care about the outcome of a task, you will have better recall of that task if it remains incomplete, than if completed. (This certainly is a bit like the concept of "unfinished business" in gestalt therapy.) Third, Wertheimer's "phi-phenomenon," wherein the illusion of movement can be achieved via two or more stimuli which are not moving; for example a neon sign that has a moving arrow. **(a)**

377. Gestalt therapy emphasizes

    a.   cognitive-behavioral issues.
    b.   transference issues.
    c.   traumatic childhood memories.
    d.   awareness in the here and now and dream work.

Choice "a" is incorrect. The gestalt mode does not believe that a client can "think" one's self out of unhappiness. The person must experience awareness for growth. **(d)**

378. The gestalt dialogue experiment generally utilizes the concepts of

     a.   behavioral self-control.
     b.   choice theory.
     c.   top dog, underdog, and the empty chair technique.
     d.   the rehearsal experiment.

The exam you are taking could refer to choice "c" as "games of dialogue." In addition to the top dog/underdog split in the personality, empty chair dialogue also could be used for other opposing tendencies, such as feminine versus masculine attributes. Gestalt assumes that anxiety is often actually "stage fright." By this the gestalt therapist assumes the client has internally rehearsed a situation and is worried that his or her "performance" will not be up to snuff. This "rehearsal" is said to get in the way of spontaneity and healthy personal experimentation. The rehearsal technique especially lends itself to group work as group members can share their rehearsals with one another, and thus awareness of stage fright (e.g., worrying about not saying or doing the right thing) and fear of not being accepted by others can be illuminated. And if you marked choice "b," review the questions on reality therapy, as choice theory is associated with this brand of treatment. Glasser's choice theory postulates that behavior is really an attempt to control our perceptions to satisfy our genetic needs—survival, love, and belonging, power, freedom, and fun.                          **(c)**

379. Critics assert that gestalt therapy is an effective treatment that

     a.   often fails to emphasize the importance of dreams.
     b.   ignores nonverbal behavior.
     c.   often fails to emphasize cognitive concerns.
     d.   uses the making the rounds technique, which is not appropriate for group work.

Quite the antithesis of REBT and related cognitive therapies, gestalt is considered a bit, well, anti-intellectual if you will. Perls once asserted that if you lose your mind you can come to your senses! **In gestalt therapy the emphasis is on increasing psychological as well as bodily awareness.** Another charge is that it is too confrontational if practiced in the manner Perls demonstrated. **Today gestalt therapists are a bit gentler, softer, and less abrupt than Perls.** Confrontation occurs when the therapist points out discrepancies or incongruencies between the client's verbal and nonverbal behaviors. The "making the rounds" strategy mentioned in choice "d" alludes to a popular group exercise in which the client is instructed to say the same message to everyone in the group. And oh yes, the word *affective* in the question means emotional. Some experts have branded gestalt and existential psychotherapy as "affective" paradigms since they urge clients to purge emotions in order to feel better about themselves. Gestalt has traditionally been a popular modality for group work. **(c)**

380. Most experts would agree that the peak period of competition between the various schools of counseling and therapy (e.g., gestalt, behavioristic, reality therapy, etc.) was during

    a.   the late 1970s.
    b.   the late 1960s.
    c.   the 1980s.
    d.   the mid-1950s.

    In the 1950s, counseling—not testing—became the key guidance function. Moreover, the 1950s marked a golden age for developmental psychology. In the late 1960s the field was literally inundated with competing psychotherapies. In the 1970s biofeedback, behavior modification, and crisis hotlines flourished. And in the 1980s professionalism (e.g., licensing and improvement in professional organizations) was evident. **(b)**

381. The relationship a client has with a gestalt therapist would most likely progress _____ than the relationship a client would have with a Rogerian counselor.

    a.   faster
    b.   slower

c.    at the same pace
d.    a and b

Because gestalt therapists are generally rather confrontational, theorists assume that the client–counselor relationship will progress at a slower rate. If you marked choice "d" I'd like to suggest that you read the answers more carefully. Answer "d" is a synthesis of choice "a" and "b," and choices "a" and "b" are contradictory.   **(b)**

382.  The school of counseling created by Carl R. Rogers, Ph.D., has undergone three name changes. Initially it was called _____, then _____, and in 1974 it changed to _____.

a.    nondirective; client-centered; person-centered.
b.    directive; nondirective; client-centered.
c.    person-centered; Rogerian, nondirective.
d.    client-centered; person-centered; nondirective.

A word to the wise: Expect to see any of these names in regard to questions on Rogers's theory. The initial name, nondirective counseling, was intended to set the approach apart from the directive and analytic models which were popular during the 1940s. In 1951, the process took on its new name, client-centered therapy, which emphasized Rogers's theory of personality and, of course, the fact that the client was not viewed as a "sick patient." In 1974, the approach took on its current name, person-centered, to emphasize the power of the person and Rogers's growing interest in group behavior. **Hint:** Although I've just given you three key names for this approach, **Rogers's method could also be known as "self theory." When his approach is used in career counseling the role of the self-concept in terms of career choice is illuminated.**          **(a)**

383.  Rogers's approach is characterized as a(n) _____ approach.

a.    existential or humanistic
b.    cognitive
c.    cognitive-behavioral
d.    neodynamic

Some exams will call humanistic psychology "third force psychology" because it was a reaction to behaviorism and psychoanalysis, the two initial forces at the time. In regard to choices "b" and "c," it can be pointed out that cognitive approaches are generally more directive and do not give the client–counselor relationship as much emphasis as the Rogerians.    **(a)**

384. Which statement is true of the person-centered approach?

    a.    Reflection is used a lot yet the counselor rarely gives advice.
    b.    Advice is given a lot.
    c.    Reflection is rarely utilized.
    d.    Closed-ended questions keep the sessions moving at a fast pace.

A strict Rogerian would generally not give the client specific techniques for behavioral change or instruct the person "how to think." **Giving advice is one of the most debated issues in counseling. Some texts classify advice giving (along with preaching, lecturing, and excessive questioning) as a nonhelpful behavior. In fact, many experts insist that lecturing/preaching is merely a variation of advice giving and can foster a power struggle between the counselor and the client. Advice giving in the initial sessions can keep a client from working through his or her feelings. Nevertheless, in crisis or emergency situations, advice giving is generally considered an appropriate intervention. Multicultural experts wisely point out that some groups (e.g., certain Asian cultures) view counseling as a last resort in which immediate direction is given to the client. In such cultures Rogerian counseling is clearly not the treatment of choice.** When I was writing my book *Favorite Counseling and Therapy Techniques* I asked a famous person-centered therapist to contribute. He wrote me back and said, "I'm a Rogerian, I don't do techniques."    **(a)**

385. In the person-centered approach, an effective counselor must possess

   a.   the skill to be confrontational.
   b.   the ability to give advice.
   c.   the ability to do formal psychological testing.
   d.   empathy, congruence, genuineness, and demonstrate unconditional positive regard to create a desirable "I–Thou relationship."

Rogerians speak of "conditions for growth" and a therapeutic atmosphere which produces a "climate for growth." The counselor helps produce the climate via genuineness (or congruence, which indicates the counselor can be real in the relationship), unconditional positive regard (nonjudgmental acceptance or nonpossessive warmth), and empathic understanding. Rogers has an optimistic view concerning human nature, believing that we have an inborn tendency toward self-actualization. Overall, the research does not support the notion that these therapeutic factors are necessarily related to positive therapeutic outcomes. Some studies indicate that the client's traits have an even greater impact on the success of psychotherapy.     **(d)**

386. Rogers viewed man as

   a.   basically evil.
   b.   driven by instincts.
   c.   a product of reinforcement.
   d.   positive when he develops in a warm, accepting, trusting environment.

Here is a wonderful little review regarding the manner in which the major modalities of counseling view clients. Expect to see several questions of this ilk on any major exam:     **(d)**

**Rogers (person-centered)**—individual is good and moves toward growth and self-actualization.

**Berne (transactional analysis)**—messages learned about self in childhood determine whether person is good or bad, though intervention can change this script.

**Freud (psychoanalysis)**—deterministic; people are controlled by biological instincts; are unsocialized, irrational; driven by unconscious forces such as sex and aggression.

**Ellis (rational-emotive behavior therapy)**—people have a cultural/biological propensity to think in a disturbed manner but can be taught to use their capacity to react differently.

**Perls (gestalt)**—people are not bad or good. People have the capacity to govern life effectively as "whole." People are part of their environment and must be viewed as such.

**Glasser (reality therapy)**—individuals strive to meet basic physiological needs and the need to be worthwhile to self and others. Brain as control system tries to meet needs.

**Adler (individual psychology)**—man is basically good; much of behavior is determined via birth order.

**Jung (analytic psychology)**—man strives for individuation or a sense of self-fulfillment.

**Skinner (behavior modification)**—humans are like other animals: mechanistic and controlled via environmental stimuli and reinforcement contingencies; not good or bad; no self-determination or freedom.

**Bandura (neobehavioristic)**—person produces and is a product of conditioning. Observation and modeling are extremely important.

**Frankl (logotherapy)**—existential view is that humans are good, rational, and retain freedom of choice.

**Williamson (trait-factor)**—through education and scientific data, man can become himself. Humans are born with potential for good or evil. Others are needed to help unleash positive potential. Man is mainly rational, not intuitive.

387. A person-centered therapist would

    a.  treat clients with everyday problems differently from psychotics.
    b.  treat all diagnostic categories of the *DSM* using the same principles.
    c.  use more closed-ended questions with adjustment reactions.
    d.  use contracting with clients who are not making progress.

The person-centered model puts little stock in the formal process of diagnosis and psychological assessment. People are people, and when they are labeled they are debased to "patients." Moreover, traditionally, strict adherents to this model do not ask a large number of questions (choice "c"). (Some years ago it was considered a cardinal sin if a graduate student serving a counseling practicum asked a client a question while engaging in the practice of person-centered counseling. Today, the practice of asking clients questions is more common; nevertheless, open-ended questions are highly recommended whenever possible.) Choice "d," contracting, is more popular with behavioristic counselors and "directive" methods rather than "nondirective" strategies. **(b)**

388. Rogers emphasized congruence in the counselor. Congruence occurs when

    a.  external behavior matches an internal response or state.
    b.  the counselor uses silence.
    c.  the counselor reflects emotion.
    d.  the counselor summarizes at the end of the session.

When the counselor has the ability to be "real" in the relationship, we say that he or she is genuine or congruent. Rogers insists that three key factors are needed for an effective helping climate. The counselor's attitude must include *genuineness* (again, also called congruence), *unconditional positive regard* (also referred to as nonpossessive warmth), and *empathic understanding*. Congruence is a condition where the counselor is very aware of his or her own feelings and accurately expresses this to the client. Of the three elements, Rogers suggested that congruence—which really implies that the counselor is genuine, authentic, and does not put on a professional front—is the most important. **(a)**

389. Rogers felt that _____ for client change to occur.

    a.    conditions must be in accordance with the problem
    b.    three conditions are necessary
    c.    nine conditions are necessary
    d.    two conditions are necessary

If you missed this one, take a break. You've been studying too long. When you're refreshed, review the answer to question 388. **(b)**

390. Person-centered counseling would prove least effective with

    a.    a bright verbal male.
    b.    a bright verbal female.
    c.    a graduate student who had a knowledge of phrenology.
    d.    a client who is not very verbal.

In choice "c," the term *phrenology* refers to an early pseudoscientific psychological doctrine which asserted that one's personality could be determined by the shape and configuration of the skull. **(d)**

391. Critics of the Rogerian approach feel that

    a.    it does not emphasize relationship concerns.
    b.    some degree of directiveness is needed after the initial phase of counseling.
    c.    more confrontation is necessary, though Rogers did encourage caring confrontations.
    d.    b and c.

I have heard counselors humorously say that Rogerian counseling is like a joke without a punch line! Many counselors now believe that some degree of directiveness is needed after the relationship is built; otherwise treatment merely goes in circles. Some books and exams refer to the process after the relationship is built as the "action phase" of counseling. J. O. Prochaska is very critical of the research which supposedly indicates the effectiveness of the Rogerian model, as some of the studies lacked a control group, failed to take the placebo effect into account, did not use the best statistical technique, or relied on self-reports of the client.                                                                    **(d)**

392. Counselors who work as consultants

    a.   generally adhere to reality therapy.
    b.   generally adhere to one single theory.
    c.   generally adhere to consultation theory.
    d.   generally do not adhere to one single theory.

Now hear this! I fully expect that you will see several questions on your exam related to consultation. Many counselors tell me they have never studied this topic. Read this answer over several times. Choice "c" is not the best answer inasmuch as no integrated theory of consultation exists at this time. Consultation can target organizational concerns or service delivery. Several major consultation models exist. First is Gerald Caplan's psychodynamic mental health consultation in which the consultant does not see the client directly but advises the consultee (i.e., the individual in the organization who is receiving the consultant's services). This model is interesting because it recommends that the consultant—not the counselor/consultee— be ethically and legally responsible for the client's welfare and treatment. Second is the "behavioral consultation" or "social learning theory model" associated with Albert Bandura, in which the consultant designs behavioral change programs for the consultee to implement. Third is the process consultation model by Edgar Schein, which is said to be analogous to the "doctor–patient" model. The consultant is paid to diagnose the problem (i.e., the consultee is not certain what it is) and prescribe a solution. The focus is on the agency or organization, not the individual client. With process consultation, the focus is not—I repeat—is not on the content of the problem, but rather the process used to solve the problems. Schein also mentions the purchase of expertise model in which the consultee says: "Here's the problem; you fix it." This is similar to the doctor–patient model except that the consultee knows what is wrong. Fourth is triadic consultation in which the consultant works with a mediator to provide services to a client.                    **(d)**

393. Counseling generally occurs in a clinical setting while consultation generally occurs in a _____ setting.

  a.   group
  b.   work/organizational
  c.   continuing care
  d.   residential

Here again, the other answer choices are not necessarily incorrect; it is just that this choice "b" is the best answer. Counselors generally focus on a person or a group, while consultants focus more on issues. Another key factor is that in consultation work, empathy—although important—is overshadowed by genuineness and respect.            **(b)**

394. Attending behavior that is verbal is also called

  a.   verbal tracking.
  b.   clarifying.
  c.   reflection.
  d.   paraphrasing.

Here is a nice little memory device. The word *attending* is similar to the word *attention*. Attending behavior occurs when you give your clients your complete attention. Helpful "nonverbal" behavior would include leaning forward slightly, eye contact, and appropriate facial expression, such as smiling. Nonhelpful nonverbals would be frowning, yawning, sitting far away from the client, repeatedly closing your eyes, shaking a finger at the client, acting as if you are in a hurry, or talking extremely fast or slow. Some exams may speak of task-facilitative behavior versus abstractive behavior in regard to the process of attending. When the counselor's thoughts are in relation to the client, this is said to be task-facilitative. When the counselor is thinking about his or her own concerns (e.g., how much money he or she is making that day or where to go for lunch) then it is seen as abstractive behavior.    **(a)**

395. The counselor's social power is related to

a. age.
b. expertise, attractiveness, and trustworthiness.
c. sex and age.
d. degree of directiveness.

Some exams will call social power "social influence." My memory technique here is what I call the "EAT" formula; the "E" is for expertness, the "A" for attractiveness, and the "T" for trustworthiness. The three factors first made an impact on the counseling profession in 1968 when Stanley Strong wrote a landmark article which suggested that counselors perceived as expert, attractive, and trustworthy would not be discredited by the client. Expertness here refers to the manner in which the client perceives the counselor rather than the way the counselor perceives himself or herself. A counselor's self-perception is technically known as "competence." E. Fuller Torrey, author of *The Death of Psychiatry*, suggested that a wall full of degrees and an impressive office can help to ensure that the counselor will be perceived as an expert. Thus, a counselor who is seen as an expert may not actually be competent. Attractiveness implies that positive feelings and thoughts regarding the counselor are helpful. One hypothesis states that if the client and counselor have had similar experiences, the client will view the counselor as attractive. Clients who say "I like my counselor" are demonstrating that the counselor has been perceived as attractive. The chemical dependency (CD) addictions model, in which a recovering addict helps a practicing addict, is based on this principle. In regard to trust, it is felt that a violation of confidentiality will nearly always eliminate this factor.    **(b)**

396. Key areas that often cause problems for the counselor's self-image are

   a.    choice of a modality and a learning disability.
   b.    age and the lack of a doctoral degree.
   c.    lack of NCC.
   d.    competence, power, and intimacy.

Competence, power, and intimacy are all factors that impact the counselor's "social influence." Competence reflects a counselor's feelings regarding his or her adequacy. A counselor who feels incompetent could directly or indirectly (e.g., tone of voice or body posture) communicate this to the client. In counseling, power is seen as a positive trait used to enhance the client's growth. Counselors struggling with their own feelings in regard to a lack of power may become rigid, coercive, or even belligerent toward the client. Others may become overly nondirective. A counselor who has personal issues revolving around intimacy also could be extremely nondirective or afraid to confront clients for fear of rejection. Clearly, such a counselor stays at arm's length from clients and could personally benefit from treatment.    **(d)**

397. A counselor who is genuine

   a.    does not role-play someone he or she is not, so as to be accepted by the client.
   b.    does not change his or her true values from session to session.
   c.    is not empathic.
   d.    a and b.

Gerard Egan stressed that clients are indeed more open and expressive with counselors who seem genuine. Egan is well-known for his books which teach a systematic approach to effective helping (e.g., *The Skilled Helper*). **Note:** Egan has referred to competence in some of his literature as "accomplishment-competence," feeling that an accomplishment (e.g., helping abate a client's depression) can impact upon one's feelings of competence, or the client's perception of the helper's expertise. In other words, the counselor must be able to deliver the goods and truly help the client.    **(d)**

398. Allen E. Ivey has postulated three types of empathy:

    a.   positive, negative regard, and cognitive.
    b.   reflective, micro-empathy, and forced choice.
    c.   basic, subtractive, and additive.
    d.   micro-empathy, basic, and level 8 empathy.

    In **basic empathy** the counselor's response is on the same level as the client's. In the case of **subtractive empathy**, the counselor's behavior does not completely convey an understanding of what has been communicated. **Additive empathy** is most desirable since it adds to the client's understanding and awareness.                          **(c)**

399. _____ and _____ created a program to help counselors learn accurate empathy.

    a.   Truax; Carkhuff
    b.   Rogers; Berenson
    c.   Rogers; Brill
    d.   Carkhuff; Satir

    Robert Carkhuff has been quoted time and time again for his statement that, "all helping is for better or worse." Or as he says, "no helpee is left unchanged by any helping interaction." Charles Truax worked very closely with Robert Carkhuff.        **(a)**

400. The human relations core for effective counseling includes

    a.   power, competence, and trustworthiness.
    b.   expertise, attractiveness, and trustworthiness.
    c.   empathy, positive regard (or respect), and genuineness.
    d.   self-image, self-talk, and attending behavior.

    Choice "b" (remember?) is the social influence core. The purpose of this question is to make certain you are able to distinguish between the social influence core and the human relations core.                                          **(c)**

# 6

## Group Counseling and Group Work

*Never doubt that a small group of thoughtful, committed citizens*
*can change the world. Indeed, it is the only thing that ever has.*
— Margaret Mead, cultural anthropologist

401. Prior to the 1960s most counseling took place

   a.   in a group setting.
   b.   with the entire family present.
   c.   in a dyadic relationship.
   d.   in behavior therapy clinics.

A **dyad** is a unit of two functioning as a pair. In this case the counselor and the counselee form the pair. The popularity of family therapy and behavior therapy was not evident in the 1950s. I cannot forego mentioning that counselors often confuse the word *dyadic* with *didactic* which means to teach. **Special note: Despite my aforementioned remarks, group leaders often put members in smaller groups during experiential experiences and this practice is often labeled as pairing. (c)**

402. A group has

   a.  a membership which can be defined.
   b.  some degree of unity and interaction.
   c.  a shared purpose.
   d.  all of the above.

Put the choices together and you have a fine definition of the word *group*. A group is really a cluster of people in a recognizable unit. An alternative definition of a group would be: three or more people who meet with a conscious cause or purpose. **Exam point saver: Although group work is very beneficial, preliminary meta-analysis research indicates that individual counseling still generally produces better results for depressed clients. At this time, however, the data are by no means 100% convincing. In general, group counseling is approximately as effective as individual work.** **(d)**

403. The term *group therapy* was coined in 1931 by

   a.  Frank Parsons, the father of guidance (also referred to as vocational guidance).
   b.  Jacob Moreno, the father of psychodrama.
   c.  E. G. Williamson, associated with the Minnesota Viewpoint.
   d.  Fritz Perls, the father of gestalt therapy.

First, although Frank Parsons did not coin the term *group* therapy, his work did help set the stage for this practice since he relied on groups to conduct group work related to career and vocational choice, and thus he has indeed been considered a mover, a shaker, and a serious player in the history of the group movement. Jacob Moreno is the correct answer. Ten years before psychiatrist Jacob Levy Moreno coined the term *group therapy* he noted that individuals in Vienna involved in theatrical productions without scripts experienced a cathartic reaction which seemed to be curative. In psychodrama the client expresses spontaneous feelings via role-playing. Hence the literature often talks about Moreno's **Theatre of Spontaneity** in the 1920s, which relied on improvisation and drama as healing forces. Psychodramatic techniques are appropriate for family therapy as well as group work. Perls, although he did not coin the term *group therapy* either, is considered a major figure in the history of group therapy; especially his work at Esalen Institute in Big Sur, California when he began practicing gestalt therapy in 1964. The name Joseph H. Pratt might also find its way onto your exam. Pratt, a top Boston physician, formed what might well be the first counseling/therapy groups from approximately 1905 to 1923. The groups dealt with the issue of tuberculosis. Freud's *Group Psychology and the Analysis of the Ego* was published in 1921; however, his interest in individual treatment seemingly kept him from becoming a major player in the history of groups and from creating a comprehensive model of group therapy. **Key hint: The first mutual aid, self-help support group, AA (Alcoholics Anonymous), was founded in 1935 by a stock broker, Bill Wilson (aka Bill W) and Dr. Bob Smith (aka Dr. Bob) in Akron, Ohio. Membership of AA worldwide is now thought to top two million. Counseling exams often refer to AA as a 12-step group.** **(b)**

404. Noted psychotherapy author and scholar Raymond Corsini once referred to the early 1940s as the "modern era" of group work. In the 1940s the two organizations for group therapy were created and group work became a legitimate specialty. The groups are

    a.    NASW and NBCC.
    b.    ASGW and AAS.
    c.    the American Society for Group Psychotherapy and Psychodrama (ASGPP) spawned by the work of Jacob Moreno in 1942 and the American Group Psychotherapy Association (AGPA) which resulted from the effort of Samuel Richard Slavson in 1943.
    d.    AACD and APA.

Abbreviations, acronyms, or so-called alphabet soup language seems endless in our field. Choice "b" mentions the ASGW (Association for Specialists in Group Work). This is the division of the ACA that focuses primarily on group intervention. The ASGW journal, *The Journal for Specialists in Group Work*, is the publication you will need to keep you updated in this area. Other abbreviations are the National Association of Social Workers (NASW), established in 1955, and the American Association of Suicidology (AAS). By now you should be familiar with the others.                                           **(c)**

405. Which theorist's (or theorists') work has been classified as a preface to the group movement?

    a.   Sigmund Freud.
    b.   C. G. Jung.
    c.   Alfred Adler and Jesse B. Davis.
    d.   Marsha Linehan, who created dialectical behavior therapy (DBT), originally used to deal with suicidal behaviors.

Dr. Jesse Buttrick Davis (a high school principal in Grand Rapids, Michigan) is cited as a pioneer in school guidance counseling and often as America's first school guidance counselor. In 1912 Davis had each high school student attend a class each week where he relied on groups to explore careers and values. His systematic work resulted in the National Vocational Guidance Association (today named the National Career Development Association or NCDA.) Adler (known for his individual psychology) was actually engaging in group treatment during the early 1920s at his child guidance facilities located in Vienna. His rationale for group work was simply that "man's problems and conflicts are recognized in their social nature." Marsha Linehan created dialectical behavior therapy (DBT), originally used to deal with suicidal behaviors.       **(c)**

406. Primary groups are

    a.   preventive and attempt to ward off problems.
    b.   always follow a person-centered paradigm.
    c.   generally utilized for long-term psychotherapy.
    d.   always focused on the client's childhood.

Examinations and literature in the area of group processes will often classify groups using a model popularized by community mental health experts such as Gerald Caplan, a pioneer in the crisis intervention movement. The three classifications are primary, secondary, and tertiary. A primary group stresses a healthy lifestyle or coping strategies which can reduce the occurrence of a given difficulty. Primary groups are often labeled as prevention groups. A terrific little memory device you can rely on is that primary starts with a "p" and so does the word prevention. Memory devices don't get much easier than that folks! **A primary group attempts to stop a problem before it occurs.** A group which teaches birth control to prevent teen pregnancy would be a fine example. **In a secondary group a problem or disturbance is present but not usually severe.** The secondary group works to reduce the severity or length of a problem and generally includes aspects of prevention. Thus, a group that deals with grief or shyness might fall into this category. **The tertiary group deals more with individual difficulties that are more serious and longstanding**. (The word *tertiary* literally means the third rank.) Choices "c" and "d" would apply mainly to groups categorized as tertiary. The terms primary, secondary, and tertiary can often be used to classify community prevention programs.

**A note on graduate preparation: According to CACREP, a student should participate in a small group activity within the program for at least 10 clock hours during a given semester.** **(a)**

407. A group is classified as secondary. This implies that

    a.    it is preventive and attempts to ward off problems.
    b.    a difficulty or disturbance is present.
    c.    two therapists are utilized.
    d.    all of the above.

Choice "a" is not entirely false since a secondary group does have preventive qualities. Nevertheless, this is not the major feature; hence, this is not the best answer. When two counselors are used in a group setting the procedure is known as "coleadership" or "cofacilitation."                    **(b)**

408. When comparing a tertiary group with a primary or secondary group

   a.    the tertiary group focuses less on individual members.
   b.    the tertiary group focuses more on the here and now.
   c.    the tertiary group is less likely to deal with severe pathology.
   d.    the tertiary group is more likely to deal with severe pathology.

Choice "a" stands incorrect because the tertiary group focuses more on the individual than the primary or secondary group. In reference to choice "b," a counselor dealing with the here and now often relies on the skill of "immediacy," which takes place (in a group or an individual session) when the counselor explores the client–counselor relationship as it is transpiring right at that moment. Immediacy relates to the counselor's ability to convey what is happening between the counselor and the client.     **(d)**

409. Group norms

   a.    exist only in encounter groups.
   b.    exist only in career counseling groups.
   c.    are not related to group cohesiveness.
   d.    govern acceptable behavior and group rules.

Let's not make this complicated. Norms are explicit and implicit (i.e., not verbalized) rules which tell group members how to behave and how not to behave in a given situation. Group specialists are quick to point out that all groups have norms, though often they are not formally presented to group members. Singing loudly while taking the NCE or CPCE would be violating a norm, although I doubt whether anyone will specifically tell you not to sing at the onset of the exam! **Norms actually refer to "expected behaviors."** Now of course norms vary depending upon your role in a group. In an educational class group, for example, the norms for the teacher may indeed be different than for the student. **(d)**

410. Group therapy initially flourished in the United States due to

   a. Freud's lectures in this country.
   b. a shortage of competent career counselors.
   c. a shortage of individual therapists during World War II.
   d. pressure from nondirective therapists pushing encounter groups.

During World War II, as well as after the war, many soldiers were plagued with severe psychological problems, yet a personnel shortage made it impossible for each and every person to be treated using individual therapy. Jacob Moreno had brought the idea of group therapy to the United States in 1925, but the supply and demand issues sparked by the war effort were the catalysts which generated this idea, whose time had come. **(c)**

411. Group content refers to material discussed in a group setting. Group process refers to

   a. analysis of the unconscious.
   b. analysis of the ego.
   c. the T-group paradigm.
   d. the manner in which discussions and transactions occur.

**Group content refers to what the group is discussing. Group process refers to analyzing the communications, interactions, and transactions.** The process is the way in which the discussion takes place. Choice "c," or T-group, merely means "training group." The first T-group was conducted in 1946. Originally, T-groups were used in industrial and organizational settings to process personnel interactions and improve efficiency. A wealth of work in this area was done by National Training Laboratories (NTL) in Bethel, Maine, created by Leland Bradford, Kenneth Benne, and Ronald Lippitt. **(d)**

412. Group cohesiveness refers to

     a.   forces which tend to bind group members together.
     b.   an analysis of group content.
     c.   a common coleadership style.
     d.   a style of leadership.

Cohesiveness is a sense of caring for the group and the other group members. The term *cohesiveness* is associated with Kurt Lewin's "field theory" in which cohesiveness was seen as a binding force among group members. Lewin called the binding force between group members "positive valence." When cohesiveness goes up, absenteeism and other negative factors go down. High cohesiveness leads to high group productivity and commitment. Lewin was a key player in the T-group movement in the United States. And here's a helpful tidbit of information. Often when a group displays little or no cohesiveness the group will be viewed as "fragmented." Just for review, you will recall that choice "c" (coleadership) is implemented when two persons lead the group.             **(a)**

413. Some theorists feel that group therapy differs from group counseling (which is also called an interpersonal problem-solving group) in that

     a.   group counseling would be of longer duration.
     b.   group therapy, also dubbed as a personality reconstruction group, would be of longer duration.
     c.   group counseling requires far more training.
     d.   group therapy addresses a less-disturbed population of clients.

George Gazda proposes a typology of three distinctive types of groups: guidance, counseling, and psychotherapy. A guidance group is a primary group in the sense that it is mainly preventive. Listen carefully, however. Some exams and texts no longer use the term *guidance group*. Instead, you may see the term *affective education group* or *psychological education group*, or even *psychoeducational group*. Guidance groups, which originated in the public school system, do not deal with remediation of severe psychological pathology. Guidance/psychoeducational groups are preventative and provide instruction about a potential problem; for example, drug abuse or improving study skills. In most cases they are time limited and occasionally use videos and guest speakers to enhance the experience. **Exam hint: In the last several years the term *psychoeducational group* has replaced the term *guidance group* since the term *guidance group* has become associated with negative practices such as excessive advice giving.** Here is another **key point**: In individual treatment the words *counseling* and *therapy* are often used interchangeably. However, in the context of group work, therapy is implied when the problem is more severe and more individual work is needed for a longer duration. Psychotherapy groups are commonly used in inpatient psychiatric hospitals and residential facilities for patients with in-depth psychological problems. The psychotherapy group is tertiary and may emphasize the role of the unconscious mind and childhood experiences more than a counseling group. A counseling group would not tend to be psychodynamic and therefore would focus primarily on conscious concerns. A counseling group generally has less structure than a guidance group. In terms of education, the assumption is that the leader of a counseling group needs more training than an individual running a guidance group. That being said (and yes this sounds a bit contradictory) experts will concede that at times a counseling group may overlap with the features of a guidance/psychoeducational group. The group therapy leader must have the most training because he or she may need to treat people who are not functioning in the range of "normality."    **(b)**

414. Most experts would agree that overall

   a. structured exercises are more effective than unstructured techniques.
   b. structured exercises are less effective than unstructured techniques.
   c. all well-trained therapists favor structured exercises over unstructured techniques.
   d. ethical guidelines must forbid unstructured techniques because they can be dangerous to the depressed or anxious client.

A structured group exercise is like an assignment for group members. The leader says, "today we will do so and so...." The benefit is that the exercise helps to speed up group interaction and can help the group focus on a specific issue. Although structured group exercises are very popular and beneficial, they are generally not as effective as unstructured methods. This answer could surprise you if you are new to group work. The well-known existentialist and group theorist Irvin Yalom pointed out that structured exercises can create a situation where group stages are passed over. In addition, the exercise itself often serves to purge feelings too rapidly when members are not emotionally equipped to handle this. Also keep in mind that the excessive use of structured exercises can cause the group to lean on or rely too strongly on the leader for support and direction. Perhaps the crowning blow in regard to relying too heavily on structured group exercises came out of an encounter group project by Lieberman, Yalom, and Miles. The project demonstrated that leaders who utilized many structured exercises were more popular than leaders who did not; nevertheless, the outcome for the group participants was lower! **Here is an excellent rule of thumb:** Group exercises must correspond to the level of group development. In a beginning group, for example, exercises which build openness and trust are desirable. In the later stages, the focus of the exercises ideally switches to critical feedback. **(b)**

415. One advantage of group work is that a counselor can see more clients in a given period of time. One disadvantage is that a counselor can be too focused on group processes and

   a.   individual issues are not properly examined.
   b.   the group becomes too behavioristic.
   c.   a and b.
   d.   the group focuses too much on content.

Choice "a" is especially apt to occur if the leader is process oriented. **Remember: Content is the material discussed, while process focuses on the way it is being discussed. A word to the wise:** The word *process* can also refer to a type of program review (conducted while a study or a program is in progress or ongoing) and a type of note taking (i.e., psychotherapy notes). You'll need to zero in on the context of the question on your exam. Choice "d" is certainly not the best answer since a leader focusing on content would not be process oriented.   **(a)**

416. According to the risky shift phenomenon, a group decision will

   a.   be less conservative than the average group member's decision, prior to the group discussion.
   b.   be more conservative than the average group member's decision, prior to the group discussion.
   c.   often be aggressive or illegal.
   d.   violate the group's confidentiality norms.

Perhaps what I'm about to suggest is a bit scary to think about but bear with me anyway. Think back for a moment to when you were a teenager. (If you can't remember that far back, think of a teenager with whom you are currently familiar, such as a relative or a client.) For the most part, your decisions and behavior were probably fairly rational—conservative if you will. Now think about your behavior when you got together with a bunch of your friends, say for a party or a night out on the town. Wouldn't you have to admit that the group's decisions and behavior were not as conservative as your views prior to the group interaction? In other words, weren't group decisions, well, just a bit more "risky"? If your answer to the aforementioned questions was "yes," then you have the social psychology theory of the "risky shift phenomenon," to explain (not condone!) the behavior of your wild and crazy teen peer group. The risky shift phenomenon dispels the popular notion that groups are very conservative. Some newer research indicates that the group behavior is not necessarily more risky, but does at least shift more toward the social norm than an individual decision made prior to group participation. Social psychology research also indicates that the group experience can polarize decisions such that they are more in line with members' initial views. This tendency is known as "group polarity" or "group polarization." In essence, group polarization predicts a person's views may become more extreme after they participate in a group. **(a)**

417. T-groups often stress ways employees can express themselves in an effective manner. The "T" in T-groups merely stands for

    a. techniques.
    b. taxonomy.
    c. training.
    d. testing.

The "T" merely stands for "training." It is not unusual for T-groups (i.e., training groups) to be called "laboratory training groups" or even at times "sensitivity groups." Such a group will focus not on mental health issues but rather on human relations processes between personnel in a business setting. Shared leadership is a common area of concern. Occasionally, a short encounter group or sensitivity group will be termed a "microlab." Taxonomy (choice "b") is the science of classification. In the field of counseling, the most common method of determining a client's classification (which is termed a *diagnosis*) is to compare the client's symptoms with those listed in the American Psychiatric Association's *Diagnostic and Statistical Manual* (*DSM*). The *DSM*, combined with the *International Classification of Disease* (*ICD*), is generally used for third-party and insurance payments or research purposes so that mental health professionals will mean the same thing when referring to a client with a given diagnosis. **Hint:** The exam you will be taking may use the word *nosology* in place of the word *taxonomy*, since nosology is the classification of disease. **(c)**

418. A counselor suggests that her client join an assertiveness training group. Most assertiveness training groups are

    a. unstructured.
    b. psychodynamic or person-centered.
    c. focused heavily on existential concerns.
    d. behavioristic and highly structured.

Groups that rely on numerous exercises are considered "structured" groups, while those which have few exercises or tasks are often known as "unstructured." Behavioral groups such as an assertiveness training group are generally highly structured. You should be aware that some experts shy away from the term *unstructured*, stating that a group cannot "not" possess structure. Such theorists would simply say that a given group has a low degree of structure or "less structure." Nondirective groups, psychodynamic groups (choice "b"), and existential groups (choice "c") generally would lean toward a low degree of structure. Therapies that stress directive techniques and concrete treatment objectives generally have a high degree of structure. Some theorists use the term *structured group* only when discussing a group which focuses on a specific topic or theme, for example, assertiveness training, stress management, or coping with test anxiety. **(d)**

419. Weight Watchers is a

   a.   T-group, also called a training group.
   b.   self-help or support group, as is AA.
   c.   psychotherapy group.
   d.   marathon group.

A self-help group (also known as a "mutual aid group") is composed of a group of people who are all attempting to cope with a given issue (e.g., alcoholism, gambling addiction, or weight control). These groups have become much more popular in the last 25 years. Members have a common goal or problem and learn from each other. The group is not led by a professional, though a self-help group may indeed rely on a professional for consultation purposes. And believe me, self-help groups are extremely popular. It is currently estimated that over 500,000 self-help groups exist in the United States and serve the needs of approximately 15 million members. Most self-help groups are voluntary and make an excellent adjunct to professional counseling. Many of these groups follow the 12 steps in Alcoholics Anonymous and therefore are referred to as "12-step groups." **What in the world is thirteenth stepping? Good**

**question! The term suggests that established members in AA and other 12-step groups sometimes exploit new members for sexual purposes.** The term *marathon group* introduced in choice "d" is an easy one to remember. A marathon race is a long race, and a marathon group is one long group. A marathon group—somewhat like a marathon race—plays on the theme that after an extended period of time defenses and facades will drop and the person can become honest, genuine, and real. A marathon group generally lasts a minimum of 24 hours and may be conducted over a weekend or a period of several days. The marathon group paradigm is usually credited to Frederick Stoller and George Bach, who created the idea in the 1960s. **Splitting hairs—well—maybe? Some advanced exams will split hairs and make you discern a self-help group from a support group although the terms are generally synonymous. The distinction is that a support group is conducted by an organization (say AA or Weight Watchers) and might charge fees, while a self-help group (say a group of neighbors getting together to brainstorm ways to clean up after a flood) would not have either or both of these features.** **(b)**

420. The ACA and the ASGW division recommend screening for potential group members

   a.   for all groups.
   b.   only when the group is in a hospital inpatient setting.
   c.   only when the group is composed of minors.
   d.   only if the group deals with chemical dependency.

Screening is easy enough to define. A professional counselor uses a screening process in order to determine who is appropriate and who will not be appropriate for a given group. Simply put, the membership of a group can determine the success or failure of that particular group. If a prospective group member is undergoing individual counseling and therapy, the group leader, after securing the client's permission, should contact the person performing the individual treatment before making a final decision. **(a)**

421. A counselor is conducting a screening for clients who wish to participate in a counseling group which will meet Tuesday nights at his private practice office. Which client would most likely be the poorest choice for a group member?

    a. A shy librarian.
    b. An anxious salesman with no group experience.
    c. An extremely hostile and belligerent construction worker.
    d. A student with 16 hours toward her M.Ed in counseling.

    Let me help you think this one through. First, the individual's occupation and the time of the group (i.e., Tuesday nights) are irrelevant. The key factor in answering the question is to identify a personality pattern which may not lend itself to group work. Hostile individuals who act out aggressively (choice "c"), persons who are actively suicidal or homicidal, paranoid clients, those who are totally self-centered, or psychotic individuals (psychotic implies that the person is not in touch with reality) are not appropriate for most counseling groups. I have purposely hedged and used the word *most* since there are certainly psychotherapy groups which cater to the aforementioned populations (e.g., a group for hospitalized schizophrenics, an anger management group, or a group for suicide attempters). Remember that psychotherapy groups focus more on individual concerns, deal with remediation of more serious pathology, and are of longer duration. Nevertheless, it is still possible that if an individual is too dysfunctional in one of the aforementioned areas, he or she would be inappropriate even for a psychotherapy group and the treatment of choice should be an individual modality. **Clients who are very verbal, open to feedback from others, and believe in group therapy often make excellent group members.** **(c)**

422. A counselor is screening clients for a new group at the college counseling center. Which client would most likely be the poorest choice for a group member?

    a. A first-year student who is suicidal and sociopathic.
    b. A second-year student who stutters.

c.    A graduate student with a facial tic.

d.    A fourth-year student with obsessive-compulsive (OCD) tendencies.

If you missed this one then you failed to read the answer from the previous question. I can't stress strongly enough that you will need to understand the practical application of counseling theory—in all eight areas, not just groups—to do well on your exam! Questions of this nature require understanding rather than just rote memory to answer correctly.          **(a)**

423. A screening for group members can be done in a group or privately. Although private screening interviews are not as cost effective or as time efficient as group screening, many group leaders feel that private screening sessions are superior

a.    because they intensify transference.

b.    because they encourage catharsis.

c.    because they intensify abreaction.

d.    in terms of counselor–client interaction.

A pre-group interview for screening and orientation can be very beneficial. In essence, the client's needs must match the goals for the group. Ethical standards and guidelines do not, however, discuss specific selection processes. An individual screening interview allows the client to voice concerns regarding what he or she wants from the group and the procedures that will be implemented. The person also can ascertain whether he or she has faith in the leader's ability. Some of the literature emphasizes that screening is a two-way process (i.e., the leader can decide whether the member is appropriate and the member can decide whether the group and the leader are appropriate). Individual screening modalities also can serve to build trust. However, I'm sure you've come across clients as well as acquaintances whose behavior is markedly different in a group as opposed to an individual situation.          **(d)**

424. Most experts in the field of group counseling would agree that the most important trait for group members is the ability

    a.   to open up.
    b.   to listen.
    c.   to trust.
    d.   to convey empathy.

Expert Irvin Yalom feels that the main factor in selecting participants for a group is that members can feel cohesive (a sense of we-ness, if you will). Research indicates that high denial, low motivation, and low intelligence are associated with premature termination from group therapy.             **(c)**

425. Groups can be open or closed. The two differ in that

    a.   open groups are limited to hospital settings.
    b.   in an open group, members can socialize between group meetings.
    c.   closed groups always employ coleaders.
    d.   closed groups allow no new members after the group begins.

You absolutely must be familiar with this important distinction in group work if you want to do well on your exam. A closed group can be likened to a room with a closed door—no new persons can enter. In a closed group the decision is made initially that no new members can join for the life of the group. So, here's a simple little memory device: "closed groups" have "a closed door policy" regarding new members. Most of your graduate classes would fall into this category. Would a new student be permitted to join your group practice class 8 weeks into a 16-week semester? Hey, in most cases I'd have to say, I don't think so! An open group simply abides by an "open door policy," if you will, by allowing new members to join.             **(d)**

426. One major advantage of a closed group versus an open group is

    a.   cost effectiveness.

b.    it promotes cohesiveness.
c.    it lessens counselor burnout.
d.    it allows the members to meet less frequently.

Generally a closed group will have more cohesiveness or "unity" since the membership is more stable (i.e., new members are not joining) and members get to know each other. Nevertheless, a closed group is not a panacea. Since the closed group does not accept new members after the group is up and running individuals may drop out, and this lessens the overall amount of group interaction. In terms of cost effectiveness (choice "a"), the closed group is at a disadvantage. The agency or private practitioner loses revenue when clients leave and are not replaced.          **(b)**

427.  One major disadvantage of a closed group versus an open group is that

a.    if everyone quits, you will be left with no group members.
b.    closed groups cannot provide depth therapy.
c.    it promotes paranoid feelings in group members.
d.    closed groups are much more structured.

It doesn't take a mathematician to discern that if you have six group members and six members quit you are left with no group! In reference to choice "b," there is no evidence to demonstrate that a closed group could not provide excellent in-depth therapy. Since the closed group promotes cohesiveness (yes, I'm repeating myself, but I want to be certain you grasp this concept) and trust (well, that eliminates choice "c" because trust reduces paranoid ideation in many cases) it could be an excellent modality for intensive therapy. And although a closed group could be more structured than an open group, this is not always the case: So much for choice "d."          **(a)**

428.  The number of people in an open group is generally

a.    more stable than in a closed group.
b.    much smaller after an extended period of time than in a closed group.

c.  significantly larger than in a closed group.
d.  more dependent on the group leader's marketing skills than in a closed group.

This is the type of question you might quibble with on an exam; however, it would be mighty difficult to defend any answer except choice "a." Yes, I agree that some of the literature uses the term *stability* to describe the membership in a closed group. The stability, of course, comes from the policy of not allowing new members. If you read this particular question very, very carefully it speaks of the "number of people in an open group." Remember the hypothetical situation discussed in the last answer. You have a closed group of six members and six members leave the group. You are left with nobody. I'd hardly call that stability, would you? This question is asking you to choose the group strategy, open or closed, which would keep that number of six members stable. In the open group, if six people drop out you could replace them with six new members. I rest my case. Remember that regardless of which exam you must tangle with, a word could be used in a different context than you have encountered in the past.                                    **(a)**

429.  One distinct disadvantage of an open group is that

a.  new members are not accepted after the first meeting.
b.  the leader does not control the screening process.
c.  a member who begins after the first meeting has missed information or experiences.
d.  the group is generally too behavioristic for depth therapy to occur.

Open groups have changing membership, and thus different members have been present for different experiences. Choice "a" is obviously incorrect since new members could indeed enter the group after the first session. **A word to the wise: Sometimes the context of the question is everything! Although most exam questions should relate to my usage of open and closed groups thus far, there is another possible distinction. Agency board meetings are said to be open when people**

**who are not on the board are able to attend (such as the general public). On the flip side of the coin, a closed board meeting (say a meeting to eliminate the counseling staff ... horrors!) would often occur in a closed board meeting populated only by board members. The same goes for Alcoholics Anonymous meetings. In a closed meeting only those with a drinking problem populate the group. In an open meeting, family, friends, and yes even students attending to satisfy an assignment for their group practice class may be present.** **(c)**

430. When a group member is speaking, it is best for the counselor to

   a.   try to face the group member.
   b.   not face the group member, as this does not appear genuine in a group setting.
   c.   smile while listening.
   d.   suppress genuine emotion.

Choice "a" is often difficult to accomplish as groups are frequently set up such that members sit in a circular fashion; yet when it is possible, it fosters good "attending behavior" on the part of the group leader. In reference to choice "d," the qualities which enhance individual counseling are also beneficial when doing group work. Genuineness, which is also known as congruence or authenticity, is advisable in *all* therapeutic settings. **(a)**

431. A group setting has a flexible seating arrangement in which clients are free to sit wherever they wish. In this setting it is likely that

   a.   an African American client and a white leader would sit close together.
   b.   a Latino/a client and an African American leader would sit close together.
   c.   an Asian American client and an African American leader would sit close together.
   d.   an Asian American leader and an Asian American client would sit close together.

Generally persons who are similar will sit next to each other. In this case, choice "d" is the only choice that mentions two persons of the same race. Now I want to introduce you to two important terms which are related to group composition. In a group where the members are very similar or alike the group composition displays what is known as "homogeneity." Weight Watchers would be a case in point. Groups which have "homogeneity" are said to be "homogeneous." Since everybody really has the difficulty or concern (e.g., weight control in this case or alcoholism in AA) people often feel a greater degree of "we-ness" or cohesiveness. Some experts are convinced that homogeneity in terms of intelligence and level of development is desirable. In children's groups, this would mean an age span of no more than two years (e.g., 10–12-year-olds). A "hetero-geneous" group or a group which has "heterogeneity" has members who are dissimilar. A general therapy group which has clients with various problems and backgrounds would be an example. Although homogeneous groups have higher attendance rates, the heterogeneous group is more like a microcosm of the social system most of us live in. Moreover, when you combine people you discover that people can learn from each other and this is said to facilitate personality change. **(d)**

432. A group setting has a flexible seating arrangement in which clients are free to sit wherever they wish. In this setting it is likely that

   a.  a male client in a designer suit and a female client in cutoff jeans will sit close together.
   b.  a Cuban male client in a designer suit and an Asian male client in another brand of designer suit will sit close together.
   c.  a white female client in a designer outfit and a white male client in a pair of old jeans and an undershirt will sit close together.
   d.  a male client in a designer suit and a female client in a jogging suit and old tennis shoes with holes in them will sit close together.

Forget the poles of a magnet; in groups "likes" attract. The likelihood is that people who are similar or believe they have "something in common" initially will sit together. **Some evidence points to the fact that social class means more than race in terms of group seating.**    **(b)**

433. Which statement made by a doctoral-level counselor is illustrative of a leader focused on process rather than product?

    a.    "Jim seems more relaxed today."
    b.    "Sally seems a bit self-critical this evening."
    c.    "I hear a lot of sadness in Betty's voice."
    d.    "You wince whenever Jane raises her voice."

    The counselor's level of education is totally irrelevant. Process focuses on the "process," or manner in which the communication transpires. All of the other choices focus primarily on the analysis of the client's material, or what is called "content."    **(d)**

434. Which statement made by a group leader in a residential center for adolescents focuses on product rather than process?

    a.    "Ken has not stolen for a week and thus is eligible for supplementary tokens."
    b.    "Karen looks down when Bill discusses relationships."
    c.    "It sounds like there is a deep sense of hurt...."
    d.    "Oh, so you fold your arms and sort of close up when Carey mentions the angry side of your personality."

    Can you guess what is irrelevant in terms of answering this question?    **(a)**

435. Groups promote the concept of universality, which suggests that

    a.    we are unique and so are our problems.
    b.    there is a universal way to solve nearly any difficulty.
    c.    a and b.
    d.    we are not the only ones in the world with a given problem.

It is therapeutic just to know that you are not the only person in the world who has a given problem! In this respect the group model has an advantage over individual treatment. **There is a likely possibility your exam might substitute the word** *mutuality* **for** *universality*.                                        **(d)**

436. In the late 1930s researchers identified three basic leadership styles:

    a.   directive, nondirective, and semi-passive.
    b.   autocratic, democratic, and laissez faire.
    c.   relaxed, anxious, and tense.
    d.   assertive, nonassertive, and aggressive.

The classic study regarding leadership styles was conducted by Lewin, Lippitt, and White in 1939. The importance of the study was that it demonstrated that leadership styles do make a difference. In this famous study, 10- and 11-year-old children met with an adult who behaved in an autocratic (authoritarian), democratic (participative), or laissez faire fashion. The French term *laissez faire* implies that group members can do as they please without leader interference or direction. Children displayed the best behavior when treated in a democratic fashion, while aggressive behavior occurred in response to the other two leadership styles. Generally, the autocratic style where leaders often gave orders, proved to be the style members liked least. The study revealed that hostility was 30 times greater in autocratic groups than it was for the other two. This study set the stage for the National Training Laboratories (NTL) mentioned in a previous question. Do not, however, assume that the democratic style is always best. It is not. The autocratic mode seems to be superior when an immediate decision is necessary. When a group has made a decision, and is committed to it, the laissez faire style is usually the leadership model with the most merit. It is interesting to note that although member satisfaction is often highest in response to democratic leadership, this style does not necessarily lend itself to high productivity, according to Ralph Stogdill, who reviewed the major research studies related to this topic. Your exam might also mention the charismatic leadership style in which the leader uses his or her personal power, charisma, and attractiveness to foster facilitation. Just for review purposes, choice "d" describes the three communication modes used by assertiveness trainers to determine or discriminate (as it is often called) client response patterns. **A legitimate criticism of the famous Lewin, Lipptt, and White findings would be that the study was not a counseling group, but rather an after school activity group, and all the leaders were male.**

**On rare occasions your exam might mention:**

- **Impersonal leaders who are distant, but aggressive.**
- **Energizers, leaders who emotionally stimulate group members and are charismatic.**
- **Managers or leaders who exert executive control.**
- **Providers are very high in caring.** **(b)**

437. The autocratic or authoritarian leader may give orders to the group, while the laissez faire leader

    a.   assigns a group member as the authoritarian.
    b.   has a hands-off policy and participates very little, with the group basically taking responsibility for itself.
    c.   has the most desirable style of leadership.
    d.   nearly always run open-ended groups.

Laissez faire counselors are nonthreatening. Choice "d" refers to a group that does not sport a given number of sessions or an ending date. If you missed this question please review the previous answer. **Stick this sentence on your mirror at home and read it every morning: Effective leaders have discovered that modeling appropriate behaviors improves group participation, even when the members are resistant.** **(b)**

438. When comparing the autocratic, democratic, and laissez faire styles,

    a.   the autocratic is the most desirable.
    b.   the laissez faire is the most desirable.

c.    the democratic, or what Sam Gladding called a facilitator, is the most desirable.

d.    there is no discernible difference in effectiveness.

Here is every test taker's nightmare. The question is vague. It decidedly does not delineate the specific group situation. Hence, the best way to answer this question is to think in terms of "most situations." Again, the democratic style is not the most effective in every case; however, it probably lends itself to more situations than the other two. Leaders that focus primarily on the here and now are now being called "speculative leaders" on some exams.                                                                    **(c)**

439.  A group with more than one leader is said to utilize coleaders. Coleadership is desirable because

a.    the group can go on even if one leader is absent.

b.    two leaders can focus on group dynamics better than one leader since two individuals will have better observational skills.

c.    leaders can process their feelings between sessions.

d.    all of the above.

Coleadership (i.e., the use of two group leaders) has a number of advantages. In addition to those listed in choices "a," "b," and "c," I could add that two leaders can supply more feedback (two points of view) to group members than one leader. They can learn from each other and can model effective communication for the group.                                                                    **(d)**

440.  Coleadership

a.    reduces burnout and helps ensure safety.

b.    increases burnout.

c.    has no impact on burnout.

d.    should not be used for open groups.

Noted authors on group practice Marianne Schneider Corey and her husband Gerald Corey mention their preference for coleadership but indicate that many leaders do in fact work best on their own. Coleaders work best when each leader has a similar philosophy and group style. It is generally accepted that it is best for coleaders to physically sit on opposite sides of the group rather than next to each other.                                **(a)**

441. Coleadership

     a.   is helpful when one leader is experiencing counter-
          transference.
     b.   exacerbates the harm of countertransference.
     c.   has no impact on the issue of countertransference.
     d.   eliminates all difficulties associated with counter-
          transference.

     If you have an issue that is unresolved and it is having a negative impact on your intervention (i.e., countertransference) then your coleader can deal with this particular person or issue. A coleader also provides a second role model for participants. **Reminder: Transference refers to a client's issue, while countertransference implies that the helper has issues that are interfering with the treatment process.**         **(a)**

442. Coleadership, also referred to as cofacilitation, can be a disadvantage when

     a.   leaders are working against each other; this can fragment
          the group.
     b.   leaders are intimate with each other.
     c.   leaders question each other's competence.
     d.   all of the above.

     It is generally accepted that if there are problems between coleaders, it is best if such difficulties are aired in a format that models effective conflict resolution during the session rather than "pretending everything is wonderful." The best advice is to pick your coleader wisely and meet with this person before and after sessions whenever possible.                            **(d)**

443. Coleaders are apt to work at cross purposes when

    a.   they do not meet between group sessions.
    b.   they do meet between group sessions.
    c.   they are master's-level practitioners.
    d.   they are doctoral-level practitioners.

Choice "b" is recommended for coleaders, while choices "c" and "d" are irrelevant. Coleadership is an excellent way for new leaders to learn the ropes, if they can be paired with a seasoned professional.                                                      **(a)**

444. Gerald Corey, who has written extensively on group therapy, believes _____ is necessary for an effective group leader.

    a.   a master's degree in guidance and counseling
    b.   a doctorate in counselor education
    c.   participation in a therapeutic group and participation in a leader's group (even if the individual is well-educated and is licensed and certified)
    d.   three credit hours in a graduate course in group theory

Sorry folks, but according to some experts a wall filled with degrees, plaques, and certifications is not enough; specific training in group work is necessary in order to become a group leader. The 2016 CACREP guidelines addressing the issue of professional identity in counseling stipulate "direct experiences in which students participate as group members in a small group activity, approved by the program, for a minimum of 10 clock hours over the course of one academic term" are required. Moreover, a group practice course is generally required prior to taking a licensing exam. A training group for future group leaders is one solution to this dilemma. A training group is composed of "leader trainees," and unlike a therapeutic group it is focused on leadership skills. Irvin Yalom has gone on record as saying that self-exploration (e.g., personal therapy) is generally necessary for potential group leaders to help them deal with issues which could cause countertransference.                               **(c)**

445. Most experts would agree that an effective adult counseling group has _____ members.

    a.   9 to 12
    b.   3 to 5
    c.   11 to 16
    d.   5 or 6 to 8

An ideal group would have about eight adults. An adolescent group might be slightly smaller, perhaps five or six members. Some experts feel that a group conducted over a long period of time (say six months) can safely have as many as 10 members. **(d)**

446. Most experts would agree that an effective counseling group for children has

    a.   more members than an adult group.
    b.   less members than an adult group.
    c.   at least two group leaders.
    d.   9 to 12 members.

Three or four children is usually recommended, versus about eight people in an adult group.                                          **(b)**

447. Although the length of group counseling sessions will vary, most experts would agree that _____ is plenty of time even when critical issues are being examined.

    a.   three hours per session
    b.   one hour per session
    c.   six hours per session
    d.   two hours per session

One and a half to two hours is sufficient for adult group work. Longer groups often beget fatigue in the group members. With children, the group leader should note the members' attention span, which is generally shorter than for adults. Since a children's group will have shorter sessions, it is often best to rely on more frequent group sessions.                                          **(d)**

448. In terms of group risks

    a.    an ethical leader will discuss them during the initial session
          with a client.
    b.    an ethical leader should never discuss risks with a client.
    c.    research has demonstrated that the less said about them,
          the better the group will interact.
    d.    an ethical leader allows the group to discover risks and
          work through them at their own pace.

Choices "b" and "d" are not desirable. According to ACA ethics,
safeguarding clients is a must in the sense that the adept leader
takes reasonable precautions to protect clients against
psychological, emotional, and physical trauma. **Hint:** Although
group confidentiality is desirable, leaders should inform
participants that they *cannot guarantee confidentiality*. Lack of
confidentiality is a risk of group intervention.                    **(a)**

449. An adept group leader will

    a.    attempt to safeguard clients against risks.
    b.    work to reduce risks and dangers.
    c.    a and b.
    d.    let the group handle the dangers on their own.

Professional counselors should give clients "information"
regarding the group so the clients can make "informed" decisions
regarding whether or not the group is appropriate (e.g., the
purpose of the group, the risks involved, and the leader's
qualifications). This practice technically is known as "informed
consent," and it is very likely that you will see an exam question
related to this issue. Ideally, informed consent occurs during
screening before the initial group session, although in the real
world this is not always possible.                    **(c)**

450. A group participant wants to drop out of a group. Since the group is "closed" most experts would agree that

    a.   the leader must insist that the client stay.
    b.   the client is allowed to withdraw.
    c.   the leader should allow other members to put pressure on the participant to stay.
    d.   a and c.

The fact that the group is open or closed would have no impact on the answer. In the past, group leaders informed members that participation was voluntary and they could exit the group at any time. But was this guideline realistic? Consider a client who is "required" by the court to attend your group because he has perpetrated sexual abuse. In the literal sense this client is not a "voluntary participant." When a client is required to go to counseling or therapy it is known as "mandatory treatment." Today, textbooks are more apt to stress that leaders discuss the impact of participation with members. **Quick quip:** When a client is referred for treatment and is not enthusiastic about the intervention, the term *reluctant client* is usually applied.     **(b)**

451. During the initial session of a group the leader explains that no smoking and no cursing will be permitted. This is known as

    a.   setting ground rules.
    b.   ambivalent transference.
    c.   blocking.
    d.   scapegoating.

When ground rules become the standard of behavior then it is known as a "norm." The leader can specify the ground rules early in the group. Examples might be no cussing or hitting another group member. The term *ambivalent transference*, choice "b," is a psychoanalytic notion often thrown out in multicultural circles which suggests that a client will treat a therapist with ambivalence, as he or she would any person viewed as an authority figure. (**Note**: Ambivalence implies that the client will experience contradictory emotions, such as love and hate, alternating from one to the other.) Choice "c," *blocking*, is a term often used in group work. Blocking occurs when a leader uses an intervention to stop—or block if you will—a negative or counterproductive behavior which could hurt another member or the group. Choice "d," scapegoating, is precisely the type of behavior a leader would want to block. In scapegoating, members gang up on a single group member.                                                    **(a)**

452. Group norms refer to

   a.   a statistically normal group composed of 8 to 12 members.
   b.   a statistically normal group composed of 12 to 14 members.
   c.   a normal group with no cultural differences.
   d.   the range of acceptable behavior within the group.

Norms are the written or unwritten do's and don'ts of the group.                                                                **(d)**

453. The study of group operations is often called

   a.   group desensitization.
   b.   the hot seat technique.
   c.   group dynamics.
   d.   structuring the group.

Group dynamics refers to the study of the interrelationships and interactions between group members. Group stages, cohesiveness, leadership style, and decision making are prime examples of group dynamics. Any factor that has an impact on the group can be referred to legitimately as a dynamic. The *hot seat*, choice "b," is a term popularized by Fritz Perl's gestalt therapy groups. A person who is the target of the therapist's interventions in the here and now is said to be on the "hot seat." Choice "d," or the structuring of the group, is determined by the presence (or lack of) structured tasks or exercises given to members by the group leader. **Important point:** Often when an exam uses the term *structured group* (not to be confused with the term *group structure*) it connotes a group which focuses on a given theme, such as a group for veterans.         **(c)**

454. The word *dynamic* means the group is

    a.    normal.
    b.    always changing.
    c.    static.
    d.    defined in an operational manner.

Choice "d" is used quite a bit in the social sciences. In order to "operationally define" something you must demonstrate the concrete steps necessary to illuminate the concept. It sounds complex, yet it really isn't. To operationally define, say, positive reinforcement, you would first note how often a behavior is occurring. Then you might give the client a reward every time he or she performs a desirable behavior, and tabulate the fact that the behavior is occurring more often than before you instituted the procedure. To operationally define the action of writing the letter "t," you could tell the person to first draw a vertical line of 1 inch in length and then draw a horizontal line 0.5 inch in length, perpendicular to and one third of an inch from the top of the vertical line. The idea of the operational definition is that another person can duplicate your actions (i.e., the exact steps) for therapeutic, research, or testing purposes. Behaviorists have emphasized the notion of operational definitions more than other therapeutic schools.    **(b)**

455. Experts firmly believe that a common weakness in many groups is

    a.    setting too many goals.
    b.    using a male and a female coleader.
    c.    that the leader uses a democratic style.
    d.    a lack of goal setting.

Most experts see choice "b," the use of a male and a female coleader, as a distinct advantage. Often goals are defined yet they are too vague.    **(d)**

456. A group leader who utilizes an abundance of group exercises is

   a.  probably not running an assertiveness training group.
   b.  is running an unstructured group.
   c.  is running a structured group.
   d.  is invariably running a self-help group.

   Look closely at choice "a." An assertiveness training group would indeed generally use a lot of structured exercises. Choice "d" is also incorrect since a self-help group would not necessarily utilize a lot of structured exercises.                          **(c)**

457. Some theorists object to the word *unstructured* in group work because

   a.  a group cannot not have structure.
   b.  only structured groups are effective.
   c.  unstructured groups are hardly therapeutic.
   d.  unstructured refers only to counseling and not to therapy groups.

   Some research indicates that structured exercises in the initial stages of the group can facilitate better communication.      **(a)**

458. Some research demonstrates that

   a.  structured exercises early in the group impaired later communication between group members.
   b.  structured exercises with feedback early in the group served to improve communication between group members.
   c.  autocratic or authoritarian leadership styles promote communication best.
   d.  structured exercises are never appropriate.

   If you marked choice "c," then stop this very moment and review the answer to question 436. So far as choice "d" goes, beware of any answer which relies on adverbs like "always" or "never."

Answers sporting the word *always* are almost always incorrect, and those using *never* are almost never correct!    **(b)**

459.  In some literature, group cohesiveness, or "we-ness," is known as

   a.   group unity.
   b.   a sociogram.
   c.   Karpman's triangle.
   d.   the transition stage.

The unity is actually a feeling of belonging, oneness, or togetherness. A sociogram (choice "b") is simply a pictorial account of a group which serves to diagram member interaction. Choice "c," Karpman's drama triangle, is used most often in conjunction with transactional analysis (TA) as a teaching device to illuminate the roles of persecutor, rescuer, and victim in interpersonal relationships. The final choice, the transition stage, is the group stage which occurs after the first or so-called initial stage. In the initial stage members get acquainted and learn norms. In the second or transition stage members are often judgmental, resistant, or involved in a struggle for power to establish a hierarchy or "pecking order."    **(a)**

460.  Group members assume roles within a group. Which of the following is not a group role?

   a.   Energizer.
   b.   Scapegoat.
   c.   Gatekeeper.
   d.   Reactive schizophrenia.

In counseling the term *reactive* means that a given condition is the result of environmental stress. Hence, reactive schizophrenia would imply that the person experienced a psychotic episode following a traumatic experience. This would be in contrast to an individual who was seemingly always schizophrenic, and the pathology could not be traced to any given set of circumstances. Choices "a," "b," and "c" are common roles individuals will play in a group setting. The energizer stimulates enthusiasm in the group (e.g., "Come on folks this will be a lot of fun; and besides we'll really learn a lot"). The scapegoat is the person everybody blames. He or she is invariably the target of severe anger and hostility (e.g., "Look Marv, we all agree that if it weren't for you we would have solved the problem two weeks ago"). The gatekeeper tries to make certain that everyone is doing his or her task and is participating. This person may "secretly" or "unconsciously" want to lead the group and could even attempt to establish norms. The danger is that a gatekeeper often does not work on his or her own personal issues (e.g., "From now on I'd like everybody to bring a journal to the group and write down at least one positive thing which happened during the week"). Is that the leader speaking out or the gatekeeper blowing off steam? Only the group members know for sure!    **(d)**

461. A group member who insists on asking other members inappropriate questions is known as a Peeping Tom or

   a.   an energizer.
   b.   a scapegoat.
   c.   an interrogator.
   d.   a follower.

The interrogator asks a never-ending string of questions, while the follower goes along with the rest of the group.    **(c)**

462. The follower goes along with whatever the rest of the group thinks. From a personality standpoint the follower is

   a.   aggressive.
   b.   assertive.
   c.   practicing excitation.
   d.   nonassertive.

Choice "c" relates to Andrew Salter's conditioned reflex therapy in which "excitation" or the practice of spontaneously experiencing and expressing true emotions (even negative ones) is seen as necessary in order to attain a state of positive mental health. "Inhibition," or constipation of emotions, is seen as the opposite of excitation. Salter said: "However, in psychotherapy we need have no fear. The diagnosis is always inhibition."     **(d)**

463. The _____ may secretly wish that he or she was running the group.

   a.  follower
   b.  gatekeeper
   c.  social isolate
   d.  harmonizer

I joke with my students about adding a note to the university course catalog under my groups course which says "only former gatekeepers need to apply." See answer 460 if you fail to see the humor! Choice "d" introduces the harmonizer role. Some books and exams bill this as the "conciliator," or the person who tries to make certain that everything is going smoothly.     **(b)**

464. Everybody picks on

   a.  the gatekeeper.
   b.  the harmonizer, also known as the conciliator.
   c.  the scapegoat.
   d.  the storyteller, the intellectualizer, the attacker, and the joker.

The storyteller, choice "d," monopolizes a wealth of group time telling endless (often irrelevant) tales. A group leader will sometimes need to help this person get to the point or will need to ask the person precisely how the story is productive in the context of the group setting. This choice also lists a bevy of other self-explanatory roles members can play.     **(c)**

465. A female group member is obviously not participating. A group member playing the _____ is most likely to mention this and urge her to participate.

   a.  gatekeeper
   b.  interrogator

c.    scapegoat
d.    storyteller

One popular notion is that these roles relate to the person's pattern of behavior in his or her nuclear family, and if appropriate the group leader can explore this hypothesis. In addition to the popular aforementioned roles is the "isolate role." The isolate is ignored by others. Isolates generally feel afraid to reach out or do reach out and are genuinely rejected—for exam purposes keep in mind that the isolate is not the same as the scapegoat. Scapegoats receive attention, although it is not by any means overwhelmingly positive. Isolates—a negative group role often referred to as the "silent one"—on the other hand, receive little or no attention.                                                              **(a)**

466.  Cohesiveness, or group unity, is desirable. It promotes bonding and a sense of "we-ness" between group members. When cohesiveness is strong, nevertheless, it also can be negative as

a.    it can stunt creativity.
b.    it can boost conformity.
c.    a and b.
d.    it can cause the group to split into factions.

Cohesiveness can stunt creativity or boost conformity since members want to fit in and go along with the wishes of most other group members. The word *faction* in choice "d" describes a clique or a group of people within a group. You might, for example, have a faction which does not wish to go along with a certain task or group exercise. The sociogram mentioned earlier can help identify group factions. A faction also may be called a "subgroup."                                                              **(c)**

467.  In a healthy group, members

a.    assume a role and never change it.
b.    have no roles.
c.    are flexible and can change roles.
d.    spend a great deal of time practicing role reversal.

In order to meet the "changing needs" of the group, members often need to "change roles." Choice "d," or role reversal, is a common behavioral role-playing technique. A client who is having difficulty communicating with another person in his or her life role-plays the person with whom he or she is having difficulty. Another group member (or the leader) plays the group member with the problem. This valuable technique gives the group member a new perspective on the situation and allows the person to learn via modeling alternative ways of behaving.    **(c)**

468. In a group, task roles

   a.    help solve problems.
   b.    aid in terms of goal setting and keep the group focused.
   c.    are seen as positive.
   d.    all of the above.

Here is a **key concept**: Group specialists classify member roles as: task roles, maintenance roles, and self-serving roles. (On some exams, self-serving roles will be identified as "individual roles.") The distinctions are actually fairly easy to remember. In everyday life when we refer to a "task" we mean a job or something which needs to be accomplished. A task role (e.g., an information giver or a clarifier) simply helps the group carry out a task. A maintenance role (e.g., the follower, mentioned earlier, or an encourager) helps "maintain" or even strengthen group processes. The final category (i.e., the self-serving role) is seen as negative. The person who falls into this category meets his or her own "individual needs" at the expense of the group. A person who downright refuses to participate or a person who criticizes or disagrees with others would be a prime example. **An entire group could be classified as a task group or perhaps a task/work group. A group of this nature focuses on accomplishing work goals. According to former ACA president, textbook author, and group expert Sam Gladding, an athletic team would fall into this category, as would a quality-circle-employee-run group attempting to improve a business.** If you have a group of very immature participants, then the so-called **situational leadership style** is recommended. Here the leader tells members what to do and does not emphasize relationships among members.    **(d)**

469. Maintenance roles, like task roles, are positive since such roles

a. help to maintain the group.
b. are self-serving.
c. help promote autocratic leadership.
d. always stress the importance of the here and now.

**Remember:** Maintenance really implies that the role maintains group interaction. Maintenance roles support the group's livelihood and hence are seen as positive. Paul Hersey and Kenneth Blanchard point out that leader activities generally fall into "task actions" and "maintenance actions" (i.e., relationship concerns). Hersey and Blanchard believe that the most effective leadership approach depends on the group situation. The researchers speak of "maturity" in regard to a specific task. If a group member has low maturity—which is really a lack of achievement motivation—then the leader should use "high task" and "low relationship" behaviors. As maturity gets better, a "high task" and "high relationship" paradigm is ideal. And when group members display very high maturity, then a "low task" and "low relationship" leadership format would be desirable. Now listen closely: Task action leadership is said to be indicative of one-way communication (i.e., the leader tells the members about a task to accomplish) while relationship behavior is said to be the result of two-way communication (i.e., the leader provides emotional support for members). Hersey and Blanchard suggest that it is not atypical for a member to display maturity on one task and a distinct lack of maturity on the next. **Now I want to stress two very important points here**: When you see the words *task* and *maintenance* on your exam, the concepts could refer to either a group member's role or the leader's behavior. The other concept I want you to be familiar with is that conflict between group members can often be abated by having the leader prescribe a "task" on which all the members must work together in order to accomplish it.    **(a)**

470. Self-serving or individual roles are negative inasmuch as

     a.   they promote democratic leadership.
     b.   they work against the group.
     c.   they serve the individual and not the group.
     d.   b and c.

     Self-serving or so-called individual roles are counter-
     productive.                                                    **(d)**

471. Although task roles and maintenance roles are indeed positive,
     the group can suffer if the group is not flexible and remains in
     one or the other role too long since

     a.   an effective group needs some self-serving roles.
     b.   if a group gets stuck in task roles, interaction suffers.
     c.   if a group gets stuck in maintenance roles, little work (or
          tasks) will be accomplished.
     d.   b and c.

     I believe this clarifies the point made earlier that group members
     ideally will be flexible and able to change roles.              **(d)**

472. Group specialists define role conflict as

     a.   tension between two group members who have assumed
          different roles.
     b.   a situation in which there is a discrepancy between the way
          a member is expected to behave and the way he or she
          actually behaves.
     c.   tension between the group leader and a group member.
     d.   members criticizing other members between group
          sessions.

     The word *conflict* comes from the Latin word *conflictus*, which
     means "striking together with force." Please do not confuse "role
     conflict" with the group term *conflict of interest*, which occurs
     when a group member maximizes his or her needs and interests
     at the expense of someone else.                                **(b)**

473. A major group dynamic is group development. This is usually expressed in terms of

    a.   the number of hours of group conflict.
    b.   theories of group stages.
    c.   the Rosenthal effect.
    d.   the Hawthorne effect.

    Here is a very helpful hint. Do not—I repeat—do not attempt to memorize every single group stage theory ever invented. First, because you have better things to do with your time (I would hope!) and second because there are far too many. Most of the theories are very similar and thus if you know the basic format you will have a very good chance of answering the question correctly. The first stage generally is known simply as the "initial stage." (Now there's one that's so simple you won't need a memory device!) Others have termed this stage as "orientation and exploration," or "preaffiliation," or "forming." The next stage usually is designated as the "transition stage," though you will often see it termed "power and control" or "storming," which logically comes after "forming." The third major stage is the "working stage," "norming stage," "cohesion stage," or "negotiation, intimacy, and frame of reference." The final stage is sometimes known as the "separation stage," the "termination stage," "the closure stage," or "adjourning." Choices "c" (no relation to yours truly!) and "d" will be covered in the sections on research.     **(b)**

474. Irvin Yalom is a famous existentialist therapist and a pioneer in the group movement. He suggested these four group stages: orientation, conflict, cohesion, and termination. In 1977 Tuckman and Jensen reviewed 25 years of research and came up with five stages: forming, storming, norming, performing, and adjourning. Which stage in Tuckman and Jensen's paradigm is similar to Yalom's orientation stage?

    a.   Forming.
    b.   Storming.
    c.   Norming.
    d.   Performing.

Okay, you deserved an easy one. Note that different group theories have differences in the number of stages. Your best bet on the exam is to try to note the similarities between the major theories. For example, the initial "group formation" stage examined in this question (i.e., orientation, forming, preparation, engagement, and who knows what some creative theorist will dare call it next!) is focused on the establishment of norms and approach–avoidance behavior of group members. Members will be tentative and size up other members. Members will identify or get acquainted with others based on culture, language, mode of dress, or occupation. **(a)**

475. The final stage suggested by theories of group stages generally deals with issues of

    a.  group tasks.
    b.  transition.
    c.  power and control.
    d.  separation and termination.

The final stage is said to represent a time of breaking away, or in plain, simple, everyday English: saying goodbye. Group members can experience loss and need to establish bonds outside of the group setting. The ideal situation would be that termination takes place after the group and its members have reached their goals (e.g., greater insight, improved self-esteem, accomplishment, and awareness) and have no further unfinished business. Certainly, in reality (such as when a client needs to leave a hospital group because his or her insurance has run out) this is not always the case. Additional referrals may be necessary. **(d)**

476. The initial group stage has been called forming, orientation, or the preaffiliation stage. This stage is characterized by

    a.  avoidance–avoidance conflicts.
    b.  a tendency for members to compete with the leader for power.
    c.  approach–avoidance behavior.
    d.  members working on the interpretation of unconscious behavior.

Yes, I'm being redundant with the words I'm using in my questions and my answers, but this will help you become more accustomed to the lingo of group work, and I've got this uncanny suspicion that it's working! In the first stage people want to be accepted but are scared to participate: Now, what about choice "a"? Well, an avoidance–avoidance conflict exists when you have two alternatives which are both unattractive, such as when your boss says you can either take a pay cut or lose your job. The approach–avoidance situation taking place in the initial group stage is a conflict wherein you are attracted and repelled by the same goal. In an analogous situation: You want to meet group members, but it's scary to think about the fact that you could be rejected.                    **(c)**

477. A client would generally feel the most suspicious of others in

    a.    the final stage of separation or termination.
    b.    the intimacy stage.
    c.    the group formation/exploratory stage.
    d.    a group with coleadership, also known as cofacilitation.

Safety comes from seeking common ground. That is to say, the new group member seeks out others of similar social status. Like Erikson's first psychosocial stage of development, the initial group stage hosts the "trust versus mistrust" drama.    **(c)**

478. Fights between subgroups and members showing rebellion against the leader generally occur in

    a.    the second stage known as the control stage or the transition stage.
    b.    the first stage known as the orientation stage or formation stage.
    c.    the separation stage.
    d.    the intimacy stage.

Garland, Jones, and Kolodny appropriately called stage 2 "power and control." This is the stage in which the fireworks fly as group members verbally attack one another, not to mention the group leader.                    **(a)**

479. A hierarchy, or pecking order, among members occurs in

    a.    the stage of storming, also known as the power–control stage.
    b.    the orientation stage.
    c.    the separation stage.
    d.    the intimacy stage.

Ditto! This is the stage movies are made of. Members rank themselves in terms of status and factions (mentioned earlier). Isolated members who are not protected by the strong subgroup (faction) sometimes drop out. It should come as no surprise that some authors have called this the "high-anxiety" or "struggle for control stage." And how is a leader to handle this turmoil? Corey and Corey appropriately suggest that the leader learns to distinguish between a "challenge" and an "attack." Do not assume, say the Coreys, that every confrontation is an attack on your integrity as a leader. Leaders can model responsible assertive confrontation with open and truthful expression.    **(a)**

480. Group planning occurs

    a.    in the initial stage.
    b.    in the stage after the transition or conflict stage.
    c.    in the final stage, also known as the termination stage.
    d.    before the group begins and continues throughout the life of the group.

The term *ecological planning* has been used to describe the process of obtaining information to determine whether a group is the most desirable form of treatment and, if it is, to decide the exact nature of the group experience. The counselor needs to look at demographics, community needs, and social considerations. After the group begins, program development or session-by-session planning is recommended. Planning can also include: (a) Whether to use a single facilitator or coleadership; (b) an assessment of the best surroundings (i.e., the room or rooms where the group will be held); (c) how the group will receive funding or payment for the group (e.g., will insurance pay for the service?); (d) whether a marketing or recruitment strategy is necessary; (e) what information can be useful from books, journals, or the Internet; (f) how the clients will be screened and prepared for the group; and (g) providing clients with informed consent documents. **(d)**

481. The final group stage (also called the termination stage) is geared toward

   a.  developing intimacy.
   b.  working through power and control issues.
   c.  exploration.
   d.  breaking away.

This phase has been called "consolidation" and occurs *after* the working stage. The leader helps members make plans for the future. I must point out that group specialists feel that every group does not necessarily pass through every stage (even after an extended period of time) and that there is not always a clear-cut discernible line of demarcation separating one group stage from another. **(d)**

482. A group therapist is constructing a diagram to better understand the dynamics between subgroups and members. This is called

   a.  sculpturing.
   b.  ego state analysis.
   c.  charting a pictorial sociogram.
   d.  charting the variance.

The study of measuring person-to-person relationships regarding what members in a group think or feel is known as "sociometry." In essence, sociometry is a quantitative study of relationship concerns in a group. The sociogram, credited to Moreno and Jennings, graphically displays group members' affiliations and interactions. Choice "a," or family sculpturing, is a family therapy technique in which the family members are instructed to arrange themselves spatially to create a live representation of family members' bonds, feelings of closeness (or lack of it), and sense of alliances. Choice "b" is a common practice in transactional analysis in which the counselor helps the client discern out of which ego state (i.e., Parent, Child, or Adult) he or she is primarily operating in a given situation.    **(c)**

483. A group leader who asks each group member to recapitulate what he or she has learned during a given session is promoting

   a.    summarization, the act of briefly stating what has transpired or discussed.
   b.    clarification, the act of making certain that the leader and the group truly understand the key factors related to what a member is attempting to communicate.
   c.    blocking, the act of putting a halt to a group member's actions that might have a negative impact on other group members.
   d.    linking, the act of pointing out similarities between clients.

Summarization, which is also appropriate in individual work, is merely the act of bringing together a number of important thoughts, insights, feelings, or transactions.    **(a)**

484. A leader who wishes to stop inappropriate discussion should rely on

   a.    summarization.
   b.    clarification.
   c.    blocking.
   d.    linking.

Blocking in groups is very much like blocking a punch in a boxing match. Blocking is used by the leader to stop (or block if you will) a hurtful behavior. Blocking in therapy is often necessary for the protection of group members. Blocking can be used in cases of gossiping or breaking confidentiality. Choice "b," clarification, is another important skill group leaders must possess. A leader uses clarification to ferret out the important points in a client's message. Clarification brings out the gist of a message and illuminates what was really said to lessen any confusion. Choice "d", linking, is used to promote cohesion. A link is an attempt to bring together common patterns or themes within the group. **Helpful hint on group verbiage: When a leader allows each group member to weigh in on a given topic we say that the leader is "making the rounds."** (c)

485. When a leader attempts to relate one person's predicament to another person's predicament, it is known as

    a.   summarization.
    b.   clarification.
    c.   blocking.
    d.   linking.

When used properly, linking illuminates areas of mutual concern. This often enhances group interaction. **(d)**

486. Strategies that approach the group as a whole are known as

    a.   vertical interventions.
    b.   horizontal interventions.
    c.   crossed transactions.
    d.   parallel transactions.

When working in a group setting, the leader needs to decide whether to work with the group as a whole (called a horizontal intervention) or with individuals within the group (called a vertical intervention—note choice "a"). Of course by now you realize how valuable memory devices are in terms of helping you to remember distinctions. Here's the one I have found valuable in this case. If you picture a group in your mind it appears spread out "horizontally." On the other hand, if you picture yourself doing counseling with an individual in a group, the individual is usually sitting up in a "vertical" position. In the case of the vertical intervention the leader is providing individual counseling in a group work setting. Techniques which focus on group relationships, processes, tasks, and interactions are said to be horizontal intervention strategies. The horizontal approach is often called the "interpersonal" method since it focuses on interactions. The vertical approach has been termed "intrapersonal" leadership. Shapiro, who suggested the intrapersonal–interpersonal leadership distinction, feels that a leader does not really choose one or the other but tends to behave on a continuum in this respect.

**Key point:** You would do well to remember that interpersonal leaders favor here-and-now interventions while intrapersonal leaders are more likely to work on the past, sometimes employing psychodynamic notions. An effective counselor should rely on both types of interventions. If, for example, a leader stresses vertical intrapersonal interventions, members may be hesitant to speak or react in a spontaneous manner. In this case the group member might literally think, "It's not my turn to speak yet Dr. X is working with Jane now." The other side of the coin, however, is that the horizontal interpersonal leader may lose some power as an expert who can model or reinforce appropriate behavior.    **(b)**

487. Strategies that focus on an individual member of the group are known as

    a.    vertical interventions.
    b.    horizontal interventions.
    c.    crossed transactions.
    d.    parallel transactions.

Again, use your memory device. See that individual sitting or standing—she's in a vertical position, of course. Choices "c" and "d" relate to transactional analysis (TA). A crossed transaction between two persons' ego states is said to be dysfunctional, while a parallel transaction promotes healthy communication. Although quite frankly TA is a bit, well, let's just say dated, it is conceivable that a question or two could still pop up on your exam.    **(a)**

488. A group therapist must make

    a.    fewer decisions than an individual therapist.
    b.    the same number of decisions as an individual therapist.

c.    modality changes for each group.

d.    more decisions than an individual therapist.

Thus, most experts would agree that it is more difficult to do productive group work than it is individual work. Nevertheless, in many settings the only way to reach all the people who need counseling in a finite period of time is to use group work.    **(d)**

489. When a counselor reads the journals in this field, it becomes evident that

a.    group counseling has more research than individual counseling.

b.    researchers and practitioners are working very closely to provide accurate and effective group strategies.

c.    a researcher/practitioner split exists in group work.

d.    no journals focus solely on group work.

Practical research about what exactly works best in a group setting is scarce. Moreover, many studies in the field of group work have not been well controlled. In many studies, the independent variable (i.e., the experimental variable) has not been scientifically defined. Say, for example, the independent variable in a study is a "T-group intervention." This indeed could create a problem since a T-group to leader A might not seem like a T-group to leader B.    **(c)**

490. Experts predict that in the future

a.    group leaders will be more like life-skills trainers.

b.    group leaders will become more person-centered.

c.    group leaders will return to a psychodynamic viewpoint.

d.    groups will lose their popularity and eventually die out.

The position has been taken that in the past groups have emphasized a narrow focus (e.g., a group for nonassertive bosses) and in the future groups should begin to deal with a broad spectrum of issues or what some call a "comprehensive model" of group work. A comprehensive educational life-skills model could stress preventive mental health skills, hopefully lowering the need for "therapeutic groups." Therefore, ultimately the counselor of the life-skills group would act more like a trainer than a therapist.                                                      **(a)**

491. According to researchers, groups are effective

    a.    although researchers cannot pinpoint precisely why this is true.
    b.    due to increased transference in group work.
    c.    due to better morale in a group setting.
    d.    due to the emphasis on cognitive restructuring.

Research in the area of group work is sometimes classified as "outcome research" or "product research." Outcome research addresses the question of whether the group was able to reach a given set of goals or simply the desired "outcome." An outcome study attempts to answer the question of whether or not the group was successful (i.e., does the group work). Process research is aimed at the question of "how groups work." Process research asks, "What allows the group to reach a target outcome?"                                                      **(a)**

492. A major limitation related to group work is that

    a.    REBT cannot be utilized in group therapy.
    b.    it is not really cost effective.
    c.    gestalt therapy cannot be used in a group setting.
    d.    a group leader can lose control and members could experience emotional harm.

Let me make certain that the purpose of this question is perfectly clear: You must know the strengths and limitations of group work for almost any comprehensive exam. Choice "d" depicts a major limitation. Other limitations include: (a) that a client may need individual therapy before he or she can benefit from group work; (b) that a client may not be capable of trusting others enough to reveal key material since he or she fears others may find it unacceptable; (c) that the group could become a substitute experience for the real world; (d) that the group counselor may not be as effective with a whole group of people as he or she is with just one person in individual treatment; (e) that some clients may feel pressure to replace their personal norms with those of the group; and (f) that disappointment can set in if the group is not helpful and the person loses faith in treatment without experiencing individual sessions. **Group work can often be intimidating and this can squelch client disclosure. Clients also receive less time working with the counselor than in individual counseling. In today's fast-paced world, the lack of flexibility in terms of meeting times for the sessions may prohibit someone from attending a group. Finally, lack of trust related to confidentially often sways clients to opt for individual treatment.** Group therapy generally is not the treatment of choice when the client is in a state of crisis, needs an interpretation of his or her psychological tests, needs confidentiality for protection (groups are notorious for having more problems with confidentiality than individual treatment), or is phobic in regard to public speaking. Choices "a," "b," and "c" are totally false. P.S. If your client is seeing an individual therapist, that therapist needs to know that his or her client is planning to join your group.                                      **(d)**

493.  A major advantage of group work versus individual work is that

   a.  members learn to give help in addition to receiving it and group sessions generally cost less (i.e., they are more economical) than individual counseling sessions.
   b.  the leader has a less complex role than that of an individual counselor.
   c.  the group leader nearly always possesses more training than an individual counselor.
   d.  all of the above.

Group advantages include: (a) that group work allows for "in vivo" interpersonal work with a sense of belonging; (b) that it is cost effective and allows a trained counselor to help a greater number of people in a smaller amount of time; (c) that it promotes universality; (d) that it can be an effective support system; (e) that members get multiple feedback; and (f) that members can model successful communication and coping skills. **Groups are like a microcosm of society that offers vicarious learning and support.** And oh yes, although it would be nice if choice "c" were true (since group leaders generally need more training than individual helpers) the truth is that some people are running groups without any training whatsoever in group work.                                    **(a)**

494. Which statement best depicts a major advantage of group work?

    a.    Group work usually focuses on the here and now.
    b.    Group work is always time limited.
    c.    Group work is always superior for career counseling.
    d.    The group setting is somewhat analogous to the communication and interaction of everyday life.

Overall, research would support the notion that groups *work*, and yes, they have advantages. However—and this is one important point folks—there is no body of research which would say that in general group work is superior to other forms of treatment. Please reread the previous sentence—yes, it's that important! Pressure to conform, confidentiality, and unhealthy relationships with others in the group provide classic examples of the disadvantages of the group model.                    **(d)**

495. Which of these factors is *not* delineated by Irvin Yalom as a curative factor?

    a.    Altruism, universality, and existential learning.
    b.    Manifest dream content and insight into the unconscious mind.
    c.    Catharsis, cohesiveness, and instillation of hope.
    d.    Imitative behavior and reenactment of family experiences.

Yalom is an existential therapist. Choice "b" is psychoanalytic. **(b)**

496. In terms of research and the group leader's personality,

    a.   extroverts are the most effective leaders.
    b.   introverts are the most effective leaders.
    c.   qualities such as flexibility, enthusiasm, and common sense may be helpful to a very small degree.
    d.   qualities such as flexibility, enthusiasm, and common sense have a tremendous positive impact.

Unfortunately, overall studies have turned up little in terms of "special characteristics" of group leaders' personalities. So much for the concept of super leaders!                                    **(c)**

497. R. K. Conyne suggested that group intervention is intended to

    a.   ferret out unconscious material.
    b.   enhance rational self-talk.
    c.   illuminate dysfunctional nonverbal behavior.
    d.   prevent, correct, or enhance behavior.

Conyne's "group work grid" model includes four intervention levels: individual, interpersonal, organization, and community population. The intervention can be prevention, correction, or enhancement oriented for either personal or task functions.   **(d)**

498. A group leader who wishes to assess the impact of the group ideally would

    a.   hand out a written evaluation form during the final session.
    b.   hold a follow-up session so members can share experiences.
    c.   have an outside "observer" sit in during group sessions and consequently rate the level of behavioral change.
    d.   give each member a pretest and a posttest utilizing a projective measure.

Keep in mind that you are looking for the best answer here. All of the choices are correct; however, choice "c" is superior to the other three. Research in the area of group work has been criticized for not using independent observers. When taking your exam be aware that "member-specific measures" are designed to assess change (or lack of it) in an individual group member. Most member-specific measures, such as a self-rating or (better still) a rating by an outside observer, are not standardized. In contrast to the "member-specific measure," researchers speak of "group-specific measures," which are intended to measure the degree of change (or again, lack of it) in all persons participating in the group. Lastly, the so-called "global measures," such as standardized tests, may well assess traits and factors not specifically addressed in the group. For example, giving members of a Weight Watchers group a pre- and post-MMPI-2 would constitute a global measurement. **(c)**

499. A group leader who is counseling children under 10 years of age could best enhance the treatment process by

    a.    involving parents and asking them for input.
    b.    keeping the parents uninvolved.
    c.    reminding the children to speak softly at all times
    d.    b and c.

Corey and Corey suggest that parental involvement can reduce resistance and improve cooperation. They also warn counselors not to take sides with a child against a parent or institution.  **(a)**

500. When an adolescent complains about his or her parents in the group it is best to

    a.    jump on the bandwagon and agree with the child.
    b.    avoid taking sides but help him or her see the parents' point of view via a therapeutic technique such as role-playing.
    c.    talk only about positive experiences.
    d.    immediately put the child on the hot seat.

This principle is true for adolescents as well as children under 10 years old. When working with children and adolescents be careful what you say about confidentiality, since in the case of child abuse, sexual abuse, neglect, or exploitation you will be required ethically and legally obligated to break confidentiality (just as you would if you saw an elderly individual who is being abused). In addition, ethics would dictate that you do likewise if a child is suicidal or plans to seriously harm another individual. Of course, these last two points would apply to all age brackets, in group or individual treatment. In closing this section I can share the fact that literally hundreds of studies attest to the effectiveness of group work. **(b)**

# 7

## Career Development

*If you love what you do, you will never work another day in your life.*

—Confucius

*It is better to choose a career than merely to hunt a job.*
—Frank Parsons, founding father of guidance

## 10 MAJOR CAREER THEORIES ON THE HEAD OF A PIN

**Trait-and-factor-matching theory.** E. G. Williamson based on his knowledge of Frank Parsons, the father of guidance. Relies on tests and assessments to match traits, aptitude, and interests with a given occupation.

**John Holland's six personality and six work environments career typology is** visually depicted with a hexagon that includes six personality types/work environments: realistic (machine shop worker or dog walker), investigative (researcher or chemist), artistic (singer or book author), social (teacher or counselor!), enterprising (sales personnel or business owner), and conventional (secretary or file clerk). RIASEC, if you will. Congruence between the person and the job is emphasized. Person is categorized using three digit codes such as SEC.

**Donald Super's self-concept and developmental stage theory.** Also referred to as a life span, life-space model. Self-concept, as well as career/vocational maturity, influences one's career throughout the life span. His life rainbow helps clients conceptualize their roles as a child, student, leisurite, citizen, worker, spouse, homemaker, parent, and pensioner. Super initially didn't believe he created a theory, but felt his work might be the basis for segments of future theories. He felt mislabeled.

**Anne Roe's early childhood needs-theory approach.** Vocational choice is related to personality development at a young age. Is the client person-oriented (teaching) or nonperson-oriented (computer programming)? Roe was influenced by Freudian psychoanalytic doctrines (the importance of the parent–child relationship) as well as Maslow. Roe's work has generated a wealth of research. Studies do not totally support this approach, however, it is extremely difficult to control the longitudinal variables involved. The Vocational Interest Inventory (VII) and the Career Occupational Preference System make use of Roe's fields and levels taxonomy.

**John Krumboltz's learning theory of career counseling (LTCC).** Initially dubbed as a social learning theory. Four factors can be used to simplify the career development process: (1) genetic endowment and unique abilities; (2) environmental conditions and life events; (3) learning experiences (either Pavlovian, social learning theory, or Skinnerian); and (4) task approach skills (problem solving, cognitive responses, and emotional patterns). Research validates the original social learning theory, but additional studies are needed to back up the newer learning theory of career counseling.

**Ginzberg, Ginsburg, Axelrad, and Herma's developmental approach ... aka the Ginzberg Group ... or Ginzberg and Associates.** Created by an economist, a psychiatrist, a sociologist, and a psychologist. The first developmental approach to occupational choice. The developmental stages are: ages 11 and under—fantasy; early adolescence, ages 11 to 17—tentative; and age 17 into early adulthood—realistic. Original hypothesis was that career choice was irreversible was later dropped.

**Mark Savickas' career construction postmodern theory.** Savickas, who worked with Donald Super, is critical of most traditional theories. His work is heavily rooted in narrative therapy in which the client's life is viewed as a story he or she has constructed, and intervention focuses on recurring themes to re-author the story.

**Social cognitive counseling theory (SCCT).** Focuses on how one's belief system impacts career choice.

**Linda Gottfredson's theory of cicumscription** (phase one: rule out certain jobs not acceptable for gender, stereotypes, and social class) **and compromise** (phase two: change mind, major etc. if career path is not truly realistic). This is a developmental approach taking one's childhood into account. Social space refers to the zone or territory of jobs where he or she fits into society.

**Edgar H. Schein's eight career anchors theory.** Career anchors manifest approximately 5 or 10 years after a person begins work and guide future career choices. Career anchors are based on the self-concept, abilities, and what the person is good at. Originally, Schein identified five anchors, but now eight are used: (1) autonomy/independence; (2) security/stability; (3) technical/functional competence; (4) general managerial competence; (5) entrepreneurial creativity; (6) service/dedication to a cause; (7) pure challenge; (8) lifestyle.

501. Lifestyle and career development have been emphasized

    a.    only since the late 1950s.
    b.    only since the late 1960s.
    c.    only since nondirective counseling became popular.
    d.    since the beginning of the counseling and guidance movement and are still major areas of concern.

Several former ACA presidents (e.g., Sam Gladding and Mark Pope) wisely posit that counseling is the only mental health profession with proficiency in the area of career counseling. In fact, the beginning of the guidance movement has often been associated with the work of Frank Parsons, who started the Boston Vocation Bureau on January 13, 1908 just nine months prior to his death. He was a Cornell graduate who later became Boston's chief law clerk and then the Dean of the Liberal Arts College at Glen Ellyn, Illinois. His landmark work, *Choosing a Vocation*, was published posthumously, thus it is doubtful that he ever knew the true impact he had on the field. Parsons served as the Bureau's director as well as a vocational counselor. The Bureau was set up at the Civic Service House though Parsons also had office hours in branch offices at the YMCA, the Economic Club, and the Women's Educational and Industrial Union. This explains why historians insist that the guidance movement in the United States began with vocational guidance. John M. Brewer, a director of the Bureau during World War I and the author of the 1942 work *History of Vocational Guidance*, speculated that as a bachelor Parsons could have been drawn to the Civic Service House in search of friendship. **How do neophyte counselors *really* feel about conducting career counseling? In a nutshell: not that great! Most of the literature suggests that grad students and beginning counselors sport a negative attitude toward the career counseling and see the work of performing personal counseling as having more prestige. Interestingly enough, career counseling trailblazer John O. Crites feels that the need for career counseling exceeds the need for therapy. Moreover, according to Crites, career counseling (which he feels is more difficult than performing psychotherapy) can be therapeutic since a positive correlation between career counseling and personal adjustment is evident. Although not all counselors would agree with Crites's assertions, it seems safe to say that in reality, the two disciplines overlap.** **(d)**

502. One trend is that women are moving into more careers that in the past were populated by males. Women workers are often

impacted by the "glass ceiling phenomenon." Assuming that a counselor's behavior is influenced by the phenomenon, which statement would he most likely make when conducting a career counseling session with a female client who wants to advance to a higher position?

a.   "Your ability to advance in the corporate world is generally based on your mother's attitude toward work. Can you tell me a little about that?"

b.   "Actually, women can advance quite rapidly in the corporate world. I support you 100%. I'd say you should be optimistic and go for the position."

c.   "Let's be rational: A woman can only advance so far. You really have very little if any chance of becoming a corporate executive. I'm here to help you cope with this reality."

d.   "In most cases a female will work in a position that is at the same level as her father. Did your dad ever work as a corporate executive?"

Women now form nearly 60% of the U.S. workforce or approximately 72 million women, so statistically speaking lots of women can benefit from career counseling. Women now own half of all businesses. This number has risen dramatically since 1900. **The glass ceiling phenomenon suggests that women are limited in terms of how far they can advance in the world of work. The glass ceiling effect is a form of occupational sex-role stereotyping that can limit women's careers. This concept is somewhat analogous to the lavender ceiling which purports that the same basic notion is true for gay, lesbian, bisexual, and transgender individuals. Gender-aware career counseling is a must.** Okay, back to the subject of female workers. One notion is that the high divorce rate (which currently impacts nearly one out of two marriages) created the phenomenon of the "displaced homemaker." **A displaced homemaker is a woman with children who was a homemaker but is currently in need of work to support her family.** Women who have made the transition from homemaker to jobs outside the home could very well be referred to as "reentry women" on your exam. It has been estimated that 75% of all divorces occur in families with children. As adults, kids who grew up in divorced families experience more depression and have more marital problems. **In roughly the last 35 years, career counseling experts have begun to focus on women's issues. Most scholars believe that the focus on minorities is still lagging behind.** **(c)**

503. Most research in the area of career development and its relationship to students indicates that

    a.   a very high proportion of students in high school and at the junior high or middle school level wanted guidance in planning a career. Career interests are more stable after college.

    b.   students did not want career guidance despite its importance.

    c.   many students were too inflexible to benefit from career guidance.

    d.   high school students wanted career guidance but junior-high school- or middle school-level students did not.

Simply put: except for the current generation of college students who seem to be avoiding career counseling, K-12 students seem to want the service. Three-fourths of the eleventh graders wanted help with career planning and the number who wanted help in the eighth grade was nearly as high, rendering choice "d" incorrect. **Most studies indicate that students would like more help in the area of career planning, including the fact that 50% of all college students have career difficulties. This information is especially important in regard to young African Americans who have fewer positive work role models. Why limit our discussion to just young people? Perhaps you've heard the statistic floating around which suggests that one in five workers snares a job based on chance factors and that 60% of all workers would like more information about the world of work if they had to do it all over again.** *Some brief comments on decision making, job performance, and career counseling*: **Another key issue is pervasive indecisiveness. This label describes** a person who has a lifelong pattern of severe anxiety related to decision making. Needless to say, this affliction makes the act of deciding on a career that much more difficult. Victor Vroom's motivation and management expectancy theory throws another mix of factors into the ring that is relevant once the individual is employed. He suggests that an employee's performance is influenced by valence (will the work provide rewards such as money, a promotion, or satisfaction?); expectancy (what does the person feel he or she is capable of doing?); and instrumentality (will the manager actually give the employee the promised reward such as a raise?).          **(a)**

504. A dual-career family (or dual-worker couple) is one in which both partners have jobs to which they are committed on a somewhat continuous basis. Which statement is true of dual-career families?

    a.    Surprisingly enough, dual-career families have lower incomes than families in which only one partner works.

    b.    Dual-career families have higher incomes than the so-called traditional family in which only one partner is working.

    c.    Dual-career families have incomes which are almost identical to families with one partner working.

    d.    Surprisingly enough, no research has been conducted on dual-career families.

Common sense prevails here as two incomes are indeed usually better than one. Nevertheless, since both partners are working there are more problems related to household chores and responsibilities. Competition between the partners can also be an issue that may need to be dealt with in counseling. **Today over 54% of all marriages are dual-wage earner marriages making them the majority. The figure hovers around the 60% mark when we examine families with children. Compare this to the 1950 statistic of 20.4%. Simply put: Dual-career couples are now the norm.** **(b)**

505. In the dual-career family, partners seem to be more self-sufficient than in the traditional family. In a dual-career household, the woman

   a.    generally has children before entering the workforce.
   b.    rarely if ever has children.
   c.    is not self-reliant.
   d.    is typically secure in her career before she has children.

Choice "a" is true of the traditional family while choice "d" describes the dual-career family. Choice "c" contradicts research which insists that partners in a dual-career family are more self-sufficient than in the traditional family.    **(d)**

506. Studies indicate that

   a.    students receive ample vocational guidance.
   b.    most parents can provide appropriate vocational guidance.
   c.    students want more vocational guidance than they receive.
   d.    career days meet the vocational guidance needs of most students.

If you missed this question please review question 503. **Hint:** Some exams will distinguish between career counseling and vocational guidance. Guidance is seen as a developmental and educational process within a school system while career counseling is viewed as a therapeutic service for adults performed outside an educational setting. Semantics? Perhaps, but you may need it to boost your exam score!    **(c)**

507. Statistics reveal that

   a.    on average, a worker with a bachelor's degree earns over $10,000 a year more than a worker with a high school diploma.
   b.    fewer workers possess a high school diploma than ever before.
   c.    blue-collar jobs are growing faster than white-collar jobs.
   d.    older workers are slower than younger workers and have fewer skills.

Roughly speaking, a bachelor's level worker brings in about $57,000 per year in comparison with a worker who has a high school diploma who will earn an average of $33,500 yearly. Asian Americans/Pacific Islanders have the highest percentage of individuals with a bachelor's degree, followed by whites, African Americans, and Latino/as. The good news is that all of the aforementioned groups have raised their graduation rates since 1990. Choice "b" is blatantly false. The number of workers in the labor force with a high school diploma has increased. The same could be said of choice "c": blue-collar jobs have not increased as rapidly as white-collar positions. These changes may be based partially on the fact that the United States has become a service economy rather than focusing primarily on the production of goods. Some exams—as well as many textbooks—will mention the "changing view of work." This phrase generally indicates that in the past work was seen as drudgery, while today it is seen as a vehicle to express our identity, self-esteem, and status. In the past work was primarily a way to pay the bills. Today, the rewards of a career are often conceptualized as fulfilling emotional needs. This would seem to indicate that people who don't need to work will still continue to do so. Is this really the case? According to a 1978 text on lottery winners by H. R. Kaplan, million dollar winners who quit their jobs felt dissatisfied. A Dutch study confirmed his findings. (We should all be lucky enough to be included in a study like this!) And did you by any chance mark choice "d"? Well if you did, you need to know that experience impacts job performance more than age does. Some research demonstrates that older workers are actually more adept than younger ones in terms of skill as well as speed! This phenomenon disproved a notion in psychology known as "decrement," which suggested that speed, skills, and retention would decrease as one entered old age.    **(a)**

508. When professional career counselors use the term *leisure* they technically mean

   a.   the client is having fun at work or away from work.
   b.   the client is relaxing at work or away from work.

    c.    the client is working at less than 100% capacity at work or away from work.

    d.    the time the client has away from work which is not being utilized for obligations.

Leisure time is defined as time away from work in which the individual has the freedom to choose what he or she would like to do. Leisure time is said to be "self-determined." Leisure can sometimes help compensate for dissatisfaction in the work place. **Career is sometimes defined as the total work one does in a lifetime plus leisure.** A leisure activity that one engages in for pleasure rather than money is often referred to as an **avocation**. Dual-career couples often report a lack of leisure time which can in turn foster additional stress for both partners.　　　　**(d)**

509.　In terms of leisure time and dual-career families/couples,

    a.    dual-career families/couples have more leisure time.
    b.    dual-career families/couples have the same amount of leisure time as families/couples with one wage earner.
    c.    dual-career families/couples have less leisure time.
    d.    dual-career families/couples have more weekend leisure time.

Both partners in the single-career relationship have more leisure time. Some books and exams are already using the term *leisure counseling*, which should alert you to the emphasis which is being placed on this topic. Fortunately, research shows that in most cases, dual-career households manage to spend as much time with their children as households with a single wage earner.　　**(c)**

510.　A client who says, "I feel I cannot really become an administrator in our agency because I am a woman" is showing an example of

    a.    gender bias.
    b.    counselor bias.
    c.    the trait-and-factor theory.
    d.    developmental theory and career choice.

Here is an agency that makes "biased" employment choices based on one's "gender." The ideal answer to this dilemma was set forth in 1964 when Title VII of the Civil Rights Act (amended in 1972) stated that women would have equal work opportunities and equal job pay. I purposely used the word *ideal* inasmuch as some statistics demonstrated that in 1964 a man was earning a buck for every 59 cents earned by a woman. Since 1964, however, progress has been slower than a tortoise with ankle weights, with women now bringing in about 76 cents for each dollar a man earns. The Equal Employment Opportunity Commission (EEOC) is the watchdog for Title VII guidelines that prohibit discrimination on the basis of color, sex, religion, race, or national origin. Since 1978, EEOC has enforced "Uniform Guidelines on Employee Selection Procedures." The procedures speak of "adverse impact." A test or selection process is said to have adverse impact if it does not meet the "80% Four-fifths Rule." Here, the hiring rate for minorities is divided by the figure for nonminorities. If the quotient is less than 80% (4/5), then adverse impact is evident. Thus, a typical exam question might inform you that a firm's selection process is such that 60 of the employees hired are African American, while 80 are white. You would then be asked to determine whether the selection process was plagued via adverse impact. Your computation would be: 60/80 = 75%. Since 75% is less than 80%, the process would indeed have an adverse impact. This formula also is used for promotion situations. The fact that minorities ought to be moved "up" more in jobs could be used as a memory device that the minority or subgroup rate is placed "up" or on the top (i.e., the numerator) of the equation. The uniform guidelines also discuss "differential validity," which is evident when a selection process (e.g., a test) is valid for one group, yet less valid or totally invalid for another group. (**Note**: This is not the same as "discriminant validity." See question 627 for a discussion of this term.) Tests plagued by differential validity should not be utilized for hiring or promotion purposes. Incidentally, choice "b" or "counselor bias" might be used to describe a counselor who was sympathetic with the agency's position. As for choices "c" and "d" be prepared to see them a lot. The chances are extremely good that you will see a question related to "trait-and-factor theory" and "developmental theory" on any major exam. The trait-and-factor theory assumes that via psychological testing one's personality could be matched to an occupation which stresses those particular personality traits. Some industrial psychology exams will speak of "profile matching." In this approach, a job candidate's personality or skills profile is matched to that of successful workers. The decision to hire is then based on the closeness or similarity of the match based on a pattern of predictor scores. The developmental approach, choice "d," views career decisions as longitudinal and reversible. **(a)**

511. One major category of career theory is known as the trait-factor (also called the trait-and-factor) approach. It has also been dubbed the actuarial or matching approach. This approach

    a.   attempts to match conscious and unconscious work motives.

    b.   attempts to match the worker and the work environment (job factors). The approach thus makes the assumption that there is one best or single career for the person.

    c.   attempts to match career behavior with attitudes.

    d.   attempts to match cognition with the workload.

Historically speaking, the trait-and-factor theory is considered the first major and most durable theory of career choice. The term *actuarial* used in the question means that empirical statistical data (such as the results from a test) is used rather than simply relying on subjective clinical judgment. Parsons's work mentioned earlier (i.e., *Choosing a Vocation*) stressed a careful self-analysis conducted "under guidance" and then put down on paper to determine your personal "traits." The traits could then be matched to occupations using advice from individuals who had "made a careful study of men and vocations of the conditions of success." Also familiarize yourself with the name Edmund Griffith Williamson, the chief spokesperson for the so-called Minnesota Viewpoint, which expanded upon Parsons's model to create a theory of counseling which transcended vocational issues. Choice "a" would be indicative of a psychoanalytic theory of career counseling. **Exam hint:** Most popular career theories are based on middle-class or upper-middle-class white males who are heterosexual and not disabled.                                    **(b)**

512. The trait-and-factor career counseling, actuarial, or matching approach (which matches clients with a job) is associated with

   a.   Parsons and Williamson.
   b.   Roe and Brill.
   c.   Holland and Super.
   d.   Tiedeman and O'Hara.

The trait-and-factor model is sometimes classified as a "structural" theory since it emphasizes individual differences or what your exam might call structural differences. **Note:** Some exams may ask you if the trait-and-factor model is grounded in "differential psychology," which is the study of individual differences. The answer is a resounding "yes," of course. The assumption in this approach is that human beings are rational. Hence, when the proper information (e.g., from tests) is available, the individual can make a proper or wise choice of career. C. F. Patterson, from the University of Minnesota, was the other major proponent of this approach and thus, his name could easily be added to choice "a." The theory has been accused of being oversimplified because it subordinated personal choice making and advanced the idea of "a single job for life." In other words, **the theory assumes that an individual's traits can be measured so accurately that the choice of an occupation is a one-time process. Computer career guidance programs often adhere to the trait-and-factor model.** Experts began to question the notion that a single "right occupation" existed for each personality profile. Choice "b" mentions Anne Roe and A. A. Brill, who espoused personality theories of career choice. In choice "c," John Holland suggested that a person's personality needs to be congruent with the work environment, while Donald Super emphasized career development rather than career choice. As for choice "d," David Tiedeman and Robert O'Hara support a decision-making theory.                          **(a)**

513. The trait-and-factor or actuarial approach asserts that

    a.    job selection is a long-term development process.
    b.    testing is an important part of the counseling process.
    c.    a counselor can match the correct person with the appropriate job.
    d.    b and c.

Parsons suggests three steps to implement the trait-and-factor approach. (a) Knowledge of the self and aptitudes and interests. (b) Knowledge of jobs, including the advantages and disadvantages of them. (c) Matching the individual with the work. Though today's career counselors generally do not practice from a pure trait-factor base, experts insist, nevertheless, that remnants of the trait-and-factor approach are still evident in some of the modern theories such as those suggested by John O. Crites, Donald Super, and John Holland. **(d)**

514. In 1909 a landmark book entitled *Choosing a Vocation* was released. The book was written by Frank Parsons. Parsons has been called

    a.    the father of lifestyle.
    b.    the father of modern counseling.
    c.    the father of vocational guidance.
    d.    the fourth force in counseling.

What's that: You felt you could have answered this one in your sleep? Well don't scold me for being redundant. Instead, why not thank your lucky stars that the repetition could save you a point on the test? The phrase "the fourth force in counseling" referenced in choice "d" has been suggested to describe "multiculturalism." Third force psychology usually refers to humanistic approaches. **(c)**

515. Which statement is not true of the trait-and-factor approach to career counseling?

    a.  The approach attempts to match the person's traits with the requirements of a job.
    b.  The approach usually relies on psychometric information.
    c.  The approach is developmental and thus focuses on career maturity.
    d.  The approach is associated with the work of Parsons and Williamson.

    **Developmental approaches delineate stages or specify vocational choice in terms of a process which can change throughout the life span.** Thus, vocational development parallels psychosocial, cognitive, and personality development. Eli Ginzberg, an economist, Sol Ginsburg, a psychiatrist, Sidney Axelrad, a sociologist, and John Herma, a psychologist, are often cited as pioneers in this area, questioning the premise that career choice was a single event. The theories proposed by Super and Tiedeman and O'Hara are also derived from developmental psychology.                                                                    **(c)**

516. Edmund Griffith Williamson's work (or the so-called Minnesota Viewpoint) purports to be scientific and didactic, utilizing test data from instruments such as the

    a.  Rorschach and the Thematic Apperception Test (TAT).
    b.  Binet and the Wechsler.
    c.  Beck Depression Inventory (BDI) and the Minnesota Multiphasic Personality Inventory (MMPI).
    d.  Minnesota Occupational Rating Scales.

    Suggested memory devices: Minnesota means matching or Minnesota and matching both begin with an "M." Williamson was associated with the University of Minnesota for over 40 years. Remember that you are looking for the best answer. All of the tests listed might be used by a modern-day counselor of the trait-factor persuasion; nevertheless, choice "d" mentions a test specifically aimed at enhancing the actuarial approach to career choice. The Myers–Briggs Type Indicator (MBTI), the Guilford–Zimmerman Temperment Survey (GZTS), the Adjective Checklist, BDI, and MMPI-2 would probably be the choice of counselors who favor a personality theory of career selection. The model is not overly popular with our current crop of counselors and it has been sarcastically referred to as the "test-and-tell" paradigm of career counseling.    **(d)**

517. The trait-and-factor approach fails to take _____ into account.

    a.    individual change throughout the life span
    b.    relevant psychometric data
    c.    personality
    d.    job requirements

Choice "b," psychometric data, refers to the use of test results in counseling, a practice which is stressed by trait-and-factor practitioners. The correct answer (choice "a") has been a major criticism of this model and perhaps accounts for some of the popularity of developmental theories.    **(a)**

518. Anne Roe suggested a personality approach to career choice

    a.    based on cognitive-behavioral therapy.
    b.    based on a model of strict operant conditioning.
    c.    based on the premise that a job satisfies an unconscious need.
    d.    based on the work of Pavlov.

The American clinical psychologist Anne Roe was one of the first individuals to suggest a theory of career choice based heavily on personality theory. Some exams refer to Roe's work as the "person–environment" theory. The theory is primarily psychoanalytic, though it also draws on Maslow's hierarchy of needs. Roe's major propositions are that needs which are satisfied do not become unconscious motivators; that higher-order needs will disappear even if they are rarely satisfied, but lower-order needs (such as safety) will be the major concern;

and that needs which are satisfied after a long delay will become unconscious motivators. Roe emphasized that early child-rearing practices influence later career choices since a job is a major source of gratification for an unconscious need. P.S. If you answered "d," salivate and crack open your old career counseling text! You're rusty!                                            **(c)**

519. Roe was the first career specialist to utilize a two-dimensional system of occupational classification utilizing

    a.   unconscious and preconscious.
    b.   fields and levels.
    c.   yin and yang.
    d.   transactional analysis nomenclature.

The eight occupational "fields" include: service, business contact, organizations, technology, outdoor, science, general culture, and arts/entertainment. The six "levels" of occupational skill include: professional and managerial 1, professional and managerial 2, semiprofessional/small business, skilled, semiskilled, and unskilled.                                            **(b)**

520. All of the following are examples of Anne Roe's "fields" *except:*

    a.   Service.
    b.   Science.
    c.   Arts and entertainment.
    d.   Unskilled.

See the previous answer. "Unskilled" refers to a "level" of occupational skill or responsibility rather than an "occupational field."                                            **(d)**

521. All of the following are examples of Anne Roe's "levels" *except:*

    a.   Outdoor.
    b.   Semiskilled.
    c.   Semiprofessional/small business.
    d.   Professional and managerial.

Review the last two questions and answers unless you chose choice "a." All of the other alternatives describe "levels."    **(a)**

522. Roe spoke of three basic parenting styles: overprotective, avoidant, or acceptant. The result is that the child

   a.   experiences neurosis or psychosis.
   b.   will eventually have a lot of jobs or a lack of employment.
   c.   will develop a personality which gravitates (i.e., moves) toward people or away from people.
   d.   will suffer from depression in the work setting or will be highly motivated to succeed.

   Some texts and exams will refer to the avoidant child-rearing style as "rejecting." It is an emotionally cold or hostile style. The acceptant style is "democratic." If the person moves "toward" people, he or she would choose the "fields" of service, business, organization, or general cultural while an individual who moves away from people would gravitate toward outdoor, science, or perhaps technology. Research tends to support the contention that an individual raised in a warm, accepting family where person-to-person interaction was rewarded would tend to seek out careers emphasizing contact with others. A cold, "avoiding" family of origin would thus be more likely to produce an individual who would shun person-oriented careers.    **(c)**

523. Roe's theory relies on Abraham Maslow's hierarchy of needs in the sense that in terms of career choice

   a.   lower-order needs take precedence over higher-order needs.
   b.   self-actualization needs take precedence over lower-order needs.
   c.   all needs are given equal consideration.
   d.   the need for self-actualization would overpower a physical need.

   The job meets the "most urgent need."    **(a)**

524. Some support for Roe's theory comes from

    a.   the BDI.
    b.   the Wechsler Adult Intelligence Scale-Fourth Edition (WAIS-IV).
    c.   the Rorschach and the TAT.
    d.   the gestalt therapy movement.

    Suggested memory device: Roe begins with an "r" and so does Rorschach. The Thematic Apperception Test (TAT) is similar in that it is a projective test.                                          **(c)**

525. In terms of genetics, Roe's theory would assert that

    a.   genetics play a very minor role in career choice.
    b.   genetics help to determine intelligence and education, and hence this influences one's career choice.
    c.   genetics are important while upbringing is not.
    d.   genetics are important while the unconscious is not.

    **Time for a Roe Review (hey was that great alliteration or what?):** career choice is influenced by genetics, parent–child interaction, unconscious motivators, current needs, interests (people/things), education, and intelligence.          **(b)**

526. According to Anne Roe, who categorized occupations by fields and levels,

    a.   the decision to pursue a career is purely a conscious decision.
    b.   using the *Strong* is the best method of explaining career choice.
    c.   early childhood experiences are irrelevant in terms of career choice.
    d.   the choice of a career helps to satisfy an individual's needs.

    Roe determined that choice "c" was incorrect and early childhood experiences are indeed important.                              **(d)**

527. A 37-year-old white male states during a counseling session that he is working as a clerk at Main Street Plumbing. This verbalization depicts the client's

    a.    career.
    b.    lifestyle.
    c.    job or position.
    d.    occupation.

Technically, a *job* refers to a given position or similar positions within an organization. An *occupation* is broader and refers to similar jobs occupied via different people in different settings (e.g., psychotherapists). *Career* is the broadest category because it depicts a person's lifetime positions plus leisure. Possible memory device to recall the order from most specific to most general: Joc (which sounds like the word Jock).     **(c)**

528. Roe recognized the role of the unconscious mind in terms of career choice. Another theorist who emphasized the unconscious processes in this area of study was

    a.    Krumboltz.
    b.    Schein.
    c.    Super.
    d.    Bordin.

Choice "a" is decidedly incorrect as John Krumboltz worked with a behavioristic model. Choice "b" refers to Edgar H. Schein who proposed an approach using eight so-called anchors. The goal is to find an anchor that encompasses your career values, motives, and competence. This model lends itself to helping a worker who has been in the workforce for a few years. Edwin Bordin, though, felt that career choices could be used to solve unconscious conflicts. Psychoanalytic approaches—used in regard to career choice or other issues—have never been extremely popular with helpers trained in counseling departments since short-term, time efficient modalities are stressed. Choice "c" refers to Donald Super, who created a five-stage life-span theory emphasizing that career choice is a developmental process based on the individual's self-concept.     **(d)**

529. Edwin Bordin felt that difficulties related to job choice

    a.   are indicative of neurotic symptoms.

    b.   are indicative of inappropriate reinforcers in the environment.

    c.   are related to a lack of present moment awareness.

    d.   are the result of irrational cognitions.

This is the kind of exam question you literally could answer correctly via the process of elimination. In the previous question, it was noted that Bordin analyzed career choices using the unconscious mind. Needless to say, this is a psychoanalytic assumption. Hence, choice "b" can be eliminated since "reinforcers" are seen as modifiers in the behaviorist school. Choice "c" also can be eliminated inasmuch as analysis is not a present moment approach. Lastly, "irrational cognitions" are stressed in rational-emotive behavior therapy and some related cognitive schools of intervention. Krumboltz's approach to career counseling is considered a cognitive approach.     **(a)**

530. Another career theorist who drew upon psychoanalytic doctrines was A. A. Brill. Brill emphasized _____ as an ego defense mechanism.

    a.   subliminal

    b.   sublimation

    c.   repression

    d.   rationalization

Choice "a" is not a defense mechanism. Sublimation occurs when an individual expresses an unacceptable need in a socially acceptable manner. A person, for example, who likes to cut things up might pursue a career as a butcher or perhaps a surgeon. **Review the counseling theories and helping relationship section if you do not know the definitions of the four alternatives.**     **(b)**

531. A client who becomes a professional football player because he unconsciously likes to hurt people would be utilizing _____ according to Brill's theory of career choice.

    a.  subliminal
    b.  sublimation
    c.  suppression
    d.  introjection

    See the explanation to the previous question.                    **(b)**

532. Today, the most popular approach to career choice reflects the work of

    a.  Anne Roe.
    b.  Donald Super.
    c.  John Holland.
    d.  Jane Loevinger.

    Choice "d" is the most outlandish—at least, if you marked any other choice you chose a career theorist. Loevinger is noted for her seven-stage transition continuum theory of ego development. John Holland's theory can be best described by his four assumptions. First, in our culture, there are six basic personality types: realistic, investigative, artistic, social, enterprising, or conventional. Second, most work environments correspond to six personality types. Third, people search out an agreeable environment which lets them express their personality type. Fourth, the individual's behavior is determined by an interaction of the personality and the environment. Possible memory device for the six types of personality/environments: "as rice." Holland's Self-Directed Search (SDS) is designed to measure the six personality types.                                           **(c)**

533. Holland categorized _____ personality orientations which correspond to analogous work environments.

    a.  two
    b.  five

c.   three
d.   six

In this theory the counselor attempts to find a job for the client in which the personality–environment interaction is congruent. Holland felt that people try to avoid environments which are disagreeable. A host of studies lends support to his theory of personality types.                                            **(d)**

534.  Most experts in the field of career counseling would classify Roe, Brill, and Holland as _____ theorists.

a.   behavior modification
b.   ego psychologists
c.   experiential
d.   personality

**Remember:** your exam could use the term *structural theory* in place of the term *personality theory*. Don't let it throw you!   **(d)**

535.  Counselors who support John Holland's approach believe that

a.   an appropriate job allows one to express his or her personality.
b.   stereotypes cannot be considered relevant.
c.   four major personality categories exist.
d.   sublimation is the major factor in job selection.

Choice "b" is incorrect: Holland did indeed believe in stereotypes, and some critics have thus said his theory is too simplistic and somewhat sexist. Choice "c" would need to read "six major personality categories" to be accurate.                      **(a)**

536.  Holland mentioned six modal orientations: artistic, conventional, enterprising, investigative, realistic, and social. A middle school counselor is most likely

a.   artistic.
b.   social.

c.  enterprising.
d.  realistic.

Teachers, counselors, speech therapists, and social workers would fit into the social category. John Holland said that the person in the "social" category prefers to solve problems using interpersonal skills and feelings.                                    **(b)**

537.  Holland's theory would predict that the vice president of the United States would be

a.  artistic.
b.  social.
c.  enterprising
d.  realistic.

The "enterprising" person likes to sell to others or perform leadership tasks. He or she tends to value power and status. Other enterprising occupations would include real estate agents, business owners, television producers, and hotel managers.  **(c)**

538.  A client who wishes to work on an assembly line would fit into Holland's _____ typology.

a.  artistic
b.  conventional
c.  social
d.  realistic

The "realistic" or "motoric" person likes machines. This individual might become a truck driver, an auto mechanic, or might fancy plumbing.                                             **(d)**

539.  Holland's psychological needs career personality theory would say that a research chemist is primarily the _____ type.

a.  investigative
b.  social
c.  enterprising
d.  artistic

The "investigative" personality type likes to think his or her way through a problem. Occupations congruent with this type include scientists, design engineers, geologists, mathematicians, and philosophers. **Reader-generated, super-cool memory device: Most textbooks recommend the memory device RIASEC to recall the six vocational personalities/work environments, but a clever reader suggested *Rosenthal Is A Successful Educator Counselor*. You've got to love it!** (Turn to the Graphical Representations section of the text for a visual picture of this paradigm.)    **(a)**

540. Holland's artistic type seems to value feelings over pure intellect or cognitive ability. Which of the following clients would *not* be best described via the artistic typology?

    a.   A 72-year-old part-time, male ballet instructor.
    b.   A 29-year-old female fiction writer.
    c.   A 33-year-old female drill press operator.
    d.   A 41-year-old singer for a heavy metal rock band.

    **Hint:** The typist on the NCE or other major exam will probably not be kind enough to type the word "not" in italics, so read the questions carefully. The "artistic" type shuns conformity as well as structure. The emphasis is on self-expression. The drill press operator would be a "realistic" type who likes physical labor and enjoys working with tools.    **(c)**

541. Holland did indeed believe in career stereotypes. In other words the person psychologically defines himself or herself via a given job. Thus, a bookkeeper or a clerical worker would primarily fit into the _____ category.

    a.   artistic
    b.   conventional
    c.   realistic
    d.   social

    The "conventional" type values conformity, structure, rules, and feels comfortable in a subordinate role. Statisticians, bank clerks, and controllers fit this stereotype. By the way, "conventional" and "conformity" both begin with a "c." Nice memory device, huh? Although Holland's theory is usually dubbed as a personality theory, it has been viewed as a trait-and-factor approach. Since most exams won't mention the trait-and-factor category, the answer they are usually looking for is that Holland created a personality approach to career counseling.                                              **(b)**

542. In regard to an individual's behavioral style or so-called modal orientation, Holland believed that

    a.    every person has a pure or discrete orientation that fits perfectly into one of the six categories.
    b.    occupational measures like the Strong Vocational are for the most part useless.
    c.    most people are not pure personality types and thus can best be described by a distribution of types such as Realistic, Social, Investigative (RSI).
    d.    a and b.

If you marked "b" try again; the Strong Interest Inventory (SII) is based on Holland's model. Although each individual has a primary direction or type, the person can be described best using a "profile" over three areas also known as a three digit code. Graphically, the six types generally are placed on a hexagon such that adjacent or consistent types are next to each other on the geometric figure. Thus RIA (Realistic, Investigative, Artistic) would be "consistent" while RAE (Realtistic, Artistic, Enterprising) would be "inconsistent" (see the Graphical Representations section of this book).                                **(c)**

543. Holland believed that

    a.    a given occupation will tend to attract persons with similar personalities.
    b.    a given occupation will tend to attract persons with a very wide range of personality attributes.

c.   one's personality is, for the most part, unrelated to one's occupational choice.

d.   b and c.

Like Roe, Holland felt that early childhood development influences adult personality characteristics.                    **(a)**

544. Holland relied on a personality theory of career choice. Robert Hoppock's theory, based on the work of _____ is also considered a personality approach.

a.   Donald Super
b.   Robert Rosenthal
c.   David Wechsler
d.   Henry Murray

Henry Murray created the "needs-press" theory and the TAT (along with Christina Morgan) projective test. The occupation is used to meet a person's current need. Rosenthal (choice "b," no relation to me) is famous for his research regarding the "experimenter effect," while David Wechsler (choice "c") is well-known for creating the Wechsler intelligence scales.     **(d)**

545. Developmental career theorists view career choice as an ongoing or so-called longitudinal process rather than a single decision made at one point in time. The pioneer theorists in this area— who were the first to forsake the matching models—were

a.   Super and Roe.
b.   Hoppock and Holland.
c.   Ginzberg, Ginsburg, Axelrad, and Herma.
d.   Brill and Bordin.

Until 1950 the trait-and-factor or matching model was king. Then in early 1951 Ginzberg and his associates began to emphasize developmental factors related to occupational choice. Based on a small research sample they concluded that occupational choice takes place over a 6–10-year period; the choice is irreversible; and always has the quality of compromise.

The theory postulated three stages: fantasy—until age 11, based strongly on impulses; tentative—ages 11–17, where interests and abilities are examined; and realistic—age 17 to early twenties, where a choice is made by weighing abilities and needs and making a compromise. Exploration was said to lead to crystallization. By 1972, Ginzberg modified his position by stating that the process of choice is open-ended and lifelong. This, of course, refuted the notion of irreversibility. He also replaced "compromise" with the concept of "optimization," meaning that individuals try to make the best of what they have to offer and what is available in the job market.          **(c)**

546. Ginzberg and his colleagues now believe in a development model of career choice which asserts that

    a.   the process of choosing a career does not end at age 20 or adulthood.
    b.   career choice decisions are really made throughout the life span.
    c.   career choice is reversible.
    d.   all of the above.

    See the question and answer to 545.          **(d)**

547. Initially, Ginzberg and his associates viewed career choice as irreversible and the result of compromises between wishes and realistic possibilities. This theory identified three stages of career development:

    a.   informal, formal, and concrete.
    b.   fantasy (birth to age 11), tentative (ages 11–17), and realistic (age 17 to early twenties).
    c.   sensorimotor, formal, and concrete.
    d.   oral, anal, and phallic.

    See the question and answer to 545.          **(b)**

548. The most popular developmental career theorist is Donald Super. Super emphasizes

    a.  id impulses.
    b.  the Critical Parent.
    c.  the self-concept.
    d.  ego strength.

    Super and self-concept both begin with an "s." How convenient! The assumption here is that the individual chooses a career which allows the self-concept to be expressed. **(c)**

549. Super's life-span theory emphasizes _____ life stages.

    a.  five
    b.  four
    c.  three
    d.  nine

    The stages are: first, Growth (birth to age 14); second, Exploration (ages 15–24); third, Establishment (ages 24–44); fourth, Maintenance (ages 44–64); and fifth, Decline (age 65+). Suggested memory device: GEE MD. (Note, so far as the two "Es" are concerned, common sense would dictate that exploration would come before establishment.) **Developmental theories like Donald Super's emphasize longitudinal career-related behavior.** **(a)**

550. Super's life-span theory includes

    a.  the life-career rainbow.
    b.  the life-career stars.
    c.  the life-career moon.
    d.  the life-career psychosis.

    The person can play a number of potential roles as he or she advances through the five stages mentioned in the previous question; they are parent, homemaker, worker, citizen, leisurite, student, or child. Super called the graphic display of the roles unfolding over the life span, the "career rainbow." The roles are played out in the "theaters" of the home, community, school, and work. **So far as Super is concerned, career can include student, employee, pensioner, retirement, civic duties, avocations, and even family roles.**                    **(a)**

551. Research into the phenomenon of career maturity reflects the work of

    a.    John Crites.
    b.    Anne Roe.
    c.    John Holland.
    d.    Nancy Schlossberg.

Career maturity might be referred to as "vocational maturity" on your exam. Choice "d" mentions the work of Schlossberg, who has focused heavily on adult career development. She suggested five noteworthy factors: behavior in the adult years is primarily determined by social rather than biological factors; behavior can either be a function of one's life stage or one's age at other times; sex differences are actually more powerful than age or stage differences; adults continually experience transitions which require adaptation and self-assessment; identity, intimacy, and generativity are recurring themes in adulthood.          **(a)**

552. The decision-making theory, which refers to periods of anticipation and implementation/adjustment, was proposed by

    a.    John O. Crites.
    b.    John Holland.
    c.    David Tiedeman and Robert O'Hara.
    d.    Donald Super.

Tiedman and O'Hara suggested that the decision process is best explained by breaking it down into a two-part process. In the anticipation stage the individual imagines himself or herself in a given career. In the implementation phase (also sometimes called accommodation or induction) the person engages in reality testing regarding his or her expectations concerning the occupation. **All decision-making theories contend that the individual has the power to choose from the various career options.**                                           **(c)**

553. John Krumboltz postulated a social learning approach to career choice. This model is based mainly on the work of

   a.   Joseph Wolpe.
   b.   Albert Bandura.
   c.   Donald Super.
   d.   Karen Homey.

**The purpose of this question is straightforward: You must know something about the concept of social learning theory in order to do well on your exam!** Anita Mitchell, G. Brian Jones, and John Krumboltz utilized the work of Albert Bandura to explain career choice. Bandura emphasized the role of modeling in the acquisition of new behaviors. The theory states that people learn not only from the consequences of their own behavior but also from observing the consequences of others. Learning which takes place by watching others is sometimes called "vicarious learning." Krumboltz felt that interests are the result of "learning," such that changes in interests can be "learned." Thus, actual exposure to a wide range of work settings (i.e., site visits) is highly desirable. Occupational indecisiveness is seen as an indication of an information deficit rather than a lack of career maturity. **Two popular behavioral techniques (though they are not necessarily just related to the work of Krumboltz) include the RJP (realistic job preview) and guided imagery. To conduct a RJP the student, usually in college, would contact a worker in the field and then interview the worker. Guided imagery, effective for adults and adolescents, can be implemented by having the client imagine a day in the future working in the job or even receiving an award for outstanding performance in the position.**                    **(b)**

554. The model Krumboltz suggested is

    a.    a human capital theory.
    b.    an accident theory of career development.
    c.    a status attainment theory.
    d.    a behavioristic model of career development.

Okay, let's review the incorrect choices (i.e., "a," "b," and "c") since they are terms that could conceivably pop up on your exam. The human capital theory purports that individuals secure training and education to get the best possible income. This theory, however, doesn't seem valid when applied to folks of lower economic status. The accident theory simply suggests that chance factors influence one's career. For example, a student liked his history teacher so he decided to become a history teacher himself. The so-called status attainment theory posits that the child will eventually secure a job commensurate with his or her family status. This notion will not hold water with a child who has exceptionally low or high career aspirations (e.g., a lower-class child who insists she will become a physician). Some textbooks and exams may categorize Krumboltz's theory as a decision-making theory or even a cognitive one. Krumboltz believed that decision making—in terms of career options as well as noncareer options—is a skill which can be learned. Krumboltz acknowledged the role of genetics and the environment but focused on what can be changed via learning.    **(d)**

555. A counselor who favors a behavioristic mode of career counseling would most likely

    a.    analyze dreams related to jobs and/or occupations.
    b.    give the client a standardized career test.
    c.    suggest a site visit to a work setting.
    d.    a and b.

Choice "a," come on—you didn't really choose it, did you? It sounds like something out of a primer on Freudian analysis. Ideally, all individuals should be exposed to as many learning experiences as possible. Another behavioristic strategy known as the "job club" has been suggested by Nathan Azrin who created the approach in the 1970s to help returning Vietnam vets and went on to write the book *Job Club Counselor's Manual: A Behaviorial Approach to Vocational Counseling*. The job club operates like a behaviorist group in which members share job leads and discuss or role-play specific behaviors (e.g., interviewing skills) necessary for job acquisition. The club helps members learn from each other. The original model also utilized a classroom model for dispensing information. You may recall from grad school that Azrin was one of the leading pioneers who created the specific guidelines for running a behavior modification token economy (i.e., giving plastic tokens which could be turned in for actual reinforcers such as food).    **(c)**

556. A fairly recent model to explain career development is the decision approach. The Gelatt Decision Model created by Harry B. Gelatt refers to information as "the fuel of the decision." The Gelatt Model asserts that information can be organized into three systems:

    a.    predictive, value, and decision.
    b.    internal, external, and in-between.
    c.    predictive, external, and internal.
    d.    internal and external.

    Decision-making theory asserts that although occupational choice is an ongoing process, there are times when a key decision must be made. In the Gelatt Model the **predictive system** is concerned with the probable alternatives, actions, and possibilities. The person's **value system** is concerned with one's relative preferences regarding the outcomes, while the **decision system** provides rules and criteria for evaluating the outcome.    **(a)**

557. In the Gelatt Model the predictive system deals with

    a.    personal likes, dislikes, and preferences.
    b.    personal rules.
    c.    alternatives and the probability of outcomes.
    d.    the Self-Directed Search.

Choice "a" would be the value system while choice "b" refers to the decision system. Prediction focuses on the probability of an outcome. Choice "d," abbreviated SDS, is a self-administered, self-scored interest inventory based on John Holland's theoretical notions.    **(c)**

558. Linda Gottfredson's developmental theory of career focuses on

    a.    fields and levels.
    b.    circumscription and compromise theory.
    c.    the career rainbow.
    d.    on the concept of career maturity, mainly.

Choice "a" is associated with Anne Roe, choice "c" with Donald Super, and choice "d" with John O. Crites, leaving "b" as the only valid choice. You won't find tons of information on this theory yet, and thus I wouldn't expect more than a question or so related to this modality. According to Gottfredson people do restrict choices (circumscription) and when people do compromise in regard to picking a job (and indeed she feels they do) they will often sacrifice the field of work before they sacrifice sex-typed behavior or prestige.    **(b)**

559. The most effective method adults use to find jobs in the United States is

    a.    to see a state employment counselor for job leads.
    b.    to visit a private practice career counselor for job leads.
    c.    surfing the Web to find job leads.
    d.    securing information via ads in the newspaper.

Surprisingly, according to a 2015 report by the Bureau for Labor Statistics, newspaper ads were still number one. What about the Internet? Well, career experts still aren't sure! **Some research indicates that only 15% of the population has found a job from job boards. Some exams are calling the process of finding a job on the Internet "job-netting." This is the type of question that could change rapidly. I suggest you do your own research prior to taking the exam.**    **(d)**

560. When career counselors speak of the *OOH* they are referring to the

     a.    *Occupational Options Handbook.*
     b.    *Occupational Outlook Handbook.*
     c.    *Career Options Occupational Titles.*
     d.    *Optional Occupations Handbook.*

The *OOH* was originally published by the U.S. Department of Labor in 1949 to aid World War II veterans. The original edition sold for just $1.75 and sold 40,000 copies. The *Occupational Outlook Handbook* is revised every two years and highlights the salient factors of the job, necessary training, earnings, and even advancement opportunities. It also discusses job prospects for the future. Since 1994, information in the *OOH* can also be accessed online and the web page gets about seven million monthly hits! Check it out at www.bls.gov./ooh/ by the Bureau of Labor Statistics (BLS) of the U.S. Department of Labor. Today, the *OOH* is the top career-information source in the country.    **(b)**

561. At its zenith the *DOT* listed

     a.    approximately 10,000 job titles.
     b.    nearly 5,000 job titles.
     c.    approximately 20,000 job titles.
     d.    nearly 100,000 job titles.

This is the largest, most comprehensive source and it was used more than any other printed resource in the field. As with the *OOH* you can thank the U.S. Department of Labor, which began publishing the *DOT* (*Dictionary of Occupational Titles*) in 1938. The *DOT* was similar to the *DSM* (*Diagnostic and Statistical Manual*). While the *DSM* provides a classification system for mental health workers, the *DOT* ... 13 years earlier, I might add ... provided a system a classification system for career counselors. **The Occupational Information Network O\*NET (www. online.onecenter.org) became a virtual replacement for the *DOT* in 1991. The new O\*NET lists far fewer occupations than the old *DOT*. Many highly specialized**

**jobs that only a small number of individuals worked as were dropped.** Since O*NET is an online program it will have the advantage of being easier and quicker to update. There are current books using *DOT* in the title; however, at this point in time these works *do not* appear to be published by the U.S. Department of Labor. **(c)**

562. In the *Dictionary of Occupational Titles* each job was given a _____ digit code.

   a.  nine
   b.  eight
   c.  six
   d.  five

The first three digits designated the occupational category and divisions, whereas the middle three described tasks in relation to data, people, and things respectively. The final digits helped alphabetize the titles. **(a)**

563. The *DOT* was first published by the U.S. Department of Labor in 1938. The first three digits in a *DOT* code referred to

   a.  an occupational group.
   b.  career options.
   c.  *OOH* data.
   d.  the transfer of skills.

The first digit in the *DOT* designated one of nine occupational categories: 0/1 professional, technical, and managerial careers; 2 clerical and sales careers; 3 service careers; 4 agricultural, fishery, forestry, and related Careers; 5 processing careers; 6 machine trade careers; 7 bench work careers; 8 structural work careers; and 9 miscellaneous. Thus, in the code for counselor (045.107-010) the first digit (0) is from the professional, technical, and managerial occupations category. The second digit (4) refers to occupations in life sciences; while the third digit defines the occupational group. In this case, 045 is "occupations in psychology." The final three digits alphabetize titles designated by the first six-digit code groups. Choices "b" and "d" would require information from the middle three digits of the code. **(a)**

564. You are working as a counselor for a major university. A student wants detailed statistics about the average wages in her state. The best resource would be

    a.  Richard N. Bolles's *What Color Is Your Parachute?*
    b.  the Bureau of Labor Statistics website.
    c.  any professional journal related to career counseling is inundated with articles of this nature.
    d.  *Choices* and the System of Interactive Guidance and Information known as SIGI.

    Choice "a" depicts the bestselling job hunting book of all time while choice "d" mentions two of the most popular computer-assisted career guidance programs. *Choices* is a software program for high school students that provides information to help them make informed decisions about career and transition planning. A middle school edition, *Choices Explorer*, is also available. SIGI 3 is a self-assessment software and web-based program that helps college students and adults pick a major and a career based on their own values, interests, and education. SIGI allows users to compare job choices and fine tune decisions. If you go to the Bureau of Labor Statistics website (the correct answer) at www.stats.bls.gov you will truly be amazed at the amount of career data you can find. **(b)**

565. A counselor who is interested in trends in the job market should consult the

    a.  State Department of Economic Regulation or the Department of Insurance, Financial Institutions, and Professional Regulations.
    b.  *SOC*.
    c.  *SIC*.
    d.  *OOH*.

Choice "a" is the state department that often handles counselor licensing. The other division that might handle mental health licensing would be the board of healing arts. Remember that licenses are conferred by each state and *not* the federal government. Next, let's look at choices "b" and "c," which are incorrect in terms of this answer yet excellent resources for the adept career counselor. The *SOC* (choice "b") is the *Standard Occupational Classification Manual*, which codes job clusters (e.g., teachers, librarians, and counselors) via similar worker function. Thus, it is very useful for a counselor who wants to find additional occupations that a worker might already be trained for or could consider with additional training. Federal agencies use *SOC* to collect, classify, and report data. You can scope it out at www.bls.gov/soc/. The *SIC* (choice "c"), the *Standard Industrial Classification Manual*, classified businesses in regard to the type of activity they are engaged in (i.e., the type of service or product). "Hopefully, working in industry won't make you sic" is a rather pessimistic, yet useful memory device here! Industry growth was often computed on *SIC* codes, but it was last revised in 1987 due to criticism. The replacement system is the *National Industry Classification System* (*NAICS*). The *OOH*, as its name implies, focuses on "outlook" and useful trends or predictions (hence the word *Outlook* in the title) in the labor market.                                                          **(d)**

566. Gender issues impact career counseling such as career segregation. Men are overrepresented in _____ positions while women often have _____ .

    a.  nursing; physician's positions
    b.  pink-collar; executive positions
    c.  CEO; positions as financial advisors
    d.  labor and executive positions; pink-collar jobs

The gender career gap might be getting a tad more narrow, but it is by no means closed! As an example, over 90% of nurses are women, while only 34% are physicians. The U.S. service economy is often classified as white collar (professional and administrative); blue collar (skilled manual labor); and pink collar (jobs dominated by women such as waitressing, secretary, child-care worker, K- middle school teacher, or beautician). Some point their finger at the fact that the service economy has helped spawn the feminization of poverty since some, but certainly not all, pink-collar jobs pay less. Females dominate the counseling and social work professions with the percentages running at about 70% and 80% respectively. **(d)**

567. A counselor with a master's degree who is working for minimum wage at a fast-food restaurant due to a lack of jobs in the field is a victim of

    a.    unemployment.
    b.    underemployment.
    c.    the phi phenomenon.
    d.    the risky shift phenomenon.

Underemployment occurs when a worker is engaged in a position which is below his or her skill level. This phenomenon can occur when an abundance of educated people floods a labor market which does not have enough jobs that require a high level of training. Hence, as more people go to college the rate of underemployment is expected to increase. **(b)**

568. According to the *OOH*, the highest-paying profession would be

    a.    a social worker.
    b.    a counselor.
    c.    a psychiatrist.
    d.    an I/O psychologist.

You might need to guess if confronted with a question of this ilk on the exam. I mean come on now … you can't commit to memory every statistic imaginable. So how would you make an educated guess? Simple, psychiatrist is the only helper with a medical school education and nearly all the top-paying jobs listed on the *OOH* are types of physicians such as surgeons or internists. The current *OOH* lists a psychiatrist's salary at approximately $173,000, while the median figure for a master's level counselor is $50,000. But money can't buy happiness. Physicians now have the highest suicide rate of any profession with dentists running a close second. In the general population males commit suicide about four times as much as females, but across physicians the number is roughly the same. It is noteworthy that industrial organizational psychologists (choice "d") was rated as the fastest growing. **(c)**

569. In a lifetime the average person has

    a.  10 to 15 jobs.
    b.  two jobs.
    c.  a single job and stays with it for his or her entire career.
    d.  about five jobs.

The actual figure is a hairline over 11 for men or women. Different sources often sport slightly different figures. Advocates of the constructivist approaches such as Savickas point to this as a sign that the old trait factor or matching where a career prescription is proposed is outdated. **(a)**

570. Self-efficacy theory is based on the work of

    a.  Anne Roe.
    b.  John Holland.
    c.  H. B. Gelatt.
    d.  Albert Bandura.

Bandura proposed that one's belief or expectation of being successful in an occupation causes the individual to gravitate toward that particular occupation. Bandura felt that "chance factors," such as accidentally being exposed to certain situations, influence career development. **(d)**

571. The System of Interactive Guidance and Information (SIGI) and *Choices* are

    a.  computer-assisted career guidance systems (CACG).
    b.  paper and pencil career tests.

c.    career theories proposed in the 1940s.

d.    computer systems which are slower to use than traditional texts such as the *DOT* or the *OOH*.

**Note: Your exam could use computer-based career information systems (CBCISs) in place of CACG.** Choice "d" is obviously incorrect since computer programs often speed up information retrieval. Just a reminder: Although web-based and online career counseling is a growing trend it is not as effective as the traditional face-to-face model.    **(a)**

572.    A client who likes her flower-arranging job begins doing flower arranging in her spare time on weekends and after work. This phenomenon is best described as

a.    the contrast effect.

b.    sublimation.

c.    the compensatory effect.

d.    spillover.

Let me introduce you to three key terms in the field of career counseling: the contrast effect (choice "a"), the compensatory effect (choice "c"), and spillover (choice "d"). In psychology, *contrast* refers to a heightened sense of awareness regarding the difference between the successive juxtapositions of two stimuli. The word *juxtaposition* simply means to put side by side. Hence, in career placement settings the term has been used to suggest that an interviewer's impression of an interviewee is often affected by previous interviewees. Thus, a typical applicant would look more impressive if she is interviewed after a string of applicants who are ill qualified for the job. Unfortunately, the converse is also true. An average applicant whose interview comes after several highly qualified (or overqualified) applicants will not be judged as favorably by the person who is doing the interviewing. The **compensatory effect** suggests that a worker compensates or makes up for things he or she can't do on the job. Thus, a librarian who must be quiet from 8.00 to 5.00 may go out after work and get wild, crazy, and most importantly **loud**. Work can also help folks compensate for things missing in one's family life. When work and family are kept separate the term **segmentation** can be utilized. **Spillover**, on the other hand, is like a glass of water spilling over onto the table. Here, the individual's work spills over, if you will, into his or her time off the job. When spillover takes place the person can talk about work with other family or household members and engages in activities similar to work during periods of leisure. The aforementioned florist or an engineer who is building a satellite in his or her basement would be a victim of spillover. The connection between family and work is known as **work interface**. This question clearly shows why it is imperative for career counselors to have adept family therapy skills.    **(d)**

573. A male client who hates his job is trying desperately to be the perfect father, husband, and family man. This phenomenon is best described as

   a.   the recency effect.
   b.   the leniency/strictness bias.
   c.   the compensatory effect.
   d.   spillover.

In some instances, textbooks and exams will refer to the compensatory effect in a psychodynamic fashion, which infers that an individual might tend to compensate for poor job satisfaction by excelling in his or her activities outside of work. My advice: although the definition given in the previous question is the most common, you should read questions of this ilk very carefully to ascertain the context in which the term *compensatory effect* is being used. Choices "a" and "b" are terms utilized to describe subjective biases of individuals who rate employee performance. The **recency effect** occurs when a rater's judgment of an employee reflects primarily his or her most recent performance. This is, of course, undesirable inasmuch as the employee's performance over the entire rating period should be duly noted. The term was borrowed from memory experiments in psychology demonstrating that numbers toward the end of a list are more likely to be recalled than those in the middle. The **leniency/strictness bias** occurs when a rater tends to give employees very high/lenient or very low/strict ratings while avoiding the middle or so-called average range. Raters who do the opposite (i.e., rate almost everybody in the average range) are said to display a **central tendency bias**.               **(c)**

574. The National Vocational Guidance Association was founded in 1913. It was fused with other organizations in 1952 to become the

    a.   APA.
    b.   AACD.
    c.   APGA.
    d.   NASW.

Did you choose "b"? If so, give yourself a pat on the back for an A answer. You see, AACD was actually the American Personnel and Guidance Association (APGA) until 1983, making choice "c" an even better response—say an A+. In 1983 APGA changed its name to AACD (American Association for Counseling and Development), which was changed in 1992 to ACA (American Counseling Association).               **(c)**

575. Lifestyle includes

    a.   work.
    b.   leisure.
    c.   style of living.
    d.   all of the above.

*Lifestyle* is a broad term which describes the overall balance of work, leisure, family, and social activities. Some exams will use the term *avocational* in place of the term *leisure*.               **(d)**

576. The Strong Interest Inventory (SCII) is based on John Holland's theory. The test assumes that a person who is interested in a given subject will experience

    a.   satisfaction in a job with workers who have different interests.

b.     satisfaction in a job with workers who have similar interests.
c.     generalized anxiety if he or she is placed in a job where people have similar interests.
d.     the best results if he or she finishes the inventory in one hour or less.

The interest inventory first appeared on the scene in 1927 when E. K. Strong, Jr., developed the *Strong Vocational Interest Blank* (SVIB) for men. The test indicated how an examinee's likes and dislikes were similar to the likes and dislikes of workers in various occupations. Later, in 1933, women's occupations were examined in the same manner using the SVIB for women. Strong died in 1963, and in 1974 the inventory was expanded by David P. Campbell. The inventory has been the subject of over 1,700 papers and studies. Recent efforts have focused on eliminating sex bias from the instrument. The test, which consists of 291 items and takes 30–45 minutes, is based on John Holland's typology (discussed earlier), and is untimed (in other words choice "d" is incorrect). The examinee responds to questions using a forced choice format of "strongly like" "like," "indifferent," or "dislike" or "strongly dislike" to each item. (Each occupational scale for the inventory was created by examining 200–300 happily employed men and women in an occupation.) It takes most adults about 30 minutes to finish the inventory. The inventory is suited to high school, college, and adult populations and must be computer scored. **Keep in mind that the SII measures interests, not abilities.**                                   **(b)**

577. The Self-Directed Search (SDS) is

a.     based on the work of Holland and yields scores on his six types.
b.     self-administered.
c.     self-scored and self-interpreted.
d.     all of the above.

John Holland introduced the SDS in 1970 to help those who did not have access (or could not afford) professional career counseling. The test takes about 20 minutes and is suitable for ages 15 and older. The measure provides a three-letter code (such as EIR or ISC) to describe the individual's career personality type. Holland warned that the test is **not suitable for grossly disturbed, uneducated, or illiterate persons, although an easy form (known as Form "E") is available for those with limited reading skills or those who lack a high school education. Form "E" is shorter than the regular SDS and uses no words beyond the fourth-grade level. The SDS is specifically not recommended for those who have a great deal of difficulty making decisions.** **(d)**

578. At a case staffing, one career counselor says to another, "The client's disability suggests she can only physically handle sedentary work." This technically implies

   a.   the client will not need to lift over 10 pounds.
   b.   the client will not need to lift over 100 pounds.
   c.   the client will be standing a lot.
   d.   the client could walk or stand up to six hours daily.

   **Sedentary:** maximum lifting is 10 pounds. **Light work:** maximum lifting is up to 20 pounds. **Medium work:** maximum lifting is 50 pounds. **Heavy work:** maximum lifting is up to 100 pounds. **Very heavy work:** maximum lifts exceed 100 pounds. The stipulation in choice "d" applies to the "light work" category. **(a)**

579. The notion of the hidden job market would suggest that

   a.   most jobs will appear on college bulletin boards.
   b.   most jobs will appear in supermarket tabloids.
   c.   most jobs will appear in daily newspaper classified ads.
   d.   most jobs are not advertised.

   Perhaps you are shocked, but experts insist it is true! A high percentage of jobs (over 76%!) are **not advertised and that is why networking is so important**. Experts also praise networking as an effective tool for finding **gay-friendly employers**. **(d)**

580. The SDS (available online or in print) score will reveal

    a.    career aptitude.
    b.    the personality via projective measures.
    c.    the individual's three highest scores based on Holland's personality types.
    d.    spillover personality tendencies.

Just for review: The SDS provides the user with a three-letter code that indicates the three personality types the examinee most resembles. A Spanish version is available. An occupational finder describes numerous occupations in order to ascertain which occupations best match the personality type. A special occupational finder is available to investigate careers and occupations for the military and veterans.    **(c)**

581. As you walk into a professional seminar on career counseling you note that the instructor is drawing a hexagon on the blackboard. The instructor is most likely discussing

    a.    David Tiedeman.
    b.    John Holland.
    c.    Anne Roe.
    d.    John Crites.

Was this just an easy question, or could it be that now you really know this material? Come on, how about giving yourself credit for all your knowledge! (See the Graphical Representations section of this book for a pictorial display of the hexagon.)    **(b)**

582. The Kuder Career Planning System (KCPS) would be appropriate for

    a.    K-12, postsecondary, and even adults.
    b.    children who have not completed the sixth grade.
    c.    kids who have taken the Peabody Picture Vocabulary Test (PPVT).
    d.    high school students.

KCPS offers career planning and online education for virtually any age bracket. The Kuder Galaxy program is for elementary students, the Kuder Navigator targets secondary students, while the Kuder Journey rounds out the choices by providing information to the postsecondary and adult population. The PPVT-4 noted in choice "c" is a measure of hearing or receptive vocabulary and a screening test of verbal ability that can be used for kids under 3 years to those over 90 and it takes 15 minutes or less. The PPVT requires no reading skills. **(a)**

583. Some exams will split hairs and distinguish a dual-earner household from a dual-career household or family. All the statements below are false *except:*

    a.  Dual-earner families have a better chance for advancement than dual-career families.
    b.  Dual-earner families are more likely to have managerial or administrative jobs than dual-career families.
    c.  Dual-career families earn more than dual-earner families.
    d.  Dual-career families have less competition.

    Generally speaking, the dual-career family has a job where advancement is possible versus the dual-earner family which is characterized by job positions where moving up the line is not possible or at best minimal. Statistically, dual-wage earning couples are now the norm. Authors have humorously called single-income families an endangered species! **(c)**

584. Occupational aptitude tests such as the Differential Aptitude Test (DAT), the Armed Services Vocational Aptitude Test Battery (ASVAB), and the O*NET Ability Profiler grew out of the

    a.  cognitive therapy movement.
    b.  humanistic psychology movement.
    c.  individual psychology movement.
    d.  trait-and-factor movement related to career counseling.

    The primary purpose of any aptitude test is to predict future performance, though career placement should never rest solely on a single source of data such as the aforementioned tests. **Must-know fact: An aptitude test does not imply that you are adept at the skill (say math, music, or principles taught in law school) at the present moment. That, my dear reader, is the province of an achievement test. The aptitude test merely speculates about whether or not you could capture these skills with proper training and experience. Aptitude tests attempt to measure potential.** **(d)**

585. A client says she has always stayed home and raised her children. Now the children are grown and she is seeking employment. She is best described

    a.   as a displaced homemaker.
    b.   as a victim of underemployment.
    c.   by conducting a job analysis.
    d.   as a victim of the hidden job market.

This is the definition of a displaced homemaker who also could be divorced or widowed. Just a reminder that gender bias (i.e., any factor that might rule out a job or career choice due to gender) must be avoided when conducting career counseling with women. **Tough terminology: Note job analysis in choice "c." This refers to a procedure where tasks, duties, skills, required education, safety issues, and other data are examined.**

**A job evaluation rates the value of the job within the organization to decide what it should pay. It does not rate the person performing the job in question! A job analysis leads to a job description or what can be known as job specifications.** **(a)**

586. According to the concept of sex-wage or gender-wage discrimination

    a.   women make more than men for doing the same job.
    b.   women make less than men for doing the same job.

    c.    men and women make identical salaries thanks to legislation.

    d.    women who are seen as attractive still make 6% more than men for doing the same job.

Although in a fair world choice "c" would be true, choice "b" still depicts reality.                                                   **(b)**

587.  According to the concept of occupational sex segregation

    a.    most women hold high-paying executive jobs.
    b.    most women hold low-paying jobs with low status.
    c.    most women hold jobs which require a college degree.
    d.    men still make considerably less than women.

The concept of "occupational sex segregation" suggests that female occupations generally pay less and lack the status of male occupations.                                                 **(b)**

588.  A counselor advises a female to steer clear of police work as he feels this is a male occupation. This suggests

    a.    positive transference.
    b.    negative transference.
    c.    counselor bias based on gender bias.
    d.    sex-wage discrimination.

But wait, don't jump to conclusions here. It's not just male counselors who are the culprit here! Not by a long shot. Research indicates that female counselors urge females to seek out traditionally feminine occupations, and worse yet some tests and inventories used in the area of career counseling are guilty of gender bias!                                                 **(c)**

589.  Most research would suggest that a woman who has the same intelligence, skills, and potential as a man will often

    a.    make the same job choice as a man.
    b.    choose a supervisory position more often than a man.

c.    have lower career aspirations than a man.

d.    choose a career well above her ability level.

Louise Fitzgerald and John Crites discovered that even when girls manifest higher career maturity than boys, their aspirations are lower.    **(c)**

590.  A displaced homemaker might have grown children or

a.    be widowed and seeking employment.

b.    be divorced and seeking employment.

c.    a and b.

d.    none of the above.

See question 585. The high divorce rate and the declining birth rate have increased the number of women seeking employment in recent years. Another related exam term is **dislocated worker**. It refers to an individual who loses his or her job because a company downsizes or relocates. It can also refer to a person who has an obsolete set of job skills.    **(c)**

591.  Midlife career change

a.    is not that unusual.

b.    is often discussed, but in reality is very rare.

c.    would be extremely rare after the death of a spouse.

d.    would be extremely rare after all the children leave home.

This generally takes place between ages 35 and 45 and additional training is often needed. Precipitating factors for the change include divorce, having a baby, caring for a disabled child, empty nest syndrome, and perhaps most important, job dissatisfaction. Choices "c" and "d" are typical motivators and thus constitute incorrect answer choices.    **(a)**

592.  The term *reentry woman* would best describe

a.    a 32-year-old female police officer promoted to sergeant.

b.   a 22-year-old female teacher who becomes a school counselor.
c.   a 59-year-old female administrative assistant who switched positions for two years and will return to her job.
d.   a 29-year-old female who was babysitting in her home but is currently working at a fast-food restaurant.

The term *reentry women* refers to women who go from working within the home to working outside the home. Counselors need to be aware of the fact that reentry women typically experience an extremely high degree of career indecision. **My prediction: In the coming years expect to see more and more questions on the career area of comprehensive and licensing exams related to women, older adults, minority groups, and persons with disabilities**.                    **(d)**

593. A counselor doing multicultural career counseling should be aware

a.   of his or her own ethnocentric biases.
b.   that Asian Americans rarely choose scientific careers.
c.   that African American males will often choose enterprising jobs in terms of Holland's typology.
d.   that career inventories have eliminated cultural biases.

Actually, Asian Americans (see choice "b") are the only minority that has a large number of individuals in the scientific community. African American males are highly represented in realistic rather than enterprising occupations (see choice "c"). Thus the counselor has to be aware of his or her own stereotypical attitudes (e.g., African American women make good housekeepers or Latino women are best off working in secretarial jobs).        **(a)**

594. In terms of the labor market

a.   music is very effective in increasing the workers' output.
b.   the number of employees that employers want to hire goes down as salary goes up.

c. the number of employees willing to work for an employer goes up as the salary increases.
d. b and c.

Choice "a" is false. Music is generally ineffective in terms of significantly boosting a worker's level of production. The lack of effectiveness is thought to be the result of "habituation." Habituation—which will be referred to as "adaptation" on some exams—indicates a decrease in response to a constant stimulus or a stimulus that is repeated too frequently. Thus, as the music becomes a familiar stimulus, the employees will not really notice it, and its positive effects are minimal. Career counselors often refer to the phenomenon described in choices "b" and "c" as the "supply and demand curve," a concept borrowed from economics. **(d)**

595. The career anchor theory was espoused by

a. Roe.
b. Tiedman and Ohara.
c. Schein.
d. Super and Savickas.

Choice "b" Tiedman and Ohara proposed a decision-making developmental theory based on Erikson's psychosocial stages. Every decision is characterized by anticipation and implementation. **(c)**

596. A career counselor who is helping a client design a resume

a. should downplay the value of the cover letter.
b. should emphasize that a lengthy resume is invariably more effective.
c. should emphasize the importance of listing height and weight data.
d. should emphasize the importance of a cover letter.

Choices "a," "b," and "c" all would be considered counter-productive. The resume should always be accompanied by a cover letter. Many personnel workers will not read a resume which is received without a cover letter. The letter should be brief (i.e., generally about three short paragraphs) and ideally the paper and type should match the resume and be of excellent quality. Counselors routinely recommend the bestselling job hunting book of all time *What Color Is Your Parachute?* by Richard Bolles, to clients who are seeking employment or a change in employment.                                                    **(d)**

597. The in-basket technique would be best

    a.   when you are on a hiring committee and assessing candidates for a managerial position.

    b.   when you are counseling an elementary school child in regard to future job choices and careers.

    c.   when you are counseling a senior in high school who is unsure whether to go to college.

    d.   when you are counseling a senior in college who is contemplating graduate school.

The in-basket technique is a job simulation in which the job candidate is given a basket (or package of materials) including memos, e-mails, phone messages, requests for presentations, data reports, and, yes, even complaints, that a manager would typically encounter after being off work for a period of time. The person making the hiring decision then monitors how the candidate makes decisions, prioritizes, pays attention to detail, delegates, and responds to the correspondence. This technique is very popular with formal assessment centers and the job applicant is generally expected to communicate why he or she is choosing the various responses. The strategy is also recommended for trainees.

**Should a hiring committee put much stock in reference letters?** The short answer appears to be: not really! First, how many people do you know who use reference letters that are negative? Probably about the same number of folks you can list who have won the lottery at least five times: None. In addition, providers of reference letters don't want applicants to be angry at them or worse yet, have the job seeker contact their favorite lawyer on the highway billboard ad to file a defamation suit.   **(a)**

598. The concept of job clubs as promoted by Azrin et al.

   a.   is very behavioristic.
   b.   is indicative of a client-centered approach.
   c.   is psychodynamic.
   d.   is appropriate, but not with disabled populations.

   **Choice "b" is roughly the opposite of the so-called selective placement philosophy.** In the client-centered approach to career counseling the counselor lets the client find his or her own leads and job contacts. A counselor who believes in the "selective placement" philosophy may give the client job leads and may take an active stance in terms of working with the client. The selective approach is preferable with clients who lack the concrete skills necessary to land a job. The job-finding club is an example of a behavioristic group strategy in that the clients share job leads and work on actual skills (e.g., interviewing) which are necessary in order to secure work. Job clubs are highly recommended for the disabled.   **(a)**

599. Which counselor would most likely say that we choose a job to meet our needs?

   a.   Albert Ellis.
   b.   John O. Crites.
   c.   John Krumboltz.
   d.   Robert Hoppock.

   Crites (choice "b") is well-known for his Career Maturity Inventory (CMI) that measures attitudes and competencies related to the career choice process. Hoppock, the correct theorist here, feels that to make an accurate career decision you must know your personal needs and then find an occupation that meets a high percentage of the needs. Lastly, as your personal needs change you might need to secure a different occupation.   **(d)**

600. All of the following are difficulties with career testing *except:*

    a.   Stereotyping.
    b.   The tests all take at least three hours to administer.
    c.   The counselor may rely too heavily on test results.
    d.   Many tests are biased in favor of white middle-class clients.

Most instruments take less than an hour to complete.    **(b)**

# 8

## Assessment and Testing

*The IQ is an intelligent test.*
　　　　—David Wechsler, creator of the Wechsler intelligence tests

601. Appraisal can be defined as

    a.　the process of assessing or estimating attributes.
    b.　testing which is always performed in a group setting.
    c.　testing which is always performed on a single individual.
    d.　a pencil and paper measurement of assessing attributes.

*Appraisal* is a broad term which includes more than merely "testing clients." Appraisal could include a survey, observations, or even clinical interviews. Choices "b," "c," and "d" are thus too limited. A test is simply an instrument which measures a given sample of behavior. When we use the term *measure* it merely connotes that a number or score has been assigned to the person's attribute or performance. On your exam an appraisal could be billed as an assessment or an evaluation. Psychometrics is the study of psychological measurement and thus a helper who primarily administers and interprets tests often has the job title of psychometrician. **An effective counselor will always inform clients about the limitations of any test that he or she administers. Some evidence indicates that neophyte counselors are sometimes tempted to administer tests merely to boost their credibility. I think it is safe to say this is not a desirable practice.**                                    **(a)**

602. A test can be defined as a systematic method of measuring a sample of behavior. Test format refers to the manner in which test items are presented. The format of an essay test is considered a(n) _____ format.

    a.    subjective
    b.    objective
    c.    very precise
    d.    concise

A "subjective" paradigm relies mainly on the scorer's opinion. If the rater knows the test taker's attributes, the rater's "personal bias" can significantly impact upon the rating. For example, an attractive examinee might be given a higher rating. (This is the so-called halo effect.) In job settings, peers generally rate their colleagues higher than do their supervisors. In an "objective" test (choice "b") the rater's judgment plays little or no part in the scoring process.                                    **(a)**

603. The National Counselor Exam (NCE) is a(n) _____ test because the scoring procedure is specific.

    a.    subjective
    b.    objective
    c.    projective
    d.    subtest

Since the NCE uses an a, b, c, d alternative format the rater's "subjective" feelings and thoughts would not be an issue. Ditto for the CPCE.                                    **(b)**

604. A short answer test is a(n) _____ test.

    a.   objective
    b.   culture-free
    c.   forced choice
    d.   free choice

Some exams will call this a "free response" format. In any case, the salient point is that the person taking the test can respond in any manner he or she chooses. Although free choice response patterns can yield more information, they often take more time to score and increase subjectivity (i.e., there is more than one correct answer). **I should mention that although testing is often controversial, schools now employ psychoeducational tests more than at any time in history. Recently there has been a strong push against this practice so keep your eyes peeled to see what transpires.** **(d)**

605. The NCE and the CPCE would be examples of a(n) _____ test.

    a.   free choice
    b.   forced choice
    c.   projective
    d.   intelligence

"Forced choice" items are sometimes known as "recognition items." This book is composed of forced choice/recognition items. On some tests this format is used to control for the "social desirability phenomenon" which asserts that the person puts the answer he or she feels is socially acceptable (i.e., the test provides alternatives that are all equal in terms of social desirability). The MMPI-2 (Minnesota Multiphasic Personality Inventory), for example, uses forced choices to create a "lie scale" composed of human frailties we all possess. This scale, therefore, ferrets out those individuals who tried to make themselves look good (i.e., the way they believe they "should" be). **(b)**

606. The _____ index indicates the percentage of individuals who answered each item correctly.

    a.   difficulty
    b.   critical
    c.   intelligence
    d.   personal

The higher the number of people who answer a question correctly, the easier the item is—and vice versa. A 0.5 difficulty index (also called a difficulty value) would suggest that 50% of those tested answered the question correctly, while 50% did not. Most theorists agree that a "good measure" provides a wide range of items that even a poor performer will answer correctly.      **(a)**

607. Short answer tests and projective measures utilize free response items. The NCE and the CPCE uses forced choice or so-called _____ items.

    a.   vague
    b.   subjective
    c.   recognition
    d.   numerical

See the answer to question 605. Recognition items give the examinee two or more alternatives.      **(c)**

608. A true/false test has _____ recognition items.

    a.   similar
    b.   free choice
    c.   dichotomous
    d.   no

"Dichotomy" simply means that you are presented with two opposing choices. This explains why choice "a" is definitely incorrect. When a test gives the person taking the exam three or more forced choices (e.g., the NCE, the CPCE, or this book) then psychometricians call it a "multipoint item." Choice "b" describes a situation in which the examinee can respond in any way he or she chooses. **(c)**

609. A test format could be normative or ipsative. In the normative format

    a.   each item depends on the item before it.
    b.   each item depends on the item after it.
    c.   the client must possess an IQ within the normal range.
    d.   each item is independent of all other items.

**Ipsative measures compare traits within the same individual; they do not compare a person to other persons who took the instrument.** The Kuder Career Planning instruments are often cited as falling into this category. The ipsative measure allows the person being tested to compare items. **(d)**

610. A client who takes a normative test

    a.   cannot legitimately be compared to others who have taken the test.
    b.   can legitimately be compared to others who have taken the test.
    c.   could not have taken an IQ test.
    d.   could not have taken a personality test.

First, forget about choice "a," it's ipsative. Technically, a normative interpretation is one in which the individual's score is evaluated by comparing it to others who took the same test. A percentile rank is an excellent example. Say your client scores 82 on a nationally normed test and this score corresponds to the percentile rank of 60. This tells you that 60% of the individuals who took the test scored 82 or less. If it's still a bit fuzzy don't sweat it! There's more where this one came from in the next section! **(b)**

611. In an ipsative measure the person taking the test must compare items to one another. The result is that

    a.    an ipsative measure cannot be utilized for career guidance.
    b.    you cannot legitimately compare two or more people who have taken an ipsative test.
    c.    an ipsative measure is never a forced choice format.
    d.    an ipsative measure is never reliable.

Since the ipsative measure **does not reveal absolute strengths**, comparing one person's score to another is relatively meaningless. The person is measured in response to his or her own standard of behavior. The ipsative measure points out the highs and lows that exist within a single individual. Hence, when a colleague tells you that Mr. Johnson's anxiety is improving, she has given you an ipsative description. This description, however, would not lend itself to comparing say Mr. Johnson's anxiety to Mrs. McBee's. Choice "c" is a no go since ipsative assessments are generally composed of forced choice items. **The ipsative approach yields a within-person analysis.**                 **(b)**

612. Tests are often classified as speed tests versus power tests. A timed typing test used to hire secretaries would be

    a.    a power test.
    b.    neither a speed test nor a power test.
    c.    a speed test.
    d.    a fine example of an ipsative measure.

In terms of difficulty, a speed test is really intended to be fairly easy. The difficulty is induced by time limitations, not the difficulty of the tasks or the questions themselves. (Try giving your secretary a timed keyboarding test and give him or her three hours to complete it and you'll see what I mean.) **A good timed speed test is purposely set up so that nobody finishes it.** A "power test" (see choice "a") is designed to evaluate the level of mastery *without* a time limit. **A timed test is really a type of speed test, but a high percentage of the test takers**

**complete it and it is usually more difficult and has a time limit (think CPCE or NCE).** **(c)**

613. A counseling test consists of 300 forced response items. The person taking the test can take as long as he or she wants to answer the questions.

    a.  This is most likely a projective measure.
    b.  This is most likely a speed test.
    c.  This is most likely a power test.
    d.  This is most likely an invalid measure.

Like the speed test, it will ideally be designed so that nobody receives a perfect score. Choice "a," projective measure, stands incorrect since the projective tests rely on a "free response" format. **In a power test time is not an issue.** **(c)**

614. An achievement test measures maximum performance or present level of skill. Tests of this nature are also called attainment tests, while a personality test or interest inventory measures

    a.  typical performance.
    b.  minimum performance.
    c.  unconscious traits.
    d.  self-esteem by always relying on a Q-Sort design.

I'm not crazy about the terms *typical* and *minimal performance*, but hey don't blame me, I'm just the messenger of what is often cited in the counseling literature. Interest inventories are popular with career counselors because such measures focus on what the client likes or dislikes. The Strong Interest Inventory (SII) is an excellent example. Choice "d," the Q-Sort, often used to investigate personality traits, involves a procedure in which an individual is given cards with statements and asked to place them in piles of "most like me" to "least like me." Then the subject compiles them to create the "ideal self." The ideal self can then be compared to his or her current self-perception in order to assess self-esteem. **(a)**

615. In a spiral test

    a.   the items get progressively easier.
    b.   the difficulty of the items remains constant.
    c.   the client must answer each question in a specified period of time.
    d.   the items get progressively more difficult.

Just remember that a spiral staircase seems to get more difficult to climb as you walk up higher. **(d)**

616. In a cyclical test

    a.   the items get progressively easier.
    b.   the difficulty of the items remains constant.
    c.   you have several sections which are spiral in nature.
    d.   the client must answer each question in a specified period of time.

In each section the questions would go from easy ones to those which are more difficult. **(c)**

617. A test battery is considered

    a.   a horizontal test.
    b.   a vertical test.
    c.   a valid test.
    d.   a reliable test.

**In a test battery, several measures are used to produce results that could be more accurate than those derived from merely using a single source.** Say, this can get confusing. Remember, that in the section on group processes I talked about vertical and horizontal interventions. In testing, a vertical test would have versions for various age brackets or levels of education (e.g., a math achievement test for preschoolers and a version for middle school children). A horizontal test measures various factors (e.g., math and science) during the same testing procedure. **(a)**

618. In a counseling research study, two groups of subjects took a test with the same name. However, when they talked with each other they discovered that the questions were different. The researcher assured both groups that they were given the same test. How is this possible?

    a.    The researcher is not telling the truth. The groups could not possibly have taken the same test.
    b.    The test was horizontal.
    c.    The test was not a power test.
    d.    The researcher gave parallel forms of the same test.

When a test has two versions or forms that are interchangeable they are termed *parallel forms* or *equivalent forms* of the same test. From a statistical/psychometric standpoint each form must have the same mean, standard error, and other statistical components.    **(d)**

619. The most critical factors in test selection are

    a.    the length of the test and the number of people who took the test in the norming process.
    b.    horizontal versus vertical.
    c.    validity and reliability.
    d.    spiral versus cyclical format.

**Validity refers to whether the test measures what it says it measures while reliability tells how consistent a test measures an attribute.**    **(c)**

620. Which is more important, validity or reliability?

    a.    Reliability.
    b.    They are equally important.
    c.    Validity.
    d.    It depends on the test in question.

**Experts nearly always consider *validity* the number one factor in the construction of a test. A test must measure**

**what it purports to measure.** Reliability, choice "a," is the second most important concern. **A scale, for example, must measure body weight accurately if it is a valid instrument. In order to be reliable, it will need to give repeated readings which are nearly identical for the same person if the person keeps stepping on and off the scale.**          **(c)**

621.  In the field of testing, validity refers to

   a.    whether the test really measures what it purports to measure.
   b.    whether the same test gives consistent measurement.
   c.    the degree of cultural bias in a test.
   d.    the fact that numerous tests measure the same traits.

**To be valid the test must measure what you want it to measure!** Incidentally, a test which is valid for one population is not necessarily valid for another group. **There are five basic types of validity you should familiarize yourself with for your exam:** First, **content validity** or what is sometimes called rational or logical validity. Does the test examine or sample the behavior under scrutiny? An IQ test, for example, that did not sample the entire range of intelligence (say the test just sampled memory and not vocabulary, math, etc.) would have poor content validity. In this case a savant might truly score higher than a well-rounded individual with a gifted level of intelligence. Second, **construct validity**, which refers to a test's ability to measure a theoretical construct like intelligence, self-esteem, artistic talent, mechanical ability, or managerial potential. Third is **concurrent validity**, which deals with how well the test compares to other instruments that are intended for the same purpose. Fourth, **predictive validity**, also known as empirical validity, which reflects the test's ability to predict future behavior according to established criteria. On some exams, concurrent validity and predictive validity are often lumped under the umbrella of "criterion validity," since concurrent validity and predictive validity are actually different types of criterion-related validity. Fifth, a small body of literature speaks of **consequential validity**, which simply tries to ascertain the social implications of using tests.     **(a)**

622. A counselor peruses a testing catalog in search of a test which will repeatedly give consistent results. The counselor

    a.    is interested in reliability.
    b.    is interested in validity.
    c.    is looking for information which is not available.
    d.    is magnifying an unimportant issue.

**Beware:** A test can indeed be reliable yet not valid. A highly reliable test could conceivably prove invalid. A scale that invariably reads 109 lb when you weigh 143 lb would hardly be providing you with a valid assessment of your true weight! The score, nevertheless, is consistent (reliable). **Thus, a test can have a high reliability coefficient but still have a low validity coefficient. Reliability places a ceiling on validity, but validity does not set the limits on reliability.**    **(a)**

623. Which measure would yield the highest level of reliability?

    a.    A TAT, projective test popular with psychodynamic helpers.
    b.    The WAIS-IV, a popular IQ test.
    c.    The MMPI-2, a popular personality test.
    d.    A very accurate postage scale.

In the real world physical measurements are more reliable than psychological ones.    **(d)**

624. Construct validity refers to the extent that a test measures an abstract trait or psychological notion. An example would be

    a.    height.
    b.    weight.
    c.    ego strength.
    d.    the ability to name all men who have served as U.S. presidents.

**Any trait you cannot "directly" measure or observe can be considered a construct.**    **(c)**

625. Face validity refers to the extent that a test

    a.    looks or appears to measure the intended attribute.
    b.    measures a theoretical construct.
    c.    appears to be constructed in an artistic fashion.
    d.    can be compared to job performance.

Okay, so I lied—well, kind of lied on the answer to question 621 when I told you there were five basic types of validity. You see most experts technically no longer list "face validity" as a sixth type of validity. Face validity—like a person's face—merely tells you whether the test looks like it measures the intended trait. Does your therapist look like a therapist? Does the Wechsler appear to be an IQ test? The obvious answer is "In most cases who cares, it's not that important"! And if a therapist looks like a good therapist, does that necessarily mean he is an adept therapist? Of course not. And the same is true of testing.    **(a)**

626. A job test which predicted future performance on a job very well would

    a.    have high criterion/predictive validity.
    b.    have excellent face validity.
    c.    have excellent construct validity.
    d.    not have incremental validity or synthetic validity.

Here you are concerned that the test will measure an independent or external outside "criterion," in this case the "future prediction" of the job performance. (**Note**: Choice "a" would be incorrect on a question such as this if the question specified current job performance. If this were the case then technically only the term *criterion* would apply.) Choice "d" introduces you to the terms *incremental validity* and *synthetic validity*. Although incremental validity and synthetic validity are not considered two of the five or six major types of validity, don't be too surprised if they pop up on an advanced exam question. The term *incremental validity* has been used to describe a number of testing phenomena. First and foremost, incremental validity has been used to describe the process by which a test is refined and becomes more valid as contradictory items are dropped. Incremental validity also refers to a test's ability to improve predictions when compared to existing measures that purport to facilitate selection in business or educational settings. When a test has incremental validity, it provides you with additional valid information that was not attainable via other procedures. Synthetic *validity* is derived from the word *synthesized*. Synthetic validity was popularized by industrial organizational (I/O) psychologists who felt the procedure had merit, especially when utilized for smaller firms who did not hire a large number of workers. In synthetic validity, the helper or researcher looks for tests that have been shown to predict each job element or component (e.g., typing, filing, etc.). Tests that predict each component (criterion) can then be combined to improve the selection process.          **(a)**

627. A new IQ test which yielded results nearly identical to other standardized measures would be said to have

    a.    good concurrent validity.
    b.    good face validity.
    c.    superb internal consistency.
    d.    all of the above.

Criterion validity could be "concurrent" or "predictive." Concurrent validity answers the question of how well your test stacks up against a well-established instrument that measures the same behavior, construct, or trait. Evidence for reliability and validity is expressed via correlation coefficients. Suffice to say that the closer they are to 1.00 the better. You also should be familiar with the terms *convergent* and *discriminant* validity. These terms relate to both criterion validity and construct validity. The relationship or correlation of a test to an independent measure or trait is known as convergent validity. Convergent validity is actually a method used to assess a test's construct/criterion validity by correlating test scores with an outside source. Say, for example, that a measure purports to measure phobic responses. A client, who has a snake phobia, is then exposed to a snake and experiences extreme panic. If the client scores higher on the test than he would in a relaxed state, then this would display convergent validity. The test also should show discriminant validity. This means the test will **not reflect** unrelated variables. Hence, if phobias are unrelated to IQ, then when one correlates clients' IQ scores to their scores on the test for phobias, this should produce a near zero correlation. Similarly, if discriminant validity is evident, a counselor who is genuinely qualified to sit for a state licensing exam should score higher on the exam than a student who flunked an introductory counseling course. When a researcher is engaged in test validation, both convergent and discriminant validity should be thoroughly examined.                                                      **(a)**

628. When a counselor tells a client that the Graduate Record Examination (GRE) will predict her ability to handle graduate work, the counselor is referring to

    a.   good concurrent validity.
    b.   construct validity.
    c.   face validity.
    d.   predictive validity.

The Graduate Record Examination (GRE), the Scholastic Aptitude Test (SAT), the American College Test (ACT), and public opinion polls are effective only if they have high predictive validity, which is the power to accurately describe future behavior or events. Again the subtypes of criterion validity are concurrent and predictive.                                                      **(d)**

629. A reliable test is _____ valid.

    a.   always
    b.   90%
    c.   not always
    d.   80%

**Again shout this one out loud: A reliable test is not always valid.** Reliability, nonetheless, determines the upper level of validity.                                                      **(c)**

630. A valid test is _____ reliable.

    a.    not always
    b.    always
    c.    never
    d.    80%

**A valid test is always reliable.** Choice "b" is correct because a test that measures a given trait well does so repeatedly. Remember that a reliable test, however, is not necessarily always valid. After all, a depression scale that was invalid and really measured anxiety could produce consistent reliable anxiety data.           **(b)**

631. One method of testing reliability is to give the same test to the same group of people two times and then correlate the scores. This is called

    a.    test–retest reliability.
    b.    equivalent forms reliability.
    c.    alternate forms reliability.
    d.    the split-half method.

All right, I've got to hand it to you—you're very perceptive. You've figured out that I'm banking on the fact that your exam will spring a few reliability or validity questions on you. The well-known test–retest method discussed here tests for "stability," which is the ability of a test score to remain stable or fluctuate over time when the client takes the test again. When using the test–retest paradigm the client generally takes the same test after waiting at least seven days. The test–retest procedure is only valid for traits such as IQ which remain stable over time and are not altered by mood, memory, or practice effects.           **(a)**

632. One method of testing reliability is to give the same population alternate forms of the identical test. Each form will have the same psychometric/statistical properties as the original instrument. This is known as

    a.    test–retest reliability.

b.    equivalent or alternate forms reliability.
c.    the split-half method.
d.    internal consistency.

Here a single group of examinees takes parallel forms of a test and a reliability correlation coefficient is figured on the two sets of scores. **Counterbalancing** is necessary when testing reliability in this fashion. That is to say, half of the individuals get parallel form A first and half get form B initially. This controls for variables such as fatigue, practice, and motivation.         **(b)**

633.    A counselor doing research decided to split a standardized test in half by using the even items as one test and the odd items as a second test and then correlating them. The counselor

a.    used an invalid procedure to test reliability.
b.    was testing reliability via the split-half correlation method.
c.    was testing reliability via the equivalent forms method.
d.    was testing reliability via the inter-rater method.

In this situation the individual takes the entire test as a whole and then the test is divided into halves. The correlation between the half scores yields a reliability coefficient. When a researcher does not use even versus odd questions to split the test, he or she may do so using random numbers (merely dividing a test according to first half versus second half could confound the data due to practice and fatigue effects).         **(b)**

634.    Which method of reliability testing would be useful with an essay test but not with a test of algebra problems?

a.    Test–retest.
b.    Alternate forms.
c.    Split-half.
d.    Inter-rater/inter-observer.

Using choice "d," several raters assess the same performance. This method is also called "scorer reliability" and is utilized with subjective tests such as projectives to ascertain whether the scoring criteria are such that two persons who grade or assess the responses will produce roughly the same score.          **(d)**

635. A reliability coefficient of 1.00 indicates

   a.   a lot of variance in the test.
   b.   a score with a high level of error.
   c.   a perfect score which has no error.
   d.   a typical correlation on most psychological and counseling tests.

As stated earlier, this generally occurs only in physical measurement.          **(c)**

636. An excellent psychological or counseling test would have a reliability coefficient of

   a.   50.
   b.   .90.
   c.   1.00.
   d.   −.90.

Ninety percent of the score measured the attribute in question, while 10% of the score is indicative of error.          **(b)**

637. A researcher working with a personality test discovers that the test has a reliability coefficient of .70 which is somewhat typical. This indicates that

   a.   70% of the score is accurate while 30% is inaccurate.
   b.   30% of the people who are tested will receive accurate scores.
   c.   70% of the people who are tested will receive accurate scores.
   d.   30% of the score is accurate while 70% is inaccurate.

Seventy percent of the obtained score on the test represented the true score on the personality attribute, while 30% of the obtained score could be accounted for by error. Seventy percent is true variance while 30% constitutes error variance.          **(a)**

638. A career counselor is using a test for job selection purposes. An acceptable reliability coefficient would be _____ or higher.

    a.   .20
    b.   .55
    c.   .80
    d.   .70

This is a tricky question. Although .70 is generally acceptable for most psychological attributes, for admissions for jobs, schools, and so on, it should be at least .80 and some experts will not settle for less than .90. **(c)**

639. The same test is given to the same group of people using the test–retest reliability method. The correlation between the first and second administration is .70. The true variance (i.e., the percentage of shared variance or the level of the same thing measured in both) is

    a.   70%.
    b.   100%.
    c.   50%.
    d.   49%.

Here's the key to simplifying a question such as this. To demonstrate the variance of one factor accounted for by another you merely square the correlation (i.e., reliability coefficient). So .70 × .70 = .49 and .49 × 100 = 49%. Your exam could refer to this principle as the **coefficient of determination**. **(d)**

640. IQ means

    a.   a query of intelligence.
    b.   indication of intelligence.
    c.   intelligence quotient.
    d.   intelligence questions for test construction.

A quotient is the result when you perform division. The early ratio formula for the Binet IQ score was MA/CA (i.e., mental age divided by your chronological age) × 100. The score indicated how you compared to those in your age group. Memory device: An MA is a high degree so put it on top of the equation as the numerator. **IQ testing has been the center of more heated debates among experts than any other type of testing.**   **(c)**

641. _____ did research and concluded that intelligence was normally distributed like height or weight and that it was primarily genetic.

   a.   Spearman
   b.   Guilford
   c.   Williamson
   d.   Galton

Francis Galton felt intelligence was a single or so-called unitary factor.                                                              **(d)**

642. Francis Galton felt intelligence was

   a.   a unitary faculty.
   b.   best explained via a two factor theory.
   c.   best explained via the person's environment.
   d.   fluid and crystallized in nature.

Sir Francis Galton of England has been recognized as one of the major pioneers in the study of individual differences. A half-cousin of Charles *"Origin of Species"* Darwin, he believed that exceptional mental abilities were genetic and ran in families, and said just that in his 1869 work *Hereditary Genius*. Choice "b" illuminates the position of Charles Spearman, who in 1904 postulated two factors—a general ability G and a specific ability S which were thought to be applicable to any mental task. (Wasn't psychological theory simple in those days?) As for choice "d," it pops up on exams from time to time. Fluid intelligence is flexible (terrific they both begin with an F), culture-free, and adjusts to the situation, while crystallized is rigid and does not change or adapt.                                                              **(a)**

643. J. P. Guilford isolated 120 factors which added up to intelligence. He also is remembered for his

    a.    thoughts on convergent and divergent thinking.
    b.    work on cognitive therapy.
    c.    work on behavior therapy.
    d.    work to create the first standardized IQ test.

Using factor analysis, Guilford determined that there were 120 elements/abilities which added up to intelligence. Two of the dimensions—convergent and divergent thinking—are still popular terms today. Convergent thinking occurs when divergent thoughts and ideas are combined into a singular concept. Divergent thinking is the ability to generate a novel idea. Choice "d" would reflect primarily the work of Alfred Binet and Theodore Simon. **(a)**

644. A counselor is told by his supervisor to measure the internal consistency reliability (i.e., homogeneity) of a test but not to divide the test in halves. The counselor would need to utilize

    a.    the split-half method.
    b.    the test–retest method.
    c.    the Kuder–Richardson coefficients of equivalence.
    d.    cross-validation.

Internal consistency or homogeneity of items also is known as "inter-item consistency." In plain everyday verbiage, the supervisor wants the counselor to find out if each item on the test is measuring the same thing as every other item. Is performance on one item truly related to performance on another? This can be done by using the Kuder–Richardson reliability/item consistency estimates, which are often denoted on exams as the KR-20 or KR-21 formulas. Another statistic, Lee J. Cronbach's alpha coefficient, also has been used in this respect. Choice "a" is incorrect. Yes, the split-half method does investigate internal consistency reliability, but it relies on (as its name implies) splitting the test in halves (e.g., even versus odd scores). Cronbach's alpha and the KR-20 or KR-21 are alternatives to the split-half method. Choice "d," "cross-validation," is another popular term used in this area of study. Cross-validation takes place when a researcher further examines the criterion validity (and in rare instances, the construct validity) of a test by administering the test to a new sample. This procedure is necessary to ensure that the original validity coefficient is applicable to others who will take the exam. This method helps guard against error factors, which are likely to be present if the original sample size is small. **In most cases a cross-validation coefficient is indeed smaller than the initial validity coefficient. This phenomenon is called "shrinkage."** **(c)**

645. The first intelligence test was created by

   a.   David Wechsler.
   b.   J. P. Guilford.
   c.   Francis Galton.
   d.   Alfred Binet and Theodore Simon.

The year was 1904 and the French government appointed a commission to ferret out feeble-minded Parisian children from those who were normal. Alfred Binet led the committee and the rest is history. By 1905, Binet, along with his coworker Theodore Simon, created a 30-question test with school-related items of increased difficulty. Binet used his own daughters as test subjects in order to investigate mental processes and also is cited as one of the pioneers in projective testing based on his work with inkblots. After testing nearly 3,000 children in the United States in 1916, Lewis M. Terman of Stanford University published an American version of the Binet that was translated into English and adapted to American children. And in case you haven't already guessed, the word "Stanford" was added to the name. **(d)**

646. Today, the Stanford–Binet IQ test is

   a.   a nonstandardized measure.
   b.   a standardized measure.
   c.   a projective measure.
   d.   b and c.

The Stanford–Binet is standardized because the scoring and administration procedures are formal and well delineated. Measures which are not standardized (choice "a") lack procedural guidelines for scoring or administration and do not include quantitative information related to "standards" of performance. **(b)**

647. IQ stands for intelligence quotient, which is expressed by

    a.    CA/MA × 100.
    b.    CA/MA × 100.
    c.    MA/CA × 50.
    d.    MA/CA × 100.

The test is Binet's, but the famous formula was created by the German psychologist, William Louis Stern. The formula produced what is known as a "ratio IQ." Today, a "deviation IQ" is utilized which compares the individual to a norm (i.e., the person is compared to others in his or her age group). Thus, the present score indicates "deviation" from the norm. Okay, now just to be sure that you are really picking this up let me say it in a slightly different way: **Although we still use the term *IQ*, the Binet today actually relies on a standard age score (SAS) with a mean of 100 and a standard deviation of 16.** So then you see, the IQ isn't really an IQ after all—right?    **(d)**

648. The Binet stressed age-related tasks. Utilizing this method, a 9-year-old task would be one which

    a.    only a 10-year-old child could answer.
    b.    only an 8-year-old child could answer.
    c.    50% of the 9-year-olds could answer correctly.
    d.    75% of the 9-year-olds could answer correctly.

A 9-year-old task was defined as one in which one half of the 9-year-olds tested could answer successfully.    **(c)**

649. Simon and Binet pioneered the first IQ test around 1905. The test was created to

    a.   assess high school seniors in America.
    b.   assess U.S. military recruits.
    c.   discriminate children without an intellectual disability from children with an intellectual disability.
    d.   measure genius in the college population.

    The Minister of Public Instruction for the Paris schools wanted a test to identify children with an intellectual disability so that they could be taught separately. The assumption was made that intelligence was basically the ability to understand school-related material. In regard to choice "d," some experts believe that the Wechsler is a better test for those who fall in the average range, while the Stanford–Binet is more accurate for assessing extremes of intellect. **Today the terms intellectual disability (ID) and Intellectual Development Disorder (IDD) have replaced the terminology used at the time, which carried negative connotations.**                                                          **(c)**

650. Today the Stanford–Binet is used from age 2 to adulthood. The IQ formula has been replaced by the

    a.   SAS.
    b.   SUDS.
    c.   entropy.
    d.   KR-20 formula.

    Review question 647. SAS stands for "standard age score." Choice "c," *entropy*, is a popular family therapy/systems theory term that means that dysfunctional families are either too open or too closed (i.e., letting too much information in or not enough information in). The healthy family is said to be in a balanced state known as negative entropy.                                   **(a)**

651. Most experts would agree that the Wechsler IQ tests gained popularity, as the Binet

    a.    must be administered in a group.
    b.    favored the geriatric population.
    c.    didn't seem to be the best test for adults.
    d.    was biased toward women.

Choice "a" is incorrect—both the Binet and the Wechsler are individual tests which require specific training beyond that required for a group IQ test. David Wechsler felt the Binet was slanted toward verbal skills and thus he added "performance" skills to ascertain attributes which might have been cultivated in a background which did not stress verbal proficiency. Choice "c" is correct since the Binet was initially created for children.    **(c)**

652. The best IQ test for a 22-year-old single male would be the

    a.    WPPSI-III.
    b.    WAIS-IV.
    c.    WISC-IV.
    d.    any computer-based IQ test.

Choice "a," the WPPSI (Wechsler Preschool and Primary Scale of Intelligence), is suitable for children ages 2 years and 6 months to 7 years and 7 months. Choice "b," the WAIS-IV (Wechsler Adult Intelligence Scale), is intended for ages 16–90 years. Choice "c," the WISC-IV (Wechsler Intelligence Scale for Children), is appropriate for kids ages 6–16 years and 11 months. Choice "d" is indicative of a paper and pencil test that has been modified so that the client can take the test via computer.

**Quick hints for dealing with WAIS-IV questions:**

- **The test is based on neurocognitive research and the Cattell–Horn–Carroll leading theory of human intelligence.**
- **It can be administered and scored online.**
- **The exam takes 60 to 90 minutes to complete.**

- When compared to the previous version of the exam, object assembly and picture arrangement have been dropped.
- Ten subject areas, also called subtests on some exams (with a mean of 10 and a standard deviation of 3) make up four index scores: verbal comprehensive index (VCI), perceptual reasoning index (PRI), working memory index (WMI), and processing speed index (SPI).
- FSIQ merely stands for full scale IQ. FSIQ and indexes sport a mean of 100 with a standard deviation of 15.
- Less emphasis than the previous version on crystallized intelligence.
- Can measure IQ from 40 to 160. Since the Stanford–Binet 5 has a wider range (e.g., it can measure an IQ up to 180) it would be a better instrument than the Wechsler for measuring extremely low IQs or giftedness.    **(b)**

653. The best intelligence test for a sixth-grade girl would be the

   a.   WPPSI-IV.
   b.   WAIS-IV.
   c.   WISC-IV.
   d.   Merrill–Palmer.

The WISC-IV is recommended for children from ages 6–16 years and 11 months. The Merrill–Palmer Scale of Mental Tests is an intelligence test for infants and children below age 7 years. Counselors who have been in the field for an extended period of time might be surprised that **the WAIS-IV and the WISC-IV no longer provide verbal and performance IQ scores. On any test the lowest possible score is known as the "floor" while the "highest possible score" is referred to as the "ceiling."**    **(c)**

654. The best intelligence test for a kindergartner would be the

    a.    WPPSI-IV.
    b.    WAIS-IV.
    c.    WISC-IV.
    d.    Myers–Briggs Type Indicator.

    Since the child most likely would be between 2 years of age and 7 years and 7 months, the WPPSI-IV would be the only possible choice. Choice "d," the MBTI is a personality inventory based on Carl Jung's analytic psychology. The MBTI uses dichotomous types: extraversion versus introversion, sensing versus intuition, thinking versus feeling, and judging versus perceiving. The test results in a four-letter type score such as ISFJ (i.e., introversion, sensing, feeling, judging). (**Note**: Intuition, though it begins with an "I," is coded using an "N" since Introversion begins with an "I.") **Important exam hint: When a test is guided via a theory it is known as a theory-based test or inventory.**                    **(a)**

655. The mean on the Wechsler and the Stanford–Binet Intelligence scales (SB5) is _____ and the standard deviation is _____.

    a.    100; 100
    b.    100; 15 Wechsler, 16 Stanford–Binet
    c.    100; 20
    d.    100; 1

    IQs above 100 are above average and those shy of 100 are below average.                    **(b)**

656. Group IQ tests like the Otis–Lennon, the Lorge–Thorndike, and the California Test of Mental Abilities are popular in school settings. The advantage is that

    a.    group tests are quicker to administer.
    b.    group tests are superior in terms of predicting school performance.
    c.    group tests always have a higher degree of reliability.
    d.    individual IQ tests are not appropriate for school children.

World War I provided the impetus for the group testing movement. Approximately two million men were tested using the Army Alpha for literates and the Army Beta for illiterates and those from other countries. School districts, government, and industry prefer tests which can be administered to many individuals simultaneously. The catch is that group tests are less accurate and have lower reliability.                          **(a)**

657. The group IQ test movement began

    a.   in 1905.
    b.   with the work of Binet.
    c.   with the Army Alpha and Army Beta in World War I.
    d.   with Freudian psychoanalysis and the psychodynamic movement.

Note the word *group*.                          **(c)**

658. In a culture-fair test

    a.   items are known to the subject regardless of his or her culture.
    b.   the test is not standardized.
    c.   culture-free items cannot be utilized.
    d.   African Americans generally score higher than whites.

The culture-fair test attempts to expunge items which would be known only to an individual due to his or her background. **Key exam hint: Ethics now consider it unethical to administer a test to a client from a given population unless that particular test or inventory has been normed on that specific population! As an example, if you gave an African American client a test that had not been normed on African Americans this would be considered a violation of ethics.**                          **(a)**

659. The black versus white IQ controversy was sparked mainly by a 1969 article written by _____.

    a.    John Ertl
    b.    Raymond B. Cattell
    c.    Arthur Jensen
    d.    Robert Williams

Here are four names with which to be familiar. Choice "a," John Ertl, claimed he invented an electronic machine to analyze neural efficiency and take the place of the paper and pencil IQ test. The device relies on a computer, an EEG, a strobe light, and an electrode helmet. The theory is that the faster one processes the perception, the more intelligence he or she has. I might add that thus far, counselors don't seem to be buying the idea! Choice "b," Raymond B. Cattell, is responsible for the fluid (inherited neurological that decreases with age and is not very dependent on culture) and crystallized intelligence (intelligence from experiential, cultural, and educational interaction). Crystallized intelligence is measured by tests that focus on content. Fluid intelligence is tested by what has been called "content-free reasoning" such as a block design or a pictorial analogy problem. Jensen, choice "c" mentioned earlier, sparked tremendous controversy—actually that's putting it mildly— when he suggested in a 1969 *Harvard Educational Review* article ("How Much Can We Boost IQ and Scholastic Performance?") that the closer people are genetically, the more alike their IQ scores. Adopted children, for example, will sport IQs closer to their biological parents than to their adopted ones. Jensen then leveled the charge that whites score 11 to 15 IQ points higher than African Americans (regardless of social class). His theory stated that due to slavery it was possible that African Americans were bred for strength rather than intelligence. He estimated that heredity contributed 80%, while environment influenced 20% of the IQ. Urie Bronfenbrenner, who could be included here if we had a choice "e," claimed that Jensen relied on twin studies with poor internal validity. Other researchers (e.g., Newman, Freeman, and Holzinger; Fehr) felt that genetic influences contributed less than 50% to IQ. In the final choice, the African American psychologist Robert Williams created the Black Intelligence Test of Cultural Homogeneity (BITCH) to demonstrate that African Americans often excelled when given a test laden with questions whose answers would be familiar to members of the African American community. Williams charged that tests like the Binet and the Wechsler were part of "scientific racism." Williams—a victim of the system himself—scored an 82 on an IQ test at age 15 and his counselor suggested bricklaying since he was good with his hands! Williams rejected the advice and went on to put PhD after his name! IQ tests, though controversial to say the least, are, however, excellent predictors of school success in most cases since schools emphasize values that have been heavily influenced by European cultures.

**1979 *Larry P. v. Wilson Riles*, Superintendent of Public Instruction, State of California: The Wechsler and Binet on Trial!** In this now oft-quoted court battle, it was initially ruled that IQ tests were racially biased against African American children who were overly represented in EMR (educable mentally retarded) classes (proper terminology at the time) based on IQ scores.                                        **(c)**

660. The MMPI-2 is

   a.   an IQ test.
   b.   a neurological test.
   c.   a projective personality test.
   d.   a standardized personality test.

The original version of this instrument was created in 1940. The Minnesota Multiphasic Personality Inventory-2, the current version used since 1989, is known as a "self-report" personality inventory. The client can respond with "true," "false," or "cannot say" to 567 questions (10 more than the traditional MMPI, which was the most researched test in history as well as the most useful for assessing emotional disturbance). The "new" MMPI, designated via the 2, is intended to help clinicians diagnose and treat patients. The test is said to have retained the best factors of the MMPI, while updating the test and eliminating sexist wording.

The MMPI-2 is suitable for those over age 18. A sixth-grade reading level is required and testing time varies from 60 to 90 minutes. The test restandardization committee reported that the norming sample for the MMPI-2 is larger and more representative than the old measure. The MMPI offers computer report packages for specialized settings such as college counseling, chronic pain programs, or outpatient mental health centers. Wikipedia calls the MMPI, "the gold standard in personality testing." The MMPI-A is a 478-question version suitable for 14-to-18-year-old adolescents. **My advice: Thumb through a few major testing catalogs before taking the exam. The major testing catalogs are available online.** **(d)**

661. The word *psychometric* means

    a. a form of measurement used by a neurologist.
    b. any form of mental testing.
    c. a mental trait which cannot be measured.
    d. the test relies on a summated or linear rating scale.

Psychometrics literally refers to the branch of counseling or psychology which focuses on testing. Choice "d" is used to describe answer scales in which various values are given to different responses. For example, on a Likert Scale a "strongly agree" might be given a 5, yet an "agree response" might be rated a 4. The clients score is the "sum" of all the items. **(b)**

662. In a projective test the client is shown

    a. something which is highly reinforcing.
    b. something which is highly charged from an emotional standpoint.
    c. a and b.
    d. neutral stimuli.

The idea here is that the client will "project" his or her personality if given an unstructured task. More specifically, there are several acceptable formats for projective tests: First, **Association**—such as "What comes to mind when you look at this inkblot?" Second,

**Completion**—"Complete these sentences with real feelings." Third, **Construction**—such as drawing a person. The theory is that self-report inventories like the MMPI do not reveal hidden unconscious impulses. In order to accomplish this the client is shown vague, ambiguous stimuli such as a picture or an inkblot. Some counselors believe that by using projective measures a client will have more difficulty faking his or her responses and that he or she will be able to expand on answers. It should be noted that examiner bias is common when using projectives and a therapist using projective measures needs more training than one who merely works with self-report tests.    **(d)**

663. The 16 PF reflects the work of

    a.    Raymond B. Cattell.
    b.    Carl Jung.
    c.    James McKeen Cattell.
    d.    Oscar K. Buros.

The 16 PF (16 Personality Factor Questionnaire), developed by Raymond B. Cattell, is suitable for persons age 16 and above and has been the subject of over 2,000 papers or other communications! The test measures key personality factors such as assertiveness, emotional maturity, and shrewdness. A couple can even decide that each party will take the 16 PF, and both an individual and joint profile will be compiled, which can be utilized for marital counseling. Choice "c" is another Cattell, who coined the term *mental test* and spent time researching mental assessment and its relation to reaction time at the University of Pennsylvania. James McKeen Cattell had originally worked with Wilhelm Wundt and later Francis Galton. **Tests and inventories like the 16 PF, which analyze data outside of a given theory, are called factor-analytic tests or inventories rather than theory-based tests.**    **(a)**

664. The Myers–Briggs Type Indicator reflects the work of

    a.    Raymond B. Cattell.
    b.    Carl Jung.

c.    William Glasser.
d.    Oscar K. Buros.

Review question 654. Buros, mentioned in choice "d," is noted for his *Mental Measurements Yearbook* (*MMY*), which was the first major publication to review available tests. After his death, the University of Nebraska set up the Oscar K. Buros Center, which continued his valuable contribution to the field by producing MMY series books packed with professional reviews to help counselors pick appropriate tests. I mean you peruse reviews before you purchase a vehicle or a new computer, right? Why not examine the tests you will be using with your clients?    **(b)**

665.  The counselor who favors projective measures would most likely be a

a.    Rogerian.
b.    strict behaviorist.
c.    TA therapist.
d.    psychodynamic clinician.

Choices "a," "b," and "c" all reflect positions that do not rely heavily on the unconscious mind (especially the behaviorists, who believe that if you can't directly measure the behavior, it is not meaningful). However, some theorists (e.g., Allport) would contend that even if it is true that unconscious impulses exist, they are not very important.    **(d)**

666.  An aptitude test is to _____ as an achievement test is to _____.

a.    what has been learned; potential
b.    potential; what has been learned
c.    profit from learning; potential
d.    a measurement of current skills; potential

An aptitude test assesses "potential" and "predicts." A person, for example, who scores high on a music aptitude test is not necessarily a skilled musician at the time he or she takes the test. The test, however, is predicting that this individual could excel in music if he or she received the proper training and practice. An achievement test examines what you know or how well you currently perform (e.g., the NCE or how fast you can run the 100-yard dash). **Predictive validity is particularly important when choosing an aptitude test.**                                                        **(b)**

667. Both the Rorschach and the Thematic Apperception Test (TAT) are projective tests. The Rorschach uses 10 inkblot cards while the TAT uses

   a.   a dozen inkblot cards.
   b.   verbal and performance IQ scales.
   c.   pictures.
   d.   incomplete sentences.

The TAT consists of 31 cards. The test, which is intended for ages 4 and beyond, uses up to 20 cards when administered to any given individual (i.e., 19 selected to fit the age and sex of the client, plus one blank card). The pictures on each card are intentionally ambiguous, and the client is asked to make up a story for each of them. Choice "d" would describe a projective test such as the Rotter Incomplete Sentence Blank (RISB) in which the subject completes an incomplete sentence with a real feeling.                                                        **(c)**

668. Test bias primarily results from

   a.   a test being normed solely on white middle-class clients.
   b.   the use of projective measures.
   c.   using whites to score the test.
   d.   using IQ rather than personality tests.

This bias should be communicated to the client when the results are explained.                                                        **(a)**

669. A counselor who fears the client has an organic, neurological, or motoric difficulty would most likely use the

    a.   Bender Gestalt II.
    b.   Rorschach.
    c.   Minnesota Multiphasic Personality Inventory-2.
    d.   Thematic Apperception Test.

    The Bender Visual Motor Gestalt Test (named after psychiatrist Lauretta Bender) is actually an expressive projective measure, though first and foremost it is known for its ability to discern whether brain damage is evident. Suitable for age 4 years and beyond, the client is instructed to copy 16 geometric figures which the client can look at while constructing his or her drawing.   **(a)**

670. An interest inventory would be least valid when used with

    a.   a first-year college student majoring in philosophy.
    b.   a third-year college student majoring in physics.
    c.   an eighth-grade male with an IQ of 136.
    d.   a 46-year-old white male construction worker.

    Interest inventories work best with individuals who are of high school age or above inasmuch as interests are not extremely stable prior to that time. Interests become quite stable around age 25.   **(c)**

671. One major criticism of interest inventories is that

    a.   they have far too many questions.
    b.   they are most appropriate for very young children.
    c.   they emphasize professional positions and minimize blue-collar jobs.
    d.   they favor jobs that will require a bachelor's degree or higher.

    **Also take note of the fact that contrary to popular opinion interests and abilities are not—that's right, not—highly correlated.** A client, for example, could have tremendous musical ability in music yet could thoroughly dislike being a musician.                                                                    **(c)**

672.  Interest inventories are positive in the sense that

   a.   they are reliable and not threatening to the test taker.
   b.   they are always graded by the test taker.
   c.   they require little or no reading skills.
   d.   they have high validity in nearly all age brackets.

   Generally, an interest inventory would be the least threatening variety of test.                                                          **(a)**

673.  A counselor who had an interest primarily in testing would most likely be a member of

   a.   HS-BCP.
   b.   AARC.
   c.   NASW.
   d.   ACES.

   The AARC (Association for Assessment and Research in Counseling) is one of 20 ACA divisions. Can you name the other choices?                                                               **(b)**

674.  The NCE is

   a.   an intelligence test.
   b.   an aptitude test.
   c.   a personality test.
   d.   an achievement test.

   The NCE is testing your knowledge and application of material in the counseling profession.                                               **(d)**

675.  The _____ are examples of aptitude tests.

   a.   O*NET Ability Profiler and the MCAT
   b.   GZTS and the MMPI-2

c.   CPI and the MMPI-2
d.   Strong and the LSAT

Plenty of alphabet soup here! Here I've teamed up the O*NET Ability Profiler with the new Medical College Admission Test (MCAT). Choice "b," the Guilford–Zimmerman Temperament Survey (GZTS), is a personality measure for persons who do not have severe psychiatric disabilities. Ditto for the California Personality Inventory (CPI), which shares questions with the MMPI. Last, the final alternative introduces you to the new Law School Admission Test (LSAT), which of course qualifies as a bona fide aptitude test. So why is choice "d" incorrect? Well, if any portion of a response is incorrect, then the entire choice is erroneous. If you marked choice "d" you can blame it on the Strong! **Exam Hint: School selection tests assess *aptitude*.**                                                      **(a)**

676. One problem with interest inventories is that the person often tries to answer the questions in a socially acceptable manner. Psychometricians call this response style phenomenon

a.   standard error.
b.   social desirability (the right way to feel in society).
c.   cultural bias.
d.   acquiescence.

The converse of choice "b" occurs when an individual purposely, or when in doubt, gives unusual responses. This phenomenon is known as "deviation." Choice "d" manifests itself when a client always agrees with something.                                              **(b)**

677. An aptitude test predicts future behavior while an achievement test measures what you have mastered or learned. In the case of a test like the _____ the distinction is unclear.

a.   Binet
b.   Wechsler
c.   GRE
d.   Bender

Sure, the GRE attempts to predict graduate school performance, but it also tests your level of knowledge. Some exams will refer to tests like the GRE, MAT, MCAT, SAT, etc., as "aptitude-achievement tests." Now here's where a counselor's life gets really complicated. Say your exam presents you with one of the aforementioned tests and gives you "aptitude" as one choice, and "achievement" as another, but does not give you "aptitude achievement" as an alternative (yipes!). Well, I certainly won't condone the practice, but based on my investigation of the textbook taxonomy of tests I'd opt for the "aptitude" option and latch onto the first good four-leaf clover I could get my hands on. **(c)**

678. Your supervisor wants you to find a new personality test for your counseling agency. You should read

    a.    professional journals.
    b.    the *Buros Mental Measurements Yearbook*.
    c.    classic textbooks in the field as well as test materials produced by the testing company.
    d.    all of the above.

Moreover, it has been discovered that if the counselor involves the client in the process of test selection it will improve his or her cooperation in the counseling process. **(d)**

679. The standard error of measurement tells you

    a.    how accurate or inaccurate a test score is.
    b.    what population responds best to the test.
    c.    something about social loafing.
    d.    the number of people used in norming the test.

Any chance you chose choice "c"? Well, social loafing is a term you can bank on seeing in comprehensive exams, but trust me when I say it has zilch to do with this question! Social loafing describes a phenomenon in which a person in a group puts forth less effort than if he or she were attempting to accomplish the same goal individually. Now for the answer to this question: If a client decided to take the same test over and over and over again you could plot a distribution of scores. This would be the standard error of measurement for the instrument in question. Suffice it to say, the lower the better. A low standard error means high reliability. Say, that's a pretty important concept; I better explain it again with a slightly different twist in the Research and Program Evaluation section of this book. **(a)**

680. A new IQ test has a standard error of measurement (SEM) of 3. Tom scores 106 on the test. If he takes the test a lot, we can predict that about 68% of the time

   a.  Tom will score between 100 and 103.
   b.  Tom will score between 100 and 106.
   c.  Tom will score between 103 and 109.
   d.  Tom will score higher than Betty who scored 139.

Calculated simply by taking: 106 − 3 = 103 and 106 + 3 = 109. **Hint:** Your exam could refer to this as the "68% confidence interval" (i.e., 103 to 109). Classical test theory suggests the formula, $X = T + E$, where X is the obtained score, T is the true score, and E is the error. Hence, psychometricians know that if a client takes the same test over and over, random error (i.e., E in the formula) will cause the score to fluctuate. **(c)**

681. A counselor created an achievement test with a reliability coefficient of .82. The test is shortened since many clients felt it was too long. The counselor shortened the test but logically assumed that the reliability coefficient would now

   a.  be approximately .88.
   b.  remain at .82.
   c.  be at least 10 points higher or lower.
   d.  be lower than .82.

**Increasing a test's length raises reliability. Shorten it and the antithesis occurs. Note:** The Spearman Brown formula is used to estimate the impact that lengthening or shortening a test will have on a test's reliability coefficient. **(d)**

682. A counselor can utilize psychological tests to help secure a
_____ diagnosis if third-party payments are necessary.

    a.    CPT
    b.    *DSM* or *ICD*
    c.    percentile
    d.    standard error

Diagnosis is a medical term which asserts that you classify a
disease based on symptomatology. CPT (Current Procedural
Terminology Codes) are used to let insurance companies,
managed care firms, etc. know which service you provided, such
as individual therapy or family therapy.                            (**b**)

683. A colleague of yours invents a new projective test. Seventeen
counselors rated the same client using the measure and came up
with nearly identical assessments. This would indicate

    a.    high validity.
    b.    high reliability.
    c.    excellent norming studies.
    d.    culture fairness.

This is known as "inter-rater" reliability.                        (**b**)

684. Counselors often shy away from self-reports since

    a.    clients often give inaccurate answers.
    b.    ACA ethics do not allow them.
    c.    clients need a very high IQ to understand them.
    d.    they are generally very lengthy.

Say a client is monitoring her behavior and does not wish to
disappoint her therapist. The report could be biased. This is a
"reactive effect" of the self-monitoring.                          (**a**)

685. In most instances, who would be the best qualified to give the Rorschach Inkblot Test?

    a.    A counselor with NCC after his or her name.
    b.    A clinical psychologist.
    c.    A D.O. psychiatrist.
    d.    A social worker with LCSW after his or her name.

Generally, a clinical psychologist would have the most training in projective measures while the social worker would have the least education regarding tests and measurements. **(b)**

686. Your client, who is in an outpatient hospital program, is keeping a journal of irrational thoughts. This would be

    a.    an unethical practice based on NBCC ethical guidelines.
    b.    considered a standardized test.
    c.    an informal assessment technique.
    d.    an aptitude measure.

Self-reports, case notes, checklists, sociograms of groups, interviews, and professional staffings would also fall into the informal assessment category. **(c)**

687. You are uncertain whether a test is intended for the population served by your not-for-profit agency. The best method of researching this dilemma would be to

    a.    contact a local APA clinical psychology graduate program.
    b.    e-mail the person who created the test.
    c.    read the test manual included with the test.
    d.    give the test to six or more clients at random.

The manual should specify the target population for the test in question. **(c)**

688. Clients should know that

    a.    validity is more important than reliability.

b.    projective tests favor psychodynamic theory.
c.    face validity is not that important.
d.    a test is merely a single source of data and not infallible.

Although the first three choices are important to the counselor, the final statement should be explained to the client. An extremely high score—say on a mechanical aptitude test—does not automatically imply that the client will prosper as a mechanic. **(d)**

689.  One major testing trend is

a.    computer-assisted testing and computer interpretations.
b.    more paper and pencil measures.
c.    to give school children more standardized tests.
d.    to train pastoral counselors to do projective testing.

But don't take my word for it. Pick up any modern testing catalog and you might erroneously think you've picked up a computer software directory! And speaking of choice "c," as a write this there seems to be a nationwide push to eliminate the number of standardized tests given.     **(a)**

690.  One future trend which seems contradictory is that some experts are pushing for

a.    a greater reliance on tests while others want to rely on them less.
b.    social workers to do most of the testing.
c.    psychiatrists to do most of the testing.
d.    counselors to ban all computer-assisted tests.

It seems we counselors just can't agree on anything. Many counselors would like to see a greater emphasis in the future on tests which assess creative and motivational factors.     **(a)**

691.  Most counselors would agree that

a.    more preschool IQ testing is necessary.
b.    teachers need to give more personality tests.

c.    more public education is needed in the area of testing.

d.    the testing mystique has been beneficial to the general public.

Again, the public needs to know the limitations of testing (i.e., that they are fallible). If you've been doing counseling for any length of time then you've surely come in contact with clients who have been harmed by hearing a score (e.g., their IQ) and then reacting to it such that it becomes a negative, self-fulfilling prophecy.                                                                    **(c)**

692.  _____ would be an informal method of appraisal.

a.    IQ testing

b.    Standardized personality testing

c.    GRE scores

d.    A checklist

Unlike choices "a," "b," and "c," the informal method does not use standard administration or scoring procedures. I might tell a client to do her checklist or diary one way and you would go about it in a totally different manner.                                               **(d)**

693.  The WAIS-IV is given to 100,000 individuals in the United States who are picked at random. A counselor would expect that

a.    approximately 68% would score between 85 and 115.

b.    approximately 68% would score between 70 and 130.

c.    the mean IQ would be 112.

d.    50% of those tested would score 112 or above.

I know, I see it too, a question with numbers—lots of numbers, but don't panic. Let's walk through this one together. First, the Wechsler IQ test has been administered to a very large group of people so chances are the distribution of scores will be normal. This tells you that the mean score will be 100 (i.e., the average IQ) and the standard deviation will be 15 (if the question were asked about the Binet you'd use 16 as the standard deviation). In a normal distribution approximately 68% of the population will fall between +/-1 standard deviation of the mean. With a standard deviation of 15 you simply subtract 15 from 100 to get the low score (i.e., 85) and add 15 to 100 to get 115. Choice "b" would be correct if the 68% was changed to 95%, since about 95% of the people in a normal distribution fall between +/-2 standard deviations of the mean. (You simply subtract 30 from 100 to get 70 and add 30 to 100 to yield the upper IQ score of 130.) Keep in mind that choice "c" should read 100 while choice "d" ought to indicate that 50% would score above 100.    **(a)**

694. A word association test would be an example of

   a.   a neuropsychological test.
   b.   a motoric test.
   c.   an achievement test.
   d.   a projective test.

Although it is rare, some texts and exams take issue with the archaic word *projective* and refer to such tests as "self-expressive."    **(d)**

695. Infant IQ tests are

   a.   more reliable than those given later in life.
   b.   more unreliable than those given later in life.
   c.   not related to learning experiences.
   d.   never used.

These "toddler tests" are sometimes capable of picking up gross abnormalities such as severe intellectual disabilities.    **(b)**

696. A good practice for counselors is to

   a.   always test the client yourself rather than referring the client for testing.
   b.   never generalize on the basis of a single test score.
   c.   stay away from culture-free tests.
   d.   stay away from scoring the test yourself.

Also, although choice "c" represents an ideal measure, most experts believe that as of this date no such animal exists.     **(b)**

697. You want to admit only 25% of all counselors to an advanced training program in psychodynamic group therapy. The item difficulty on the entrance exam for applicants would be best set at

    a.    0.0.
    b.    .5 regardless of the admission requirement.
    c.    1.0.
    d.    .25.

In most tests the level is set at .5 (i.e., 50% of the examinees will answer correctly while 50% will not). However, in this case the .25 level would allow you to ferret out the lower 75% you do not wish to admit. Item difficulty ranges from 0.0 (choice "a") to 1.0 (choice "c"). The higher the index number, the greater the number of examinees who will answer the question correctly. Or simply: The higher the number, the easier the question is to answer.     **(d)**

698. According to Public Law 93–380, also known as the Buckley Amendment, a 19-year-old college student attending college

    a.    could view her record, which included test data.
    b.    could view her daughter's infant IQ test given at preschool.
    c.    could demand a correction she discovered while reading a file.
    d.    all of the above.

Persons over age 18 can inspect their own records and those of their children. The Family Educational Rights and Privacy Act (FERPA) also stipulates that information cannot be released without adult consent.     **(d)**

699. Lewis Terman

    a.    constructed the Wechsler tests.
    b.    constructed the initial Binet prior to 1910.

c.    constructed the Rorschach.

d.    Americanized the Binet.

Since Terman was associated with Stanford University the test became the Stanford–Binet.                          **(d)**

700. In constructing a test you notice that all 75 people correctly answered item number 12. This gives you an item difficulty of

a.    1.2.

b.    .75.

c.    1.0.

d.    0.0.

The item difficulty index is calculated by taking the number of persons tested who answered the item correctly/total number of persons tested. Hence, in this case 75/75 = 1.0. This maximum score for item 12 tells you it is probably much too easy for your examinees.                          **(c)**

# 9

## Research and Program Evaluation

*There are three kinds of lies: lies, damn lies, and statistics.*
—Benjamin Disraeli, British Prime Minister

## 11 Current Trends in Counseling Research

1. More studies seem to be sporting multiple authors and female authors.
2. Increased attention is being paid to multicultural issues.
3. Field-based professionals and practitioners are submitting *fewer* contributions.
4. Meta-studies are being used to summarize findings related to a given topic or a theme. Cohen's *d* effect size (ES) statistic is used to gauge how strong a relationship exists (i.e., small 0.2, medium 0.5, or large 0.8).
5. A majority of studies rely on graduate students and adults as subjects.
6. Qualitative (non-numerical) research popularized by luminaries such as Freud and Piaget seems to be making a comeback.

Graduate programs are emphasizing qualitative procedures and research.

7. N = 1 single-subject designs seem to be making a comeback due to a number of advantages of this paradigm. First, only one person is required and counselors are very interested in individual change. The setting is usually a real-world situation rather than a laboratory setting. Finally, it is generally easier for consumers of mental health services to understand studies of this type since they generally need fewer complex statistical analyses. A type of single-subject (N = 1) numerical experiment using the ABABA design is common once again. This model, popularized in the 1970s by the behavior modification rage, tracks the client with an extended baseline, through treatment, to the outcome. Single-subject research is dubbed as *idiographic*, while studies using groups of individuals to discover general principles are called *nomothetic*.

8. Counselors and graduate students feel they need more training in APA publication guidelines in order to feel comfortable making journal submissions.

9. Kurt Lewin's concept of action research is popular because it is intended to improve the situation (not just advance knowledge) with local people/clients who will be better off at the end of the research. Self-surveys are often used to conduct Action Research. Action research bridges the gap between research and application/practice.

10. Using the Internet to conduct an experiment. Advantages can include rapid data collection, lower research costs, and very often the ability to secure very large sample sizes.

11. Neuroscience is being used to help guide diagnostic and treatment procedures. More females are being used in such studies since most traditional neuroscience findings are biased toward male humans and other mammals. The microbiome gut–mental health connection is emerging, especially in regard to bad bacteria and good bacteria (think probiotics such as organic yogurt or kefir) in the gastrointestinal tract.

701. The most valuable type of research is

    a.    always conducted using a factor analysis.
    b.    conducted using the chi-square.

c.   the experiment, used to discover cause-and-effect relationships.

d.   the quasi-experiment.

**A mini pep talk from me to you: Just think of statistics and research as another area on the test—no easier and no harder. Most of the students I've spoken to who used this book to study for major exams were surprised to find that questions related to this section of the test were not that difficult! I shall try to keep my explanations simple and will vary the presentation of the material so that if you don't understand it in one way, you'll comprehend it when it is explained in a different manner. And lastly, I promise repetition, repetition, and more repetition!**

Experimental research is the process of gathering data in order to make evaluative comparisons regarding different situations. An experiment must have the conditions of treatment controlled via the experimenter and random assignments (also called randomization) used in the groups. An experiment attempts to eliminate all extraneous variables. In the quasi-experiment (choice "d") the researcher uses preexisting groups, and hence the IV (independent variable) cannot be altered (e.g., gender or ethnicity). In a quasi-experiment you cannot state with any degree of statistical confidence that the IV caused the DV (dependent variable). One popular type of quasi-experiment is known as the "ex post facto study." Ex post facto literally means "after the fact," connoting a correlational study or research in which intact, preexisting groups are utilized. In the case of the ex post facto study, the IV was administered before the research began. When conducting or perusing a research study a counselor is very concerned with "internal and external validity." Threats to internal validity include maturation of subjects (psychological and physical changes including fatigue due to the time involved), mortality (i.e., subjects withdrawing), instruments used to measure the behavior or trait, and statistical regression (i.e., the notion that extremely high or low scores would move toward the mean if the measure is utilized again). **Internal validity refers to whether the DVs were truly influenced by the experimental IVs or**

**whether other factors had an impact. External validity, on the other hand, refers to whether the experimental research results can be generalized to larger populations (i.e., other people, settings or conditions).** Thus, if the results of the study only apply to the population in the study itself then the external validity is said to be low. P.S. If it's been a while and you've forgotten terms like IV and DV just hold your pants on; we'll get to you in a minute. As for the other incorrect choices, a "factor analysis" (choice "a") refers to statistical procedures that use the important or underlying "factors" in an attempt to summarize a lot of variables. Hence, a test which measures a counselor's ability may try to describe the three most important variables (factors) that make an effective helper, although literally hundreds of factors may exist. Using factor analysis procedures, a brief test that measures the three major factors may be able to predict who will be an effective counselor as accurately as 10 other tests that examine hundreds of variables or so-called factors. Choice "b" mentions the "chi-square." The chi-square is a nonparametric statistical measure that tests whether a distribution differs significantly from an expected theoretical distribution.  **(c)**

702. Experiments emphasize parsimony, which means

    a.    interpreting the results in the simplest way.
    b.    interpreting the results in the most complex manner.
    c.    interpreting the results using a correlation coefficient.
    d.    interpreting the results using a clinical interview.

Parsimonious literally means a tendency to be miserly and not overspend. A parsimonious individual is said to be overly economical and stingy. In research, we strive for parsimony in the sense that the easiest and less-complex explanation is said to be the best; an economical description if you will. Simply put, the simplest explanation of the findings is always preferred. The factor analysis mentioned in the previous answer is parsimonious in the sense that 10 tests which measure the dimensions of an effective counselor can be explained via a short measure which describes three underlying variables. Factor analysis, then, is concerned with data reduction.  **(a)**

703. Occam's Razor suggests that experimenters

    a.    interpret the results in the simplest manner.
    b.    interpret the results in the most complex manner.
    c.    interpret the results using a correlation coefficient.
    d.    interpret the results using a clinical interview.

A word to the wise: Exams often refer to parsimony as Occam's Razor, the principle of economy, or Lloyd Morgan's 1894 Canon (canon in this sense means "law"). Conway Lloyd Morgan was an English psychologist/physiologist, while William of Occam was a fourteenth-century philosopher and theologian. The early behaviorists (e.g., Watson) adhered closely to this principle. **Key point:** Have you ever placed a sticker on your car and tried to smooth it out? No matter how many times you attempt to do this the sticker usually retains a few trapped air bubbles. This analogy has often been used in conjunction with research, in the sense that flaws in research are often called **bubbles**.    **(a)**

704. A counselor educator is running an experiment to test a new form of counseling. Unbeknownst to the experimenter one of the clients in the study is secretly seeing a gestalt therapist. This experiment

    a.    is parsimonious.
    b.    is an example of Occam's Razor.
    c.    is confounded/flawed.
    d.    is valid and will most likely help the field of counseling.

The experiment is said to be invalid (so much for choice "d") due to an extraneous independent variable (IV) (e.g., the gestalt therapy). Variables which are undesirable confound or "flaw" the experiment. The only experimental variable should be the IV—in this case the new form of counseling. The IV must have the effect on the dependent variable (here the DV would be some measure of the client's mental health). In this experiment any changes could not be attributed with any degree of certainty to the new form of counseling since DV changes could be due to the gestalt intervention (an extraneous confounding variable). All correlational research is said to be confounded.     **(c)**

705. Nondirective is to person-centered as

   a.   psychological testing is to counseling.
   b.   confounding is to experimenting.
   c.   appraisal is to research.
   d.   parsimony is to Occam's Razor.

A simple analogy question. Nondirective and person-centered therapy are synonymous; both refer to names given to Rogerian counseling. Parsimony is roughly synonymous with Occam's Razor. **Important exam reminder:** Most counselors see themselves as practitioners rather than researchers. Research, nevertheless, helps the entire field of counseling advance. It has been pointed out that we know about the work of many famous counselors and career counselors because of their published research not because of what transpired in their sessions. **Test hint: The APA's *Journal of Counseling Psychology* publishes more counseling research articles than any other periodical in our field.**     **(d)**

706. An experiment is said to be confounded when

   a.   undesirable variables are not kept out of the experiment.
   b.   undesirable variables are kept out of the experiment.
   c.   basic research is used in place of applied research.
   d.   the sample is random.

I hope you didn't mark choices "b" and "d" since they are necessary for a proper experiment. Confounding is said to occur when an undesirable variable which is not controlled by the researcher is introduced in the experiment. **Hint: Your exam could refer to this as a contaminating variable.** If you missed this one, fess up and review question 704. Take a good hard look at choice "c." **Basic research** is conducted to advance our understanding of theory, while **applied research (also called action research or experience-near research)** is conducted to advance our knowledge of how theories, skills, and techniques can be used in terms of practical application. Often counselors assert that much of the research is not relevant to the actual counseling process and indeed they are correct.    **(a)**

707. In experimental terminology IV stands for _____ and DV stands for _____.

    a.    independent variable; dependent variable
    b.    dependent variable; independent variable
    c.    individual variable; dependent variable
    d.    independent variable; designer variable

Variables in an experiment are categorized as independent variables (IVs) or dependent variables (DVs). A variable is merely a behavior or a circumstance that can exist on at least two levels or conditions. In plain, simple, everyday English, a variable is a factor that "varies" or is capable of change. In an experiment **the IV is the variable that the researcher manipulates, controls, alters, or wishes to experiment with**. A neat little memory device is that IV begins with an "I," so imagine yourself as the researcher and remember "I manipulate the IV" or "I experiment with the IV." **The DV expresses the outcome or the data.** Here the memory device is a cinch: DV begins with a "D" and so does the word *data*. The DV expresses the data regarding factors you wish to measure. IVs and DVs—the variables of the experimental trade—can be discrete (e.g., a brand of counseling or occupation) or continuous (e.g., height or weight). **Exam score booster: If your exam describes a true experiment—such as the biofeedback research described in the next several questions—except for the fact that the groups were not randomly assigned, then the new exams are calling this a causal comparative design. Expect to see this term on the exam. Data gleaned from the causal comparative ex post facto or after the fact design can be analyzed with a test of significance (e.g., a *t* test or ANOVA) just like any true experiment.**    **(a)**

708. A professor of counselor education hypothesized that biofeedback training could reduce anxiety and improve the average score on written board exams. If this professor decides to conduct a formal experiment the IV will be the _____, and the DV will be the _____.

    a.    professor; anxiety level
    b.    anxiety level; board exam score
    c.    biofeedback; board exam score
    d.    board exam score; biofeedback

Ah, here we have it: the old standby in the field of comprehensive exams. The examinee is given an experiment to ferret out the IV and DV. Now I've got this uncanny feeling that you won't be caught by surprise when you see it! Okay, time to plug in your memory devices. "I manipulate… or I experiment with, well, *the biofeedback training*, of course." The "I" statement here gives you your "IV." For your "DV" (remember DV begins with a "D" like "data") your data are provided by the board exam score. True, the researcher here hypothesized that the training lowers anxiety, but you won't have any direct data regarding this trait. Hence it will not be your DV in this experiment.          **(c)**

709. Experimenters should always abide by a code of ethics. The variable you manipulate/control in an experiment is the

    a.    DV.
    b.    dependent variable.
    c.    the variable you will measure to determine the outcome.
    d.    IV or independent variable.

**Again, repeat after me: "I am the researcher so I manipulate or experiment with the IV."** Choices "a," "b," and "c" all mention the DV, which deals with outcome "data." Now, in any experiment the counselor researcher is guided by ethics: this suggests first, that subjects are informed of any risks; second, that negative after-effects are removed; third, that you will allow subjects to withdraw at any time; fourth, that confidentiality of subjects will be protected; fifth, that the results of research reports will be presented in an accurate format that is not misleading; and sixth, that you will use only techniques that you are trained in. Research is considered a necessary factor for professionalism in counseling.    **(d)**

710. In order for the professor of counselor education (see question 708) to conduct an experiment regarding his hypothesis he will need a(n) _____ and a(n) _____.

     a.   biofeedback group; systematic desensitization group
     b.   control group; systematic desensitization group
     c.   control group; experimental group
     d.   control group with at least 60 subjects; experimental group with at least 60 subjects

     The control group and the experimental group both have the same characteristics except that members of the control group will not have the experimental treatment applied to them. In this case, for example, the control group will not receive the biofeedback training. **The control group does not receive the IV. The experimental group receives the IV.** The basic presupposition is that the averages (or means) of the groups do not differ significantly at the beginning of the experiment. Choice "d" would also be a correct answer if it said 15 per group instead of 60. **Remember that if you cannot randomly assign the subjects to the two groups then your exam will consider the research a quasi-experiment.** Most experts suggest that you need at least 30 people to conduct a true experiment. Correlational research requires 30 subjects per variable while a survey should include at least 100 people.    **(c)**

711. In order for the professor of counselor education to conduct the experiment suggested in question 708 the experimental group would need to receive

     a.   the manipulated IV.
     b.   the biofeedback training.
     c.   a and b.
     d.   the organismic IV.

The experimental group receives the IV, which in this case is the biofeedback training. An organismic variable is one the researcher cannot control yet exists, such as height, weight, or gender. To determine whether an organismic IV exists you simply ask yourself if there is an experimental variable being examined which you cannot manipulate. In most cases, when you are confronted with IV/DV identification questions, the IV will be of the "manipulated variety." **(c)**

712. Hypothesis testing is most closely related to the work of

   a.   Robert Hoppock.
   b.   Sigmund Freud.
   c.   Lloyd Morgan.
   d.   R. A. Fisher.

Hypothesis testing was pioneered by R. A. Fisher. A hypothesis is a hunch or an educated guess which can be tested utilizing the experimental model. A hypothesis might be that biofeedback raises board exam scores; or that reality therapy reduces dysfunctional classroom behavior in high school students; or perhaps that cognitive therapy relieves depression in males in the midst of a divorce. **A hypothesis is a statement which can be tested regarding the relationship of the IV and the DV.** **(d)**

713. The null hypothesis suggests that there will not be a significant difference between the experimental group which received the IV and the control group which did not. Thus, if the experiment in question 708 was conducted, the null hypothesis would suggest that

   a.   all students receiving biofeedback training would score equally well on the board exam.
   b.   systematic desensitization might work better than biofeedback.
   c.   biofeedback will not improve the board exam scores.
   d.   meta-analysis is required.

The null hypothesis asserts that the samples will not change (i.e., they will still be the same) even after the experimental variable is applied. Let me say that in a slightly different way: According to the null hypothesis the control group and the experimental group will not differ at the end of the experiment. **The null hypothesis is simply that *the* IV *does not affect the DV*.** Null means "nil" or "nothing." Null is a statement of "no difference." Choice "d" introduces the term *meta-analysis*, which is a study that analyzes the findings of numerous studies. Hence, a study of reality therapy that looked at the results of 20 reality therapy studies would be a meta-analysis.                          **(c)**

714. The hunch is known as the experimental or alternative hypothesis. The experimental hypothesis suggests that a difference will be evident between the control group and the experimental group (i.e., the group receiving the IV). Thus, if the experiment in question 708 were conducted, the experimental hypothesis would suggest that

     a.  the biofeedback would raise board scores.
     b.  the control group will score better on the board exam.
     c.  there will be no difference between the experimental and the control groups.
     d.  the experiment has been confounded.

     An alternative hypothesis—which may be called the "affirmative hypothesis" on your exam—asserts that the IV has indeed caused a change.                                                     **(a)**

715. From a purely statistical standpoint, in order to compare a control group (which does not receive the IV or experimental manipulation) to the experimental group the researcher will need

     a.  a correlation coefficient
     b.  only descriptive statistics.
     c.  percentile rank.
     d.  a test of significance.

Let's go through each possible alternative here. Choice "a" or correlational research does not make use of the paradigm in which an IV is experimentally introduced. Descriptive statistics (choice "b"), as the name implies, merely describes data (e.g., the mean, the median, or the mode). In order to compare two groups, "inferential statistics," which infer something about the population, are necessary. Choice "c," percentile rank, is a descriptive statistic that tells the counselor what percentage of the cases fell below a certain level. Hence, if Joe's score puts him at the 50th percentile, then 50% of the people had raw scores lower than his particular score. **Do not confuse percentiles with percentage scores. A percentage score is just another way of stating a raw score. A percentage score of 50 could be a very high, a very low, or an average score on the test. It merely says that the examinee got half of the answers correct.** Graphically speaking, a distribution of percentile scores will always appear rectangular and flat. The correct answer is that the researcher in this experiment will need a test of significance. Such statistical tests are used to determine whether a difference in the groups' scores is "significant" or just due to chance factors. In this case a $t$ test would be used to determine if a significant difference between two means exists. This has been called the "two-groups" or "two-randomized-groups" research design. In this study, the two groups were independent of each other in the sense that the change (or lack of it) in one group did not influence the other group. Thus, this is known as an "independent group comparison design." If the researcher had measured the same group of subjects without the IV and with the IV, then the study would be a "repeated-measures comparison design." **Exam hint:** When a research study uses different subjects for each condition, some exams refer to the study as a "between-subjects design." If the same subjects are employed (e.g., such as in repeated measures) your exam could refer to it as a "within-subjects design." To state it in a different manner: In a between-subjects design, each subject receives only one value of the IV. In a within-subjects design, two or more values or levels of the IV are administered to each subject.                                        **(d)**

716. When you see the letter $P$ in relation to a test of significance it means

    a.    portion.
    b.    population parameter.
    c.    probability.
    d.    the researcher is using an ethnographic qualitative approach.

    Don't be surprised if the word *parameter* makes its way into your exam. A parameter is technically a value obtained from a population while a statistic is a value drawn from a sample. A parameter summarizes a characteristic of a population (e.g., the average male's height is 5'9"). The correct answer is choice "c" which refers to the probability or the level of significance. Traditionally, the probability in social science research (often indicated by a $P$) has been set at .05 or lower (i.e., .01 or .001). The .05 level indicates that differences would occur via chance only five times in 100. The significance level must be set before the experiment begins! And oh yes, ethnographic research involves research that is collected via interviews, observations, and inspection of documents.                                    **(c)**

717. In the social sciences the accepted probability level is usually

    a.    .05 or less.
    b.    1.0 or higher.
    c.    .0001 or less.
    d.    .05 or higher.

    The two most popular levels of significance are .05 and .01.   **(a)**

718. $P = .05$ really means that

    a.    five subjects were not included in the study.
    b.    there is only a 5% chance that the difference between the control group and the experimental groups is due to chance factors.
    c.    the level of significance is .01.
    d.    no level of significance has been set.

**Important note:** Many experts in the field feel it is misleading when many exams still refer to this as the "95% confidence interval," meaning that the results would be due to chance only five times out of 100. When $P = .05$, differences in the experimental group and the control group are evident at the end of the experiment, and the odds are only one in 20 that this can be explained by chance. So once more for good measure (no pun intended!) your exam could refer to the "level of significance" as the level of confidence or simply the confidence level. The meaning is intended to be the same. **(b)**

719. $P = .05$ really means that

    a.    differences truly exist; the experimenter will obtain the same results 95 times out of 100.
    b.    differences truly exist; the experimenter will obtain the same results 99 times out of 100.
    c.    there is a 95% error factor.
    d.    there is a 10% error factor.

Review the previous three questions and answers if you missed this question. **(a)**

720. The study that would best rule out chance factors would have a significance level of $P =$

    a.    .05.
    b.    .01.
    c.    .001.
    d.    .08.

The smaller the value for $P$ the more stringent the level of significance. Here, the .001 level is the most stringent level listed, indicating that there is only one chance in 1,000 that the results are due to chance, versus one in 20 for .05, and one in 100 for .01. In plain, everyday English it is easier to get significant results using .08, .05, or .01, than it is using .001. **(c)**

721. Type I and Type II errors are called _____ and _____ respectively.

    a.   beta; alpha
    b.   .01; .05
    c.   a and b
    d.   alpha; beta

If it sounds a little like Greek, that's because it is. Alpha and beta are the first and second letters of the Greek alphabet. A Type I (alpha error) occurs when a researcher rejects the null hypothesis when it is true; and a Type II error (beta error) occurs when you accept null when it is false. The memory device RA (as in "residence advisor") works well here so you can remember the principle as well as the sequence. Let "R" signify "reject when true" and "A"—which comes after "R"—signify "accept when false." If that memory device leaves you feeling apprehensive, here's another one using the "RA" abbreviation. Let "RA" be your first error (i.e., alpha, Type I) and remember this error occurs when you "R" (reject) null when you should "A" for accept it. Or better still use both "RA" devices. **The probability of committing a Type I error equals the level of significance mentioned earlier. Therefore, the level of significance is often referred to as the "alpha level." 1 minus beta is called "the power of a statistical test." In this respect, power connotes a statistical test's ability to reject correctly a false null hypothesis.** Parametric tests have more power than nonparametric statistical tests. Parametric tests are used only with interval and ratio data.    **(d)**

722. A Type I error occurs when

    a.   you have a beta error.
    b.   you accept null when it is false.
    c.   you reject null when it is true.
    d.   you fail to use a test of significance.

Okay, here it is: Time to plug in your handy dandy memory formula—"RA" or "reject when applicable/true." Since all statistical tests rely on probability there is always the possibility that the results were merely chance occurrences. Researchers call these chance factors "errors."    **(c)**

723.  A Type II error

   a.   is also called a beta error.
   b.   means you reject null when it is applicable.
   c.   means you accept null when it is false.
   d.   a and c.

Although lowering the significance level (e.g., .01 to .001) lowers Type I errors, it "raises" the risk of committing a Type II or beta error. Simply think of the Type I/Type II relationship as a seesaw in the sense that when one goes up the other goes down. Hence, in determining an alpha level, the researcher needs to decide which error results in the most serious consequences. The safest bet is to set alpha at a very stringent level and then use a large sample size. If this can be accomplished, it is possible to make the correct decision (i.e., accept or reject null) the majority of the time.    **(d)**

724.  Assume the experiment in question 708 is conducted. The results indicate that the biofeedback helped raise written board exam scores but in reality this is not the case. The researcher has made a

   a.   Type I error.
   b.   Type II error.
   c.   beta error.
   d.   b and c.

Questions like this can be very difficult. Be sure to utilize scratch paper to write down your thoughts if your exam allows you to do so! First, write down (or mentally picture) the null hypothesis regarding the experiment in question. In this case null would indicate that biofeedback did not raise board exam scores. This question tells you that the experimental results revealed that biofeedback did raise board scores, so you will reject the null hypothesis. The question then goes on to say that in reality the biofeedback did not really cause the results. Therefore, you have rejected null when it is true/applicable. This is the definition of a Type I or alpha error. Since the experimenter sets the alpha level, he or she is always cognizant of the probability of making a Type I error.                                                         **(a)**

725. A counselor educator decides to increase the sample size in her experiment. This will

    a.   confound the experiment in nearly every case.
    b.   raise the probability of Type I and Type II errors.
    c.   have virtually no impact on Type I and Type II errors.
    d.   reduce Type I and Type II errors.

    Raising the size of a sample helps to lower the risk of chance/error factors. Simply put: Differences revealed via large samples are more likely to be genuine than differences revealed using a small sample size.                                                      **(d)**

726. If a researcher changes the significance level from .05 to .001, then

    a.   alpha and beta errors will increase.
    b.   alpha errors increase but beta errors decrease.
    c.   alpha errors decrease; however, beta errors increase.
    d.   this will have no impact on Type I and Type II errors.

    Review question 723. Let me mention as an aside that research can evoke fear, hostility, and anxiety in counselors. Why? Well, many counselors view research as cold, sterile, impersonal, and not related to the actual counseling process. There is also the fear of negative results related to the way one practices his or her craft.                                                         **(c)**

727. A counselor believes that clients who receive assertiveness training will ask more questions in counseling classes. An experimental group receives assertiveness training while a

control group does not. In order to test for significant differences between the groups the counselor should utilize

a.    the student's $t$ test.
b.    a correlation coefficient.
c.    a survey.
d.    an analysis of variance (ANOVA).

When comparing two sample groups the $t$ test, which is a simplistic form of the analysis of variance, is utilized. The $t$ test is used to ascertain whether two sample means are significantly different. The researcher sets the level of significance and then runs the experiment. The $t$ test is computed and this yields a $t$ value. The researcher then goes to a $t$ table found in the index of most statistics' texts. If the $t$ value obtained statistically is lower than the $t$ value (sometimes called "critical $t$") in the table, then you accept the null hypothesis. **Your computation must exceed the number cited in the table in order to reject null.** If there are more than two groups, then the analysis of variance (choice "d") is utilized. The results of an ANOVA yield an $F$-statistic. The researcher then consults an $F$ table for a critical value of $F$. If $F$ obtained (i.e., computed) exceeds the critical $F$ value in the table, then the null hypothesis is rejected. The other major statistical tests likely to show up on your exam include the following six: the analysis of covariance (ANCOVA), which tests two or more groups while controlling for extraneous variables that are often called "covariates"; the Kruskal–Wallis, which is used instead of the one-way ANOVA when the data are nonparametric; the Wilcoxon signed-rank test, used in place of the $t$ test when the data are nonparametric and you wish to test whether two correlated means differ significantly (use the "co" to remind you of "correlated"); the Mann–Whitney $U$ test, to determine whether two uncorrelated means differ significantly when data are nonparametric (the "$u$" can remind you of "uncorrelated"); the Spearman correlation or Kendall's tau, which is used in place of the Pearson $r$ when parametric assumptions cannot be utilized; and the chi-square nonparametric test, which examines whether obtained frequencies differ significantly from expected frequencies.

**Note that statisticians have created nonparametric tests that parallel the popular parametric measures.** **(a)**

728. The researcher in question 727 now attempts a more complex experiment. One group receives no assertiveness training, a second group receives four assertiveness training sessions, and a third receives six sessions. The statistic of choice would be the

    a. mean.
    b. *t* test.
    c. two-way ANOVA.
    d. ANOVA.

    This is a tough question. A one-way analysis of variance is used for testing one independent variable, while a two-way analysis of variance is used to test two independent variables. When a study has more than one DV the term *multivariate analysis of variance* (MANOVA) is utilized. **The answer is choice "d" since the simple ANOVA or one-way analysis of variance is used when there is more than one level of a single IV, which in this case is the assertiveness training.** **(d)**

729. If the researcher in the previous question utilized two IVs then the statistic of choice would be the

    a. median.
    b. *t* test.
    c. two-way ANOVA or MANOVA.
    d. ANOVA.

    Two IVs requires a two-way ANOVA, three IVs, a three-way ANOVA, etc. **(c)**

730. To complete a *t* test you would consult a tabled value of *t*. In order to see if significant differences exist in an ANOVA you would consult

    a. the mode.
    b. a table for *t* values.

c.    a table for $F$ values.

d.    the chi-square.

More elaborate tests (e.g., Tukey's, Duncan's multiple range, and Scheffe's test) can determine whether a significant difference exists between specific groups. Group comparison tests such as these are called "post hoc" or "a posteriori" tests for ANOVA calculations.                                                                                    **(c)**

731. Which level of significance would best rule out chance factors?

a.    .05

b.    .01

c.    .2

d.    .001

Some researchers refer to the level of significance as where "one draws the line" or the "cutoff point" between findings that should or should not be ascribed to chance factors. The significance level must be set low. If, for example, a researcher foolishly set the level at .50, then the odds would be 50–50 that the results were due to pure chance. I guarantee you a reputable journal would never touch an article with statistics like that! If you marked anything other than choice "d," you also should review question 720.                                                                                    **(d)**

732. When a researcher uses correlation, then there is no direct manipulation of the IV. A researcher might ask, for example, how IQ correlates with the incidence of panic disorder. Again, nothing is manipulated; just measured. In cases such as this a correlation coefficient will reveal

a.    the relationship between IQ and panic disorder.

b.    the probability that a significant difference exists.

c.    an $F$ test.

d.    percentile rank.

**A statistic that indicates the degree or magnitude of relationship between two variables is known as a**

**"correlation coefficient" and is often abbreviated using a lower-case *r*.** A coefficient of correlation makes a statement regarding the association of two variables and how a change in one is related to the change in another. Correlations range from 0.00, no relationship, to 1.0 or -1.0 which signify perfect relationships. **Important: A positive correlation is not a stronger relationship than a negative one of the same numerical value. A correlation of -.70 is still indicative of a stronger relationship than a positive correlation of .60. The minus sign merely describes the fact that as one variable goes up the other goes down.**                    **(a)**

733. If data indicate that students who study a lot get very high scores on state counselor licensing exams, then the correlation between study time and LPC exam scores would be

    a.    positive.
    b.    negative.
    c.    0.00.
    d.    impossible to ascertain.

    **A positive correlation is evident when both variables change in the same direction. A negative correlation is evident when the variables are inversely associated; one goes up and the other goes down.** In the scenario for this question the relationship is positive since as study time increases, LPC exam scores also increase. A negative correlation (choice "b") would be expected when correlating an association like the number of dental cavities and time spent brushing one's teeth; as brushing time goes up dental cavities probably go down. Choice "c" or a zero correlation indicates an absence of a relationship between the variables in question. **Note:** Your exam could throw the term *biserial correlation* at you. This merely indicates that one variable is continuous (i.e., measured using an interval scale) while the other is dichotomous. An example would be evident if you decided to correlate state licensing exam scores to NCC status (here the dichotomy is licensed/unlicensed). If both variables are dichotomous (i.e., two valued) then a phi-coefficient correlation is necessary. Imagine a researcher who wants to correlate NCC status with CCMHC status or perhaps gender with certification status (has certification/does not have certification).                                                              **(a)**

734. Which of the following would most likely yield a perfect correlation of 1.00?

    a.    IQ and salary.
    b.    *ICD* diagnosis and salary.
    c.    Length in inches and length in centimeters.
    d.    Height and weight.

    In the real world, correlations may be strong (e.g., choice "d"), yet they are rarely 1.00. Correlation is concerned with what statisticians call "covariation." When two variables vary together statisticians say the variables "covary positively," and when one increases while the other decreases they are said to "covary negatively."                                                         **(c)**

735. A good guess would be that if you would correlate the length of CACREP graduates' baby toes with their CPCE scores the result would be

    a.    close to 0.00.
    b.    close to a perfect 1.00.
    c.    close to a perfect negative correlation of -1.00.
    d.    be about +.70.

    There is an absence of association here because as one variable changes the other variable varies randomly. The variation of one variable is most likely totally unrelated to the variation of the other.                                                                       **(a)**

736. Dr. X discovered that the correlation between therapists who hold NCC status and therapists who practice systematic desensitization is .90. A student who perused Dr. X's research told his fellow students that Dr. X had discovered that attaining

NCC status causes therapists to become behaviorally oriented. The student is incorrect because

a.   systematic desensitization is clearly not a behavioral strategy.
b.   this can only be determined via a histogram.
c.   the study suffers from longitudinal and maturational effects.
d.   correlation does not imply causal.

**Shout it out: Correlation does not mean causal!** Correlational research is quasi-experimental, and hence, it does not yield cause–effect data. A major research study, for example, might discover a very high correlation between the number of college students in a given geographical area and number of smart devices owned. Yet it would certainly be misleading to conclude that owning a lot of smart devices causes one to become a college student. **Exam hint:** When correlational data describe the nature of two variables, the term *bivariate* is utilized. If more than two variables are under scrutiny, then the term *multivariate* is used to describe the correlational paradigm.          **(d)**

737. Behaviorists often utilize N = 1, which is called intensive experimental design. The first step in this approach would be to

a.   consult a random number table.
b.   decide on a nonparametric statistical test.
c.   take a baseline measure.
d.   compute the range.

"N," or the number of persons being studied, is one. This is a "case study" of one approach. This method is popular with behaviorists who seek overt (measurable) behavioral changes. The client's dysfunctional behavior is measured (this is called a baseline measure), the treatment is implemented, and then the behavior is measured once again (i.e., another baseline is computed). Exams sometimes delineate this paradigm using upper-case As and Bs and Cs such that As signify baselines, Bs intervention implementation, and Cs a second or alternative form of intervention. Single case investigations are often called "idiographic studies" or "single-subject designs." The original case study methodology was popularized by Freud, though needless to say, unlike the behaviorists, Freud did not rely on numerical baseline measures. Case studies are often misleading because the results are not necessarily generalizable.          **(c)**

738. In a new study the clients do not know whether they are receiving an experimental treatment for depression or whether they are simply part of the control group. This is, nevertheless, known to the researcher. Thus, this is a

    a.   double-blind study.
    b.   single-blind study.
    c.   baseline for an intensive N = 1 design.
    d.   participant observer model.

In the single-blind study the subject would *not know* whether he or she is a member of the control group or the experimental group. This strategy helps eliminate "demand characteristics" which are cues or features of a study which suggest a desired outcome. In other words a subject can manipulate and confound an experiment by purposely trying to confirm or disprove the experimental hypothesis. Let us say that in the above-referenced experiment a subject is fond of the researcher. And let us further assume that a score on a standardized depression inventory will be used as the DV. Our subject might purposely answer the questions as if he is less depressed than he really is. A subject who disliked the researcher could present himself as even more depressed. Just in case you erroneously chose choice "c," please notice that the question used the word *clients* which is plural. N = 1 designs rely on a single individual for investigation purposes. Choice "d" describes a study in which the researcher actually participates in the study, while making observations about what transpired.          **(b)**

739. A large study at a major university gave an experimental group of clients a new type of therapy that was intended to ameliorate test anxiety. The control group did not receive the new therapy.

Neither the clients nor the researchers knew which students received the new treatment. This was a

a.    double-blind study.
b.    single-blind study.
c.    typical AB design.
d.    case of correlational research.

A double-blind study goes one step beyond the single-blind version by making certain that the experimenter is also unaware of the subjects' status. In fact, in the double-blind situation the persons assigned to rate or judge the subjects are often unaware of the hypothesis. This procedure helps eliminate confounding caused by "experimenter effects." **Experimenter effects can flaw an experiment because the experimenter might unconsciously communicate his or her intent or expectations to the subjects.** Choice "c," though incorrect, is a must-know concept. **An AB or ABA time-series design is the simplest type of single-subject research and was initially popularized by behavior modifiers in the 1960s and 1970s.** (You will recall that Freud used the case study paradigm, but needless to say, did not rely on the AB or ABA model.) **Single-subject case studies of various types are once again gaining in popularity.** Okay, back to the AB and ABA models that rely on "continuous-measurement." A baseline is secured (A); intervention is implemented (B); and the outcome is examined via a new baseline (A) in the case of the ABA design. In order to improve the research process, an ABAB design can be utilized to better rule out extraneous variables. If the pattern for the second AB administration mimics that of the first AB, then the chances increase that B (the intervention or so-called treatment) caused the changes rather than an extraneous variable. Some exams will refer to ABA or ABAB paradigms as "withdrawal designs." The rationale is that the behavior will move in the direction of the initial baseline each time the treatment is withdrawn if the treatment IV is responsible for the change. The ethical counselor must forego using a withdrawal or reversal design (as they are sometimes called) if the removal of the treatment variable could prove harmful to the subject or those who come in contact with the individual. Here, a simple AB or ABA must suffice. Remember that when a researcher employs more than one target behavior, the term *multiple-baseline design* probably will be used on your exam.    **(a)**

740. Experimental is to cause and effect as correlational is to

    a.    blind study.
    b.    double-blind study.
    c.    N = 1 design.
    d.    degree of relationship.

**A correlation coefficient is a descriptive statistic which indicates the degree of "linear relationship"** between two variables. Statisticians use the phrase "linear relationship" to indicate that when a perfect relationship exists (i.e., a correlation of 1.0 or -1.0) and it is graphed, a straight line is formed (see the Graphical Representations section of this book). The Pearson Product-Moment Correlation $r$ is used for interval or ratio data while the Spearman rho correlation is used for ordinal data. Correlational research is not experimental and hence does not imply causality. So what do you do if your exam sneaks in a question regarding the type of data which must be used with the Pearson $r$ versus the Spearman rho? I'd opt for a memory device. Pearson $r$, the most common correlation coefficient, uses I and R (interval and ratio data) as in "information and referral." Spearman rho ends in "o" as in ordinal. **Yes you can do well on questions related to this section of the exam!**    **(d)**

741. In a normal curve the mean, the median, and the mode all fall precisely in the middle of the curve. From a graphical standpoint the so-called normal or Gaussian curve (named after the astronomer/mathematician K. F. Gauss) looks like

    a.    a symmetrical bell.
    b.    the top half of a bowling ball.
    c.    the top half of a hot dog.
    d.    a mountain which is leaning toward the left.

The normal curve is a theoretical notion often referred to as a "bell-shaped curve." The bell is symmetrical. Most physical and psychological traits are normally distributed. In other words, if enough data are collected in regard to a given trait, and a frequency polygon is constructed, it will resemble the bell-shaped curve. Curves that are not symmetrical (i.e., those which are asymmetrical) are called "skewed distributions." (See the Graphical Representations section of this book.) **Hot hint: I want you to commit to memory the fact that the 68-95-99.7 rule (the empirical rule) states that in a normal distribution 68% of the scores fall within +/-1 standard deviation (SD) of the mean; 95% within 2 SDs of the mean; and 99.7% within 3 SDs of the mean. The verdict: almost all the scores will fall between 3 SDs of the mean.**      **(a)**

742. The most common measures of central tendency are the mean, the median, and the mode. The mode is

   a.   the most frequently occurring score and the least-important measure of central tendency.
   b.   always 10% less than the mean.
   c.   the arithmetic average.
   d.   the middle score in the distribution of scores.

The mode is the highest or maximum point of concentration. The French phrase *à la mode* means "in style" or "in vogue." The mode is the score that is most "in style" or occurs the most. Just remember that pie à la mode has a "high concentration of calories." **The modal score is the highest point on the curve.** Hence, a test might tell you that a population of schizophrenics consists of 400 whites, 60 Asian Americans, and 100 African Americans and ask you to pick out the so-called modal category, rather than the modal score. In this case the highest value is held by the white population. Statisticians refer to choice "c" as the "mean" and choice "d" as the "median."      **(a)**

743. A bimodal distribution has two modes (i.e., most frequently occurring scores). Graphically, this looks roughly like

    a.    a symmetrical bell-shaped curve.
    b.    a camel's back with two humps.
    c.    the top half of a bowling ball.
    d.    a mountain which is leaning toward the left.

Come on, admit it now, the camel's back makes a nice little memory device doesn't it? If you decided to give the NCE to first-year counseling students and counselor educators teaching in CACREP programs, the distribution of scores would probably be bimodal. So would a distribution of men's and women's heights. Chances are that in both of the aforementioned situations two peaks would be evident. When a curve exhibits more than two peaks it is known as a "multimodal" distribution. This can be contrasted to the curve with just a single peak (e.g., the normal curve) which is said to be "unimodal" (see the Graphical Representations section of this book).     **(b)**

744. In a basic curve or so-called frequency polygon the point of maximum concentration is the

    a.    mean.
    b.    median.
    c.    mode.
    d.    range.

Say your exam provides you with a list of test scores such as this: 1, 10, 19, 1, 10, 19, 19, 19, 6, 54. You are then asked to delineate the mode. Your answer will simply be determined by finding the score that appears the most, which in this example would be 19 since four individuals scored 19. The mean, choice "a," would be computed by adding the numbers provided (i.e., the scores) and then dividing by the number of scores which in this case is 10. Here the sum of the scores equals 158 divided by 10 which yields a mean value of 15.8. The median, choice "b," is defined as the score which is the exact middle of the distribution. (Just remember that the median is in the middle of the highway.)

Choice "d," the range, which is a measure of variability, is the distance between the largest and the smallest scores (i.e., 54 and 1). To compute the range, you would take 54 – 1 and get a range of 53. **The larger the range the greater the dispersion or spread of scores from the mean.** Since the computation of the range is based solely on the computation of two scores, the variance and the standard deviation (the square root of the variance) are more stable statistics.                                    **(c)**

745. The most useful measure of central tendency is the

     a.   mean, often abbreviated by an X with a bar over it.
     b.   median, often abbreviated by Md. or Mdn.
     c.   mode, often abbreviated by Mo.
     d.   point of maximum concentration.

In everyday life when we use the word *average* we are referring to the "mean." Perhaps this is because in most instances it is the most useful of the three measures of central tendency. Nevertheless, if a distribution is plagued with extreme scores then the "median" is the statistic of choice. The median is best for skewed distributions. If a counselor decides to figure the average income of incoming undergraduate freshmen in a crisis-intervention class, and one of the students is a millionaire, then the median will be a more valuable statistic than the mean since the mean would be raised significantly by the millionaire's income. And of course, you were able to discern that choice "d" is a definition of choice "c," mode, which researchers consider the least-important measure of central tendency.                       **(a)**

746. In a career counseling session an electrical engineer mentions three jobs he has held. The first paid $10 per hour, the second paid $30 per hour, and the third paid a higher rate of $50 per hour. The counselor responds that the client is averaging $30 per hour. The counselor is using

     a.   a Pearson Product-Moment Correlation coefficient.
     b.   a factorial design.
     c.   the harmonic mean.
     d.   the mean.

The mean is the sum of scores divided by the number of scores: $10 + $30 + $50 = $90; $90 divided by three jobs = $30. A factorial design has virtually nothing to do with this question! The term *factorial design*—which can easily be confused with the term *factor analysis*—can be used when there are two or more independent variables. Choice "c," the harmonic mean, refers to a central tendency statistic that is the reciprocal of the arithmetic mean of the reciprocals of the set of values. Say, for example, that your exam asks you to calculate the harmonic mean for three scores of: 2, 2, and 4. First you would convert them to reciprocals: ½, ½, and ¼. The arithmetic mean then is ½ + ½ + ¼ = 1¼ or 1.25/3 = .4166. The reciprocal of this gives you a harmonic mean of 1/.4166. The statistic has limited usage; however, it is occasionally called for if measurements were not made on an appropriate scale (e.g., data revealed the number of behaviors per hour, when the number of minutes per behavior would be more useful). The harmonic cannot be utilized with negative numbers or if the data include a score of zero.     **(d)**

747. From a mathematical standpoint, the mean is merely the sum of the scores divided by the number of scores. The mean is misleading when

    a.   the distribution is skewed.
    b.   the distribution has no extreme scores.
    c.   there are extreme scores.
    d.   a and c.

    See question 745 for an explanation.     **(d)**

748. When a distribution of scores is not distributed normally, statisticians call it

    a.   Gauss's curve.
    b.   a symmetrical bell-shaped curve.
    c.   a skewed distribution.
    d.   an invalid distribution.

Your exam might show you a graphic representation of a distribution and ask you whether the distribution is skewed. **In a skewed distribution the left and right side of the curve are not mirror images. In a skewed distribution the mean, the median, and the mode fall at different points. In a normal curve they will fall at the same point** (see the Graphical Representations section of this book).    **(c)**

749. The median is

    a.    the middle score when the data are arranged from highest to lowest.

    b.    the arithmetic average.

    c.    the most-frequent value obtained.

    d.    never more useful than the mean.

Use your memory device: the median is the exact "middle of the highway"—it is the "middle score." In studies measuring variables with extreme scores (e.g., family size or income), the median would be the best statistic. Your exam could specify a distribution of scores and ask you to name the median score. Say, for example, your exam provides these scores: 1, 90, 12, 90, 6, 8, 7. First rank the scores from the lowest to the highest: 1, 6, 7, 8, 12, 90, 90. In this case, the median score is 8 since there are three scores above 8 (12, 90, 90) and three scores below it (1, 6, 7). Now let's assume that the test-construction committee isn't so kind. In fact, maybe they are feeling a little sadistic that day. This time they add another score so there are eight scores rather than seven in the distribution. Now the distribution has an even rather than an odd number of scores. Assume the score of 10 was added. Thus when you rank order the distribution, it now looks like this: 1, 6, 7, 8, 10, 12, 90, 90. Do I hear some head-scratching here—maybe even a tinge of panic? What's that you say? You can't find a value that has an equal number of scores above and below it. Well you're correct—it doesn't exist. The trick here is to know that the median is a score or a "potential score" that divides the distribution in half. Therefore, when a distribution has an even number of scores, you take the arithmetic mean of the two middle scores and use this as the median. In this case: 8 + 10 = 18 and 18/2 = 9. The median of 9 lies midway between the middle scores of 8 and 10. In some cases, your computation could legitimately yield a fraction (e.g., 9½).   **(a)**

750. In a new experiment, a counselor educator wants to ferret out the effects of more than one IV. She will use a _____ design.

    a.    Pearson Product-Moment $r$.
    b.    Spearman rank order rho
    c.    factorial
    d.    Solomon four-group

In a factorial experiment, several experimental variables are investigated and interactions can be noted. Factorial designs, therefore, include two or more IVs. Sometimes the IVs in a factorial design are called levels. Experts admonish you not to let the term *levels* throw you. It does not connote hierarchy. You could have two levels of the IV such as "individual therapy" and "group therapy" but this does not mean that one is better than another. Choices "a" and "b" are not considered pure experimental. Now even though choice "d" is incorrect, it is indeed a must-know term. In the Solomon four-group design (design created by psychologist Richard L. Solomon) the researcher uses two control groups. Only one experimental group and one control group are pretested. The other control group and experimental group are merely posttested. The genius of the design is that it lets the researcher know if results are influenced by pretesting. The two control groups as well as the two experimental groups can then be compared.   **(c)**

751. Regardless of the shape, the _____ will always be the high point when a distribution is displayed graphically.

    a.    degrees of freedom (df)
    b.    mean
    c.    median
    d.    mode

The mode will be highest because it is the point where the most frequently occurring score falls.   **(d)**

752. A group of first-semester graduate students in counseling took an experimental counseling exam that was much more difficult than the NCE. All of the students scored very low. A distribution of their scores would

    a.    always be a bimodal distribution.
    b.    be positively skewed.
    c.    be negatively skewed.
    d.    produce a curve with a long tail to the left side of the graph.

Try to imagine this in your mind or roughly graph it on scratch paper. Most of the scores would fall on the left or the low side of the distribution. Graphically then, the "tail" of the distribution would point to the right or the positive side. **Memory device: The tail indicates whether the distribution is positively or negatively skewed** (see the Graphical Representations section of this book). **(b)**

753. Nine of the world's finest counselor educators are given an elementary exam on counseling theory. Needless to say, all of them scored extremely high. The distribution of scores would most likely be

    a.    a bell-shaped curve.
    b.    positively skewed.
    c.    negatively skewed.
    d.    indicative that more information would be necessary.

Since high scores pack the right side of the distribution, this gives you a long tail that points to the left, which indicates a negative skew. The tail points you in the direction of the correct answer! (See the Graphical Representations section.) **(c)**

754. Billy received an 82 on his college math final. This is Billy's raw score on the test. A raw score simply refers to the number of items correctly answered. A raw score is expressed in the units

by which it was originally obtained. The raw score is not altered mathematically. Billy's raw score indicates that

a.  he is roughly a B student.
b.  he answered 82% correctly.
c.  his percentile rank is 82.
d.  more information is obviously necessary.

Don't get burnt on a question like this; the fact that Billy scored an 82 tells you next to nothing. Raw data is like a raw piece of meat; it is uncooked and nothing has been done to it. How many questions are on Billy's test? Well, you don't know, do you? So, you couldn't choose choice "b" since you don't have enough information to figure out the percentage. The question doesn't specify this critical fact. You see, if Billy scored an 82 on a test with 82 questions, then he had a perfect score. If, however, the exam had several thousand items, his score may not have been all that high. I say "may not have been all that high," since a raw score of 82 might have been the highest score of anybody tested. You would need a "transformed score" or "standard score" (such as choice "c") to make this determination. **Okay, now memorize this: The benefit of standard scores such as percentiles, t-scores, z-scores, stanines, or standard deviations over raw scores is that a standard score allows you to analyze the data in relation to the properties of the normal bell-shaped curve.** **(d)**

755. A distribution with class intervals can be graphically displayed via a bar graph also called a

a.  histogram.
b.  sociogram.
c.  genogram.
d.  genus.

Most bar graphs are drawn in a vertical fashion. When the bars are drawn horizontally it is sometimes called a "horizontal bar chart." A "double-barred histogram" can be used to compare two distributions of scores such as pre- and posttest scores (see Chapter 13). **(a)**

756. When a horizontal line is drawn under a frequency distribution it is known as

    a.   mesokurtic.
    b.   the y axis.
    c.   the ordinate.
    d.   the x axis.

    Choice "a" is from the Latin root "meso" or middle, and kurtic refers to the peakedness of a curve. The normal Gaussian curve is said to be mesokurtic since the peak is in the middle. **When graphically representing data, the "x axis" (also called the abscissa) is used to plot the independent variable. The x axis is the horizontal axis. The "y axis" (also called the ordinate) is the vertical axis which is used as a scale for the dependent variable.**                                        **(d)**

757. The x axis is used to plot the IV scores. The x axis could also be called the _____ on your exam.

    a.   y axis
    b.   abscissa
    c.   DV
    d.   vertical axis

    Again, it is the horizontal axis which plots the IV—the factor manipulated via the experimenter.                          **(b)**

758. The y axis is used to plot the frequency of the DVs. The y axis could also be called the _____ on your exam.

    a.   ordinate
    b.   abscissa
    c.   IV
    d.   horizontal axis

    The ordinate plots the DV or experimental data. **A simple memory device might be that the y axis is vertical like the letter "y."** It works for me and a lot of students.          **(a)**

759. If a distribution is bimodal, then there is a good chance that

    a.    the curve will be normal.
    b.    the curve will be shaped like a symmetrical bell.
    c.    the researcher is working with two distinct populations.
    d.    the research is useless in the field of counseling.

    Imagine if you will that you are plotting the average weights of adult men and boys under the age of 10. In all probability, two distinct points of concentration would be evident on the curve (see Chapter 13).    **(c)**

760. If an experiment can be replicated by others with almost identical findings, then the experiment is

    a.    impacted by the observer effect.
    b.    said to be a naturalistic observation.
    c.    the result of ethological observation.
    d.    said to be reliable.

    Choice "a" refers to a situation in which the person observing in a participant observer research study influences/alters the situation. You will recall that the term *reliability* in the social sciences is also used in regard to testing to indicate consistency in measurement. Choice "b" occurs when clients are observed in a "natural" setting or situation. Choice "c" relates to the observation of animals.    **(d)**

761. The range is a measure of variance and usually is calculated by determining the difference between the highest and the lowest score. Thus, on a test where the top score was a 93 and the lowest score was a 33 out of 100, the range would be

    a.    61.
    b.    77.
    c.    59.
    d.    more information is necessary.

**The range is the simplest way to measure the spread of scores.** Technically, statistics that measure the spread of scores are known as "measures of variability." **The range is usually calculated by subtracting the lowest score from the highest score** (e.g., 93 - 33 = 60). But wait: horrors, 60 is not a choice! Well, I purposely gave you this example to point out that some tests and statistics books define the range as the highest score minus the lowest score plus 1. If the test specifies the "inclusive range" then use the formula with plus 1. If not, I'd go with the "exclusive range" formula, which does not include it. My guess is that most counseling tests would give you either 60 or 61 as a choice (probably 60) but not both.               **(a)**

762. A sociogram is to a counseling group as a scattergram is to

    a.   the normal curve.
    b.   the range.
    c.   a correlation coefficient.
    d.   the John Henry effect.

**A scattergram—also known as a scatterplot—is a pictorial diagram or graph of two variables being correlated** (see the Graphical Representations section of this book). And yes, my dear reader, choice "d" is for real. There really is a John Henry effect. The John Henry effect (also called compensatory rivalry of a comparison group) is a threat to the internal validity of an experiment that occurs when subjects strive to prove that an experimental treatment that could threaten their livelihood really isn't all that effective. (An old railroad song asserts that John Henry died with a steam drill in his hand to prove he could outwork the machine.) Say, for example, that counselor educators were asked to use computers as part of the teaching experience but were worried that the computers might ultimately take their jobs! The counselor educators in the comparison control group might purposely spend more time preparing their materials and give students more support than they normally would. One way for the researcher to handle this problem is to make observations before the experiment begins. Another control group phenomenon that threatens internal validity in research is the "Resentful

Demoralization of the Comparison Group" (also called "compensatory equalization"). Here, the comparison group lowers their performance or behaves in an inept manner because they have been denied the experimental treatment. When this occurs, the experimental group looks better than they should. If the comparison group deteriorates throughout the experiment while the experimental group does not, then demoralization could be noted. This could be measured via a pretest and a posttest.    **(c)**

763. A counselor educator is teaching two separate classes in individual inventory. In the morning class the counselor educator has 53 students and in the afternoon class she has 177 students. A statistician would expect that the range of scores on a test would be

   a.    greater in the afternoon class than the morning class.
   b.    smaller in the afternoon class.
   c.    impossible to speculate about without more data.
   d.    nearly the same in either class.

**The range generally increases with sample size.**    **(a)**

764. The variance is a measure of dispersion of scores around some measure of central tendency. The variance is the standard deviation squared. A popular IQ test has a standard deviation (SD) of 15. A counselor would expect that if the mean IQ score is 100, then

   a.    the average score on the test would be 122.
   b.    95% of the people who take the test will score between 85 and 115.
   c.    99% of the people who take the test will score between 85 and 115.
   d.    68% of the people who take the test will score between 85 and 115.

Statistically speaking 68.26% of the scores fall within + or -1 SD of the mean; 95.44% of the scores fall within + or -2 SD of the mean; and 99.74% of the scores fall within +/-3 SD of the mean.    **(d)**

765. Using the data in question 764 one could say that a person with an IQ score of 122 would fall within

    a.    + or -1 SD of the mean.
    b.    the average IQ range.
    c.    an IQ score which is more that 2 SD above the mean.
    d.    + or -2 SD of the mean.

    Two SD would be IQs from 70 to 130 since 2 SD would be 30 IQ points. Please note that if everybody scored the same on the test then the SD would be zero. An SD, for example, of 1.8 has scores closer to the mean (i.e., not as spread out or scattered) than an SD of 2.8. **The greater the SD, the greater is the spread.**                                                    **(d)**

766. The standard deviation (SD) is the square root of the variance. A z-score of +1 would be the same as

    a.    1 SD above the mean.
    b.    1 SD below the mean.
    c.    the same as a so-called t-score.
    d.    the median score if the population is normal.

    **Z-scores are the same as standard deviations! In fact, z-scores are often called standard scores. Write it on your wrist and don't wash it off for a week.** A z-score is the most elementary type of standard score. It is possible your exam will refer to it merely as a standard score. Just say it in slang: "z-score" (sounds rather like saying "the score") is simply the SD. A z-score of +1 or 1 SD would include about 34% of the cases in a normal population. For those with a fear of negative integers, the normal distribution also can be described using t-scores sometimes called "transformed scores." The t-score uses a mean of 50 with each SD as 10. Hence, a z-score of -1.0 would be a t-score of 40. A z-score of -1.5 would be a t-score of 35 and so on. If double digit figures intimidate you, then you might want to analyze the normal distribution using a "stanine" score which divides the distribution into nine equal parts with 1 the lowest and 9 the highest portion of the curve. (See Chapter 13).    **(a)**

767. Z-scores (also called standard scores) are the same as standard deviations, thus a z-score of -2.5 means

    a.    2.5 SD below the mean.
    b.    2.5 SD above the mean.
    c.    a CEEB score of 500.
    d.    –.05% of the population falls within this area of the curve.

This would be a t-score of 25. Now, let's examine choice "c" which expresses the abbreviation for the College Entrance Examination Board (CEEB) scores. This standard score is used for tests such as the GRE or the SAT. The scale ranges from 200 to 800 with a mean of 500. CEEB scores use a standard deviation of 100. Scores lower than 200 or above 800 are simply rated as end-point scores. A score of 200 corresponds to 3 SD below the mean with 800 landing at a point 3 SD above the mean. Therefore, in this case, choice "c" would need to read "a CEEB score of 250" to be accurate. (That is to say, you would take the CEEB mean of 500 and subtract 2½ SD. Since each SD on the CEEB scale is 100 you would subtract 250 from 500 which gives you a CEEB score of 250.) **It is conceivable that your exam could refer to a CEEB score as an ETS score and the scale was created to eliminate negative scores.** (See Chapter 13) **(a)**

768. A t-score is different from a z-score. A z-score is the same as the SD. A t-score, however, has a mean of 50 with every 10 points landing at a SD above or below the mean. Thus a t-score of 60 would equal +1 SD while a t-score of 40 would be

    a.    –2 SD.
    b.    –1 SD.
    c.    a z-score of +2.
    d.    a z-score of +1.

Note that the t-score isn't as mathematically threatening since it is never expressed as a negative number. Choice "a" would be a t-score of 30, choice "c" a t-score of 70, and choice "d" a t-score of 60. Here again, a look at the normal curve displayed in the Graphical Representations section of the book should be helpful. **(b)**

769. An IQ score on an IQ test which was 3 SD above the mean would be

 a.  about average.
 b.  slightly below the norm for adults.
 c.  approximately 110.
 d.  very superior.

Think of it this way. Over 99% of the population will score between + or -3 SD of the mean. Therefore, less than 1% of the population would score at a level 3 SD above the mean. Now that would be a very high IQ score; 145 on the WAIS-IV to be exact. Lewis M. Terman, a pioneer in the study of intelligence, classified any children with IQs over 140 as "geniuses."  **(d)**

770. A platykurtic distribution would look approximately like

 a.  the upper half of a bowling ball.
 b.  the normal distribution.
 c.  the upper half of a hot dog, lying on its side over the abscissa.
 d.  a camel's back.

**If you see the word *kurtosis* on your exam, it refers to the peakedness of a frequency distribution. A "platykurtic" distribution is flatter and more spread out than the normal curve.** This is easy to remember if you consider that "plat" sounds rather like "flat." When a curve is very tall, thin, and peaked it is considered "leptokurtic." **Suggested memory device: A leptokurtic distribution leaps tall buildings in a single bound.** Well, Superman fans, how about it; does that do it justice? (See Chapter 13.)  **(c)**

771. Test scores on an exam that fell below 3 SD of the mean or above 3 SD of the mean could be described as

    a.   extreme.
    b.   very typical or within the average range.
    c.   close to the mean.
    d.   very low scores.

    If you graph this situation you will note that these scores would be unusually high (which negates choices "b," "c," and "d") or very low.                                                                                   **(a)**

772. In World War II the Air Force used stanine scores as a measurement. **Stanine scores divide the distribution into nine equal intervals with stanine 1 as the lowest ninth and 9 as the highest ninth. In this system 5 is the mean.** Thus a Binet IQ score of 101 would fall in stanine

    a.   1.
    b.   9.
    c.   5.
    d.   7.

    Stanine is the contraction of the words *standard* and *nine*. The mean or average score on the Binet is 100, so a Binet score of 101 would fall in stanine 5. (See Chapter 13.)                          **(c)**

773. There are four basic measurement scales: the nominal, the ordinal, the interval, and the ratio. The nominal scale is strictly a qualitative scale. It is the simplest type of scale. It is used to distinguish logically separated groups. Which of the following illustrates the function of the nominal scale?

    a.   A horse categorized as a second-place winner in a show.
    b.   A *DSM* or *ICD* diagnostic category.
    c.   An IQ score of 111.
    d.   The weight of an Olympic barbell set.

The order of complexity of S. S. Stevens's four types of measurement scales can be memorized by noting the French word *noir* meaning black (**n**ominal, **o**rdinal, **i**nterval, **r**atio). Parametric tests rely strictly on interval and ratio data, while nonparametric tests are designed only for nominal or ordinal information. The nominal scale is the most elementary as it does not provide "quantitative" (measurable) information. The nominal scale merely classifies, names, labels, or identifies by group (choice "b" is thus correct). **A nominal scale has no true zero point and does not indicate order.** Other examples would be a street address, telephone number, political party affiliation, brand of therapy, or number on a player's uniform. Adding, subtracting, multiplying, or dividing the aforementioned nominal categories would prove meaningless.    **(b)**

774. The ordinal scale rank orders variables, though the relative distance between the elements is not always equal. An example of this would be

   a.   a horse categorized as a second-place winner in a race.
   b.   an IQ score of 111.
   c.   the weight of an Olympic barbell set.
   d.   a temperature of 78 degrees Fahrenheit.

This is the second level of measurement. Nominal data do not rank order the data like ordinal data. The rank does not indicate absolute differences. Thus, you could not say that the first-, second-, and third-place horses were equidistant apart. **The ordinal scale provides relative placement or standing but does not delineate absolute differences.** Again, adding, subtracting, multiplying, or dividing is a no-no with this scale. Ordinal sounds like "order" so you should have no problem committing this scale to memory.    **(a)**

775. The interval scale has numbers scaled at equal distances but has no absolute zero point. Most tests used in school fall into this

category. You can add and subtract using interval scales but cannot multiply or divide. An example of this would be that

a.    an IQ of 70 is 70 points below an IQ of 140, yet a counselor could not assert that a client with an IQ of 140 is twice as intelligent as a client with an IQ of 70.
b.    a 20 lb weight is half as heavy as a 40 lb weight.
c.    a first-place runner is three times as fast as the third-place finisher.
d.    a baseball player with number 9 on his uniform can get 9 times more hits than player number 1.

Since the intervals are the same, the amount of difference can be stipulated (e.g., three IQ points). Using this scale, distances between each number are equal yet it is unclear how far each number is from zero. Division is not permissible inasmuch as division assumes an absolute zero. (If you had an absolute zero then you could in fact assert that a person with an IQ of 140 would be twice as smart as someone with an IQ of 70. But of course, zero on an IQ test does not equal zero knowledge; hence, **IQ tests provide interval measurement**.)          **(a)**

776. A ratio scale is an interval scale with a true zero point. Ratio measurements are possible using this scale. Addition, subtraction, multiplication, and division all can be utilized on a ratio scale. In terms of counseling research

a.    the ratio scale is the most practical.
b.    all true studies utilize the ratio scale.
c.    a and b.
d.    most psychological attributes cannot be measured on a ratio scale.

If you remember your memory device "noir" you'll recall that the final letter "r" stands for the ratio scale, which is the highest level of measurement. Time, height, weight, temperature on the Kelvin scale, volume, and distance meet the requirements of this scale. Please note the word *most* in the correct choice (i.e., choice "d"). Occasionally, a trait such as GSR (galvanic skin response) biofeedback could be classified as a ratio scale measurement. Since most measurements used in counseling studies do not qualify as ratio scales, choices "a" and "b" are misleading. **(d)**

777. Researchers often utilize naturalistic observation when doing ethological investigations or studying children's behavior. In this approach

   a.   the researcher manipulates the IV.
   b.   the researcher manipulates the IV and the DV.
   c.   the researcher does not manipulate or control variables.
   d.   the researcher will rely on a 2 × 3 factorial design.

**When utilizing naturalistic observation the researcher does not intervene.** Preferably, the setting is "natural" rather than an artificial laboratory environment. Historically speaking, this is the oldest method of research. Choice "d" indicates a study using two independent variables. The 2 × 3 is called *factorial notation*. The first variable has two levels (e.g., male or female) and the second independent variable has three levels. **(c)**

778. The simplest form of descriptive research is the _____, which requires a questionnaire return or completion rate of _____ to be accurate.

   a.   survey; 5%
   b.   survey; 10–25%
   c.   survey; 50–75%
   d.   survey; 95%

Unfortunately, it has been estimated that in most surveys the return rate hovers around the 40% mark. In a survey, the researcher attempts to gather large amounts of data, often utilizing a questionnaire or an interview, in order to generate generalizations regarding the behavior of the population as a whole. Ideally, the sample size will be at least 100. (Compare this to an experimental study which can generally get by with a sample size of 15 per group.) A public opinion poll such as the

Gallup is an example of a survey. **Survey problems include: poor construction of the instrument, a low return rate, and the fact that often subjects are not picked at random and thus are not representative of the population.**    **(c)**

779. A researcher gives a depressed patient a sugar pill and the individual's depression begins to lift. This is known as

   a.    the Hawthorne effect.
   b.    the Halo effect.
   c.    the placebo effect.
   d.    the learned helplessness syndrome.

   A student once told me that while he was preparing for final exams his roommate suggested that he "pop a couple uppers" for energy. The student did indeed pop the pills, studied like a whirlwind, and aced all his finals. He was sold on the pills until his roommate discovered that the two amphetamine capsules were still sitting on the table—the student had swallowed two ordinary breath mints lying next to the drugs! The student thought the pills would work and so they did. Researchers often give clients involved in studies an inert substance (i.e., a placebo such as a gelatin capsule) so it can be compared with the real drug or treatment procedure. **A nocebo, on the other hand, has a negative effect such as when a doctor comments that a person with such and such condition has only six weeks to live.** If this happens to you or one of your clients always remember that a statistic may not apply to you personally. The fact that the average counselor at your agency wears a size 9 shoe is meaningless to you if you wear a size 7.    **(c)**

780. A researcher notes that a group of clients who are not receiving counseling, but are observed in a research study, are improving. Her hypothesis is that the attention she has given them has been curative. The best explanation of their improvement would be

   a.    the Hawthorne effect.
   b.    the Halo effect.
   c.    the Rosenthal effect.

d. a Type II error in the research.

Ah yes, this relates to the famous study by Australian psychologist Elton Mayo and Fritz Roethlisberger and colleagues that took place from 1924 to 1932 at the Hawthorne Works of the Western Electric Company, Cicero, Illinois. The research indicated that work production tended to increase with better lighting or worse lighting conditions. The verdict: Simply that if subjects know they are part of an experiment—or if they are given more attention because of the experiment—their performance sometimes improves. When observations are made and the subjects' behavior is influenced by the very presence of the researcher, it is often called a "reactive effect" or "reactivity" of observation/experimentation. The subject is said to be **reacting to the presence of the investigation. As I mentioned in question 760, this is sometimes known as an observer effect.** A comprehensive test without at least one question on the Hawthorne effect—no way! **(a)**

781. An elementary school counselor tells the third-grade teacher that a test revealed that certain children will excel during the school year. In reality, no such test was administered. Moreover, the children were unaware of the experiment. By the end of the year, all of the children who were supposed to excel did excel! This would best be explained via

a. the Hawthorne effect.
b. the Halo effect.
c. the Rosenthal effect or the experimenter expectancy effect.
d. observer bias.

Well, forget the Hawthorne effect this time around since the kids don't even know an experiment is in progress. Here the "Rosenthal effect" or experimenter expectancy effect is probably having the impact. The Rosenthal effect, named after noted psychologist Robert Rosenthal, and no relation to this author, asserts that the experimenter's beliefs about the individual may cause the individual to be treated in a special way so that the individual begins to fulfill the experimenter's expectations.

**Hint:** When you see the Hawthorne effect question on your exam you can bet that the Rosenthal effect question is within shouting distance. Choice "d" is self-explanatory. The observer has perceptions regarding the research that are not accurate. **(c)**

782. A panel of investigators discovered that a researcher who completed a major study had unconsciously rated attractive females as better counselors. This is an example of

    a.   the Hawthorne effect.
    b.   the Halo effect.
    c.   the Rosenthal effect.
    d.   trend analysis.

    The Halo effect occurs when a trait which is not being evaluated (e.g., attractiveness or how well he or she is liked) influences a researcher's rating on another trait (e.g., counseling skill). Choice "d," trend analysis, refers to a statistical procedure performed at different times to see if a trend is evident. Some exams use the term to describe an application of the ANOVA to see if performance on one variable mimics the same trend on a second variable. Say you have arranged three groups of subjects in regard to their ability to respond to reality therapy (i.e., poor clients, average clients, and good clients). Your hypothesis is that clients at each level also will respond better to REBT than will those on the level below them. (For example, good reality therapy clients will be better REBT clients than average or poor reality therapy clients.) Here the ANOVA allows you to statistically test this hypothesis. **(b)**

783. All of the following describe the analysis of covariance technique *except:*

    a.   It is a correlation coefficient.
    b.   It controls for sample differences which exist.
    c.   It helps to remove confounding, extraneous variables.
    d.   It statistically eliminates differences in average values influenced by covariates.

Just what is the analysis of covariance or the ANCOVA/ ANACOVA as they say in statistical circles? First and foremost, the ANCOVA is similar to the ANOVA yet more powerful because it can help to eliminate differences between groups which otherwise could not be solely attributed to the experimental IVs. In other words, although ideally each random sample will be equal to every other random sample this is not always the case. A so-called COVARIATE, which correlates with the DV, could be present. Let's take this very simple example. Imagine that you are using an ANOVA to test the null hypothesis regarding three groups of college students. First, a random sample of college students is selected. Next, the sample is randomly divided into three groups. Group A receives biofeedback, Group B receives meditation, and Group C receives instruction in self-hypnosis. All are intended to reduce test anxiety. At the end of the semester a test which measures test anxiety will be administered to all three groups. The ANOVA would then be applied to test the null hypothesis. Null, of course, would be rejected if a significant difference between the three groups' means was evident on the test anxiety measure. Here comes the problem, however; your random groups, as pointed out earlier, may not really be all that identical. You might suspect, for example, that athletic training is a covariate and thus impacts upon the measure of test anxiety; your DV. The ANCOVA allows you to correct for the differences in the groups (possibly due to prior athletic training). By making the groups more alike upfront, it will enhance the possibility that the IVs (biofeedback, meditation, and self-hypnosis instruction) rather than a covariate, such as athletic training, caused the differences (i.e., the DVs) in the groups. In summary, the ANCOVA tests a null hypothesis regarding the means of two or more groups **after the random samples are adjusted to eliminate average differences**. It is often referred to as an "adjusted average" statistical procedure. **The ANCOVA is an advanced technique and thus there *might* be one question on it on an exam like the NCE or CPCE hence, I wouldn't waste a great deal of time attempting to master all the nuances of this procedure.** **(a)**

784. Three years ago an inpatient addiction treatment center in a hospital asked their clients if they would like to undergo an archaic form of therapy created by Wilhelm Reich known as "vegotherapy." Approximately half of the clients stated they would like try the treatment while the other 50% stated that they would stick with the tried-and-true program of the center. Outcome data on their drinking was compiled at the end of seven weeks. Today—three years later—a statistician compared the two groups based on their drinking behavior at the end of the seven weeks using a $t$ test. This study could best be described as

   a.    correlation research.
   b.    a true experiment.
   c.    a cohort study.
   d.    causal comparative research.

   Since the groups were not randomly assigned and the current researcher did not truly control the IV in the study (since it took place three years ago), "d" is the best answer. Just for the record a cohort study examines people who were born at the same time (or shared an event; for example, fought in Vietnam) in regard to a given characteristic. For example, one might wish to discover how many women born during the Great Depression that began in 1929 committed suicide.    **(d)**

785. The WAIS-IV IQ test is given to 100 adults picked randomly. How many of the adults most likely would receive an IQ score between 85 and 115?

   a.    7.
   b.    99.
   c.    95.
   d.    68.

   This is really an easy question to answer if you remember that in a normal distribution approximately 68% of the population will fall between +/-1 SD of the mean. One SD on most popular IQ tests is 15 or 16, and the mean score is generally 100. Choice "c" is indicative of +/-2 SD, while choice "b" approximates +/-3 SD.    **(d)**

786. A researcher creates a new motoric test in which clients throw a baseball at a target 40 feet away. Each client is given 100 throws, and the mean on the test is 50. (In other words, out of 100 throws the mean number of times the client will hit the target is 50 times.) Sam took the test and hit the target just two times out of the 100 throws allowed. Jeff, on the other hand, hit the target an amazing 92 times out of 100 trials. Using the concept of statistical regression toward the mean the research would predict that

    a.   Sam's and Jeff's scores will stay about the same if they take the test again.
    b.   Sam and Jeff will both score over 95 next time.
    c.   Sam's score will increase while Jeff's will go down.
    d.   Sam will beat Jeff if they both are tested again.

Statistical regression is a threat to internal validity. Statistical **regression predicts that very high and very low scores will move toward the mean if a test is administered again**. This concept is based on "the law of filial regression," which is a genetic principle that asserts that generational traits move toward the mean. If a father is 7 feet tall, then the chances are that his son will be shorter (though still much taller than the average person), whereas if a father is 4 feet, 10 inches, chances are his son will have a few inches on his father. The statistical analogy suggests that extremely low scores on an exam or a pretest will improve while the unusually high scores will get lower. Statistical regression results from errors (i.e., lack of reliability) in measurement instruments and must be taken into account when interpreting test data. Now as for alternative "d" I can only say don't bet on it. Most scores don't change that much, and although Sam's score will probably inch up a bit and Jeff's will lose a little ground, Sam will probably still be in the lower quartile and Jeff the upper quartile. **You must know the statistical lingo: the term *quartile* is common and refers to the points that divide a distribution into fourths. This indicates that the 25th percentile is the first quartile, the second quartile is the median, and the third lies at the 75th percentile. The score distance between the 25th**

**percentile and the 75th percentile is called the interquartile range.** **(c)**

787. Standardized tests always have

    a.  formal procedures for test administration and scoring.
    b.  a mean of 100 and an SD of 15.
    c.  a mean of 100 and a standard error of measurement of 3.
    d.  a reliability coefficient of +.90 or above.

    Standardization implies that the testing format, the test materials, and the scoring process are consistent. **(a)**

788. There are two distinct types of developmental studies. In a cross-sectional study, clients are assessed at one point in time. In a longitudinal study, however,

    a.  the researcher has an accomplice pose as a client and act in a certain manner.
    b.  the same people are studied over a period of time.
    c.  the researcher relies on a single observation of a variable being investigated.
    d.  all of the above.

    Some exams refer to the cross-sectional method as the "synchronic method" and the longitudinal as the "diachronic method." The longitudinal study is beneficial in the sense that age itself can be used as an IV. In a longitudinal study, data are collected at different points in time. In the cross-sectional method, data are indicative of measurements or observations at a single point in time, and thus it is preferable in terms of time consumption. The person in choice "a" is known as a "confederate" or a "stooge." Social psychology studies routinely employ "confederates" or "stooges," who are not real participants but in reality work with the researcher. **(b)**

789. A counselor educator, Dr. Y, is doing research on his classes. He hypothesizes that if he reinforces students in his morning class by smiling each time a student asks a relevant question, then

more students will ask questions and exam grades will go up. Betty and Linda accidentally overhear Dr. Y discussing the experiment with the department chair. Betty is a real people pleaser and decides that she will ask lots of questions and try to help Dr. Y confirm his hypothesis. Linda, nevertheless, is angry that she is being experimented on and promises Betty that Dr. Y could smile until the cows came in but she still wouldn't ask a question. Both Linda and Betty exemplify

a.    internal versus external validity.
b.    ipsative versus normative interpretation of test scores.
c.    the use of the nonparametric chi-square test.
d.    demand characteristics of experiments.

**Ipsative implies a within-person analysis (was your jog today faster than yesterday?) rather than a normative analysis between individuals.** In other words, are you looking at an individual's own patterns revealed via measurement (e.g., highs and lows) or whether his or her score is compared to others evaluated by the same measure. The former is "ipsative" while the latter is "normative." Choice "c" mentions what is perhaps the most popular nonparametric (i.e., a distribution which is not normal) statistical test, the chi-square. The chi-square— threatening as it sounds—is merely used to determine whether an obtained distribution differs significantly from an expected distribution. A chi-square might answer the question whether being a counseling major or a social work major determines if you will seek therapy for an elevator phobia. You must be able to have mutually exclusive categories to use the chi-square (such as "will seek therapy" or "won't seek therapy"). The answer to this question, nevertheless, is choice "d." A demand characteristic relates to any bit of knowledge—correct or incorrect—that the subject in an experiment is aware of that can influence his or her behavior. **Demand characteristics can confound an experiment.** Deception has been used as a tactic to reduce this dilemma.                                                    **(d)**

790. If an ANOVA yields a significant $F$ value, you could rely on _____ to test significant differences between group means.

    a.    one- and two-tailed $t$ tests
    b.    percentile rank
    c.    Duncan's multiple-range, Tukey's, or Scheffe's test
    d.    summative or formative evaluation

Choice "a" refers to whether a statistical test places the rejection area at one end of the distribution (one-tailed) or both ends of the distribution curve (two-tailed). A two-tailed test is often called a "nondirectional experimental hypothesis," while a one-tailed test is a "directional experimental hypothesis." In a one-tailed test your hypothesis specifies that one average mean is larger than another. So, a two-tailed hypothesis would be, "The average patient who has completed psychoanalysis will have a statistically *different* IQ from the average patient who has not received analysis." The one-tailed hypothesis would be, "The average patient who has completed psychoanalysis will have a statistically significantly *higher* IQ than the average patient who has not received analysis." When appropriate, one-tailed tests have the advantage of having more "power" than the two-tailed design (i.e., the statistical ability to reject correctly a false hypothesis). In choice "d" you should be aware that summative evaluation is used to assess a final product (e.g., how many high school students are not indulging in alcoholic beverages after completing a yearly program focusing on drug awareness education?). Summative research attempts to ascertain how well the goal has been met. Formative process research, on the other hand, is ongoing while the program is underway (e.g., after three weeks of a proposed year-long drug awareness education program how many high school students are taking drugs?). The correct answer to this question, of course, is alternative "c." An $F$ test for the ANOVA is analogous to the student's $t$ test table when performing a $t$ test. In order to further discriminate between the ANOVA groups the post hoc measures mentioned in choice "c" would be appropriate.　　**(c)**

791. Switching the order in which stimuli are presented to a subject in a study is known as

    a.   the Pygmalion effect.
    b.   counterbalancing.
    c.   ahistoric therapy.
    d.   multiple treatment interference.

Let choice "a" come as no surprise if it shows up on your exam. The Rosenthal/Experimenter effect often shows up wearing this name tag. The experimenter falls in love with his or her own hypothesis and the experiment becomes a self-fulfilling prophecy. Choice "b," the correct answer, is used to control for the fact that the order of an experiment could impact upon its outcome. The solution is merely to change the order of the experimental factors. Choice "c," "ahistoric therapy," connotes any psychotherapeutic model that focuses on the here and now rather than the past. This of course has nothing to do with answering the question. Choice "d" warns us that if a subject receives more than one treatment, then it is often tough to discern which modality truly caused the improvements.     **(b)**

792. A doctoral student who begins working on his bibliography for his thesis would most likely utilize

    a.   SPSS.
    b.   ERIC, for primary and secondary resources.
    c.   O*NET.
    d.   a random number table or random number-generation computer program.

Here's a must-know question for anyone seriously contemplating a thesis or dissertation. The Educational Resources Information Center (ERIC), www.eric.ed.gov/, is a resource bank of scholarly literature and resources to help you complete your literature search before you begin writing. So what's the scoop on the primary and secondary stuff? Glad you asked! If you say that Ellis said such and such and reference a book Ellis wrote then the resource or documentation is primary. If you say that Ellis said such and such and quote a general counseling text then the resource is considered secondary. The Statistical Package for the Social Sciences (SPSS) is a popular computer software program that can ease the pain of computing your statistics by hand in case you happen to have an aversion to numbers (e.g., a *t* test, correlation, or ANOVA). Actually, most large studies do rely on computers since they are faster and more accurate than scratch paper calculations. And if you marked choice "c" then you must have slept through my chapter on career development!    **(b)**

793. In a random sample each individual in the population has an equal chance of being selected. Selection is by chance. In a new study, however, it will be important to include 20% African Americans. What type of sampling procedure will be necessary?

   a.   Standard (i.e., simple) random sampling is adequate.
   b.   Cluster sampling is called for.
   c.   Stratified sampling would be best.
   d.   Horizontal sampling is required.

   **Remember:** Random sampling (choice "a") is like sticking your hand in a fish bowl to pick a winning ticket. In the random sample each subject has the same probability of being selected, and the selection of one subject does not affect the selection of another subject. The simple random sampling procedure eliminates the researcher's tendency to pick a biased sample of subjects. In this case, nevertheless, a simple random sampling procedure will not suffice, since a "stratum" (plural "strata") or a "special characteristic" needs to be represented. In this case it is race. In other studies it might be gender, educational degree, age, or perhaps therapeutic affiliation. The stratification variable in your sample should mimic the population at large. Thus, if 20% of all Rogerian counselors are African Americans, then your study on Rogerian counselors should have 20% African American counselors in your sample. In a research situation where a specific number of cases are necessary from each stratum, the procedure often is labeled as "quota sampling." Quota sampling is merely a type of stratified sampling procedure. The "cluster sample" (choice "b") is utilized when it is nearly impossible to find a list of the entire population. The cluster sample solves the problem by using an existing sample or cluster of people or selects a portion of the overall sample. A cluster sample will not be as accurate as a random sample yet it is often used due to time and practical considerations. Imagine trying to make a list of everybody in the United States who is securing treatment for heroin addiction so you can pick a random sample utilizing a random number generator. Instead, you might rely on the population in your home town chemical dependency unit. And yes there really is a procedure called "horizontal sampling," mentioned in choice "d." Horizontal sampling occurs when a researcher selects subjects from a single socioeconomic group. Horizontal sampling can be contrasted with "vertical sampling," which occurs when persons from two or more socioeconomic classes are utilized. **Since this question does not specify socioeconomic factors, you could have eliminated choice "d."**

**What if your exam asks about snowball sampling? Relax, I've got you covered. A snowball sample or a chain-referral sample uses subjects to … well … drum up other subjects for your study. Imagine you were studying heroin addicts living on the streets in a given location. It is possible you could not find them without the help of others in the same predicament.** **(c)**

794. A researcher wants to run a true experiment but insists she will not use a random sample. You could safely say that

    a. she absolutely, positively cannot run a true experiment.
    b. her research will absolutely, positively be casual comparative research.
    c. she could accomplish this using systematic sampling.
    d. her research will be correlational.

All good things come to an end. For years and years researchers relied on random sampling. Today researchers are slowly but surely embracing systematic sampling, since it is often easier to use. Here's how it works. With this approach you take every nth person. Say you have a list of 10,000 folks. You want 1,000 in your study. You pick the first person between one and 10 at random and then use every 10th person. According to some statisticians your results will be virtually the same as if you used good old random sampling. Still the random versus systematic sampling debate rages on with the majority embracing the old tried and true random approach. **Must-know exam concept: sampling error. One problem is that small samples intended to mimic the population sometimes do not! The average or mean IQ is 100. This is known as the population parameter. But say you took the mean IQ in a counseling class with 20 students. It could turn out to be 100, but there also is a good chance it might not. (I know, counselors have much higher IQs right!) The margin of error stated in political poll results is based on this concept.**      **(c)**

795. An operational definition

   a.   outlines a procedure.
   b.   is theoretical.
   c.   outlines a construct.
   d.   is synonymous with the word *axiom*.

Choice "d" or **axiom**, unlike a theory, is a universally accepted idea needing no additional proof (e.g., hence REBT is a theory; gravity exists on planet earth is an axiom). It is very important that researchers "operationally define" procedures so that other researchers can attempt to "replicate" an experimental procedure. Replication implies that another researcher can repeat the experiment exactly as it was performed before. In most cases, counselors would not accept a finding as scientific unless an experiment has been replicated. This means that a researcher should never say something like, "we reinforced children for good classroom behavior." Instead, the procedure must be delineated into specific values and exact terminology. For example: "We reinforced each child with 25 cents within 30 seconds after he or she answered five addition problems on the ABC Test correctly."      **(a)**

796. In a parametric test the assumption is that the scores are normally distributed. In nonparametric testing the curve is not a normal distribution. Which of these tests are nonparametric statistical measures?

    a.    Mann–Whitney $U$ test, often just called the $U$ test.
    b.    Wilcoxon signed-rank test for matched pairs.
    c.    Soloman and the Kruskal–Wallis $H$ test.
    d.    All of the above are nonparametric measures.

All of the above-referenced tests are categorized as "nonparametric." Many exams refer to nonparametric statistical tests as "distribution-free" tests. Before I explicate their differences I want to familiarize you with the term *matched design*. **In a matched design the subjects are literally "matched" in regard to any variable that could be "correlated" with the DV, which is really the post-experimental performance.** If you wanted to test a hypothesis concerning a new treatment for bipolar disorder but felt that IQ might be correlated with the DV, then you would try to match subjects based on IQ. This procedure is logically termed "matched sampling." Hence, whether the experiment concluded that the IV did or did not have an impact, the researcher could breathe a little easier knowing that the IQ variable did not confound the study. A special kind of "matched subjects design" is the "repeated-measures" or "within-subjects" design in which the same subjects are used, once for the control condition and again for the experimental IV conditions. The theory here is that ultimately a subject is best matched by him- or herself assuming that counterbalancing is implemented. Now the Mann–Whitney $U$ test (choice "a") is used to determine whether two uncorrelated/unmatched means differ significantly, while the Wilcoxon signed-rank test examines whether two correlated means differ significantly from each other. By employing ranks, it is a good alternative to the correlated $t$ test. Why not remind yourself that the $U$ in Mann–Whitney $U$ is like the $u$ in uncorrelated/unmatched to help you distinguish it from the Wilcoxon? (**Note: Unmatched/uncorrelated groups could be termed independent groups on your exam.**) The $U$ test, like the Wilcoxon, is an alternative to the *t* test when parametric precepts cannot be accepted. Now think back for just a moment and you will recall that if you were using a parametric test to examine a null hypothesis for two means, you could rely on the *t* test. If, however, you had three or more groups, then the ANOVA and the *F* test would be required. A similar situation is in order here. If parametric assumptions are in doubt, the Mann–Whitney *U* test or the Wilcoxon can be used for two groups; however, when the number of groups reaches three or above, the Kruskal–Wallis one-way ANOVA *H* test noted in choice "c" is utilized. The Solomon, you will recall, controls for pretest effects. **Hint: Most comprehensive counseling exams will have several questions in which the examinee is given the basic factors concerning a research study and then is asked to pick the appropriate statistical test.**          **(d)**

797. A researcher studies a single session of counseling in which a counselor treats a client's phobia using a paradoxical strategy. He then writes in his research report that paradox is the treatment of choice for phobics. This is an example of

   a.   deductive logic or reasoning.
   b.   inductive logic or reasoning.
   c.   attrition or so-called experimental mortality.
   d.   construct validity.

   **This is inductive since the research goes from the specific to a generalization. Deductive—which sounds a bit like "reductive"—reduces the general to the specific.** This question would have been answered using "deductive" if the researcher observed many clients being cured of their phobias via paradox and so he assumed that Mr. Smith's phobia would be cured in the same manner. Choice "c" refers to subjects that drop out of a study.          **(b)**

798. A client goes to a string of 14 chemical dependency centers that operate on the 12-step model. When his current therapist

suggests a new inpatient program the client responds with, "What for, I already know the 12 steps?" This client is using

a.    deductive logic.
b.    inductive logic.
c.    an empathic assertion.
d.    an I statement.

Review the previous question if you missed this one. Here the client assumes that the general (his experience in 14 treatment facilities) can be reduced (deduction—remember your memory device) to the specific (the new treatment program).        **(a)**

799.  Mike takes a math achievement test. In order to predict his score if he takes the test again the counselor must know

a.    the range of scores in his class.
b.    the standard deviation.
c.    the standard error of measurement (SEM).
d.    the mode for the test.

The standard error is all you need to know. **The SEM tells the counselor what would most likely occur if the same individual took the same test again.** The question does not ask how well he did on the test, nor does it ask you to compare him to others.                                              **(c)**

800.  A researcher performs a study that has excellent external or so-called population validity, meaning that the results have generalizability. To collect his data the researcher gave clients a rating scale in which they were to respond with strongly agree, somewhat agree, neutral, somewhat disagree, or strongly disagree. This is

a.    a projective measure.
b.    unacceptable for use in standardized testing.
c.    a speed test.
d.    a Likert Scale.

Created by Rensis Likert in the early 1930s, this scale helps improve the overall degree of measurement. Response categories include such choices as strongly agree, agree, disagree, or strongly disagree. (Hmmm, that's easy enough to remember: How much do you like/Likert something?) **(d)**

# 10

## Professional Orientation and Ethical Practice

*I never let ethics get in the way of good treatment.*
—Jay Haley, pioneer in strategic therapy

ACA/NBCC ethical standards are stressed on most-comprehensive counseling exams. In 2005, ACA created a new code of ethics that was radically different from anything in the past. The revision took place over a three-year period and was the first in a decade. Then in 2014, ACA released another new code which has numerous updates that were not covered in the 2005 document. It took 11 committee members three years to complete the project and receive what they determined was ample feedback from over 100 counselors, most of which was supportive. All ACA members are expected to adhere to the guidelines and over 20 state licensing boards now use this document for adjudicating complaints of an ethical nature. **It is imperative that you also peruse the ACA and NBCC code prior to your exam.** Readers must note that ethical standards are updated routinely and some states have exams predicated on state ethics guidelines not covered in this text. You should contact your state licensing committee prior to your exam to ascertain if this is the case.

# QUICK GUIDE TO THE 2014 ACA CODE OF ETHICS

1.  The code includes a preamble (sets the tone for the document and the purpose of the code), a mission statement, a contents, a glossary of terms, as well as an index.
2.  The new code lists five values. Codes in other countries often list values. The values are: to enhance human development for the entire life span, embrace diversity and multicultural factors since clients are unique, promote social justice, safeguard the integrity of the counselor–client relationship, and to practice counseling in an ethical/safe manner.
3.  Six foundational principles for ethical behavior are set forth that are similar to the medical and health professions: **autonomy** or the notion that a client has a right to control his or her own life; **maleficence**, meaning the counselor never uses strategies/interventions or other behavior that could cause harm; **beneficence**, meaning the counselor practices for the good of society as well as the client; **justice**, or the idea that all clients are treated fairly and there is equality; **fidelity**, meaning the counselor keeps promises, and finally, **veracity**, the helper is truthful (e.g., provides an accurate diagnosis).
4.  The code sets expectations for all counselors, though to be sure, ACA has no power over counselors who are not members. (At this time ACA boasts approximately 55,000 members.)
5.  Major additions: social media, technology, and distance counseling. All are infused throughout the entire code as well as occupying their own special sections.
6.  Chronic suicidal clients are *not* a good fit for electronic counseling intervention.
7.  In reference to Facebook and hundreds of other social media sites, do not make clients "friends." Doing so goes beyond professional boundaries. Explain social media policies to client and **do not follow clients online as this constitutes an invasion of their privacy**.
8.  If a counselor has a social media file, the counselor should have separate professional and personal pages ... and make sure clients can discern the difference.

9. Never post information about clients on social media and never ask for assistance with a difficult client on LinkedIn forums, since this could possibly leak confidential information to the public.

10. Counselors should give Tarasoff warnings in cases where serious and foreseeable harm is possible.

11. Tarasoff warnings/exceptions to confidentiality can apply to a medical situation if your client has a contagious life-threatening disease which could harm somebody else. Verification of the medical condition (required in the 2005 Code) has been removed based on the fact that the practice just wasn't realistic.

12. Some states do not have a duty to warn/inform and so laws and ethics are not always in agreement.

13. The definition of pro bono has been expanded. In the past pro bono occurred when a counselor saw a client for free. The new code includes behaviors like free lectures, offering a reduced fee, or providing post-trauma/disaster services.

14. If your normal fee would cause a client a financial hardship adjust the fee if possible.

15. Fee splitting has been deemed unethical. Yes, this would include using a percentage of the fee for the use of an office. (Just thinking out loud folks, but I'm guessing thousands of counselors reading this nationwide will be impacted by this, buy hey, I could be wrong!) Charging a set office fee is ethical.

16. A counselor can engage in bartering with a client if, and only if, the practice will not cause harm or exploitation. When bartering is used, a written contract and cultural considerations should be taken into account.

17. A counselor may accept or decline a small gift from a client. The ethical guidelines don't stipulate precisely what constitutes a small gift, but I have heard experts quote the figure of $20 or less. Cultural factors and the client's rationale should also be a part of the decision.

18. Counselors only use theories grounded in science and research. If you have a developing, innovative theory, this should be shared with the client upfront in an informed consent disclosure statement.

19. Conversion and reparative therapies attempting to change the sexual orientation of a client are still unethical regardless of the

name of the therapy. These techniques, and any others sporting substantial evidence of harm, should not be used.

20. Ethical consultations are highly recommended in difficult situations.

21. If necessary, you can schedule an appointment to speak with an ACA representative by phone who is familiar with the Code.

22. The new Code prohibits counselors from discriminating based on sexual orientation or gender identity. Hence, a counselor cannot say, "I will not counsel you because you are gay," or "I won't discuss gay relationships because of my religious beliefs." Major controversy: Several states such as Arizona and Mississippi actually have bills that do *not* support ACA's new code on this issue. ACA's response is that all counselors should tell law makers what constitutes efficacious counseling—not the other way around. Politicians should not be dictating behavior to counselors.

23. A counselor can refer a client due to a lack of knowledge, but not because of his or her personal values.

24. When practicing distance counseling, the counselor should make decisions based on the laws of the state he or she practices in, as well as the state where the client resides.

25. Distance counselors should have an informed consent statement describing technology failure issues, response time (e.g., you only read your e-mail in the evening), risks, time zones, and emergency protocol.

26. For distance counseling use a client verification process such as a special number or code word. A unique graphic is also acceptable since a client can lie about identity issues.

27. Even records stored in the cloud must be backed up and secure. It is imperative that you explain to the client that you are using electronic storage procedures, if this is the case.

28. Inform the client if a third party, such as computer-support staff, software vendors, or supervisors/colleagues, could have access to their electronic file.

29. Encryption is a procedure in which a message is encoded so only a designated or authorized person or persons (often just the client and the counselor) have the ability to read or listen to it.

30. It is expensive and thus not necessary for counselors to encrypt their entire website, although the contact form page should be encrypted.

31. A large number of counselors will need to update their websites since the website should sport a link to licensing and certification boards. The website should be accessible to individuals with disabilities and, whenever possible, those who speak a different primary language. Translation programs are available, however, they are far from perfect and this should be stated clearly on the site.

32. PHI stands for public health information. PHI should be encrypted. According to the Health Insurance Portability and Accountability Act (HIPAA), a client can request unencrypted PHI, but the counselor must explain the risks related to privacy and confidentiality. In such instances, a statement delineating these issues should be give to the client and the client should sign the document.

33. Inform clients of security risks such as weak passwords or public Wi-Fi connections.

34. Since Skype is not encrypted it is not considered HIPAA compliant at this point in time.

35. Virtual relationships with clients are considered a no-no! A virtual relationship is defined as any relationship that is not face to face, such as those cultivated using social media.

36. Removed end-of-life exception rule. In plain everyday English: You cannot refer a client because he or she is terminally ill or considering a physician's assisted suicide.

37. You must wait five years after the last session before having a sexual or romantic relationship with a client, family member of a client, or the client's romantic partner. This holds true for face-to-face as well as electronic relationships. After five years a written statement should be prepared to explain why the relationship would not hurt or exploit the former clients. (**Note**: NBCC ethics use two years as the line of demarcation.)

38. Do not counsel family or friends where your objectivity could be impacted.

39. When working for a school or a counseling agency do not refer the client to your own private practice. This is known as a "self-referral." Granted there are rare situations where an organization will allow self-referral, but most do not.

40. When using an interdisciplinary team approach rely on informed consent to educate the client regarding the composition of the team and their purpose.
41. Get the client's permission before recording a session or allowing somebody to observe the session.
42. Counselors should rely on continuing education to maintain their competence and stay up to date.
43. Media presentations must follow the ACA Code of Ethics.
44. Do not harass or dismiss an employee or colleague for attempting to expose the inappropriate practices of a counseling agency or organization.
45. Do not use assessment data from outdated tests.
46. Never evaluate current or former clients, their romantic partners, or the client's family members for legal/forensic purposes. Moreover, do not counsel individuals if you are evaluating them. (Typical example: You are evaluating a client for the court system. She has been accused of committing a crime. You should *not* be counseling her as well.)
47. Counselor educators should include relevant multicultural diversity material and information regarding ethical standards into all their courses and workshops for counselors including online and hybrid courses.
48. When using case examples you must have permission from the client, supervisee etc., or you must modify the story so the true person's identity is not revealed.
49. Counselor educators should provide advice related to the student's career and related opportunities.
50. Counselor educators do not take fees or payments for placing a student in a given setting.
51. Counselor educators should recruit and attempt to retain a diverse faculty and student body.
52. A prospective client who has an appointment for counseling receives the same confidentiality as clients in your caseload.
53. A counselor should have a plan in each situation if he or she becomes incapacitated, dies, closes the practice, or retires. The plan relates to the client and client records.
54. Counselors explain the limitations and benefits of distance/technology counseling such as the fact that vocal inflections or nonverbal behavior might not be evident.

55. Violating an ethical principle does not necessarily mean you have broken the law. Legal liability can only be established by a court of law.
56. The principal researcher has the ultimate responsibility for ethical research. Anybody else involved in the research is responsible for their own behavior.

801. Which group was most instrumental in opposing counselor licensure?

    a.   Social workers.
    b.   Psychiatrists.
    c.   Psychologists.
    d.   AAMFT members.

Some hypothesize that psychologists wanted a monopoly on nonmedical mental health services, especially the right to collect third-party payments. Others point out that at one time psychologists were debased and called "junior psychiatrists," and therefore the psychologists did to counselors what psychiatrists had done to them. In any case, the tide appears to be turning as "mental health coalitions" are popping up in which psychiatrists, psychologists, counselors, social workers, and related specialists (e.g., choice "d," the American Association for Marriage and Family Therapy) meet to discuss mutual professional concerns. Psychologists have now secured prescription medication privileges in several parts of the country and both psychologists and social workers in some states are challenging counselors' rights to diagnose clients and perform other services. **(c)**

802. In the late 1970s, AACD (known as ACA since 1992) began to focus very heavily on professional credentialing. This led to the formation of the

    a.   CCMHC.
    b.   NBCC.
    c.   CACREP, formed in 1981.
    d.   APGA, formed in 1952.

In 1982, the American Association for Counseling and Development (AACD), now the American Counseling Association (ACA), formed the National Board for Certified Counselors (NBCC). If you meet the educational/skill requirements and pass an exam (come on now you remember, probably the exam you are studying for this very minute!) you can use the title NCC—National Certified Counselor. This is a generic certification. The designation lasts for five years at which time the counselor must have 100 approved hours of continued professional development (e.g., workshops) or sit for the test again. (For some strange reason, I'm guessing you'll choose the first option.) Other alphabet soup acronyms include choice "a," Certified Clinical Mental Health Counselor; a specialty certification you might wish to snare by taking another exam(!). Choice "c," the Council for the Accreditation of Counseling and Related Educational Programs, which is an ACA affiliate formed in 1981 that certifies counselor programs rather than individual counselors; and choice "d," the major counseling organization, the American Personnel and Guidance Association, which later became the AACD and is now the ACA. **(b)**

803. By passing the NCE, a counselor can attain the _____, given via NBCC.

   a.  NCC, a generic certification for counselors
   b.  NCC, a specialty mental health certification for counselors
   c.  NCC, national certification for school counselors
   d.  MAC, master addictions counselor

Again, here is one of those must-know concepts, especially since many readers are striving to put NCC after their names. The NCC credential constitutes a "generic" certification. The word *generic* literally means "general" or "referring to all types of counselors." Look at choice "c" and ask yourself: What is incongruent about this item? The answer is simply that the acronym for National Certified School Counselor is NCSC. NBCC offers another specialty certification, the MAC (see choice "d"). **Key reminder: You can only secure specialty certificates such as CCMHC and NCSC after you secure**

**the NCC credential.** And, oh yes, one more very, very **important point**: Just because you are certified does not mean you can call yourself a licensed counselor. **National certifications can (as the name suggests) be used on a national basis unlike licenses, which tend to be primarily state specific. Licenses are conferred by the individual state and not the federal government.**                              **(a)**

804. Which choice would most likely violate the counseling ethic or law termed "scope of practice"?

    a.   A counselor who is using good, accurate empathy with a client, but fails to confront her about her excessive drinking.
    b.   A licensed counselor who gives the client a *DSM* diagnostic code for insurance.
    c.   A counselor who is too active-directive with a client.
    d.   A counselor who is conducting a strict Freudian psychoanalysis with the client.

The "scope of practice" concept suggests that counselors should only practice using techniques for which they have been trained. Most counselors are not trained in classical analysis. This concept also implies that a counselor should not attempt to treat clients for which he or she has no training. Your state counseling law could stipulate that you disclose your "scope of practice" to all potential clients.                              **(d)**

805. Ethical guidelines were first created for the helping professions in 1953 when the American Psychological Association (APA) published their first code of ethics. The National Association of Social Workers (NASW) created their code in 1960, and in 1961, the organization that is now ACA adopted ethics for counselors. Ethics always describe

    a.   laws.
    b.   universal principles which apply to all helpers.
    c.   standards of conduct imposed by the ACA and NBCC.
    d.   all of the above.

Let's examine precisely why choices "a," "b," and "d" are incorrect. In regard to choice "a," the state in which you practice may not have a law on the books that explicitly states that you can't date a counselee, yet I can almost guarantee that your licensing board will see it as a so-called dual relationship, which could be an ethics violation. Ethics define standards of behavior set forth by organizations and certification bodies. Ethics are not state- or federally mandated laws. Unlike many laws, ethical guidelines generally do not spell out penalties for violations. Hence, the aforementioned counselor who is dating a client might lose his or her license but will not be serving time in a city jail or a federal penitentiary. Choice "b" is misleading since ethics are not universal. That is to say, the ethics set forth by one organization may not be identical to those spelled out by another organization. **Exception to the aforementioned explanation! I wish life were a little simpler but often it is not. I just explained that ethics are not always identical or equal to laws; however, if your state sends you ethical guidelines that are state statutes after you secure your license, then in this instance your guidelines will be the law. Since approximately 20 states use the ACA ethical code, in these states the Code would likely qualify as the law.**          **(c)**

806. Most ethical dilemmas are related to

   a.   confidentiality.
   b.   testing.
   c.   diagnosis.
   d.   research.

Confidentiality implies that the counselor will not reveal anything about a client unless he or she is given specific authorization to do so. Some of the literature in the field refers to confidential material as "entrusted secrets." What goes on in the counseling relationship remains private and not shared rather than being public. Helpers must, nevertheless, be aware that there are exceptions to this principle. The exceptions illuminate the fact that confidentiality is relative to the situation. **When does confidentiality end? According to ACA ethical guidelines,** counselors have an obligation to protect the confidentiality of the deceased and this should be stated clearly in your informed consent document given to the client at the beginning of treatment. *Counseling Today Online* once asked several ACA ethics task-force members about some issues related to this topic. Say an elderly person dies and said some nice things about surviving family members. Could you break confidentiality and tell them generally what the elderly person said? Yes! However, assume that a young man commits suicide and after his death his mother wanted to know if he hated her. The answer the experts give is that you would attempt to uphold what the son would have wanted based on documentation. If this is not clear (and very often it is not!) then it should be kept private. Can a counselor attend a funeral? You ask yourself whether it might be beneficial just as you would if you decided to attend a client's wedding. If somebody approaches you at the funeral you can say that you knew the deceased professionally. **(a)**

807. The landmark 1969 case, *Tarasoff v. the Board of Regents of the University of California* illuminated

    a.    difficulties caused when a counselor has sex with a client.

    b.    ethical issues in relation to research.

    c.    the duty to warn a client in imminent danger.

    d.    the impact of an impaired professional.

For the most part, I wouldn't go around memorizing court cases for exams; however, the *Tarasoff* case is now so well known in the behavioral sciences that it is an exception to the rule. In 1969 a student named Prosenjit Poddar at Berkeley was receiving counseling on an outpatient basis. During the course of the treatment he revealed that he was going to kill a woman (Tatiana Tarasoff) when she returned from Brazil. The therapist consulted with other professionals and called the campus police. The therapist wanted Poddar hospitalized. Campus police spoke with Poddar but did not hospitalize him. A letter also was sent to the chief of campus police regarding this dangerous situation.

Despite all the actions taken, Poddar did indeed kill Tarasoff, and Ms. Tarasoff's parents filed suit against the Board of Regents as well as the University employees. The charge was failure to warn an intended victim. Although a lower court dismissed the suit, the parents appealed the decision, and the California Supreme Court ruled in favor of the parents in 1976. **This case is often cited as an example of a professional helper's "duty to warn" a person of serious and foreseeable harm to him- or herself or to others. ACA chose to replace the phrase "clear and imminent danger" which appeared in the previous version of their ethical code with "serious and foreseeable harm." The newer terminology is seen as indicating that there is a broader scope of circumstances where confidentiality may need to be broken such as a client with a terminal illness who has no medical options and wishes to end his or her own life. Nevertheless, no matter what terminology is used, if another party needs to be contacted to prevent a dangerous situation then the counselor should ethically take this action even if it means violating confidentiality. Recently, some states (e.g., Illinois) have literally gone beyond *Tarasoff* and now stipulate that when there is "clear or present danger" (yet another way of describing a serious situation) to themselves or the community, a report must be made to a designated state agency within a brief period of time, generally 24 hours.** Choice "d," impaired professional, connotes a helper who has personal issues (e.g., substance abuse or brain damage) that would hinder the quality of services rendered. **(c)**

808. A counselor reveals information that is extremely damaging to a client's reputation. This counselor could be accused of

   a.  beneficence.
   b.  justice.
   c.  nonmaleficence
   d.  defamation

Hold on folks, this is starting to sound a lot like law school! That's because I think there is a good chance that you may see one or all of the above terms on your exam. **Beneficence means the counselor is working for the good of the client or the group. Justice (usually applied to group situations) means that the counselor treats all members fairly. Nonmaleficence means that the counselor will do no harm. The correct answer—defamation—describes behavior that can damage one's reputation. It is known as libel if it is written and slander if the defamation refers to verbal remarks.**

A plaintiff can win a case against a counselor even if the communication was *not intended as malicious*. Some experts suggest that counselors should avoid psychological jargon and only communicate with others regarding a client when it is necessary (e.g., a duty to warn or responding to a request for a release of information) to avoid defamation allegations.      **(d)**

809. State laws can govern title usage and practice, however, they do not govern

   a.   accreditation.
   b.   counselor licensure.
   c.   psychologist licensure.
   d.   involuntary commitment to state psychiatric facilities.

State laws regulate "licensing" of professionals such as choice "b," counselors, and choice "c," psychologists, and commitment procedures (choice "d"). Accreditation, however, is not the law. In fact, you need to be aware of the fact that many counselor-preparation programs are not accredited. Accreditation is a process whereby an agency or school (not an individual) meets certain standards and qualifications set forth by an association or accrediting organization. The organization that grants the accreditation usually requires site visits for the purpose of evaluating the institution initially and on an ongoing basis. Thus, programs in psychology will boast accreditation via the APA (American Psychological Association) while counseling programs can be accredited by CACREP, mentioned earlier. CACREP boasts that counselors who graduate from accredited programs score higher on the NCE. **Important reminder:** The term *accreditation* applies to programs, not individual counselors. Moreover, experts warn that accreditation is not without disadvantages. Disadvantages include that being accredited is very costly for the institution; that faculty are busy teaching required courses and thus often don't have time to teach creative alternative courses; that the accreditation organization and not the school determines the curriculum; that faculty credentials are determined via accreditation guidelines, and this does not necessarily mean such individuals have the best teaching, clinical, or research skills; and that the program approval can be misleading inasmuch as the program could be accredited yet ineffective. **Despite the aforementioned issues beginning January 1, 2022, applicants for the NCC credential will need to be graduates of CACREP institutions with a master's degree or beyond. The new policy should improve portability so your credentials are more likely to be accepted if you move to another state.** **(a)**

810. An exception to confidentiality, or what is termed as relative confidentiality, could occur when a client is suicidal. Suicidal warning signs include

    a.    repeatedly joking about killing one's self.
    b.    giving away prized possessions after one has been depressed for an extended period of time.
    c.    a previous suicide attempt and a very detailed suicide plan for the future.
    d.    all of the above.

Lately, suicide has been checking in as the tenth leading cause of death in the United States (higher than homicide!); and among those aged 15–24 suicide is the second or third leading killer. The rate for older adults is two to three times what it is for the general population. Firearms account for more suicides than all the other methods put together. Suicides are more likely to occur in rural areas that are not highly populated and in times of economic recession or depression. When a famous person commits suicide the national rate will show an increase. Most suicides occur in the spring at the end of April or May and about 75–80% of your clients will give warning signs.     **(d)**

811. A statement of disclosure could include all *except:*

   a.   A list of the courses the counselor took in graduate school.
   b.   The counselor's qualifications, office hours, and billing policies.
   c.   Emergency procedures and therapy techniques utilized.
   d.   A statement that confidentiality is desirable, but cannot be guaranteed in a group setting.

Some states now require a statement of disclosure be given to all potential clients. The procedure of giving the client this document and having him or her read it and sign it is sometimes referred to as "informed consent." The client has the information to consent to the treatment.     **(a)**

812. Privileged communication refers to the fact that anything said to a counselor by a client

   a.   can be revealed in a court of law if the counselor decides it is beneficial.
   b.   can be revealed only if a counselor testifies in court.
   c.   is protected by laws in every state.
   d.   will not be divulged outside the counseling setting without the client's permission.

By definition *privileged communication* is a legal term that implies that a therapeutic interaction (verbal or written) will not be available for public inspection. A counselor–client relationship protected by privileged communication is one in which **the client—not the counselor or the court—can choose not to have confidential information revealed during a legal proceeding (generally on the witness stand). Repeat after me out loud: the client is the holder of the privilege. Say it again!** Simply put—and this is a fine memory device—it is the "client's privilege" to reveal. In relation to choice "c," the law varies from state to state. In some states, one mental health provider will be covered by the law (e.g., a psychologist or psychiatrist) while another provider (often a counselor, social worker, or caseworker) will not be covered.               **(d)**

813. In regard to state law and privileged communication, counselors must be aware that

    a.    privileged communication exists in every state in the union for LPCs.
    b.    laws are unclear and may vary from state to state.
    c.    there are no laws which govern this issue.
    d.    state psychology laws are applicable in this respect.

Privileged communication is a legal concept that protects clients, not counselors. If a client decides to waive his or her right to privileged communication, then the counselor must reveal the information. Privileged communication legislation varies from state to state (so much for choices "a" and "c"). Check your state laws if you are taking an exam for state licensure. As of this time, some states do not have privileged communication for the licensed counselor/client relationship. **Privileged communication is not applicable in cases of child abuse, neglect, or exploitation; suicide or homicide threats; criminal intentions; clients in dire need of hospitalization; or in cases where a counselor is the victim of a malpractice lawsuit. In addition, privileged communication does not apply to minors (although their legal guardians generally hold the privilege) or those who are mentally incompetent.** As for choice "d," state psychology laws would not govern the behavior of licensed professional counselors.               **(b)**

814. When counselors state that privileged communication is "qualified," they actually mean that

    a.    the counselor must have certification before privileged communication applies.
    b.    privileged communication applies only to doctoral-level counselors.
    c.    exceptions may exist.

d.    all of the above.

See the answer to question 813 for exceptions. In regard to choices "a" and "b," it is important to note that privileged communication is based on licensure status rather than one's graduate degree or certification credentials.                    **(c)**

815. You are a counselor in a state that does not legally support privileged communication. You refuse to testify in court. In this situation

   a.    ACA will back you for doing the ethical thing.
   b.    NBCC will back you if, and only if, you have attained NCC status.
   c.    you need not testify if your case was supervised by a licensed psychologist and/or psychiatrist.
   d.    you could be held in contempt of court.

Your client in this situation would <u>not</u> have the "privilege" to say no if you are asked to testify.                    **(d)**

816. An 11-year-old child comes to your office with a black eye and tells you she can't remember how she received it. You have reason to suspect abuse. You should

   a.    be empathic and discuss her feelings regarding the matter.
   b.    drop the matter as it could embarrass her.
   c.    refer her to a medical doctor of your choice.
   d.    call the child abuse/neglect hotline.

**Counselors are mandated reporters for child abuse. It is legal and ethical to break confidentiality in such cases. You must report child abuse, it's the law! The word** *mandated* **means that a counselor does not have a choice in the matter.** Your state may have a legal penalty for failure to report child abuse, sexual abuse, neglect, or exploitation. Check your state laws. Generally, counselors report incidents via the state child abuse hotline. Some exams may refer to this area of concern as "protective services," or "children's services." Other

**exceptions** or **limitations** to maintaining confidentiality include:

a. Client is a danger to self or others.
b. Client requests a release of information.
c. A court orders a release of information.
d. The counselor is engaged in a systematic supervision process.
e. Clerical assistants who process client information and papers.
f. Legal and clinical consultation situations.
g. Client raises the issue of the counselor's competence in a malpractice lawsuit.
h. The client is less than 18 years of age. (If a client is a minor, a parent or guardian can demand that information be disclosed that was revealed during a session.)
i. An elderly person is abused.
j. An insurance company or managed care company requests a diagnosis and/or relevant clinical information.

Is a counselor always on duty? I mean, what about the old "I saw a child being abused in the grocery store" dilemma? As of this writing counselors are only mandated reporters while they are performing professional duties. If you are in the grocery store tapping on watermelons and you spy a parent abusing his child, you can make the decision to report it, or not report it, just like anyone else in the store. You are not acting as a mandated reporter at that point in time. Statistically speaking, perpetrators of sexual abuse are primarily males, and perpetrators of physical abuse are generally females. **(d)**

817. During a counseling session a 42-year-old male client threatens suicide. You should

a. keep it a secret as the client is not a minor.
b. call the state child abuse/neglect hotline even though he is an adult.
c. call his wife and mention that a serious problem exists but be very careful not to discuss the issue of suicide since to do so would violate the client's confidentiality.

d.    contact his wife and advise her of possible suicide precautions.

Most experts would agree with choice "d." Ethics guidelines will usually say something like this: When a client's condition indicates that there is a clear and imminent danger or serious and foreseeable harm to the client and others, the counselor must take reasonable personal action or inform responsible authorities. This may seem a bit vague (i.e., specific words such as *suicide* and/or *homicide* are not mentioned). Indeed, ethics guidelines are often not nearly as specific as counselors would like them to be.                                                    **(d)**

818. A 39-year-old female secretary you are seeing in your assertiveness training group reveals that she is plotting to shoot her husband. Based on the *Tarasoff* case you should

a.    warn the husband.
b.    keep it confidential because an assertiveness training group is decidedly not the same as one-to-one counseling.
c.    make a police report in the city in which the husband resides.
d.    tell a supervisor, administrator, or board member if one exists, but do not contact her husband.

*Tarasoff* implies that a responsible helper will warn an intended victim. **Professionals generally adhere to the principle of minimal disclosure, which suggests that you reveal only what is necessary.** Another landmark case, the *Hedlund* case, suggests that therapists should warn others (i.e., third parties) who also may be in danger. *Tarasoff* is controversial and based on a California court decision that may or may not apply to your state. Again, I recommend checking your state's laws if your exam is for licensure status. Choice "d" also might have been appropriate had the phrase "do not contact her husband" been eliminated.                                                    **(a)**

819. You pass your exam and now have NCC status. You perform a battery of tests on your client. After you complete the testing

you discover your client is in imminent danger. You receive a legal court order to turn over the test scores. You

a.  must get a signed release from the client.
b.  you must turn over the test records complete with the test scores.
c.  turn over the test records without the scores.
d.  should recall that according to "aspirational ethics," your client comes first and so you will do nothing.

The answer is choice "b." Skeptical? Then please read NBCC's Certified Counselor's Code of Ethics. In this regard we are told that normally you would <u>not</u> release a client's test or assessment results without prior written consent. The exception: When there is clear and imminent danger or when legally required to do so by a government agency or a court order. Aspirational ethics (answer "d") means that a practitioner adheres to the highest possible ethical standards. **(b)**

820. One impetus for counselor licensing was that

a.  Academy of Certified Social Workers (ACSW) wanted to restrict counselors.
b.  politicians demanded that counselors be licensed.
c.  psychology licensure bodies sought to restrict the practice of counselors so counselors could not receive third-party payments from insurance and managed care companies.
d.  insurance companies pushed strongly for it.

Many—if not most—counselors were not able to be licensed as psychologists because one popular requirement was—and still remains—that the graduate program had to be "primarily psychological in nature," which basically meant that persons who attended counseling programs were considered inappropriate. Licensing for counselors was needed as psychologists attained licensing (and had somewhat of a monopoly on nonmedical treatment services) in every state in the United States. **(c)**

821. A counselor who possesses a graduate degree wishes to become a licensed psychologist. Which statement most accurately depicts the current situation?

    a.    Any counselor can easily become a psychologist if he or she can pass the EPPP.

    b.    A counselor can become a licensed psychologist by taking three graduate credit hours in physiological psychology and then passing the EPPP.

    c.    In nearly every case, individuals trained in counseling departments would not be allowed to sit for the EPPP and thus could not become licensed psychologists.

    d.    A counselor with a doctorate in counseling could be licensed as a counseling psychologist if he or she has a degree from a recognized department of counseling.

Choice "c" (the correct response) provides a good rationale why counselors needed a license to call their own. EPPP stands for Examination for Professional Practice in Psychology. Roughly speaking, the EPPP is to psychologists as the NCE is to counselors. Choice "d" would be incorrect in most cases as the applicant would still generally need a degree from a psychology rather than a counseling department. **(c)**

822. A woman who is in private practice mentions in her phone book advertisement that she is a licensed counseling psychologist. This generally means that

    a.    she has a doctorate from a counselor education program.

    b.    she has a graduate degree from a psychology department.

    c.    she has a degree from a CACREP program.

    d.    she has a degree in counseling but is trained in projective testing.

The trick to answering this question is to remember that the term *psychology* can only be used if the helper is a licensed psychologist, even if the person specializes in counseling. Hence, the degree would need to be from a program which is primarily psychological, a psychology rather than a counseling department (rendering choice "a" incorrect). For review purposes, pertaining to choice "c" you will recall that CACREP is the Council for Accreditation of Counseling and Related Educational Programs, which is ACA's accrediting agency. CACREP, which set up shop in 1981, currently has approximately 715 programs from 185 public and 77 private institutions. Critics charge that the number of programs sporting CACREP accreditation is still too low. **Some oh-so-good news for CACREP graduate readers! CACREP accredits master's degree programs in career counseling, college counseling, community counseling, gerontological counseling, marital, couple, and family counseling/therapy, mental health counseling, school counseling, student affairs, counselor education and supervision, and doctoral degree programs. The largest number of CACREP programs is in school counseling with community counseling not that far behind. Gerontological counseling is lacking at this time. If you have a CACREP degree under your belt and you wish to become an NCC, the two years of supervised experience is waived! You simply take the NCE and pass it and presto you've snared NCC credentials after your name. In addition, some states will waive a portion of the supervised experience for licensure.** **(b)**

823. One major difference between the psychology versus the counseling movement seems to be that

    a.    the psychologists are working to eliminate practitioners with less than a doctorate, while the counselors are not.

    b.    counselors are working to give up tests for licensure.

    c.    psychology boards are made up primarily of psychiatrists.

    d.    in most states psychologists do not need to take an exam.

Counselors and social workers seem comfortable with master's level practitioners. In an early study in which ACES members were asked to comment on the minimum level of education necessary for licensure, over 45% of the respondents felt comfortable with master's level practitioners. A little over 41% insisted that a doctorate was necessary. **(a)**

824. APA is to psychologist as ACA is to

    a.   APGA.
    b.   certified clinical mental health counselor.
    c.   counselor.
    d.   NCC.

Here is a straightforward example of an analogy item. First, recall that the APA (in the context of this question) refers to the American Psychological Association, which is the major professional body for psychologists. ACA plays the same role for counselors.                                            **(c)**

825. You have achieved the status of NCC. NBCC, nevertheless, feels you have violated professional ethics. NBCC can do any of the following *except:*

    a.   Revoke your state counseling license.
    b.   Remove your name from the list of NCCs in the U.S.
    c.   Revoke your NCC status.
    d.   Note in their newsletter that your NCC status has been revoked.

Here is the key point: Certification is not the same as licensing. Thus, a certified reality therapist cannot legally use the title counselor unless he or she is licensed by the state. A certification is given to an individual via an organization which is not part of the state or federal government. A counseling license is granted by the state government. Nevertheless, you must (yes must) be certified to call yourself a certified counselor. You could, however, call yourself a professional counselor if you are not certified. A certification is a title mastered by living up to certain standards. Does the fact that choice "d" is true surprise you? It shouldn't! NBCC is very open and upfront about this fact and specifically states that certification violations (e.g., using the title MAC when you have not fulfilled the requirements) may be published in NBCC's newsletter. Believe me, this is one situation where you certainly don't need the notoriety! And oh yes, I almost forgot; this is what makes this such a difficult question.

Although a certification board cannot revoke your license for an ethics violation, they do indeed reserve the right to contact your state licensing board (or other certification boards, for that matter) and your state board may well decide to take your license. The certification organization also could deny you further certification and take legal action against you. **Important exam reminder:** Ethical guidelines drafted via your state licensing board may indeed be at odds with your national organization's standards (e.g., ACA, NASW).                    **(a)**

826. A counselor who is alcoholic and suffering from burnout could best be described as

   a.   a mesomorph.
   b.   an impaired professional.
   c.   a paraprofessional.
   d.   a counselor who is wise enough to use his own experiences to help others.

The term *impaired* is used here to mean a deterioration in the ability to function as a counselor. The counselor described in this question definitely meets the criteria. Choice "a" is derived from an old theory of personality proposed by Sheldon, which suggested three basic temperaments based on one's physical build. The mesomorph or muscular type was said to be assertive, courageous, and willing to take risks. The ectomorph, characterized by a slender or frail build, was thought to be sensitive and inhibited. The endomorph, or soft rotund individual, was inclined to love food, comfort, and relaxation. Choice "c," paraprofessional, is used to describe a helper who does not possess the education and experience necessary to secure professional credentials.       **(b)**

827. Counselor certification

   a.   is synonymous with licensure.
   b.   is synonymous with program certification.
   c.   recognizes that you have reached a given level of competence and thus are authorized to use a title.
   d.   is primarily a legal process.

If you marked anything other than choice "c," review the explanation given in answer 825. **(c)**

828. A woman comes to you for help with an eating disorder. You have no experience or training in this area. Ethically you should

    a.   refer this client to a colleague who is indeed trained and experienced with this type of client.

    b.   keep the client and work on her general lack of self-esteem.

    c.   tell the client you will do a comprehensive Internet search on the topic and then begin seeing her.

    d.   explain to the client that a symptom such as eating or not eating is not the real problem and that counseling focuses on real underlying issues.

Would you do psychosurgery on somebody's brain without the correct training? I didn't think so. Choice "d" is very psychodynamic. **(a)**

829. Virginia was the first state to license counselors in 1976. The APGA (later AACD and now ACA) division that was initially the most instrumental in pushing for licensing was the

    a.   American College Personnel Association.

    b.   American School Counselor Association.

    c.   Association for Specialists in Group Work.

    d.   American Counselor Education and Supervision.

Known as ACES, the APGA set up a licensure commission in 1975. **What's in a name? Why in the world did the American Personnel and Guidance Association (APGA), founded in July of 1952, change the organization's name to AACD (American Association for Counseling and Development) in 1983? Well, the story goes that during the late seventies and early eighties members expressed a dislike for the words *personnel* and *guidance*, as these terms did not accurately depict the work of counselors. The current nameplate, the American Counseling Association (ACA), was adopted in July 1992, after the members voted by**

**mail. The new name was intended, once again, to clarify what members really did.** **(d)**

830. The problem with income-sensitive or sliding fee scales (based on the client's ability to pay) is that

    a.  scales of this kind are unethical.
    b.  scales of this nature are illegal.
    c.  it is difficult to administer them in a fair manner.
    d.  scales like this are used frequently; however, they are unethical and illegal.

Sliding fee scales, which are ethical and legal, are quite popular with not-for-profit agencies. Different insurance companies pay different amounts for the same service and pay different fees for different providers. Hence, the psychologist or social worker next door could very well be making a different amount than you for the same service. Hey, Albert Ellis warned us that life isn't fair!**(c)**

831. One possible negative aspect of counselor licensure is that

    a.  counselors would receive more third-party payments.
    b.  counselors might be accepted as providers by insurance companies.
    c.  counselors may not be as creative during their graduate work and simply take courses aimed at fulfilling the requirements to take the licensure exam.
    d.  it will take business away from psychologists.

Choices "a" and "b" mean basically the same thing and are anything but negative, and in fact constitute two excellent reasons why counselors fought for licensure. Licensing generally adds prestige to a profession and can serve to protect the public; nevertheless, students often take precisely what is required for licensing or certification. **(c)**

832. A client wants his records sent to a psychiatrist he is seeing. You should

   a.  advise against it based on current research.
   b.  refuse to do so based on ethical guidelines.
   c.  first have the client sign a dated release of information form that stipulates whether the information can be released once (or for what period of time it can be released) and then you can send the information.
   d.  call the psychiatrist to discuss the case but explain that state law prohibits a counselor from sending anything in writing about the client.

   Clients have a right to "privacy." Do not use a xerox or photocopy of the client's signature on any release of information form. **Exam hint:** If you or your agency didn't collect the information in the record then don't send it even with a release form. What's that you say? That doesn't make sense. Okay, let's assume that your client was seen at the local homeless shelter. You had him sign a release and now have information from that particular shelter. Now the information from the homeless shelter is part of your record file. But, as you well know from the question, a psychiatrist wants the client's record from you. You should not send what you acquired from the homeless shelter. Can the psychiatrist secure this information? After all, it might prove clinically valuable. Of course, but the psychiatrist will do precisely what you did. The psychiatrist can procure it simply by having the client sign a release which the psychiatrist will send to the homeless shelter. **Exam hint: Your exam might refer to a release of information as consent to disclose or transfer records. Also note that you may not record or observe sessions without permission of the client.**    **(c)**

833. You are a licensed professional counselor in one state but will soon relocate to another state. The new state informs you that they will grant you reciprocity or so-called endorsement. You will thus

   a.  simply need to take the licensing test in the new state.

b.    be permitted to practice in the new state based on your current credentials without taking another exam.
c.    need to take numerous graduate courses.
d.    not be allowed to practice until you serve an internship.

**Reciprocity occurs when one state or organization accepts the license or credentials of another state or organization.** Cool huh? Yeah, well don't get your hopes up! State requirements for licensure differ and thus one state does not always accept credentials snared in another state. When that occurs we merely say that the state the counselor is moving to will not grant the counselor reciprocity. **The profession, especially CACREP, is working diligently to enhance portability (the ease that something can be transferred) so that one state would accept another's credentials.**                        **(b)**

834.    According to the Family Educational Rights and Privacy Act (FERPA) of 1974 (also known as the Buckley Amendment)

a.    a parent can see his or her daughter's middle school record.
b.    an 18-year-old college student can view his or her own educational record.
c.    a and b.
d.    a and b are both illegal.

Although the act applied to educational files (often called student cumulative record files) rather than counseling records, most agencies and ethical bodies created procedures so clients who wish to can view their records. In order to abide by FERPA, school counselors are urged to keep their counseling notes separate from the rest of the student's file and to make certain other teachers do not have access to the files. However, school counselors should be aware that a court of law can still subpoena the actual counseling notes or request that the counselor testify.                        **(c)**

835. You are a school counselor who wishes to refer a student with an orthopedic disability to a private therapist. In general, the best referral would be to

    a.    a CRC.
    b.    a MAC.
    c.    a licensed clinical psychologist.
    d.    a licensed social worker.

    CRC stands for Certified Rehabilitation Counselor. CRCs will need at least a master's in rehabilitation counseling from a dually accredited CACREP, CORE (Council on Rehabilitation and Education) program, acceptable experience in the field, and a passing score on a 175-question multiple-choice examination. CACREP and CORE have now merged. Choice "b" is a certification specialty of NBCC known as master addictions counselor.                                                                    **(a)**

836. A registry would be

    a.    a list of licensed psychologists in the state of Illinois.
    b.    a list of CRCs in the United States.
    c.    a and b.
    d.    the registration process for counselor licensure in the state of Missouri.

    A registry is always a list of providers. A person whose name is included in a state counseling registry can sometimes use the title "registered professional counselor" or RPC.                          **(c)**

837. A counselor wins the lottery and closes her practice without telling her clients. This counselor's course of action is best described as

    a.    a multiple relationship.
    b.    defamation.
    c.    abandonment.
    d.    nonmaleficence.

In most situations, ethics frown on multiple or dual relationships such as counseling a client you are dating! Imagine how objective you will be when the client divulges during the next session that he or she is dating somebody he or she likes better! **Are ethical guidelines becoming—dare I say it—a bit more humanistic? Perhaps! The first major change in the tide began in 2005 when ACA dropped the term** *dual relationships* **from their ethical guidelines because they felt that in** *some* **instances a relationship of this nature could be beneficial (such as attending a client's graduation or visiting them in the hospital). In the newer 2014 ACA Codes, the phrase "noncounseling roles and relationships" is used. The counselor is advised to include in his or her counseling notes why such action would be beneficial. The counselor should also discuss any potential benefits and harm that could occur. Whenever possible, the notation should appear prior to the actual event. Sexual or romantic activity with any current client is unethical under the new or the old set of ethics!** Defamation occurs when a counselor says something (i.e., slander) or writes something (i.e., libel) that damages a client's reputation. Nonmaleficence means to do no harm. **The client in this question is the victim of abandonment, which occurs when a counselor stops providing services and does not refer the client to another helper.** **(c)**

838. You are counseling your first cousin for depression. This is

    a.  ethical.
    b.  not actually an ethical issue.
    c.  ethical if you continue to counsel her and refer her to a psychiatrist for an antidepressant.
    d.  generally unethical as it would constitute a dual or so-called multiple relationship.

A dual relationship, multiple relationship (NBCC's term for this behavior), or noncounseling relationship results when a counselor has another significant relationship with the client that hinders objectivity. A dual relationship is also said to exist when a supervisor accepts a subordinate or administrator as a client. **A gentle reminder: If you have had a previous sexual or romantic relationship with an individual you should not be that person's counselor or therapist.**    **(d)**

839. A counselor who sports NCC after her name

    a.   will need not concern herself with continuing education.
    b.   will need to complete three graduate courses every 10 years.
    c.   will never receive credit for workshops but should attend for her own personal growth nevertheless.
    d.   will need a specified amount of continuing education contact hours before she can be recertified, or she will need to take the NCE again.

One hundred hours of professional development are needed during a five-year period. Recently, home study programs and online courses have made this process more convenient.    **(d)**

840. You find yourself sexually attracted to a client. This is known as

    a.   countertransference.
    b.   ambivalent transference.
    c.   negative transference.
    d.   positive transference.

A typical manifestation of countertransference would be romantic or sexual feelings toward a client. Countertransference is an indication of unresolved problems on the part of the helper.    **(a)**

841. Your sexual attraction toward your client is hindering the counseling process. You should

    a.   continue treatment but be honest and empathic with the client.
    b.   ignore your feelings; after all you are a professional.
    c.   explain this to the client and then refer the client to another provider.
    d.   continue to see the client but ignore psychosexual topics.

The word *hindering* is critical to answering the question correctly. If the counselor felt a sexual attraction which had "not" as yet hindered the treatment process, then personal therapy/professional supervision for the counselor would be the most desirable plan of action. Moreover, prior to the point where the counselor's attraction interfered with the treatment, most experts would advise against discussing the attraction with the client. **According to the NBCC code, even one inappropriate behavior on the part of the helper constitutes sexual harassment.** **(c)**

842. A malpractice or liability insurance company is least likely to defend you if

   a.    you are sexually involved with a client.
   b.    you violate confidentiality.
   c.    you do not have a client sign a release of information and send a record to another agency or provider.
   d.    you call a state child abuse hotline and a client takes legal action since the child was actually the victim of an accident.

Some states will revoke your license for sexual misconduct even if it occurs outside the session and even if the client has consented! In addition, your license may be revoked even if the client is not damaged or harmed by the experience. The fact that a client seduced you is irrelevant even if it is true. Some insurance companies pay smaller settlements or no settlement in cases where you are found guilty of sexual harassment or misconduct. Let me share with you what my current professional liability insurance occurrence form states. It says: "A smaller limit of liability applies to judgments or settlements when there are allegations of sexual misconduct." In addition, if a counselor is found guilty most insurance companies will cancel the insurance and the possibility of finding another company to insure a counselor in this situation is very difficult. **A counselor should never have a sexual relationship with a current client. It is even considered illegal in most areas of the country. NBCC ethics stipulate that you should not engage in sexual intimacies with a former client within a minimum** of two years after terminating the counseling relationship. If you engage in such a relationship after the two-year period you must be able to document that the relationship was not exploitative in nature. ACA ethics indicate that a minimum of 5 years must pass before the counselor can have a romantic relationship with the client. Hint: If your ethics exam is created via your state board, check state regulations regarding nonerotic touching; some states stipulate that behaviors such as hugging a client are unethical. **(a)**

843. Computers are now being used in various counseling settings. Counselors speak of computer-assisted counseling (CAC) and computer-managed counseling (CMC). An office that employs a computer to schedule clients would be an example of

    a.    CMC.
    b.    CAC.
    c.    an ethical violation.
    d.    the misuse of computers, though the practice is ethical.

    When a computer helps manage your practice (yes, just like a manager) then it is known as CMC. CMC would include tasks such as bookkeeping, client scheduling, printing billing statements, and compiling referral sources. CAC is like having a counseling "assistant" do the counseling for you. A computer software program that attempts to counsel clients is an example of CAC in action. CAC is controversial and most experts agree computers can never provide the compassion of a human doing counseling. **(a)**

844. A college student who suffers from panic disorder types his symptoms and concerns onto a PC screen and then waits for the computer program to respond or question him further. The student engages in this practice for a 40-minute session per week. This is an example of

    a.    CAC.
    b.    CMC.
    c.    computer-managed counseling.
    d.    b and c.

Again, the computer "assists" in the actual practice of counseling; hence the term *computer-assisted counseling*, a humanistic counselor's worst nightmare! **(a)**

845. A counselor educator has created a research study. He is using students as research subjects. This is commonplace.

   a.  Student participation can be mandatory as part of a counseling course.
   b.  Student participation can be mandatory for students who have finished their coursework and are completing a dissertation, thesis, or required scholarly paper.
   c.  Participation or lack of it cannot impact the student's academic standing.
   d.  According to ethics the student cannot participate in the research if he or she is not currently enrolled in the counselor educator's class.

   Likewise, NBCC's code tells us that if you use clients you **may not** stipulate that they must participate in order to receive counseling services **(c)**

846. Which statement best describes the counseling profession's reaction to computer-assisted counseling and computer-managed counseling?

   a.  Counselors are very humanistic and seem to dislike CMC and CAC technology.
   b.  Counselors have welcomed both forms of computer technology with open arms.
   c.  CMC has been well received since it cuts down time on paperwork, scheduling, and record keeping, but there is a mixed reaction to CAC as some feel it depersonalizes counseling.
   d.  Counselors dislike CMC but praise CAC highly.

   Work around any agency, school counseling office, or private practice and you'll surely hear counselors complaining about paperwork, ergo the enthusiasm over CMC procedures. CAC, nevertheless, seems a bit cold and depersonalizing in a field which emphasizes concepts like empathy and positive regard. Besides, when computers display warmth they tend to electronically shut down! **(c)**

847. You secure a state license and NCC status and open a private practice. Your cousin comes to the agency for supervision to get his state license.

   a.   You would supervise him just like anybody else.
   b.   You could supervise him if he is your second cousin, but not your first cousin.
   c.   Consultation is very important in today's world. You could supervise him if you receive a consultation and the consultant approves of it.
   d.   It would be unethical to supervise him.

   Surprise! The answer is choice "d." NBCC ethics keep it very simple: "Supervisors should not supervise relatives." **(d)**

848. A counseling journal article should use documentation (i.e., references) that is based on

   a.   APA style.
   b.   MLA style taught in most English composition classes.
   c.   a or b.
   d.   none of the above.

   Counseling journals conform to the standards of the **Publication Manual of the American Psychological Association.** The reality is, however, that many of us took only English composition courses that taught MLA, rather than APA style. **(a)**

849. A 14-year-old male threatens to blow up his parents' garage because he has been grounded. You believe his threat is genuine. You should

   a.   ask the child if he will sign a release of information so you can talk to his parents.

b.   not talk to the parents since this would weaken the bond of trust you have with the client.

c.   have the child sign a contract stating he will not blow up the garage but mention nothing to the parents.

d.   warn the parents that their property is in danger.

There is little evidence to suggest a right or a wrong answer to this question. Nevertheless, a case tried in the Supreme Court of Vermont suggested that a mental health agency was negligent for not warning parents that their son, who was in therapy, threatened to burn down their barn—which he did. So until further notice, a warning is in order.                          **(d)**

850.  A 16-year-old girl threatens to kill herself and you fail to inform her parents. Your behavior as a counselor is best described as

a.   an example of a multiple relationship.

b.   an example of informed consent.

c.   an example of negligence, which is a failure to perform a duty, and in this instance is an obligation to protect the client.

d.   multiple submission.

Here is a myriad of terms related to counseling ethics. A dual relationship, also called a multiple relationship or noncounseling relationship (choice "a"), occurs when a counselor has a relationship with the client in addition to being his or her counselor (e.g., a sexual relationship or a business deal with the client). As stated earlier, in many instances ethics frown on this practice, claiming that it prevents professional objectivity. **A referral to another professional might be necessary to avoid this in some instances.** Informed consent, on the other hand, is an example of a desirable counselor behavior that can actually reduce the chances of a malpractice suit. Informed consent is roughly the opposite of mystifying the counseling process. The counselor "informs" the client what will take place so the client will have the necessary information to decide whether he or she wants to "consent" to the procedure. **Informed consent applies to research (e.g., a fair explanation of**

**benefits, discomfort, freedom to withdraw from the study at any time, etc.) as well as counseling!** Multiple submission (choice "d")—a violation of ethics—transpires when a journal article is submitted to more than one journal at a time. Negligence (choice "c") is evident when a counselor "neglects" or fails to perform a required behavior.                                    **(c)**

851. NBCC has developed a code of ethics to help counselors behave in a professional manner. The Code warns against stereotyping and discrimination. All of the following would be examples of stereotyping and discrimination *except:*

   a.   Advising an African American client to avoid graduate school because you believe the Jensen research regarding African Americans and IQ scores.
   b.   Advising a client to consider switching his college major based on your clinical judgment as well as the results from an extensive test battery.
   c.   Advising a female client to avoid taking a management position because you feel women are generally nonassertive.
   d.   Advising a female client to avoid taking a management position because you feel women managers are generally too aggressive.

   Discrimination is the practice of not treating all clients in an equal manner especially due to religious, racial, ethnic, sexual, or cultural prejudice on the part of the therapist. Stereotyping occurs when a counselor views all persons of a given classification or group in a biased manner (e.g., all women are too nonassertive to hold management positions; or all therapists are crazy—I knew that one would get your attention even after pondering 851 questions!).                                    **(b)**

852. NBCC ethics caution counselors against sexual harassment. An example of an ethics violation in this respect would be

   a.   a female counselor who tells a male client how sexy his hairy chest looks when he leaves his shirt unbuttoned. The male client blushes and appears uncomfortable.

b.    a male counselor who smiles to reinforce a female client (who is overly critical of her looks) who has just said that she is beginning to accept her feminine qualities.

c.    a female career counselor who tells a male client that she feels his gray flannel suit would be the most appropriate for a given job interview.

d.    when a client who has been very depressed and neglecting her looks comes into the therapy session looking much better and the counselor comments, "You certainly look nice today."

A 1977 study by Holroyd and Brodsky of 1,000 Ph.D. licensed psychologists (500 females and 500 males) found that when erotic contact did occur it was usually between male therapists and female clients. And of those therapists who had intercourse with patients, 80% repeated the act. Of male therapists, 5.5% reported having intercourse with a patient, while the female therapist rate was 0.6%. Most of the therapists in the study felt erotic contact is never beneficial to clients. Response "a" is illustrative of a sexually inappropriate comment on the part of a helper. Ethics warn that a single or multiple occurrence of verbal, nonverbal, or physical actions that are unwelcome or perceived as harassment by a "reasonable person" would fall into the unethical category.                                                    **(a)**

853.  You are a well-known cognitive behavior therapist who heads up a private practice in New Jersey. For the next two years you will be in Canada conducting a research project. Your practice has six other counselors. The practice is sending brochures to schools, agencies, and hospitals in an attempt to boost referrals. Your name appears on the front of the brochure as if you are available for referrals. This is

a.    totally ethical.

b.    unethical.

c.    possibly ethical and possibly unethical. Not enough information is given to answer this question.

d.    irrelevant since ACA and NBCC ethics do not address private practice.

The verdict: unethical. Ethics do address private practice and suggest that persons who hold leadership roles not allow their names to be used in professional notices when they are not practicing counseling unless this is clearly stated in the practice's literature.    **(b)**

854. A colleague of yours who is <u>not</u> a certified counselor behaves in an unethical manner. The ethical thing for you to do is

    a.    ignore it; unfortunately you have no rights in this situation.
    b.    consult the school the person graduated from.
    c.    attempt to rectify the condition via institutional channels, and if this fails report it to regulatory organizations.
    d.    all of the above are considered ethical.

According to NBCC the counselor in question could be any mental health professional.    **(c)**

855. A client asks you (and you have NCC status) for classical psychoanalysis yet you have no training whatsoever in this area. If you agree to analyze the client, you are

    a.    violating the duty to warn.
    b.    still ethical if you possess LPC or NCC.
    c.    unethical as this is misrepresentation.
    d.    still ethical if, and only if, you have a doctorate.

Six doctorates and a wall covered with LPC and NCC credentials will not change the situation. The NBCC's Code of Ethics states: "NCCs provide only those services for which they have education and qualified experience." The same goes for tests and assessments. Now assuming the above counselor had extensive training, say via an analytic institute, then he or she could perhaps provide this service ethically.    **(c)**

856. In your initial disclosure statement it was clearly explained to the client that she must pay her bill in a timely manner. She did not. According to ACA ethical guidelines you can terminate her.

    a.  This practice was ethical at one time, but now it is not ethical under any circumstances.
    b.  This practice was not mentioned, but experts have been very critical of this omission.
    c.  This practice is ethical whether you revealed this to the client in the initial disclosure statement or not.
    d.  This practice is ethical if you revealed this to the client in the initial disclosure statement.

    Counselors are allowed to adjust fees when it is legally permitted.                                                  **(d)**

857. Dr. X recommends to his clients at the agency where he practices that he would rather counsel them in his private practice. Ethically speaking

    a.  Dr. X has every right to do this.
    b.  Dr. X is diverting agency clients to his practice and this is unethical.
    c.  guidelines do not address this practice.
    d.  NBCC and ACA actually encourage this method for private practitioners who wish to increase the number of clients they can assist.

    This is also a great way to get yourself fired from the agency!  **(b)**

858. You wish to use an experimental treatment strategy. According to NBCC

    a.  this is a blatant ethics violation.
    b.  you can do it since you are advancing the profession in a scientific manner.
    c.  this could be ethical if you explain this to the client and the client agrees.

d.   it could be ethical, but since it is experimental you must make an audio or video recording of the interview.

Certified counselors will clearly inform clients of the purposes, goals, and techniques utilized. Some textbooks in the field may have inadvertently given counselors the *false* notion that it is best to mystify the counseling process such as when prescribing paradoxical interventions. **Must-know principle:** Paradoxical interventions—in which a client is told to exaggerate a symptom—are contraindicated in cases with homicidal or suicidal clients.                                                        **(c)**

859.  A counselor is counseling an executive secretary. The counselor is writing a book and mentions this to the client. The counselor suggests that as paying for the counseling might be a hardship for the client so the client could type the counselor's manuscript. This is

a.   known as bartering and unethical as described here.
b.   known as bartering and ethical.
c.   known as bartering and is highly recommended for clients with limited income.
d.   is known as bartering and ethics encourage this practice whenever possible.

And what happens to the counselor's objectivity if the secretary is doing a poor job or worse yet not completing the manuscript? The practice of "bartering" is discouraged. Bartering occurs when a client exchanges goods or service for treatment or testing (e.g., I'll paint your car if you provide me with six sessions of therapy). **Currently, ethics allow the practice of bartering if the client requests it, a written contract is drafted, it does not result in any harm, and the relationship is not exploitative.**     **(a)**

860.  Ethics state that a counselor should _____ all clients for group counseling.

a.   diagnose
b.   test

c.    screen

d.    a and b

Some clients are inappropriate for group work.    **(c)**

861. You are a middle school counselor at a public school. A child is threatening to kill another student and admonishes you to keep it a secret. According to the ethical principle of minimal disclosure the best course of action would be to

a.    try to talk the client out of his plan of action but do not violate his confidentiality by telling anyone else.

b.    call the major radio and television stations as research clearly indicates that publicity can stop school tragedies.

c.    call the police and give them a complete blow-by-blow description of the counseling session.

d.    inform the parents of the student in danger, inform the principal, and call the police immediately, discussing only material related to the threat.

**An important mini-review here:** Minimal disclosure means that if you must break confidentiality you reveal only what is necessary (i.e., a minimal amount) and when possible inform the client that you are going to disclose confidential information. In reality, there is no perfect answer to a question such as this.    **(d)**

862. Your agency uses a collection agency when clients don't pay their bills. You should

a.    not take a chance on degrading the therapeutic relationship by mentioning it.

b.    explain to the client that ethically the agency can do this; however, a private practitioner is not allowed to use a collection agency and thus a private counselor might be a wiser choice.

c.    inform the client of this before the counseling begins.

d.    never do this as it is unethical in our field.

The ethical principle of informed consent dictates that the counselor should give the client this information upfront.    **(c)**

863. You have just made a landmark discovery which you feel could literally change the entire field of counseling and thus you write an article which depicts your findings. The next step would be to

    a.    submit the article to no more than two journals simultaneously.
    b.    submit the article to every major APA and ACA journal published.
    c.    submit the article to one publication at a time despite your conviction that the article must get published.
    d.    write your state licensing board and request permission for multiple submission privileges.

The NBCC code sets the record straight: "Counselors submit manuscripts for consideration to one journal at a time." **In our field, multiple or duplicate submissions are unethical in relation to journal articles. Exam hint:** Once your article is published you may not have it republished elsewhere without the express permission of the first publisher.    **(c)**

864. Consulting is included in ethical guidelines. Consultation can best be defined as

    a.    a voluntary relationship between a professional helper and a help-needing individual that is generally longer than supervision.
    b.    a brand or paradigm of long-term psychotherapy.
    c.    a systematic process based on classical conditioning.
    d.    a voluntary relationship between a professional helper and a help-needing individual, group, or social unit in which the consultant helps define or solve problems related to clients, the client system, or work-related issues.

One ethical consideration here is that the consulting relationship encourages growth and self-direction for the consultee. The consultant should not become a decision maker for clients or create a dependent relationship. If choices "b" and "c" are unclear, reread the questions and answers in this book in the Counseling and Helping Relationship sections. **In most instances consultation services do not go on as long as supervision services.** **(d)**

865. NBCC's Code of Ethics describes ethical issues related to private practice. Which of these situations is clearly an ethics violation?

   a. A private practitioner who advertises in the *Yellow Pages*.
   b. A private practitioner who advertises in a daily newspaper.
   c. A counselor who terminates a professional relationship with a client because she feels it is no longer productive for her client. She refers the client to another helper.
   d. An executive director of a private practice who has his name listed on the practice's website as a counseling provider despite the fact that he is out of the country and is engaged in a research project for the next two years.

I hope I am getting my message across here: Expect to see a host of questions related to the practical application of all the major areas of counseling—not just ethics—on your exam. The helping professions have become more liberal about advertising practices and thus, based on the information in choices "a" and "b," you cannot say they are unethical. Counselors in executive leadership roles should not allow their names to be used in professional notices at times when they are not performing counseling. **(d)**

866. Nosology refers to a system of classification. Name the nosological system(s) utilized by professional counselors who diagnose clients.

   a. *DSM.*
   b. *ICD.*
   c. a and b.
   d. The Rogerian classification system.

Did you mark choice "a"? Well give yourself an A- because that's not really a bad answer. In fact, it is not even an incorrect answer. The answer I wanted you to mark, nevertheless, was choice "c" since some third-party payers have begun asking for *ICD* (*International Classification of Disease*) codes (choice "b"). Strict Rogerians, choice "d," frown on formal diagnosis.   **(c)**

867. *The Diagnostic and Statistical Manual of Mental Disorders* (*DSM*) was created by the American Psychiatric Association (APA). *The Manual of the International Statistical Classification of Diseases, Injuries, and Causes of Death* (*ICD*) was created by the World Health Organization (WHO). Which counselor would most likely be required to utilize one of these guides to diagnose a client?

   a.   A counselor who wishes to secure insurance (i.e., third-party) payments.
   b.   A school counselor discussing a child with a teacher.
   c.   A multicultural counselor who is seeing a client who grew up in another country.
   d.   A counselor leading a T-group.

   Some experts (e.g., Jay Haley and Carl Rogers) have noted that the formal process of diagnosis is not necessarily a good thing. Giving the client a diagnosis may bias the counselor or cause the counselor to stereotype the individual. Diagnosis has been seen as dehumanizing, and a given diagnosis does not necessarily imply a given cure. Despite all the aforementioned difficulties, insurance companies/managed care organizations ask for a diagnosis before paying for a service; this is a remnant of the so-called medical model. Remember: The *DSM* is produced by a medical organization, the American Psychiatric Association (yes unfortunately, there's another APA to commit to memory).   **(a)**

868. Traditionally, _____ counseling has caused the most ethical concerns.

   a.   behavioral
   b.   person-centered
   c.   humanistic
   d.   reality therapy

The concern has been that behavior therapists can control, manipulate, and shape behavior. Is it ethical, for example, to use aversive conditioning such as electrical shocks, drugs, or paralysis to eliminate smoking, alcoholism, or gambling? Some clients in token economy behavior modification systems have questioned the legality of using contingencies in the form of reinforcement to get them to talk, work, behave, dress, or interact in a certain way. **(a)**

869. Insurance payments are also called

    a.   mandated payments.
    b.   third-party payments.
    c.   optional payments.
    d.   psychometric payments.

Keep in mind that third-party payments do not always cover the entire counseling fee. An insurance policy, for example, could pay only 50% or 80%. Other third-party systems have a maximum fee for services which could conceivably be less than your normal rate. When a client pays for a portion of the service it is known as a "copayment." **(b)**

870. The *DSM-5* no longer uses a multiaxial classification system or GAF scale. Diagnostic codes have _____ digits.

    a.   four or five
    b.   two
    c.   nine (which correspond to the DOT)
    d.   12

Examples: 300.3 Obsessive-compulsive disorder or 305.50 Opiod use disorder. Mild. On occasion, the first digit can be a letter such as V62.3 Academic or educational problem. **(a)**

871. Identify the *DSM* code.

    a.   29622
    b.   29.622

c.   296.99

d.   2962.2

You would not need to know that this is the code for "Disruptive mood dysregulation disorder" to answer this question. In fact let me give you some friendly advice: **Do not waste one second of your time memorizing the code numbers for diagnoses for the NCE or the CPCE. The idea of these questions is to familiarize you with the format of the diagnostic process.** Choice "c" is correct. As mentioned in the answer to the last question, the decimal point occurs after the third digit.          **(c)**

872. A counselor educator is giving a seminar on the *DSM-5*. She gives the students a handout and it lists hoarding disorder and obsessive-compulsive disorder as both having the same 300.3 code. This most likely explanation is:

     a.   that this could be correct since two diagnoses can share a single code.
     b.   it is a typo on the handout.
     c.   this is a trick question since the counselor educator must be quoting an *ICD* code.
     d.   she is a researcher and thus does not realize all disorders have unique codes.

     **Because of the fact that a single code *can* truly represent multiple conditions it is imperative that you list the name of the condition in the client's chart or medical record.  (a)**

873. During a counseling session your client tells you in great detail how he robbed a convenience store six months ago. He got away with a huge sum of money and shot the owner. His descriptions are extremely specific and you believe every word he says. In reality, you are very familiar with the case because the police never solved it and it has been all over the radio and television stations in your town. There is even a huge reward to anybody

who can help law enforcement agencies solve the case. Ethically, you should

a.    call the police and tell them everything you know.
b.    urge the client to call the police and turn himself in.
c.    call the anonymous crime tips line since as a counselor you would not be permitted to reveal your true identity.
d.    just keep it confidential.

I'm not a betting man, but if I were I would bet this question will be the most controversial in this entire tome! Let's look at each answer stem. Remember that the question says "ethically." It is possible your state *laws* dictate something different. Okay, first this client's actions—horrific as they might seem to you—occurred in the past. Based purely on the information in the question there is no reason to believe this client is going to harm himself or anybody else in the future … so don't read things into the question which do not exist. Therefore, a *Tarasoff* duty to warn or protect is decidedly *not* applicable. Choice "a" would violate the client's confidentiality. Choice "b" should be avoided because you are not the client's attorney. He might take legal action against you if he turns himself in and doesn't like the consequences! Choice "c" is still breaching confidentiality. So, at least as of this writing, choice "d" is the undisputed correct answer although I would be mighty surprised if you didn't have some extremely powerful feelings about doing nothing with the information in this situation. **(d)**

874. All of the conditions below are V code diagnoses *except:*

a.    Acculturation problem.
b.    Occupational problem.
c.    Post-traumatic stress disorder.
d.    Academic problem.

In addition to the three V codes listed above, others include: malingering (which is avoiding life's work or duties by intentionally exaggerating or feigning physical symptoms or illness), parent–child problems, occupational problems, noncompliance with medical treatment, other interpersonal problems, and a phase of life or circumstances problem (such as enduring a divorce). In essence, these are what the average person might consider day-to-day problems rather than a psychiatric or psychological difficulty. Survivors of a trauma such as an abduction, airplane crashe, flood, often experience post-traumatic stress disorder (PTSD), however, persons who experienced combat are statistically the most likely. Often PTSD symptoms are said to be delayed in the sense that they do not manifest themselves immediately following the trauma. Reliving the event via flashbacks and dreams is somewhat typical.     **(c)**

875. Formal diagnosis, also known as nosology, is most closely related to the _____ model.

   a.   behavioral
   b.   medical
   c.   cognitive-behavioral
   d.   rational-emotive behavior therapy

The behaviorist, choice "a," is looking for an operational definition (remember, I mentioned this term earlier) of the problem. A *DSM* diagnosis such as 300.23, social anxiety disorder, is vague and meaningless for the behaviorist. Instead, a diagnosis like "I cry whenever I have to give a presentation in my Counseling 502 class" is the type of specific information in which the behaviorist is interested. Rational-emotive behavior therapists and other cognitive behavior therapists are generally more interested in the client's self-talk than in the *DSM* category. The medical model of medicine or psychotherapy begins with a formal label or diagnosis of the problems.     **(b)**

876. Which treatment match-up is incorrect?

   a.   Vivitrol for alcoholism.
   b.   Lithium for bipolar disorder.
   c.   Suboxone for opiod dependence.
   d.   Narcan for schizophrenia.

Narcan or Naloxone is all over the news right now because it can block the effects of opiods such as heroin and painkillers such as morphine, codeine, and oxycodone. By impacting the same portions of the brain as opiods, it can stop or reverse overdoses to save lives. Narcan has virtually no serious side effects and will not make the person high.                                        **(d)**

877. The type of mental health service provided to the client is coded via _____ and is generally required for insurance payments.

   a.   the *DSM*
   b.   the *ICD*
   c.   the AMA's Current Procedural Terminology (e.g., CPT 90844)
   d.   the *Psychiatric Dictionary*

If you want to accept insurance payments you will generally need to specify a CPT code in addition to the *ICD* code on your billing statement. The CPT code will specify the exact nature of the treatment being utilized to help your client (e.g., psychotherapy, hypnosis, biofeedback, or group psychotherapy). A CPT code also can specify the length of the service unit, such as "psychotherapy over 30 minutes." At the end of each session, a client seeking insurance or third-party benefits is given a statement which is sometimes called a "superbill." The superbill verifies the nature of the counselor–client interaction. At the very least, an acceptable superbill usually lists the client's name, the date, the *ICD* diagnosis, the CPT code, and the provider's name and license. It is misrepresentation to list someone else as a direct service provider to secure third-party payments if you provided the service yourself. If an insurance company only reimburses a psychiatrist or a licensed clinical psychologist, then you are not allowed to put the psychologist's or psychiatrist's name on the superbill as if he or she were the service provider. The psychiatrist's or psychologist's name could, however, be clearly noted as a supervisor. This can help to secure insurance payments in some cases. Third-party providers can and have taken legal action against therapists for such misrepresentation. Moreover, therapists have been required to pay back funds received in this manner. My advice is to play it straight. Your bank account may not be quite as large, but I guarantee you'll sleep a lot better.                                                            **(c)**

878. You refer a client to Dr. Smith. Ethically, Dr. Smith

   a.   may not pay you a referral fee for sending her the client.
   b.   may pay you a referral fee if you have a written contract with her.
   c.   may pay you a referral fee if she has expertise in the client's area of concern and you don't and the client gives you written permission.
   d.   can pay you a referral fee if, and only if, she is a psychiatrist.

Save your nickels; counselors cannot ethically accept referral fees.                                                            **(a)**

879. You have written a very popular book on reality therapy. Now you are teaching a graduate course on counseling at a local university. Ethically, you

   a.   may not use the textbook in your class.
   b.   may not use the textbook in your class, but other teachers at the university may indeed use your book as a textbook.
   c.   may use the book as a textbook in your class; however, the royalties you receive must be donated to the institution.
   d.   may use the book as a textbook in your class.

It's ethical! Nevertheless, your school could have a policy against it or a policy similar to choice "c."                       **(d)**

880. An elementary school counselor is giving a child a standardized test. On several occasions the child says he does not understand what the counselor has said. The counselor should

   a.   refuse to repeat the question.
   b.   tell the child to answer the question nevertheless.
   c.   repeat the question, but talk more slowly.
   d.   ignore the child's verbalizations.

A word of caution is in order here. The counselor should always attempt to use the recommended wording. Changing the wording could alter the impact of the test question, possibly confounding the results. **(c)**

881. The most popular paradigm of mental health consultation has been proposed by

    a.    Satir and Minuchin.
    b.    Schein.
    c.    Caplan.
    d.    Bandura.

Mental health consultation occurs when a consultant works with a consultee regarding clients or administrative/program issues. **When the ultimate goal is to help a client, it is known as a "client-centered" consultation.** When your licensing supervisor suggests a plan of action for a given client, then you as a consultee are the recipient of "client-centered" consultation (not to be confused with client-centered therapy). **The exam you will take also may mention "consultee-centered" consultation. Here, the focus is on helping the consultee develop improved techniques or skills.** Thus, when your licensing supervisor explains a better way for you to implement a hypnotic induction with one of your clients, then you are the recipient of "consultee-centered case consultation." **A variation of this is the "consultee-centered administrative consultation" in which your supervisor's or consultant's intention is to sharpen up your administrative skills (e.g., making you a better presenter at your agency board meeting). Finally, there is the "program-centered administrative consultation." As the name suggests, the emphasis here is on creating, designing, or evaluating the program in question.** These four basic types of mental health consultation have been proposed by Gerald Caplan. Choice "a" identifies two well-known names in the family therapy movement, while Albert Bandura (choice "d") is well-known for his work in modeling and vicarious learning by observation (sometimes known as "social learning theory"). In this approach, the consultant helps the consultee set up behavioral management programs for the clients. **(c)**

882. The doctor–patient consultation model relies on four distinct stages: entry, diagnosis, implementation, and evaluation. In order for the doctor–patient structure to work, the consultee (i.e., the person receiving the consultation) must accurately depict symptomatology, trust the consultant's diagnosis, and carry out the consultant's directives. This model is associated most closely with the work of

    a.   Caplan.
    b.   Freud.
    c.   Adler.
    d.   Schein.

**Consultants can focus on process (what is happening from a communications standpoint) or content (knowledge imparted from the consultant to the consultee).** **(d)**

883. _____ are the leading causes of malpractice actions taken against counselors, therapists, and mental health providers.

    a.   Confidentiality and dual relationships
    b.   Termination
    c.   Failure of the duty to warn
    d.   Inferior record keeping

Sexual issues also make it into the top ten slots and indeed I have even seen research that puts it in the number one spot. It has been estimated that over 95% of those clients who were sexually involved with their therapists have been harmed, and that in about one third of the cases, treatment literally ended as soon as sexual intimacy began. **Important reminder many counselors are not aware of: Excessive self-disclosure on the part of the helper can be considered malpractice. If it doesn't help the client and is seemingly intended to help the counselor then it is inappropriate.** **(a)**

884. Your client was seeing Dr. Doyle for counseling for three years. The client has now stopped seeing Dr. Doyle and has an appointment to see you. You should

    a.    refuse to see the client unless she will sign a release so you can secure the information Dr. Doyle compiled.

    b.    call Dr. Doyle. In this situation no release of information or consent form is necessary.

    c.    counsel the client.

    d.    put something in writing and send it to Dr. Doyle prior to the second session of counseling.

Treat this client in the same manner as you would treat any other client! To be sure, you might decide that information amassed via Dr. Doyle would be helpful and then you would secure the client's written permission to contact him. Nevertheless, this certainly isn't required to begin the counseling process. Moreover, it is possible that the client will not sign for the release. **(c)**

885. You are treating a man who suffers from panic disorder. His panic attacks are so severe he cannot drive to work. After just three sessions he is not only driving to work but has taken up sky diving to demonstrate his progress over his fear. You would love to put his testimonial on your brochure to show how adept you are at treating this affliction. You should

    a.    ask him if he will write you a few sentences to place on the brochure with his name at the end.

    b.    ask him if you can write the testimonial for him and place it on the brochure.

    c.    not ask him for a testimonial since it would constitute an ethics violation.

    d.    ask him if he will write you a few sentences to place on the brochure but assure him that his name will not appear.

Ethics guidelines clearly state that the counselor should not solicit testimonials from clients. **(c)**

886. Ethical dilemmas rarely have clear-cut answers. Thus when a complex ethical situation manifests itself, it is best to

   a.  consult only ethical codes and not colleagues.
   b.  consult with colleagues as well as ethical codes inasmuch as legal standards are very often based on the methods of fellow professionals in analogous situations.
   c.  consult ACA but not your colleagues.
   d.  consult your state licensing bureau but not your colleagues.

Legal standards and cases regarding malpractice suits are often decided by the behavior of your fellow professionals. If I were you, I'd check to make certain you're not the one soldier marching in the opposite direction! In malpractice cases you are often judged by what your peers would do in the situation.  **(b)**

887. You have attempted to help a client for over two years with little or no success. You should

   a.  always refer the client to a board-certified psychiatrist.
   b.  terminate the relationship and initiate an appropriate referral.
   c.  change therapeutic modalities and see the client for another six months.
   d.  change therapeutic modalities and see the client for at least another year.

Ethics guidelines suggest that when a counselor feels he or she is unable to help a potential or existing client, then the relationship should not be initiated, or the existing one should be terminated. In either case, the counselor is responsible for providing alternative referral sources to the client.  **(b)**

888. Assume that you have decided to refer a client elsewhere because you were unable to help her. Upon you mentioning this, the client insists that she has seen several other therapists and you are the finest one. Ethics guidelines would dictate that

   a.  you must see her; your duty is to the client.

   b.   you must refer her to a medical practitioner.

   c.   you must ask her to consider hospitalization.

   d.   you are not obligated to continue the relationship.

You are acting in the best interest of the client.       **(d)**

889.  Counseling is a relatively new profession. The first counselors in the United States were not called counselors. They were

   a.   psychoanalysts practicing short-term therapy.

   b.   behaviorists practicing short-term therapy.

   c.   deans and advisors employed after the Civil War in college settings to watch over young women.

   d.   humanistic psychologists.

                                                    **(c)**

890.  Historically speaking, the first psychology laboratory was set up by

   a.   Frank Parsons, who set up community centers to help individuals in search of work.

   b.   Sigmund Freud, the father of psychoanalysis.

   c.   Wilhelm Wundt, in 1879 in Leipzig, Germany.

   d.   E. G. Williamson.

Wundt was convinced that psychology could be accepted as a science if consciousness could be measured. Wundt's school of thought is termed *structuralism* because his interest was in the "structure" of consciousness. German psychologists—and I'm certain you'll find this humorous in terms of our emphasis today on pragmatic strategies—were convinced that Wundt's theory was indeed pure science because it had no practical applications! **Parsons, choice "a," has been called the father of guidance. Some historians insist that the profession of counseling officially began when Parsons founded the Vocational Guidance Bureau of Boston and published the book *Choosing a Vocation* in 1909.**   **(c)**

891. Counseling became popular after the 1931 publication of

    a.    *Workbook in Vocations* by William Proctor, Glidden Ross Benefield, and Gilbert Wrenn.
    b.    *The Interpretation of Dreams* by Sigmund Freud.
    c.    *Behaviorism* by John B.Watson.
    d.    *Counseling and Psychotherapy* by Carl Ransom Rogers.

These are all landmark books in the field. Choice "a" is the correct answer because it set the stage for the popularization of the word *counseling*. Prior to 1931, the word *guidance* was used for educational and vocational guidance. This work, as well as an earlier one by William Proctor in 1925 entitled *Educational and Vocational Guidance*, began to conceptualize counseling as a psychological process. Choice "b" is considered Freud's most influential work, while choice "c" described the tenets of behaviorism, which was born in 1912. Watson's behaviorism asserted that the only subject matter for psychology was observable behavior. Choice "d" is the 1942 classic in which Rogers emphasized a theory of intervention in which the counselor was not an authoritarian figure such as in psychoanalysis, trait-factor analysis, or directive schools of helping. Rogers was also known as one of the first theorists to employ audio recordings to improve practicum supervision.        **(a)**

892. PL 94-142 (the Education for All Handicapped Children Act) states that

    a.    all children between ages 5 and 21 are assured free education.
    b.    handicapped persons are placed in the least-restrictive environment (LRE).
    c.    an Individualized Education Plan (IEP) is developed for each child
    d.    all of the above.

**Note:** The term *disabled* is now preferred over the antiquated term *handicapped*. The Act was passed in 1975—a year before Virginia passed the first counselor licensure law—after a congressional finding that the United States had over eight million children who were disabled. Over half were not receiving appropriate education while one million were excluded from public education. Enforcement relied on funding. That is to say, if a state did not meet the guidelines mentioned in choices "a," "b," and "c," funding was denied. Section 617 (c) of PL 94-142 (another stipulation for funding) gave individuals the right to read their own records and files if they were over 18, as well as the records of their children. In 1990, the Americans with Disabilities Act (ADA) prohibited employers with 15 or more employees from discriminating against the disabled.    **(d)**

893. The major trend that impacted upon the counseling movement in the 1980s

   a.   was reality therapy.
   b.   was behavior modification.
   c.   included an emphasis on professionalism, certification, and licensing.
   d.   was the group movement.

Credentialing helped counseling become a specific and separate profession such as psychology or psychiatry. Although group work is still very popular, it emerged as a driving force in the 1970s.    **(c)**

894. The APGA and APA had joint ethics guidelines for counselors and psychologists. This changed during the 1970s when

   a.   Psy.D. programs were introduced.
   b.   the APA did not wish to credential master's level counselors or psychologists.
   c.   psychologists were doing more testing.
   d.   joint ethics became illegal in the United States.

Separate ethics were thus developed, which helped discern counseling from psychology as a profession. Psy.D., or doctor of psychology programs (choice "a"), generally focus more on practitioner skills and less on research and experimental skills than Ph.D. programs in clinical psychology.                    **(b)**

895. The 1950s was the age of tremendous strides in

    a.   analysis.
    b.   developmental psychology.
    c.   behavior modification.
    d.   group work.

Piaget, Erikson, and Havinghurst were very influential. In addition, thanks primarily to the work of Carl R. Rogers, counseling rather than testing became the major task for professionals.                    **(b)**

896. The _____ movement began in the late 1960s.

    a.   testing
    b.   Rogerian
    c.   group
    d.   developmental psychology

Groups would remain popular in the 1970s. Some of the literature in the field refers to the 1960s and 1970s as "decades of variation," in which we became "therapy of the month consumers"! Jerome Frank hypothesized at the time that the sudden flood of new therapies was due to the current upheaval in society. Gestalt, transactional analysis, primal scream therapy, encounter groups, marathon groups, and yes, even naked encounter groups became popular!                    **(c)**

897. In the 1960s C. Gilbert Wrenn's book, *The Counselor in a Changing World*, urged counselors to

    a.   use biofeedback.
    b.   rely more heavily on projective testing.
    c.   emphasize developmental concerns rather than merely focusing on crises and curing emotional illness.
    d.   stick to proven nondirective techniques.

This 1962 APGA publication was an attempt to steer counseling away from merely providing remedial services to students.    **(c)**

898. One of the primary problems of counseling in the early 1960s was that it wrongly emphasized

    a.    social issues.
    b.    intrapsychic processes.
    c.    referrals to secure antidepressant medicine.
    d.    career counseling.

Choice "b" is correct, intrapsychic processes (i.e., processes within one's mind or psyche). This was not entirely a negative thing; nevertheless, social issues such as Vietnam, civil rights, and women's issues could have been emphasized to a greater degree.    **(b)**

899. The significance of the 1958 National Defense Education Act was that it

    a.    provided financial aid for graduate education in counseling.
    b.    expanded school guidance services.
    c.    improved guidance for gifted children.
    d.    all of the above.

Many pilot programs developed as a result of the funding. Gradually, the funding found its way into helping counselors prepare to work with economically disadvantaged youth. Thus, the Act eventually helped all types of young people secure better counseling and guidance services. Some exams may use the abbreviation NDEA when referring to this act.    **(d)**

900. A man has a rare, highly contagious disease that is fatal. He is keeping it a secret and insists that he will never tell his wife. You should

    a.    break confidentiality and tell his wife.
    b.    honor the man's decision not to tell his wife for therapeutic reasons.

    c.    honor the man's decision not to tell his wife in order to maintain ethical confidentiality.

    d.    handle it based on your clinical intuition since ethical guidelines fail to address this emotionally charged issue.

Ethics tell us that if a client has a contagious fatal disease the counselor is justified in telling a third party who would be at serious and foreseeable risk. Of course, the counselor must ascertain that the client has not already informed this person or that the client does not intend to inform the third party in a reasonable period of time. **(a)**

# 11

## Counseling Families, Diagnosis, Neurocounseling, and Advanced Concepts

*Perhaps the greatest social service that can be rendered by anybody to this country and to mankind is to bring up a family.*
—George Bernard Shaw, satirist, social commentator, and playwright.

## 27 HINTS FOR TACKLING *DSM-5/ICD* QUESTIONS ON YOUR EXAMS

1. The first *Diagnostic and Statistical Manual of Mental Disorders (DSM)* was released in 1952 with approximately one hundred diagnostic categories. The *DSM* was, and is, a book of nosology, or the classification of disorders. It allows you to identify and name the disorder resulting in a differential diagnosis.

2. The *DSM-III*, released in 1980, moved the focus from psychodynamic to the medical model of disease and mental health. The *DSM* grew in size and by the year 2000 the *DSM-IV-TR* listed 297 disorders. Most helpers felt the *DSM-IV-TR* was not user-friendly. The chapters did not flow in a sensible order

and most mental health experts didn't relish the multiaxial system. Multicultural scholars lamented that the text was shy on taking cultural factors into account. A *DSM-5* was released May 18, 2013 by American Psychiatric Association Press at the annual meeting of the American Psychiatric Association.

3. The *DSM-5* is the result of 14 years of revisions. Sadly, for the most part, the profession of counseling was not given the opportunity to impact changes in the new edition. The profession of social work, a huge mental health provider in the United States, also had very little input. Note the title is the *DSM-5* and not the *DSM-V*. It is possible that the roman numerals showcased in past editions were dropped so that minor updates in future editions such as *DSM-5.2* or *DSM-5.3* might be used. Time will tell if this approach is actually implemented.

4. Internet sites went on record as saying there had never been a book in history that has had as much criticism as the *DSM-5* prior to its release! Some clinicians supported the text, pointing out that the new guide would urge third-party payers to fork out funds for better treatment. Others, criticized the new edition. A good example would be Allen Francis, M.D.—who chaired the *DSM* task force and wrote the final draft for the *DSM-III*—who quipped, "The publication of *DSM-5* is a sad moment for psychiatry and a risky one for patients. My recommendation for clinicians is simple. Don't use the *DSM-5* … ." Francis noted that he was worried that millions of normal people would be mislabeled as having a disorder. Other experts charged that the pharmaceutical industry had way too much input into the context of the book. Another point of contention was that there was way too much secrecy surrounding the process of updating the *DSM*.

5. The *DSM-5* does not predict treatment outcomes nor does it provide insight into the etiology of the mental disorders. The book uses 20 chapters— each chapter is a classification of similar disorders or spectrum of disorders—that match or link to the structure of the *International Classifications of Diseases (ICD)*. Chapters roughly follow age-related or developmental patterns. Thus, disorders of childhood come first with the chapters near the end of the book applying more or less to disorders seen in older adults.

6. Again, the multiaxial system that first appeared in the *DSM-III* way back in 1980 is gone, eliminated, defunct! **The new *DSM* is nonaxial.** It seems that many, if not most clinicians, never really understood why a disorder needed to be on say Axis I rather than Axis II or vice versa. Ditto for the GAF (global assessment of functioning) scale. It too has been eliminated.

7. In a chapter called "Substance Related and Addictive Disorders," gambling disorder is included. The term pathological gambling has bit the dust. The *DSM-5* has incorporated alcohol abuse disorder and alcohol dependence disorders into one disorder known as alcohol use disorder (AUD). "Cravings" has been added as a criterion. Again: The *DSM-5* does not separate diagnoses of substance abuse and dependence! Cannabis withdrawal, caffeine disorder, and tobacco use disorder are included in this chapter.

8. Neurodevelopmental disorders are caused by pathological brain development, while the "Disorders Diagnosed in Infancy, Childhood, or Adolescence" have been eliminated.

9. The term "mental retardation" has been eliminated and replaced with a new diagnosis of intellectual disability (ID) specifying mild, moderate, severe, or profound. The *ICD* will use an alternate term, intellectual developmental disorder.

10. Stuttering is now billed as childhood-onset fluency disorder and is considered a communication disorder.

11. Autism spectrum disorder (ASD) now takes the place of autistic disorder, Asperger's disorder, childhood disintegrative disorder and pervasive developmental disorder-not otherwise specified (PDD-NOS). Again, all of the aforementioned diagnoses are consolidated under the umbrella of ASD. This one is very controversial.

12. Attention deficit hyperactivity disorder (ADHD) is also housed in the neurodevelopmental category chapter. With the new guidelines it is easier to be diagnosed with ADHD.

13. The depressive disorders includes disruptive mood dysregulation disorder (DMDD). This diagnosis is intended to reduce the number of children under age 10 who are diagnosed, and hence treated for bipolar disorder. The word dyscontrol in this category implies that an individual cannot control his or her behavior.

14. Dysthymia (a low-level depression) will now fall under the category of persistent depressive disorder as well as chronic major

depressive disorder (MDD). Premenstrual dysphoric disorder which appeared in the index of the *DSM-IV* now graces the main pages of the *DSM-5*. Dysphoria is a vague term that conveys a state of sadness, depression, distress, and uneasiness or anxiety. Naysayers wonder if the new *DSM* is making a normal part of womanhood appear abnormal.

15. Another controversial change is that the bereavement exclusion disorder for depressive episodes has been omitted. In the previous *DSM* symptoms of grief less than two months following the death of a loved one would not be diagnosed with a major depressive disorder (MDD) episode. Some experts charge that the new *DSM* has made normal grief seem pathological or abnormal, while others feel that removing the exclusion is a good therapeutic move as fewer clients will be denied a diagnosis and thus can receive treatment.

16. The new chapter on Obsessive-Compulsive and Related Disorders includes hoarding disorder, excoriation (picking on your skin), and hair pulling (formerly trichotillomania).

17. Post-traumatic stress disorder (PTSD) has new criteria with additional symptoms. A pre-school PTSD subtype for kids under age 6, and a dissociative type for clients who have feelings of being detached from their body and mind or if the world seems dreamlike, distorted, and unreal.

18. Since the label hypochondriasis had negative connotations, it was eliminated with the new diagnosis being somatic symptom disorder.

19. In the "Feeding and Eating Disorders" chapter, bulimia nervosa can be diagnosed with one weekly bout of binge eating and inappropriate compensatory behavior. The old *DSM* required two bouts per week. Binge eating disorder is now a recognized label.

20. The term "gender identity disorder" has been ousted with gender dysphoria listed as a new diagnostic category. The new term describes a difference between an individual's assigned gender and one's experienced gender for at least six months. There are other indicators, such as a wish to be treated as the other gender, and a desire for primary and secondary sexual characteristics of the other gender, to name a few.

21. Sleep disorders have now morphed into sleep wake disorders.

22. A category of paraphilic disorders distinguishes between paraphilias and paraphilic disorders. Confusing! You bet. If a sexual behavior does not hurt others, and does not cause impairment or distress to the client then it is not a disorder and need not be treated. It would be a paraphilia, but not a paraphilic disorder. It only becomes paraphilic if there is distress to the client, or others are being harmed. Also, the term "retarded ejaculation" gives way to the new term "delayed ejaculation."

23. Lastly, the *DSM-5* has more ratings (often called specifiers) than any previous edition to describe severity. Some exams use the term "dimensionality" to describe severity indicators.

24. **Beginning midnight October 1, 2015 all counselors were required to submit *ICD-10* codes, not *DSM* codes, to get paid by Medicare, Medicaid, and all private insurance carriers. This is a HIPAA requirement. So, I know it sounds a tad strange because *so* much emphasis has been placed on the *DSM*, and yes the *DSM* should be used to make your diagnosis, but that said, your billing code must be from the *ICD-10* if you wish to get paid! I would reread those last couple of sentences several times if I were you. The *DSM-5* sets diagnostic criteria, while the *ICD-10* provides billing codes.**

25. V codes (important for treating the client, **but not mental disorders** stemming from situations such as extreme poverty, academic or educational problems, victims of crime, or problems related to abuse and neglect) have *ICD-10* Z codes (say Z59.0 Homelessness). Lastly, remember to use the *DSM* in conjunction with other appropriate assessment tools, such as the clinical interview and appropriate tests.

26. **Benefits of a formal diagnosis:** The *DSM* is the most popular diagnostic system for counselors. It gives counselors a shared language to communicate with other practitioners, clients, families, and the health system. Putting a label on a person's condition/behavior can sometimes be a good thing. The client might feel better knowing he or she is not the only person with a given condition. Family and friends might be more compassionate toward the person.

27. **Negative factors of a formal diagnosis:** The diagnosis becomes a part of the client's identification ("I can't help it, I suffer from

ADHD."). Diagnostic labels make the client feel like the difficulty is outside of his or her control and therefore, he or she is not responsible for various behaviors and could become the scapegoat for family problems or coddled and not allowed to be independent.

## WHAT YOU NEED TO KNOW ABOUT THE EMERGING NEUROSCIENCE AND COUNSELING REVOLUTION

1.  According to Allen Ivey, Mary Bradford Ivey, and other experts, the client's *and* the counselor's brain change during counseling. **Neuroscience focuses on the science of brain function, and the nervous system rather than just overt behavior. A major premise:** To be effective a counselor must know what is going on in the brain. This can change the way we do therapy. A 2008 book, *Being a Brain-Wise Therapist* by marriage and family therapist Dr. Bonnie Badenoch, helped convince the field that a neuroscientific mindset would be beneficial. **In this area of counseling functional magnetic resonance imaging (fMRI) scans are used to measure blood flow in the brain to gauge activity in different brain sites. Positron emission tomography (PET) scans can do this as well using radioactive tracer dyes.**

2.  A key concept is **neuroplasticity** or the concept that the human brain can change and new neural connections can be made even in later life regardless of our genetics or life experience. It is as if the brain is rewiring itself.

3.  **Neurogenesis** suggests that new neurons can be formed. Hence the notion that we always go downhill with age is flawed. Exercise, for example, can boost serotonin release to fight depression.

4.  Counseling techniques that focus too much on the negative can have an undesirable impact by influencing the interaction between the amygdala and the frontal cortex. Cognitive therapy (e.g., REBT) or reframing does roughly the opposite and can increase serotonin, ergo positive thoughts, just like prescription antidepressants.

5.  Empathy can be measured in the brain and thus it is no longer merely a psychological construct. The **mirror neuron concept indicates that a neuron or neurons fire if you perform a**

**behavior and that the *same* neuron or neurons fire if you witness that behavior in somebody else**. A client describes the painful loss of a spouse and you feel empathy. If a bear chases us we feel fear. Likewise, if we see someone else chased by a bear we feel fear. The response is automatic or involuntary. No thinking is required. **These examples highlight IPNB (interpersonal neurobiology)**.

6. The brain fires at a high level when we see a face similar to our own. This finding seemingly illuminates our cultural conditioning and can be incorporated into training when teaching counselors how to work with clients from other cultures.

7. Children growing up in impoverished settings have higher than desirable levels of stress hormones (such as cortisol). This hinders performance in a number of areas and lessens the chance that this person will escape poverty.

8. Functional MRI (fMRI) allows us to peer into the brain's neural network in instantaneous *real time*. fMRI technology shows which areas of the brain have the most activity and blood flow.

9. Cognitive enchancement therapy (CET) is included in the evidence-based neurocounseling modalities. Here, the clients, often diagnosed with schizophrenia, use neurocognitive video-type games and coaching to improve functioning.

10. The National Institute of Mental Health (NIMH) has embraced neuroscience to the extent that our field might be moving away from the traditional *DSM* diagnostic system.

11. Politically speaking, if counselors do not gravitate toward neurocounseling when psychiatry and psychology embraces the technology, our profession could be left behind.

12. Some counselors are very disturbed with this new trend pointing out that our counseling grew out of a humanistic tradition and this neurobiological approach fails to look into the whole human experience.

13. Another criticism is that counselors and researchers might be attaching too much significance to increased blood flow in various regions of the brain.

14. Although most experts tell us that fMRI and PET scans are safe, a number of researchers do not agree. What might be absolutely necessary to decide on a course of medical intervention might not be wise for research, diagnostic, or counseling purposes. At this

point in time fMRI and blood tests are not accurate enough for diagnosis. (Some neurofeedback methods such as EEG, EMG, and temperature training biofeedback are perfectly safe.)

901. A married couple brings their two children to counseling for behavioral problems. The 14-year-old daughter stays out late and their 17-year-old son is using drugs. According to most marriage and family therapists the identified patient would be

    a.    the 17-year-old son.
    b.    the 14-year-old daughter.
    c.    the family.
    d.    both children.

Most family counselors believe that the entire family system, which is really a natural social system, is dysfunctional. **Hence the entire family is the identified patient and in need of treatment.** Traditionally, the identified patient (IP) was seen as the person who was having a problem. **(c)**

902. You are seeing a husband and wife for marriage counseling. During one of the sessions you decide to see them separately. The husband tells you he has seen an attorney because he is filing for divorce. He has not told his wife and indicates that he will not do so. You feel the wife has a right to know this because it will help her plan for the future. You should

    a.    only tell his wife if he gives you permission.
    b.    communicate his intent to his wife since ethics guidelines state you may do so when a member of the couple is contemplating divorce.
    c.    not tell the wife since research indicates that women respond more positively to divorce when they have less time to think about it.
    d.    terminate the husband unless he tells her.

According to ethics guidelines counselors must not disclose information about one family member in counseling to another without prior consent. Could this situation happen in your caseload? Consider this: In the United States, getting married could be likened to playing the ponies—approximately 50% of all marriages end in divorce, while about 65% of second marriages end in divorce. By the third marriage the figure tops 70%. In general, family therapy seems to be briefer than counseling or therapy provided to individuals.           **(a)**

903. You are supervising a licensing candidate who is primarily interested in marriage and family counseling. You are very attracted to her and have sex with her. According to ethics guidelines

    a.   this is perfectly ethical, since this is a student and not a client.
    b.   this is unethical.
    c.   this is perfectly ethical, since this is a supervisee and not a client.
    d.   a and c are both correct.

    There's a clear-cut answer here folks: **Counselors should never engage in sexual or romantic relationships with current students or supervisees. Likewise for sexual harassment. This refers to in-person as well as electronic relationships.** The fact that the supervisee is interested in marriage and family counseling is totally irrelevant.           **(b)**

904. The fastest growing clientele for professional counselors are persons

    a.   experiencing bipolar disorder.
    b.   experiencing suicidal ideation.
    c.   experiencing marriage and family problems.
    d.   who abuse their children.

    Philosophical differences between organizations are evident. The American Association for Marriage and Family Therapy (AAMFT) sees marriage and family therapy as a separate profession in and of itself. The International Association of Marriage and Family Counselors (IAMFC)—a division of ACA and adheres to CACREP guidelines—believes that marriage and family counseling is a specialty mastered by an individual who has experience and generic training in counseling. **Coursework areas between CACREP programs and those set forth to meet AAMFT curriculum are similar, though certainly not identical.** **(c)**

905. Family counselors generally believe in

a. circular/reciprocal causality (e.g., dynamics of family members).
b. linear causality.
c. random causality.
d. dream analysis.

Linear causality is where you assume $a$ causes $b$. For example, a person was physically abused as a child so now that person becomes an abusive parent. Linear causality is generally accepted as a valid concept in individual counseling; however, marriage and family therapists usually prefer the notion of circular causality. Anthropologist Gregory Bateson became interested in cybernetics (the analysis of information interactions and how the flow of information regulates and controls a system) after World War II and launched the concept of circular causality. Bateson was fond of explaining the new paradigm by taking the example of a man who kicks a stone versus a man who kicks a dog. When a man kicks a stone a linear or Newtonian physics model is appropriate. That is to say, if we know the weight of the stone, the angle it was kicked, the air density, and so on we can calculate the result of the kick. If a man kicks a dog, however, the dog's behavior may control the man's next response. Hence, the dog might bark and merely sit there; howl and run; or perhaps growl and attempt to bite the man. The man is influencing the dog; nevertheless, the dog is influencing the man. **Thus, since everybody is influencing everybody else the problem resides in the family rather than a given individual. The distinction between linear causality and circular causality is a must-know concept for most exams in this field. Performing family therapy often seems to resemble group**

**therapy more than individual work; however, most group models do not work well with families since they are a very special type of group.**                                          **(a)**

906.  Cybernetics is a concept used by family therapists. It is usually associated with the work of

   a.   Sigmund Freud and Albert Ellis.
   b.   Norbert Wiener.
   c.   Virginia Satir.
   d.   behavioral family therapists and cognitive family therapists.

Cybernetics was pioneered in the early 1940s and named (from the Greek word for steersman) by MIT mathematician Norbert Wiener. Wiener was asked to investigate how guns could be aimed to hit moving targets. He teamed up with mathematician John von Neumannn, who worked on the Manhattan Project in Los Alamos, New Mexico, the site of the first U.S. nuclear weapons production. This information, which initially related to machines, was used to analyze family systems thanks to Gregory Bateson. In family therapy, cybernetics suggests that the family has **feedback loops** to self-correct a family system.          **(b)**

907.  A family that is stable and reaches an equilibrium is in a state of

   a.   adaptability.
   b.   enmeshment.
   c.   nonsummativity.
   d.   homeostasis.

**The best answer is choice "d," homeostasis—and that can be good or bad— which refers to maintaining a balanced state.** A thermostat that controls the temperature in your home is a device that monitors and controls homeostasis as is a guidance system on a missile or a smart bomb. A balanced state is not necessarily healthy! The family will attempt to hold onto a given pattern of functioning that could indeed be dysfunctional. Choice "a" describes a family's ability to change or display flexibility in order to change. Choice "b," enmeshment, occurs when family members are overinvolved with each other and thus lose their autonomy. Nonsummativity, choice "c," is a concept suggesting that any system including the family is greater than the sum of its parts (the individuals in it) and therefore it is necessary to examine patterns rather than merely each individual's behavior.                                    **(d)**

908.  Adaptability is the ability of the family to balance

    a.   ego strength.
    b.   stability and change.
    c.   morphostasis and morphogenesis.
    d.   b and c.

Morphostasis is the ability of the family to balance stability while morphogenesis refers to the family's ability to change.     **(d)**

909.  A family wants to see you for counseling; however, they have a very limited income and can't afford to pay. You therefore agree to see the family for free (i.e., pro bono). The term that best describes your actions would be

    a.   aspirational ethics.
    b.   mandatory ethics.
    c.   empathy.
    d.   all of the above.

**Exam hint:** The answer to this question would be the same whether the question was asking about individual, group, or family treatment. Ethics guidelines are documents that sometimes contain two types of ethics: mandatory and aspirational. The literature describes mandatory ethics as guidelines that are strictly enforced. If you violate a mandatory ethic there are consequences for your actions. **Your exam may call mandatory ethics, standards of practice.** Mandatory ethics are often very clear-cut and have no gray areas (e.g., you should never have sex with a current client). Aspirational ethics, on the other hand, describe ideal or optimal practice. Pro bono services would fall into this category because it would be difficult to win an ethics' violation charge against a counselor because he or she would not see the client for free. **Indeed, counseling ethics currently mention pro bono work, but the ethics do not stipulate the principle as limited to "seeing a client for free," so the best answer seems to be aspirational. Expect to see a number of vague questions like this on the actual exam.** **(a)**

910. Experiential conjoint family therapy is closely related to the work of

   a. Virginia Satir.
   b. Albert Ellis.
   c. Jay Haley.
   d. Salvador Minuchin.

Satir was a social worker who began seeing families in private practice in 1951. She felt that the family could be healed via love while Minuchin, the father of structural family therapy, felt that family therapy was a science requiring therapeutic interventions well beyond warmth. These two family therapy titans clashed during a 1974 meeting in Venezuela, and Satir—who felt Minuchin was speaking for the entire movement—went her own way for the rest of her career. She died of pancreatic cancer in 1988. **The term *conjoint* merely implies that two or more family members are in the therapy session at the same time.** **(a)**

911. Virginia Satir felt that a major goal of therapy was to improve intrafamily communication (i.e., communication between family members). According to Satir, four basic patterns prevented good communication under stress. These defensive postures or stress positions are: placating, blaming, being overly reasonable, and being irrelevant. Placating means

   a. you disagree with all the other family members.
   b. you pick a favorite family member and agree with him or her.
   c. you ignore the other family members.
   d. you try to please everybody out of a fear of rejection.

The placating style causes the individual to sacrifice his or her own needs as a way of dealing with stress.    **(d)**

912.  The placater is a people pleaser under stress while the blamer

    a.    will sacrifice others to feel good about himself.
    b.    will often say "if it weren't for you…."
    c.    will point the finger at others to avoid dealing with his or her own issues.
    d.    all of the above are typical behaviors of the blamer.

The blamer basically asserts that, "It's your fault I'm the way I am."    **(d)**

913.  The person who becomes overly reasonable

    a.    practices excitation.
    b.    cries a lot during therapy sessions.
    c.    is likely to engage in the defense mechanism of intellectualization.
    d.    has a high degree of emotion.

Choice "a" is an old term for expressing true emotion—basically the opposite of what the overly reasonable person does! Some of the literature describes the overly reasonable individual as "functioning like a computer" to keep his or her emotions in check. The person is emotionally detached. **Exam hint:** Your test could refer to the overly reasonable client as the **responsible analyzer**.    **(c)**

914.  According to Virginia Satir, the individual displaying an irrelevant style

    a.    will distract the family from the problem via constantly talking about irrelevant topics.
    b.    will become a people pleaser.
    c.    will analyze the situation more than most.
    d.    all of the above.

Choice "a" is typical of this dysfunctional type of communication. Choice "b" is clearly the pattern of the placater, while choice "c" describes the overly reasonable client. **(a)**

915. Virginia Satir is considered a leading figure in experiential family therapy. _____ is sometimes called the dean of experiential family therapy.

    a.   Ludwig von Bertalanffy
    b.   Gregory Bateson
    c.   Carl Whitaker
    d.   Murray Bowen

Okay, calm down! Nobody is asking you to learn to spell von Bertalanffy's name—yet! His name often comes up in discussions of family therapy since Ludwig von Bertalanffy was the biologist who popularized the notion of the connectedness of all living things or the so-called **systems theory model**. The analogy is that the family is more than merely the separate persons but rather a system with rules, patterns that connect members, and so on. Murray Bowen based his family therapy on systems theory. The correct answer to this question is Carl Whitaker, who was fond of saying that experience, not education, changes families. Experience goes beyond consciousness, according to Whitaker and the best way to access the unconscious is symbolically. **Exam reminder:** Your exam may refer to Whitaker's approach as **experiential symbolic family therapy**. **(c)**

916. Carl Whitaker's interaction with the family could best be described as

    a.   quiet and empathic.
    b.   joining the family and experiencing it as if he were a family member.
    c.   a reality therapist.
    d.   a cognitive behavior therapist.

Whitaker, a psychiatrist by training, intentionally minimized the importance of theory, noting that therapeutic interaction is more of an art. **Note:** Although some theories created for individual counseling (e.g., reality therapy or Adlerian) can be used with families and couples, other approaches, such as Whitaker's that emphasize systems, are unique and generally not covered in sources and courses that focus only on individual models.     **(b)**

917.  According to Carl Whitaker,

    a.    a co-therapist is helpful.
    b.    a co-therapist should never be used.
    c.    a co-therapist should be used only with blended families.
    d.    all of the above could be true.

Whitaker felt that a co-therapist can provide meaningful feedback and allows the therapist to be an active participant in the therapy rather than merely a teacher.     **(a)**

918.  Psychotherapy of the absurd is primarily related to the work of

    a.    Virginia Satir.
    b.    Carl Whitaker.
    c.    Maxie C. Maultsby, Jr.
    d.    William Glasser.

Whitaker could be wild at times. A couple who was in a power struggle, for example, might be asked to have a tug of war in order to prove who really had control. In today's world with an attorney's billboard on every corner, I'd probably not recommend an activity of that nature! Maultsby—the psychiatrist in choice "c"—is noted for creating rational self-counseling that is similar to Ellis's REBT.     **(b)**

919.  A behavioristic marriage and family therapist is counseling the entire family together. She turns to the 18-year-old son who is attending community college and says, "You must complete your sociology essay before you can use the family car and go out with

your friends." Which theorist is primarily guiding her intervention strategy?

a.  David Premack's principle or law.
b.  Ivan Pavlov and John B. Watson.
c.  B. F. Skinner.
d.  all of the above.

Behaviorists who practice marriage and family therapy rely on the same theorists as individual practitioners of this persuasion. All of the theorists listed are behaviorists. Premack's work, nevertheless, suggests that a family member must complete an unpleasant task (known as a low-probability behavior; LPB) before he or she would be allowed to engage in a pleasant task (known as a high-probability behavior; HPB). This is known as Premack's principle.                                          **(a)**

920.  A behavioristic marriage and family counselor is counseling the entire family together. She turns to the 18-year-old son who is attending community college and says, "I know you like to play golf. Therefore, every time you cut the grass your father will take you to play golf. I am going to have you and your dad sign a contract confirming that you agree with this policy." Which principle is primarily guiding her strategy?

a.  Negative reinforcement.
b.  Thought stopping.
c.  Shaping with successive approximations.
d.  Quid pro quo.

In Latin quid pro quo means "one thing for another," "something for something," or "this for that." Gee, I knew there was some reason I spent two years studying a dead language in high school! Anyway, this technique, which generally makes use of a behavioral contingency contract, is based on the notion that one person in the family will do something as long as the other member agrees to do something comparable. Just for the record, all of the choices are behavioristic.                        **(d)**

921. A male is supervising a female counselor for state licensing. He tells her that he will continue to supervise her as long as she has sex with him. This is an example of

    a.   quid pro quo.
    b.   a legal but not an ethical violation.
    c.   a and b.
    d.   none of the above.

    Surprise! The correct answer is choice "a." Here the term (i.e., quid pro quo) is being used (in a different context to question 920) in a negative manner that constitutes sexual harassment. Needless to say, the term still has "something for something" or "you do this for me and I'll do this for you" connotations. Expect to see it in either context on your exam. Choice "b" is incorrect since this is clearly an ethical violation.                    **(a)**

922. A behavioristic family counselor suggests that the family chart the number of times that 6-year-old Billy says "no" when he is told to do something. The baseline of the chart would refer to the period

    a.   when positive reinforcement is being implemented.
    b.   when negative reinforcement is being implemented.
    c.   when quid pro quo is being implemented.
    d.   before the behavior modification begins.

    In behaviorism, a baseline is merely a measure of the behavior prior to the treatment or when treatment is not being implemented. **What's with the A and the B stuff?** On some exams the baseline is signified via the upper-case letter A while the behavior modification treatment is written with an upper-case B.     **(d)**

923. The family counselor explains to Mrs. Smith that the next time that 9-year-old Sally hits her little brother she must sit in the family room by herself. The counselor is using

    a.   shaping.
    b.   shaping with successive approximations.

c. reciprocity.

d. time-out, a procedure that most behaviorists feel is a form of extinction.

Time-out occurs when a family member (usually a child) is isolated or removed from an environment for a specified period of time so as to ensure that he or she does not receive reinforcement for dysfunctional behavior. **(d)**

924. Mrs. Chance tells a family therapist that she pays all the bills, does all the cleaning, and brings in 90% of the family's income. Moreover, Mrs. Chance is convinced that her husband does not appreciate her or show her affection. According to the behavioristic principle of family therapy known as reciprocity

a. there is a good chance that Mrs. Chance will consider leaving the marriage.

b. it may seem paradoxical; nevertheless, Mrs. Chance will be more committed to making the marriage work.

c. it may seem paradoxical; nevertheless, there is a good chance Mr. Chance will consider leaving the marriage.

d. this situation will have virtually no impact on this couple's marriage.

Yes, reciprocity can mean that one state accepts another state's license or credential but that obviously isn't what it means in this respect. In fact, if that crossed your mind, take a break, you've been studying too darn long! The concept of reciprocity in marriage asserts that in most cases two people will reinforce each other at about the same level over time. When this doesn't happen marital discord may result. **(a)**

925. A couple is having sexual problems that stem from anxiety. A marriage counselor who is a strict behaviorist would most likely

a. dispute the couple's irrational thinking.

b. prescribe thought stopping.

c. rely on systematic desensitization procedures.

d. rely primarily on paraphrasing and reflection.

Joseph Wolpe's systematic desensitization pairs feared mental imagery with relaxation to eliminate the fear. Choice "a" isn't necessarily a poor choice since it refers to rational-emotive behavior therapy (REBT; formerly known as rational-emotive therapy—RET) that does employ behavioristic techniques. Nevertheless, a strict behaviorist would be more likely to rely on a *purist technique* such as systematic desensitization.    **(c)**

926. A family counselor notices that the husband in a blended family is having obsessive sexual thoughts about a woman living down the street. A strict behaviorist would most likely

    a.   analyze the man's dreams.
    b.   have him chart the incidence of the behavior, but do little else.
    c.   practice thought stopping.
    d.   rely primarily on Wolpe's systematic desensitization.

Behavioral family therapy first appeared on the scene in the late 1960s, initially focusing on kids in the family who had problems. Psychologist Gerald Patterson (who popularized behavioral parent training in the family's home), psychiatrist Robert Liberman, and social worker Richard Stuart (who created operant interpersonal therapy) are generally cited as the pioneers of this approach. Thought stopping is intended to do just what it sounds like—stop thoughts! The man would be taught to yell in his mind **stop!** as loudly as possible every time he experienced a sexual thought related to his neighbor.    **(c)**

927. You secure a job as the executive director of a family counseling agency. As you go through your files you discover that five years before you took the job the agency selected 100 families and counseled them using a strict behaviorist model. The agency took the next group of 100 families and counseled them using Satir's experiential conjoint family therapy model. Each family received 12 sessions of therapy and each family took a before and after assessment that accurately depicted how well the family was functioning. You decide to run a $t$ test to examine

whether or not a statistically significant difference is evident between the two approaches. This is

a.   an ex post facto (i.e., after the fact) correlation study.
b.   causal comparative or ex post facto (i.e., after the fact) research.
c.   a true experiment.
d.   simple survey research.

**Since the research occurred in the past and the researcher did not have control over the independent variable this qualifies as causal comparative research. The fact that a *t* test was used would allow you to eliminate choices "a" and "d." Causal comparative and correlational research and surveys are called nonexperimental designs.      (b)**

928.   All of the techniques listed below would be used by a behavioristic family therapist *except:*

a.   Family sculpting.
b.   A functional analysis of behavior followed by operant conditioning.
c.   Modeling.
d.   Chaining and extinction.

Family sculpting, popularized by Virginia Satir, is an experiential/ expressive technique in which a family member places other family members in positions that symbolize their relationships with other members of the family. Finally, the member places him- or herself. This helps the therapist understand family dynamics that might be missing from a mere discussion of family issues.      **(a)**

929.   Which statement is true of families?

a.   The divorce rate has decreased markedly in the last several years.
b.   Remarriage today is uncommon.
c.   Remarriage today is common.
d.   The divorce rate in the United States hovers at about 10%.

Four in ten new marriages are remarriages. Choices "a" and "d" are incorrect inasmuch as the divorce rate is rather stable at about 50%.                                                         **(c)**

930. Which statement is true?

   a.   Single life is short-lived for divorced persons. About 30% of all divorced persons are remarried within 12 months of being divorced.
   b.   Most persons who are divorced do not remarry.
   c.   Most persons who are divorced wait a minimum of five years to remarry.
   d.   Women remarry quickly, however, men do not.

The average divorce takes place after eight years. On average, after the marriage ends the partners will remarry in three or four years.                                                          **(a)**

931. The theory of psychodynamic family counseling is primarily associated with

   a.   William Glasser.
   b.   Sigmund Freud.
   c.   Virginia Satir and Carl Whitaker.
   d.   Nathan Ackerman.

Although Freud is the father of psychoanalysis, it was Ackerman—an analytically trained child psychiatrist—who as early as 1938, recommended studying the family and not just the child who was brought into treatment as the identified patient. Some experts consider this the true beginning of the family therapy movement. **Because he was analytically trained, Ackerman—unlike many family therapists—was concerned with the internal feelings and thoughts of each individual as well as the dynamics between them. Prior to Ackerman it was considered inappropriate to include family members in analytic treatment sessions.**          **(d)**

932.  In psychoanalytic family therapy the word *object* means

   a.   a dream.
   b.   a significant other with whom a child wishes to bond.
   c.   transference.
   d.   countertransference.

This is the notion that an individual (or the individual's ego) attempts to establish a relationship with an object—often a person or a part of the body—to satisfy needs. When this does not occur anxiety is manifested.                    **(b)**

933.  In psychoanalytic family therapy the term *introjects* really means that the client

   a.   unconsciously internalizes the positive and negative characteristics of the objects within themselves.
   b.   possesses internal verbalizations.
   c.   possesses a finite number of problem-solving options.
   d.   possesses the internal motivation to solve his or her own difficulties.

Eventually, these introjects (taking in personality attributes of others that become part of your own self-image) determine how the individual will relate to others.                    **(a)**

934.  Pick the best example(s) of the psychoanalytic concept of splitting.

   a.   A client who realistically perceives her therapist as a very empathic person.
   b.   A client who realistically perceives her therapist as only having good qualities.
   c.   A client who sees her therapist as all bad.
   d.   b and c.

Splitting occurs when the client sees an object (another person) as either all good or all bad. Splitting allows one to keep anxiety in check by making objects predictable. This tendency begins in childhood, usually by categorizing one's mother as all good or all bad. Removing dysfunctional introjects from childhood is curative. **(d)**

935. A 72-year-old woman you are counseling in a family reminds you of your mother and this is bringing up unresolved childhood issues for you as the counselor. This is an example of

    a.   positive transference.
    b.   negative transference.
    c.   countertransference.
    d.   ambivalent transference.

Yes, I realize that I have introduced you to these concepts earlier in the text, nevertheless, repetition can help ensure that you truly understand the concepts. Countertransference occurs when a counselor has an unresolved issue that impacts treatment. A strict psychodynamic theorist would assert that the counselor has an unconscious reaction to the family or to the 72-year-old woman that is similar to a reaction he or she experienced in a previous situation; often his or her own childhood. **(c)**

936. A family actually changes the structure of their family system. According to Watzlawick, Weakland, and Fisch the family has achieved

    a.   second-order change that is more desirable than first-order change.
    b.   first-order change that is more desirable than second-order change.
    c.   mediation.
    d.   a Greek chorus.

**Second-order change is indeed more desirable than first-order change. Why? The answer is easy. First-order change can be defined as changes that are superficial. That is to say, behavioral changes do occur; however, the organization or structure of the system does not change. Therefore, first-order change often ameliorates symptoms but the**

**changes are often temporary. Second-order change involves an actual change in the family structure that alters an undesirable behavioral pattern.** Mediation—a term that is becoming more popular—refers to a procedure used by attorneys and trained mental health professionals to settle disputes between couples getting a divorce without going to court. Yes, my dear reader, choice "d" is a real bona fide must-know exam term. Peggy Papp's Greek chorus refers to a consultant or supervisory team that observes a session from behind a one-way mirror and sends messages to the therapist or the family. This so-called treatment-team approach is very popular with strategic therapists. Keep in mind that the counselor may accept or reject notions put forth via the Greek chorus. **(a)**

937. A woman sees her husband as all good sometimes and all bad at others. An analytically trained family therapist who believes in object relations would see this as

   a.  ambivalent transference.
   b.  splitting.
   c.  persistent depressive disorder.
   d.  psychotic behavior.

Here is another type of splitting (the first type is depicted in question 934). As a child this woman internalized an image of her mother as all good at times and all bad at others. She now adheres to this pattern as an adult. **You old pros reading this will know that choice "c" was formerly dysthymia but goes under the label of persistent depressive disorder in the *DSM-5*. Both terms refers to a low-level chronic depression that occurs for more days than not, for two years or more.** **(b)**

938. Nathan Ackerman is considered a famous psychoanalytic family therapist; so are

   a.  Carl Rogers and Albert Ellis.
   b.  Arnold Lazarus and Joseph Wolpe.
   c.  William Glasser and Robert Wubbolding.
   d.  James Framo and Robin Skynner.

Here's a very brief mini-review: Rogers is person-centered; Ellis is rational-emotive behavior therapy; Lazarus is multimodal therapy based on his BASIC-ID structure; Wolpe is systematic desensitization (behavior therapy); and Glasser and Wubbolding are reality therapy. Framo believes that important objects (usually parents) often fuel "love–hate" feelings in kids. The more pathological the early life experiences are the more that person as an adult will make all relationships fit the internal "love–hate" scenario from childhood. Skynner (not Skinner!) is a British psychoanalyst who feels that kids who had poor role models as children possess **protective systems**. This simply means that such individuals harbor unrealistic expectations of people in current relationships carried over from childhood.          **(d)**

939.  Cloe Madanes and Jay Haley are associated with the _____ school of family counseling.

a.    strategic
b.    behavioral
c.    psychodynamic
d.    object relations

Haley is the name we associate most with this area. Haley was impacted by the late great Milton Erickson (not Erik Erikson) who believed in "designing a strategy for each specific problem." It has been said that Haley helped alter Erickson's work so that it helped families as much as individuals. Haley actually coined the term **strategic therapy** to explain Erickson's method.   **(a)**

940.  When Jay Haley began investigating psychotherapy he

a.    was already trained as a Freudian analyst like so many other pioneers in the field.
b.    was already trained as a behaviorist.
c.    had studied REBT with Albert Ellis.
d.    had a degree in the arts and communication rather than the helping professions.

Could it be that Haley viewed his lack of formal training in the counseling field as an advantage? Possibly! While at the Philadelphia Child Guidance Clinic he and pioneer Salvador Minuchin trained people with virtually no background in psychotherapeutic intervention. Since these individuals did not harbor preconceived notions of what therapy should or should not be they were seemingly more open to innovative ideas.    **(d)**

941.    Jay Haley believes in giving clients directives. You are counseling a family and during the session the 14-year-old daughter exclaims that she is suicidal. The best example of a directive would be

a.    you turn to the 14-year-old daughter and say, "You seem to be saying that living is too painful."

b.    you turn to the 14-year-old daughter and say, "Could it be that you want to hurt yourself because your boyfriend no longer wishes to see you?"

c.    you turn to the family and say, "If your daughter threatens suicide this week I want the entire family—including your daughter—to stay home and nobody leaves for the day."

d.    you turn to the family and say, "Could this be a family problem rather than a difficulty for your daughter?"

A directive or prescription is when the therapist tells a client or family what to do.    **(c)**

942.    Which of these responses is the best example of the double-bind concept used in Haley's strategic therapy? You are trying to help a client stop smoking:

a.    You hypnotize her and tell her she will never smoke another cigarette again. After you awaken her you admonish her to smoke as many cigarettes as she can for the first three days.

b.    You recommend that the client chart the number of cigarettes she smokes.

c.    You tell her to mentally visualize herself as a nonsmoker whenever she has the desire to smoke.

d.    All of the above.

A double bind is a **no-win situation characterized by contradictory messages such as never smoke again and then smoke as much as you want**. It constitutes a paradox in the sense that the client is told he or she can engage in a behavior that the person wishes to abate. Although it is used therapeutically, Gregory Bateson (mentioned previously) believed that when parents repeatedly double-bind children the result could be schizophrenia. Yes, my dear reader, a therapeutic technique resulted from studying pathological behavior. Choice "b" represents a behavioristic ploy. Choice "c" is also a possible mode of intervention. I have personally used the correct answer (choice "a") and it tends to work well with smokers. A person who has just been hypnotized will do anything to prove that he or she can still smoke!                                    **(a)**

943. The directive or prescription given to the smoker in the previous question could best be described as

    a.   a paradoxical intervention.
    b.   a cognitive intervention.
    c.   an object relations intervention.
    d.   a behavioristic intervention.

    **A directive is really a therapeutic task or command.** When a person follows a paradoxical directive the symptoms are under therapeutic control. So if the client in the previous question called the counselor and said, "Hey you hypnotized me and I smoked five cigarettes after the session," the therapist could remark, "Well of course you did, I told you to smoke as many cigarettes as you could." One definition of paradox is that the helper prescribes what the client or family *would probably do anyway* and can even tell them to exaggerate it! **Paradox is roughly the direct antithesis of common sense and is a must-know concept for your exam!**                    **(a)**

944.    A couple tells a therapist using strategic family therapy that they have a quarrel at least once every evening. The therapist says, "Between now and the next time I see you I want you to have a serious quarrel at least twice every evening." This is an example of

a.    relabeling, which is commonly used in this form of therapy.
b.    reframing, which is commonly used in this form of therapy.
c.    prescribing the symptom.
d.    a directive that is not paradoxical or a double bind.

Choices "a" and "b" mean roughly the same thing and *are* used by Jay Haley and his followers. Choice "d" stands incorrect since prescribing the symptom is a paradoxical strategy.    **(c)**

945.    Strategic family counselors often rely on relabeling or reframing. A client says his girlfriend yells at him every time he engages in a certain behavior. The best example of reframing or relabeling would be

a.    a counselor who remarks, "Research seems to show that when she yells at you it is because she loves you so much. A woman often feels foolish if she hugs or kisses you in a situation like that."
b.    a counselor who remarks, "Can you tell me about it in the present moment, as if she is yelling at you this very minute?"
c.    a counselor who remarks, "You are upset by her verbal assaults."
d.    a counselor who remarks, "Are you really hurt by your girlfriend's remarks or is it the fact that you are telling yourself how catastrophic it is that she said these things?"

**Reframing occurs when you redefine a situation in a positive context (i.e., make the situation or behavior seem acceptable to the client).** The situation is described in a positive light to evoke a different emotional response. Choice "c" is a technique used by Rogerian therapists while choice "d" would be a common response for an REBT family therapist.    **(a)**

946. In strategic family counseling the person with the power in the family

    a.   has the authority to make rules and enforce them.
    b.   is usually extremely aggressive.
    c.   is usually not willing to follow a family therapist's prescriptions or directives.
    d.   is the one who talks the most.

Jay Haley believes you enhance the power of a family member within the context of therapy by speaking to him or her first during the initial session of therapy.                    **(a)**

947. Psychoanalytic practitioners do not attack symptoms directly. Strategic therapy

    a.   does not attack the symptoms directly either.
    b.   is pragmatic and often focuses on abating symptoms.
    c.   does not take a position on whether a counselor should attempt to ameliorate symptoms or not.
    d.   takes the position that if you can change each family member's unconscious, then symptoms will gradually disappear.

Haley's therapy is solution/symptom focused and very action oriented.                    **(b)**

948. Cloe Madanes insisted that symptoms serve a function. A child, for example, sees that her mother is depressed. The daughter throws a glass cup to the floor to break it. This brings her mother out of the depressed state and makes her mother angry and powerful. This is known as

    a.   symptom substitution.
    b.   the perverse triangle.
    c.   incongruous hierarchy.
    d.   latency.

Madanes believed that one of the keys to family functioning is to help children find more direct ways to help their parents so that their symptoms (in this case breaking one of the family's cups!) no longer serve a viable purpose. **In a normal family hierarchy, the mother controls her daughter; however, in this case, since the daughter is in control, the term incongruous hierarchy is evident. Haley has stated that a malfunctioning hierarchy is evident in most dysfunctional families. The strategic approach asserts that a symptom controls a situation when everything else has failed. A symptom is sometimes viewed as a metaphor for a difficulty being expressed by another family member.** **(c)**

949. Madanes advocated pretend techniques that are somewhat paradoxical. An example might be

   a. a child who has panic attacks pretends he has a mental bullhorn in his head and shouts "stop."
   b. a child who has panic attacks pretends in his mind that a therapist is counseling him.
   c. a child who has panic attacks pretends his dad is a therapist during the actual family therapy session.
   d. a child who has panic attacks pretends to have one during the session and the parents pretend to help him.

In the pretending, the family enacts a make-believe scenario of the problem. Most experts maintain that the pretend technique is more gentle and less confrontational than traditional paradoxical interventions. **(d)**

950. A strategic family therapist says to a family, "I don't know what else you can do to stop the bickering and fighting in your house." This is an example of

   a. restraining.
   b. quid pro quo.
   c. pretending.
   d. interpretation.

In restraining a therapist may warn the family or individual about the negative consequences of change. The counselor might tell the family to take it very slow or expect a relapse. **Restraining helps overcome resistance by suggesting that it might be best if the family does not change!**    **(a)**

951. A client remarks that her depression is extremely intense. Her strategic counselor remarks, "It is very possible your depression is hopeless. It is possible you will never get over it." Her comment is an example of

    a.  a blatant ethical violation.
    b.  positioning.
    c.  cohesion.
    d.  behavioral disputation.

Who knows, at some point in time choice "a" could be the correct answer, however, choice "b" is currently correct. **Positioning occurs when a helper accepts the client's predicament and then exaggerates the condition.** Positioning paints an even more negative picture of the situation for the client than restraining, mentioned in the previous question. **The strategic techniques of restraining, positioning, prescribing the symptom, and relabeling (also called redefining and reframing on some exams) are all examples of paradoxical interventions since they defy common sense.** Choice "c" refers to the degree of bonding between family members or members in a counseling group. Choice "d" is associated with Albert Ellis's REBT. In REBT, the primary goal is to dispute and change the client's cognitions. In behavioral dispute, the client tries to behave in a way that is markedly different from his or her normal, though undesirable, pattern.    **(b)**

952. A family counselor treats an Asian American family exactly like he treats the Arab American families in his caseload. He also imposes values from his own culture on them. This counselor has been described in the literature as

    a.  culturally sensitive.

b.   lacking cultural sensitivity.
c.   culturally encapsulated.
d.   b and c.

**Cultural encapsulation** (a term suggested by counseling pioneer Gilbert Wrenn) **results in a counselor imposing goals from his or her own culture on people from another culture. This is a no-no in counseling.** Counselors who treat all families the same ignore key cultural differences.   **(d)**

953.  Which statement is true of African American families?

a.   They are the largest minority in the United States.
b.   Fewer African Americans are getting married.
c.   African Americans are less likely to be concerned about gender roles (e.g., men and women can cook meals or work outside of the home).
d.   b and c.

Choice "a" is false since as of this writing African Americans constitute the second largest minority. Latino/as constitute the largest minority group.   **(d)**

954.  When working with an African American family, the best approach would probably be

a.   Bowen's family therapy; Minuchin's structural family therapy; or Haley's strategic family therapy.
b.   cognitive family therapy.
c.   Ackerman's psychoanalytic approach to family therapy.
d.   a strict reality therapy approach based on the work of psychiatrist William Glasser.

Several studies indicate that African American families are less likely to seek professional treatment because they often rely on the extended family and the church for support and guidance. This is viewed as a strength. When family counseling is utilized, problem-focused, brief, or multigenerational approaches mentioned in the first choice seem to fare best.   **(a)**

955.  When counseling Asian American families the best approach would most likely be

   a.   Ackerman's psychoanalytic approach.
   b.   behavioral family therapy.
   c.   solution-focused/problem-focused modalities.
   d.   a, b, and c.

Remember that there are huge differences between one cultural group and another, however, no culture is purely homogeneous. That said, when a study by P. Wang et al. looked at Asian Americans, the researchers found that Asian Americans might be mentally healthier than the general population (8.6% had mental health symptoms compared to 17.9% for the population at large). Moreover, those with a *DSM* diagnosis were less likely to seek treatment (34.1% for the Asian Americans versus 41.1% for the general population).   **(c)**

956.  Which statement is true of Latino/a families?

   a.   They have a high unemployment rate, often live in poverty, and rarely earn high school diplomas or college degrees.
   b.   They have higher than average incomes but usually don't finish high school or college.
   c.   They have college degrees, but still generally live in poverty.
   d.   They prefer long-term treatment in therapy.

In general, Latino/as tend to have a higher unemployment rate than whites, are more likely to live in poverty, and earn high school diplomas or college degrees less frequently. Let me address choice "d." In a high percentage of the cases Latino/a clients expect mental health treatment to mimic the treatment they receive from their medical doctors. Short-term behavioral family therapy or structural approaches appear to work well.   **(a)**

957.  A model by Olson, Sprenkle, and Russell suggests that family functioning can be described in two dimensions—cohesion and adaptability. The family therapy term *cohesion* refers to the level

of emotional bonding between family members. Adaptability refers to

a.    a family's level of enmeshment or disengagement.
b.    a family's ability to adapt to the therapist's personality.
c.    a family's ability to adapt to the theoretical persuasion of the therapist.
d.    how rigid, structured, flexible, or chaotic the family is.

Choice "a" is incorrect since it clearly describes the family's level of cohesion. Adaptability refers to the family's balance between stability, **known as morphostasis** and change, **known as morphogenesis**. According to this model the key factor is that the family should have balance in cohesion as well as adaptability. This is the so-called circumplex family model. A word to the wise: Since a number of popular texts include information on this topic it is likely that you will see a question on one or more of the terms included in this question.    **(d)**

958.  Which statement is true regarding Native American families?

a.    They are a very diverse group as they belong to over 550 state-recognized tribes, with over 220 in Alaska.
b.    Extended family and the tribe are very significant.
c.    A high percentage of children have been placed in foster care homes, residential facilities, or adoption homes that are non-Native American.
d.    All of the above are true.

Most theorists agree that the result of choices "a," "b," and "c" (all true, by the way) has been identity confusion.    **(d)**

959.  The statement "Native Americans, also called American Indians in some of the literature, have a problem with alcoholism and suicide" is

a.    false.
b.    true as far as alcoholism is concerned, however, false where suicide is concerned.

    c.    true.

    d.    true regarding the suicide rate, however, false regarding their use of alcoholic beverages.

The Centers for Disease Control and Prevention (CDC) statistics indicate suicide is the second leading cause of death among Native Americans/Alaska Natives between the ages of 10 and 34. Alcohol is involved in 69% of the suicides for all age brackets in this cultural group, topping all other groups tabulated. The high rates of suicide and alcoholism create issues with suicide bereavement (people mourning a suicide are known as "survivors of suicide"), fetal alcoholism, and cirrhosis of the liver.     **(c)**

960.   Murray Bowen is known for his work in intergenerational family therapy. When Bowen refers to triangulation he means

    a.    that most people have three ego states (i.e., the Parent, the Adult, and the Child) in their personality.

    b.    that most people have a personality structure composed of the id, the ego, and the superego.

    c.    when a dyad (i.e., two individuals) is under stress a third person is recruited to help stabilize the difficulty between the original dyad. This could even be a child placed in the middle of the conflict.

    d.    therapy has three distinct phases.

Choice "a" is postulated via transactional analysis while choice "b" is the darling of the Freudians. Choice "c" is the correct answer. Unfortunately, the ploy usually makes the situation between the original pair worse!     **(c)**

961.   One of the primary goals of Bowen's intergenerational family therapy is differentiation. Differentiation is

    a.    the extent that one can separate one's intellect from one's emotional self.

    b.    the extent that one is different from one's peers.

    c.    the extent that one is different from one's childhood.

    d.    the same as fusion.

Did you mark choice "d"? If so, you'd be going back a space or two if this were a board game since fusion is the direct opposite of differentiation. It occurs when the intellectual and emotional aspects of the personality merge. A person who does not possess differentiation does not have a clear sense of the self and others.                                              **(a)**

962. Bowen popularized a three-generational pictorial diagram as a therapy tool. This is known as

    a.    an histogram.
    b.    a sociogram.
    c.    a genogram.
    d.    family sculpting.

A genogram is a family tree of sorts that relies on lines, words, and geometric figures (e.g., squares for males, circles for females, horizontal lines for marriages, and vertical lines for children). If you've ever studied electronics you will note that a genogram looks a bit like a schematic. Bowen suggested that the genogram should depict three or more generations.                   **(c)**

963. An intergenerational family therapist says she is concerned with the nuclear family emotional system. She is referring to

    a.    the fact that although the current family in therapy has an emotional system, this emotional system is influenced by previous generations whether they are alive or dead.
    b.    the fact that a genogram should depict a single generation.
    c.    the fact that emotional discord is a function of the unconscious mind.
    d.    the miracle question.

The "miracle question" introduced in choice "d" is a common term popping up on exams these days. The miracle question is a brief-therapy technique in which the therapist asks, "Suppose one night, while you were asleep, there was a miracle and this problem was solved. How would you know? What would be different?" The miracle question, popularized by the solution-oriented therapy of Steve de Shazer, allows clients to look beyond the problem. Bowen originally referred to the nuclear family emotional process as an "undifferentiated family ego mass" since families with difficulties display a high degree of fusion. **(a)**

964. Albert Ellis is to REBT as Salvador Minuchin is to

a. the MRI model.
b. structural family therapy.
c. intergenerational family counseling.
d. behavioral family counseling.

Note that choice "a" uses the abbreviation MRI for Mental Research Institute in Palo Alto, California. Haley's strategic model has also been called the MRI model or the communications model. To answer the question you would need to know that Ellis is the father of rational-emotive behavior therapy while Minuchin is the founder of action-oriented structural family therapy. This approach posits that an individual's behavior can only be interpreted by analyzing family interaction. Moreover, a change in the family's patterns of communication and interaction must occur to create a healthy family. Here again, play with a memory device like "Salvador begins with an S and so does structural." **(b)**

965. An important technique in structural family therapy is joining. Which statement most accurately depicts this intervention?

a. The therapist meets, greets, and attempts to bond with the family. The therapist will use language similar to that of the family and mimesis which means that he or she will mimic communication patterns.
b. The therapist is professional but distant.
c. The therapist joins the family and sympathizes with their difficulties.
d. Joining is used during the final session of therapy.

Joining occurs during the initial session to boost the family's confidence in the treatment process and reduce resistance. In subsequent sessions the therapist will challenge the dysfunctional communication patterns and the structure of the family.    **(a)**

966. A family is seeing a structural family therapist because there is a huge argument every time the subject of the 16-year-old daughter's boyfriend comes up. The therapist says, "Okay, I want you to play like you are at home and act out precisely what transpires when the subject of your daughter's boyfriend is mentioned." The structural family therapist is using a technique called

   a.  joining.
   b.  reframing.
   c.  enactment.
   d.  cognitive disputation.

Enactment is a strategy that allows the counselor to see an instant replay, if you will, of what genuinely transpires in the family. Although "c" is the correct answer here structural therapists do employ reframing (defined as an alternative way of describing or perceiving an event) and relabeling discussed in earlier questions.    **(c)**

967. When a structural therapist uses the term *boundaries* he or she really means

   a.  the limits of the human mind.
   b.  the limits of behavior in the family.
   c.  the separation of the family members from their family of origin.
   d.  the physical and psychological entities that separate individuals and subsystems from others in the family.

When structural therapists attempt to help the family create healthy boundaries it is known as **changing boundaries** or the **boundary marking** technique. In this technique the family seating is often altered and family members are placed at a different distance from each other.    **(d)**

968. In Minuchin's structural approach, clear boundaries are

    a. pathological.
    b. rigid.
    c. also called diffuse boundaries.
    d. ideal—firm yet flexible.

Clear boundaries are considered healthy. When boundaries are clear persons in the family are supported and nurtured, but each has the freedom to be his or her own person (i.e., individuate). **(d)**

969. A woman is having difficulties at her place of employment. Her husband turns to her in a session and says, "You're on your own, I've got my own problems." A structural family therapist would assert that the boundaries between this couple are

    a. rigid.
    b. clear.
    c. diffuse.
    d. a combination of a and c.

Rigid boundaries are characterized by individuals or subsystems being disengaged. What will the wife do in this situation? Well, according to this theory she will seek support outside of the family system. **(a)**

970. A mother insists on accompanying her 20-year-old daughter on a date. A structural therapist would assume that the family

    a. has clear boundaries.
    b. has rigid boundaries.
    c. has diffuse boundaries.
    d. supports individuation.

Okay, so some of you overprotective moms out there thought I should have included a choice "e"—cautious! Very funny. The answer I was looking for, nonetheless, was choice "c," diffuse boundaries. Minuchin does not feel that the "I devote my life to my children" mentality is a healthy one. In fact, he believes that if the spousal subsystem becomes obsessed with parenting the child will be afraid to experiment and thus could mature slowly. This child will often have trouble making friends outside of the home. When such individuals get married they rely far too much on their family of origin. Such children often grow up to not feel comfortable when they are alone. **(c)**

971.  Minuchin would often mimic the family's style. This is known as

    a.   cognitive disputation.
    b.   the structural map.
    c.   permeable boundaries.
    d.   none of the above.

Minuchin did rely on a so-called structural map with symbols to diagram the structure of the family, but of course, choice "b" is not the correct answer. Choice "d" is correct. The correct term is **mimesis** and it implies that the therapist copies the family's style. This helps the therapist **join** the family and helps the family accept him or her as a helper. **(d)**

972.  Ackerman is psychodynamic. Haley is strategic. Minuchin is structural. Bowen is intergenerational. Another well-known intergenerational family therapist would be

    a.   Alfred Adler.
    b.   Ivan Boszormenyi-Nagy (enunciated Naahge).
    c.   Andrew Salter.
    d.   Mara Selvini-Palazzoli.

Boszormenyi-Nagy—thank your lucky stars you need not know how to spell it for the exam—is a Hungarian analytically trained psychiatrist who discusses the importance of give and take fairness or relational ethics in the family. According to the notion of **relational ethics** a healthy family can negotiate imbalances and preserve a sense of fairness and accountability. Boszormenyi-Nagy introduced the term **family legacy**, which refers to expectations handed down from generation to generation. He is also known for his **family ledger** technique. The ledger is a multigenerational balance sheet or accounting system, if you will. The ledger outlines who gave what to whom and who owes what to whom. Mara Selvini-Palazzoli is associated with Milan systematic family therapy.                                    **(b)**

973.  A family member who is emotionally distant is

   a.   disengaged.
   b.   enmeshed.
   c.   an example of equifinality.
   d.   a placater.

Disengagement is often defined as an isolated lack of connectedness between family members.                       **(a)**

974.  During the course of a family session you discover that the man and his 14-year-old son are putting pressure on mom to quit her job. Mom very much likes her work. In Haley's theory this set of dynamics would be called

   a.   reframing.
   b.   equifinality.
   c.   the perverse triangle.
   d.   paradox.

The perverse triangle is a situation when two members who are at different levels of the family hierarchy (usually a coalition between parent and a child) team up against another family member. The alliance between the parent and the child may be overt or covert. In any event, the alliance against the other parent undermines his or her power and authority.       **(c)**

975.  _____ was a pioneer in the early history of family therapy.

   a.   Carl Jung
   b.   David Wechsler
   c.   Alfred Adler
   d.   Franz Anton Mesmer

Adler opened over 30 child guidance clinics in Vienna in the 1920s that were later eliminated by the Nazi Party in 1934. These clinics would often perform **open forum therapy** in which Adler worked with the family as well as the open forum audience. **(c)**

976. Which therapist could best be described as atheoretical?

   a. Jay Haley.
   b. Carl Whitaker.
   c. Alfred Adler.
   d. Nathan Ackerman.

Whitaker asserted that theory is often used as an excuse to keep therapists emotionally distant from the family. Whitaker promoted "craziness" (not a typo!) and creativity of family members. **(b)**

977. Solution-oriented therapy as practiced by William O'Hanlon, Insoo Kim Berg, Steve de Shazer, and Michelle Weiner Davis focuses primarily on

   a. the past.
   b. the present.
   c. the future.
   d. dream analysis.

This approach puts little or no emphasis on understanding the problem. The therapist's verbalizations center on the future. The therapist co-formulates a plan of action with the client or family. There may be more than one appropriate course of action. **(c)**

978. Narrative therapy (NT), which highlights stories in counseling, is associated with the work of

   a. William O'Hanlon.
   b. William Glasser.
   c. Milton H. Erickson.
   d. Michael White, his wife Cheryl White, and David Epston.

Narrative therapy fits in a new category of treatment known as postmodernism or constructivism. **Constructivism or social constructivism asserts that a client constructs or invents the way he or she perceives the world.** Clients come up with a story about their lives and they can reauthor these stories in therapy. Simply put: Reality is invented or constructed; it is not objective. The Whites and Epston believe that every country and culture espouses viewpoints or social narratives. Social narratives dictate what a family ought to be like. In narrative therapy the therapist asks questions or uses language to externalize the problem. Externalize, in this case, means to separate the problem from the person. The therapist utilizing this approach teams up with the family to take on the enemy (i.e., the problem). Thus, a therapist working with a family with an abusive spouse might say to the abuser, "I know you want to put an end to this violence. Tell me about a time when you stopped a violent episode that keeps you from being the wonderful, loving husband you want to be."

**Quick hint: In cases of intimate partner violence (IPV), verbal abuse typically takes place prior to physical abuse.** **(d)**

979. Postmodernist Tom Anderson, a psychiatrist from Norway, became disenchanted with traditional family therapy. He began using a radical approach based primarily on

    a.   a one-way mirror and a reflecting treatment team.
    b.   three therapists.
    c.   the gestalt empty chair technique.
    d.   homework assignments.

**Postmodernism is a key concept that assumes that there are no fixed truths in the world, only people's individual perceptions of what constitutes reality or the truth.** This technique was discovered when Anderson asked a family if they would like to hear what the team was saying about them. The family said "yes." The family and the family therapist listen as the team (called a reflecting team) discusses the case. Finally, the therapist processes the family's reaction to the team's observations. A number of schools of family therapy have now incorporated this technique. **Constructivism is not really a unified therapy based on a single individual but rather the theorists mentioned in this question as well as the trailblazers mentioned in the previous two questions. The theory stresses that therapy should be less hierarchical. A helper does not treat a client. Instead the client and the therapist have a conversation to work together in a collaborative effort.** **(a)**

980. Feminist therapy criticizes traditional therapies

    a.    because they are androcentric (i.e., they use male views to analyze the personality).

    b.    because they are gendercentric (i.e., they assume that there are two separate psychological developmental patterns—one for men and one for women).

    c.    because they emphasize heterosexism and debase same-sex relationships.

    d.    all of the above.

Feminist counselors often wisely note that a psychological difficulty can be located in the environment or the political system, rather than in the person (i.e., intrapsychic). A woman who is depressed because she is being beaten by her partner would be an excellent example. In the case of a woman who is making less money than a man for the same job, the phrase "the personal is political" rings true. In a nutshell, feminist therapies are said to be "gender free," in the sense that differences between men and women are seen to be the result of socialization—not whether they are male or female. Like the postmodernists, the feminist therapists attempt to have an egalitarian relationship with the client. Bibliotherapy, appropriate therapist disclosure, and assertiveness training are often used. This modality tends to dispute sex-role stereotypes (e.g., women are less assertive and less aggressive than men). **Feminists strive for equality in human relationships and the counselor can help in this area by avoiding complex clinical jargon. Many feminist**

**practitioners have a person-centered slant to their work.** Can a male be an effective feminist therapist? Well, as it now stands, the feminists themselves are not in agreement on this issue. It is common, nevertheless, for feminist therapists to work with male batterers. **Your exam might refer to feminist counseling as gender-fair counseling. One interesting fact related to the women's counseling movement and its emphasis on abating sexism is that it helped illuminate the special issues in counseling men, masculinity, and men's psychology. Since the early to mid-1980s, counseling and clinical services for men have become much more commonplace.** Another interesting finding is that parents and society are more tolerant of girls who adopt masculine behaviors, than of boys who take on feminine behaviors. In childhood, young girls are often reinforced for showing emotions. This is generally not the case with boys, who are reinforced for physical pursuits and *not* showing affective/emotional expression. **Men are therefore less likely to seek out counseling services and may do so only when they are experiencing a crisis. When men do engage in counseling services their competitiveness can help them work hard to succeed.** **(d)**

981. The term *skeleton keys* as used in Steve de Shazer's brief solution-focused therapy (BSFT) indicates

   a. a standard or stock intervention that will work for numerous problems.
   b. a technique where the client goes home to see his or her family of origin.
   c. a technique that works for one specific problem, but usually will not work with other difficulties.
   d. a technique in which the therapist hands the client or clients a sheet of paper with a compliment on it.

Choice "d," although it is not the correct answer, is a de Shazer technique that has been dubbed simply as a **compliment**. When using a similar technique known as **past successes** the therapist may also compliment past successes without specifically relating them to the current obstacles. **Brief therapy is sometimes abbreviated as BT.**                                                (a)

982.  One criticism of using cognitive-behavioral methods like REBT with families or individuals in multicultural counseling would be

a.    that the theory is not intended to be used with diverse populations.
b.    the theory suggests that the therapist must have ethnic or racial ties with the client in order for efficacious treatment to occur.
c.    that it ignores present moment problems.
d.    that the cognitive disputation could go against cultural messages.

Another criticism is that Albert Ellis views dependency as unhealthy and some cultures see interdependence as a positive attribute.                                                               **(d)**

983.  Most experts predict that in the twenty-first century, theories of counseling and psychotherapy will

a.    become more integrative, since about 30–50% of all therapists say they are eclectic.
b.    become more behavioristic, since this is the approach that uses statistical outcomes.
c.    become more Rogerian, since the world as a whole is becoming more humanistic.
d.    not tolerate eclecticism, since it is not scientific.

Will we see an end to therapy wars as we know them? Is the battle between psychotherapeutic and counseling modalities winding down? It would seem that the answer is yes. The trend is clearly toward integration. Theorists and practitioners alike have discovered that one theory is never extensive enough to include all behaviors. In addition, studies often indicate that one approach is not necessarily superior to another, or to put it very simply: Most approaches are equal in terms of their therapeutic value. Persons who pay allegiance to one school of psychotherapy are now incorporating approaches from other (sometimes rival!) modalities. So much for the therapy wars of the twentieth century. Expect to see the term **integrative psychotherapy** more frequently in the coming years. **One notion is that theories of counseling are helpful because they have elements that are common to all approaches. This is called a "common factor approach." Another theory about why integrative counseling works is that regardless of the paradigm there are "common stages of change."**       **(a)**

984.  Pick the most accurate statement.

    a.    Brief solution-oriented therapy requires the use of a one-way mirror with a treatment team behind the mirror.

    b.    Brief solution-oriented therapy does not utilize a treatment team behind a one-way mirror.   -

    c.    Brief solution-oriented therapy sometimes uses a treatment team behind a one-way mirror, nevertheless, it is not required.

    d.    Brief solution-oriented therapy does not utilize paradoxical interventions.

This therapy often relies on paradox; hence, choice "d" is incorrect. **On brief strategic/family therapy questions on your exam, the term ecosystems refers to the fact that larger systems often impact client and family functioning (e.g., the schools, church, or health care system). An ecosystemic approach always takes these larger systems into account.**       **(c)**

985.  A researcher takes a group of clients and gives them a depression inventory. He then provides each client with two sessions of brief solution-oriented therapy and gives them the same depression inventory. A $t$ test is used to compare the two sets of scores on the same people (i.e., the before and after measures of depression). This would be

    a.    a between-groups design.

    b.    a correlation coefficient.

c.    a related measures within-subject design.
d.    survey research.

In the within-subjects design, each subject acts as his or her own control. The between-groups design (which relies on separate people in the control and experimental groups) is a much more popular form of research. **When a single group is used in research or two groups that are not equivalent, your exam will probably refer to this situation as a pre-experimental design.**                                                                    **(c)**

986.  A question on the NCE or CPCE regarding a pre-experimental design uses the letters XO. The letters stand for

a.    treatment (X) and observation, measurement, or score (O).
b.    the mean (X) and no treatment was given (O).
c.    the median (X) and other group (O).
d.    treatment (X) and the number of observations taken (O).

**Experimental designs are often diagrammed. The most popular abbreviations are: O for observation, measurement, or score—O is the dependent variable (DV) in the experiment; X for treatment; E for experimental group; C for control group; R for random sampling; and NR for no random sampling of groups. Hence, the pre-experimental design in the group in question 985 could be connoted by:**

**Group: E**
Subject Assignment: NR
Pretest: O (since a score was accrued)
Treatment: X (in this case two sessions of brief-solution oriented therapy)
Posttest: O (since another score was accrued)

**If you were not acquainted with these abbreviations in graduate school I highly recommend you reread this question several times!**                                                    **(a)**

987. Another type of pre-experimental design is the one-group only posttest design. This is best depicted by

     a.    OXO.
     b.    XO.
     c.    OX.
     d.    XX.

Okay, let's walk through this quagmire together. The group only receives treatment (remember a capital X) and a score (that would be O) so the correct answer is choice "b." What would the correct sequence be for the previous question? Choice "a" since the group received a test (O), treatment (X), and then another test (O). Geez! I wonder if researchers stay up all night trying to come up with abbreviations and nomenclature to make exams more difficult. We should get together and do a study on that one! If the results are significant I'm certain we can find a journal dealing with psychopathology that will be more than happy to put our findings in print.      **(b)**

988. A time-series design is a quasi-experimental design

     a.    that utilizes two randomly chosen groups; a control group and an experimental group.
     b.    without randomly chosen control and experimental groups, which relies on multiple observations of the dependent variable (i.e., the thing you are measuring) before and after the treatment occurs.
     c.    a and b.
     d.    is not depicted by any of the answers above.

Choice "a" is incorrect since two randomly chosen groups would constitute a true experiment. Using our abbreviations this design would look something like this: O1, O2, O3, X, O4, O5, O6.     **(b)**

989. The Solomon four-group is considered a true experimental design since each group is chosen via a random sample. When using this design

    a.   all groups receive a pretest.
    b.   there is no pretest.
    c.   one control group receives a pretest and one experimental group receives a pretest; the other control group and experimental group do not.
    d.   there is no posttest.

In this design one pair of control/experimental groups receives a pretest while the other pair does not. This design helps weed out the impact of a pretest. **(c)**

990. John Gottman is known for

    a.   setting the level for intoxication driving while under the influence (DUI) or driving while intoxicated (DWI) at .08 or higher in most states.
    b.   creating a paradigm to predict which marriages would likely end in divorce.
    c.   demonstrating that physical biomarkers of older adults can be reversed if they are placed in an environment from the past and told to act like they are living in the past.
    d.   popularizing the notion of propinquity.

Let's survey our choices. Although Gottman had nothing to do with it, the legal limit in most states for blood alcohol concentration or blood alcohol content (BAC) is set at .08. The limit for commercial vehicle operators, say truck drivers, will be more stringent or lower such as .04. The same often holds true for those under the age of 21. Just for the record, at .3 you lose consciousness and at .4 some people will die. Gottman's claim to fame is depicted in choice "b." **He postulates six predictors of divorce:** (1) The marriage got off to harsh "start up." (2) The relationship is characterized via negativity which includes criticism, contempt, defensiveness, and stonewalling. (3) There is flooding" in the sense that the negativity comes on suddenly and is overwhelming. (4) "Body language" changes such as a pulse rate between 110 and 165. (5) Attempts to repair the marriage fail. (6) A lack of fond memories from the early days of the relationship. Detractors are quick to point out that Gottman did not rely on true experiments to come up with his theories. Choice "c"—also a must-know—depicts the work of Dr. Ellen Langer. When she placed 70–80-year-old men in an environment commensurate with the one they lived in 20 years ago and told them to act like it was 20 years earlier, their biomarkers of aging actually went backwards! People even thought they looked younger at the end of the research. Her book on this fascinating study, *Counter Clockwise*, has become a classic in the mindfulness movement. Finally, the term propinquity, often pops up on exams. It also goes under the name of the "mere exposure effect," indicating that the more you are around a person the greater the likelihood is you will become attracted to them. Emerging research suggests this is even true, though to a lesser degree, for virtual relationships such as via e-mail or instant messaging.                    **(b)**

991.  The newest career theory would be

a.    constructivist and cognitive approaches.
b.    the trait-and-factor approach.
c.    the developmental and psychoanalytic approaches.
d.    the transactional analysis approach.

Career experts wonder if traditional theories are applicable now since the majority of theories were based on research using white, middle-class males, which is hardly representative of the work market today that includes more people of color, a large number of women and teens, and more persons from lower socioeconomic classes.                                 **(a)**

992.  A popular TWA career counseling model by René V. Dawis and Lloyd Lofquist uses the abbreviation PEC. This stands for

a.    person emotion consequence.
b.    person education consequence.

   c.    person environment correspondence.

   d.    person environment consequence.

Wait a minute! What in the world does TWA stand for? It stands for Theory of Work Adjustment or what Dawis considers his "greatest accomplishment" (with the help of Lofquist, whom he admits had equal input). This theory posits that the person must fit the job (i.e., the correspondence or congruence between the individual and the work must be high), and also that the work must meet the needs of the person. **In other words the relationship works both ways. This theory therefore espouses that higher work satisfaction generally results in greater productivity. Work adjustment is basically the match between the expectations of the employee and the expectations of the place he or she is working.** Tests are routinely used in this model to assess one's work personality, abilities, and needs. Criticisms? Well pundits charge that the theory does not take into account the fact that the individual changes over time. So does the work environment. **(c)**

993.  Most experts believe that the number of multigenerational families with a child, a parent, and a grandparent living together will

   a.    decrease.

   b.    increase.

   c.    remain static.

   d.    will continue to go up and down on a fairly regular basis.

The number of families of this ilk nearly doubled between 1980 and 1990. When the economy goes into a recession and young adults can't afford to live on their own they often live with their family. In addition, as more people live longer, the number will go up since many of the older folks are incapable of caring for themselves. And just in case your exam asks, the number of single adults in the United States is also increasing. **(b)**

994.  A researcher wants to prove that structural family therapy is the most effective modality. She conducted a study a year ago using

a significance level of .05. Several colleagues felt her significance level needed to come down. She thus ran the same basic experiment again with new people using a significance level of .01. Her chances of making a Type I error or so-called alpha error reduced. Now assume you compare her new research to her old research. What could you say about the possibility that her results will indicate that structural family therapy was not significantly different when in reality it truly is significant?

a.    Statistically, nothing.
b.    The chance of this occurring will go down when compared to the first experiment.
c.    The chance of this occurring increases when compared to the first experiment.
d.    It would totally depend on the sample size.

The situation described in this question is a Type II error or so-called beta error. When the chance of making a Type I error goes down (as stated in the question) then the probability of making a Type II error goes up. **Type I and Type II errors are like a see-saw—as one goes up the other goes down.** Why do you think I called this section *advanced*?    **(c)**

995.    A question on your comprehensive exam asks you to compute the coefficient of determination. You are given a correlation coefficient of .70. How would you mathematically accomplish this task?

a.    You would subtract .70 from a perfect correlation of 1.00.
b.    You would multiply the mean of the population by .70.
c.    You would add .70 to a perfect correlation of 1.00.
d.    You would square the .70.

The coefficient of determination is computed by squaring the correlation coefficient. Thus, in this case the variance would be 49%.    **(d)**

996.    A correlation coefficient between variables X and Y is .60. If we square this figure we now have the coefficient of determination

or true common variance of 36%. What is the coefficient of nondetermination that shows unique rather than common variance?

a.   There is no such concept.
b.   You would subtract 36 from 100.
c.   It would still be 36%.
d.   It would be 64%.

You subtract the coefficient of determination from 100.    **(d)**

997.  John Krumboltz proposes a _____ model of career development.

a.   social learning behavioristic
b.   trait-and-factor
c.   developmental
d.   psychoanalytic

Krumboltz builds on the social learning theory of Albert Bandura. Krumboltz insists that learning, not *interests*, guides people into a certain occupation. In addition, changes of interest, hence jobs, occur due to learning. This theory notes that career decisions are influenced by: (a) genetic endowment and special abilities (e.g., a certain physique); (b) environmental conditions and events (e.g., a government policy or an earthquake); and (c) instrumental learning (e.g., positive reinforcement for solving math problems) and/or association learning (e.g., a client wants to go to medical school because everyone in the family loves her uncle who is a physician).    **(a)**

998.  Krumboltz's social learning theory is sometimes referred to as a cognitive theory because it emphasizes beliefs that clients have about themselves as well as the world of work. When Krumboltz speaks of self-observation generalizations he really means

a.   generalizations regarding a given occupation and how successful the client would be in the occupation.
b.   Pavlov's principle of stimulus generalization.

c.   Skinner's principle of operant conditioning.
d.   in career counseling your primary concern is the manner in which people view themselves and their ability to perform in an occupation.

Choice "a," though incorrect, is what Krumboltz calls **worldview generalizations** that are also important when counseling a client.                                                              **(d)**

999.  SCCT stands for

a.   social cognitive career theory.
b.   social cognitive family therapy.
c.   self-control career theory.
d.   self-contained career therapy.

Social cognitive career theory asserts that self-efficacy beliefs can influence one's career decisions. A woman, for example, may have very good math skills, nevertheless, she might not consider the field due to the belief that women are not as proficient in math as men. **Self-efficacy really deals with the personal question of, "Can I really do this and what will happen if I try to do this?"**                                      **(a)**

1000. Career counselors refer to job shadowing and volunteering as _____ activities, while reading the job hunting book *What Color Is Your Parachute?* is _____.

a.   noninteractive; interactive
b.   interactive; noninteractive
c.   interactive; interactive
d.   noninteractive; noninteractive

With noninteractive activities and media (e.g., reading a book, hearing a speech, or watching a video regarding a job or career) the client has some control over the process. Noninteractive approaches to career decisions have been called **linear**. On the other hand, interactive approaches (e.g., a field visit to a business, interviewing a worker in a given field, or a computer-based career guidance system) are said to be **nonlinear**. Interactive approaches are often more expensive and reduce the influence or control that the client has over the process. A counselor could decide that she no longer wishes to read a job pamphlet, however, she cannot control the hours of employment of the agency she is visiting. **(b)**

1001. Urie Bronfenbrenner is one of the codevelopers of the National Head Start Program. He proposed a theory of development that is

    a.    essentially the same as Piaget's constructivism.
    b.    almost identical to Watson's behaviorism.
    c.    an ecological systems theory.
    d.    based on 12 discrete stages.

Although choice "a" is incorrect, Piaget's approach is a constructivism theory of cognitive development. Bronfenbrenner, born in Russia, is credited with creating the theory of human ecology. **Hint: Bronfenbrenner's theory is not a stage theory!** The theory stresses the microsystem (any immediate or close relationships or organizations the child interacts with); the mesosystem (the way microsystems work together such as family and school); the exosystem (i.e., the school, church, neighborhood, parents' places of employment, in essence other places the child interacts with but not as often); and the macrosystem (i.e., the largest and most remote system which includes, culture, wars, the federal government, and customs). **(c)**

1002. Before _____ child psychologists studied the child, sociologists studied the family, anthropologists studied society, economists analyzed the economic framework, and political scientists investigated the political structure.

    a.    James W. Fowler
    b.    Daniel Levinson
    c.    Urie Bronfenbrenner
    d.    Nancy Chodorow

Various forms of this statement, which refers to Bronfenbrenner, are alive, well, and living in a glut of books, journal articles, and scholarly Internet sites; hence, it occurred to me that it could rear its head on a professional exam. Levinson, you will recall, postulated that the human life span has several stressful transition periods. He also postulated the now popular term *midlife crisis*; however, research indicates that the majority of people do not experience it. Fowler's name is associated with faith development, while sociologist Nancy Chodorow is a psychoanalytic feminist. Chodorow feels that the domestic ideal caused oppression in women.    **(c)**

1003. The school psychometrician refers Katie to you for individual counseling. She indicates that Katie's IQ is at the 50th percentile. Katie's IQ

   a.   indicates she has an intellectual disability.
   b.   cannot be estimated based on this statistic.
   c.   is approximately 100.
   d.   is well above the norm for children her age.

   See Figure 13.1 of the normal curve in the Graphical Representations section of the book. **Note that the 50th percentile is directly in the middle of the normal curve.** Since an average IQ is approximately 100, this would be the best answer.    **(c)**

1004. The psychometrician calls you to tell you that she has another student, who has an IQ that falls near the 84th percentile. This student's IQ

   a.   is somewhere in the gifted range, say 140.
   b.   is most likely near 105.
   c.   is approximately 115.
   d.   is between 75 and 80.

   Here again, take a look at the normal curve. The 84th percentile is about a standard deviation above the mean. A standard deviation above the mean is roughly 15 IQ points above the mean, thus 100 plus 15, so an IQ of 115. Again I ask you, why do you think we call it the advanced section?    **(c)**

1005. An exam has a mean of 50 and a standard deviation of 20. Phil has a score of 90. His score would fall

    a.    at the 40th percentile.
    b.    at the 5th stanine.
    c.    near the 98th percentile and the 9th stanine.
    d.    in the 6th stanine.

Some folks who have taken their comprehensive exams claim that it helps to draw a watered-down version of the normal curve with a few percentages, $z$-scores, t-scores, and stanines on scratch paper (provided at the exam site) before beginning the exam. Needless to say, you'll need to practice drawing the curve *before sitting for the exam* or else your numbers could be wrong, resulting in a string of incorrect answers! In any event, if you take Phil's score of 90 you can see that it is 2 standard deviations above the mean since 1 standard deviation is 20. Looking at the normal curve you can see that this is an exceptionally high score, placing it in the top or 9th stanine.                                 **(c)**

1006. Mrs. Kim wanted her daughter to attend a private school for gifted children who have very high intelligence. Mrs. Kim's daughter took the Otis–Lennon IQ test. Her t-score was 80. Kim's counselor knew that

    a.    Mrs. Kim would be very upset because her daughter's low score would not allow her to be admitted.
    b.    Mrs. Kim would be elated because her daughter scored exceptionally high and would be admitted.
    c.    she could not give Kim's mother any feedback since a t-score tells you nothing about one's actual IQ score.
    d.    a t-score of 80 is very average.

Take a look at the normal curve and wow, Mrs. Kim's daughter blew the lid off the test with a superb IQ score of nearly 150. Since a gifted or very superior IQ is generally around 130 you can bet your bottom dollar she will be admitted to the school.        **(b)**

1007. The mean score on a new counseling exam is 65. The standard deviation is 15. Tanja scored a 35. This tells us that

    a.   she had a z-score of +1.
    b.   she had a z-score of -1.
    c.   she had a t-score of 40.
    d.   she had a z-score of -2.

The z-score is the same as the standard deviation. In this case Tanja scored 2 standard deviations below the mean. **(d)**

1008. Kia was given a new client with a morbid fear of heights. Her supervisor emphasized that he wanted her to use the most high-tech form of treatment available. Kia should use

    a.   VRT.
    b.   William Glasser's new reality therapy with choice theory.
    c.   Joseph Wolpe's systematic desensitization (also known as reciprocal inhibition), a form of behavior therapy that works well with fears
    d.   REBT, created by Albert Ellis, which was once called RET.

If you've been out of grad school for eons of time—and I include myself in this category—then VRT would be totally unfamiliar. Virtual reality therapy (VRT) has been dubbed in many sources as "the next best thing to being there." Clients are hooked to a computer by wearing headgear. The computer simulates a real-life situation such as being high up in a glass elevator (or whatever the problem is). This is termed *virtual reality*. Dr. Barbara Rothbaum created this behavioristic approach. **The client experiencing the virtual environment (VE) generally has the same physiological reactions as he or she would experience in an actual situation such as a higher heart rate and sweaty palms.** Initial research on VRT with clients who have a fear of flying shows that it is as effective as treatment using exposure to the actual feared stimuli and that VRT clients do make more progress than those in a control group. Could this be the next big thing? Stay tuned! **(a)**

1009. The *DSM-5* provides diagnostic criteria for intellectual disability (ID), formerly billed as mental retardation. It states that

    a.    the client must have an IQ score of 70 or below on an individually administered IQ test and the onset of the condition must be prior to age 18. The client's ability to adapt to normal life in school, work, or family at home must also be impaired.

    b.    the client must have an IQ score below 70 on any group administered IQ test.

    c.    The client must have an IQ score on an individually administered IQ test and the onset of the condition must be prior to age 21.

    d.    the client must have an IQ score of 70 or below on an individually administered IQ test.

Choice "d" stands incorrect because an IQ score is not enough to make the diagnosis. Contrary to popular belief, intellectual disability is not always present throughout the life span. Training is capable of raising IQ scores. **Exam reminder: Group IQ tests are not considered as accurate as individually administered tests. The individual IQ test is the gold standard; however, IQ testing is a very controversial topic.**     **(a)**

1010. Measures of central tendency are used to summarize data. A counseling researcher wants to use a measure of central tendency which reacts to every score in the distribution. He will thus

    a.    use the median, or middle score when the data are ranked from lowest to highest. The median divides the distribution in half since half the scores will fall above the median, while half the scores will fall below the median.

    b.    use the mode, which is the most frequently occurring score or category.

    c.    use the mean, which has been termed the arithmetic average.

    d.    use the median or the mode.

Repeat after me three times aloud: The mean is the *only measure of central tendency which reacts to every score in the distribution*.

Although the mean has been called the most useful average, it has the mixed blessing of being misleading when a distribution contains very high or abnormally low scores—sometimes even a single extreme score. Take this common example that has been used a thousand times before, but illustrates this nicely. Bill Gates decides to take one of your graduate courses in counseling (fat chance, right). If you were to figure the mean income for the class it would suggest that the average student was a multimillionaire! Case closed. **Exam hint:** The median would generally be superior to the mean when you have a skewed distribution with a glut of high or low extreme scores.       **(c)**

1011. Which theorist would most likely assert that EQ is more important than IQ?

   a.   David Wechsler
   b.   Alfred Binet
   c.   Charles Spearman
   d.   Daniel Goleman

   EQ, incidentally, stands for emotional intelligence. EQ would encompass traits such as empathy, impulse control, motivation, and the ability to love. According to Daniel Goleman in his popular book *Emotional Intelligence: Why It Can Matter More Than IQ*, it is EQ rather than IQ that determines success.   **(d)**

1012. A counseling agency decides to pay their employees once a week. The agency is using a

   a.   fixed interval (FI) schedule of reinforcement.
   b.   a variable interval (VI) schedule of reinforcement.
   c.   a fixed ratio (FR) schedule of reinforcement.
   d.   a variable ratio (VR) schedule of reinforcement.

   This question is as old as the hills (yes even older than the Bill Gates example, in fact Bill probably didn't own a computer when this one first surfaced) but that means there is an excellent chance it will pop up (or at least a version of it) on your comprehensive exam. Since the employee gets paid every seven days this must be a fixed schedule. Moreover, since it involves time it must be an interval scale. Forget about this question for a moment. In everyday life when we refer to the passage of time we say "time interval." **Hence, your handy dandy memory device can be that all interval scales deal with time**.    **(a)**

1013. As a gambling addiction counselor Laura is well aware that slot machines operate on a

    a.    variable ratio schedule of reinforcement.
    b.    variable interval schedule of reinforcement.
    c.    fixed ratio schedule of reinforcement.
    d.    reinforcement system that counselors truly cannot explain.

Another good old typical reinforcement question. Since the slot machine does not operate on time (e.g., it won't pay out every 20 minutes) then it is not an interval scale. Instead, it is based on the opposing or ratio scale. Remember my explanation in the previous question? And, since the slot machine does not always pay out every so many times (say every 10 times you put in a token) you play it (otherwise you could just count the number of times you played and make a serious chunk of change betting big when you know you will win—wouldn't that be awesome) then you know it is a variable scale.    **(a)**

1014. Pick the most accurate statement.

    a.    Behavior therapies based on classical conditioning are used primarily with clients who have bipolar disorder. Lithium is no longer used.
    b.    Behavior therapies based on classical conditioning are much more effective than CBT when treating mood disorders.
    c.    Behavior therapies based on classical conditioning are commonly used to treat phobias, but are also utilized for clients with obsessive-compulsive disorders (OCD).
    d.    Behavior therapy is never based on classical conditioning.

One of the most popular forms of behavior therapy based on classical conditioning, Wolpe's systematic desensitization is an excellent therapy for phobic clients in individual and group therapy and it has its roots in Pavlov's classical conditioning. In terms of choice "a," psychiatrists and other physicians are still prescribing lithium for bipolar disorder. Clients must be monitored since high dosages can lead to medical problems such as kidney damage or even death.                                       **(c)**

1015. Ken's supervisor told Ken to do a meta-analysis related to treating children with sleep disorders.

    a.   Ken can use a correlation coefficient.
    b.   Ken can set up a true experiment with a control group and an experimental group.
    c.   Ken can use a single subject N = 1 intensive design.
    d.   Ken will use statistics based on numerous studies to investigate the issue.

Karl Pearson—also associated with the concept of correlation—created the first statistics department in a university in 1911. In 1904 he unleashed the technique of meta-analysis. **Meta-analysis or meta-research occurs when several studies on the same topic are utilized in order to examine a hypothesis.** The results of several studies—or tons of studies if they are available—are then synthesized. The technique was originally used to overcome the severe limitations of a small sample size that often occurs when a researcher performs a single experiment. Needless to say, the drawback to this technique is that it may be relying on a glut of poorly designed studies which in turn will yield inaccurate results.        **(d)**

1016. You gave your client, Ester, a personality test and then shared your interpretation of the test with her. Your client was amazed at how accurate the test results were in terms of depicting her personality. She readily accepted the interpretation. The next day you discovered that you had interpreted the wrong test! The test you were analyzing was not Ester's but rather belonged to another client! Ester's behavior could best be explained by

a.    the obvious fact that she is psychotic, which means that she is not in touch with reality.
b.    the Barnum effect.
c.    negative transference.
d.    the placebo effect.

In psychometrics, the Barnum effect (which can also be dubbed the Forer effect after the psychologist who discovered it, Bertram R. Forer) refers to the fact that clients will often accept a general psychological test report, horoscope, or palm reading and believe it applies specifically to them! And no you need not be psychotic (choice "a") to be influenced by this effect. You'll recall that P.T. Barnum was quoted (or according to some misquoted) when he quipped that "there is a sucker born every minute."                                                              **(b)**

1017.    Approximately 40% of all elementary schools have shortened recess or student playtime. Counselors

a.    are excited about this change because U.S. children are behind other countries academically and thus need more study time.
b.    believe the change will actually have little or no impact on the children.
c.    are concerned because some research indicates that recess can have a positive impact since children are less fidgety on days when they have recess; especially if they are hyperactive.
d.    are not concerned as boys have better concentration on days when they do not have recess.

Choice "d" is patently false. Boys showed less concentration on days when normal recess was delayed. Choice "c" stands correct as research indicates that fourth graders were less fidgety on days with recess playtime. Good attention requires periodic novelty.                                                              **(c)**

1018. Neuroscience supports

    a.   the analytic notion that focusing on negative emotions is helpful.

    b.   the medical model, and thus it is not truly relevant to counselors.

    c.   the notion that the concept of neuroplasticity is merely a myth.

    d.   the notion that empathy and exercise could benefit depressed individuals.

According to the burgeoning field of neuroscience and neuroimaging the first three choices are clearly incorrect. In terms of choice "a," talking incessantly about negative experiences triggers a sad response from the amygdala and the frontal cortex and this is not our goal in counseling. Choice "b" is incorrect since neuroscience seems to provide us with research that will be helpful to counselors and has improved our knowledge of human growth and development. Finally, choice "c" or the concept of neuroplasticity suggests that the actions of the client as well as the environment do change the brain. **(d)**

1019. Neuroscience seems to show that

    a.   cognitive therapy does not impact one's brain.

    b.   cognitive therapy could raise serotonin, the feel good chemical in the brain, just like antidepressant pharmaceuticals.

    c.   cognitive therapy raises cortisol to an extremely high level.

    d.   cognitive therapy has virtually no impact on the frontal cortex.

Cognitive therapy (as set forth by Albert Ellis and Aaron T. Beck) works like a prescription medicinal and raises serotonin without the side effects! Cortisol has been dubbed the stress hormone, and we would not want to increase it through cognitive therapy. **(b)**

1020. Which statement best reflects the position of neurogenesis?

    a.    A 76-year-old man signs up for a course in chess and generates more neurons.

    b.    A 9-year-old girl falls off her bicycle and now has a learning disability.

    c.    A 32-year-old man uses temperature/thermal biofeedback to help ward off headaches.

    d.    A 32-year-old man uses EMG biofeedback to help ward off headaches.

Learning, such as counseling, generates neurons even in older adults.    **(a)**

1021. _____ seemingly is related to serotonin in the brain. Deficits of serotonin are thought to cause depression.

    a.    Vitamin B5, also known as pantothenic acid,

    b.    L-Arginine, an amino acid,

    c.    Tryptophan, an amino acid,

    d.    Omega 3 from sources such as fish oil, krill oil, or algae,

All of the above nutrients *might* be distantly related to serotonin levels, however, when tryptophan is removed from the diet memory, anxiety, sleep, and mood go south. Aggression, on the other hand rises.    **(c)**

1022. At the last count, approximately 43,000 U.S. citizens committed suicide during a single year making suicide the tenth leading cause of death. Worldwide the figure is an alarming 800,000 per year. Suicide often checks in as the second- or third-leading killer of young people in the 15–24-year-old age bracket. Men commit suicide more frequently than women, however, women attempt suicide far more often than men. It is accurate to say that

    a.    10–15% of all claims handled by the ACA liability insurance programs are related to suicide.

    b.    nearly 100% of the claims handled by the ACA liability insurance programs are related to suicide.

    c.    ACA liability insurance will not cover you if a client commits suicide.

    d.    African American females have an extremely high rate of suicide.

First, choice "d" is blatantly false since the African American female rate is very low (about two females per 100,000 compared to about 12.5 females per 100,000 for the general public). According to *Counseling Today*, about 40% of all expenditures for the ACA liability insurance programs relate to suicide, thus raising the premiums. Suicide rates of rescue workers increased after the September 11, 2001 terrorist attacks. The suicide rate for U.S. veterans is also up. Most legal difficulties related to suicide revolve around negligence. You can avoid negligence by making certain that as a counselor you adhere to the ethical principle of practicing within your *boundaries of competence* and providing appropriate referrals when requested or needed. Always use a suicide-prevention or so-called "no suicide" safety plan contract. The safety plan contract, among other things, will stipulate that the client will contact you or a suicide hotline/helpline if an uncontrollable urge to commit suicide is manifested. And finally: If you think consultation is in order, just do it!                                          **(a)**

1023. Statistically speaking, males typically use _____ and females use _____ to commit suicide.

    a.    poison; firearms
    b.    heroin; alcohol
    c.    firearms; poison
    d.    heroin; jumping off a building or bridge

The most commonly used methods are firearms for men in approximately 57% of the cases and poison in about 35% of the instances for women.                                          **(c)**

1024. Neurocounseling research indicates that the _____ is dominant _____.

    a.   left hemisphere; in most people
    b.   right hemisphere; in most people
    c.   left hemisphere; in right-handed people
    d.   left hemisphere; in 50% of the population

The left hemisphere of the brain is dominant in over 95% of the population. Although the percentage is higher in right-handed persons, it is still dominant in most left-handers. Damage to the left hemisphere often results in issues with the right side of the body. P.S. The self-help psychology notion that the left side is logical and the right side is creative has *not* been substantiated. This notion is so pervasive an exam question may <u>only</u> give you the pop psychology choices! If that is the situation, then go with left brain logical/rational and right brain creative. What can I say?                                                                                 **(a)**

1025. Matt was diagnosed with a somatic symptom disorder (SSD), with predominant pain. It is safe to say that

    a.   Matt is at least 40 years of age.
    b.   Matt has never had a physical exam in regard to his pain.
    c.   no physiological basis or medical condition can be found to explain his reaction.
    d.   Matt's pain can be carefully traced to a precise physical cause.

Somatic symptom disorders must have a physical exam in order for the SSD diagnosis to be valid. **The key factor here is that emotional factors can cause somatic (bodily) complaints and health concerns.** Choice "a" is incorrect since SSD often begins early in life (often in one's teens) and can literally last an entire lifetime. It is often overlooked by mainstream medicine.                                                         **(c)**

1026. Millie has a panic attack whenever she drives across a bridge. She has

   a.    situationally bound panic attacks.
   b.    cued panic attacks.
   c.    a and b.
   d.    predisposed panic attacks.

Okay, folks. To answer this question you need to discern an uncued attack, also termed an "unexpected" attack, from a cued attack, also called a "situationally bound attack." **Simply put: situationally bound or cued attacks have a cue or an environmental trigger.** In this case it is obviously the bridge. **On the other hand, an uncued or unexpected attack seemingly occurs out of nowhere and no internal or external trigger can be identified. Women experience panic attacks more often than men.**    **(c)**

1027. Sybil was a famous client who had 15 personalities. At the time Sybil was said to suffer from multiple personality disorder (MPD). Today her diagnosis would be

   a.    dissociative identity disorder.
   b.    a mood disorder.
   c.    related to RS issues.
   d.    a personality disorder.

In any dissociative disorder, the client attempts to avoid stress by dissociating or escaping from the situation. Cases of amnesia (i.e., the inability to recall) fall into this diagnostic category. In the case of dissociative identity disorder formerly known as multiple personality disorder (MPD), the client has often been sexually abused as a child. Counseling can be efficacious in terms of integrating the personality into a single entity. Just for review purposes, in choice "c" RS means religious and spiritual. **Experts, I might add, do not agree on a single definition of spirituality. Generally, the term describes a unique personal experience related to feelings of self-actualization, a better understanding of the meaning of**

**life, and an awareness of a divine or Higher Power.** One theory is that 12-step programs such as Alcoholics Anonymous (AA) promote a brand of what has been called "informal spirituality" which has made RS issues more popular with the general public. Another major impetus for the spirituality movement was Scott Peck's landmark 1978 book *The Road Less Traveled*. This work helped religion and psychotherapy gel. Research indicates that religion can be a double-edged sword for clients. In general, religion generally has a positive impact on clients (e.g., improved well-being, better marital satisfaction, and less depression). On the negative side of the coin, clients who harbor religious strain—such as difficulty forgiving God— suffer from more stress, depression, and even suicidal feelings. Because of the contradictory evidence, counselor educators do *not suggest* that counselors urge clients to be more spiritual or have more religious involvement. This seems ironic since one survey of ACA-affiliated counselors revealed that the majority of these helpers valued spirituality in their own lives even more than they did organized religion. I think it goes without saying that your personal views may differ!                    **(a)**

1028. Bulimia is classified as

    a.   an eating disorder which occurs equally in both men and women.
    b.   an eating disorder that occurs primarily in women.
    c.   an anxiety disorder.
    d.   a narcissistic personality disorder.

Anorexia nervosa and bulimia nervosa are eating disorders. **Bulimia is more prevalent.** Statistically speaking, about 90% of anorectics and bulimics are female. The onset of these disorders often occurs in adolescence. In anorexia, the client refuses to eat enough to maintain a healthy body weight. Bulimia nervosa is characterized by binge eating (eating a tremendous amount of food) and then compensating for the binge eating by purging (vomiting, enemas, diuretics, or laxative abuse), fasting, or excessive exercise. **Low body weight is typical in anorexia, but not in bulimia or binge-eating disorder.**                    **(b)**

1029. Binge-eating disorder (BED)

    a.   is not a valid *DSM* diagnosis.
    b.   occurs mainly in men.
    c.   results in vomiting and extreme bouts of exercise.
    d.   is the most common type of eating disorder.

Clients with BED often eat alone (solitary dining), and eat very rapidly, often to the point of pain even if they are not hungry. **(d)**

1030. A counselor can assume that, in general

    a.   women make less money than men for the same job.
    b.   most complaints against counselors for exploitation come from women complaining about male counselors.
    c.   women are not as comfortable as men when they are involved in competitive situations
    d.   all of the above.

According to the Department of Health and Human Services, all of the above statements are right. They also add that women (in general, of course) are more compassionate and more likely to adhere to traditional moral values. The old adage that "women are more comfortable expressing their feelings" is only partially true. Women are more comfortable expressing sadness, intimacy, and nurturing behavior, nevertheless, they are *less comfortable* expressing anger and being assertive. Thus, men—who are more aggressive—are more likely to die via accidents, suicide, homicide, war, or an act of violence. **(d)**

1031. Intersexuality

    a.   describes an individual with male and female sexual characteristics and possibly male and female internal or external sex organs.
    b.   describes a person who is always gay.
    c.   describes a person who is always heterosexual.
    d.   describes a person who is a cross-dresser.

Several definitions have been accepted by the literature in our field so it would be nearly impossible to create an answer stem here which covers the entire topic. An intersex individual (in the past known as a hermaphrodite) sometimes has male and female genitalia, but by definition will have atypical sexual/reproductive development, chromosomes, or hormones. In some cases, the genitals cannot clearly be classified as male or female. Physicians do give the individual a gender even if this occurs at birth. Choice "d," a cross-dresser, wears clothes generally worn by the opposite sex and has been called a transvestite in some of the earlier literature. Choices "b" and "c" are incorrect inasmuch as intersex individuals, or cross-dressers for that matter, are <u>not</u> exclusively heterosexual or homosexual. **(a)**

1032. Gay men and women

    a.    primarily live the gay or lesbian lifestyle.
    b.    basically have the same range of gender-role behaviors as do male and female heterosexuals.
    c.    cannot be characterized in terms of lifestyle due to a distinct lack of research.
    d.    are always transgender.

Choice "a" is way off base: **There is no single gay, lesbian, bisexual lifestyle!** Choice "d," transgender, is used to describe a person who does not identify with his or her birth sex. **Transsexuals are generally regarded as being in a separate category or at least subcategory from transgender individuals—persons who do not identify with their gender assignment based on biology at birth—because transsexuals resort to the use of medical interventions including hormones and plastic surgery in order to better express their identity. Save yourself an e-mail! Sexual identity terms change at the speed of light and after the last *Encyclopedia* was released I received numerous correspondence about my definitions being incorrect. My response, "I know, it transpired after the book was released." The moral of the story: Check the definitions of terms in this category before you take the exam.** **(b)**

1033. Warren needs to conduct a study. His supervisor wants him to use a parametric inferential statistic. This means that

   a.   he will need to use random sampling and the distribution is normal.
   b.   he will need to use a convenience sample or a volunteer sample.
   c.   his distribution will be positively skewed.
   d.   his distribution will be bimodal.

By definition, parametric statistics are used when the distribution is normal (i.e., the mean, the median, and the mode are the same) and random sampling has been utilized. Convenience samples and volunteer samples are not picked randomly. Moreover, a bimodal or multimodal curve is not the same as a bell-shaped normal curve. **Parametric designs use interval and ratio data, while nonparametric designs rely on nominal and ordinal data.**                                    **(a)**

1034. A counselor has an answering machine in her office. Which statement most accurately depicts the ethical guidelines related to this situation?

   a.   Ethical guidelines forbid the use of answering machines.
   b.   Ethical guidelines allow answering machines, but forbid speaking with clients via a cell phone.
   c.   Ethical guidelines allow answering machines, but experts insist that unauthorized staff should not be allowed to listen or retrieve such messages.
   d.   Ethical guidelines are clear that a pager should be used rather than an answering machine.

According to experts, there are additional guidelines which apply to counselors who use the telephone for messages. First, never give out information to an unknown caller—in fact don't even tell such a caller whether a client is receiving services or not! Remember that anything you say to a client over the phone could end up in court. Be very careful about leaving personal messages for clients on their answering machines. You never know who is in the household and will be listening to the messages. When using a cell phone never forget that the call might be monitored by an unauthorized third party, horrors! When sending a message via a pager use the same precautions listed above for telephone messages. Finally, if you aren't technologically challenged and decide to send a confidential fax, it is the counselor's responsibility (yes you!) to make certain the fax is secure. Hence, prior to sending a fax check to see if the appropriate person will be receiving it. As of this writing, "text" or "texting" does not appear in ACA or NBCC ethical codes. **(c)**

1035. The law requires clinicians to

    a.    keep process notes.
    b.    keep progress notes.
    c.    keep process and progress notes.
    d.    keep the client's name and address, but no other information.

As a neophyte in the field I remember storming into my supervisor's office to complain that I did all these wonderful things for my clients and still didn't get a raise. When I stopped ranting and raving my supervisor gave me some sage advice, "Rosenthal," she quipped, "I want to tell you something and I never want you to forget it during your career. If you didn't write it down, you didn't do it, and it never happened!" Today, *all* competent supervisors espouse something similar. Now let's tackle the question. First you should keep accurate records on your clients. Documentation helps you provide appropriate counseling, decreases your liability (chances of being sued), and helps you or your agency get reimbursed. **There are basically two types of client records. First, there are progress notes and yes they are mandated by law. Counselors often refer to these as clinical notes.** Experts state that progress notes are behavioral because they focus on what the client does and says. Progress notes could include something about informed consent, assessment procedures or tests used, the client's *DSM* diagnosis, symptoms, the type of counseling interventions used, the goals of counseling, progress, release of information issues, the dates of the sessions, and the termination date. **Process notes (sometimes called psychotherapy notes) are not generally shared with clients or made available to them. Process notes are kept separate and intended for the counselor who created them. They are not required by law.**    **(b)**

1036. A client wants to read her record. Pick the statement which is not accurate.

    a.    You should allow her to read the record or a summary of it because she has an ethical right to do so.

    b.    You should allow her to read it, however, you should go back and change things you don't want her to see; for example, the fact that you said she was schizophrenic.

    c.    You should allow her to read the record realizing that it is best if you enter the information as soon as possible after the session and then sign and date the entry.

    d.    Since your agency inputs the client's record on a computer, each entry will be dated and have a time on it. You could then print the document for her perusal.

All of the above are excellent practices except choice "b". This choice is incorrect since a counselor cannot alter documented information in a client's file after it has become part of the record.    **(b)**

1037. A counselor is seeing a client on a managed care plan. Unfortunately, the client has used up her maximum number of sessions for the year. The counselor is convinced that the client is in need of additional counseling, however, the counselor's agency will not allow him to see her for any additional sessions. The best plan of action would be for the counselor to

    a.    refer the client for continued counseling to a practitioner who will see the client whether or not she has managed care benefits.

    b.    empathize with the client, but be sure to explain that she is catastrophizing (an irrational thought pattern delineated by Albert Ellis) and use REBT, a cognitive therapy, to help her cope with the fact that she cannot be seen again until next year.

c. threaten to sue the managed care company, since this the company's policy would be in violation of ethical care for the client.

d. see the client, but don't tell your supervisor. This is both legal and ethical.

It is also possible that the client has even reached her lifetime limit on sessions. **(a)**

1038. A career counselor who relies on the constructivist viewpoint would emphasize that

a. unconscious conflicts influence career decisions.

b. an individual's career choice is influenced by his or her personal story and attempt to construct meaning out of the world of work.

c. most career counselors do not give enough career inventories.

d. SCCT is the best theory.

Measuring traits to match a suitable career for the client's personality is minimized in the narrative/postmodern approach. SCCT is social cognitive career theory. **(b)**

1039. A gay male protests that he is unhappy with his sexual preference and wants to lead a heterosexual lifestyle. He tells you that he wants a family and children. You should

a. refer him to a psychiatrist as medicine is necessary.

b. use dialectical behavior therapy (DBT).

c. bring in other members of his family since homosexuality has its roots in the family system.

d. explain that homosexuality is not a mental disorder that needs to be changed.

Though dialectical behavior therapy (which synthesizes ideas from individual therapy, group therapy, behavior therapy, and cognitive modalities) is clearly the wrong answer, I'd be familiar with this evidence-based modality that seems to work well with borderline personality disorder. In this approach diary cards are used to make a hierarchy of treatment targets with suicidal and self-mutilating behaviors getting top attention. Now for the answer to this question. In 1998 the ACA Governing Council passed a resolution indicating that gay and lesbian individuals are not mentally ill due to their sexual orientation. Approximately 4% of the population in the United States is gay or lesbian. Harassment for these individuals generally starts early in life. **The ACA and the Association for Gay, Lesbian, and Bisexual Issues in Counseling (AGLBIC) supports counselors working in this area; however, the organization does not support trying to transform members of the LBGTQ community into heterosexuals.** You may recall that homosexuality was removed from the *DSM* way back in 1973. **The answer to this question is clear-cut: According to the new ACA ethics it would be unethical to treat this client for the purpose of changing his sexual orientation. Some counselors find ACA's position controversial. Perhaps this is fueled by the fact that the majority culture is said to have a negative view of homosexuality.** **(d)**

1040. Conversion or reparative therapy is intended to change sexual orientation and behaviors from gay to straight.

    a.    The literature in scientific and peer-reviewed journals does not indicate that a person's sexual orientation can be altered from same-sex attraction to opposite-sex attraction.

    b.    ACA prohibits counselors from practicing conversion or reparative therapies although no studies exist in this area.

    c.    Longitudinal studies with clients who have been through reparative or conversion therapy indicate that the treatment is effective, but it still remains unethical.

    d.    ACA ethics indicate that a counselor trained in conversion or reparative therapy can practice these modalities if the client insists on the treatment.

The actual findings of the ACA—when researching peer-reviewed journals to create their new ethics—was that conversion and reparative therapies can actually harm clients. Religious organizations who claim to change gay individuals to straight often use the term *transformational ministries* to describe their services.                                                                    **(a)**

1041. A lesbian client wants to become heterosexual and asks for conversion or reparative therapy. You explain that you ethically do not believe in this form of intervention. She asks you to refer her to a practitioner who will perform this type of therapy. You should

    a.   comply, since ethical counselors provide an appropriate referral.

    b.   comply, but you must provide her with at least three referrals.

    c.   tell the client you prefer not to refer her to a therapist who engages in this form of treatment. Discuss the potential harm and risks with the client emphasizing that this is an unproven form of treatment.

    d.   tell her to secure a consultation with a licensed physician prior to making a referral.

Evidence-based literature does not support the value of reparative or conversion therapy. No training in these paradigms is offered or condoned via the ACA since clients who go through such therapies function worse than before the treatment began. The ACA goes so far as to state that these forms of treatment are not providing a service within the scope of professional counseling, but rather some other profession (e.g., Christian counseling or faith-based healing).                                      **(c)**

1042. The ethical requirement to have a transfer plan in writing would apply to

    a.   a situation in which a counselor became disabled.

    b.   a situation in which a counselor died.

    c.   a situation where a counselor moved to another state.

    d.   all of the above.

A transfer plan is necessary because a counselor or researcher could become incapacitated, die, or move. Hence, the transfer plan should be set up to protect the welfare of the client as well as his or her files. Or to put it another way: If you are incapacitated (e.g., are hospitalized), leave the practice or agency, or die, your clients will have access to their records, as well as their files. The transfer will be smooth. Prior to 2005 ACA ethics did not address this issue. **All counselors should include a transfer plan in their informed consent document given to the client at the beginning of treatment. The new contact person and custodian of the records will be listed with complete contact information.** **(d)**

1043. You are counseling a 29-year-old man in your private practice who is seeing a primary care physician (PCP) for severe headaches.

   a.   You are required to contact the PCP.
   b.   You are not required to contact the PCP; however, attempting to secure permission to do so from your client would be considered the ideal course of action.
   c.   The answer would be no for headaches, but yes if the client had visited the PCP regarding a mental health complaint.
   d.   Yes, but only if the client is abusing a child or a senior citizen.

Okay, hold onto your thinking caps because this can get a tad complex to say the least! Although the best answer is "b," that you are not required to inform the primary care physician (PCP), experts recommend that you place a statement in your informed consent document asking the client to agree to or refuse such a disclosure. The client may indeed decline. Some states require you to document in writing the client's consent or refusal. In these states, if a counselor violates this then he or she has broken a state law. Experts Robert J. Walsh and Norman C. Dasenbrook give counselors another incentive for asking the client for consent to the disclosure—money! It is a golden opportunity to market your private practice since physicians spend about seven minutes with a patient in a given office visit and thus often make mental health referrals. Marketing materials related to your practice can be sent to the PCP along with your diagnosis, steps to treat the client, and progress updates. **(b)**

1044. As a private practice counselor your _____ would be most important in terms of filing claims.

    a.   graduate transcript
    b.   undergraduate and graduate transcript
    c.   NCC provider number
    d.   NPI number

The National Provider Identifier (NPI) number would be required to file claims electronically or even by mail. HIPAA rules stipulate that the NPI is your standard unique identifier as a health care provider. **(d)**

1045. A counselor is treating a woman for a mood disorder. The counselor has sex with the woman's daughter. This is considered

    a.   unethical.
    b.   ethical.
    c.   ethical only after the counselor terminates the client's sessions and then waits two years.
    d.   debatable since ACA guidelines fail to deal with sexual issues of this nature.

**Counselors are prohibited from engaging in sexual relationships with current clients, with the client's family members, or clients' romantic partners. An exam reminder for those who have been out of grad school for a while ... this changes everything:** Since 2005 The ACA Ethical Code Revision Task Force was adamant that *some nonsexual* dual relationships are beneficial to the client and therefore not prohibited or banned via newer codes. Hence, it might be ethical to attend a client's wedding, graduation, or even visit a client in the hospital. The counselor should document in the record why he or she feels the interaction would be beneficial prior to the event when possible. If a negative or harmful situation does occur the counselor is expected to take reasonable action to rectify the situation. The same guidelines would apply to a supervisee. Remember that sexual harassment is not only unethical, but illegal.                                           **(a)**

1046. You have impeccable training and experience as a counseling supervisor. One of your supervisees comes in for her session and she is crying uncontrollably because her boyfriend told her he was breaking up with her. It is clear counseling would be beneficial and she asks you for counseling. You should

    a.    provide appropriate crisis counseling and then assist her in finding an appropriate counselor.

    b.    begin counseling her immediately as she needs it, but refer her to another supervisor.

    c.    assist her in finding an appropriate counselor.

    d.    begin counseling her immediately as she needs it, but make her sign a statement saying there could be issues and if she begins to feel the sessions are exploitative in any way, you will refer her to another colleague.

Ethical guidelines are clear that supervisors do not provide counseling services to supervisees. Case closed!                 **(c)**

1047. ACA ethical guidelines stipulate that a counselor can refrain from making a diagnosis if the counselor believes the diagnosis could harm the client or others.

    a.    Therefore, a counselor could ethically diagnose all clients as having an adjustment disorder to secure insurance since this diagnosis is somewhat benign and not likely to harm the client.

    b.    A counselor could refrain from making a diagnosis if it is in the best interest of the client.

    c.    A decision to refrain from making a diagnosis is ideally made in collaboration with the client, although the counselor has the final say.

    d.    Choices "b" and "c" are both correct.

Choice "a" stands as incorrect because counselors should never intentionally misdiagnose a client, although I have seen this practice recommended by top figures in our field in the past! A counselor could refrain from making a diagnosis according to recent ethics. From a thought-provoking interview that appeared on the ACA website here are several reasons that members from the ACA ethical task force, which created the ethical code, gave for not making (i.e., refrained from making) a diagnosis.

- You are seeing a 9-year-old boy and have insufficient data to diagnose him as having ADHD. If you were to diagnose him as such he could have longstanding identity problems based on the misdiagnosis. The boy might even be inappropriately medicated for normal energetic behaviors.
- In some cultures a person will hear voices as part of the grieving process related to death. A psychotic diagnosis would be a misdiagnosis in this respect.
- A client meets all the criteria for borderline personality disorder, yet the counselor refrained from making diagnosis, knowing that this particular client might look the term up on the Internet and might feel doomed to a life of unhealthy relationships.
- An individual with top security clearance in either the government or the military might lose his or her clearance based on a diagnosis.

**(d)**

1048. The agency you work for insists that you diagnose every client. Since this is in violation of the newer ACA ethics this would qualify as "negative conditions." You could handle this by

a. meeting with your supervisor and executive director of the agency and discussing other ways to secure funding that go beyond *DSM* reimbursement.
b. advocate for the client by explaining to the insurance company asking for the diagnosis that in some cases it is best that a diagnosis not be given. You could even teach the client to advocate for herself by having her inform the

insurance company that a diagnosis might not be in her best interest.

c.    show your supervisor, executive director, or insurance company/managed care firm the actual ACA Code of Ethics so they can see it in writing that the Code stipulates that "Counselors may refrain from making and/or reporting a diagnosis if they believe it would cause harm."

d.    All of the above.

Hmmm, choice "d" seems to be becoming a popular correct answer choice lately! Now although your well-meaning supervisor or insurance company representative may not agree, experts have cited *all of these* as viable ways to deal with this situation. Every counselor is responsible for educating agencies, insurance companies, managed care firms, and mental health professionals in related disciplines about the information in the new code. To those realistic readers who are saying to themselves "my agency won't get paid for that client," at this stage of the game I can only quip, "You may be right!" We can only hope that in the future, reality and ethics will be 100% on the same wave-length.                                                              **(d)**

1049. You leave your practice to study mental health treatment in another country. Dr. Kline, another licensed counselor, is now the custodian of your records. This was clearly explained in your informed consent brochure given to the client during the first visit. The clients have Dr. Kline's contact information. Ethically

a.    Dr. Kline should contact each client when he receives the record.

b.    you should contact each client even though you are residing in another country.

c.    the client is totally responsible for contacting Dr. Kline since he or she was given an informed consent document.

d.    neither you nor Dr. Kline would be obligated to contact the client.

Remember to give transfer plan information to appropriate staff members such as administrative assistants or another counselor in your practice since a client might lose the statement of informed consent (again, usually in the form of a brochure). If you are in private practice a colleague you use for back-up or so-called on-call situations would be ideal. **(a)**

1050. In terms of the previous question:

    a.   A certified public accountant (CPA) would be preferable to a mental health professional such as Dr. Kline to use as a custodian for the records.

    b.   An attorney would make the best custodian for the records.

    c.   Using a mental health professional on staff or at another facility is preferable to using a lawyer or a CPA.

    d.   A CPA, an attorney, or a mental health professional would be an excellent choice.

Whether you are using your own staff or somebody outside the agency or practice, it is imperative that you put the transfer arrangement in writing! A gentleman's or gentlewoman's agreement with a handshake is not enough! Finally, remember that after you retire you will still need a custodian, although to be sure you may personally provide their records if you are capable of doing so. This, needless to say, means that your clients will need your contact information after retirement. The bottom line: **Transfer plans protect the client's welfare in unforeseen circumstances including death or incapacitation of a helper.** **(c)**

1051. During a counseling session Mrs. Sander's 13-year-old daughter Jamie tries to speak. Mrs. Sanders says, "I told you not to say anything." Her daughter wants to know why she cannot talk. Mrs. Sanders replies, "Because I'm the parent, end of discussion young lady." According to the parenting typology of Diana Baumrind, Mrs. Sanders is

    a.   an authoritative parent.

    b.   an authoritarian parent.

    c.   a permissive parent.

    d.   a nonpunitive parent.

For starters, you could eliminate the final two answer choices. The permissive parent *is* nonpunitive and rarely says "no" to a child. A parent operating out of this style is highly affectionate, and at times is more like a friend. The permissive parent makes few demands on the child. The key to answering this question correctly is to know that the authoritative parent (choice "a") does champion give and take verbal exchanges with the child, while the authoritarian parent (choice "b") does not. **An authoritarian parent expects his or her child to follow orders without explanations.** In most situations the authoritative parent will produce a happy child with desirable social skills. Not so much for the authoritarian and permissive styles, which often correlate with alcoholism, drug abuse, and other antisocial behaviors. Now the night prior to the exam the authoritative and authoritarian styles will sound suspiciously similar and nearly impossible to distinguish. One way to put your finger on the difference might be to recall that an authoritarian leader is generally not the best facilitator for most groups. But, let's be honest, what works for me might not work for you. Come up with something that provides you with total recall.        **(b)**

1052. A counselor identifies herself as an ABA practitioner. The technique she would be least likely to use would be

   a.   VR reinforcement.
   b.   FR reinforcement.
   c.   asking the client to talk about his dreams as if the dream is occurring in the present.
   d.   thinning.

First, remember what I taught you in the FAQ section of this text. On the actual exam you will often see question, after question, after question, using "most likely" or "least likely." And just when you think you have spied all you could possibly see, yep, the exam authors will likely hit you with still another question following this pattern. The key to mastery is *not* for me to give you thousands of questions precisely like this, but rather to learn the theories, theorists, and general principles related to the question. So, in this instance the counselor is an ABA (applied behavior analysis) practitioner. This is basically the new terminology for behavior modification. The choices "a," "b," and "d" are right out of the ABA helper's playbook so you can eliminate them in a nanosecond. Your answer: Choice "c" is an approach favored by gestalt therapists. **(c)**

1053. A counselor is working with a client suffering from post-traumatic stress disorder (PTSD). Which counselor would be most concerned about inducing REM/EM during the sessions?

 a. A counselor who is performing systematic desensitization as set forth by Joseph Wolpe.
 b. A counselor who is using Francine Shapiro's EMDR.
 c. A counselor who is using existential strategies popularized by Irvin Yalom.
 d. A counselor who relies on brief strategic therapy (BST).

EMDR (eye movement desensitization and reprocessing) is a popular modality for helping those with PTSD. The technique attempts to produce rapid eye movement/eye movement (REM/EM) during the actual course of the sessions. **Exam point saver:** There seems to be a rumor floating around the Internet and infiltrating some of the literature in our field that EDMR pioneer Francine Shapiro felt that this approach could generally treat the client in a single session. She was indeed misquoted and her verbiage pulled out of context meaning that EMDR is not, and never was, intended to be one session therapy. **(b)**

1054. A counselor is using the memory device: IS PATH WARM? He is most likely working with

 a. a client with bipolar disorder.
 b. a client with test anxiety.
 c. a client diagnosed on the autism spectrum disorder.
 d. a client whom he feels could be suicidal.

If you were thinking, "Oh no, not another Rosenthal mnemonic device," chill out, this isn't one I created! This one (IS PATH WARM?) was created via the American Association of

Suicidology (AAS) to assist folks in terms of assessing the risk of suicide: **I** = ideation, **S** = substance abuse, **P** = purposelessness, **A** = anxiety, **T** = trapped, **H** = hopelessness, **W** = withdrawal, **A** = anger, **R** = recklessness, **M** = mood changes. Because of the popularity of this concept, I can only assume the chance is high it will appear on a number of comprehensive exams.            **(d)**

1055. Child-centered play therapy (CCPT) is experiencing rapid growth in popularity and spawning research. This modality was created by

    a.    Virginia Mae Axline, an associate of Carl R. Rogers who penned *Dibs In Search of Self*.

    b.    Carl R. Rogers, who created client-centered/person-centered counseling.

    c.    Gerard Egan, author of the well-known text, the *Skilled Helper.*

    d.    Anna Freud, daughter of Sigmund Freud.

Although Anna Freud was a mover and shaker in the field of child therapy, as well as play therapy, it was Virginia Axline who took Rogerian principles and applied them to play therapy. CCPT advocates that a therapist should be friendly, warm, as well as accept the child as he or she is. A CCPT does not direct the child's topics of conversation or behavior and recognizes that the process should not be rushed since the child leads and the therapist follows. It makes sense that this approach is often called nondirective child play therapy since it has a lot in common with the person-centered, nondirective Rogerian approach. Violet Oaklander, influenced by Axline, has added gestalt therapy ideas to play therapy.            **(a)**

1056. In a children's career counseling group, the group will help the children

    a.    have a sense of belonging.

    b.    share feelings and ideas.

    c.    engage in desirable peer interaction.

    d.    in all the ways listed above.

Since the NCE, the CPCE, and comprehensive exams cover both *career counseling* and *group counseling* it would be foolhardy to assume that these exams would not have questions that apply to both areas. It might even be safe to say these questions will start popping up like out-of-control weeds. I've thus included a few simple tutorial questions to help you learn the specifics you could encounter on an actual exam. Ready? Let's do this.                                                                    **(d)**

1057. In terms of adolescents and career group counseling

    a.    the literature indicates such groups just don't work.

    b.    such groups are cost effective and promote peer identification.

    c.    textbook authors such as Dr. Samuel T. Gladding insist that adolescents can only be assisted in individual sessions.

    d.    it may be true that such groups work, but they do not help adolescents with other aspects of their lives.

Choice "c" is way off base as Dr. Gladding feels groups are the natural environment for adolescents to learn. Ditto for choice "d." Truth be told, often the lessons learned in a career counseling group apply to other aspects of the participant's life.          **(b)**

1058. The concept of universality (also called mutuality) applies to group treatment. In career groups we can safely say

    a.    the group allows the members to see that others can be struggling with similar issues related to work, vocation, and career.

    b.    these terms are rarely, if ever, utilized.

    c.    other members of the group are in similar situations.

    d.    choices a and c are both correct.

Mutuality/universality is a curative factor in counseling as well as career counseling groups.          **(d)**

1059. If you compare group career counseling to noncounselor interventions

   a.  you will discover that group career counseling is more effective.
   b.  you should know this is not a valid question. Because there is no counselor in noncounselor interventions, career counseling cannot take place! The question defies common sense.
   c.  you will find out that no studies exist in this area.
   d.  you will find that they are equal in terms of helping persons who are wrestling with career and vocational issues.

Okay, yes my spellcheck balked at the word *noncounselor*, but indeed it is a valid term you will see used in our field. A noncounselor intervention could be the use of a computer or a software program. Noncounselor implies a counselor is not present for the session. A meta-analysis (i.e., looking at a boatload of studies in the field) clearly reveals that career counseling with a warm body (it could be you!) is more effective. It's nice to know we are needed, but indeed most of us already knew that.    **(a)**

1060. When you conduct group career counseling

   a.  unstructured groups work best.
   b.  structured groups work best.
   c.  gestalt groups work best.
   d.  the group must be based on the concepts set forth by motivational interviewing.

Structured career counseling groups *and* structured career counseling workshops seem to be superior.    **(b)**

1061. Special career counseling groups can be set up. Some examples include a group with displaced homemakers or persons receiving public assistance. Groups of this nature

   a.  are discriminatory and are not recommended.
   b.  have been used, but are rarely desirable.

c.   can be very helpful.

d.   are never a good choice if individual sessions are available.

Special career counseling groups for specific populations work quite well.                                                   **(c)**

1062. Group career counseling

a.   is an international phenomenon. It is used in China with college students.

b.   is not used in any other country except the U.S. We are clearly the world leader in this area.

c.   is more expensive to conduct than providing individual sessions.

d.   is rarely used in the U.S. for college students; however, it is used with K-12 students.

Group career counseling is an international modality. But let's quickly look at choice "c." I humorously tell my students, "When I ask a question in class and you don't know the answer, the answer is almost always money." Ah yes, follow the money! Group career counseling is much more cost effective than individual career counseling. In K-12, as well as college settings, it is not realistic to think that a counselor could do individual career counseling with every student due to huge caseload sizes. If you are shaking your head, yes, I can safely say you are a school, college, or university counselor.                         **(a)**

1063. The main purpose of a career group is

a.   to promote insight.

b.   to provide catharsis related to job and career issues.

c.   to release pent up emotions related to frustrations surrounding work-related issues.

d.   to provide information to participants.

Since you have literally wrestled with over 1,050 questions, I thought I'd throw in an easy one. Another key purpose is to help folks explore vocations and to enhance their decision-making skills.                                                      **(d)**

1064. According to expert John Krumboltz

    a.   career groups with a psychodynamic slant are the most effective.

    b.   group career counseling is important, but will not have an impact on your happiness.

    c.   career decision issues are crucial in terms of one's happiness.

    d.   career groups should focus primarily on developmental issues.

It makes sense that your career and work would influence your overall mood and happiness. Even Freud once quipped, "Love and work are the cornerstones of our humanness." Choice "a" could be eliminated by remembering that Krumboltz is a behaviorist. I recall using a text he authored for a behavior modification class early in my own educational career. **Once again: More and more exams are referring to behavior modification as applied behavior analysis (ABA).**        **(c)**

1065. An advantage of group career counseling over individual career counseling is

    a.   other clients in the group can help you to rev up your motivation.

    b.   you get to help other clients and they get to help you.

    c.   participants can role-play situations such as how to answer questions during a job interview.

    d.   All of the above statements are correct.

Choice "d" stands out since choices "a," "b," and "c" all depict ways in which the group is helpful.        **(d)**

1066. Richard Nelson Bolles penned the bestselling job hunting manual in history titled *What Color Is Your Parachute?* The book, updated yearly, has sold over 10 million copies and is published in over 20 languages.

a.    Bolles champions the idea of securing a network of persons who can help you with your job search.
b.    Bolles likes groups if the group uses the trait-and-factor theory.
c.    Bolles likes groups if the group uses Donald Super's theory.
d.    Bolles likes groups if the group uses the concepts set forth by Nathan Azrin.

Surprisingly, when I interviewed Dick Bolles for my book *Therapy's Best* he told me he was not really enamored with any of the existing career theories. **Bolles is a major fan of networking. If possible, your clients should try to pick the job he or she will enjoy the most.**                                    **(a)**

1067. Nathan Azrin studied with B. F. Skinner. His job club groups are based on

a.    REBT.
b.    narrative therapy.
c.    behaviorism based somewhat on positive reinforcement.
d.    DBT.

The fact that Azrin studied with Skinner should have tipped you off that he is a behaviorist. Make no mistake: Azrin's job clubs were **not intended for career exploration! The individual in the club had a good idea of the type of job he or she intended to secure.** The group was action oriented ... a vehicle where the individual was urged to forge forward in his or her job hunting goals (such as calling possible job sites each day and going for the actual interview). Azrin created job clubs way back in the 1970s. The club/group did provide support, but also helped participants build skills, and provided networking ("Do you know of any job openings?"). If you didn't know what DBT means, you've been out of grad school for a while. DBT, created by psychologist Marsha Linehan, stands for dialectical behavior therapy and it is a popular intervention for working with suicidal

individuals, clients who are self-abusive, and those who have
addiction issues.                                                    **(c)**

1068. Career groups are often considered a theme group. The best
intervention in a structured career group would be

    a.    promoting psychodynamic insight.
    b.    paraphrasing as often as possible.
    c.    using activities such as a game.
    d.    changing the client's internal verbalizations as stressed by
        REBT, the model created by Albert Ellis.

None of the answers would be entirely wrong. That said, the
question tells you very little and the only technique that you can
be sure is structured is using a game as part of the career sessions.
                                                                     **(c)**

1069. You create a career group to examine the clients' roles in life as
a child, student, citizen, homemaker/parent, worker, citizen,
and time spend participating in leisure activities (leisurite). You
should use

    a.    the MBTI based on the work of psychiatrist Carl Jung.
    b.    Nathan Azrin's job club model, based on behaviorism.
    c.    John Holland's SDS or so-called Self-Directed Search.
    d.    Donald Super's life career rainbow.

The career rainbow helps group members answer the question:
Where have you been in life and where are you going? It opens
the door to discuss a career crisis such as a layoff.              **(d)**

1070. According to the fetal origins hypothesis, adult heart disease,
some emotional disorders, and type 2 diabetes could be related
to

    a.    lack of stimulation (i.e., nurture) during the first year of life.
    b.    nature.
    c.    in utero malnutrition
    d.    undiscovered factors related to the human genome.

Experts believe that "fetal origins" my be the "third arm" or missing link in the longstanding nature–nurture debate. Or to put it a different way, genetic endowment and environmental influences after birth, along with what happens to the fetus <u>during</u> gestation (conception to birth), determine our behavior and risks for developing physical diseases and emotional disorders. In utero merely means in the womb, should you see it on your exam.                                                    **(c)**

1071. According to the human growth and development notion of plasticity every client you see

   a.   can alter his or her traits at any point in the life span.
   b.   has his or her behavior governed by critical periods.
   c.   must be aware of the fact that change is not an ongoing process.
   d.   must be aware that most processes of change are merely random.

The concept of plasticity drives home the point that every trait within a given individual can be altered throughout the course of the life span. Change is ongoing, and not random—thus negating choices "b" and "c"—nor necessarily easy.                            **(a)**

1072. Two 18-year-olds are given the exact same dosage of an antidepressant medication. One indicates that the medicine makes her feel "great" while the other insists the intervention makes her "very tired." This can most likely be attributed to

   a.   differential sensitivity.
   b.   the fact that medical practitioners, including psychiatrists, overmedicate and should use smaller doses of antidepressants.
   c.   the fact that both clients are impacted by the placebo effect.
   d.   the fact that antidepressants are intended to make clients extremely tired, but do help with mood disorders.

Differential sensitivity is a term which is making the rounds in our field so I wouldn't be at all surprised if you catch a glimpse of it on your version of the exam. The term illuminates the idea that some people are more vulnerable than others to a particular experience, yes even prescription pharmaceuticals, due to genetic differences. **(a)**

1073. You are conducting a program evaluation (PE) for your 501(c)(3) nonprofit counseling agency. You should begin by

a. getting the support of the staff, administration, and clients.
b. writing a grant to fund the study.
c. asking United Way for help.
d. taking the steps in choices b and c.

You didn't really mark choice "c," did you? Seriously? A lot of counselors make the mistake of adding information to the question that does not exist. The agency *could* be a United Way member, but, since the question doesn't tell you that, I certainly would not make that assumption. A common misconception I hear is that all nonprofit agencies have United Way membership. There are *lots of not-for-profit agencies which are not funded by United Way*. Choice "a" is the best answer. Since the agency does have nonprofit status you would also want to garner support from your board of directors. **(a)**

1074. Program evaluation (PE) helps agencies, organizations, and centers make wiser decisions. PE takes place in a natural, rather than a laboratory or controlled, setting and helps _____ answer questions posed via _____.

a. researchers; staff
b. programs; researchers
c. programs; staff
c. staff; researchers

Program evaluations help the program and are generally not intended to gear toward hypotheses or theories. An adept program evaluation answers several questions including: Is this program actually necessary? If so, which clients should receive the services from the program and for what duration of time?

What are the outcomes of the program? In the majority of cases, stakeholders such as staff, the board, clients, and administrators pose the questions and conduct the research—not researchers. **A key hint: When performing PE use existing data whenever possible to keep the cost down.** **(c)**

1075. A cost–benefit analysis (CBA) answers the question:

   a.   Should the counseling organization become a private practice or a 501(c)(3) nonprofit?
   b.   Should a counseling center opt to do brief strategic therapy?
   c.   Was the money wisely spent or does the counseling center need a new program?
   d.   Which clients should receive pro bono services?

Counselors often find it difficult to talk about CBA because it deals with the issue of whether or not it is worth the price to assist people. As counselors, we routinely take the position that you can't put a price tag on helping others. **(c)**

1076. You are the owner of a counseling practice. You make the sole decision which counselor receives the new referrals. According to new ACA ethics on fee splitting

   a.   you can charge counselors 50% of the agency counseling fee for office space.
   b.   you can charge counselors one third of the agency counseling fee for office space, but it must never exceed one third.
   c.   fee splitting is totally ethical and the director could set the fee split at any cost he or she feels is appropriate.
   d.   although many counselors believe this is controversial, it is unethical based on the fact that charging a percentage of the payment rate per client appears to be a kickback scheme similar to accepting a referral fee.

ACA has taken the position that this could be a problem since you might be apt to refer the clients to staff who are paying a greater fee to the agency, rather than assigning clients based on a rotational basis or the competency of the clinicians on staff. This would go against the ethical notion that we always should consider what is best for clients. **Making referrals based on financial outcomes is not, I repeat not, ethical!** The practice of referring to employees who are paid less, say a licensed provisional counselor versus a licensed practitioner, would also not be appropriate. Make no mistake about it, however, the owner (or for that matter anybody assigning the clients) *could* charge each helper a set amount for office use.    **(d)**

1077. You are supervising a counselor-in-training and focusing on the OARS core skills. You are teaching her how to perform

   a.    psychodynamic group therapy.
   b.    gestalt therapy created by Fritz Perls.
   c.    motivational interviewing (MI) created mainly by William Miller and Stephen Rollnick.
   d.    career counseling using directive techniques.

Motivational interviewing is really hot right now, especially in the area of addictions, since the strategy was initially used with problem drinkers. It is even used beyond the borders of the U.S. Most experts see it as an offshoot of Rogerian counseling, though to be sure it is much more goal directed. OARS, by the way, stands for Open questions (e.g., how is your gambling addiction impacting your life?), Affirmations (any positive factors the counselor sees in the client's life such as awards, achievements, or successes), Reflection (you know this one by now), and Summaries (again, you've got this one down). MI is a brief form of therapy often implemented in five sessions or less. Despite all the excitement over MI, and certainly some positive literature to support this approach, a few studies have given this modality mixed reviews.    **(c)**

1078. The order of the four processes that MI uses is

   a.    engaging, focusing, evoking, and planning.
   b.    engaging, evoking, focusing, and planning.

c.    evoking, focusing, engaging, and planning.
d.    planning, engaging, focusing, and evoking.

Engaging is used first to create a relationship with the client. In MI the counselor is not intended to be an expert, but rather a partner. Focusing simply means that the conversation should be limited to the patterns of behavior the client wishes to change. Evoking stresses the client should use his or her own motivation to make changes, and planning is the act of creating a smart, measurable plan (if possible!) that works. **Rosenthal reminder: In MI the change comes from the client and not an outside source. The client must overcome his or her ambivalence toward change (e.g., "I guess I could give up smoking, but then I might gain weight"). Aggressive confrontation, giving advice, and persuasion are not part of the MI process. The helper is never punitive and would not insist the client has a problem and therefore must change. Miller and Rollnick are adamant that MI should not be confused with traditional brief therapy.**    **(a)**

1079. According to existential therapist Irvin D. Yalom

a.    most therapists do a superb job of interacting with clients who bring up the topic of death.
b.    most therapists are afraid of their own mortality and avoid the topic of death.
c.    discussing dreams related to death is not very therapeutic.
d.    helping the client put death out of one's mind aids the client's growth.

Yalom notes that since therapists are often afraid of their own mortality they will wrongly avoid the topic with verbalizations such as, "Look, there is really nothing anybody can do about death, so let's move on." Choice "c" is incorrect since Yalom feels that dreams can be quite important in therapy. **Yalom is convinced that we are all hardwired to have anxiety about death. Nevertheless, when it crosses over to terror and immobilizes our life it is not healthy. He believes life can be richer by keeping death in mind. He uses the example**

**that cancer patients faced with death would sometimes comment that they were sorry they waited so long to learn how to live. Yalom is the author of the book *Staring at the Sun: Overcoming the Terror of Death*.**    **(b)**

1080. Pick the most accurate statement regarding patients diagnosed with cancer.

   a.    Since January 1, 2015 there is official recognition that a diagnosis of cancer will affect a patient's mental health.
   b.    Physicians are required by law to give all cancer patients a referral for counseling or psychotherapy.
   c.    Paradoxically, although a diagnosis of cancer is often very serious there is virtually no evidence that cancer patients have any more mental health issues than prior to the diagnosis.
   d.    Counselors have always been the primary workers in the medical system when compared to social workers and psychologists and thus traditionally have counseled most patients diagnosed with cancer.

Let me say right off the bat that choice "d" is misleading because social workers and psychologists *have* been at the forefront of the medical treatment for years. Now counselors need to step up to the plate and become more involved in this area. Cognitive behavior therapy (CBT), groups, and mindfulness seemingly work well for clients diagnosed with cancer. **Okay, big news folks: Beginning in 2015, the American College of Surgeons Commission on Cancer (ACoS) created a new rule that any center their organization accredits would need to screen for psychosocial stress. Theoretically, this will help more patients who need to secure mental health services.**    **(a)**

1081. Transgender individuals have an attempted suicide rate which is approximately 25 times higher than the rate for the general population. A high percentage of transgender youth experience oppression and are physically assaulted. A transgender does not identify with the gender they were given at birth or the person's expression differs from societal expectations. What is cisgender?

a.  All females.
b.  All males.
c.  The same as genderfluid.
d.  A person who identifies with the gender they were assigned at birth and hence by definition this person is not a transgender individual.

Choice "c" is a key term and describes an individual who changes from one gender (or no gender) to another (or several others) often very rapidly ... say multiple times per day. So as an example, the person might feel like a girl, then a boy, then no gender whatsoever. Persons who consider themselves bi-gender (e.g., alternating between a female and a male) would fall into this category. Finally, another term of note is cisnormative or cisnormativity, which describes an individual who has a gender identity that matches their sex assigned at birth. Cis comes from Latin meaning "to this the near side." A cisgender privilege would connote any unearned advantage a person gains from identifying with their gender assigned at birth.          **(d)**

1082. A correlation/association between variables x and y is .50. According to the notion of effect size (ES)

a.  the correlation is medium.
b.  the correlation is small.
c.  the correlation is large.
d.  the correlation would not be applicable to this statistic.

**Listen up counseling fans: The effect size (ES) statistic has come of age and will likely be coming to a comprehensive exam in your future. A small association is .20 or less; medium is .50 or less; and large, strong, or big (yes all these terms are used) checks in at .80 or higher. P.S. Although this concept is hardly new, I am well aware that if you have been out of school for an extended period of time the ES concept was not covered in many statistics**

**and research classes. Initially it was applied to meta-analyses, generally a host of studies in the same area, but now its use has expanded.**                                              **(a)**

1083. You conduct a true experiment. The results between the several groups are statistically significant. You have rejected the null hypothesis.

    a.    You should still provide an effect size (ES) statistic.

    b.    You would not need to provide the effect size (ES) since the data indicate there is a statistical significance.

    c.    You would not need to provide the effect size (ES) since the ES only applies to correlations and this is a true experiment.

    d.    You could provide the effect size (ES), but since it is a true experiment this information could be very misleading.

**When describing a statistically significant result—in plain everyday English you have rejected the null hypothesis— it is the researcher's duty to provide the ES statistic. Again, the ES is required. Why? Well simply put, although the results of the experiment most likely did not occur via chance, it is still important to find out how large/strong the effect is in this situation. For instance, if the ES was 3.15, then the difference between the means of the two groups was very high (since .8 or above is large) so we have a *very* large effect. Unlike correlations, the ES, based on a statistic called Cohen's d, can exceed 1.00. Choice "c" is downright incorrect since the ES can apply to tests of significance. So just for review: The ES helps us analyze the magnitude of the differences when looking at correlations, tests of significance, or even a meta-analysis.**                      **(a)**

1084. A major meta-analysis (a term coined by researcher Gene V. Glass) of 375 outcome studies using effect size (ES) by Mary Lee Smith, Gene V. Glass, and Thomas I. Miller revealed that

    a.    psychotherapy is approximately as effective as antidepressants, about .31.

b.   psychotherapy is less effective than antidepressants, about .22.

c.   psychotherapy was too hard to define to come up with an ES statistic.

d.   psychotherapy had a strong or so-called big effect, checking in at a .85.

**This must-know meta-analysis is frequently quoted or referenced.** Choice "a" depicts the results of 74 studies looking at FDA-registered antidepressants approved between 1987 and 2004. The *New England Journal of Medicine* quoted ESs of .31 for Lexapro, .26 for Prozac, .24 for Zoloft, and .3 for Cymbalta. Keep these stats, as well as the the answer to this question, in the back of your mind, when you gaze at all those ads for psychiatric medicinals! Psychotherapy was vindicated after this 1980 analysis appeared in the classic book *Benefits of Psychotherapy* by the three authors mentioned in the question. No key differences were discovered between the different modalities of therapy.     **(d)**

1085. According to the *DSM-5*

a.   pathological gambling is not a disorder.

b.   pathological gambling is a disorder and is listed with Obsessive-Compulsive and Related Disorders just like trichotillomania (now called hair pulling).

c.   pathological gambling is a disorder and is listed with Substance-Related and Addictive Disorders.

d.   pathological gambling is a conduct disorder.

Hair pulling, showcased in choice "b," *is* listed in the *DSM-5* as an Obsessive-Compulsive Disorder. Disorders of this nature are often called impulse disorders. Gambling addiction, nevertheless, is listed with Substance-Related and Addictive Disorders. Since gambling addiction is often treated via addiction and substances abuse centers, this makes logical sense to a lot of counselors.     **(c)**

1086. All of the statements below are true about bullying *except:*

a.   More girls are bullied than boys.

b.    More whites are bullied than minorities.

c.    Fewer students claim they are being bullied in recent years.

d.    More students are harassed in the hallways than on social media.

Cyber-bullying usually takes place via unwanted text messages and to a lesser degree via Internet posts that contain negative or hurtful information. One surprise is that some research indicates that sibling bullying is a more common variety of school bullying.    **(d)**

1087. Wilderness therapy falls under the auspices of adventure-based therapy. There is no one set model for wilderness therapy. All of the statements below are true about wilderness therapy *except*:

a.    Effective wilderness therapy occurs when a boot camp model is used in the wilderness.

b.    Most counselors believe stricter regulations should be put in place to avoid abuses.

c.    Effective wilderness therapy settings use little or no force, confrontation, or point level systems.

d.    Reports of abuse and even death of youth have surfaced.

Boot camps, under the guise of doing wilderness therapy, often use a military paradigm and turn to employees with little or no therapeutic background, while good wilderness therapy programs rely on trained staff and well-established theories of psychology, counseling, and change. **Therefore, before you make referrals to wilderness programs, check out the program in question very carefully (see choice "d" which is true).** Some programs send the young adults home after the program, but others use aftercare centers or treatment-oriented boarding schools.    **(a)**

1088. The 1974 Family Educational Rights and Privacy Act (FERPA) could be called the Buckley Amendment on your exam since

Senator James K. Buckley was a strong supporter. All of these facts are true regarding FERPA *except*:

a. Parents have access to a minor child's educational records. Children over age 18 can view their own records.
b. A parent is able to have the educational record amended.
c. A counselor working in a private educational institution which does not receive federal funding would still be required to follow FERPA guidelines.
d. In situations involving imminent danger, a counselor could release information to protect the client, others, or ward off harm.

Surprised? Perhaps! Counselors working in schools and universities not receiving federal funds from appropriate government programs are *exempt* from FERPA guidelines. **What's the scoop on school directories?** The student's name, dates of attendance, place of birth, address, phone number, and even awards or honors can indeed be revealed *without* parental consent. However, the parents and students must be contacted once a year to let them know that they *can* elect to prevent their information (and that of their children) from being released. **(c)**

1089. Mr. Donald is seeing you for a gambling addiction problem. Several years ago he won a huge amount of money at the casino from a slot machine. As soon as he pulled the handle he snapped his fingers. Now he always snaps his fingers after he pulls a slot machine handle. His superstition can best be explained by

a. accidental reinforcement.
b. contingent reinforcement.
c. shaping with successive approximations.
d. the fact that he has savant tendencies.

In many instances when you encounter a question with two opposite answer stems and you are certain one is dead wrong, then there is nearly a 100% chance the other is the correct answer! Thus, you could immediately eliminate choices "c" and "d" even if you don't know or recall what they mean. In this case you probably figured out that most of the time when we use reinforcement it is contingent (think dependent) on a given behavior. Hence, your dog knows that you provide a treat—as a reinforcer—when she comes to the door after you call her. Accidental reinforcement, on the other hand, can occur regardless of the behavior (think independent). B. F. Skinner discovered this when he reinforced pigeons with food for no special reason and discovered that whatever the pigeon was doing (say spinning around or pecking) they tended to repeat the behavior. Clearly Mr. Donald's finger snapping has zilch to do with the outcome of the slots.    **(a)**

1090. Pick the incorrect statement.

   a.   Men commit suicide more than women.
   b.   Women suffer from depression more than men.
   c.   Alcoholism occurs more in women than men.
   d.   Autism occurs more in men than women.

   A common question on exams pertains to whether popular disorders or diagnoses occur more in men or women. This question showcases some of the most common ones.    **(c)**

1091. You are supervising a graduate student. The client she is discussing was raped and robbed several days prior to your session with this student. When you ask your supervisee for more information she says, "Well, I'm certain the fact that she was carrying a very expensive handbag and wearing tight clothes was an issue." Based on gestalt psychologist Fritz Heider's concept of attribution theory

   a.   your supervisee is relying on situational attributions.
   b.   your supervisee is relying on dispositional attributions.
   c.   paradoxically, the expensive handbag and tight clothes would ward off crime.
   d.   the tight clothes were an issue, but not the expensive handbag.

Attribution theories assign a cause, explanation, or reason for a behavior or outcome of an event. **When the cause or outcome is generated by the person it is said to be a dispositional or internal attribution.** For example, Melissa flunked her comps because she didn't study. In a similar fashion, the grad student—even if she is completely wrong—seems to be blaming her client for being robbed and raped. **When the cause is attributed to factors outside the individual, it is an example of situational or external attribution.** For example, Wesley flunked his comps because the department created an exam so difficult nobody could pass it. Fritz Heider is the father of attribution theory.                                          **(b)**

1092. Based on the information in the previous question, the best example of a fundamental attribution error (also called a fundamental attribution bias) would be:

   a.   The graduate student blames the woman for carrying an expensive handbag and wearing tight clothes.
   b.   The graduate student blames the man who committed the rape and the robbery.
   c.   The graduate student blames the police force for not patrolling the area better.
   d.   The graduate student becomes so emotional, she cannot discuss the incident with you as her supervisor.

   **The fundamental attribution error occurs when a person attempts to look at somebody else's negative behavior, failure, or undesirable event (never your own!) and come up with an explanation. The tendency is to put more stock in dispositional (think personality, judgment, and ability) explanations than situational ones. The problem is attributed to the person. Interestingly enough, most people attribute their own negative outcomes in life to situational/external attributes, but assess other people's as dispositional/internal.**                          **(a)**

1093. According to attribution theory and the self-serving bias, if you pass your exam _____ and if you fail your exam _____.

    a.    it is because of external issues; it is because of internal issues

    b.    it is because of situational issues; it is because of dispositional issues

    c.    it is because of dispositional issues; it is because of situational issues

    d.    you lucked out; the authors of the exam chose poor exam questions

So according to the self-serving bias, if *you* failed your exam, the exam questions were stupid etc.... . Well, you get my point! But, if *you* passed ... you are one smart counselor! If somebody else passed, it was just an easy exam. **This tendency is called the self-serving bias. A positive event occurred because you are so wonderful etc.! A negative event occurred because of the situation or external circumstances! It had nothing to do with you.**                                        **(c)**

1094. You are performing career counseling with a client. This client is extremely depressed. The client goes on a job interview and doesn't get the job. Based on research related to attribution theory

    a.    in most instances this client will begin having suicidal ideation within 24 hours.

    b.    the client's view of reality will be swayed due to his depression and thus he will insist that the interviewer was a total jerk.

    c.    he will blame himself for his poor performance during the interview.

    d.    he will make a joke out of the fact that he did not get the job.

A depressed client will typically do the opposite of a person who is not depressed and will blame himself. In a situation like this the self-serving attribution bias would *not* apply. In terms of choice "b" hold onto your seat; research shows that depressed individuals often harbor a more accurate view of reality, but that isn't always a good thing! Or to put it a different way, the person who is <u>not</u> depressed might have been totally inept in the interview, but using a self-serving bias, will insist the interviewer was a jerk. **(c)**

1095. A counselor is using telephone coaching with a client. The counselor is most likely to base her treatment on

    a.   William Glasser's reality therapy with choice theory.
    b.   REBT as set forth by Albert Ellis.
    c.   DBT as set forth by Marsha M. Linehan.
    d.   systematic desensitization.

Dialectical behavior therapy (DBT) is an evidence-based form of counseling that was initially used in the late 1980s with suicidal clients as well as those with borderline personality disorder and is now used with an array of mental health issues. It is classified as a type of cognitive behavior therapy (CBT). This model relies on four modes: (1) skills training; (2) phone counseling; (3) therapist consultation team; (4) individual treatment. **When DBT is adapted to a setting or situation where it is not possible to use all four modes, the term DBT-informed is used. As a simple example, if a counselor was only going to use telephone coaching due to time restraints or cost restrictions, then the term "DBT-informed" would be appropriate. So you will hear helpers talk about standard DBT (the entire kit and caboodle with all four steps) or abbreviated DBT-informed practices.** **(c)**

1096. A counselor is utilizing a thought log—also known as a thought record—with an anxious client. She is practicing

    a.   psychodynamic therapy.
    b.   career counseling based on the work of Donald Super.
    c.   cognitive behavior therapy (CBT).
    d.   the transtheoretical model which draws from all of the available theories to help the client change.

CBT is now the most popular modality in the United States as well as several other countries such as the United Kingdom. It has been called the dominant force in psychotherapy. Why? Most likely because CBT has been deemed effective in hundreds of studies and therefore can be viewed as a valid form of evidence-based practice (EBP). CBT counselors often use thought records to help clients see how their thoughts are impacting their lives. The thought record is merely a chart depicting an activating event, the actual thought, the emotional consequence and/or behavior, and an alternative thought or perspective. On rare occasions the log will include the new emotional response based on the alternative thought. Granted choice "d" *might* be correct, but in a case where there are two viable choices, pick the one that is most likely to be the appropriate choice.                                    **(c)**

1097. You are conducting a session using CBT; however, you are incorporating mindfulness as well as ACT into the session. Strictly speaking you are

    a.   performing second wave CBT.
    b.   third wave CBT.
    c.   first wave CBT.
    d.   operant conditioning.

Steven C. Hayes is generally cited as coming up with the first, second, and third wave categories of behaviorist treatment. **First wave** treatments were based on operant and classical conditioning such as the work of B. F. Skinner and Ivan Pavlov. **Second wave** interventions focused heavily on cognitions depicted by the work of Albert Ellis and Aaron T. Beck. **Third wave** or contemporary approaches incorporate DBT, motivational interviewing, and ACT (pronounced just like the word act), which stands for acceptance and commitment therapy.                                    **(b)**

1098. A counselor is performing CBT. He believes his client is not dealing with the real or core issue causing the difficulty. The most effective ploy would be to

   a.   change his approach to narrative therapy.
   b.   give the client a projective personality test.
   c.   use the downward arrow technique, created by David D. Burns, M.D.
   d.   prescribe rational imagery (RI), often advocated by Albert Ellis.

The downward arrow technique is highly recommended to ferret out what the client is truly upset about and make the client aware of this issue. Say a client is upset because he forgot to buy his wife a birthday gift. The therapist could ask him, "What is the worst thing that could happen?" He might say (or write), "She might be very upset on this special day." The counselor asks for yet another response and gets, "She might be so upset she would leave and go out with her girlfriends." Finally, he keeps asking what might happen next and gets to the real issue known as the **core belief**, "She might be so upset she would divorce me."          **(c)**

1099. Classical conditioning is based on paired learning, whereas operant conditioning is predicated on rewards or punishment. In a classical conditioning experiment a dog was trained to salivate to a bell which was originally presented about 0.5 second before the meat. The bell is

   a.   a CS or conditioned stimulus.
   b.   an NS or neutral stimulus.
   c.   a UR or unconditioned response.
   d.   a CR or conditioned response.

When I tell you that the correct response is choice "a" many of you will be ready to e-mail me to say it is a misprint in the book since I taught you earlier in this text that many exams use the terms CS or NS in an interchangeable manner. Well, I didn't call this the advanced section for nothing! Recently, some exams are splitting hairs and do make a distinction between a CS and an NS. This means the answer choices could list both! What's the deal? Well in some of the newer literature the neutral stimulus terminology is only used until a CR occurs. When the bell without the meat produces a CR (salivating) then the dog is conditioned and the bell is now technically a CS or conditioned stimulus. At that moment in time a UR becomes a CR because it is learned. Ergo, if the question suggested that the dog had not yet acquired the response to salivate then choice "b" would be the right on target.                                          **(a)**

1100. Your supervisor insists you rely on a teleological approach with a client. Pick the correct statement.

    a.    You would simply talk to the client about her childhood.
    b.    You would prescribe a homework assignment related to her childhood.
    c.    You would focus exclusively on the here and now.
    d.    You would focus on the client's goal to become a stock broker in four years when she finishes her business degree.

Some approaches are historic and dwell on the past. Others are present moment oriented and focus on the here and now. And still others are said to be teleological in the sense that a *future event* is responsible for the client's current behavior.          **(d)**

**GOOD LUCK!**

# 12

## Final Overview and Last-Minute Super-Review Boot Camp

Review this material *after* you have completed the entire *Encyclopedia of Counseling*. **Do not skim over this review: it is a very powerful learning device.** I've even added a few last-minute concepts that can be explained in a sentence or two as exam insurance! You should begin scanning this chapter at least a week or so before the exam, and even peruse it the night before or the morning of the exam. Ideally, combine this review with the Boot Camp program in my audio program. Here is your mini-review on a little more than the head of a pin! Best wishes!

### HISTORIC NBCC ANNOUNCEMENT

On November 17, 2014, NBCC President and CEO, Dr. Thomas W. Clawson, sent a communication revealing that NCC applications received after **January 1, 2022,** will only be accepted if the applicant possesses a master's degree or higher from a program accredited by the Council for Accreditation of Counseling and Related Programs (CACREP). This will reduce the difficulty of securing a license when a counselor moves. This will *not* affect anybody who currently has NCC status. ACA is backing this position.

# NONPROFIT COUNSELING ORGANIZATIONS

Nonprofits must adhere to the **IRS 501(c)(3)** guidelines and will be exempt from paying federal income taxes. The organization will have a **board of directors** and this board will be legally responsible for the agency's actions. In most states you must have at least three founding board members. The board sets policies, generally is not paid, and the staff will implement the policies.

# ROSENTHAL'S 44 KEY RULES FOR AVOIDING LAWSUITS, ETHICAL VIOLATIONS, AND MALPRACTICE DIFFICULTIES

1.  Get a medical diagnosis on clients to rule out physical and organic problems. You never want to treat a problem as a purely psychological (functional) disorder when it is organic.
2.  Don't break confidentiality unless legal and ethical guidelines stipulate you should do so. Confidentiality lives on after the client is deceased.
3.  Inform the client upfront that there are times when you need to break confidentiality, for example, you are subpoenaed and asked to provide information about a client. This is known as "relative confidentiality" or the "limitations of confidentiality." Your informed consent information statement should also delineate freedom of choice issues, fees, techniques you utilize, and your qualifications.
4.  If you haven't been properly trained to treat a problem, don't treat it.
5.  If you haven't been properly trained to use an approach, don't use it.
6.  Never promise or guarantee that you will cure the client.
7.  Never have sex or become romantically involved with a current client, a client's partner, family member, or supervisee, or use the relationship for monetary gains. According to ACA you may have

a romantic or sexual relationship with a former client if you wait five years after the last contact. NBCC states two years after termination. The relationship cannot be exploitative.

8. If you don't know how to handle a case, get supervision or seek out a consultation. The "standard of practice or care" concept refers to the fact that competent peers would have handled the situation in the same usual or customary manner as you.

9. Document your work by keeping good, accurate records. Computerized or so-called electronic records require restricted access so only appropriate staff can view them.

10. Breech confidentiality if a client threatens to hurt himself, herself, or someone else, relying on the principle of "minimal disclosure."

11. Always contact a hotline regarding child abuse and abuse of the elderly or a disabled adult. Counselors are mandated reporters.

12. Counselors and counselors-in-training should peruse current NBCC Code of Ethics related to Face-to-Face Counseling, Technology Assisted Distance Counseling (i.e., Internet counseling, telephone counseling) and also peruse ACA's Code of Ethics.

13. Practice fidelity by keeping promises and being loyal to clients. Lying, not keeping appointments, and breaking confidentiality for no good reason are examples of behavior that violates fidelity.

14. Always ask a client before you record (audio or video) the session and explain how the recording will be utilized. Clients are not obligated to agree to this practice. Allowing supervisees and students to take recordings home could be detrimental to confidentiality.

15. Always secure malpractice (liability) insurance.

16. Initially provide the client with a written informed consent/disclosure statement with a transfer plan (in case you become ill, incapacitated, retire, die, or leave the practice) for the record and treatment.

17. Do not perform conversion or reparative therapy to convert members of the LBGTQ community to heterosexuals since LBGTQ lifestyles are not considered abnormal.

18. If you are running a group, let the group know that confidentiality is crucial, but you cannot guarantee it.

19. Refrain from giving the client a diagnosis in cases where the diagnosis might harm the client.

20. Steer clear of dual/multiple relationships with current or former clients unless the relationship is beneficial to the client (e.g., attending a graduation or visiting the client in the hospital). Document why you feel the interaction is beneficial in advance whenever possible. If a nonprofessional situation or relationship is targeted at meeting your needs and not the client's, then you should avoid it!

21. If you are a counselor educator you must infuse multicultural and diversity material into all courses and workshops.

22. Never use a test, inventory, or assessment tool on a population unless that particular instrument has been normed on that population.

23. Never use a test or inventory that is obsolete or make client decisions based on obsolete test scores.

24. Use the title "Dr." only if your doctorate is in counseling or a closely related field. If a degree is an honorary degree (versus a degree which is earned) this must be disclosed.

25. Do not use your regular counseling job to recruit clients for your private practice.

26. NCCs keep records for at least five years, unless the law says otherwise.

27. Do not make multiple or so-called duplicate submissions to professional journals.

28. If you are working with a terminally ill client who wishes to hasten his or her death you have a right to break or not break confidentiality after you consult with appropriate professional and legal sources.

29. Work with your clients to jointly devise a counseling plan and review the plan on a regular basis.

30. If you are using a treatment team you must inform the client. In addition, you should reveal the composition of the team.

31. If a client gives you a small gift based on the client's cultural norms, you could accept the gift if you feel the monetary value of the gift is appropriate ($20 or less according to most experts) and the motivation for giving the gift is acceptable. It should not be a recurrent event and should promote, not endanger, the client's welfare.

32. Counselor educators who are book authors are permitted to use their books for classes and workshops.

33. A wealth of new technology-related ethical imperatives now exist. If you provide technology-assisted services (e.g., telephone counseling,

software, online counseling, websites, online assessments etc.) use encrypted websites and e-mail communications. If this is not possible, only use communications that are not client specific. Check legal regulations and the licensing bureau of the state where the client resides to determine if you must be licensed in that particular state. Provide language translation services for clients who communicate in a different language. Also, establish a password or set up a webcam system at the beginning of each session to verify the identity of the client. Consider taking NBCCs training to become a Distance Credentialed Counselor (DCC).

34. If you provide technology-assisted services, give the client emergency procedures in case technology fails and let the client know what services are covered under insurance. Moreover, ensure that technological accessibility meets the Americans with Disabilities Act (ADA).

35. If you are using a technique or treatment modality that is not proven via empirical evidence or a proven scientific foundation, always inform the client that the intervention is "unproven" or "developing." Discuss the possibility of harm with the client. If you are unsure whether or not a treatment modality is unscientific, consult with a former professor, colleagues, or other expert. Keep up with the latest research by reading textbooks, journals, and attending professional workshops. Moreover, if you do harm a client unintentionally you need to show that you attempted to remedy such harm.

36. Counselor supervisors should not counsel their supervisees.

37. Counselor supervisors should provide an on-call supervisor to assist supervisees in his or her absence.

38. A supervisor can legitimately recommend that a supervisee be dismissed from a training program or a professional setting.

39. Either a supervisor or a supervisee can legitimately terminate a supervisory relationship. A referral should be given to the supervisee.

40. Whenever possible, do not use deception with subjects in research studies. If you cannot find an alternative, then debrief the subjects as soon as possible.

41. Avoid fee-splitting and never accept a referral fee for a client.

42. Beware: Ignorance of ethical guidelines is not considered a valid excuse to violate them!

43. NBCC says you should not solicit testimonials from current clients. Wait two years. ACA also agrees you should not solicit testimonials from current clients or from others who might be "vulnerable to undue influence." ACA does not mention any waiting period.
44. Excessive self-disclosure pertaining to your own problems which will not help the client could be an ethics violation.

Ethical codes protect counselors and their clients. Moreover, such codes provide an outline for professional accountability and acceptable practice. These codes are not static and therefore do change over time.

# HUMAN GROWTH AND DEVELOPMENT

The application of human growth and development theories to the practice of counseling became popular in the 1980s. In 1981, CACREP included this as a core content area. In 1983 APGA (now ACA) changed its name to American Association for Counseling and Development to help emphasize the developmental aspects of our profession. Development is ongoing, systematic, orderly, sequential, and is said to build upon itself. The term *continual* implies that development occurs throughout the life span.

There is speculation as to whether individuals are active or passive in terms of influencing their development. Another issue centers on the nature or nurture debate. Is behavior the result of inborn tendencies/heredity (i.e., nature) or the environment (i.e., upbringing, nurture, and learning)? Current theorists insist it is both, but disagree on the amount of impact exerted. The third arm may be **fetal origins**, referring to what happens to the fetus during gestation.

Changes can be **quantitative** (measured) or **qualitative** (change in organization or structure).

Many theorists stress the notion of **critical periods (also called sensitive periods or all or nothing periods)** where a behavior or developmental process, for example language or types of visual acuity, can be acquired; or it is nearly impossible to develop at a later time of life.

Ironically, young children have **more neural connections than adults**.

If **genetics** play such a strong role in development, why are children from the same family often so much different? The current notion is that **shared experiences/influences** (all family members attended the same family functions, went on identical vacations, etc.) have less impact than **nonshared individual experiences/ influences** (siblings may have different teachers, friends, etc.). Also, individuals may perceive the same event in totally different ways.

## MAJOR THEORIES AND THEORISTS

### G. Stanley Hall

Founder of psychology in the U.S. and the first president of the American Psychological Association. He popularized the study of the child and child guidance. He wrote seminal works on adolescence.

### Behaviorism

Behaviorism was outlined by John B. Watson, Ivan Pavlov, Joseph Wolpe, and B. F. Skinner. Initially the mind is a blank slate and the child learns to behave in a certain manner. This is basically a passive theory. The mind is like a computer that is fed information. This model relies on empiricism—John Locke's view that knowledge is acquired by experience. All behavior is the result of learning.

### Erik Erikson's Eight Psychosocial Stages

Erikson's stages are delineated in his classic 1963 work *Childhood and Society*. The stages are based on ego psychology and the epigenetic principle that states that growth is orderly, universal, and systematic. The stages are: **trust versus mistrust** (birth to 1.5 years); **autonomy versus shame and doubt** (1.5–3 years); **initiative versus guilt** (3–6 years); **industry versus inferiority** (6–11 years); **identity versus role confusion** (12–18 years); **intimacy versus isolation** (18–35 years); **generativity versus stagnation** (35–60 years); and **integrity versus despair** (age 65 and beyond).

## Jean Piaget's Qualitative Four Stages of Cognitive Development (Genetic Epistemology)

**Theory: sensorimotor** (birth to 2 years); **preoperational** (2–7 years); **concrete operations** (7–12 years); and **formal operations** (11/12–16 years).

- Patterns of thought and behavior are called **schema** or the plural, schemata.
- **Adaptation** occurs *qualitatively* when the individual fits information into existing ideas (also known as assimilation) and modifies cognitive schemata to incorporate new information (this is called accommodation).
- **Assimilation** and **accommodation** are said to be complementary processes. The ages in the Piagetian stages can vary, the order is static.
- **Object permanence** occurs in the sensorimotor stage (an object the child can't see still exists).
- **Centration** is the act of focusing on one aspect of something. It is a key factor in the preoperational stage.
- **Conservation** takes place in the concrete operations stage. The child knows that volume and quantity do not change, just because the appearance of an object changes (e.g., pouring a short glass of water into a tall skinny glass does not alter the amount of the liquid). The child comprehends that a change in shape does not mean a change in volume.
- **Abstract scientific thinking** takes place in the formal operations stage.

## Keagan's Constructive Developmental Model

Keagan's model emphasizes the impact of interpersonal interaction and our perception of reality.

## Lawrence Kohlberg's Three Levels of Moral Development

**Preconventional level**—behavior governed by consequences; **conventional level**—a desire to conform to socially acceptable rules; **postconventional level**—self-accepted moral principles guide behavior. Each level has two stages.

## Carol Gilligan's Theory of Moral Development for Women

Gilligan's 1982 book, *In a Different Voice*, illuminated the fact that Kohlberg's research was conducted on males. Women have a sense of caring and compassion.

## Daniel Levinson's Four Major Eras/Transitions Theory

In a 1978 classic book titled *The Seasons of a Man's Life*, Levinson depicted the changes in men's lives throughout the life span. The four key eras include: childhood and adolescence, early adulthood, middle adulthood, and later adulthood.

## Lev Vygotsky (1896–1934)

Vygotsky proposed that cognitive development is not the result of innate factors, but is produced by activities that take place in one's culture. His **zone of proximal development (ZDP)** refers to the difference in the child's ability to solve problems on his own and his capacity to solve them with some help from others.

## Sigmund Freud's Psychoanalytic/Psychodynamic Five Psychosexual Stages

Freud's stages are: **oral** (birth to 1 year), **anal** (1 to 3 years), **phallic (Oedipal/Electra complex** (3–7 years), **latency** (3–5 years until age 12), and **genital** (adolescence and adulthood).

    **Libido** is the drive to live and the sexual instinct that is present even at birth. It is said to be sublimated in the latency stage as the individual has little interest in sex. This ends when puberty begins.

- **Regression** is the return to an earlier stage caused by stress.
- **Fixation** implies that the person is unable to move to the next stage.
- Freud is criticized for focusing on sex and not including the entire life span in his theory.

## Abraham Maslow's Hierarchy of Needs

Maslow interviewed self-actualized people. Lower-order physiological and safety needs must be fulfilled before self-actualization can occur.

## William Perry's Three-Stage Theory of Intellectual and Ethical Development in Adults/College Students

**Dualism**—in which students view the truth as either right or wrong. **Relativism**—the notion that a perfect answer may not exist. There is a desire to know various opinions. **Commitment to relativism**—in this final stage the individual is willing to change his or her opinion based on novel facts and new points of view.

## James W. Fowler's Prestage Plus Six-Stage Theory of Faith and Spiritual Development

Fowler conducted 350 structured interviews and drew on the work of Piaget, Kohlberg, and Erikson. **Stage 0: undifferentiated (primal) faith** (infancy, birth to 4 years); **Stage 1: intuitive-projective faith**

(2–7 years, early childhood); **Stage 2: mythic-literal faith** (childhood and beyond); **Stage 3: synthetic-conventional faith** (adolescence and beyond) a stage of conformity; **Stage 4: individuative-reflective faith** (young adulthood and beyond); **Stage: 5 conjunctive faith** (mid-thirties and beyond) openness to other points of view, paradox, and appreciation of symbols and metaphors; and **Stage 6: universalizing faith** (midlife and beyond) few reach this stage of enlightenment.

- According to Fowler, faith is not identical with one's belief in religion. "Faith can be religious faith, but it can also be centered on a career, a country, an institution, a family, money, success, or even oneself." Faith grows and changes throughout the life span.

## Diana Baumrind's Typology of Parenting Styles

**Authoritative:** High expectations for the child, but is warm and nurturing. The child is **given an explanation of the rules**. Generally produces a child who is happy, does well in school, has good emotional regulation, and fine social skills.

**Authoritarian:** Characterized by bossy parenting which **champions "follow my orders" with no explanation**. Punishment and verbal insults are used liberally. Can produce anxious, withdrawn children who are likely to engage in antisocial behavior including alcohol and drug abuse, stealing, and gang activities.

**Permissive Passive Indulgent:** Parent has a low level of control and is easily manipulated. Rarely says "no" to a child and is nonpunitive. **Very affectionate and wishes to please the child like a friend.** Child can display a lack of social skills, boundaries, and can be extremely demanding. Children often use drugs and alcohol.

## Teen Pregnancy

Although the number of teen pregnancies is declining, the U.S. still sports the highest rate of any industrialized nation. Both moms and kids have more difficulties such as preeclampsia (very high blood pressure during pregnancy), prenatal addiction, children with low birth rates, and children who are delinquent and have mental health and addiction issues. Children born to teen moms are statistically more likely to become teen moms themselves.

**Family therapy** appears to be the best treatment of choice for those with eating disorders.

# SOCIAL AND CULTURAL FOUNDATIONS

**Culture** is defined as habits, customs, art, religion, science, and the political behavior of a given group of people during a given period of time. Cultures are said to be **dynamic**: each culture changing or evolving at its own rate. The dominant or major culture in a country is the **macroculture**, often contrasted with the smaller **microculture**. Learning the behaviors and expectations of a culture is known as **acculturation**. **Cultural humility** is a way to view **cultural competency** as an ongoing process and not an end product. The construct suggests you need a lifelong commitment to self-evaluation; fix power imbalances where they should not exist; and develop partnerships to advocate for others.

**Universal culture** implies that we are all genetically and biologically similar **"biological sameness"** (i.e., we all need air, food and water); **national culture** can determine our language, political views, and our laws; **regional culture** gives us the behavior for a certain region; and **ecological culture** where factors such as earthquakes, floods, and food supply may influence our behavior.

- **Racism** occurs when one race views itself as superior to others. A given race has a set of genetically transmitted characteristics such as white, African American, or Asian.
- **Ethnocentrism** means that a given group sees itself as the standard by which other ethnic groups are measured.
- **Emic versus etic** distinctions. In the emic approach the counselor helps the client understand his or her culture. In the etic approach the counselor focuses on the similarities in people; treating people as being the same.
- **Autoplastic–alloplastic dilemma**. Autoplastic implies that the counselor helps the client change to cope with his or her

environment. Alloplastic occurs when the counselor has the client try to change the environment.

- **Tests** and nosological systems such as the *DSM* can have a Eurocentric or Euro-American bias.
- **Paralanguage** implies that the client's tone of voice, loudness, vocal inflections, and speed of delivery, silence, and hesitation must be taken into consideration. It is part of the study of nonverbal communication and is usually considered more accurate than verbal communication.
- **Low context communication versus high context communication** was postulated by anthropologist **Edward T. Hall.** Low context implies that there will be a precise *explicit* verbal explanation and possibly repetition such as summarizing at the end of a class, meeting, or a group counseling session. Popular in the U.S., UK, Canada, and Germany. High context communication is *implicit*. It is common in the Middle East, Italy, Spain, and Asian countries. It relies on nonverbal over verbal, respect for tradition and the past, and is readily understood by others in the culture with a shared frame of reference.
- **Stereotyping** is the act of thinking that all people of a group are alike. Stereotypes can be good or bad.
- **Prejudice** occurs when we have an opinion based on insufficient evidence.
- **Androgynous/androgyny** is the notion that psychologically healthy people possess both masculine and feminine characteristics.
- **Proxemics** addresses the issue of personal space, also known as **spatial relations**. A counselor who sits too close to a client, for example, may make the client uncomfortable. Communication and social relations are impacted by proxemics.
- **Means tests** determine whether a client is eligible for a social program or benefit such as temporary assistance for needy families (TANF) or food stamps. Income and assets such as bank accounts are often used to make this determination. Often contrasted with **social insurance programs** such as social security for which an extremely wealthy person could still be qualified.
- **Social comparison theory**, popularized by early research conducted by **Leon Festinger**, simply postulates that we evaluate our behaviors and accomplishments by comparing ourselves to others. Festinger is also well known for his **cognitive dissonance**

**theory**, asserting that individuals will change their beliefs to match their behavior when there is a mismatch. This reduces the tension created by the initial inconsistency.

- **Confirmation bias** is to acknowledge information that supports your point of view and ignore that which does not.
- Counselors strive to understand a client's **worldview** (the way the client sees the world due to attitudes, value systems, and beliefs).
- **Socioeconomic factors** must be taken into account. Nearly 15% of the U.S. population lives below the poverty threshold set by the U.S. government.
- **Social comparison theory** means we compare ourselves with others to evaluate ourselves. **High self-monitoring individuals** care about their self-image and what others think of them.
- The affiliation statement **misery loves company (or literally miserable company!)** is often true according to **Stanley Schachter**.
- Women are more apt to talk to others (especially other women) in a social situation.
- **Anglo-Conformity Theory** asserts that people from other cultures would do well to forget about their heritage and try to become like those in the dominant macroculture.
- **The Five-Stage Atkinson, Morten, and Sue's Racial/Cultural Identity Development Model (R/CID)** aka the Minority Identity Model: (1) **conformity** (lean toward dominant culture and prefer a counselor from the dominant culture); (2) **dissonance** (question and confusion, prefer a counselor from a minority group); (3) **resistance and immersion** (reject the dominant culture while accepting one's own culture); (4) **introspection** (mixed feelings related to the previous stage, prefer a counselor from one's own racial/ethnic group); and (5) **synergetic articulation and awareness** (stop racial and cultural oppression, prefers a counselor with a similar attitude or worldview over merely a counselor who is the same race/ ethnicity, but has different beliefs). Not everyone goes through all stages and some individuals never progress beyond the second or third stage. An individual can also go backward.

## MULTICULTURAL COUNSELING

**Please keep in mind that the descriptions below are broad generalizations, since no group is truly homogenous, and attributing the below statements to every or all members of that particular group can be damaging to developing a meaningful, helpful client-counselor relationship. The trend is clearly moving away from saying this group is this way or that group is that way. I've only included these brief descriptions here and a few other places in this book inasmuch as an occasional question of this ilk may still appear on a comprehensive exam since similar ones do appear in some of the major texts.**

1. **Native Americans** (or American Indians) and **Alaska Natives** may keep their suffering private, speak with few words and hesitate often. Young males have a high suicide rate. They do not engage in eye contact while talking or listening, do not live by the clock, and tend to emphasize spirituality. Consider counseling them in their own homes. Storytelling combined with advice giving is often effective. Family therapy, and extended family therapy, are often the treatment of choice.

2. **African Americans** may like to be taught concrete skills and strategies for change. Systems-based family therapy that includes the nuclear and extended family, short-term counseling, and behavioral modalities are effective. Counselor self-disclosure, topics related to spirituality and group work may be beneficial. Multicultural experts assert that African Americans often drop out of treatment too soon and thus it is important to create trust during the initial sessions. Some experts worry that "schizophrenia has become a black disease" because of misdiagnosis/overdiagnosis.

3. **Asian Americans** have been called the most diverse group and characterized as patriarchal. Academic and professional success is valued. They may speak very low and desire assertiveness training (because Asian Americans often do not express angry thoughts and feelings) or other behavioral strategies. Family therapy is often used to take the focus off the individual and more on the family as a whole, but do whatever is possible to ensure the client will not feel shame. Ideally, the counselor is seen as a trained authority figure and this population is known to have a high dropout rate *so*

*the counselor's authority and expertise should be evident during the
initial session.* Do not joke with the client. Degrees and certificates
in the office and the use of professional titles (e.g., "I'm Dr. Lewis,
the Program Director") may be desirable. Stress is often brought
on via the idea of the **model minority**, which suggests that Asian
Americans are extremely successful and intellectual. An Asian
American therapist will help with client retention in some instances.

4.  **Latino/Latina Americans** often benefit from catharsis and
    abreaction (getting feelings out). Psychodrama techniques, active-
    directive family therapy with specific suggestions, and calling
    clients by their first names may well facilitate therapy. Separation
    from one's family of origin is not generally a goal of therapy.
    Currently the number of Latino/Latina counselors is low, as is the
    number of Latinos/Latinas who use the mental health system.
    Latino/Latina counselors, as well as counselors from other
    cultures, can feel uncomfortable counseling whites if they don't
    associate with them on a day–to-day basis or if they are not familiar
    with the dominant U.S. culture. Psychological symptoms often
    manifest themselves as physical issues. A Latino/Latina therapist
    will improve client retention in some instances.

5.  **Gay and lesbian couples** raise children who are as happy and
    possess good cognitive and social skills. In every area, including
    mental health, these children fare as well as children raised by
    heterosexual couples.

6.  **Sexual orientation, identity, and terminology related to sexual
    questions on your exam. LGBTQ** is the acronym for Lesbian,
    Gay, Bisexual, Transgender, and Questioning (unsure regarding
    source of attraction/identity). **Transgender:** Individuals whose
    gender expression or identity does not match gender assigned at
    birth. Transgender persons can be gay, asexual, bisexual, lesbian, or
    heterosexual. **Pansexual:** Attracted to persons regardless of gender.
    **Cisgender/Cissexual:** Gender assignment, body, and identity all
    match. **Homophobia/Biphobia/Transphobia:** Exaggerated,
    irrational fear of, or discrimination against, homosexual, bisexual,
    and transgender persons and behavior. **Internalized Homophobia/
    Biphobia/Transphobia:** Self-hatred and/or shame over
    homosexual, bisexual, or transgender identity and/or attraction.
    **Transgender, MTF:** Gender assigned at birth was male, but person
    identifies as a female. **Transgender, FTM:** Person was assigned a

female gender at birth, but currently identifies as male. **Crossdresser:** Wearing or dressing up in clothes worn by a different gender.

The word **machismo** may be used to describe the view that women are subservient to men and that men are expected to provide for the family.

**Colorism** is discrimination predicated on skin tone or skin color. Colorism is often perpetrated by persons of the same racial or ethnic group, for example, African American on African American.

## Five Famous Experiments in Social Psychology

1. **Phillip Zimbardo (1971 Stanford Prison Experiment):** A situation can control behavior as well as assigned roles, such as telling subjects to be a guard or a prisoner. Would not be ethical today.
2. **Muzafer Sherif (Robbers' Cave Experiment):** Two opposing groups of boys ended up working together because they were both attempting to solve the same problem (called a superordinate goal).
3. **Solomon Asch/Asch Situation (1950s studies regarding conformity based on the length of a line):** In a social or group situation people would sell out and agree with the opinions of others about the length of the line even when they knew the individuals were clearly wrong!
4. **John Darley and Bibb Latané (Bystander Effect/Apathy):** The greater the number of people in a group, the *less* likely they are to assist a person in need (and will be slower if they do intervene)! The 1964 case of Kitty Genovese is seen as the quintessential example. Also billed as "group inhibition for helping."
5. **Stanley Milgram (1963 Obedience to authority experiment):** Sixty-five percent of subjects gave painful electrical shocks to innocent victims when instructed to do so by an authority figure! None stopped even when a participant said she or he had heart trouble! Some experts insist this could explain the Holocaust.

## THE HELPING RELATIONSHIP

There are over 400 approaches to psychotherapy and counseling worldwide. Most counselors claim they use several approaches and thus would be classified as eclectic or integrative. **Very important:** Research illuminates that the therapeutic relationship contributes to 30% of the client outcome.

## The Helping Myth

Research demonstrates that having a counselor and a client of the same gender and ethnicity does not necessarily produce a better therapeutic relationship. The data are not strong and clearly more research is necessary.

## Happiness

Most people overestimate the impact an event will have on their degree of happiness or unhappiness. For example, individuals believe that marriage or winning the lottery will make them happy. The happiness boost for marriage lasts roughly two years, while the increase from winning the lottery spans about six months. In general, people are poor at forecasting affective/ emotional reactions.

## Psychotherapy and Counseling are Cost Effective

**Cost–Benefit Analysis (CBA)** reveals that therapy reduces mental health expenditures in the community. Unfortunately, insurance and managed care firms primarily push medication as a first line of treatment for mental health issues.

## Sigmund Freud's Psychodynamic Psychoanalysis

Psychoanalysis is a theory of personality and a form of psychotherapy. It is a long-term form of treatment often lasting three to five years or more. In classical analysis the patient (the analysand) is seen four of five times per week. This form of therapy is said to be historic since it focuses on the past.

- Patient is asked to engage in **free association**, which is saying whatever comes to mind.
- **Dreams** are very important and generally viewed as a process for wish fulfillment. Research does not support the Freudian wish fulfillment notion.
- **Unconscious material** is examined.
- **Freud emphasized ego defense mechanisms: repression** (most important)—something that is too painful to face is totally forgotten; **displacement**—taking your anger out on a safe target rather than the source of your anger; **projection**—you can't accept a quality about yourself so you attribute it to others (i.e., you think that you are looking out a window but you are really looking in a mirror); **reaction formation**—you deny an unacceptable unconscious impulse by acting in the opposite manner; **sublimation** (often cited with career counseling)—you express an unacceptable impulse in a socially acceptable manner; **rationalization**—when a person overrates or underrates a reward or outcome; **identification**—joining a feared person (such as a gang) to relieve your anxiety; **suppression or denial** (not unconscious or automatic)—occurs when you purposely don't think of a situation.
- **Transference** is also a key principle. The analysand (client) behaves as if the analyst is a parent or caretaker from the past.
- The discharge of repressed emotions is called **abreaction or catharsis**.
- According to Freud's structural theory, the personality has three systems: a **superego** (the moral seat of the mind housing two entities the conscience and the ego ideal); **the ego** or reality principle that balances the id and the superego; and **the id**, which houses biological forces, especially sex and aggression: The id operates on the pleasure principle striving for immediate gratification and tension reduction.
- **Eros** is the life instinct; **thanatos** the death instinct.
- Critics charge that Freud used only case studies to test analysis rather than using true scientific experiments.

## Carl Jung's Analytic Psychology

Carl Jung broke away from Freud in 1914 because he felt Freud overemphasized the role of sexuality. His approach, like Freud's, is psychodynamic.

- The unconscious has two parts: a **personal unconscious** (very similar to what Freud postulated) and **the collective unconscious** (an unconscious that one inherits which is common to all individuals). The collective unconscious is composed of archetypes passed down through the ages.
- Archetypes include the **persona**: a social mask the person wears. To explain gender, Jung cites the **animus** or the masculine side of the female and the **anima** or feminine side of the male. Individuals are said to be **androgynous**, having both male and female characteristics. He also speaks of the shadow or the so-called dark side of the personality related to animal instincts. **The self** is symbolized via a mandala (a magic circle in Sanskrit) or a balance between the personal unconscious and the collective unconscious.
- Jung created the **extroversion/introversion typologies**. Jung felt that we possess both; however, one is dominant. The Myers–Briggs Type Indicator (MBTI) has its roots in Jung's work.
- *Individuation* was Jung's term for becoming a unique human being.

## Alfred Adler's Individual Psychology

Alfred Adler broke away from Freud to create his own theory. Adler's individual psychology is a psychodynamic approach that focuses on the fact that behavior is one's unconscious attempt to compensate for feelings of inferiority. An individual constructs a lifestyle which is chosen.

- Adler stressed the **"will to power"** to generate feelings of superiority.
- The theory adheres to the principle of fictional finalism or the notion that behavior is motivated primarily by future opportunities rather than the past.

- Adler felt **birth order** (also called place in the family constellation) was important. First-born children are conservative leaders. Second-born kids tend to be more competitive and rebellious. Sibling interaction can have a greater impact than parent–child interaction. Since Adler felt behavior is highly influenced by future goals rather than one's past, this is a **teleological theory**.

## Behaviorism, Behavior Modification, and Behavior Therapy

**Key reminder:** Newer exams often refer to **behavior modification** as **applied behavior analysis (ABA)**. ABA looks at observable behavior, rather than hypothetical constructs. **The key concept is that behavior is learned and not pathological.**

John B. Watson coined the word *behaviorism* while Arnold Lazarus created the term *behavior therapy*. Counselors who use these approaches assume that behavior is based on learning rather than insight into the unconscious mind. The criticisms of behavior therapy are that it does not yield insight, it treats symptoms not the root cause, and it can be manipulative and often changes behavior but not underlying feelings.

- **B. F. Skinner's radical behaviorism** purports that behavior is molded solely by its consequences. This paradigm is known as operant or instrumental conditioning.
- **A positive reinforcer** is a stimulus that raises the probability that a behavior will be repeated. The reinforcer must come after the behavior (or operant).
- **Negative reinforcers** also raise behavior. For example, a recruit in the military makes a bunk bed to avoid being yelled at by a drill instructor. All reinforcers, whether positive or negative, raise behavior. All reinforcers are said to follow or come *after* a behavior (e.g., a youngster gets a prize after she completes a math problem).
- **Albert Bandura** speaks of **social learning theory**. Here the person's own behavior increases when he or she sees somebody else getting reinforced for it; also referred to as vicarious learning or modeling.
- **Punishment** is intended to lower behavior by suppressing it.

- Behaviorists champion role-playing (e.g., assertive behavior).
- **Extinction** (such as time-out) will lower behavior after an initial extinction burst or response burst.
- **Ratio schedules of reinforcement** rely on work output whereas **interval schedules** rely on time. **Ratio schedules are more effective than interval schedules.**
- **Continuous reinforcement** occurs when each behavior is reinforced. Good when first learning a new behavior.
- **Intermittent reinforcement or variable reinforcement** occurs some of the time, but not all of the times the desired behaviors are reinforced (e.g., a child gets a treat for every third math problem he completes). **Variable reinforcement is more effective than a fixed schedule where you always reinforce in the same manner (e.g., after every instance of the behavior).**
- **Shaping with successive approximations** is reinforcing small chunks of behavior that lead to the desired behavior.
- **Differential reinforcement of other behaviors (DRO)/ differential reinforcement of alternative behavior (DRA)** takes place when the helper reinforces behaviors other than the dysfunctional behavior to reduce the dysfunctional **target behavior** (e.g., you want a child to quit talking in class so you give him a gold star only when he is doing his work and not talking). Procedure relies on reinforcement and extinction.
- In Skinnerian **operant conditioning**, the behavior is affected by the consequences that come after the behavior.
- **Ivan Pavlov** popularized what is now known as **classical conditioning**. **John B. Watson's** work was also significant. Behavior modification/applied behavior analysis is generally based on **Skinner**, while behavior therapy usually has its roots in **Pavlov**. **Interventions based on classical conditioning include: sensate focus, systematic desensitization, flooding (aka in vivo exposure with response prevention or deliberate exposure with response prevention), implosive therapy, and assertiveness training.**
- **Classical or respondent conditioning = learning by pairing things together.**

- **Operant conditioning based on the work of Skinner and Thorndike = learning by consequences occurring after a behavior.**
- **Joseph Wolpe's systematic desensitization** can be conducted individually or in a group to curb fears and abate anxiety. Wolpe believed his technique of counterconditioning was based on Pavlov and relied on relaxation and imagining feared stimuli. That said, newer research using dismantling (which deconstructs a procedure) revealed that relaxation is not necessary and therefore it is extinction and not counterconditioning that is making the difference. Along those same lines, it has also been discovered that Dr. Francine Shapiro's **eye movement desensitization and reprocessing therapy (EMDR)** can be effective for ameliorating conditions caused by trauma or disturbing events *without the eye movement*, once again indicating that extinction is likely the curative factor.
- Behaviorists may also use **implosive therapy** where the client imagines scary or feared stimuli in the safety of the counselor's office.
- **Biofeedback** devices are used to enhance the client's self-control of the autonomic nervous system. Examples include heart rate, brain waves, or warming cold hands with thermal training for migraine headaches or Raynaud's Phenomenon. This is a form of operant conditioning. Biofeedback is popular in **neurocounseling** in which the practitioner attempts to understand the brain's role as it relates to counseling.
- **Criticisms of behavior therapy:** Does not yield insight; mechanistic; treats symptoms and not the cause; can be manipulative; generally ignores developmental stages; often changes behavior but not underlying feelings. This approach deals with behaviors rather than the whole person.
- **Hint:** A great way to determine whether a question is referring to reflexive classical conditioning or Skinner's operant conditioning is to ask yourself a simple question: Is there a reflex with every member of the species who is not disabled? If the answer is *yes*, then it is most likely Pavlovian conditioning (e.g., all dogs salivate (an unconditioned/unlearned response or UR) when they see meat (an unconditioned stimulus or US)—so it's Pavlovian).

## Carl R. Rogers's Person-Centered Humanistic Therapy

This approach has also been called client-centered, Rogerian, nondirective, or self-theory. The basic notion (a very positive one) is that human beings can self-actualize and reach their full natural potential in a therapeutic setting that fosters growth; classified as an optimistic form of therapy.

- **Three conditions for effective helping:** The therapist must show empathy; be genuine/congruent; and display unconditional positive regard (UPR).
- **Empathy is not sympathy! It is the ability to subjectively understand the client's world in the here and now—to walk in his or her shoes—and convey this to the client. Robert Carkhuff** created a five-point empathy scale with a level-five response as the best response.
- The counselor must be genuine/congruent. The counselor cannot be a phony. Words must match (i.e., be congruent) with actions.
- The counselor accepts the client regardless of his or her behavior. This does not imply that you necessarily agree with the client. This is called **unconditional positive regard**.
- The counselor will often use reflection or open-ended questions.
- Counselor strives to improve congruence so that the person is more like his or her ideal self.
- Rogerians are not big fans of traditional diagnosis and testing. Moreover, they do not believe in the unconscious. Humans can control their own behavior. Critics are concerned that this approach is too optimistic and may not be the treatment of choice for severely disturbed individuals or very young children. **Natalie Rogers**, daughter of Carl Rogers, created **person-centered expressive arts therapy (PCEA)**. This method strives to generate a creative connection with inner feelings via such things as movement, sound, art, writing, and journaling, which are shared with the helper.

## Albert Ellis's Active-Directive Rational Emotive Behavior Therapy (REBT)

Previously known as RET, this is a cognitive-behavioral (CBT) form of therapy. Change your thinking (cognitions) and you can change your life. Essence of the treatment captured in the saying of Epictetus, a first-century Stoic philosopher, "Men are disturbed not by things, but of the view which they take of them." Irrational beliefs (IBs) are replaced by rational beliefs (RBs) via the counseling process.

- Uses the **ABC or ABCDE model of personality**. A is an activating event. B is the client's belief system. C is the emotional consequence. At D the counselor disputes the irrational belief at B. E is a new emotional consequence that occurs when B becomes rational.
- Humans have an innate tendency to think in an irrational, illogical, unscientific manner. Thought is referred to as self-talk or internal verbalizations.
- Shoulds, oughts, musts, terriblizing, and awfulizing causes irrational thought.
- This is an active directive form of therapy utilizing lots of homework, **bibliotherapy** and even **rational imagery (RI)**.
- Critics charge that the approach does not emphasize feelings, the counselor client relationship, and that REBT is mechanistic or even sterile. It may be too complex for those with psychosis or thought disorders.

## Aaron T. Beck's Cognitive Therapy

Beck's cognitive therapy is similar to REBT, emphasizing that the client has **automatic thoughts which are distortions of reality** such as polarized black or white thinking, overgeneralizing based on a single event, personalization—wrongly attributing an event to yourself and drawing conclusions without real evidence. Not as confrontational as Ellis. Socratic questioning is sometimes employed. Clients are urged to keep a record of dysfunctional thoughts.

## Fritz Perls's Gestalt Therapy

This **experiential/existential** approach focuses on the **here and now** in an attempt to help the client become whole again. Gestalt is an experiential form of therapy and it relies on dream work, role-playing, confrontation, the top dog/underdog concept, hot seat, and the empty chair technique. Modern gestalt therapists are not as abrupt with clients as Perls. The therapy is now considered a softer gentler treatment.

- **Gestalt** is a German word that basically means "**organized whole**." The view of human nature is that humans want to be self-actualized and complete (whole).
- **Dreams** are the royal road to integration. Counselor asks client to recount the dream as if it is occurring in the present moment.
- **What and how questions** are used more than why questions (e.g. "What is your foot doing now?").
- **Goal** is for the client to take responsibility and achieve *awareness* in the here and now. **Doing is emphasized over just talking about problems.**
- **Laura Perls** (Fritz Perls's wife) helped develop the approach and made it more popular with women in therapy.

Critics charge that this approach is "gimmicky," puts little or no stock in diagnosis and psychological testing, and at times is "antitheoretical." On occasion, the approach can lead to self-centeredness.

## Eric Berne's Transactional Analysis (TA)

A here-and-now approach that took Freudian terminology and made it fun and easy to understand. The theory took into account transactions between individuals. It is often combined with gestalt. Critics charge this is like mixing water and oil since TA is cognitive and gestalt is experiential. Others say this is desirable since the two complement each other. The person unconsciously develops a life plan at an early age called a **life script**. **Script analysis** assumes the person is at least partially living the preprogrammed script. The script concept is also used in narrative therapy.

- **Ego states** are the **Parent, Adult, and Child (PAC)**. These states roughly correspond to Freud's superego, ego, and id.
- Uses **Tom Harris's life positions**. I'm OK, you're OK (healthy); I'm OK, you're not OK; I'm not OK, you're OK; and I'm not OK, you're not OK.
- Games are played to avoid intimacy. Somebody is always hurt in a game.
- **Stephen B. Karpman's drama triangle (aka Karpman's triangle).** A person changes his or her position from victim to persecutor to rescuer during the discussion.

Critics note that TA promotes game calling.

## William Glasser's New Reality Therapy with Choice Theory

This therapy focuses on present behavior. Clients are taught that they create their own personal reality with the behaviors they choose. Glasser believes that "**Behavior is the control of our perceptions**" and that a **success identity** is the result of being loved and accepted. Glasser has been criticized for downplaying the role of the environment in terms of impacting ethnic minorities. Reality therapy has also been deemed "weak" in terms of not dealing with dreams, the past, or traumatic memories. According to Glasser, psychiatric medicines or "brain drugs" are not the answer. **This paradigm challenges the medical model of psychiatry.**

- **The eight steps of reality therapy**: build a relationship with the client; focus on present moment behavior; help the client to evaluate his or her current behavior; develop a contract with an action plan; have the client commit to the plan; accept no excuses; do not use punishment; and refuse to give up on your client. The approach emphasizes short-term treatment and is very concrete.
- **Psychological needs include** belonging, power, freedom, and fun.
- When Glasser contributed to my book *Favorite Counseling and Therapy Techniques* he said, "We are responsible for what we do, and we choose all we do."

- **Robert Wubbolding** expanded the theory of reality therapy with his introduction of **WDEP**. **W** for **wants** (belonging, freedom, fun, belonging, power, and independence), **D** for **direction and doing** (is the client doing something to take him or her in the best direction?) **E** for **evaluation or self-evaluation** (how is the behavior working for the client?), and finally, **P** for **plan**. Plan should be immediate, attainable, and measurable.

Critics charge that reality therapy is a bit too simplistic, does not take into account developmental stages, and has changed its focus over the years.

## Lynn P. Rehm's Self-Control Therapy

This is a self-control behavioristic paradigm of therapy which relies on self-monitoring, evaluation, and self-reinforcement.

## Hypnosis

Helpful for pain, insomnia, anxiety, and habit control such as overeating and smoking. Can also be used to elicit repressed memories, however, the memories are often dubbed as "pseudomemories," meaning they are not accurate. Hypnosis is a controversial modality.

## Feminist/Non-Sexist Therapy

No single theorist is the founder. Has its origins in the women's movement of the 1960s. Some similarities to multicultural counseling. A strong focus on women's rights, sex-role stereotyping, and the oppression of women. Approach postulates that most therapies have an **androcentric bias** (centered on men) and are not ideal and sometimes harmful to women.

## Postmodern Social Constructivist Theories

Social constructionism emphasizes that realities are socially constructed. Brief therapy and narrative therapy are constructivist approaches.

### *Narrative Therapy (NT) by Michael White (Australia) and David Epston (Auckland, New Zealand)*

Narrative therapy postulates that individuals construct their lives by stories they tell about themselves and stories others create about them. Stories create meaning and this becomes the client's identity.

- Therapy consists of the client describing his or her life experiences and then rewriting or reauthoring the narrative in a new way.
- A narrative therapist externalizes the problem in his or her progress notes and sends it to the client as a letter between sessions.
- Rather than saying "You are a cocaine addict," a narrative therapist will tell the client, "Cocaine has been trying to wreck your life." Again, clients reauthor their lives with new stories and fresh language.
- The narrative therapist sees him- or herself as a consultant or collaborator with the client. Some cultures want an expert therapist, and thus (at times) this can create a problem for multicultural counseling.
- Often recommended—with or without CBT—for working with **refugees** (those forced to leave their home country to escape a natural disaster, war, or persecution) and **immigrants** (persons who make a voluntary decision to leave their native country and want to reside permanently in another country) who want to tell their stories. Journaling works well with this population and more disclosure is generally possible in individual rather than group sessions. **Bilingual counselors** should allow the clients to choose the language spoken in the interview and language switching is often appropriate.

## Solution-focused brief therapy (SFBT) Steve de Shazer and Insoo Kim Berg

SFBT focuses on solutions and *not* on an understanding of the problem. The focus is on exceptions to the rule—what is working.

- Using so-called exception questions: a client who is depressed is asked: "When aren't you depressed?"
- Goals are small and realistic. The client is also asked the miracle question: "If a miracle took place while you were sleeping, how would you know the problem was solved? How would things be different?"
- SBFT also uses formula first session task (FFST). This is a homework assignment prescribed after the first session.
- Recently, this approach has gained popularity in group treatment settings.

Brief therapy (BT) is becoming the norm in many instances since **managed care firms** (hell-bent on cutting costs!) often **restrict the number of sessions** the client can attend. Most counselors dislike managed care, feeling that the managed care company is micromanaging their practice. In some states managed care firms cannot be sued for their actions. Insurance and managed care policies are responsible for the fact that many counselors spend as much time dealing with business issues as they do actually counseling their clients. On the **positive side**, managed care forces counselors to look at outcome measures.

## Psychotherapy Integration by Frederick Thorne

Psychotherapy integration uses strategies from a number of counseling schools. Instead of merely using techniques from the approaches in eclecticism, the integrative approach assumes that using or integrating two or more theories will often produce results that are superior to a single school of therapy. Today support is mounting for this approach.

## Family Counseling

Family counseling asserts that the pathology resides in the family system and not in an individual. The client is the family and *not* the identified patient. Family therapists believe in **circular** rather than **linear** causality. **First-order change** occurs when a client makes a superficial change to deal with a problem, but the change does not alter the underlying structure of the family. **Second-order change** alters the underlying structure and thus makes a difference that is longer lasting.

**Negative feedback loops** are not necessarily bad, but keep the family in homeostasis and functioning the way the family always has. **Positive feedback loops** induce change in the family system.

## Case Integration

Case integration takes place when several helpers from the same agency or different agencies work together without duplicating services to help an individual client.

## Milieu Therapy

Milieu therapy urges helpers to change the client's entire environment (social and physical) to help the client. Hence, treatment is not limited to counseling sessions. In most instances, this takes place in inpatient treatment facilities.

## Famous Family Therapists

**Nathan Ackerman** used the psychoanalytic or psychodynamic approach.

Experimental conjoint family therapist **Virginia Satir** popularized the notion that in times of stress, family members use four inept patterns of communication. The placator (who tries to please everybody in the family); the blamer; the reasonable analyzer (who intellectualizes); and the irrelevant distracter (who interrupts and changes the topic to something irrelevant).

**Experimentalist Carl Whitaker** could be very wild, radical, and creative, and often utilized a co-therapist.

**Murray Bowen** is a key name in intergenerational therapy. His approach is often referred to as extended family systems therapy.

- **Triangulation** (also referred to as triangles) occurs when two people who are stressed, bring in a third party to reduce the dyad's stress level and restore equilibrium.
- **Genograms** are actually graphic diagrams of the family from a minimum of three generations.
- **Fusion** is a blurring of the psychological boundaries between the self and others. A person driven by fusion can't separate thinking and feeling well.
- **Differentiation** (the opposite of fusion) is the ability to control reason over emotion. People often secure their level of differentiation from a multigenerational transmission process.

**Salvador Minuchin** is the leading name behind **structural family therapy**. The technique of **joining** or blending in with the family is used. The therapist uses a popular strategy of joining, known as **mimesis**, to imitate or copy the family's communication and patterns. The therapy proposes that changes in the family system, subsystems, and family organization must take place in order for individual family members to resolve their systems. Structural therapy is directive and performed in the here and now.

**Jay Haley and Cloe Madanes** are powerful names in **strategic family counseling** (also called the **MRI model** and the **communications model**). In this paradigm, the therapist gives **directives or prescriptions**, often **paradoxical** (e.g., telling a client who is afraid he will shake, to shake as much as he can; actually prescribing the symptom). Reframing and relabeling problems is common in this modality. This approach warns us that **double-bind communication** (e.g., a parent telling a child she loves her while beating her severely) could cause serious psychopathology, even schizophrenia.

- **Other brief strategic therapists** that champion paradox or prescribing the symptom in individual or family therapy include: Milton H. Erickson, Steven de Shazer, Bill O'Hanlon, Paul Watzlawick, Don Jackson, and Michelle Weiner Davis.
- **Solution-focused brief therapists (SBFT)** speak of first-order change, which is superficial, and second-order change, which includes actual changes in the rules and structure of the organization.

**SFBT or BT, brief therapy, is not the same as crisis intervention.** Crisis intervention is used for persons who are experiencing an expected *normal* reaction to stress. Therapy on the other hand is aimed at reducing abnormal and pathological behaviors and symptoms.

**The Milan Model** uses a treatment team with a one-way mirror.

**Consultation** occurs when you voluntarily assist a counselor or counselors (known as consultees) who will be helping clients.

- Contact with the helpees is indirect.
- Gerald Caplan is known as the father of mental health consultation.
- Edgar Schein's purchase of expertise model (where you buy the person's information and knowledge); his doctor–patient model (here you aren't sure what the problem is, so you hire an expert to diagnose and treat it); and his process consultation model (where the consultant helps the consultee with the process).

**Process models** focus on the process while **content models** focus on the imparting knowledge to the consultee.

## Brain Chemicals and Neurotransmitters Related to Neuroscience

- **Serotonin** mood. Most prescription medicines given to clients for mental health issues impact serotonin (e.g., SSRI (selective serotonin reuptake inhibitor) drugs or the old tricyclic antidepressants).
- **Dopamine** excess is thought to fuel schizophrenia, while very low levels are implicated in Parkinson's disease. Some experts believe addictive behaviors such as gambling can flood the brain with dopamine.
- **Lithium** is a trace mineral or rare earth. It helps stabilize mood, especially in clients with bipolar conditions. An excess caused by prescription dosages can cause liver damage or tremors.

The **left hemisphere of the brain** is logical, verbal, and analytic, but the **right hemisphere of the brain** is emotional, creative, and artistic. This notion is still controversial.

The **microbiome** or balance of good bacteria (such as probiotics) and bad bacteria in the gastrointestinal tract can affect our mood, digestion, and general health. **This is sometimes called the gut–brain connection.**

## Popular Psychiatric Medicines

**Anxiety: Benzodiazepines**—Xanax, Librim, Klonopin Ativan, and Valium.

**Depression: Selective serotonin reuptake inhibitors (SSRIs)**—Prozac, Zoloft, Luvox, Celexa, Paxil, and Lexapro. **Selective and norepinephrine reuptake inhibitors (SNRIs)**—Cymbalta, Pristiq, and Effexor. **Tricyclics (TCAs)**—Elavil, Tofranil, and Pamelor.

**ADHD:** Ritalin and Concerta (both classified as methylphenidate), Adderall, and Vyvanse (also used for binge eating). **Note:** the CDC now recommends behavior therapy for ADHD before using medication for children aged 6 years or under.

**Bipolar:** Risperdal, Zyprexa, Lithobid, Depakote, Tegretol, and Lithium.

**OCD:** Prozac, Paxil, Luvox, Zoloft, Anafranil, and Effexor.

**Panic disorder:** Ativan and Paxil.

**Antipsychotic/schizophrenia:** Abilify, Geodon, Risperdal, Clorzaril, and Zyprexa.

# GROUP COUNSELING

## Existential Therapy Expert and Psychiatrist Irvin Yalom Outlines 11 Reasons Groups Work So Well

1. **Altruism.** Giving help to others gives members a sense of well-being.
2. **Universality.** Simply the notion that you are not the only one in the world with a particular problem.

3. **Installation of hope.** In plain everyday English, the members expect the group to work.
4. **Catharsis.** Talking about your difficulties is beneficial.
5. **Group cohesiveness** or a sense of we-ness.
6. **Imitative behavior.** As you know, behaviorist Albert Bandura's social learning theory suggests that we learn by watching others. In this situation the members copy or model the leader and the other members.
7. **Family reenactment.** The group helps abet family of origin issues and feelings and the group allows you to work through them.
8. **Imparting information.** This could be advice or even psychodynamic insights.
9. **Interpersonal learning.** Members receive feedback regarding how their behavior affects others.
10. **Socialization techniques** such as feedback and instruction are helpful.
11. **Existential factors**, for example discovering that life can have meaning even if it is seemingly unjust and unfair at times.

Yalom is a proponent of working in the here and now and emphasizes the therapeutic alliance is a powerful ingredient. A client with anger management issues will express anger in therapy if he or she is in treatment long enough.

Yalom also wrote *Staring at the Sun: Overcoming the Terror of Death*. Freud noted that denial of sexual impulses can lead to symptoms. In a similar fashion, Yalom asserts denial of death leads to symptoms as well. Nightmares are often manifestations of one's fear of death.

## Groups

- Ideal size is five or six to eight members, with eight being preferable. Groups that are conducted for a long time (e.g., six months or more) can function effectively with up to 10 members. Size should be smaller with children. **Duration** can refer to the length of the group sessions or how long the group will run.

- **Groups can be open** (new members can join after the group begins) **or closed** (no new members can join after the group begins).
- A group can have a **single leader** or be led by **coleaders. Advantages of coleaders:** having two role models (perhaps two genders), more feedback, one leader can deal with the client if there is transference and two leaders can better see what is transpiring in the group. **Disadvantages:** leaders can work at cross-purposes, may have conflicting models of therapy, could be in a power struggle, and may each decide to charge the client a different fee.
- Group work is cost effective and the counselor can see more clients in the same period of time.
- Most experts believe in the **stage models** to explain development and dynamics: The **initial stage, the forming stage, or the orientation stage**—this is kind of the "get acquainted" stage; the **transition, conflict, or storming stage**—this is characterized by power struggles for control and resistance, and some members will rate their satisfaction as lower; the **working, productive, performing, or action stage**—here the group works toward goals in a cohesive manner; the **termination, closure, completion, or mourning and adjourning stage**—members must deal with saying goodbye. Members often experience feelings of improved insight, awareness, accomplishment, and enhanced self-esteem. Referrals for additional intervention may be prescribed.

Group member roles are positive, such as helping others and being a stellar role model. Other roles, such as monopolizing the group; intellectualizing too much; being silent; or attacking others are considered negative. The scapegoat is the member who is blamed for the group's problems. This term is also used in family therapy.

## Group Leadership Styles

Adept group leaders model appropriate behavior to enhance participation. This is especially important with resistant clients.

Leaders rely on a strategy called **pacing** to determine how rapidly the group progresses.

**Autocratic or authoritarian style** advocates making decisions for members. It is appropriate during a crisis or when a quick decision is in order but in most situations it will foster resentment.

**Laissez faire or hands-off style.** Here the leader has little involvement. This approach is appropriate when all members are very committed to a group outcome or goal.

**Democratic approach** allows input from members, including input into the decisions made. This is generally the best style.

**Speculative leaders** are often seen as charismatic. They rely on their personal power and charisma to move the group in a desirable direction. They are often adored and group members look up to them, though they are not peer oriented.

**Confrontive leadership style.** The facilitator reveals the impact that his behavior has on himself as well as the impact that other group members have on him.

- Research has not shown that the speculative style is superior to the confrontive style or vice versa. Whatever style the leader utilizes, he or she must not impose his or her personal values on group members.

## Types of Groups

1. **Psychoeducational/old name guidance groups** provide members with information relevant to their situation.
2. **Counseling groups** focus on conscious issues related to personal growth and development.
3. **Group therapy** (a term coined by Jacob Moreno who founded psychodrama) can focus on unconscious material, the past, and personality change.
4. **T-groups** (training groups) are often intended for business or personal motivation.
5. **Structured groups** are centered around certain issues, such as shyness or how to prepare for a job interview.

6. **Self-help groups/mutual help/support groups** (such as AA) are not led by a professional. These groups have been dubbed as support groups and those that follow the AA model are often called 12-step groups.

**The self-serving attribution bias in relation to groups.** When the group is productive or successful the person takes credit for it, but when the group is unproductive or not successful, it is the fault of others.

 **The leader is responsible for the safety of group members.** Exercises like hitting each other with styrofoam bats, or other ways of venting anger, are not only dangerous, but research shows they often increase rather than decrease aggression! In essence, the notion that catharsis is therapeutic is largely a myth.

 **The risky shift phenomenon**. Members make more risky decisions in a group than they would on an individual basis. **Group polarity** suggests that members of a group make more extreme decisions than they would individually.

 **ASGW Best Practice Guidelines** are intended to specifically help counselors apply ACA's Code of Ethics to group work. The guidelines stipulate a leader should have an evaluation plan to meet the requirements of organizations, regulatory bodies, and insurance companies when appropriate. **ASGW** has drafted *Multicultural and Social Justice Competence Principles for Group Workers*. The leader allows members to discuss diversity, power, privilege, and why social justice/advocacy issues are important.

 **Group members are not required to participate in an exercise or experiential activity** and can quit during the experience. It is the leader's job to clarify this upfront; however, the leader should explore why a participant did not wish to participate or stopped in the middle of the exercise.

 As group members get to know each other, spontaneous touching may occur. That said, **forced touching exercises** are not recommended and could cause negative feelings in some members (e.g., those who have been sexually abused).

## Lifestyle and Career Counseling Theories

Grad students and neophyte counselors often have a negative attitude toward learning about career counseling and do not want to engage in this practice. In reality, career counseling and personal counseling overlap. Nevertheless, career counseling is commonly seen as having less prestige than personal counseling and psychotherapy.

**Trait-and-factor theory (matching or actuarial approach).** Frank Parsons (father of guidance) was the author of the seminal work in the field, *Choosing a Vocation*. A client needs to know his or her personal attributes and interests or traits; appropriate occupations should be investigated; finally, match the client's traits to the occupation. E. G. Williamson expanded this theory to six steps: analysis, synthesis, diagnosis, prognosis, counseling, and follow-up. The trait-and-factor approach makes the assumption that there is a single best career goal for everyone. Many experts disagree with this assumption.

**Anne Roe** created a psychodynamic needs approach. Jobs meet our needs determined by our childhood satisfactions and frustrations. Occupations are categorized by six levels and eight fields. Our orientation toward or away from other people can influence our career choices.

**Eli Ginzberg, Sol Ginsburg, Sidney Axelrad, and John Herma** proposed a developmental theory in the 1950s with three periods: **fantasy** (birth to 11 years) in which play becomes work oriented; **tentative** (11–17 years); and **realistic** (17 years and up).

**David Tiedeman and Robert O'Hara** rely on a developmental approach. In their model, career development is commensurate with psychosocial development as delineated by Erik Erikson's stages.

**Donald Super** is well known for emphasizing the role of the **self-concept** in career and vocation choice and his **life rainbow**.

**John Holland's personality typology theory.** The six personality types are **realistic, investigative, artistic, social, enterprising, and conventional (RIASEC)**. He is also known for his assessment tools: the **Self-Directed Search, My Vocational Situation**, and the **Vocational Preference Inventory**.

**John Krumboltz, Anita Mitchell, and G. Brian Jones** theorized that career decision was based on **social learning theory**. Today Krumboltz leans toward behaviorism in general. Four factors impact career choice: genetics and special abilities; the environment and special events; learning experiences; and task-approach problem-solving skills.

**Linda S. Gottfredson** emphasized **circumscription** (the process of narrowing the acceptable alternatives) and **compromise** (realization that the client will not be able to implement their most preferred choices). The client adjusts aspirations to accommodate such things as hiring practices, family obligations, or educational programs. People sacrifice interests rather than sex-type or prestige. Theory created in the early 1980s.

**Social cognitive career theory (SCCT)** by Robert Lent, Steven Brown, and Gail Hackett helps complement other theories emphasizing the role of self-efficacy and cognitive processes.

**Mark Savickas** uses techniques popularized by narrative therapy to create a postmodern constructivist approach.

# CAREER CHOICE

**Computer-assisted career guidance** (CAGC) such as SIGI. To use CAGC, the counselor should:

1. Screen the client to make certain this modality and computer program or online program is appropriate.
2. Give the client an orientation to describe the pros and cons of the system.
3. Follow-up to make certain an appropriate plan of action is evident.

*Dictionary of Occupational Titles (DOT)* listed over 20,000 job titles; with nine digit codes for the occupation. The *DOT* has been replaced by **O\*NET** also known as O\*NET online. A text version of O\*NET known as *O\*NET Dot* or *O\*NET Dictionary of Occupational Titles* is available; however, as of this writing it is not published by the Department of Labor.

*OOH* or *Occupational Outlook Handbook* gives job trends for the future with salaries, and can be accessed over the Internet.

**Richard Bolles's** book, *What Color is Your Parachute?* is a fine tool for job hunting.

**Eighty percent** of all jobs are not advertised and thus job seekers need to network. This is referred to as **the hidden job market**.

- Key trend: women moving into careers that were traditionally occupied by males. **Sex-wage discrimination/earnings gap**: women make $0.80 for each dollar earned by men. African American women earn $0.68, and Latina women earn $0.60 for every dollar earned by white men.
- One in five workers still secure a job based on chance factors and 60% of all workers would like more information if they had to do it all over again. However, overall **college students are avoiding career counseling services**.
- **Underemployment** occurs when a person takes a job below his or her level of skill, expertise, and training (e.g., a PhD who works in an entry-level fast food position).
- **Dislocated worker** is a term that describes a person who is unemployed due to downsizing, a company relocation, or the fact that the company closed the business.
- **Displaced homemaker** describes women who enter or reenter the workforce after being at home. This often occurs after a divorce or the death of a partner or spouse.
- **Outsourcing** takes place when U.S. companies rely on labor from another country in order to save money (i.e., the salaries would be lower). This can also result in fewer jobs in the United States.
- **Online career counseling** is a growing trend. While helpful, the practice is not as effective as the traditional face-to-face model.
- The **average worker** has nine jobs by age 36.
- **Networking** helps clients secure jobs and can help them find **gay-friendly employers**.
- In two-parent families, if both parents work this is called a **dual-career or dual-income family**. Strictly speaking: **Dual earner**—there is no chance for advancement; **dual career**—consists of a managerial or professional position with the possibility for advancement.

**Supervisors** who rate workers often suffer from **rater bias**.

- When a supervisor erroneously rates the majority of workers as average, it is called the **central tendency bias**.
- **The recency effect** occurs when the rating reflects primarily the worker's recent performance (rather than the entire rating period) since this effect suggests we remember best things that are presented last.
- A supervisor generalizing about an employee based on a single characteristic (e.g., giving a worker who is kind a higher rating than a worker who is just as good but isn't kind) is the **halo effect**. Positive and negative halo effects are possible.
- Supervisors often rate workers higher if the supervisor hired that particular worker.
- **Quality circles.** Employees with identical or similar jobs meet as a group to solve problems and come up with solutions to help management.

**Job interviews, personality tests, and reference letters** are *not* excellent predictors of whether a person will do well in a job. **Structured job interviews** usually fare better than **unstructured job interviews**. The **contrast effect** suggests that if a job seeker is interviewed after a superb candidate he or she will not seem as desirable. On the other hand, if a very weak candidate is interviewed it will make the next job applicant appear more competent. **Interest inventories** do not predict job success well, but they do predict **job satisfaction**.

## ASSESSMENT AND TESTING

Tests are nearly as old as the profession of counseling, but agreement over whether tests are useful has varied a great deal. According to expert Anne Anastasi, a test is an objective standardized measure of behavior. **Ideally, tests measure and provide valid and reliable data regarding your clients so you can pick the effective modalities of treatment, referral, or placement.** Critics note that tests can be faked, are mechanical, often measure irrelevant factors, and can invade privacy. Testing can also create prejudice in the sense that the counselor perceives the client in a different manner.

**Standardized tests** have uniform procedures for scoring and administration. In addition, these instruments have validity, reliability, and norm data which has been investigated and analyzed. The ***Mental Measurements Yearbook* (*MMY*)** and ***Tests in Print* (*TIP*)** from the Buros Institute provide counselors with information on thousands of tests. Online versions are now available. Approximately 2,500 of the tests have been critically analyzed by Buros.

A score is "**raw**" if it is unaltered. Raw scores can be converted to **standard scores** (e.g., **t-scores, z-scores, percentile rank, standard deviation, or stanine**) so that the scores relate to the **normal bell curve**. The **range** is the highest score minus the lowest score (some exams will add 1 to the answer).

**Percentile rank** tells the counselor the percent of scores equal to or below the score you are investigating. Hence, a client who is at the 75th percentile scored equal to or better than 75% of the people who took the exam. *It does not necessarily imply that he or she got 75% of the answers correct since a score of 20% correct might be higher than 75% of the examinees!*

**Three measures of central tendency:** the **mean** or arithmetic average (e.g., if your gas bill for a year is $144, then your mean bill per month is $12 or 144 divided by 12); the **mode** is the most frequently occurring score or category: and the **median** or middle score when the data are ranked from highest to lowest. In a **normal curve** they all have the same point in the center of the bell shape. When a curve leans, we say it is **skewed**. If the tail points to the left, the curve is **negatively skewed**; if it points to the right, it is **positively skewed**.

**Standard deviation (SD)** is a measure of **variability or dispersion of scores**. Are the scores bunched up close to the mean or are the scores spread out? A standard deviation of 1 is a z-score or standard score of one. A standard deviation of -2 is a z-score of negative 2, and so on. **T-scores** have a mean of 50 and the standard deviation is 10. If your test asks: What is a t-score when the standard deviation is 2; the answer is 70. If it asks: What is the t-score for a standard deviation of -3; the answer is 20.

**Areas under the normal curve you should commit to memory. Sixty-eight percent** of the scores will fall between +/-1

SD from the mean; **95%** of all scores will fall between +/-2 SD; and **99.7%** of all scores fall between +/-3 SD. It is safe to say that virtually all scores fall between +/-3 SD of the mean. This is known as the **empirical 68-95-99.7 normal curve rule**.

**Validity** is the most important property of a psychological test. Does the test, test what it purports to test? The validity of standardized tests in our field is said to be on a par with instruments used in the medical field.

**Reliability:** Is the test consistent? Will it give the similar results if we administer it again and again. If an IQ test yields a score of 100 today and 130 for the same client tomorrow it is not valid!

A **reliable test** is not always valid, but a **valid test** is always reliable.

**Inter-rater reliability** describes the consistency of two or more raters. If two counselors read the same test reports and come up with the same diagnosis, then **inter-rater reliability or agreement** is high. If they come up with different diagnoses then it is low.

A test or instrument that is only **normed** on the majority culture is not appropriate for cultural minorities since it is misleading and could cause discrimination.

**Tests** can give a false positive or a false negative.

**Aptitude tests** predict **potential**. For example, a high score on an aptitude test for music doesn't imply that you are a great musician but with the correct training and practice you could excel in this area.

**Achievement tests** give you the current accomplishments, what has been learned or the level of performance achieved up to this point in time (e.g., she is reading at the sixth-grade level).

**Intelligence tests or IQ tests** such as the **Wechsler** or the **Binet** attempt to measure mental abilities. IQ tests are very controversial and have been a source of debate for counselors. Individual IQ tests are generally more accurate than group-administered measures.

**Power tests.** Time (slow performance) is not a factor like it is in so-called **speed tests**.

**Projective tests.** There is no correct answer. The client merely looks at an inkblot, a vague picture, or an incomplete sentence. The client's answer is assumed to be a projection of his or her personality. Thus two clients look at the same Rorschach Inkblot Card or TAT picture and see something totally different.

- Scoring projective tests is subjective. Thus one rater could score it differently than another rater. Again, this phenomenon is called inter-rater reliability.

**Regression to the mean** states that if a client scores exceptionally low or exceptionally high on a test, then the client with the low score will go up on the next administration; while the client with the high score will go down toward the mean or average. Chance factors or everyday luck probably influenced the first score.

**Diagnosis generally implies that a label is placed on the client using a classification system, generally the *DSM* as an assessment tool.** Insurance companies virtually always require a diagnosis with an *ICD* **diagnosis** before they will pay for treatment. Moreover, most other professionals (e.g., psychologists and psychiatrists) use diagnostic terminology and thus counselors need to use the same classification system and terminology.

Assessment also helps determine admissions/selection/placement to schools (think your GRE score or perhaps an IQ score used to determine whether a child should be in a gifted class) and treatment organizations. Finally, assessment can help you determine if your client is truly making progress or not.

**Computer-based tests** generally reduce costs, can provide immediate scoring, and cut the risk of scoring errors, when compared to traditional **paper and pencil tests**. However, because the Web is expanding so rapidly many measures on the Web have low validity and reliabilty.

**High-stakes assessment** occurs when a test (say the NCE if you wish to practice counseling or the CPCE if you wish to graduate!) is used to make important decisions about the future. Licensing exams fall into this category. Thus, without passing a driver's license test you cannot drive a motor vehicle.


## RESEARCH AND PROGRAM EVALUATION

Studies clearly indicate that only a small percentage of counselors actually conduct research or use research findings in their practice. Many counselors feel that research is virtually cold, impersonal, and irrelevant to their day-to-day practice and thus say that helping, rather than research, is their top priority. A gap between research and practice is evident. A high percentage of beginning master's level students actually resent having to take research and statistics courses. It is true that a lot of studies are not helpful to counselors. What's more, it has been discovered that research articles are perused primarily by other researchers and not practitioners. Research that is considered helpful is often dubbed experience-near research or applied research. When counselors *do* integrate research into practice it is called Empirically Validated Treatment (EVT) or Empirically Supported Treatment (EST).

**Correlation** is not the same as causality. Correlation is simply an association. The correlation between people who have an umbrella open and rain is very high, but opening your umbrella does not cause it to rain.

- **Correlations go from negative 1 to 0 to positive 1.** Zero means no correlation while positive 1 and negative 1 are perfect correlations. A positive correlation of .5 is not higher than a correlation of -.5. In fact, a correlation of -.8 is stronger than a correlation of .5.
- In **a positive correlation**, when X goes up, Y goes up. For example, when you study more, your GPA goes up.
- In **a negative correlation**, when X goes up, Y goes down. For example, the more you brush your teeth, the less you will be plagued by cavities.

**Research** is quantitative when one quantifies or measure things. **Quantitative research** yields numbers. When research does not use numerical data, we call it **qualitative research**. All research has flaws, sometimes referred to as **bubbles**.

    **True experiment.** Two or more groups are used.

- True experiments must have the study participants selected randomly. **This is known as random selection.** In addition, the participants must be randomly assigned to the control and the experimental groups. **This is known as random assignment. Systematic sampling** where every *n*th person is chosen can also be used, however, researchers still prefer random sampling and random assignment.

- When the researcher cannot control the independent variable (IV), then it is a **quasi** rather than a true experiment. **Quasi-experimental research also referred to as a natural experiment does not ensure causality. When pitted against a true experiment, the quasi gains external validity, is often not as artificial, but shows a loss in internal validity.**

- The experimental groups get the **independent variable (IV)** also known as the experimental variable. **There are levels of the IV such as no counseling (the control group) and counseling (provided to the experimental group).**

- **The control group** does not receive the experimental IV.

- The outcome data in the study are called the **DV or dependent variable**. If we want to see if eating carrots raises one's IQ then eating carrots is the IV while the IQ scores at the end of the study would be the DV.

- Each experiment has a **null hypothesis**: there is no significant difference in people's IQs who eat carrots and those who don't eat carrots. **The experimental or alternative hypothesis** is: there is a significant difference between people's IQ's who do eat carrots versus those who do not.

- When a researcher rejects a null hypothesis that is true, it is a **Type I alpha error**. When a researcher accepts null hypothesis when it should have been rejected, we say that a **Type II beta error** has occurred.

- The significance level for the social sciences is usually set at .05 or less (.01 or .001). The significance level gives you the probability of a Type I error. Smaller is better!

- **N = 1** is known as a single-subject design or case study and thus does not rely on IV, DV, control group, etc. Case studies are becoming more popular.

- **Demand characteristics** are evident when subjects in a study have **cues** regarding what the researcher desires or does not desire that influence their behavior. This can confound an experiment rendering the research inaccurate.

- If subjects **know** they are being observed we refer to the process as an **obtrusive or a reactive measure**. Observers' presence can influence subject's behavior rather than merely the experimental variable or treatment modality. When subjects are

**not aware** that they are being measured we say that it is an **unobtrusive measure**.

- **Internal validity** is high when an experiment has few flaws and thus the findings are accurate. In other words, the IV caused the changes in the DV, not some other factor (known as confounding extraneous variables or artifacts). When internal validity is low, the researcher didn't measure what he thought he measured.
- **External validity** is high when the results in a study can be generalized to other settings.
- **A *t* test is a popular parametric test for comparing two means.**
- The **ANOVA or analysis of variance originally developed by Ronald Fisher (also called a one-way ANOVA) is used when you have two or more means to compare**. The *t* test and the ANOVA are parametric measures for normally distributed populations. The ANOVA provides F values and the ***F* test** will tell you if significant differences are present. Use the **MANOVA or multivariate analysis of variance** when you are investigating **more than one DV**. Use a **factorial analysis of variance** when you are investigating **more than one IV/experimental variable** (i.e., if you have two IVs it would be called a two-way ANOVA; three IVs, a three-way ANOVA, etc.).
- If the population is not necessarily normal then a nonparametric test such as a **chi-square** (the most common nonparametric test) or **Kruskal–Wallis** (similar to the ANOVA) can be used.
- If the researcher did not manipulate the variable and you are looking at after the fact data, then the research is not a true experiment but rather an **ex post facto** or so-called **causal-comparative design**.

**Descriptive statistics** are statistics that describe central tendency like the mean, median, the mode, the range, quartiles, the variance, and the standard deviation.

**Quartiles** are three data points dividing the distribution into four equal parts. **Q1** = 25th percentile or lowest 25% of scores. **Q2** = 26th–50th percentile. Remember the 50th percentile is the median. **Q3** = 75th percentile and higher (i.e., 75% of scores below this value). **Interquartile or IQR** is 25th–75th percentile or **Q3–Q1 = IQR** or where approximately the middle 50% of the scores fall. If you divide the **IQR** by two it gives you the so-called **semi-quartile statistic**.

**Statistical analyses** include correlation coefficients, $t$ tests, ANOVAs, analysis of covariance, chi-square, Kruskal–Wallis etc.

**Cohort studies** examine a group of people who have something in common (e.g., all soldiers who fought in Vietnam or all counselors who received their license in 2007).

**Longitudinal research** takes place when the same individuals are evaluated over a period of time. It is usually contrasted with **cross-sectional research** that relies on observation or data from a given point in time.

**Formative evaluation** takes place during treatment or while a program is going on while **summative or outcome evaluation** occurs at the end of a program or treatment (e.g., after the final session of counseling).

**Between-groups design** uses **different subjects** in the different groups (e.g., one group of subjects for the control group and another group of subjects for the experimental group).

In the **within groups design (also known as the repeated measures or within-subject design)** the **same subjects** for the control condition and then at a different time for the IV/experimental condition(s). **Or to put it a different way, the subject is his or her own control.**

**Institutional Research Board or IRB approval** is required prior to conducting human research. The IRB committee will determine whether your research meets ethical, legal, and institutional guidelines so no subjects are harmed. You might need to go through more than one IRB. For example, a dissertation using community college students as subjects would need the approval of your graduate institution's IRB as well as the IRB of the community college.


## PROFESSIONAL ORIENTATION AND ETHICS

The term *scope of practice* implies that you only practice if you are adequately trained in a given area or with a given population. Hence, if you have no training running a gestalt group, then don't run one. If you know nothing about clients with eating disorders, don't treat them.

**A counselor's duty to warn.** Initially based on a California supreme court case, **Tarasoff**, this principle now states that if a client is going to harm him- or herself, somebody else, or both, you will break confidentiality and contact the appropriate people (e.g., the police, the target person) to ward off this tragedy. Some states currently stipulate a counselor (even in a school) must report it to the parents if a child threatens suicide.

**Dual relationship/boundary issues** (could also be called multiple or nonprofessional relationships, on your exam). This concept implies that you are a person's helper but you also have another significant relationship with that person (maybe you are dating them or perhaps they are a relative or business partner). Such relationships, whether in-person or virtual/eletronic, get in the way of objectivity and should be avoided whenever possible unless the relationship is beneficial to the client.

**Privileged communication is set by state law. Privileged communication** asserts that you cannot reveal what a client said in a session in court unless the client allows you to do so. There are exceptions to this such as child abuse, suicide, homicide, and supervisory sessions or if a lawsuit is filed against you. You should never release information about the client outside of court (unless it is the exceptions just mentioned) unless the client signs a release of information consent form. Remember to disguise the identity of your clients when doing research, training, or in a work for publication.

- Always check the NBCC and ACA websites for the latest information on Internet Counseling and Ethics before you take your comprehensive exam. These ethics and those related to social media are changing extremely rapidly.

# 13

## Graphical Representations

Having a graphical concept is often very beneficial when answering questions. In this chapter are presented several graphical representations including the following:

Bell-shaped curve and related statistical information (Figure 13.1)

Graphical representations other than bell-shaped curve (Figures 13.2, 13.3, and 13.4)

Skewed distributions (Figures 13.5 and 13.6)

Bar graph or histogram (Figures 13.7 and 13.8)

Scattergrams showing correlations (Figures 13.9, 13.10, and 13.11)

Holland's hexagon model (Figure 13.12)

Berne's transactional analysis (Figure 13.13)

The normal Gaussian bell-shaped curve is symmetrical, unimodal, and mesokurtic. Here, the curve is matched up with an array of popular standard scores (Figure 13.1).

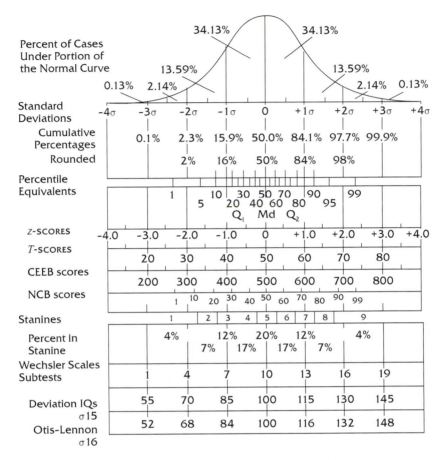

**Figure 13.1.** Bell-shaped curve and related statistical information. Reprinted courtesy of Psychological Corporation from Test Service Notebook No. 148.

The so-called bimodal curve is characterized by two peaks (Figure 13.2). When a frequency polygon sports three or more peaks, it is known as multimodal.

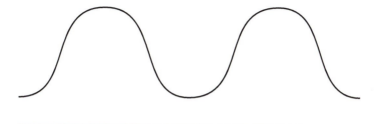

**Figure 13.2.** Bimodal curve.

Platykurtic distributions are flatter and more spread out than the normal curve. The number of persons scoring very high, very low, and in the average range would be similar (Figure 13.3).

**Figure 13.3.** Flatter curve.

The leptokurtic distribution is taller, skinnier, and has a greater peak than the normal curve (Figure 13.4).

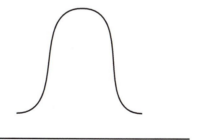

**Figure 13.4.** Leptokurtic distribution.

The positively skewed distribution has an abundance of low scores and is asymmetrical (Figure 13.5).

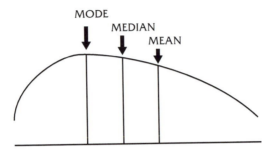

**Figure 13.5.** Positively skewed distribution.

The negatively skewed distribution reflects an abundance of high scores (Figure 13.6). The direction of the tail indicates whether the distribution is positively or negatively skewed.

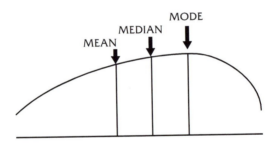

**Figure 13.6.** Negatively skewed distribution.

A bar graph, also called a histogram, can effectively represent data (Figure 13.7).

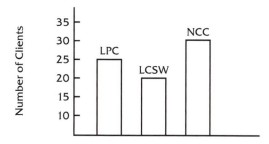

**Figure 13.7.** Bar graph or histogram.

In Figure 13.8, a double-barred histogram is utilized to compare two sets of scores. In this hypothetical example, private practice LPCs and LCSWs in a control group are compared to an experimental group of professionals who received a seminar in marketing. The DV, which is plotted on the Y axis, would seem to indicate that the marketing strategies were helpful. Therapists in the experimental group acquired more clients each week.

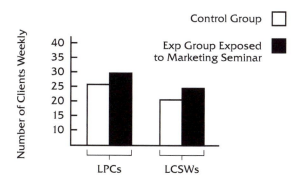

**Figure 13.8.** Double-barred histogram.

Scattergrams—also known as scatter plots or scatter diagrams—graphically depict the Pearson Product-Moment Correlation Coefficient. Representation of three scattergrams are presented in Figures 13.9, 13.10, and 13.11.

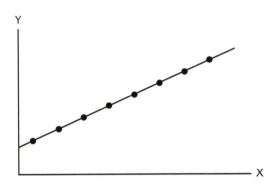

**Figure 13.9.** Scattergram of a perfect linear positive correlation. $r = +1.00$.

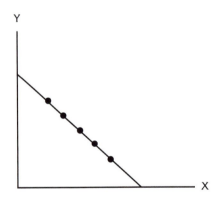

**Figure 13.10.** Scattergram of a perfect linear negative correlation. $r = -1.00$.

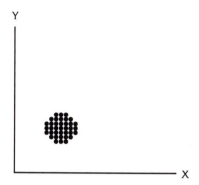

**Figure 13.11.** Scattergram showing a lack of relationship, $r$=0.00.

Career theorist John Holland proposes a hexagon model with six vocational personalities/work environments (Figure 13.12). Adjacent types are seen as consistent.

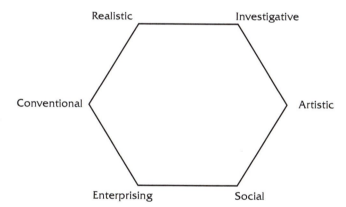

**Figure 13.12.** Holland's hexagon model.

Eric Berne's transactional analysis relies on three ego states: the Parent, the Child, and the Adult (Figure 13.13). When a message sent from a given ego state receives a predicted response, the transaction is said to be complementary. The complementary exchange is healthy. Contrast this with the crossed transaction, which occurs when a message is returned with an unexpected response. Crossed transactions foster emotional discord between the persons communicating. The person who initiated the conversation often feels discounted.

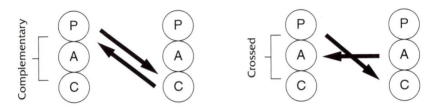

**Figure 13.13.** Schematic of Berne's transactional analysis.

# 14

## Resources

In this chapter are listed resources frequently used by counselors. The first list is of statistical tests used in counseling research. Parametric and nonparametric tests are listed alphabetically. These explanations are in brief summary form. For a more complete explanation, please refer to a statistics book.

The second list consists of major psychoeducational diagnostic tools. These are listed alphabetically. The brief explanation is to help you know the kind of instrument, the age range (in most cases), and the general construct of each. The manual for the specific diagnostic tool and/or a comprehensive psychological testing text would be excellent references for more information.

Each professional group of mental health practitioners has a code of ethics. These codes are reviewed regularly and updated frequently. Therefore, each professional needs to keep abreast with the ethical codes applicable to him or her. The third list in this chapter provides the name and address of the source for each of 10 codes.

# STATISTICAL TESTS USED IN COUNSELING RESEARCH

## Parametric Tests

**Analysis of Covariance (ANCOVA or ANACOVA).** An extension of the ANOVA which controls the impact that one or more extraneous/unstudied variables (covariates) exert on the dependent variable.

**Analysis of Variance (ANOVA).** Also called a one-way analysis of variance, this test is used to determine whether two or more mean scores differ significantly from each other. The ANOVA examines a null hypothesis between two or more groups.

**Factorial Analysis of Variance.** Used to describe an ANOVA that is used to compare two or more independent variables. When two independent variables are utilized, the term "two-way ANOVA" is used; with three independent variables, the term "three-way ANOVA" is used; and so on.

**Multivariate Analysis of Variance (MANOVA).** Used to describe an ANOVA when a researcher examines more than one dependent variable.

**Pearson Product-Moment Correlation (r).** Used with interval and ratio data, this statistic examines the direction and magnitude of two variables. Correlation describes a relationship or association between variables. When relying on correlational research, variables are merely measured, not manipulated via the researcher.

**Phi Coefficient/Tetrachoric Correlation Coefficient.** Used to assess correlation when both variables are dichotomous (i.e., binary or two-valued). Also known as a "fourfold-point correlation."

**Point Bi-Serial/Bi-Serial Correlation.** Used when one variable is continuous and the other is dichotomous (i.e., placed in two classes), for example correlating IQ with sex.

**Scheffe's S Test/Newman-Keuls/Tukey's HSD/Duncan's New Multiple Range Test.** Used after a researcher discovers a significant $F$ ratio in an ANOVA to test the differences between specific group means or combinations of group means. Such measures are known as "a posteriori tests" or "post hoc tests" for the ANOVA.

***t* test** Used to ascertain whether two means or correlation coefficients differ significantly from each other. The *t* test procedures can be employed for correlated/related/matched samples and for uncorrelated/independent/unmatched samples. The *t* test is used also to determine whether a single sample or correlation coefficient differs significantly from a population mean.

## Nonparametric Tests

**Chi-Square Test**. Used to assess whether an obtained distribution is significantly different than an expected or theoretical distribution.

**Kruskal–Wallis Test**. Used as a nonparametric one-way analysis of variance. The Kruskal–Wallis statistic is called "H"; hence researchers sometimes refer to it as the "*H* test."

**Mann–Whitney *U* Test** Used to test whether a significant difference is present between two uncorrelated/unmatched means. Can be used in place of the *t* test for uncorrelated/independent/ unmatched means when parametric assumptions cannot be met. A "Whitney extension" allows the test to be used with three samples.

**Spearman Rank-Order Correlation (rho)/Kendall's tau**. Used in place of the Pearson Product-Moment Correlation coefficient when parametric assumptions can't be met (i.e., ordinal data are involved).

**Wilcoxon Matched-Pairs/Signed-Ranks Test**. Used to determine whether two correlated means are significantly different. Can be utilized in place of the related samples *t* test when parametric assumptions cannot be met.

## MAJOR PSYCHOEDUCATIONAL, CAREER COUNSELING, AND DIAGNOSTIC TOOLS

**Bayley Scales of Infant Development (BSID-II).** A test that evaluates children from 1 month to 42 months. Test items measure responses to visual and auditory stimuli, manipulation, play with objects, and discrimination of sounds and shapes. The test is comprised of a mental scale, a motor scale, a behavior rating scale, a social-emotional scale, and the adaptive behavior scale. Preschool tests can have weak predictive validity.

**Beery Developmental Test of Visual-Motor Integration (Beery VMI).** A test consisting of geometric shapes that the person reproduces. The test, that takes about 20 minutes to administer, measures visual perception and eye–hand coordination to identify difficulties which may lead to learning and behavior problems. A Short Format for children aged 2–8 years and a Full Format for children through the age of 18.

**Bender Gestalt II Test of Visual-Motor Integration (Bender).** An expressive test with no time limit consisting of 16 stimulus cards with geometric figures that the person copies. It assesses visual perception and perceptual motor integration. It can be used also to detect the presence of underlying emotional difficulties, brain damage, and memory. Suitable for ages 3 or 4 years and beyond. When a client rotates a figure in his or her copy then organicity (i.e., a neurological difficulty) may be present.

**California Psychological Inventory (CPI).** A test intended for reasonably well-adjusted individuals that focuses on the assessment of personality characteristics that are important for social living and interaction. It has been used with age 12 years and older. The inventory relies on 434 test items (or 260-statement short form) that yields 20 scales of individual differences.

**Career Decision Scale (CDS).** This is a 19-item, self-reporting measure suitable for high school and college-aged students. It can be used in both individual and group settings.

**Children's Apperception Test (CAT).** A downward extension of the TAT that is utilized with children ages 3–10 years. It consists of 10 picture cards depicting animals in various situations that a trained examiner uses to reveal dominant drives, emotions, sentiments, and personality characteristics.

**Comprehensive Test of Nonverbal Intelligence (CTONI).** A language-free measure of intelligence and reasoning. It consists of 50 abstract symbols in patterns with a variety of problem-solving tasks presented. The tasks increase in difficulty. The administration does not require reading, writing, listening, or speaking on the part of the individual evaluated. The test is suitable for those aged 6 years and over, and takes about one hour to administer. The CTONICA version is computer administered.

**Draw-A-Person Test (DAP).** A norm referenced projective/expressive test in which the person is asked to draw human figures. It is a nonverbal measure of intellectual ability and can be used as a projective measure of personality. Suitable for ages 3–16 years.

**General Aptitude Test Battery (GATB).** A multi-aptitude test battery consisting of 12 tests developed specifically for vocational counseling in schools and job placement settings. The test focuses on in-depth measurement of aptitude and skills that relate to potential occupational success. The test takes about 2.5 hours to administer and is designed for use with students in grades 9 through 12, as well as with adults.

**Guilford–Zimmerman Temperament Survey (GZTS).** This personality inventory is designed to be used with normally functioning individuals aged 16 years and older, measuring 10 traits. It was initially developed to assess Carl Jung's constructs of introversion and extroversion. It can be used in a variety of settings, but it has been used most frequently with the college-aged population.

**Halstead–Reitan Neuropsychology Battery (HRNB).** This test is used not only to diagnose neuropsychological dysfunction but to establish a baseline of function against which to measure future functioning. It consists of three batteries: one for children ages 5–8 years, one for children ages 9–14 years, and one for adults.

Each battery includes a minimum of 14 separate tests, which are scored as 26 variables. Helps detect brain damage and severity.

**Holtzman Inkblot Technique (HIT).** Initially developed in an attempt to improve the reliability of the Rorschach Test. There are two parallel forms (A and B), each consisting of 45 inkblot cards. There are two practice blot cards that are identical for each test. The client is encouraged to give only one response for each card. Parallel forms allow for test–retest reliability. Suitable for age 5 years through adulthood.

**House-Tree-Person (HTP).** A projective/expressive drawing test that provides the examiner with information pertaining to intrapersonal, interpersonal, and environmental adjustment of the individual evaluated. It is often used with children and adolescents.

**Kinetic Family Drawing (KFD).** This instrument is a supplement to the DAP in which the person is asked to draw everyone in his or her family doing an activity. It is used as a projective measure of personality to assess the individual's perception of himself or herself as well as his or her family.

**Kuder Career Inventories.** This is a set of interest inventories that makes the assumption that a person will find satisfaction in an occupation where workers have similar interest patterns. The Kuder Galaxy is tailored for Pre-K through fifth grade; the Kuder Navigator for grades 6 to 12; and the Kuder Journey for adults.

**Kuder Search with Person Match (Interest Inventory)** is a new generation of the well-known Kuder Occupation Interest Survey (KOIS). This is an interest survey that makes the assumption that a person will find satisfaction in an occupation where workers have similar interest patterns. Currently examines about 140 occupations and college majors. It takes about 20 minutes to complete and must be scored by computer. The survey can be administered via pencil and paper, computer, or the Internet. It is primarily suited to those in the tenth grade and beyond.

**Leiter International Performance Scale (LIPS-3).** A completely nonverbal culture-fair measure of cognitive abilities and intelligence used with individuals from age 3 to 75 years. It is most often used to evaluate individuals who are deaf, nonverbal, non-English speaking, culturally deprived, autistic, or have severe medical complications. Administration time is 20–45 minutes.

**Minnesota Multiphasic Personality Inventory (MMPI-2).** This is a test designed to assess some major personality characteristics that affect personal and social adjustments. It contains 567 true/false statements covering a range of subject matter including physical conditions, moral attitudes, and social attitudes. The test is individually administered and is suitable for persons 18 years of age who have had at least six successful years of schooling. Administration time is 60–90 minutes. The MMPI-A is a compact version of the test composed of 478 true/false questions for 14–18-year-old adolescents. It takes approximately one hour to administer.

**Myers–Briggs Type Indicator (MBTI).** This is a widely used measure of personality disposition and preferences created by psychologist Isabel Briggs Myers and her mother Katharine Cook Briggs, which utilizes 93 or more items. It is based on Carl Jung's theory of perception and judgment. Four bipolar scales are used, resulting in 16 individual personality types, each of which is given a four-letter code used for interpreting personality type. It is suitable for use with upper elementary-aged children as well as adults. Some counselors question the validity and reliability of this measure.

**O\*NET Interest Profiler (IP)** is an interest inventory with a paper and pencil, computerized, and shorter web-based version. The inventory uses 180 items to discern which occupations a client would like and find exciting. The CIP (Computerized Interest Profiler) measures interests related to over 800 occupations using John Holland's RIASEC typology and can be self-administered and self-interpreted. Administration time is just 30 minutes. Go to www.onecenter.org.

**Otis–Lennon School Ability Test (OLSAT-8).** This is a group-administered multilevel mental ability battery designed for use in grades K (kindergarten) through 12. The test results are often used to predict success in school. It takes 75 minutes or less to administer.

**Peabody Individual Achievement Test (PIAT-R).** This test is designed to measure the level of educational achievement in the areas of basic skills and knowledge in approximately 60–90 minutes. It does not require written responses and can be used with individuals in grades K (kindergarten) to 12.

**Piers–Harris Children's Self-Concept Scale 2 (PHCSCS).** This is a 60-item scale that provides a self-descriptive scale entitled, "The Way I Feel About Myself." This test yields a self-concept score as well as six subscores. It takes just 10–15 minutes to administer and can be used for ages 7–18 years.

**Portage Guide to Early Education Checklist.** A developmentally sequenced, criterion-referenced checklist used as a measure with infants, children, and developmentally disabled individuals with functional age levels from birth to 5 years. It is used to measure skills in the cognitive, language, self-help, motor, and socialization areas.

**Rorschach Inkblot Test.** A projective test created by the Swiss psychiatrist Hermann Rorschach that utilizes ten 6 × 9½ inch cards. Five of the cards are gray or black, while five are colored. The examinee is asked to describe what he or she sees or what the card brings to mind. The test is appropriate for age 3 years and beyond.

**Rotter Incomplete Sentence Blanks (RISB).** This is a projective method of evaluating personality. The person is asked to complete 40 sentences for which the first word or words is/are provided. It is assumed the individual reflects his or her own wishes, desires, and fears.

**Self-Directed Search (SDS).** A self-administered career interest assessment that is available in several forms addressing the needs of a variety of clients, both students and professionals. It is a self-scoring instrument that can be completed and scored in approximately 35–45 minutes. It is based on John Holland's RIASEC model and an SDS interactive web-based version is available.

**SIGI PLUS** is a popular software program based on research conducted by Educational Testing Service (ETS) to help with career self-assessment and information. It provides a realistic view of the finest career options for high school, college, and adult clients. Occupations can be searched for via college major or high school tech prep clusters. The program is updated on a yearly basis. Ideal for clients who want to change careers as well.

**16 Personality Factor Questionnaire (16 PF).** A 185-item, normal adult personality measure that can be administered to individuals age 16 years and above. This test assesses personality on 16 scales that are grouped into five "global factors." Can be completed in 35–50 minutes. An additional 26 questions are added to yield a couple's counseling report.

**Slosson Intelligence Test (SIT-R3).** A verbally administered measure of intelligence utilized to gain a quick estimate of intellectual ability. This test can be utilized from ages 4 to 65 years with a test time of approximately 10–20 minutes.

**Stanford–Binet Intelligence Scale (SB5).** This is a 45–90-minute intelligence test designed to measure cognitive ability as well as provide analysis of the pattern of an individual's cognitive development. The scale is used for individuals aged 2–85+ years.

**Stanford–Binet Intelligence Scale (form L-M).** The best test for ferreting out children above the 99th percentile. Since it has a higher ceiling than the Wechsler or the Binet listed above, it is the best test for the extremely gifted. An age scale using standards of performance to measure intelligence regarded as general mental adaptability. Can be used for clients aged 2 years and beyond and takes 30–90 minutes to administer.

**Strong Interest Inventory (SII).** This career inventory, which takes 30–45 minutes, is based on the career theory of John Holland and can be used with anyone who can comprehend the test items (approximately an eigth-grade reading level); that is, most people over 14 years. The SCII compares a person's interests with those of persons who have been in their occupation for at least three years and state that they enjoy their work. The test consists of 291 items. An online version is available.

**Thematic Apperception Test (TAT).** A projective test consisting of a pool of 32 ambiguous picture cards (and one blank card) for which the individual is asked to make up emotions, sentiments, complexes, and conflicts of the individual's personality. Generally, a full TAT consists of 19 picture cards and the one blank card. If more than 10 cards are used, then it is appropriate to have test sessions on different days. It is suitable for age 4 years and older. Targets unconscious processes.

**Vineland Adaptive Behavior Scale (VABS-II).** This is a survey form that assesses the individual's personal and social sufficiency. This instrument measures adaptive behavior from birth to 90 years. A popular evaluation instrument for dementia, ADHD, and brain injuries.

**Wechsler Adult Intelligence Scale (WAIS-IV).** This is the most popular adult intelligence test in the world. It is comprised of verbal and nonverbal scales designed to measure intellectual functioning of adolescents and adults based on a capacity to understand and cope with the world. The test takes 60–90 minutes to give and can be used for ages 16–90 years.

**Wechsler Intelligence Scale for Children (WISC-V).** An individual test comprised of verbal and nonverbal scales designed to measure intellectual functioning of children based on capacity to understand and cope with the world. Appropriate for ages 6–16 years and 11 months. The test takes approximately 50–70 minutes.

**Wechsler Preschool and Primary Scale of Intelligence (WPPSI III).** A test comprised of verbal and nonverbal scales designed to measure intellectual functioning of young children based on capacity to understand and cope with the world. Appropriate for ages 2 years and 6 months to 7 years and 3 months and takes about 1.5 hours to administer.

**Wide Range Achievement Test (WRAT-4).** This instrument is used to measure word reading, sentence comprehension, spelling, and mathematical computation. It is often utilized for a quick estimate of academic achievement. Suitable for ages 5–94 years and can be administered in just 15–45 minutes depending upon the age of the test taker.

# HIPAA BASICS FOR COUNSELORS

The Health Insurance Portability and Accountability Act (HIPAA) 1996 ensures privacy of the client's records and limits sharing this information. The purpose of the Title II of the Act was to protect consumer health care information (sometimes called PHI or Protected Health Information) since technological advancements could violate client security and confidentiality. HIPAA provided national standards for electronic health care transactions with administrative simplification. If the client signs a Notification of Privacy Practices form then several providers can share records and information without separate signed client consent forms for each provider. Third-party payers (e.g., insurance companies and managed care firms) could view the client's complete record. It also allows clients to view their own records. The helping organizations that were opposed to third-party payers having access to the whole file and ultimately process notes, also known as psychotherapy or counseling notes, are now the exception. Impressions, analysis of the client, or the conversations that take place in counseling are considered psychotherapy notes and thus are excluded from the aforementioned guidelines. Again, psychotherapy notes can be excluded from being released unless the client authorizes this action, but they must be kept separate from the official record. Nevertheless, prescription medication monitoring, counseling session times, treatment modalities, and frequency of intervention, treatment plans, tests, and diagnosis, prognosis, symptoms, progress of the client and prognosis are *never* considered psychotherapy notes!

The U.S. Department of Health and Human Services (HHS) and law enforcement agencies can inspect the complete record in some instances thus this would be an exception to the guidelines. Most counselors and health care providers find the regulations confusing and some experts would even assert that consumers have lost some degree of privacy due to HIPAA regulations.

Providers need to secure a National Provider Identity (NPI).

# SOURCES FOR OBTAINING ETHICAL GUIDELINES

**Counselors** can secure "ACA Ethical Standards" from the American Counseling Association. www.counseling.org

**National Certified Counselors** can secure the "NBCC Code of Ethics" from the National Board for Certified Counselors. www.nbcc.org

**Marriage and Family Therapists** can secure the "AAMFT Code of Ethics" from the American Association for Marriage and Family Therapy. www.aamft.org

**Psychologists** can secure "Ethical Principles of Psychologists" from the American Psychological Association. www.apa.org

**School Counselors** can secure "Ethical Standards for School Counselors" from the American School Counselor Association. www.schoolcounselor.org

**Social Workers** can secure the "NASW Code of Ethics" from the National Association of Social Workers. www.naswdc.org

**Sociologists** can secure the "Ethical Standards of Sociological Practitioners" from the Sociological Practice Association. Phone: 320-255-3428. www.socpractice.org

**Psychiatrists** can secure "Principles of Medical Ethics, with Annotations Especially Applicable to Psychiatry" from the American Psychiatric Association. www.psych.org

**Psychoanalysts** can secure the "Code of Ethics" from the American Psychoanalytic Association. www.apsa.org

**Human Service Workers** can secure "Ethical Standards of Human Service Professionals" from the National Organization for Human Services. www.nationalhumanservices.org

# Index

Numbers Refer to Question Numbers
Unless Otherwise Specified

# About the Author

**Dr. Howard G. Rosenthal, Ed.D.**, received his master's degree from the University of Missouri, St. Louis, and his doctorate from St. Louis University. He is the author of the bestselling counseling exam preparation audio program of all time: the *Vital Information and Review Questions* for the NCE and CPCE. He also authored the first ever *Human Services Dictionary*, which is unique since the definitions help the reader answer typical or prototype exam questions. In 2010, both of the aforementioned materials made it into the Routledge Counseling and Psychotherapy *Top Ten List* for the United States and overseas, while the previous version of this book, *The Special 15th Anniversary Edition of the Encyclopedia of Counseling, 3rd edn*, captured the number one slot.

Dr. Rosenthal's book *Favorite Counseling and Therapy Techniques* (a publisher's bestseller) and the companion book *Favorite Counseling and Therapy Homework Assignments* include contributions from many of the top therapists in the world.

Dr. Rosenthal's humorous, reader-friendly writing style landed him an interview—along with other influential authors such as Barry

Sears of *Zone Diet* books and Mark Victor Hansen, co-author of the *Chicken Soup for the Soul* series—in Jeff Herman's book, *You Can Make It Big Writing Books: A Top Agent Shows You How to Develop a Million-Dollar Bestseller.*

Some of his other popular books include *Not With My Life I Don't: Preventing Your Suicide and That of Others*; *Before You See Your First Client: 55 Things Counselors and Mental Health Providers Need to Know*; *Help Yourself to Positive Mental Health* (with Joseph W. Hollis); and *Therapy's Best, Practical Advice and Gems of Wisdom From Twenty Accomplished Counselors and Therapists.* Dr. Rosenthal has now lectured to over 100,000 people, making him one of the most popular speakers in the Midwest.

He holds the national record for winning the most "teaching tips of the year awards" given by the publication *Teaching for Success.* He has been inducted into the St. Louis Community College Hall of Fame; he is an Emerson Excellence in Teaching Award recipient; a winner of the Missouri Wayne B. McClelland Award; and most recently, a John & Suanne Roueche Excellence Award winner. He is listed in *Who's Who in America* and Samuel T. Gladding's *The Counseling Dictionary* in the "Prominent Names in the Counseling Profession" section. He has written over twenty articles alone for *Counselor, The Magazine for Addictions Professionals*, and he is one of the leading bloggers for Victor Yalom's Psychotherapy Net.

In 2014 he wrote the *Encyclopedia of Human Services, Master Review and Tutorial for the Human Services-Board Certified Practitioner Examination (HS-BCPE).*

Dr. Rosenthal currently serves as professor and coordinator of Human Services and Addiction Studies at St. Louis Community College at Florissant Valley.

His website is www.howardrosenthal.com.